Practical Art of
Motion Picture Sound
Third Edition

David Lewis Yewdall, M.P.S.E.

ELSEVIER

AMSTERDAM • BOSTON • HEIDELBERG
LONDON • NEW YORK • OXFORD
PARIS • SAN DIEGO • SAN FRANCISCO
SINGAPORE • SYDNEY • TOKYO
Focal Press is an imprint of Elsevier

Focal
Press

Acquisitions Editor: Elinor Actipis
Associate Acquisitions Editor: Cara Anderson
Publishing Services Manager: George Morrison
Project Manager: Marilyn E. Rash
Production Services: Graphic World
Marketing Manager: Christine Degon Veroulis
Cover Design: Louis Forgione
Cover Image: iStockphoto logo/Daniel Brunner/Dizzo
Text Printing: Sheridan Books
Cover Printing: Phoenix Color Corp.

Focal Press is an imprint of Elsevier
30 Corporate Drive, Suite 400, Burlington, MA 01803, USA
Linacre House, Jordan Hill, Oxford OX2 8DP, UK

∞ Recognizing the importance of preserving what has been written, Elsevier prints its books on acid-free paper whenever possible.

Library of Congress Cataloging-in-Publication Data
Yewdall, David Lewis, 1950–
    Practical art of motion picture sound / David Lewis Yewdall—3rd ed.
      p. cm.
    Includes index.
    ISBN-13: 978-0-240-80865-9
    ISBN-10: 0-240-80865-7 (alk. paper)
    1. Television broadcasting—Sound effects. 2. Sound motion pictures. 3. Television. I. Title.
    TK7881.4.Y48 2007
    778.5'2344—dc22   2006035676

British Library Cataloguing-in-Publication Data
A catalogue record for this book is available from the British Library.

ISBN-13: 978-0-240-80865-9
ISBN-10: 0-240-80865-7 (alk. paper)

For information on all Focal Press publications visit our website at
www.books.elsevier.com

    08 09 10 11   10 9 8 7 6 5 4 3 2

Printed in the United States of America

Working together to grow
libraries in developing countries

www.elsevier.com | www.bookaid.org | www.sabre.org

ELSEVIER   BOOK AID International   Sabre Foundation

To my wife
Lisa

Her patience, hard work, and support made it possible
for me to write this book.

Special Thanks and Acknowledgments

Neumann.Berlin—The Microphone Company: Georg Neumann, Gmb.H
  and Matthias Spahrmann
Schoeps Mikrofone: Ulrich Schoeps and Dagobert Schaefer
Sound Devices, Inc.: Jon Tatooles
Nuendo: Lars Baumann
Aaton, s.a.: Jean-Pierre Beauviala
DigiDesign: A Division of Avid, Danny Caccavo
Kiwa International: David Kite
Audio Mechanics, Inc.: John Polito
Legend Films, Inc.: Barry B. Sandrew, Ph.D and Susan Olney
Academy of Motion Picture Arts and Sciences: Rich Miller

And also:

Bruce Campbell
John LeBlanc
Zach Seivers
Charles Maynes
Joe Sikorski
Basil Poledoris
David Stone
Richard King
Richard Anderson
Stephen Hunter Flick
Donald Flick
Greg Hedgepath
John Larsen
R.J. Kizer
Eric Potter
Wendy Hedin
Jim Troutman
John Ross
Vanessa Ament

Roger Corman
Stuart Wilson
Rusty Amadeo
Dave Carmen
Rusty Amadeo
Roger A. Scheck
Thomas Causey
Colin Broad
Jon Johnson
Paul Jyrälä
Mark Mangini
Steve Lee
Warren Hamilton, Jr.
Coonfer Wade
Smokey Cloud
Sonny Pettijohn
Casey Crabtree
Richard Meredith
Cadac Holland

Warren Hamilton, Jr.
Dave Whittaker
Eric Karson
Robert Wise
Scott Burns
Mike Le-Mare
Karola Storr
Petur Hiddal
Mark Goldblatt
Leander Sales
Lovinder Gill
George Simpson
Lee Howell
Millie Moore
Jim Webb
Greg Bartram
Clancy Troutman
Steve Tushar
Tom Knight

Contents

A Memorial to Excellence

John Bonner

Before we begin, I wish to remember these two gentlemen. Without question, John Bonner and John Mosely had the greatest influence on my personal education in the audio arts as well as the development of my professional discipline to serve that art form.

John Bonner worked within the studio environment, serving both professionals and studios alike, always placing the good of the art form above the short-term and often artificial profit gain.

John Mosely was the classic independent maverick, willing to lay his job and reputation on the line for the things he believed in. When it came to his craft, he was unwavering and uncompromising, but also extremely inventive and innovative.

From John Mosely I learned the physics and disciplines along with his personal theology on how the ideal presentation of sound *should* be. We did not always agree on the creative applications, but no one could dispute his expertise or mastery of audio engineering.

From John Bonner I had the infusion of *practical* application, the realities of working within an industry that is forever changing, forever reinventing itself. He

John Mosely

taught me how to hold onto my own principles and creative applications in the everpresent factory-style grind that often suffers the unfortunate effects of artistic mediocrity. This book's title is derived from the *practical* approach.

To both these men I owe the success of my career and my reputation and for a benchmark standard of professional excellence to strive for that has never failed me. For this, I hope you will always remember their names and their contributions to the motion picture and television industries, as well as to our craft.

Chapter 1
The Empowerment of Sound

"It's probably not a good idea to come into this room and hear this demo—because after I finish, you will belong to me."

– David Lewis Yewdall, M.P.S.E. (playfully teasing clients who are not empowered by the art of sound as they enter the author's sound design and editorial facilities)

This book is for everyone interested in sound. It does not matter if you are in the sound business. It does not matter if you aspire to personally design and prepare your own soundtracks for the silver screen, television broadcast, or live theatre performances. This book is just as important to those not involved in the actual hands-on creative efforts, but just as responsible for the ultimate success of the soundtrack through the misunderstood and seldom considered phases of preplanning, budgeting, and scheduling. This book has been written with one objective in mind—to empower you, the reader, in ways seldom offered or available. Many years ago (and I hesitate to admit just how many), I produced numerous amateur "home-movie" productions, dreaming of the day when I would set off for Hollywood and work on feature films.

I scoured the libraries, bookstores, and technical periodicals looking for any information about the skills and techniques I would need to make more exciting and interesting films. I am not referring to the "technodata" books of engineering or the idealistic platitudes that so often fill such texts. I was starved for the real thing—the practical and experienced craftsperson who had set down his or her thoughts and advice from which others could learn. Such books were, and still are, rare. Many talk *at* their subject, but few talk *about* it with substance and experience. It is for that very reason this book has been written—for the accurate compilation of the experiences and expertise of dozens of men and women who bring some of the most exciting audio achievements to the screen, regardless of the media format.

Figure 1.1 The author is developing direct-to-picture vari-speed sound effects by interlocking his 35mm Moviola to the Magna-Tech in his transfer bay. It was the most effective way to create the hydrogen car sound effects for the picture *Black Moon Rising* (New World, 1984). (Photo by David Yewdall.)

Our world is filled with a vast amount of misinformation—by far the most damaging is the misinformation that we hear or see written by those we respect or hold in high esteem or by those who lend the perception that they should know what they are talking about, particularly books and papers written by people with PhDs. Most misinformation is born out of ignorance, drawing the wrong conclusions, or having knowledge of the front end and knowledge of the back in, then guessing or extrapolating what they think the middle is, and erring in the process. For instance, I have great respect for Ted Turner's Movie Classics cable channel. I consider it the last bastion of commercial-free presentations of great film. But they run an occasional blurb that says, "Turner Classic Movies, 30 frames a second. . . ."

I heave a sigh of disappointment every time I hear that. Thirty frames per second is a video standard. Motion pictures are shot at 24 frames per second. The extra six frames is made up by using a "drop-frame" video transfer technique, where every fourth frame of the film is repeated, thus making 24 frames per second view at 30 frames (video) per second.

Ignorance such as this by the writer (and subsequently by the narrative voice not to correct the error in the script) is how misinformation spreads throughout your daily life. And when you read it as a printed text or hear it spoken by a voice that represents a standard of respected quality, it blurs the truth and confuses the audience. I have, therefore, striven to present the material in this book as straightforwardly as possible. You will not find a bibliography note anywhere, because I do not draw upon other people's works to build my own. I will tell it like it is—as straight and honest as I can.

Back to the issue of the audio art form. Sound is sound—whether you are working on amateur film productions, commercials, student films, documentaries, multimedia presentations, CD-ROM games, interactive virtual reality, episodic long-form television, or multimillion-dollar theatrical motion picture events. The recording of dialog and sound effects, the style of editing, and the preparation of these sounds, as well as the philosophical taste and manner of mixing the sounds together, are all virtually the same.

Read this paragraph very carefully. Whether you record with an analog tape recorder, a digital DAT machine, straight to hard disk, or to liquid-helium molecular storage; whether you cut on film with a Moviola and a synchronizer; or whether you spin a trackball with a nonlinear computer platform—the techniques, procedures, technical disciplines, and creative craftspersonship of creating an acoustical event are the same. Only the tools change; the artistic and scientific principles remain the same.

Whether I cut the sound cue with a Rivas splicer and scrape the magnetic soundtrack from the edge with a degaussed razor blade or whether I use a mouse to manipulate a digital cut on a computer screen and encode a fade-in, the artistic reasons for doing it and the net results are identical.

Of course, unique application differs from one medium to another, but the art form and techniques of sound recording, sound design, dialog preparation, and sound-effect editing are identical. The reason I have taken this moment to stress the art form so vehemently is that not enough people understand this, especially those perhaps most responsible for ensuring the success of the final audio track by planning for it long before the cameras even roll.

I will refer to the term *technical disciplines* many times throughout this book, and I want you to understand why. Many of us are rather puzzled by the educational institutions that now offer film and television courses. Most of these schools are caught up in theory and raw-creativity style instruction, something they call "critical studies." Many are literally discarding and openly discounting the need for the film student to develop the technical skills and discipline necessary to create a successful project. This style of instruction is akin to a mechanic putting an engine into your car, offering creative ideas about where to go, but not giving you a steering wheel, transmission, or brakes to drive it. What good are theory and creativity when you are frustrated and floundering with the very tools that you need to bring your creative vision to fruition?

Even more important than knowing how to use the physical tools of production is knowing what is possible. I wish I had a nickel for every time I heard producers or directors say they did not know they actually had to do something or preplan the shot or action so that they could achieve something creatively that they assumed could only be achieved months later in postproduction. They were not empowered by their educational background to release their full potential and/or creative desires.

I served as the supervising sound editor on an unremarkable kickboxing picture several years ago. After the final mix, the director and producer both displayed little enthusiasm about what they had just heard during the final continuity playback. I noticed this and asked what was troubling them. The director's brow furrowed as he struggled to articulate his feelings. "I don't know, I guess I thought it would just sound . . . bigger."

I knew exactly what the problem was and what it had always been; but so seldom did I have such a receptive audience as I had right then and there. "I want you both to listen to me very carefully. We gave you the soundtrack for the movie that you made." The two men sat there waiting, as if I had not made my point yet. The director shook his head. "I don't understand." I knew he did not.

"What did you expect to hear?" I asked.

"I thought we would have stereo pan-by stuff, you know, big—broad."

"Absolutely, we can do all of that. But you first have to make the movie in such a way that we can do those kinds of things. For instance, you want all these stereo pan-by effects, but you didn't give us the cinematic opportunities to do it—because you didn't plan for it."

"Plan for it? What do you call those car-by shots?"

"A perfect example. Your film was photographed monophonically."

The producer leaned forward. "Mono-what?"

"When the car races by, your cameraman panned with the car, keeping the image in the center. If we put the sound of the car into a pan-pot joystick, where do you expect us to pan it when the action remains in the center of the screen? What your cinematographer should have done was to keep the camera anchored down, filming the car going past him, whooshing close by to the left off-screen. While the stunt driver set up the action again, you set up the second shot, turning the camera around to catch the car whooshing past, only this time from the right of the screen and throttling down the road away from the camera."

The producer started to understand. "This way they can pan the car from center to hard left and then come by hard right and go away into the center of the screen."

I smiled. "That's right, except you have to continue to plan for it when you cut the picture. Many picture editors do not understand the difference between cutting for television and cutting theatrical, between cutting monophonically and cutting for stereo. Many picture editors would cut the first shot just as the car disappeared screen left and then a frame before it appeared on the right. That's monophonic thinking. Your picture editor should give a full beat once it has disappeared screen left, and a full beat before it appears screen right, knowing that the follow-through stereo panning effect the mixer makes will yield the fullest stereophonic result, making it big—and full."

I'm sure it was a bitter revelation for the two men, but judging from their subsequent pictures I would say they learned much from that enlightenment. From that moment, they became empowered—the proverbial light bulb had gone on—and their creative planning and preparations would be forever different.

The sharing of actual "war" stories and examples like this is a vital part of this book. It is the glue that bonds the information and techniques in such a way as to give a certain vicarious experience that will serve you well in the future. Of course, you will make mistakes of your own along the way; we all do. Hopefully, though, you will learn from the mistakes described herein, and avoid making them yourself.

This book is written with real industry terms, not only technical words, but the jargon and nomenclature that is part of the language and understanding of motion picture craftspeople. For instance, one simple example that often appears is the word "sync." By proper dictionary spelling, the word is "synch," as it would be outside of postproduction industry usage. In the professional industry jargon, however, this word is spelled without the "h."

Rather than write this book with a literary correctness, I have decided to spell the words as they have come to be known in their professional applications. You will find that if you read this book in sequential order, both your vocabulary and your technical understanding of the process will grow geometrically. As you learn more terms, you will not only understand them singularly, you will quickly develop a rhythm—an ability to assimilate and comprehend. By the time you finish this book you should not only be enriched with detailed explanations of techniques and practical applications, but through the various examples and actual experiences, you should begin to understand why the industry works the way it does.

One more ingredient is vital to any kind of work you do, whether creative or mechanical. You must have passion for what you are doing. Frankly, most craftspeople today are working in jobs other than those they dreamed of doing. This is not necessarily a bad thing; in fact, it can often lead to even more interesting and fulfilling opportunities—as long as you fuel your working gas tank with passion.

Many newcomers to the industry confuse the concept of loving the idea of doing something with being passionate about actually doing it. It reflects in their work; it reflects in the attitude of how to work. Many lose their way spending untold fruitless hours trying to develop shortcuts rather than rolling up their sleeves and simply doing the work. For those of us endowed with the love and passion of our work, there is only the craftspersonship, the yearning to achieve a greater level of quality and meaning. The secret to real success and personal satisfaction is knowing you must have passion for everything you do, even for jobs for which you have disdain. You cannot work in this industry by doing only what you want to do, and you probably cannot start right away working at the job of your dreams. The quickest way to achieve promotion and advancement toward the dream career is to approach each job assignment and task with as much passion and enthusiasm as if it were your dream job.

During a spirited argument with a colleague over the creative abstractness of the sound design of a picture on which we were working, he became flustered and suddenly blurted out, "Yewdall, you know what your problem is? You have a passion for what you do, and you think it makes a difference!"

I nodded. "You're right, I do have a passion for what I do, and I know it makes a difference."

The passion you have for your work will be a double-edged sword. It will energize you and empower you to stretch, to go that extra distance to create and achieve. Unfortunately, it will also lay you open and expose you to those who would ridicule and destroy rather than inspire and challenge. You cannot have one without the other. You must choose. Are you going to be a photocopy drone of a thousand others and mindlessly turn out formula products that everyone has seen and heard over and over again? Or are you going to stretch and do something new and different? Therein lies the challenge; therein lies the passion.

You will also notice that very often I posture ideas or examples in military terms. I do this for a good reason. Making a motion picture is almost identical to a military operation. No two films are the same—you must alter and adjust your tactics for the new material and problems that arise. Good filmmaking is 5 percent creativity and 95 percent problem solving. Keep this simple axiom in the forefront of your mind, and you will become a Navy Seal commando of your craft.

Chapter 2
Our Amateur Beginnings

When I was in junior high school, I had to stay home for several weeks because of a contagious illness. My father had an old office $\frac{1}{4}''$ audiotape machine with a simple omnidirectional microphone that was really only intended for recording close-proximity voices. In a matter of days I was swept into a fantasy world of writing and recording my own performances like the radio shows I had heard. I played all the parts, moving about the room to simulate perspective, making a wide variety of sound effects and movements to conjure up mental images of Detective Ajax as he sought out the bad dealings of John J. Ellis and his henchmen.

I opened and closed doors, shuffled papers, moved chairs about. My parents had an antique wood rocking chair that creaked when you sat in it. I ignited a firecracker to make gunshots and threw a canvas sack of potatoes on the floor for body falls. It wasn't until the recording tape broke, however, and I took up scissors and tape to splice it back together, that I got the shock of my life. After I repaired the break, I wondered if I could cut and move around prerecorded sounds at will. This could remove the unwanted movement sounds—trim the mistakes and better tighten up the sound effects. Years later I came to appreciate how the early craftspeople in the infancy of motion pictures must have felt when they first tried moving shots and cutting for effect rather than repair. The power of editing had sunk in.

Late at night I would crawl under the covers, hiding the audiotape machine under the blankets, and play the sequence over and over. Though I would be embarrassed by its crudeness today, it was the germination and the empowerment of sound and storytelling for me. Clearly I had made a greater audio illusion than I ever thought possible.

Several years later I joined the high school photography club. That was when I became visually oriented. The exciting homemade radio shows became just fond memories after I found a fateful $20 bill hidden in a roll-top desk at a thrift shop. I had been eyeing a black, plastic Eastman Kodak 8-mm spring-wind camera that could be ordered from the Sears catalog for $19.95. Guess how I spent the $20?

The camera had no lens, only a series of holes in a rotatable disk that acted as f-stops. The spring-wind motor lasted only 22 seconds, so I carefully had to plan how long the shots could be—but with it my life changed forever. The visual image now

Figure 2.1 Amateur high school film *The Nuremberg Affair*. Warren Wheymeyer and Chris Callow act as German soldiers in a firefight scene with French resistance fighters. (Photos by David Yewdall.)

moved, and with a little imagination I quickly made the camera do dozens of things I'm sure the designer and manufacturer never intended for it to do.

Later that year I was projecting some 8-mm film on the bedroom wall for some of my high school friends who had been a part of the wild and frenzied film shoot the previous weekend. We had performed the action on an ambitious scale, at least for small-town high school students. We shot an action film about the French Resistance ambushing a German patrol in a canyon, entitled *The Nuremberg Affair*. We carefully buried several pounds of black powder in numerous soft-drink cups around the narrow flatland between two canyon walls of a friend's California ranch, and a couple of dozen of us dressed in military uniforms.

A hulk of a car had been hauled up from the junkyard, a vehicle identical to the operating one serving as the stunt car. We carefully filmed a sequence that gave the illusion of a French Resistance mortar shell hitting the staff vehicle, blowing it up, and sending a dozen soldiers sprawling into the dirt and shrubs of the wash. In the next set-up, they rose and charged the camera. My special effects man, sitting just off-camera, ignited each soft-drink "mortar-cup" charge, sending a geyser of dirt and debris into the air. The high school stunt actors had fun as they jumped and flung themselves about, being invisibly ambushed by the off-screen French underground.

A week later we huddled together to watch the crudely edited sequence. It happened that my radio was sitting on my bedroom windowsill and a commercial for *The Guns of Navarone* burst forth. Action-combat sound effects and stirring music were playing while the segment of our amateur mortar attack flickered on the bedroom wall. Several of us reacted to the sudden sensation—the home movie suddenly came alive, as many of the sound effects seemed to work quite well with the visual action. That year I won an Eastman Kodak Teenage Award for *The Nuremberg Affair*. The bug had really bitten hard.

Up until that time, I had been making only silent films—with an eye toward the visual. Now my visual eye grew a pair of ears. Of course, sound did not just appear on the film from then on. We quickly learned that there seemed to be much more to sound than simply having the desire to include it as part of the performance package. It also did not help much that back in the 1960s no such thing existed as home video cameras with miniature microphones attached. Super-8-mm was offering a magnetic striped film, but any kind of additional sound editing and mixing were very crude and difficult.

We did make two amateur short films with a separate $\frac{1}{4}$" soundtrack. Of course no interlocking sync mechanism existed, and the only way to even come close was to use a $\frac{1}{4}$" tape recorder that had a sensitive pause switch. I would sit and carefully monitor the sound, and, as it started to run a little faster than the film being projected, I would give the machine little pauses every so often, helping the soundtrack jog closer to its intended sync. All of this seemed very amateurish and frustrating. Yet as difficult as non-interlocking sound gear was to deal with, it had become essential to have a soundtrack with the picture.

EARLY APPLICATIONS

My first real application of custom sound recording for public entertainment occurred when I was given the sound effects job for Coalinga's West Hills College presentation of the play *Picnic*. Sound effect records of the day were pretty dreadful, and only the audiophiles building their own Heathkit high-fidelity systems were interested more in authentic realism and speaker replication than in entertainment expression.

As you work increasingly in sound, you will quickly learn the difference between reality sound and entertainment sound. I can play you a recording of a rifle butt impacting the chin of a man's skull. It is an absolutely authentic recording, yet it sounds flat and lifeless. On the other hand, I can edit three carefully chosen sound cues together in parallel and play them as one, and I promise that you will cringe and double over in empathetic pain. Therein lies the essential difference between realism, which is an actual recording of an event, and a sound designer's version of the same event, a combination brew that evokes emotion and pathos.

I soon gave up trying to find prerecorded sound effects and set out to record my own. I did not know much about how to record good sound, but I was fortunate to have acquired a monaural Uher model 1000 $\frac{1}{4}$" tape deck that I used for my amateur

16-mm filmmaking. I talked a local policeman into driving his squad car out of town and, from a couple of miles out, drive toward me at a hasty rate of speed with his siren wailing away. I recorded doorbells and dogs barking, as well as evening cricket backgrounds. At that time I was not at all interested in pursuing a career in sound, and actually would not take it seriously for another 10 years, yet here I was practicing the basic techniques I still use today.

While making a documentary film about my hometown, we had gotten permission to blow up an oil derrick on Kettleman Hills. We had shot the sequence MOS (without sound) and decided later we needed an explosion sound effect. I did not know how to record an explosion, nor did I think the explosions we made for our films would sound very good; how they looked and how they sounded in reality were two entirely different things.

I decided to experiment. I discovered that by wrapping the microphone in a face towel and holding it right up next to my mouth I could mimic a concussionary explosion with my lips and tongue, forcing air through my clinched teeth. The audio illusion was magnificent!

A few years later a couple of friends and my father joined me in making a fundraising film for Calvin Crest, a Presbyterian church camp in the Sierra Nevada mountains. It was our first serious attempt at shooting synchronous sound while we filmed. We had built a homemade camera crane to replicate Hollywood-style sweeping camera moves in and among the pine trees. The 18-foot reach crane was made of wood and used precision ball-bearing pillow-blocks for rotation pivots.

We never actually had a synchronous motor on the camera, so during the postproduction editorial phase of the project I learned how to eyeball sync. I discovered that a non-sync motor means that the sound recording drifts. I painstakingly resynced the sound every few seconds as the drift increased. Becoming extremely observant, I looked for the slightest movement and identified the particular sounds that must have come from that movement. I then listened to the track, found such audible movements, and lined the sound and action into sync. Conversely, I learned to take sound with no synchronous relationship at all with the image that I had, and, through clever cuts and manipulation, made the sound work for moments when we had no original sound recording at all.

I am the first to admit how bizarre and out of place the camera set-up in Figure 2.2 appears. Most filmmakers starting out will tell you (especially if you have no money and must work "poor-boy" style) that you must learn how to mix and match various kinds of equipment together—to make do when money to rent modern camera and sound equipment is scarce. In the photo, I am standing just to the side of the lens of the 16-mm Arriflex as I am directing the action. My partner, Larry Yarbrough, is standing just behind me, coordinating the lighting and handling the audio playback of prerecorded dialog, as we did not record very much sync sound back then. Our actors listened to a prerecorded tape played back through a speaker off-screen as they mouthed the dialog, much the same way musicals are filmed to playback. Like I said, you have to make do with what you have. It certainly was not a convenient camera platform, but boy was it rock steady!

Of course, our soundtrack was crude by professional audio standards today, but for its day and for where I was on the evolutionary scale of experience, Calvin Crest

Figure 2.2 I'm standing just behind the lens of a 16-mm Arriflex sitting atop the giant 100 Moey gear head specially designed for the giant MGM 65-mm cameras. This particular gear head was one of the set used in William Wyler's *Ben-Hur*. (Photo by David Yewdall.)

had opened a multitude of doors and possibilities to develop different ideas because of new, empowering, creative tools then in hand. With what I had learned through the "baptism by fire" of doing, I could take a simple 35-mm combat Eymo camera with a spring-wind motor and an unremarkable $1/4$" tape recorder with absolutely no sound sync relationship between them and, if I had the will to do so, I could make a full-length motion picture with both perfectly synchronized sound, and depth and breadth of entertainment value. I was, and still am, limited only by my own imagination—just as you are.

INTERVIEW WITH BRUCE CAMPBELL

Bruce Campbell is probably best known and recognized both for his grizzly cult starring role in the *Evil Dead* trilogy as well as his title-starring role on the television series *The Adventures of Brisco County Jr.* When it comes to sound, Bruce is one of the most passionate and audio-involved actor-director-producers I have ever met and had the great pleasure to work alongside.

Bruce began making amateur movies with his high school buddies Sam Raimi (who went on to direct pictures like *Crimewave* and *Darkman*, as well as the cult classics *Evil Dead*, *Evil Dead 2*, and the ultimate sequel *Army of Darkness*) and Rob Tapert (producer of movies and television shows). They grew up just outside of Detroit, where they spent increasingly more time creating their first amateur efforts. Bruce remembers:

Figure 2.3 Bruce Campbell, cult star of the *Evil Dead* trilogy, star of *The Adventures of Brisco County Jr.*, and director and recurring guest star in the number one syndicated *Hercules: the Legendary Journeys* and *Xena: Warrior Princess*.

Originally, we worked with regular 8-mm film and a little wind-up camera. The film was 16-mm in width. You would shoot one side, which was 50 feet long, then flip the roll over and expose the other side. You sent it to the lab and they developed it and slit it in half for you.

Of course, we shot those films silent; at least, as we know and understand synchronous sound recording today. Our friend, Scott Spiegel, had a cassette recorder, and he had recorded our dialog as we shot the film. Of course, there was nothing like what we have today with crystal sync and timecode. We just recorded it to the cassette, and Scott would keep careful track of the various angles and takes and re-record/transfer them later as close as he could to the final-cut 8-mm film.

Scott would also record sound effects and backgrounds, many of them from television broadcasts of Three Stooges films. The nice thing about the Stooges was that they didn't have any music during the action scenes, just dialog and loud sound effects. Scott would have all the sound effects he intended to use lined up on one cassette tape like a radio man would set up his cue list and have his sound effect source material at the ready.

We would get in a room and watch the cut 8-mm picture, then Scott would roll the original dialog cassette, playing the sound through a speaker. Scott would play the second cassette of sound effects at precise moments in the action against the dialog cassette, and we would stand around and add extra dialog lines that we had not recorded when we shot the film to begin with. All this time, Scott was re-recording the collage of speaker playback sound and our new live dialog performances onto a new cassette in a crude but effective sound mix.

It was kind of like doing live radio as we were injecting sound effects, looping dialog and mixing it all at once, the difference being that we had to keep in sync to the picture. The real trick was Scott Spiegel mastering the pause button to keep on top of the sync issues.

Scott was the master of this so we let him do it. We had a vari-speed projector, and Scott had made marks on the edges of the film that only he could see during a presentation so that he could tell how out-of-sync the cassette playback was going to be; then he would adjust the projector a little faster or a little slower to correct the sync. Sometimes Scott would have to fast-forward or rewind the cassette real quick in order for the playback to be right. You could hear the on and off clicks in the track, but we didn't care—after all, we had sound!

We would test our films at parties. If [we] could get people to stop partying and watch the movie, then we knew we had a good one. We made about 50 of these short movies, both comedies and dramas.

Then we moved up to Super-8-mm, which had a magnetic sound stripe on it so you could record sound as you filmed the action. The quality of the sound was very poor by today's standards, but at the time it was a miracle! You could either send your Super-8 film out for sound striping (having a thin ribbon of magnetic emulsion applied to the edge of the film for the purposes of adding a soundtrack later), or you could buy Super-8 film with a magnetic sound stripe on it.

There were projectors that had sound-on-sound, where you had the ability for one attempt to dub something in over the soundtrack that was already on the film. Say the action in your Super-8-mm film has two guys acting out a shootout scene, and the first actor's line, "Stick 'em up!" was already on the film. Reacting to the first guy, the second actor turned, drew his pistol, and fired, which of course is a cap gun or a quarter-load blank. If you wanted a big sound effect for the gunshot, using the sound-on-sound technique, you would only have one chance to lay a gunshot in. If you did not record it in correctly or close enough sync, then you wiped out the actor's voice and you would have to then loop the actor saying "Stick 'em up!" all over again, which on Super-8-mm film was going to be extremely difficult at best.

On the original Super-8-mm projectors you could only record on the main magnetic stripe, but when the new generation of projectors came out you could record on the balance stripe [a thin layer of magnetic emulsion on the opposite side of the film from the primary magnetic soundtrack to maintain an even thickness for stability in film transport and being wound or rewound onto a film reel]. This allowed us to record music and sound effects much easier by utilizing the balance stripe as a second track instead of messing up the original recorded track that had been recorded in sync when we originally filmed the sequence.

Our postproduction supervisor was the lady behind the counter at K-Mart. She would see us coming and say, "Okay fellas, whad'ya got now?" Whether it was developing or sending our cut film back to have a new balance stripe applied to the edge so we could record a smoother music track, she was our lab.

Sam Raimi did a 50-minute film called *The Happy Valley Kid*, the story of a college student driven insane, that he shot on the Michigan State University campus with real professors and real students, and Rob Tapert portrayed the Happy Valley Kid. The film cost about $700 to make, and they showed it at midnight showings to students. The kids loved to see the film because they got to see *The Happy Valley Kid* blow away all the evil professors. Sam actually got the professors to allow themselves to be shot and gunned down on film. They made about $3,500 bucks on it—probably some of the best vicarious therapy that frustrated students could sit down and enjoy without going postal themselves.

We actually raised the money to make a movie based on a Super-8-mm film that we had shot as a pilot, as a device to show investors the kind of motion picture that we were going to make and convince them to invest money in us. Sam Raimi had been studying some occult history in humanities class when his prolific and overactive imagination gave him a middle-of-the-night vision. I personally think it stemmed from something he had eaten for dinner earlier in the evening, but a lot of Sam's subsequent script was based on the *Necronomicon* stuff that came up in class.

We made our best Super-8-mm double-system sound film yet. We had acquired much better sound effects, using a $1/4$" reel-to-reel deck whenever we could get our hands on one. We would carefully patch directly in from a stereo system so we could control the quality of the sound transfer for music or sound effects. By this time we had gotten much better about understanding recording levels, even the concept of distortion and how to avoid it as much as possible. By the time we raised the money to make the first *Evil Dead* film, we were much better prepared, at least knowing that we wanted a really good and interesting sound, and we knew that before we went out to film the picture.

When we finished cutting the picture of *Evil Dead* and we were ready for the post-production sound process, we went to Sound One in New York City with Elisha Birnbaum. We immediately discovered that, from an audio point-of-view, it was a whole new ball game and that we weren't in Kansas anymore. We had a lot of bones and blood and carnage in the film, so Sam and I would go to a market and we would buy chickens and celery and carrots and meat cleavers and that sort of stuff to use for recording. Elisha was a one-man show. He would roll the picture, then run in and perform Foley cues on the stage; then he would run back into the back booth to stop the system.

Our supervising sound editor was Joe Masefield. Joe was extremely detail oriented. Each sound effect had a number, based on the reel it belonged to, whether it was a cue of Foley or a sound effect or dialog or whatever. He sat there in the recording booth and told us what we needed to perform. For Sam and me, we were still kind of lagging from our amateur days of how to make sounds because we would argue who could make the best gravy-sucking sound and who would twist and cut the celery while the other guy was making awful slurping noises. We heard later that it took weeks for them to get the smell of rotting cabbage and chicken out of their Foley stage.

Mel Zelniker was the mixer. He was really good for us, as he brought us up out of our amateur beginnings and helped to point us into a more professional way of doing things. Mel would teach us stage protocol and procedure through example. Sam stepped off the stage for a drink of water and returned just as Mel mixed the sound of a body being flopped into a grave. Sam asked Mel if he could mix the body fall a little hotter. Mel played the game of not touching the fader pot to see if we noticed—you know, the way mixers can do. It was so embarrassing because then he would ask Sam what he thought after he supposedly mixed it hotter, and Sam would say he liked it, and Mel would huff and reply, "I didn't touch it."

Then Mel would run it again, only this time he would push the volume until it was obviously over the top. He'd ask us, "How was that?" We'd nod our heads, 'That was fine, just fine.' Mel snapped back at us, "It's too loud!," and he would run it again and bring the volume back down. Mel knew we were a couple of hicks from Detroit, but in his own way he was trying to teach us at the same time.

At one point I asked him if he could lower one of my loop lines. Mel turned on me, "What's the matter, you embarrassed?!" I didn't know what to say. "Yeah, I am actually." Mel shrugged, "Okay, I just wanted to clear that up," and he would continue mixing. He would mix one long pass at a time, and we actually got a weird effect out of it. Their equipment had an odd, funky problem with one of the fader pots; it left an open chamber, which created a strange airy-like sound that, if he just moved that pot up a little, created the best eerie ambience for us. It was not a wind; it was almost like you were in a hollow room. That was our gift. Every so often either Sam or I would say, "Hey, stick that ambience in there!" Mel would frown, "You guys! You're usin' it too much!"

It wasn't until after the mix that Mel and his engineer discovered that a rotating fan motor vibration was being conducted through hard point contact that was leaking into the echo chamber, a clever technique that Mel quietly tucked away for future use. For our first real movie we got several gifts. Another one happened in the middle of the night when we were shooting the film in Tennessee. Sam was awakened by a ghostly wind that was coming through the broken glass window in his room. He ran down the hall and dragged the sound guy out of bed to fire up the Nagra to record it. That airy tonal wind became the signature for the film. The fact is, there are gifts around you all of the time, whether you are shooting or not—the trick is for you to recognize the gifts when they happen and be versatile enough to take advantage of them. That's when the magic really happens.

Several years later, the trio made the sequel, *Evil Dead 2*. It was their first opportunity to work with the sound in a way that they could prebuild entire segments before they got to the rerecording dubbing stage. They had progressed from the Moviola, where their sound had been cut on 35 mm mag stripe and fullcoat to 24 track using videotape and timecode to interlock the sync between picture (on videotape) and soundtrack (being assembled on 24-track 2" tape). Bruce Campbell not only reprised his character of Ash from the original *Evil Dead*, but he also handled the postproduction sound chores. He started by insisting on walking his own footsteps in the film, and one thing led to another. The attention to detail became an obsession.

We cut the picture for *Evil Dead 2* in Ferndale, Michigan, in a dentist's office. I asked the manager of the building to give me one of the offices for a month that was in the center of the building, not near the front and not near the back. I didn't want to contend with traffic noise. We got the deepest part of an office that was well insulated by the old building's thick walls. I asked a sound engineer by the name of Ed Wolfman, who I would describe in radio terms as a tonemeister, a German term for a master craftsperson mixer or recordist, to come look at this huge plaster room we had. I told him that I wanted to record wild sound effects in this room, and how could I best go about utilizing the space acoustically?

We built a wooden section of the floor, then built a downscaled replica of the original cabin set from the film. We needed the floor to replicate the correct hollowness that we had from the original cabin because we had a lot of scuffling, props falling, footsteps—a lot of movement that would have to fold seamlessly into the production recording. Ed told us to build one of the walls nonsymmetrical—angle it off 10 percent, 20 percent—so we put in a dummy wall that angled in, so that the sound would not reflect back and forth and build up slap and reverb. We did the foam-and-egg-carton routine by attaching them in regimented sheets around on sections of the wall for trapping and controlling sound waves.

While Sam [Raimi] was in a different part of the office building picture-cutting the film, I cranked up my word processor and built an audio event list—a chronological list of sounds that were going to be needed for the picture that we could replicate in our downsized cabin stage and custom record them. I guess you would consider this wild Foley. These sound cues were not performed while we watched picture or anything. We would review the list and see "things rattle on a table." Okay, let's record a bunch of things rattling on a table, and we'll record a number of variations. "Table falls over"—we recorded several variations of a table falling over, etc.

This one office of the dentist building had water damage from the radiators, and we thought, "Let's help 'em out just a little bit more." So I took an axe and recorded some really good chops and scrapes. It is so hard to find that kind of material in just that kind of condition to record. It was so crunchy, and it had these old dried wood slats from the 1920s—it was perfectly brittle. One little chop led to another. "Keep that recorder rolling!" I'd swing the axe, smashing and bashing. I felt guilty about what I was doing to the ceiling, but the recordings were priceless. It is just impossible to simulate that kind of sound any other way!

What resulted was Bruce and Sam returning to Los Angeles for formal postproduction sound-editorial work with a wealth of custom-recorded material under their arms, meticulously developed over weeks of study and experimentation.

Bruce Campbell continued his acting and directing career in the states and abroad, spending much of his time in New Zealand, writing, directing, and even appearing in the *Xena* and *Hercules* television series, as well as developing theatrical motion picture projects of his own.

Bruce admits that sound has had a tremendous effect on his professional career. It has made him a better storyteller as well as a more creative filmmaker, but he admits he misses having the luxury of the hands-on participation in custom recording and developing soundtracks. Listen to the *Xena* and *Hercules* television shows. The roots of their sound design go all the way back to those early days in Detroit when Bruce and his friends struggled not only to keep an audio track in sync with the visual image but also to create something extraordinary.

DEVELOP YOUR EYES AND EARS TO OBSERVE

I do not mean for this to sound egotistical or pompous, but, shortly after you finish reading this book, most of you will notice that you see and hear things differently than ever before. The fact is, you have always seen and heard them—you have just not been as aware of them as you now are going to become. This transition does not happen all at once. It does not go "flomp" like a heavy curtain—and suddenly you have visual and audio awareness. You probably will not be aware the change is taking place, but, several weeks or a few months from now, you will suddenly stop and recognize that your sensory perceptions have been changing. Some of you will thank me—others will curse me. Some people become so aware that they find it incredibly hard to watch movies or television again. This is a common side effect. It is really nothing more than your awareness kicking in, along with a growing knowledge of how things work. Be comforted to know that this hyperawareness appears to wear off over time. In fact, it actually does not.

Your subconscious learns to separate awareness of technique and disciplines from the assimilation of form and storytelling, the division between left-brain and right-brain jurisdictions. Regardless of whether you are aware of it, you learn how to watch a motion picture or television program and to disregard its warts and imperfections. If you did not learn this ability, you probably would be driven to the point of insanity (of course, that might explain a few things in our industry these days).

As for myself, I remember the exact moment the figurative light bulb went on for me. I was sitting in my folks' camper, parked amid the tall redwood trees near the Russian River in northern California, reading Spottiswood's book *Film and Its Techniques*. I was slowly making my way through the chapter dealing with the film synchronizer and how film is synced together when kapow!—suddenly everything I had read before, most of which I was struggling to understand conceptually, suddenly came together and made perfect sense. Those of you who have gone through this transition, this piercing of the concept membrane, know exactly to what I'm referring. Those of you who have not experienced it are in for a wonderful moment filled with a special excitement.

PROTECT YOUR MOST PRECIOUS POSSESSIONS

The world has become a combat zone for one of your most precious possessions: your ability to hear. During everyday activities, you are constantly in close proximity with audio sources with the potential to permanently impair your future ability to hear. Unfortunately, you probably give none of these sources a passing consideration.

If you hope to continue to see and hear the world around you clearly for a long time, then let go of any naive misperception that those senses will always, perfectly, be with you. This book does not address the everyday dangers and potentially harmful situations regarding loss of or impairment to your eyesight because it was not written with authority on that topic. As for protecting your ability to hear clearly, one of the most common and sensory-damaging dangers is distortion. This is not the same as volume. Your ears can handle a considerable amount of clearly produced volume; however, if the audio source is filled with distortion, the human ear soon fatigues and starts to degenerate. A common source of distortion is the device known as the "boom box." Car radios are another source of overdriven audio sources, played through underqualified amplifiers and reproduced by speakers setting up a much higher distortion noise to clear signal ratio, which begins to break down the sensitivity of your audio sensors.

In other scenario, you attend a rock concert. After a few minutes, you start to feel buzzing or tingling in your ears. This is the first sign that your ears have become overloaded and are in danger of suffering permanent and irreparable damage.

The audio signal in question does not have to be loud, however. Many television engineers and craftspeople who work in close proximity to a bank of television monitors for long periods of time discover that they have either lost or are losing their high-end sensitivity. Many of these individuals cannot hear higher than 10-kHz.

Sometimes I had groups of students from either a high school or college come to the studio to tour the facility and receive an audio demonstration. During the demos, I would put a specially made test-tone tape on a DAT machine and play a 1-kHz tone, which everyone could hear. They would see signal register accordingly on the VU meter. I would then play them 17-kHz. Only about half could hear that, but they could all see the signal on the VU meter. I would then play them 10-kHz with the same strength on the VU meter. By this time, several students inevitably would be in tears; they had lost the ability to hear a 10-kHz tone so early in life.

After asking one or two poignant questions regarding their daily habits of audio exposure, I knew the exact culprit. Almost no demonstration strikes home more dramatically than this, forcing a personal self-awareness and disallowing denial. The students could fib to me about whether they could hear the signal, but they themselves knew they could not hear it; the proof was in front of them, the visual affirmation of the strong and stable volume on the VU meter for all to see. I plead with you, before it is too late. Become aware of the dangers that surround you every day, understand what audio fatigue is, realize that length of duration to high decibels and audio distortion results in permanent hearing loss, either select frequency or total.

Someone asked me once, "If you had to choose between being blind or deaf, which would you choose?" I did not hesitate; I chose blind. As visual a person as I am, I could not imagine living in a world where I could not enjoy the sweet vibrant sound of the cello, or the wind as it moves through the pine trees with the blue jays and morning doves, or the sensual caress of the whispered words from my wife as we cuddle together and share the day's events. So protect your most precious of personal possessions—your eyes and ears.

Chapter 3
The Passing of a Tradition and Coming of Age

In the professional world of sound award achievements for film and television, the three standards are the Golden Reel Awards (Motion Picture Sound Editors Society), the Emmy (the Academy of Television Arts and Sciences), and of course the most coveted of all, the Academy Award (the Academy of Motion Picture Arts and Sciences). While the Golden Reel and the Emmy give numerous awards each year for sound for many aspects and many categories, there is only one Academy Award each year for Best Sound Editing and for Best Sound Mixing.

THE PASSING OF A TRADITION

For a quarter of a century, we had a very unique and somewhat peculiar practice of getting together on the first Tuesday of February, which was changed in the last few years to late January when the Academy Award ceremonies were moved up. We would enter the smoked-glass doors of the masonry building at Wilshire Boulevard and Almont in Los Angeles, the headquarters of the Academy of Motion Picture Arts and Sciences. The top sound craftspeople in the motion-picture industry gather, members of the Sound Branch of the Academy as well as several hundred associate observers and guests, to review those films competing for the honor of being nominated for the Academy Award for Best Sound Effect Editing, which was changed to Best Sound Editing in 2000. Only the Sound Branch Academy members are allowed to vote for the final nominations during the "bake-off" screening procedure.

Six weeks prior, the sound editor members of the Sound Branch voted by written ballot for five of their top choices from that year's nearly 400 qualifying motion pictures. Those ballots had been mailed to PricewaterhouseCoopers, at which point the seven semifinalists had been determined: those garnishing the highest number of votes by their first-through-fifth-choice ranking. Over the last few weeks, the producers of the "anxious seven" had been notified so that they could prepare a sample reel for the first Tuesday evening in February—an event affectionately known as the "bake-off," a term coined by Richard Anderson, supervising sound editor and co-sharer of the Academy Award for Best Sound Effects Editing in 1981 (along with Ben Burtt for the action-adventure sensation *Raiders of the Lost Ark*).

The sample reel would contain actual clips from the release print of the picture. The soundtrack could not be enhanced, remixed, or reprinted: it must be identical to what was exhibited in the theatres. The task of choosing the clips that comprised the allotted 10 minutes in the "bake-off" was left to the supervising sound editor, as it was he or she who honchoed the preparation of the soundtrack for the re-recording mixing stage in the first place.

In the lobby, representatives from PricewaterhouseCoopers checked off the names of the voting Sound Branch members as they stepped up to identify themselves. One representative checked the names on the list as the other representative issued each voter a ballot, each assigned with a designated number for identification. The members were also given an information sheet regarding the seven pertinent feature films.

The voters headed up the staircase to the legendary Academy's Samuel Goldwyn Theater on the second floor to see and schmooze with hundreds of colleagues, many of whom have not been seen since the sound "bake-off" the previous year. The center quadrant of seats were roped off and reserved for the award-nominating committee members, so that they could listen to and judge the sound presentation of each sample reel in the acoustically ideal section.

As everybody settled down at the appointed hour, the chairman of the Sound Effects Editing Award Rules Committee would step up to the podium to review the year's rules as well as to lend a personal word of wisdom to those of us about to sit in judgment of our fellow craftspeople. This forum was not supposed to be about politics, although politics definitely deals a few wildcards from time to time. Additionally, this forum was not supposed to be about personalities, about who we liked or disliked as individuals, although there were times that it was a challenge to separate one's personal feelings and biases from the task at hand. I gazed up to see the two massive statues of Oscar on either side of the huge screen, reverently standing vigil over the presentation—here in the greatest of all theatres in the world, and I knew that as an Academy member I needed to put aside politics and personal favor. We are there not only to judge our colleagues but also to celebrate our art form and to be challenged throughout the coming year to raise our professional standards and artistic achievements accordingly.

During a lighter moment, the chairman poked a jab at the ever-rising volume of motion-picture soundtracks as he thanked all the sound craftspeople over at Warner Brothers (some 14 miles away) who could not be here tonight, but who would hear the playback of the sample reels anyway.

After 70 minutes of high-octane audio playback from SDDS, DTS, and Dolby SR-D mastered soundtracks, the audience experienced a good dose of audio fatigue. If ever there was a litmus test for considering the responsibility to monitor more reasonable volume levels, especially through sustained sequences that truly leave your ears ringing, those "bake-off" evenings were excellent reminders. Just because sound is mixed loud does not mean that it sounds better. Just because digital and the new achievements in speaker design and amplifier clarity allow sound to be brought into the theatre at ever-increasing decibel levels does not mean that it should be done.

As you read this book, consider well the power of silence. Years ago, when I walked onto Stage D at Goldwyn for the rerecording process of *Escape From New York*, Bill Varney, the lead mixer, turned and announced to everyone that we were going to build dynamics into the mix. We all agreed enthusiastically. Of course, at the time I did not have a clue what he meant or what he was talking about, but over the next four years and 11 pictures for which I supervised the sound editorial that mixed on Stage D, I came to learn and appreciate exactly what Bill meant.

One must bring the soundtrack down; the levels should be lowered and relaxed between the high-energy action peaks. Not only does this give the audience a chance to recover from the strength and power of the action sequences, but coming down also allows the sound to go back up again. The power and volume "appear" bigger and louder than they really are if time is taken to come down and the audience's ears are allowed to rest.

If the soundtrack constantly is active and loud, the sound has nowhere to go when it must go up for the action moments. It is exactly like riding a roller coaster: you cannot enjoy the thrill of the high-drop runs unless you have come down to the bottom, paused, and anticipated the climb back up to the top again. A great classical composer also understood this principle extremely well. Beethoven, the master of mood and drama, composed a passage with notations of adagio or largo with a pianissimo delicacy, followed by a sudden explosion of power and glory at double fortissimo with a presto urgency. Those who have listened to Beethoven's legendary "Moonlight Sonata" probably only know its melodious and moody opening movement. Those who have played this seemingly passive piece on the piano, however, surely understand my point when they dash through the third movement! Seldom are the strength and precise dexterity of the pianist's hands and fingers more greatly challenged.

So, too, the motion-picture soundtrack. While conceptualizing, designing, and executing a final soundtrack of dialog, music, and sound effects into one interwoven yet fluid and continuous audio event, the entire team of audio craftspeople does well to think in terms of dynamics—the entire roller-coaster ride.

Unfortunately, the entire sound team can design and execute the most amazing soundtrack ever, but if the director and producer do not understand the philosophy of dynamics and audio dramatization, then all the skill and efforts of the entire sound collaboration are for naught. Dynamics. It seems so obvious, so simple and basic, yet so many filmmakers fall into this trap. I discuss this and other audio philosophies more closely throughout this book, especially in Chapter 20—but you might be wondering why I took this moment to bring up the philosophy of dynamics at this time, in this chapter.

As the chairman finished his review of the rules and regulations and his duty of describing how the theatre speakers had been carefully swept and balanced for the evening's presentation, we sat and thought about literally thousands of the world's foremost theatrical sound craftspeople, most of whom are unsung heroes, who made it possible for the supervising sound editor to step to the podium on Academy Award night and accept the golden statuette for Best Sound Editing.

How many production sound mixers, boom operators, cable men, audio engineers, sound effects and dialog editors, sound assistants, sound designers, sound librarians, equipment and acoustical engineers, ADR and Foley mixers and recordists, Foley artists, Walla Group and vocal mimic performers, and many others had literally wrapped their work in an embryonic envelope of this left, center, right, and split surround-sound experience? How many long and overworked hours went into moments of the picture that we probably never fully appreciated?

The lights of the theatre dimmed as the first sample reel was about to be projected. I glanced up to one of the giant statues of Oscar. He has stood vigilant for many years, holding his golden sword as he watches over the audience. I can almost imagine he was looking at me. His smooth face has an almost omnipotent presence, silently reminding me to put any personal tendentious susceptibilities aside and to view these seven presentation reels with an objectivity worthy of the fair and idealistic judgment that Oscar represents.

THE PROCESS HAS EVOLVED

In the summer of 2006, the Academy made a major change in how the Best Sound Editing awards would be considered and voted. In many respects, they reflect most of the other disciplines, such as Best Cinematography, Best Director, Best Actor, and so on.

The tradition of gathering at the Samuel Goldwyn Theatre and reviewing the seven semi-finalists came to an end. On the one hand, it was a sad decision. Many of us had enjoyed seeing each other—in fact, many of us only saw each other annually there. However, it was time to evolve and find ways to make the process more in step with how the other disciplines were doing it—and hopefully making it a fairer and more open proposition. One of the drawbacks of the "bake-off" is that most Sound Branch members who did not live in the Los Angeles area found it very difficult to attend.

Now we will be voting for our five top choices on a mailed ballot sent out right after Christmas. The Sound Branch members will list their top choices and mail their ballot back, from which PricewaterhouseCoopers will add up the votes and the top five vote pictures will become the five nominations that will appear on the final ballot that PricewaterhouseCoopers will send out to all voting Academy members for the final vote.

This will simplify the process; it will bring more Sound Branch members who not only do not live in and around L.A. but live abroad to have an equal say, deemphasizing the L.A.-based advantage which the "bake-off" could not help but encourage. Even though I will miss the getting together, the camaraderie, the catching up on the year with others, I personally feel that the change will be healthy for the art form and open up more craftspeople throughout the world in the process. I am often asked exactly how this process works and why certain individuals are considered. The following is the exact extract from the rules and regulations of the Academy.

2006—Special Rules for the Sound Editing Award
1. A reminder list of all eligible productions shall be sent with a ballot to all members of the Academy Sound Branch who shall vote in the order of their preference for not more than five productions.

2. The five productions receiving the highest number of votes shall become the nominations for final voting for the Sound Editing Award.
3. Eligibility for this award shall be limited to the Supervising Sound Editor directly involved in and primarily responsible for the planning, creation, direction and execution of the sound design and editing for each achievement. The Supervising Sound Editor must be the primary creative decision maker and principal interpreter of the director's vision to the sound editing team. The Supervising Sound Editor must approve the sound effects and their specific placement in the film, coordinate the creation of newly designed sound and Foley effects and the editing of dialogue and ADR. The Supervising Sound Editor must oversee the recording of the pre-dubs and be present to supervise the final mix. In the event the above responsibilities are divided, both co-supervisors must adhere to the above criteria.
4. Nomination eligibility of the Supervising Sound Editor responsible for the achievement shall be determined by the Sound Editing Award Rules Committee.
5. Final voting for the Sound Editing Award shall be restricted to active and life Academy members.

Special Rules for the Sound Mixing Award
1. A reminder list of all eligible pictures shall be sent with a nominations ballot to all members of the Academy Sound Branch who shall vote in the order of their preference for not more than five productions.
2. The five productions receiving the highest number of votes shall become the nominations for final voting for the Sound Mixing Award.
3. The talents of the rerecording mixers on a panel (not to exceed three) and the production mixer will be judged as contributing equally to a sound track achievement. On an Official Data Record supplied by the Academy, the producer and the sound director shall designate the eligibility of the co-rerecording mixing collaborators (not to exceed three) **who have contributed substantially to the final mix**, and the production mixer (not to exceed one) for Academy Award purposes.
4. In the event of a credits dispute, the nomination eligibility for the Sound Mixing Award shall be determined by the Sound Branch Executive Committee.
5. Following a review of the Official Data Records, determination of nomination eligibility shall be the responsibility of the Academy, as provided in General Rule Two.
6. The Theater Sound Inspection Committee shall inspect and approve the projection sound systems of the Academy's theaters at least one week prior to the annual screening of nominated achievements. No changes may be made in the sound systems after final approval by the committee. Any production that deviates from the normal sound system, or requires modification of the system, must be approved by a majority of the committee before the final check of the system. Notification of such deviation or modification requirements must be submitted to the Academy at least three weeks in advance of the inspection and approval of the sound system. Any composite release print that plays on

the normal projection sound system of the Academy's theaters requires no special approval of the committee.

7. Before screening films nominated for the Sound Mixing Award, representatives of the pictures to be shown may run **a maximum of one A/B reel** of their pictures to **audition them**. At the actual screenings, **films will be run at the Academy Standard sound level**.

8. Final voting for the Sound Mixing Award shall be restricted to active and life Academy members.

BUT HOW DID THEY GET HERE?

But how did these soundtracks get here? How did they survive the challenges and often stormy path to fruition? Let us go back, all the way back, even before the cameras start to roll. It all begins with the vision and dedication to achieve a work of audio art, an acoustical experience that stays with the audience. It starts with careful and realistic planning—a plan for success.

Chapter 4
Success or Failure
Before the Camera Even Rolls

*"If you prep it wrong, you could find yourself
in a win-win-lose situation."*

The success or disappointment of your final soundtrack is decided by you, before the cameras even roll, even before you commence preproduction!

The above 22 words constitute perhaps the single most important truth in this book. It is so important that I want you to read it again. The success or disappointment of your final soundtrack is decided by you, before the cameras even roll, even before you commence preproduction!

You not only must hire a good production sound mixer along with a supreme boom person, you must know the pitfalls and traditional clash of production's form and function to "get it in the can" and on its way to the cutting room. You must know how to convey the parameters and needs to the nonsound departments, which have such a major impact on the ability of the sound-recording team to capture a great production dialog track. If you do not allow enough money in the lighting budget to rent enough cable, you do not get the generators far enough away from the set, resulting in continuous intrusion of background generator noise. This isn't so bad if you are filming in bustling city streets, but it certainly does not bode well if you are filming medieval knights and fair maidens prancing around in a Middle Ages atmosphere. Regardless of the period or setting of the film, unwanted ambient noises only intrude on the magic of production performances.

In addition, you must know about the dangers and intrusions of cellular phones and radio-control equipment when working with wireless microphones. You must know how to budget for multiple microphone set-ups using multiple boom persons and multiple cameras. You must understand the ramifications of inclement weather and the daily cycle of atmospheric inversions that can cause unpredictable wind-buffet problems during an exterior shoot.

Figure 4.1 Sound boom operators must get into the middle of any action being created on the screen: from hurricane-driven rain, to car-chase sequences, to dangerously moving equipment. Here, two boom operators bundle up on padded-boy wraps, gauntlets, and machinist masks to protect themselves from flying bits of rock and debris, while still striving to capture the best microphone placement possible. (Photo by Ulla-Maija Parikka.)

With today's advancements in wind-control devices and numerous new mounts and shock absorbers, production mixers capture recordings with greater clarity and dynamic range than ever before, but they can't do it alone. Such a recording equipment package does not come free, included in the daily rate of the craftsperson. You must allow enough money in the equipment rental package, whether it is rented from an audio facility or whether it is the property of the sound person utilizing his or her own gear.

It is important that you consult with your director of photography. After careful consideration of the photographic challenges you must overcome, you will soon know what kinds of cameras you should rent. Three unblimped Arri-III cameras grinding away as they shoot the coverage of three men lounging in a steam room speaking their lines pose some awful sound problems—that is, if you hope to have a production track to use in the final mix! The motors of three unblimped cameras reverberating off hard tile walls will not yield a usable soundtrack. Do you throw up your hands and tell the sound mixer to just get a guide-track, conceding that you will have to loop it later in postproduction? You can, but why should you?

Of all the films I contracted and supervised, I only remember three pictures where I was brought in before the producer commenced preproduction to advise and counsel during the budgeting and tactical planning, the desired result being a successful final track.

John Carpenter set me as the supervising sound editor for *The Thing* a year before he started shooting. I helped advise and consult with both John and his production mixer, Tommy Causey, before they even left for Alaska, where they shot the "Antarctica" location sequences. By this time, I had already done two of John's pictures, on both of which Tommy had served as production mixer. Tommy used to ask if we could get together for coffee and discuss the upcoming shoot. It gave me a great opportunity to ask him to record certain wild tracks while he was there. He would tell me how he intended to cover the action and what kinds of microphones he intended to use. It never failed that after the cast and crew screening Tommy would always tell me that he really appreciated the coffee and conversation, as he would not have thought of something that I had added or that I said something that stimulated his thinking, which led to ingenious problem solving.

While John and his team shot up north in the snow, I saw dailies at Universal and went out into the countryside on custom-recording stints to begin developing the inventory of specialty sounds that were needed, months before sound teams were usually brought onto a picture. This preparation and creative foreplay gave us the extra edge in making an exciting and memorable soundtrack. (Oddly enough, the bone-chilling winds of *The Thing* were actually recorded in hot desert country a few miles northwest of Palm Springs.) To this day, I have been hired for other film projects because I did the sound for *The Thing*.

A couple years later, Lawrence Kubik and Terry Leonard sat down with us before they commenced preproduction on their action-packed anti-terrorist picture *Death Before Dishonor*. They needed the kind of sound of *Raiders of the Lost Ark*, but on a very tight budget. Intrigued by the challenge to achieve a soundtrack under such tight restrictions, coupled with Terry Leonard's reputation for bringing to the screen some of the most exciting action sequences captured on film today—sequences that always allowed a creative sound designer to really show off—I decided to take it on.

To avert any misunderstandings (and especially any convenient memory loss months later, during postproduction), we insisted that the sound-mixing facility be located where we would ultimately re-record the final soundtrack. We further insisted that the final re-recording mixers be set and that all personnel with any kind of financial, tactical, or logistical impact on the sound process for which I was being held singularly responsible meet with me and my team, along with the film's producers. Using a felt-tip marker and big sheets of paper pinned to the wall, we charted out a battle plan for success.

Because we could not afford to waste precious budget dollars, we focused on what the production recording team must come back with from location. We gave the producers a wish list of sounds to record in addition to the style of production recording. Because of certain sequences in the script where we knew the dialog would later be looped in postproduction for talent and/or performance reasons, we suggested they merely record a guide-track of the talent speaking their lines for those specific sequences. The production sound mixer should concentrate on the nearly impossible production sound effect actions taking place in nearly every action set-up, getting the actors to speak their lines as individual wild tracks whenever he could.

Hundreds of valuable cues of audio track came back, authentic to the Middle Eastern setting and precisely accurate to the action. This saved thousands of dollars of postproduction sound redevelopment work, allowing the sound-design chores for high-profile needs, rather than track building from scratch.

Because we could not afford nearly as much Foley stage time as would have been preferred, we all agreed as to what kind of Foley cues we would key on and what kind of Foley we would not detail but could handle as hard-cut effects. We placed the few dollars they had at the heart of the audio experience. This included making the producers select and contract with the re-recording facility and involving the re-recording mixers and facility executive staff in the planning and decision-making process. Each mixer listened to and signed off on the style and procedure of how we would mount the sound job, starting with the production recordings through to delivering the final-cut units to the stage to be mixed into a final track. We charted out the precise number of days, sometimes even to the hour, that would be devoted to individual processes. Also, we set an exact limit to the number of channels that would be used to perform the Foley cues, which mathematically yielded a precise amount of 35-mm stripe stock to be consumed. With this information, we confidently built in cap guarantees not to be exceeded, which in turn built comfort levels for the producers.

We laid out what kind of predubbing strategy would be expected, complete and proper coverage without undue separations, specifying a precise number of 35-mm fullcoats needed for each pass.

Mathematically and tactically, both the facility budget and dubbing schedule unfolded forthwith. It was up to us to do our part, but we could not, and would not be able to, guarantee that we could accomplish the mission unless everyone along the way agreed and signed off to his or her own contribution and performance warranty as outlined by the various teams involved. Everyone agreed, and 14 months later the Cary Grant Theatre at MGM rocked with a glorious acoustical experience, made possible by the thorough collaboration of problem-solving professionals able to lead the producers and director into the sound mix of their dreams.

In a completely different situation, I handled the sound-editorial chores on a South-Central action picture. We had not been part of any preplanning process, nor had we any say on style and procedure. As with most jobs, my sound team and I were brought onboard as an afterthought, only as the completion of picture editorial neared. We inherited a production track that was poorly recorded, with a great deal of hiss, without thought of wild-track coverage. To further aggravate the problem, the producer did not take our advice and loop what was considered to be a minimum requirement to reconstruct the track. The excuse was that the money was not in the budget for that much ADR. (This is a typical statement, heard quite often, almost always followed several months later by a much greater expenditure than would have been needed had the producers listened to and taken the advice of the supervising sound editor.)

The producer walked onto Stage 2 of Ryder Sound as we commenced rehearsing for a final pass of reel 1. He listened a moment, then turned and asked, "Why are the sound effects so hissy?" The effects mixer cringed, as he was sure I would pop my cork, but I smiled and calmly turned to the head mixer (who incidentally had just recently won an Academy Award for Best Sound). "Could you mute the dialog predub please?" I asked.

"Sure," he replied as his agile fingers flicked the mute button. The entire dialog predub vanished from the speakers. Now the music and sound effects played fully and pristinely, devoid of any hiss or other audio blemishes. The producer nodded approval, then noticed the absence of dialog from the flapping lips. "What happened to the dialog track?"

I gestured to the head mixer once more. "Could you please unmute the dialog predub?"

He flipped off the mute button, and the dialog returned, along with the obnoxious hiss. The producer stood silently, listening intently, then realized. "Oh, the hiss is in the dialog tracks." He turned to the head mixer. "Can you fix that?"

The mixer glanced up at him, expressionless. "That *is* fixed."

This made for more than one inevitable return to the ADR stage as we replaced increasingly more dialog cues—dialog we had counseled the producer to let us ADR weeks earlier. Additionally, more time was needed to remix and update numerous sequences. This experience did much to chisel a permanent understanding between producer and sound supervisor—and a commitment not to repeat such a fiasco on future films. Much to my surprise, the producer called me in for his next picture, which was a vast improvement; but it wasn't until the following picture that the producer and I bonded and truly collaborated in mounting a supreme action soundtrack.

The producer called me in as he was finishing the budget. "Okay, Yewdall, you keep busting my chops every time we do a picture together, so this time you are in it alongside me. No excuses!"

He made it clear that he wanted a giant soundtrack, but did not have a giant budget. After listening to him explain all about the production special-effects work to be done on the set, I told him that we should only record a guide-track. We decided that we would ultimately ADR every syllable in the picture. It would not only give us a chance to concentrate on diction, delivery, and acting at a later time, but also it would eliminate the continual ambience from the center speaker, which often subdues stereophonic dynamics, allowing us to design a much bigger soundtrack. In fact, the final mix was so alive and full that clients viewing dailies in the laboratory's screening facility were said to have rushed out of the theatre and out the back door, convinced a terrorist takeover was in progress. To this day, the producer calls that picture his monster soundtrack—and rightfully so.

UNDERSTANDING THE ART FORM OF SOUND

First, you must know the techniques available to you; many filmmakers today do *not*. They don't have a background in the technical disciplines; hence, they have no knowledge of what is possible or how to realize the vision trapped inside their heads. This stifles their ability to articulate to their department heads clear meaningful guidance, so they suffocate their craftspeople in abstract terminology that makes for so much artsy-sounding double-talk. They use excuse terms like "Oh, we'll loop it later" or "We'll fix it in post" or, the one I really detest, "We'll fix it when we mix it." These are, more often than not, lazy excuses that really say "I don't know how to handle this" or "Oops, we didn't consider that" or "This isn't important to me right now."

Sometimes you must step back, take a moment, and do everything you can do to capture a pristine dialog recording. The vast majority of filmmakers will tell you

Figure 4.2 Pekka Parikka, director of *Talvisota: The Winter War*, goes over the sound design concepts with Paul Jurälä, the production sound recordist, co-supervising sound editor, and rerecording mixer. Precise planning is vital when working on a *very* tight budget. (Photo by Ulla-Maija Parikka.)

they demand as much of the original recording as possible; they want the magic of the moment. Many times you know that post-sound can and will handle the moment as well if not better than a live recording, so you either shoot MOS (without sound) or you stick a microphone in there to get a guide-track. You must know your options.

THE "COLLATERAL" TERROR LURKS AT EVERY TURN

If you are making an independent film, you must have a firm grip on understanding the process and costs involved, both direct and collateral. Most production accountants can recite the direct costs like the litany of doctrine, but few understand the process well enough to judge the collateral impact and monetary waste beyond the budget line items.

For example, on an animated feature, the postproduction supervisor had called around to get price quotes from sound facilities to layback our completed Pro Tools sessions to 24-track tape. The postproduction supervisor had chosen a facility across town because its rate was the lowest and it did a lot of animation there. When making the inquiry, he had been given a very low rate and had been told that the average time to transfer a reel to 24-track was no more than 30 minutes.

The postproduction supervisor was delighted, and on his scratchpad he scribbled the hourly rate, divided it in half, multiplied it by 4 (the number of reels in the show), and then by 3 (the number of 24-track tapes the supervising sound editor estimated would be needed). That was the extent of the diligence when the decision was made to use this particular facility to do the layback work.

The first layback booking was made for Thursday afternoon at one o'clock. Based on the scanty research (due to the postproduction supervisor's ignorance about the process) and the decision made forthwith, it was decided that, since it would only take 30 minutes per reel to layback, I would not be without my hard drives long enough to justify the rental of what we call a layback or transport drive. A layback or transport drive is a hard drive dedicated to the job of transferring the edited sessions and all the sound files needed for a successful layback; this way, an editor does not need to give up the hard drive and can continue cutting on other reels.

The first error was a lack of communication from the postproduction supervisor and the facility manager in defining what each person meant by a "reel" (in terms of length) and how many channels of sounds each person was talking about regarding the scope of work to be transferred. Each had assumed they were both talking about the same parameters. Sadly, they were not. In traditional film editing terms, a theatrical project is broken down into reels of 1,000 feet or less. This means that the average 90 to 100 minute feature will be Picture Cut on 9 to 10 reels, each running an average of 8 to 10 minutes in length. After the final sound mix is complete, these reels are assembled into "A-B" projection reels (wherein edit reels 1 and 2 are combined to create a projection reel 1AB, edit reels 3 and 4 are combined to create projection reel 2AB, and so forth). Projection reels are shipped all over the world for theatrical presentation. Whether they are projected using two projectors that switch back and forth at the end of reel changeovers, or whether the projectionist mounts the reels together into one big 10,000-foot platter for automated projection, they are still shipped out on 2,000-foot "AB" projection reels.

When the facility manager heard the postproduction supervisor say that our project was four reels long, he assumed that the reels would run approximately 8 to 10 minutes in length, like the reels they cut in their own facility. We were really cutting preassembled AB-style, just like projection reels in length, as the studio had already determined that the animated feature we were doing was a direct-to-video product. Therefore, our reels were running an average of 20 to 21 minutes in length—over twice as long as what the facility manager expected.

Second, the facility manager was accustomed to dealing with his own in-house product, which was simple television cartoon work that only needed 4 to 8 sound effect tracks for each reel. For him this was a single-pass transfer. Our postproduction supervisor had not made it clear that the sound-editorial team was preparing the work in a theatrical design, utilizing all 22 channels for every reel to be transferred.

Because the facility only had a Pro Tools unit that could only play back eight dedicated channels at once, the transfer person transferred channels 1 through 8 all the way through 20 to 22 minutes of an AB reel, not 8 to 10 minutes of a traditional cut reel. Then he rewound back to heads, reassigned the eight playback outputs to channels 9 through 16, transferred that 20 to 22 minute pass, then rewound back to heads and reassigned the eight playback outputs to channels 17 through 22 to finish the reel. Instead of taking an average of half an hour per reel, each reel took an average of 2 hours. Add to that a 2 hour delay because they could not figure out why the timecode from the 24-track was not driving the Pro Tools session.

The crew finally discovered that the reason the timecode was not getting through to the computer was that the facility transfer technician had put the patch cord into the wrong assignment in the patch bay and had not thought to double-check the signal path. To add more woes to the hemorrhaging problem, the facility was running its Pro Tools sessions on an old Macintosh Quadra 800. It was accustomed to a handful of sound effects channels with sprinklings of little cartoon effects that it could easily handle. On the other hand, we ran extremely complex theatrical-designed sound with gigantic sound files, many in excess of 50 megabytes apiece. One background pass alone managed 8 gigabytes of audio files in a single session, a session twice as long as traditional cut reels. At the time, I used a Macintosh PowerMac 9600 at my workstation, and they tried to get by with only a Quadra 800. The session froze up on the transfer person, and he didn't know what was wrong. The editor upstairs kept saying the drive was too fragmented, and so they wasted hours re-defragmenting a drive that had just been defragmented the previous day.

I received an urgent call and drove over to help get things rolling again. I asked them if they had tried opening the computer's system folder and throwing out the Digidesign set-up document, on the suspicion that it had become corrupted and needed to be rebuilt. They didn't even know what I was talking about. Once I opened the system folder and showed them the set-up document, I threw it in the trash and rebooted the computer, then reset the hardware commands. The Pro Tools session came up and proceeded to work again.

Part of the reason why the facility offered such an apparently great transfer deal was that it did not have to pay a transfer technician very high wages, as he was barely an apprentice, just learning the business. He transferred sound by a monkey-see, monkey-do approach; he had been shown to put this cord here, push this button, turn this knob, and it should work. The apprentice was shoved into a job way beyond his skill level and was not instructed in the art of precise digital-to-analog transfer; nor had he been taught how to follow a signal path, how to detect distortion, how to properly monitor playback, how to tone up stock (and why), or how to problem solve.

The facility did not have an engineer on staff, someone who could have intervened with expert assistance to ferret out the problem and get the transfer bay running again. Instead, a sound editor was called down from the cutting rooms upstairs, someone who had barely gotten his own feet wet with Pro Tools, someone only a few steps ahead of the transfer person. Not only was the layback session of Thursday blown completely out, but a second session was necessary for the following day, which ended up taking 9 hours more. As a consequence, I was without my drive and unable to do any further cutting for nearly 2 days because of this collateral oversight. In addition to nearly a thousand dollars of lost editorial talent, the layback schedule that *on paper* looked like it would take 2 simple hours actually took 14, wiping out the entire allocated monies for all the laybacks—and we had just started the process!

These collateral pitfalls cause many horror stories in the world of filmmaking. Filmmakers' ignorance of the process is compounded by the failure to ask questions or to admit lack of knowledge; the most common mistake is accepting the lowest bid because the client erroneously thinks money will be saved. Much of the ignorance factor is due not only to the ever-widening gap of technical understanding by the producers and unit production managers, but by the very person producers hire to look after this phase of production—the postproduction supervisor. The old studio system used to train producers and directors, through a working infrastructure where form and function had a tight, continuous flow, and the production unit had a clearer understanding of how film was made, articulating its vision and design accordingly. Today many producers and directors enter the arena cowboy-style, shooting from the hip, flashing sexy terms and glitzy fads during their pitch sessions to launch the deal—yet they so seldom understand that which their tongue brandishes like a rapier.

Many executive-level decision makers in the studios today rose from the ranks of number-crunching accountants, attorneys, and talent agent "packagers," with little or no background in the art of storytelling and technical filmmaking, without having spent any time working in a craft that would teach production disciplines. They continue to compress schedules and to structure inadequate budgets.

A point of diminishing returns arrives where the studios (producers) shoot themselves in the foot, both creatively and financially, because they don't understand the process or properly consult supervisors and contractors of the technical crafts who can structure a plan to ensure the project's fruition.

PENNY-WISE AND POUND-FOOLISH

A frequent blunder is not adopting a procedural protocol to make protection back-ups of original recorded dailies or masters before shipping from one site to another. The extra dollars added to the line-item budget are minuscule indeed compared to the ramifications of no back-up protections and the consequent loss of one or more tapes along the way.

I had a robust discussion with a producer over the practice of striking a back-up set of production DATs each day before shipping the dailies overseas to Los Angeles. For a mere $250, all the daily DATs would have been copied just prior to shipment. He argued with me that it was an unnecessary redundancy and that he would not line anybody's pockets. Sure enough, 2 months later, the postproduction supervisor of the studio called me up. "Dave, we've got a problem."

The overseas courier had lost the previous day's shipment. The film negative had made it, but not the corresponding DAT. They had filmed a sequence at night on the docks of Hong Kong. An additional complication arose in that the scene was not even scripted, but had been made up on the spur of the moment and shot impromptu. There were no script notes and only the barest of directions and intentions from the script supervisor.

Consultation with the director and actors shed little light on the dialog and dramatic intent. After due consideration and discussion with the postproduction supervisor, we set upon an expensive and complex procedure, necessary because the producer had not spent that paltry $250 for a back-up DAT copy before lab shipments.

Two lip readers were hired to try to determine what the actors were saying. The television monitors were too small for the lip readers to see anything adequately because the footage was shot at night with moody lighting. This meant we had to use an ADR room where the film image projected much larger. Naturally, the work could not be done in real time. It took the lip readers two full days of work to glean as much as they could. Remember, these were raw dailies, not finished and polished cut scenes. The lip readers had to figure out each take of every angle because the sequence was unscripted and the dialog would vary from take to take.

Then we brought in the actors to ADR their lines as best as they could to each and every daily take. After all, the picture editor could only cut the sequence once he had the dialog in the mouths of the actors.

After the preliminary ADR session, my dialog editor cut the roughed dialog in sync to the daily footage as best as she could. This session was then sent out to have the cut ADR transferred onto a Beta SP videotape that the picture assistant could then digitize into the Avid (a nonlinear picture-editing system). It should go without saying that once the picture editor finished cutting the sequence, the entire dock sequence had to be reperformed by the actors on the ADR stage for a final and more polished performance.

All in all, the costs of this disaster ran upward of $40,000, if you include all collateral costs that would not have been expended if a duplicate DAT back-up had been made in the first place. To make matters worse, they had not secured a completion bond nor had they opted for the errors-and-omissions clause in the insurance policy.

DEVELOPING GRASS-ROOTS COMMON SENSE

Budget properly, but not exorbitantly, for sound. Make sure that you are current on the costs and techniques of creating what you need. Most importantly, even if you do not want to reveal the amount of money budgeted for certain line items, at least go over the line items you have in the budget with the department heads and vendors with whom you intend to work. I have yet to go over a budget that was not missing one or more items, items the producer had either not considered or did not realize had to be included in the process: everything from giving the electrical department enough allowance for extra cable to control generator noise, to providing wardrobe with funds for the soft booties actors wear for all but full-length shots, to allowing enough time for a proper Foley job and enough lead time for the supervising sound editor and/or sound designer to create and record the special sound effects unique to the visuals of the film.

The technicians, equipment, and processes change so fast and are still evolving and changing so quickly that you must take constant pulse checks to see how the industry's technical protocol is shooting and delivering film; otherwise, you will find yourself budgeting and scheduling unrealistically for the new generation of postproduction processes. Since 1989 the most revolutionary aspects of production have been in the mechanics of how technicians record, edit, and mix the final soundtrack—namely, digital technology. This has changed the sound process more profoundly than nearly any other innovation in the past 50 years. Today we are working with G-5s and terabyte drives with speeds that we could only dream about a decade ago.

Costs have come down in some areas and have risen dramatically in others. Budget what is necessary for your film and allow enough time to properly finish the sound processes of the picture. A sad but true axiom in this business is: there is never enough time or money to do it right, but they always seem to find more time and money to do it over!

Half the time, I don't feel like a sound craftsperson. I feel like the guy in that old Midas muffler commercial who shrugs at the camera and says, "You can pay me now—or pay me later." The truly sad thing is that it is not really very funny. My colleagues and I often shake our heads in disbelief at the millions of dollars of waste and inefficient use of budget funds. We see clients and executives caught up in repeating clichés or buzzwords, the latest hip phrase or technical nickname. They want to be on the cutting edge, they want to have the new hot-rod technologies in their pictures, but they rarely understand what they are saying. It becomes the slickest recital of technical double-talk, not because they truly understand the neat new words but because they think it will make their picture better.

While working on a low-budget action robot picture, I entered the re-recording mix stage to commence predubbing sound effects when the director called out to me, "Hey, Dave, you did prepare the sound effects in THX, didn't you?" I smiled and started to laugh at his jest, when the re-recording mixer caught my eye. He was earnestly trying to get my attention not to react. It was then that I realized the director was not jesting—he was serious! I stood stunned. I could not believe he would have made such a statement in front of everybody. Rather than expose his ignorance to his producer and staff, I simply let it slide off as an offhanded affirmation. "THX—absolutely."

An old and tired cliché still holds very true today: the classic triangle of structuring production quality, schedule issues, and budget concerns—The Great Triangle Formula: (1) You can have **good quality**. (2) You can have it **fast**. (3) You can have it **cheap**.

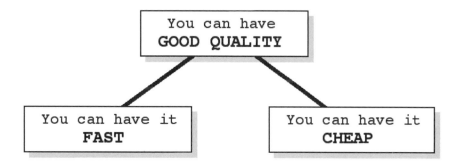

You may only pick **two** of the three. When potential clients tell me they want all three options, then I know what kind of person I am dealing with, so I recommend another sound-editorial firm. No genuine collaboration can happen with people who expect and demand all three.

One False Move is a classic example of this cliché in action. When Carl Franklin and Jesse Beaton interviewed me, we came to an impasse in the budget restrictions. I rose, shook their hands, bid them well, and left. Carl followed me down the hall and blocked my exit. "I'm really disappointed with you, Yewdall!"

"You're disappointed with ME?" I sighed. "You're the ones with no money."

"Yeah, well, I thought one Cormanite would help out another Cormanite," snapped Carl.

I grinned. "You worked with Roger Corman? Why didn't you say that to begin with? Cormanites can always work things out."

And with that, we returned to the office and told their postproduction supervisor to just sit quietly, listen, and *learn* something. First, I asked what the release date was. There was no release date. Then why the schedule that Graham had outlined? Because he had just copied it from another movie and did not know any better. All right, if you don't have much money then you must give me a lot more time. If I have to hire a full crew to make a shorter schedule work then that is "hard" dollars that I am going to have to pay out. On the other hand, if I have more time, then I can more of the work personally, making do with a smaller crew, which in turn, saves the outlay of money that I would otherwise have to make.

Carl and Jesse were able to give me six extra weeks. This allowed me to do more work personally, which was also far more gratifying on a personal level. That the picture was ready for the re-recording process during a slow time in the traditional industry schedule also helped.

Here is another point to note: In peak season, financial concessions are rare. If you hope to cut special rates or deals, aim for the dead period during the Cannes Film Festival in May.

THE TEMP DUB

A new cut version of a picture is seen as counterproductive by studio executives, as they are usually not trained to view cut picture with only the raw cut production sound. They don't fully understand the clipped words and the shifts in background presences behind the various angles of actors delivering their lines. They watch a fight scene and have difficulty understanding how well it is working without the sounds of face impacts and body punches. This has caused an epidemic of temp dubbing on a scale never before seen or imagined in the industry.

Back in the early 1980s, we called temp dubs the process of flushing $50,000 down a toilet for nothing. Today, we accept it as a necessary evil. Entire procedures and tactical battle plans are developed to survive the inevitable temp dub, and they do not come as a single event. Where there is one, there will be more. How many times has a producer assured me not to worry about a temp dub? Either there will not be one because no money is in the budget for one, the producer insists, or there will be one temp dub and that is it!

A comedy spoof, *Transylvania 6–5000*, which I supervised the sound for, is an excellent example of what can go horribly wrong with temp dubs when there is no defined structure of productorial control. Two gentlemen, with whom I had had a very fine experience on an aviation action film the previous year, were its producers. I was assured there would be no temp dub(s), as there was certainly no money in the budget for one. But the project had a first-time director, a respected comedy writer on major films who was trying to cross over and sit in the director's chair. Being a talented writer, however, did not suddenly infuse him with the knowledge, wisdom, or technical discipline about how motion pictures were made, especially about the postproduction processes.

We had no sooner looked at the director's cut of the picture when the director ordered up a temp dub. I decided not to cut my wrists just then, as I picked up the phone and called the producer for an explanation. He was as surprised as I was and told me to forget about it. I instructed my crew to continue preparing for the final. Within an hour, I received a call from the producer, apologizing and explaining that he could do nothing about it. If the director wanted a temp dub, then we needed to prepare one. I reminded the producer that no allowance had been made for the temp dub in the budget. He knew that. He had to figure things out, but for now, he said, just use budget monies to prepare the temp dub. He would figure out how to cover the overage costs. I asked the producer why he could not block the director's request. After all, I had been trained that the pecking order of command gave producers the veto power to overrule directors, especially when issues of budget hemorrhaging were the topic of conversation. The producer explained that the hierarchy was not typical on this picture; the director was granted a separate deal with the studio that effectively transcended the producer's authority over him. I reluctantly agreed to the temp dub, but reminded the producer that it would seriously eat into the dollars budgeted for the final cutting costs until he could fortify the overage.

After the first temp dub we had resumed preparations for the final when we received a second phone call from the producer. The director had ordered up a second temp dub for another series of screenings. No compensation had been made for the first temp, and now a second temp dub was being ordered? The producer sighed and told us to just continue to use budget dollars until he could figure it out. This would definitely be the last temp dub, and the nightmare would be over.

The nightmare continued for four weeks. Each week the director ordered up yet another temp dub. Each week the producer was unable to deal with studio executives and was dismissed from acquiring additional budget dollars to offset the temp dub costs.

After the fourth temp dub, the producer asked how much longer it would take us to prepare the final mix. I shrugged and said that as far as I was concerned we were already prepared. His eyes widened in disbelief as he asked how that was possible. I told him that the four temp dubs had burned up the entire sound-editorial budget due to the director's dictates. Nothing was left to pay the editors to prepare the final soundtrack unless compensation was forthcoming; therefore, the fourth temp dub would have to serve as the final mix. The producer did not believe we would really do that. To this day, the film is shown on television and viewed on DVDs with the fourth temp dub as its ultimate soundtrack.

You can easily see how a judgment error in the director/producer jurisdiction can have calamitous collateral effects on the end product. Someone, either at the studio or over at the attorney's offices, had been allowed to structure a serious anomaly into the traditional chain-of-command hierarchy. This unwise decision, made long before the cameras ever rolled, laid the groundwork for financial and quality control disasters.

The truth of the matter, this has not been a unique tragedy. I could name several major motion pictures whose supervising sound editors told me that they were so balled up by producing temp dubs nearly every week that they never had a chance to properly design and construct a real soundtrack and that those films are really just temp dubs.

Remember this one truth. No one gives you anything free. Someone pays for it; most of the time—you. If producers only knew what really goes on behind the scenes to offset the fast-talking promises given a client to secure the deal, they would be quicker to negotiate fairly structured relationships and play the game right.

READ THE FINE PRINT

Several years ago a friend brought me a contract from another sound-editorial firm. He told me the director and producer were still fighting with the editorial firm regarding the overages on their last picture. This contract was for a major motion picture, and they did not want to end up suffering a big overage bill after the final sound mix was completed. Would I read through the contract and highlight potential land mines that could blow up as extra "hidden" costs? I read through the contract.

The editorial firm guaranteed, for a flat fee, a Foley track for each reel of the picture. The cost seemed suspiciously low. When I reread it, I discovered it would bill a flat guaranteed price of "a Foley track," in other words, Foley-1 of each reel. Foley tracks 2 through (heaven knows how many) 30 to 40 would obviously be billed out as extra costs above and beyond the bounds of the contract.

All the Dolby A noise-reduction channels would be thrown into the deal free. Sounds good—except and that by this time nobody of consequence used Dolby A channels, and those who did had already amortized their cost and threw them free into every

Figure 4.3 The deal makers.

deal anyway. Of course, nowhere in the contract did it specify about the free use of Dolby SR channels, the accepted and required noise-reduction system at the time. This would, of course, appear as extra costs above and beyond the bounds of the contract.

To help cut costs, the contract specified that all 35-mm fullcoat rolls (with the exception of final mix rolls) would be rental stock, costing a flat $5 each. It was estimated, based on the director's last project and the style of sound postproduction tactics that this project would use at least 750,000 feet of 35-mm fullcoat. That would cost the budget an estimated $3,750 in stock rental.

Since the picture and client were of major importance, the sound-editorial firm wrote into the contract it would purchase all brand-new stock and guarantee to the client that the first use of this new rental stock would be on this picture. This must have sounded delicious to the producer and director. However, in a different part of the contract, near the back, appeared a disclaimer that if any fullcoat rental stock was physically cut for any reason, it would revert from rental to purchase, the purchase price in keeping with the going rates of the studio at the time. A purchase price was not specified or quoted anywhere in the contract. I happened to know that the current purchase price of one roll of fullcoat at the studios averaged $75. This would end up costing the producer over $56,000! No risk existed for the sound-editorial firm; the director was notorious for his changes and updates, so the expectation that each roll of fullcoat used would have at least one cut in it, and would therefore revert to purchase price, translated into money in the bank.

My advice to the producer was to purchase the desired-grade quality fullcoat directly from the stock manufacturer at $27 per roll. Since the production would use so much fullcoat, I suggested the producer strike a bulk-rate discount, which brought the price down to $20 per roll. This would give the producer a guaranteed line-item cost of $15,000, along with the peace of mind that any changes and updates could be made without collateral overages leaching from the budget's fine print regarding invasive use.

I then came across a paragraph describing library effects use. The contract stated that the first 250 sound effects of each reel would be free. A fee of $5 per effect would be added thereafter. First, most sound-editorial firms do not charge per effect. The use of the sound library as required is usually part of the sound-editorial contract. In the second place, no finite definition of what constituted a sound effect was given. If the same sound effect was used more than once in a reel, did that sound effect constitute one use, or was every performance of that same sound effect being counted separately each time? If the editor cut a sound effect into several parts, would each segment constitute a sound effect use? The contract did not stipulate. I might add that this picture went on to win an Academy Award for Best Sound—but industry rumors placed the overages of the sound budget well over $1 million.

BUT YOU SAID IT WOULD BE CHEAPER!

While I was working on *Chain Reaction*, a studio executive asked to have lunch, as he wanted to unload some frustrations and pick my brain about the rapid changes in postproduction. For obvious reasons, he will remain anonymous, but he agonized over his Caesar salad about how he just didn't understand what had happened. "You guys said digital would be cheaper!"

"Wait a minute," I stopped him. "I never said that to you."

"I don't mean you. But everybody said it would cost less money, and we could work faster!"

"Name me one sound editor that told you that. You can't, because it wasn't one of us who sold you this program. It was the hardware pushers who sold it to you. You deluded yourselves that it would cost less and allow you to compress schedules. Now what have you got? Compressed schedules with skyrocketing budgets."

"So let's go back to film!"

I smiled. "No. Do I like working in nonlinear? Yes. Do I think that it is better? Not necessarily. Do I want to go back to using magnetic film again? No."

"Where'd we go wrong?" he asked.

"You expected to compare apples with apples—like with like. That's not how nonlinear works. With the computer and the almost weekly upgrades of software, we can do more and more tasks. Because we can do more, the director expects us to do more. You cannot expect us to have access to a creative tool and not use it.

"Are we working faster than before? Mach four times faster. Can we ignore using the extra bells-and-whistles and use the equipment as if it were an electronic Moviola? Absolutely NOT! The sooner you stop throwing darts at the calendar as you make up these artificial schedules and listen to your craftspeople's advice, the sooner you are going to start injecting sensibility into your out-of-control postproduction budgets and start recapturing an art form that is quickly ebbing away. Otherwise, you had better take a deep breath and accept the fact that the reality of today's postproduction costs are out of control, fueled by directors who find themselves in a studio playpen with amazing creative toys at their disposal. They are going to play with them!"

BUDGET FUNDAMENTALS

One of the most frequent agonies in the birthing process of a film is the realization that the budget for the sound-editorial and/or re-recording process was inadequately structured and allocated. Since these two processes are ranked among the most misunderstood phases, they are the two that often suffer the most.

The process is not alleviated by those who strive to help the new independent producers or unit production managers (UPMs) by trying to develop "plug-in" budget forms, whether printed or via computer software developed by those knowing even less about the postproduction process. More often than not, these forms are copied from budgets acquired from someone working on another show or even from someone trained during a different era. Not understanding the process, the software writer or print-shop entrepreneur copies only what is seen, thereby carrying only those line items and detail (especially the lack thereof) of whatever is on the acquired budget breakdown, including all the mistakes.

We often have been shocked to find that the producers or UPMs did not allow certain critical line items into their own budgets because they did not see an allowance for a line item in their budget form. Not understanding the sound-editorial and mixing process themselves, they did not add their own line items as needed. The ignorance and ensuing budget disaster is carried from project to project, like bad genes in a DNA strain, photocopying the blueprints for disappointment and failure onto the next unsuspecting project.

Understanding the Budget Line Items

Following are some important budget line items to consider. Remember, these costs directly impact the soundtrack. These line items do not include creative noise abatement allowances. One must use common sense and draw upon experienced craftspeople to assist in planning a successful soundtrack.

Production Dialog Mixers vs. Custom Sound Effect Mixers

In addition to the time allocated for the production sound mixer, the smart producer budgets time for the mixer to go on a location field trip in order to see and hear the natural ambience, walk the practical location and hear the potential for echo, note nearby factories and highways, and detect the presence of aircraft flight paths. In addition, the mixer takes a quick overview of where power generators might be parked, and if natural blinds exist to help block noise or if acoustic gear should be brought to knock down potential problems.

With regard to a pristine dialog track, the boom operator is the key position. The production mixer is the head of the production sound crew, but even the mixer will tell you the boom operator is more important. If the microphone is not in the right position, what good is the subsequent recording? More often than not, the producer or UPM always underbudgets the boom-operator slot. I have seen production mixers shave some of their own weekly rates so that those extra dollars can bolster the boom operator's salary.

Most smaller pictures cannot afford the cable man (the term "cable man" has stuck, regardless of the technician's gender). The cable man also handles the second microphone boom as well as other assistant chores. On one picture the producer had not allowed the hiring of a cable man, alleging that the budget could not support one. One night, the crew was shooting a rain sequence at a train station. The production mixer was experiencing many pops on the microphone because the rain was heavier than first anticipated. Needing the rain bonnet, he asked the director for five minutes so that the boom operator could fetch one from the sound truck. The director said no, "We'll just loop his lines later in postproduction." The following night, the actor was tragically killed in a stunt crash during filming. What do you think it cost to fix the rain-pelted production track, as opposed to the cost of the requested 5-minute wait the night before?

On large productions, especially those with a great deal of specialized equipment, vehicles, or props that may be expensive or impossible to acquire later, increasingly more producers factor a production FX recordist into the budget. Usually these individuals have a reputation for knowing how to record for sound effect use and for effectively interfacing with the postproduction crew to ensure needed recordings. They often work separately from first unit, usually arranging to work with vehicles or props not being used at the time, taking them out and away to areas conducive to quality recordings.

ACCT	ACCOUNT TITLE		PREP	PROD	POST		RATE	TOTAL
3400	SOUND (Production)							
3401	SOUND MIXER		1 wk	6 wks	2 dys			
3402	BOOM OPERATOR		2 dys	6 wks	1 dy			
3403	CABLE MAN		1 dy	6 wks	1 dy			
3404	PROD. FX RECORDIST		2 dys	2 wks	2 dys			
3405	PLAYBACK OPERATOR							
3410	Equipment Package rental							
	analog/digital (for DIA)			6 wks				
3412	Equipment Package rental							
	analog/digital (for FX)			2 wks				
3415	Recording equip supplies							
3420	Purchases							
3425	Rentals							
3430	Walkie-Talkies / comm			6 wks				
3440	Repairs							
3460	Daily Transfer —Digital—							
3461	time code DAT rental			6 wks				
3462	digital transfer labor			6 wks				
3463	audio file back-ups							
3470	Daily Transfer —Film—							
3471	film mag stripe							
3472	film transfer labor			6 wks				
[____]	[_____]							
[____]	[_____]							
[____]	[_____]							
[____]	[_____]							
3480	Fringes (___%)							
3481	Sales Tax (___%)							
				Prod SOUND ACCT TOTAL:				

Figure 4.4 Production sound budget.

For instance, a Trans-Am may be the hero vehicle for the picture. The director may want the Trans-Am recorded to match the production dialog, but recorded as a stunt-driven vehicle to give the "big sound" for postproduction sound editorial. Recordings of this type are usually done off-hours, not while the shooting unit is in need of any of the special props or locations in question. Those occasions do arise, though, when the production FX recordist will record during actual shooting, such as recording cattle stampeding through a location set. It may be a financial hardship to field the cattle and wranglers after the actual shoot just to record cattle stampeding. Recordings like these are best orchestrated in a collaborative manner with camera and crew.

Each situation requires a different problem-solving approach. Common sense will guide you to the most fruitful decision. However, production effects recording during principal photography demands attentive regard for suppressing inappropriate noises often made by the production crew. Such events are incredibly challenging and seldom satisfying from the sound mixer's point of view.

The project may require that precise wild track recordings be made of an oil rig, say, or a drawbridge spanning a river. These types of sound recordings should be entrusted to a recordist who understands the different techniques of recording sound effects rather than production dialog (major differences explained later in this book). The production FX recordist is not usually on for the entire shoot of the picture, but brought on as needed, or for a brief period of time to cover the necessary recordings.

A perfect example was a major action thriller with a huge car chase scene through Paris. The sound supervisor showed me 50 minutes of the work-in-progress footage, as he wanted me to come on the picture to work with him in handling the vehicle chase scenes. It looked very exciting, a sound editor's dream! The first thing I asked was how were we going to handle custom recording these various cars? We knew that at least two of them were not even available in the United States yet. He asked for a recommendation and proposal. The next day I presented him with my plan: hire Eric Potter, who specializes in custom sound effect recording and let him recommend the sound equipment package that he feels he would need, including any assistant help that we knew he would require. Send them over to Paris where they were still filming the picture, and, as a bonus while they were there, have them record a ton of stereophonic ambiences.

A couple of days later, the sound supervisor came into the office and told me that the producer had decided against my plan. Why spend the money when he would just have the production mixer custom record the vehicles on his off time? I threw up my hands. I knew this man, a son of an ex-studio executive, a second-generation film producer. I had worked for him on another picture several years before. I knew well the fact that he did not understand and appreciate the collateral costs that he was about to waste by not following the custom-recording plan.

I thanked the supervisor for considering me to work on the film, but I knew what "postproduction hell" was coming down the pike. Another studio had recently offered to build a sound-editorial suite to my custom design to entice me over to them. I apologized to my friend and politely turned down doing the car picture to take the deal to move to the other studio.

Several months later that sound supervisor called me up and asked if he could come over and check out my new room. Sure I said, though I thought it strange because he must be knee deep in a difficult project and how could he afford to waste a valuable weekday afternoon with me? He sat down and told me the temp dub was a disaster. Everything I said would go wrong *had* gone wrong, and then some. What was the name of that recordist I had recommended? I replied that to custom record the cars now would cost a great deal more than if they had done it during the shoot, and sure enough, after shipping the cars over to California, renting an air field, trying to find cobblestone streets where they could record, etc., the sound supervisor told me the production unit spent nearly 10 times the amount of money that my original plan would have cost.

This is not a lesson about ego; this is a lesson about understanding that production dialog mixers are trained to record dialog. There is an exact discipline, technique, and approach that they are trained to utilize to capture the best production dialog track they can. It is *seldom* the technique that we utilize when we record sound effects. The two styles are completely different. That is why you need to hire a specialist such as Eric Potter, Charles Maynes, or John Fasal to custom record the sound effect requirements of your project.

The Production Sound Budget

Production recording mixers can and prefer to use their own equipment. This is of great benefit to the producer for two reasons. First, the production mixer is familiar with his or her own gear and probably yields a better-quality sound recording. Second, in a negotiation pinch, the production mixer is more likely to cut the producer a better equipment-package rental rate than an equipment rental house. Remember too that the production mixer is usually responsible for and provides the radio walkie-talkies and/or Comtech gear for crew communications. Communication gear is not part of the recording equipment basic package but handled as a separate line item.

As you consider the kind of picture you are making, the style and preference of the production recording mixer, and the budget restraints you are under, you will decide whether to record analog or digital (single-channel, two-channel, or multi-channel). This decision outlines a daily procedure protocol from the microphone to picture editorial—how to accomplish it and what you must budget.

With very few exceptions, virtually all dailies today are delivered to picture editorial digitally. There are three ways of doing this. The first two choices involve having the production mixers make daily sound tapes or removable hard drive recording storage, either digitized (if by DAT) or transferred as audio files that already exist on a removable hard drive so that they can be synced up to visual image at picture editorial.

1. You may choose to have the laboratory do the transfer. This in-lab service may be more convenient for you, as they deliver you a video telecine transfer with your sound already synced up to the picture. Sounds good? The downside is that it is a factory-style operation on the laboratory's part. Very few lab services have master craftspeople sound techs who think beyond the timecode numbers and sound report's circled takes. The precision and attention to detail are often lost with the necessary factory-type get-it-out schedule.

More importantly, you introduce, at the very least, a generation loss by virtue of the videotape and, at worst, a lot of new noise and hums depending on the quality of the telecine. I do not care what the laboratory tells you—all video transfers introduce degradation and system noise to some degree. I have also personally inherited numerous projects that producers had had the laboratories handle sound transfer in this manner and I have been underwhelmed with their level of service and expertise.

One of the underlying reasons for this is that in order to compete, the laboratories have to keep their labor costs down. Bean counters only know numbers on a page: so many technicians, working at a certain pay rate, equals a profit or loss on a foot of film processed. What is happening is that the real craftspeople who really know why they do things the way they do them, who have seen all of the freakish problems in production and have their own veteran memories so they can instantly access and problem solve the issue, are let go when their pay rate reaches a certain level. On paper, a lower paid technician makes business sense. The problem is that it usually takes three to six "newbys" to handle and turn out the work that one veteran knows how to do. This is a collateral invisible chuckhole that the studio accountants just do not understand. More mistakes are made because less experienced beginners are still learning; more and more work has to be redone because it was improperly done the first time.

2. You may choose to have your own assistant picture editor transfer (digitize) the sound straight into your nonlinear editing system (such as Final Cut Pro or Avid), then sync the digitized audio files to the digitized picture. This certainly bypasses the laboratory factory-style issues—but more importantly, it places the burden of quality control and the personal project precision on the picture-editorial team. This technique is mandatory if you hope to utilize the OMF procedure later in postsound editorial, as I have come to *never* trust any material that was handled by a film laboratory, whether telecine transfer or even digitized audio files, if I ever hoped to use OMF in the postsound edit equation. (OMF, open media framework, is covered in greater detail in Chapter 14.)

3. Your third choice is to have your production sound mixer do it, so to speak. By this I mean that the sound mixer would be recording sound to either the DEVA IV or V or to the Nagra V or several other very high-quality recorders, such as the Sound Devices 744t, the Aaton Cantar X, the Fostex PD6, or such other highly respected recording units. All these units are FAT 32 formatted to record four to eight discreet channels of audio signal, all capable of up to at least 96-kHz/24-bit recording (a few are rated to record as high as 192-kHz/24-bit) in industry standard audio formats BWF (Broadcast Wave Format) and some also record in .WAV audio format files. (Near the end of Chapter 5, we take a brief look at several of these units. Chapter 23, which is devoted to an in depth discussion of the Nagra V, is available from http://textbooks. elsevier.com/companions/9780240808659 as a downloadable file.)

Timecode and other scene/take reference data are included in the directory information of these files, making them instant "drag-and-drop" transfer items into nonlinear picture and audio workstations. As you will read in more detail later, your sound mixer will simply change out the removable hard drive (or flash memory unit) and replace it, or he or she might simply make a back-up clone out of their recording set-up and burn a DVD-R to ship straight to picture editorial, ready to simply be data-transferred into the computer.

ACCT		ACCOUNT TITLE	POST		RATE		TOTAL
4600		MUSIC					
4601		COMPOSER(s)					
4602		LYRICIST(s)					
4603		CONDUCTOR					
4605		MUSICIANS [_____]					
4605		ARRANGER/ORCHESTRATOR					
4608		COPYIST					
4609		SINGERS/CHORUS [_____]					
4610		VOCAL INSTRUCTORS					
4611		Special Instrument Rentals					
4612		Labor/Transport-Instruments					
4613		Studio Rental					
4614		Studio Equipment — Rentals -&- set-up					
4615		MUSIC RECORDIST					
4616		RECORDIST ASST.					
4620		MUSIC EDITOR					
4621		Music Editor SET-UP					
4650		Multi-track MIX-DOWN					
4651		STOCK: Digital multi-track Digital protection					
4652		Stock & Source Music License fees					
4654		Music publishing Copyright costs					
4655		Reuse Fee					
4660		Administrative expenses					
[_____]		[_____]					
[_____]		[_____]					
[_____]		[_____]					
[_____]		[_____]					
4680		Fringes (___%)					
			MUSIC ACCT TOTAL:				

Figure 4.5 Music budget.

Music Budget

Once the producer settles on the music composer and they thoroughly discuss the conceptual scope of work to be done, the composer outlines a budget to encompass the financial requirements necessary. I am not even going to pretend to be an authority about the budget requirements for music, just as I would not want a music composer to attempt to speak for sound-editorial budget requirements; therefore, you should consult your music director and/or composer for their budgetary needs.

Sound-Editorial Budget

The "Labor" line items of the sound-editorial detail illustrated in Figure 4.6 are geared toward a medium-sized feature film with a heavy action content. (I discuss the individual job slots and their contribution to the soundtrack later in this book.)

"Room Rentals" refers to the actual rooms where editorial workstations with monitors and computers are set up and used by the editorial editors and assistants as necessary for the editorial team. This cost does not reflect the equipment, but many sound-editorial firms do include at least a 200 to 300 gigabyte external drive in the use of the room. Obviously, with today's digital memory requirements for digitized picture, thousands of audio files and edit sessions will only get you started.

Each sound editor has a workstation system requirement. A sound designer has much more gear than a dialog editor. Assistant sound editors have different kinds of equipment requirements than do sound editors. The workstation system rentals obviously vary from one requirement to another.

Sound editors need more hard drives than the 200 to 300 gigabyte drive that their room rental may allow. This need is dictated by how busy and demanding the sound-editorial requirements are; again, every show is different. I have an "informal" Pro Tools set-up under the end table of my couch so that I can put my feet up on the coffee table while I spend time with my wife in the evenings, and I have 1.5 terabytes of sound library drives under the end table with two firewire cables that poke up when I want to plug in my laptop and go to work. My formal workstation room is set up entirely differently of course, where I can properly monitor in 5.1 and do serious signal analysis and mixing. It all depends on what kind of work you are doing and what set-up is structured for what purpose.

The "Custom FX Recordist" may, at first glance, look like a redundancy slot from the sound (production) budget page. It is not! The production FX recordist covered the production dialog and any sound effects that were captured during the actual filming of a scene. From time to time, good production mixers know how to take advantage of recording production vehicles, location background ambiences, and props unique to the filming process. Later, usually weeks and even months later, the sound-editorial team is up against a whole new set of needs and requirements. It may need to capture specialized backgrounds not part of the original location, but needed to blend and create the desired ambience.

A good example of this is when I supervised the sound for the 1984 version of *The Aviator* (starring Christopher Reeve). The director and producers were biplane enthusiasts and wanted exact and authentic recordings for the final film; however, they were prohibited from using the authentic Pratt-Whitney engines of 1927 because the

ACCT		ACCOUNT TITLE	POST		RATE	TOTAL
4700		SOUND EDITORIAL				
4701		Labor:				
		SUPERVISING SOUND EDITOR	12 wks			
		CO-SUPERVISING SOUND EDITOR	12 wks			
		SOUND DESIGNER	7 wks			
		DIALOG SUPERVISOR	7 wks			
		DIALOG EDITOR #2	5 wks			
		A.D.R. SUPERVISOR	9 wks			
		A.D.R. EDITOR	4 wks			
		SOUND EFFECTS EDITOR #1	6 wks			
		SOUND EFFECTS EDITOR #2	6 wks			
		SOUND EFFECTS EDITOR #3	6 wks			
		FOLEY ARTIST #1	10 dys			
		FOLEY ARTIST #2	10 dys			
		FOLEY SUPERVISOR	6 wks			
		FOLEY EDITOR #2	4 wks			
		1st ASSISTANT EDITOR	12 wks			
		2nd ASSISTANT EDITOR	9 wks			
4702		Room Rentals				
4703		Workstation Set-ups (designer)				
4704		Workstation Set-ups (editors)				
4705		Workstation Set-ups (assistants)				
4706		Hard Drive Rentals				
4710		CUSTOM FX RECORDIST	2 wks			
4711		Equipment Package rental (FX record)	2 wks			
4715		back-up media (DLT / DVD-RAM)				
4716		Expendable Supplies				
4720		Courier / Shipping				
4730		Special Edit Equipment Rentals				
4735		Other Rentals				
4740		TEMP DUB allowances				
4750		Workstation Transfer Exports				
4760		CD-ROM / DVD services to client				
4765		Transfer STOCK and/or MEDIA				
4770		Payroll taxes				
4780		Fringes (___%)				
4781		Sales Tax (___%)				
[_____]		[_____]				
[_____]		[_____]				
		SOUND EDITORIAL ACCT TOTAL:				

Figure 4.6 Sound-editorial budget.

insurance company felt that they were not strong enough, especially as Christopher Reeve did all of his own flying (being an avid biplane pilot enthusiast himself). Therefore, none of the production recordings of the aircraft that were made during the production shoot could be used in the final film. Every single airplane engine had to be custom recorded in postproduction to match how the engines should have historically sounded for 1927.

In *Black Moon Rising*, the stunt vehicle looked great on film, portrayed as a huge and powerful hydrogen jet car, but in actuality it only had a little four-cylinder gasoline engine that, from a sound point of view, was completely unsuitable. As the supervising sound editor, I had to calculate a sound design to "create" the hydrogen jet car. You will want your custom sound effect recordist to record jets taking off, flying by, landing, and taxiing at a military air base. He or she may need to have the recordist go to a local machine shop and record various power tools and metal movements. These recordings, as you can see, are completely different and stylized from the production dialog recordist, who was busy recording a controlled audio series of the real props or vehicles as they really sounded on the set.

Referring to the "back-up media" line item, back-ups can never be stressed enough. Every few days, sound editors turn their hard drives over to the assistant sound editors, who make clone drive back-up copies, depending on the amount of material, possibly making DVD-R back-ups of "Save As" sessions. Many of the larger sound-editorial firms have sophisticated servers, supplying massive amounts of drive access and redundancy. You can never be too careful about backing up your work.

To this day I can take a Pro Tools session document from any one of the sessions from *Starship Troopers* (as well as other films) and boot up the session. The software will scan the drives, find the corresponding archived material, and rebuild the fades in a few minutes. I have resurrected FX-D predub from reel 7, the invasion sequence of the planet Klendathu (one of scads of predub passes that seemed endless). Without good and disciplined habits in file identification protocols, disk management procedures, and back-up habits, resurrecting a session like this would be extremely difficult, if not impossible.

"TEMP DUB allowances" is a highly volatile and controversial line item. The fact is, directors have become fanatical about having temp dubs because they know their work is being received on a first-impression style viewing, and anything less than a final mix is painful. Studio executives want test screenings for audiences so they can get a pulse on how their film is doing—what changes to make, where to cut, and where to linger—all of which necessitate showing it with as polished a soundtrack as possible.

Extra costs may be needed to cover the preparation of the temp dubs separate from the sound preparation for final mix predubbing. Producers and supervising sound editors may want a separate editorial team to handle most of the temp dub preparation, as they do not want the main editorial team distracted and diluted by preparing temp dubs. (Temp dub philosophy is discussed later.)

"Workstation Transfer Exports" refers to the common practice of sound editorial to make "crash downs" (multichannel mixes) of certain segments of action from digital workstations and to export them as single audio files for picture editorial to load into their Final Cut Pro or Avid picture-editing systems and sync up to picture, thereby giving picture editorial few work-in-progress sections, such as action scenes, to assist the director and picture editor as work continues. Figure 4.7 illustrates the raw stock supply for the production recording mixer. Note the back-up media.

Transfers and Stock Purchase

Unless you are cutting your picture on film, the "Stripe for Transfers" line item hardly affects you. This is where you would budget your 35-mm mag stripe and fullcoat costs if you were still cutting on film.

Very few of today's postproduction facilities are still recording ADR and/or looping sessions to analog 24-track 2" tape—but you may run into one or two of them along the way, so you should understand the format. If you find that you need to use a service that still uses 2" tape, refer to the ADR "String-offs" line item. You need to consider the following: five 24-track rolls cover a 95- to 100-minute motion picture. Unless you have extremely complex and overlapping ADR, you should require only one set of 24-track rolls. You will require a second set of 24-track rolls if you are planning to record Group Walla, especially with today's stereophonic microphone set-ups. We will discuss ADR and looping techniques and the recording format options in Chapter 16.

I cannot imagine any Foley stage still recording Foley to 24-track 2" tape, but if you find that your sound facility is still using this format, you need to refer to the "Foley String-offs" line item, the same considerations apply as before. Some films require more Foley tracks than others, so you would simply allow for a second set of 24-track rolls. Sometimes Foley only requires a few extra channels, and if the Group Walla requirements are not considered too heavy you can set aside the first few channels for the overflow Foley tracks and protect the remaining channels for the Group Walla that has already been done or has yet to be performed.

In both the ADR and Foley stage-recording requirements, I am sure you have noticed that I have not yet mentioned recording straight to an editing workstation hard disk. We will talk more about this in Chapter 16 (for ADR/looping) and Chapter 17 (for Foley). The majority of your postproduction sound services for recording your ADR/looping sessions and/or your Foley sessions will be straight to a hard disk via nonlinear workstations such as Pro Tools. Though this procedure will not require a transfer cost in the traditional sense of "transferring" one medium to another medium, you will need to back up the session folder(s) from the facility's hard drive to whatever medium you require to take to your editorial service. This medium could be your own external 200 to 300 gigabyte hard drive, or you could have the material burned to DVD-Rs, or some other intermediate transport protocol you have decided to use. If that is the case, you need to budget for it under "Hard Drive Media Back-ups."

In reference to the "Fullcoat Requirements," you will probably not require fullcoat for ADR or Foley recording. I have not heard of any ADR or Foley stages using fullcoat now for several years. The 4-channel film recorders have, for the most part, been replaced by 24-track 2" analog tape and direct-to-disk workstation recording systems such as Pro Tools.

Depending on which studio you opt to handle the re-recording chores of your project, you may still require 35-mm fullcoat for some or all of the predubbing and

ACCT	ACCOUNT TITLE		POST		RATE	TOTAL
5000	TRANSFERS-&-STOCK PURCHASE					
5001	Raw Stock for Production Recording					
	DAT-and/or-1/4" (orig)					
	DAT Back-Up -or- DVD-RAM					
5005	Stripe for transfers					
	Dailies	X				
	Sound Effects	X				
	Dialog Reprints	X				
	Foley String-offs	X				
	A.D.R. String-offs	X				
	Worktrack 1:1's	X				
	Backgrounds (mono)	X				
	Temp FX — (for Pix Edit)	X				
5006	Fullcoat Requirements					
	Backgrounds (stereo)	X				
	Temp Dub Mix stock					
	Foley (4 trk) Stock	X				
	A.D.R. (4 trk) Stock	X				
	Music Transfers	X				
	Predubs (all)					
	Final Mix — Masters					
	Final Mix — Back-Up					
	Final Mix — Stems					
	M.&E. "Foreign"					
	Television Version					
5007	Stage Protection Stock					
	DAT-or-1/4" protection — Foley					
	DAT-or-1/4" protection — A.D.R.					
5010	Stock for Customization					
	DAT-or-1/4" protection — FX					
5020	Courier service					
[____]	[_____]					
[____]	[_____]					
[____]	[_____]					
5081	Sales Tax (___%)					
	TRANSFERS-&-STOCK PURCHASES ACCT TOTAL:					

IF you are cutting your picture on FILM rather than nonlinear digital

Figure 4.7 Transfer budget.

final mix processes, although most mixing is done digitally today using hard drive systems.

You must allow for protection back-up stock when you have ADR or Foley sessions (see the "Stage Protection Stock" line item). There may be a few ADR stages that still use DAT back-up, even though you are recording to a Pro Tools session. The sound facility where you contract your stage work may include this cost in its bid. You must check this—make sure to take an overview of how many protection DATs are allowed and the cost per item if you decide to use such tape protection.

Some sound facilities charge the client a "head wear" cost for using customer-supplied stock. This is nothing but a penalty for not buying facility's stock, which has obviously been marked up considerably. Find out the kind of stock the facility uses and then purchase the exact brand and type of stock from the supplier. Not only will you save a lot of money but you will pull the rug out from anyone trying to substitute "slightly" used reclaim stock instead of new and fresh. This is a common practice.

Postsound Facility

Referring to the "TEMP DUB(s)" line item (Figure 4.8), note for the purpose of discussion that we have reserved 4 days for temp dubbing in this budget sample. This can be used as 4 single temp mixing days, as 2 two-temp mixing days, or as 1 major 4-day temp mix.

We have a fairly good production track, for this budget example, but we have several segments where we need to loop the main characters to clean out background noise, improve performance, or add additional lines. We budgeted 5 days on the ADR stage. For this project, we have fairly large crowd scenes, and although we expect that sound editorial has all kinds of stereophonic crowds in its sound effects library, we want layers of specialized Crowd Walla to lay on top of the cut crowd effects. We budgeted 1 day to cover the necessary scenes (see the "A.D.R. STAGE & Group Walla" line item).

Note that you need to check your cast budget account and ensure that your budget has a line item for Group Walla. Many budgets do not, and I have encountered more than one producer who has neglected to allow for this cost. In this case, we budgeted for 20 actors and actresses, who all double and triple their voice talents. With four stereo pairs of tracks, a group of 20 voices easily becomes a chanting mob scene or terrified refugees.

Here we budgeted 10 days to perform the Foley (see "FOLEY STAGE"), giving us 1 day per reel. This is not a big budget under the circumstances—action films easily use more time—but we were watching our budget dollars and trying to use them as wisely as possible. In a preliminary meeting with the supervising sound editor, who the producer had already set for the picture, we were assured that 10 days were needed for those audio cues that must be performed on the Foley stage. Other cues that could not have been done on a Foley stage, or that could have been recorded in other ways or acquired through the sound effects library, were not included in the Foley stage scheduling.

When it comes to "PREDUBBING," one should always think in terms that more predubbing means a faster and smoother final mix; less predubbing means a slower

ACCT		ACCOUNT TITLE	POST		RATE	TOTAL
5900		POST-SOUND FACILITY				
		(stage & labor — 8-hour days)				
5901		Temp Music Transfer				
		Digital and/or Analog				
5902		TEMP DUB(s)	4 dys			
		Screening copy transfer(s)				
5903		A.D.R. STAGE — sync voices	5 dys			
5904		A.D.R. STAGE — Group Walla	1 dy			
5905		FOLEY STAGE	10 dys			
5906		Dialog Reprint Transfer				
		Digital and/or Analog				
5910		Workstation Set-up(s) (stage)	25 dys			
		[Pro Tools / Waveframe]				
5920		PREDUBBING				
		Dialog Predubbing	3 dys			
		Foley Predubbing	2 dys			
		Background Predubbing	2 dys			
		Hard FX Predubbing	3 dys			
5921		FINALS				
		Final Rerecording	8 dys			
		Run thru -&- Updates	2 dys			
		Test screening mag transfer	10,000'			
5930		POST-TEST SCREENING MIX				
		Stem Transfer for Recut				
		Stem Remixing Updates	2 dys			
5940		2-track PRINT MASTER	1 dy			
5950		Optical Sound Mix Transfer	10,000'			
5960		Dolby & Surround Channel License Fee				
5961		Digital system License Fee(s)				
5963		Digital MASTERING (SDDS/DTS/SRD)				
5970		M.&E. "FOREIGN" MIX	1 dy			
5975		TELEVISION VERSION MIX	1 dy			
[____]		[_____]				
[____]		[_____]				
[____]		[_____]				
5981		Sales Tax (___%)				
		POST-SOUND FACILITY ACCT TOTAL:				

Figure 4.8 Post-sound budget.

and more agonizing final mix with a higher certainty of hot tempers and frustration. (You will read a great deal about mixing styles and techniques as well as dubbing stage etiquette and protocol later in this book.)

This budget allowed 8 days of final (see the "FINALS" line item). The first day is always the hardest. Reel 1 always takes a full day. It is the settling-down process, getting up to speed, finding out that the new head titles are two cards longer than the slug that was in the sound videos, so the soundtrack is $12\frac{1}{2}$ feet out of sync, stuff like that. This always brings the we-will-never-get-there anxiety threshold to a new high, causing the producer to become a clock-watcher. But as reel 3 is reached, one witnesses rhythm and momentum building...8 days is enough for this picture after all.

When the primary mix is finished, one then interlocks the final stems with the digital projector and screens the picture in a real-time continuity. Dubbing reel by reel, then viewing the film in a single run, are two different experiences. Everybody always has plenty of notes for updates and fixing, so we budgeted 2 days for this process.

Now we want to take the picture out with its brand-new, sparkling soundtrack and see what it does with a test audience. Depending on how we intend to screen the film, we may need to make a screening magnetic film transfer, if we are test screening on 35-mm print. This is best accomplished by running the mix through the mixing console so it can be monitored in the full theatre environment for quality control. We take this screening copy mix and our 35-mm silent answer print and run an interlock test screening somewhere that is equipped for dual interlock (and there are many venues).

It is a good idea to have a test run-through of the interlock screening copy materials before the actual test screening. I have seen too many instances where the client cut the schedules so tight that the last couple of reels of the screening copy was actually being transferred while the first reel was rolling in the test screening—not a good idea. While *Escape From New York* started to be interlock screened during a film festival on Hollywood Boulevard, we were still finishing the final mix on reel 10 back at the studio!

After the test screening, we have notes for further changes and updates. We need to allot monies to have the dialog, music, and effects stems as well as the predubs transferred into nonlinear editing hard drives for sound editorial to update and prepare for the stage.

To save money and any potential generation loss, we remix the updates stems and predubs (see the "Stem Remixing Updates" line item) straight from Pro Tools systems on the stage and interlocked to the machine room. We budgeted 2 days to remix the updated stems and predubs. We wisely have another test screening. Once we sign off on the both the film and its sound mix, we need to make the "2-track PRINT MASTER."

Even in our digital world we still need the matrixed stereo optical soundtrack. To accomplish this, we need to make a 2-track print master. At this point, we bring in the Dolby or Ultra*Stereo engineer, who brings the matrix equipment and monitors the transfer process of folding down the multiple stereo channels into a 2-track matrix. The engineer watches the peak meters closely, ensuring that the maximum levels will make optical, that the vibrancy and dynamics of the mix is translating properly. Many independent sound facilities do not have their own optical transfer departments. They subcontract this work out to reliable and reputable specialists. We must budget for the optical track to be shot and processed.

Do not forget the license fees. Almost all distributors now cover all the audio bases in one print, putting the various digital formats (Dolby SR-D, SDDS, and DTS) as well as the traditional 2-track analog optical on the same print. No matter what format the theatre has been built for, the same print plays in all of them.

Depending on the complexity and the sound-editorial preparation for M&E considerations, the "M.&E. 'FOREIGN' MIX" can take as short as half a day to as long as 2 days. We budgeted 1 full day for the M&E mix for our film. The last thing we need is for a foreign territory to bounce our M&E track and stick us with thousands of dollars in fix-it costs. (I cover techniques of preparation and delivery requirements of the foreign M&E track later in this book.)

Sound editorial had gleaned through the picture, replacing alternate lines or looping television coverage on the ADR stage. We budgeted 1 day for mixing our "TELEVISION VERSION MIX."

THE LOST SOUND DIRECTOR

Years ago we had an individual that followed the sound from the initial budgeting and scheduling, through the final 2-track print master and M&E delivery inventory. This individual was known as the sound director, who was, in a word, the QC (quality control) gatekeeper to the film's audio experience.

We have lost this position. More is the pity. In an age of filmmaking where mismatching technologies have mushroomed out of control and when coordinating an audio track has literally become a global challenge and responsibility, we need the return of the sound director. This is not the postproduction coordinator, as some people think. This is a management overseer, richly trained in the audio arts and with experience hash-marks up both arms. Wise will be the producer who writes this position in as a budget line item.

For budgetary reasons the producer might want to structure the sound director on a consultant basis rather than as a weekly payroll position, especially as a sound director oversees more than one project at a time. However the position is structured, the project reaps the obvious creative and financial benefits.

These are only a few highlights of the pitfalls in the journey you are preparing to take. How you prepare for it determines whether you bask in the joy of success—or anguish in a battlefield strewn with could-have-beens and should-have-dones. The technology is at your disposal; fine craftspeople can be found throughout the world—it is up to you.

Chapter 5
The Challenging Battlefield of Production

"I'm sorry, David, but the #$%*!ing director won't give me
two minutes to slap a couple of wireless mikes on the actors, and
there's no room in the #$%*ing office for my boom man, so I
had to stick the mike on the floor under the desk, so don't
blame me if it sounds like #$%*!"

*– Lee Howell, commenting on production DAT-14 while
working as a production sound mixer*

Without a doubt, the most difficult and arduous recording process in the audio track development of a film is the on-camera production dialog recording. Here the lack of preparation and tactical planning rears its ugly and expensive head in the coming months of postproduction. Here the ignorance and apathy of other production-unit department heads, usually consumed by their own contracted concerns, becomes apparent; they do little to help the sound-recording team in what should be a collaborative effort to achieve ideal production audio tracks during the shoot. Only seasoned directors and producers know the loss that occurs of both real money (spent to ADR actors' lines) and of the magic of on-camera performance, rarely recaptured and seldom improved.

Some actors have it written into their contracts that they will do no postproduction looping. In other words, if the sync production track is not usable, or if the director or producer decides that a line should be read differently or replaced for whatever reason, the actor would not be available to come onto an ADR stage and reperform it. These additional contractual complexities add even more pressure to capture the most pristine production recordings possible—pressure that seldom concerns other production heads, who so often have an immediate and dramatic impact on the ability of the production sound mixer and boom operator to achieve such recordings.

I remember, while working on one film, watching the production crew filming a medium angle of Jamie Lee Curtis at MGM. I was amazed to see a crewman standing

Figure 5.1 A typical basic production sound crew of three: the production sound mixer on the right (Paul Jyrälä), the boom operator on the left (Matti Kuorti), and the cable man in the center (Olli Viskari) working on *Talvisota: The Winter War*. (Photo by Ulla-Marja Parikka.)

just off to the side of the camera's view, calmly eating an apple. The penetration of his teeth was clearly heard each time he bit into the apple's skin. An electrician stood beside him playing with the loose change in his pocket. Neither was making this "sound clutter" on purpose; both were clearly audio-ignorant. Nevertheless, I was stunned at the lack of respect and professionalism they paid to their audio craftspeople during the sequence filming. I knew that a few weeks hence, some sound editor would heave a sigh of disappointment and spend an unnecessary amount of time and extra production dollars to clean out the audible intrusions.

I talked to hundreds of various craftspeople while writing this book, and was constantly surprised and fascinated by the wide range of views and perceptions regarding sound. The vast majority agree that sound is one of the most important components of a film, and many actually rate sound as more important than the visual photography itself—yet most craftspeople not working in sound do not understand their own contributions to the success—or failure—of the production soundtrack.

THE PRODUCTION RECORDING TEAM

The Sound Mixer

Responsible for the quality of the sound recordings on the set, the head of the recording team is the sound mixer. During preproduction the sound mixer consults with the producer and director on the best ways to tackle the recording challenges of the production sound. Each project is different; each dictates its particular needs. Simple projects may have fairly straightforward requirements, so it might be agreed to record the dialog on a less expensive 2-channel digital recorder, most likely direct-to-hard disk within the machine or flash technology. Most digital dialog today is recorded at 48 kHz/24-bit, but there are projects that are seeing the wisdom to move up to 96 kHz/24-bit. Virtually every serious professional recording device today is rated at least to this level as they see this standard quickly approaching. A few units are already qualified to record at 192 kHz—decidedly prepared for future and inevitable growth. The retarding factor in this higher recording rate is the compatibility with nonlinear picture-editorial platforms such as Final Cut Pro and Avid. The incredible reduction cost in price-per-gigabyte disk space is making such leaps in improved audio file size much easier to deal with.

Most serious projects will probably require multiple-channel recording capabilities so the sound mixer can capture multiple microphone setups that will be in constant flux of different actors in constant motion on a complicated set on their own discrete channels. More and more complicated audio setups are becoming the norm, not the exception. Individual wireless microphones may be placed on each actor as well as two channels of overhead "air" mikes and two foreground boomed mikes. This could easily require at least one 8-track recorder. Such discrete control becomes vital in maintaining control in mixing the discrete channels later, and not prematurely mixing together two or more microphone sources, only to have misbalance mixing decisions made on the set and then be unable to rebalance them later.

The sound mixer must choose the right recording format for the project, rent or supply the necessary equipment to accomplish the task required, and use that equipment to the best of his or her abilities during the filming process. They not only supply picture editorial with the best possible recorded material, but also with a volume of copious notes and sound reports that help guide the picture editor, and later the sound editors, through the maze of sync recordings, wild tracks, and room tones.

The Boom Operator

The boom operator is an incredibly important position: if he or she does not get the microphone into the right position at the proper moment, the actor's voice is off-axis and sounds off-mike. There is no such postproduction "plug-in" to process off-mike dialog and correct it. Off-mike is off-mike! The boom operator must be strong and agile, as well as attentive and observant. He or she must know the exact positions of invisible boundaries below which the microphone must not dip down into camera view. The boom operator must also memorize light throws and angles so as not to allow the shadow of the microphone to be seen on any surface of the area being photographed.

For those readers who might think it cannot be any big deal dangling a microphone around over a couple of actors, try tying an unopened can of dog food to the end of an 18-foot pole and hold it (fully extended) over your head for 4 minutes. Now think about having to do this while concentrating on rotating and pivoting the pole to flip the microphone into position, first one way, then suddenly another way—all the while watching for microphone shadows and keeping it above the view of the camera lens. You must accomplish all of this without making any noise or vibration that will be telegraph low-end thumping into the microphone's diaphragm. Getting tired yet?

The boom operator must also know the delicate workings of radio microphones. He or she must know how to wire an actor quickly, yet know how to work diplomatically with performers' often unpredictable personalities and temperaments. The boom operator has a personal kit: a tool or tackle box that holds the tools, tapes, batteries, supplies, and implements that make it all work. In a matter of moments, the wireless microphone must be placed on the actor, in exactly the right spot. The wire must be carefully hidden under the clothing and run to wherever the transmitter is being hidden on the actor's body. This is an art form onto itself.

The boom operator must be constantly on the lookout for anything making unwanted noise. Good boom operators do not complain and report problems to the sound mixer or first assistant director; they assess the problem and offer solutions for dampening the offending sound down, if not completely eliminating the audio intrusions from polluting the recording.

The Cable Man

The cable man used to be known as the "third man." He or she is also known as the sound utility, and, when a second microphone boom is needed, the cable man wields it into place. The cable man literally clears the microphone cables and keeps the boom operator from backing into things or banging props or the side of the set with the fish pole when cast and crew are in motion. When a boom operator must make a backward maneuver to clear the way and reposition to capture the actors cleanly, the cable man guides the boom operator back with a hand on the belt or back, clearing cable or even silently moving things out of the way.

If a microphone cable has gone bad or is suspect, the cable man grabs another cable and changes it out instantly. The cable man is often creating an impromptu rain hat, using short sections of doweling (often precut thin lengths of branches) and wrapping it with a thin liner of plastic cover from a dry-cleaning bag and a section of air-conditioning "hog hair" filter. He or she anticipates problems before they arise and quietly solves them so the boom operator can concentrate on the job at hand.

The Sequence of Production Recording

The production mixer understands the rhythm of the production shoot. He can tell when the first A.D. (assistant director) is about to announce that they are ready to roll film for a take. The mixer sets his sound recorder into a standby, or "Test" position. This allows the electronics to power up and be warmed and ready to operate at nominal performance on command.

The production mixer's sound recorder has been parked in the pause (Test) mode, keeping the electronics live and ready to roll. The mixer activates the recorder in the Record mode. The tape turns at the designated speed, and the indicator shows a steady and dependable speed. The mixer presses his slate mike on his microphone mixing unit to verbally slate the shot, "Scene 29 Baker, take 3."

Figure 5.2 Production mixer Glen Trew with his Deva 5 and Cameo handling the chores on James Agee's classic novel, *A Death in the Family*, for Masterpiece Theater.

Verbally slating the audio tape prior to the camera rolling can save valuable film negative. Many mixers actually preslate the upcoming take prior to the first A.D.'s announcement to roll sound. The mixer will preslate and then place the recorder in pause ("Test") mode again, waiting for the first A.D. to call to "Roll sound."

Sure enough, the first A.D. calls out, "Let's have the light and bell."

The production mixer is also responsible for the warning light (the revolving red light) just outside the stage or on the perimeter of the location set. The mixer flips the warning light on, which also sounds the bell (one ring duration). Work activity stops and the crew holds their positions quietly for the shot.

Satisfied that activity has settled on the set, the first A.D. cries out, "Roll sound!"

The production mixer turns the recording machine into Record mode. Once he or she is satisfied that the machine is up to proper speed and that time code or pilot sync is true and steady the mixer will call out, "Speed."

Nothing, and I mean *nothing*, can or will proceed until the sound mixer has called out "Speed." I have seen too many beginning mixers feel so intimidated that they are holding up the shoot, that they call out "Speed" before their equipment is truly ready, especially if they had turned the recorder on from a cold start without having the electronics warmed up. This means that the first few seconds of recording will not sound clear, and on more than one occasion valuable dialog was ruined because the mixer did not take the extra few seconds to pay strict attention to the sound through the headsets and be satisfied that he or she was actually getting a proper clear and steady signal.

Just because we live in a digital world now does not mean that digital equipment does not have to be warmed up and up-to-speed and satisfaction before the mixer commits to go forward.

Once the mixer has announced "Speed," then the first A.D. cues the camera crew, "Roll camera."

The camera operator turns the camera on and gives it a moment to gain sound speed; then he or she answers, "Camera speed."

The slate assistant (who is usually the film loader) holds up the slate that has the vital information for the show and scene number written on it. For our example purposes, it reads 29 "B" TK-3.

Most camera crews have the slate assistant verbally slate the scene, "Scene 29 Baker, take 3."

Some crews forgo doing this as an excuse to save film. It is really up to the protocol desired and the concern of film stock that will dictate this choice of procedure. The slate assistant snaps the slate for sync and steps quickly out of camera view.

The first A.D. calls, "Cue background."

The second A.D. cues the background extras so that they will be in motion. The director allows the action to take a few moments so that a few precious seconds of presence with background movement will be recorded (it will match any "inter-filling" that needs to be done later by a dialog editor). Then the director cues the actors, "Action."

The preceding is the proper and ideal protocol for preslating, rolling sound, and on-screen slating by a slate assistant and for creating pre-action presence with the natural action of background extras as it will sound during the internal action of a scene. If you were to record presence tone without the background extras, the intercut presence would sound horribly out of place, cut in between actors' lines, for instance, to replace a director's cue or an unwanted sound. With audio-aware directors and assistant directors, you will achieve this level of protocol and consideration consistently, rendering the best possible audio results.

The Basic Recording Kit

Like anything else, the composition and extent of the mixer's tools at his or her disposal differ with every picture and every budget at hand. Whether the project has no money to speak of or is a multimillion-dollar blockbuster, the basic recording kit does not change much. You need the following items:

- Sound cart
- Sound recorder(s)
- Portable mixer
- Microphones
- Microphone cables
- Wireless RF microphones

- Fish pole(s)
- Shock mount pistol grip with zeppelins
- Windscreen covers
- Miscellaneous adapters, phase inverters
- Smart slate
- Communication radios/comtechs
- Voltage meter for AC tie-ins
- Battery supply
- Cables
- Extra plugs, batteries, etc.
- Plastic and/or blanket for protection from flying objects or weather

ANALOG OR DIGITAL

Whether to record digitally or analog is a decision that requires factoring numerous technical and philosophical requirements and attitudes. One must not think that just because a new technology and/or "fad buzzword" is used means that it is better or more desirable. For instance, it is nearly impossible to convince someone that analog recording can not only be preferable, but superior, unless he or she has used both a digital DAT recorder and an analog Nagra under comparative recording conditions and compared the results.

Personally, I embrace both analog and digital recording, deciding what will accomplish the desired result. In the early days of DAT recording I became weary of listening to my colleagues argue back and forth that digital was better, and others say that analog was better. So I decided that we should go out and record analog and digital formats side-by-side simultaneously, using identical microphones that were arrayed together (for precisely the same recording aspect) and identical cables. The difference would be the tape recording device—analog or digital, and what format. To help you appreciate the recording differences, review the "comparative medium recordings" on the DVD provided with this book. Check the fifth button on the main menu of the DVD, named Custom Recording FX. The second button on the submenu is named Comparison Recording.

We felt that we needed a very dynamic intense audio event to make the comparison easier to analyze, and frankly, I could think of nothing more dynamically intense than a .308 Heckler and Koch assault rifle!

Most production mixers currently use the direct-to-disk digital recorders as their primary tool; however, many still keep a $1/4$" Nagra in the sound truck. When the digital gremlins plague a recording session, and many mixers have their own "bad days" stories, they require a rugged and dependable back-up recorder until the digital gremlins have been vanquished.

For the first 10 or 12 years of production digital recording, serious audio craftspeople still preferred the fullness and warmth of analog recording, especially when they had the luxury to record on a Nagra at 15 ips. During those early days of digital production sound, very few of us disagreed with that ideal, especially those with an ear trained to harmonic subtleties. However, those of us who still recorded material in analog (for whatever practical reason) would immediately transfer the audio material into the digital environment for the postproduction process.

The question of analog versus digital recording then became an issue of the production challenges themselves, budget considerations and, of course, who handled the recording chores as mixer. I have had the pleasure of working with a handful of mixers who were extraordinary at recording digitally in the early days of DAT technology. Lee Howell (Los Angeles) is one; Paul Jyrälä (Helsinki) is another. Peter Meiselmann was, by nature a hardcore analog specialist, but was pressed into recording the production track for *Terror Tract* using a DAT recorder because the first-time producers felt they needed digital technology for some postproduction reason. It was Peter's first time using the DAT technology, but his years as a disciplined analog mixer served him well to adapt to the digital medium. In fact, I was stunned by the results, as I happened to handle this project. The usual flaws and recording mistakes that plague the digital world were not there. In fact, numerous sequences that had a screaming monkey, shotgun blasts, and other harsh concussive audio cues were not only recorded beautifully, but they were devoid of distortion and overload edginess—all of which were overcome because of Peter's analog experience and discipline know-how.

One must not be lulled into thinking that the final outcome of a film's soundtrack is reflective of the production mixer's work. It can be, but not necessarily. I have handled films where every second of production recording was ultimately stripped out of the track and every syllable of the movie was re-voiced.

BACK-UP TAPES

As discussed in Chapter 4, having back-up medium (DATs, DVD-Rs, or clone drives) may seem like an inconvenience and a waste of money, but when you first experience the shipping carrier losing the shipment on the way to the lab and sound facility, or the first time your primary DAT machine "eats" the tape at program number 88, or the audio data files on your removable drive are found to be corrupted, you will wish that back-up precautions had been a part of the budget.

The mixer should always hold on to the original material, sending the clone drive, DVD-R, or back duplicate back-up DAT back to picture editorial. The last thing you want is to ship both the original and back-up medium together (obviously all would be lost if the shipment got lost or was destroyed!). That is, after all, the whole point of the exercise.

The mixer has the original in his or her care should the director and producer have a critical question that may arise of "bad sound" or problems that actually became an issue of a bad sound transfer later at the lab or sloppy digitization by the assistant picture editor. Many a sound mixer could have avoided being the scapegoat in a finger-pointing row between the producer and sound transfer over the poor quality of a daily soundtrack. I know of several situations where the sound mixer was vindicated because an A-B comparison between the original recorded medium and the transfer was played side-by-side for the director and producer. On one particular picture, the studio was actually compelled to fire its own sound transfer department as contractor and then contract the sound transfer chores to a rival studio, all because the mixer had kept either a back-up tape (or drive) or the original, depending on which he or she sent back to picture editorial.

LINE-UP TONES

As described in greater detail in Chapter 6, it is critical that every tape, whether analog or digital, even when you are recording direct-to-disk hard drives, have a known line-up reference tone at the head of the tape or the first cue on the hard drive. The sound mixer threads up the first tape of the day onto the Nagra, or inserts the first DAT cassette into the recorder, or warms up the multichannel direct-to-disk recorder. The first thing he or she does is record an announcement of what is what and where they are and what kind of line-up tone is about to be heard.

> Good morning, we're out here today at Glacier Point for Silver Run Entertainment's production of Five Rings of Michael. The date is Tuesday, June 26th, 2007. This is drive 3. We're recording on a Sound Devices 744t with a flat-EQ mode at a sampling rate of 96 K at 24-bit. Stand by for the reference tone which is –20 dB equals "0" VU.

In this short and to-the-point pell-mell of information, you have given the most important hit points.

- Location of recording
- Production company name
- Project name
- Date of recording—month, day, and year
- The $^1/_4$" roll, DAT, or removable hard drive number
- Type/model of recording machine
- Equalization setting
- Tape speed or sampling rate being recorded at
- A clear definition of line-up tone

One must approach recording the information header of a fresh roll of recording tape, DAT, or hard drive as if the tape or drive itself will be the only thing that survives the shoot. The box will be lost, the data card will be lost, the sound report will be lost. Believe me, I know. I once had a big box handed to me that was just a huge wad of $^1/_4$" tape from a shoot in the Philippines. No box, no reports, no reels, just thousands of feet of $^1/_4$" tape. Anything and everything I was going to know about the material on it (once I unwound the scrunched up ball of magnetic ribbon) was going to be what I gleaned from the mixer's header information and verbal shot slates. With that kind of nightmare possibility looming around you, it really makes you keep in mind how vitally clear and precise vocal slates and information headers are to everyone who will work with your material.

- *Location of recording:* Though not vital to know, almost all sound mixers mention where the shoot is in the information header.
- *Production company name:* This identifies these recordings as the property of the company or individual that hired the recording mixer to do the assigned work.

- *Project name:* Always list the name of the project. In the case of episodic material, always name the project along with the production number.
- *Date of recording:* Name the date. There are numerous information data entries that will follow the shoot that use the date as a reference. Many times we will check the date of one or more shoots to satisfy what may supersede earlier versions; as well, sometimes it is vital information to be used for legal purposes.
- *Roll or drive number:* This is one of the most important pieces of information, as the roll or drive number is entered alongside the negative roll number (picture) in the code book and shows up on the EDL (Edit Decision List) of the final-cut version of the film from the nonlinear platform. It becomes the quickest way to access original roll material for reprints, alternate takes, or to make an A-B comparison between an OMF (Open Media Framework) file from the nonlinear platform to determine if a complete retransfer from source material will be required because the original digitized transfers were substandard (a subject we will discuss later in the book).
- *Type/model of recording machine:* Always tell us what kind of recording device you are using. The transfer facility will want to know this so they will not inadvertently try to transfer the material on a playback unit with the wrong head configuration.
- *Equalization setting:* It is valuable for the transfer tech or the assistant editor to know what kind of equalization setting was used, whether or not you rolled off any high or low end, etc.
- *Tape speed or sampling rate:* Tell us what tape speed (analog) or sampling rate (digital) you are recording at. Do not think that it is always obvious. You would be surprised how many times not knowing has screwed things up because someone assumed that it was obvious.
- *Line-up tone:* The line-up tone quoted above is written on the sound report as − 20 dB = "0" VU. Because there are so many variations of "0" levels that equal a prescribed peak meter level and other variations of recording equipment that use different levels and/or kinds of level protocols, it is a vital technique for the mixer to verbally tell us what kind of line-up tone he or she is about to record onto the tape or hard drive and what it means.

Once the line-up tone is defined, the mixer will lay down at least 8 to 12 seconds of line-up tone. The reference tone level quoted on the tape is interpreted to be referenced to "0" on the VU (volume unit) analog meter or is referenced to what level "0" is interpreted on a peak meter (i.e., 20 dB equals "0" VU; or if you are using a peak meter in transfer, make −20 dB equal −20 dB on the peak meter). Without this reference tone, one cannot accurately set playback levels to make exact 1:1 (one-to-one) copies at a later time.

SOUND REPORT

The sound report is the key to the mixer's hard work and efforts; it is the road map of what is on the recorded tape and where to find it. If properly filled out, the sound report also offers a wealth of information through notations made by the mixer as work progresses. Some mixers are more note-oriented than others; but if all mixers actually realized the value of their notes, they would probably pay more attention to making them.

As a supervising sound editor, I know the invaluable contribution of a mixer's notes, especially when it comes to comments about airplane noise or undesirable talking (listed as VOX) that may have marred the recording.

The most valuable of notes are those regarding wild tracks (listed as WT). When I begin a project, I immediately get a copy of the mixer's sound reports and quickly scroll through them, looking for any WTs or miscellaneous recordings that may determine what other recordings to which I may need to refer or authorize to have done.

On more than one occasion, I was required to look at the sound reports of a project before I committed a bid, and depending on the quality of note coverage (or lack thereof), I have actually rejected even bidding on a show because I could see the dialog work was going to be too much of a nightmare because of sloppy mixer notations and lack of vital information. The reverse is also true; I have accepted what appeared to be impossible edit assignments *because* the mixer's sound reports were highly detailed and had a wealth of notes regarding unwanted noise to watch out for, good production sound effect moments, as well as the presence of professional technique to record numerous WTs to help problem solve audio issues that sound editorial would eventually find invaluable.

It is equally important to list a shot where there is no sound. For one reason or another it may be decided to shoot a setup where the sound mixer is not rolling sound. He or she will list on the Sound Report the abbreviation MOS (which stands for without sound). Actually, a person could sit for hours and wonder how in the world you get the letters MOS out of "without sound," until one knows the genesis of the abbreviation.

Back in the early 1930s, during the infancy of the motion picture sound process, a famous director was shooting a picture when he decided not to have the optical sound camera roll for whatever reason. He turned to his crew and in his heavy European accent, he announced to them, "Awlright children, this vun vee do mit out sound." The continuity script girl did not ask what he meant by that, but listed the sound note of the shot as M.O.S. in the script notes, and to this day the acronym MOS has stuck.

Frankly, it is uncertain who actually coined the term. Believe me, every academic professor has his or her expert opinion, but I can guarantee you that none of them was there to witness it. I have heard of someone who claims to have been there, but when you scratch the surface of the claim it was actually hearsay. I have interviewed a number of my colleagues on this issue, several of whom date that far back, but none of them knows the answer beyond a shadow of a doubt. Many think that it was the colorful, if not legendary, Michael Curtiz who said it (*The Sea Hawk, Casablanca, The Egyptian, We're No Angels*). Curtiz certainly had an infamous reputation for mauling the English language. Others insist that it was Ernst Lubitsch (*The Shop Around the Corner, Heaven Can Wait, To Be or Not to Be, That Uncertain Feeling*) who said the immortal words; while Hal Mohr, a cinematographer who had worked with Paul Fejos many years ago, attributes the quote to Fejos himself, whose continuity script girl's abbreviation stays with us to this day.

Regardless of *who* said it, the fact remains, when the production sound mixer writes MOS on his or her sound report next to a scene/shot designation, every sound transfer facility in the world knows that the sound recorder was *not* rolling.

There is no doubt that at some point one or more of these individuals may well have slurred the pronunciation and enunciation of the directive. The truth of the matter is that that is not the genesis of the acronym, rather a romantic explanation by those who do not know the entire background. (Remember what I said in Chapter 1.)

The fact is that there is no substantiation that the curious expression spawned the acronym, whereas during the evolution of recording sound onto a 35-mm film negative, using a sound "camera" as a photographic optical medium for production sound recording, the designation MOS was well known to mean "Minus Optical Sound." When the director did not require sync sound for a particular shot, the recording mixer simply listed MOS on the sound reports.

Unlike hearsay stories, there are actual written sound report notes that explain this fascinating story. Not as romantic and fun? Sorry. Remember, back during the first 25 years of motion picture audio, production sound recordings were accomplished by "photographing" the microphone pick-up via the *optical* sound camera.

Increasingly, more mixers are adopting a full-page-width sound report, which gives considerably more room for notation. The slender version of the sound report that dominated the industry for decades was designed so that you could fold it over and simply lay it inside the box of a 5" or 7" reel of ¼" tape. Unfortunately, this convenient width also inhibited mixers from writing sufficient notations, and, believe me, we in the postproduction process will read as many notes, ideas, and warnings as the mixer will take the time to write.

As you study a typical sound report (Figure 5.3), note the types of vital information displayed there. Believe it or not, even the title of the picture is important. Too many times the transfer department is hung up trying to find a scene and take of a print only to discover that it picked up a similar-looking box assumed to belong to the same show because no markings indicated the contrary; hence, valuable time is lost as the transfer department searches for the right roll number from the wrong show title. Worse, when the "right" scene is found and the transfer department takes and prints it, it is sometimes discovered too late that it is from the wrong show.

Many times, mixers do not fully complete the information header, which has often confused transfer departments. Sometimes unusual head tone levels are utilized; these must be carefully noted.

If the mixer is using a DAT machine, he or she enters the PNO (program number) that the DAT recorder automatically assigns each time it starts a new recording. The PNO locator system has been a wonderful thing for us in postproduction. You simply enter the program number of the scene and take you want and hit the play button. The DAT machine spins at 200 times speed in search of this number, automatically stops, and aligns at the head of the recording and plays it—what a great timesaver!

Next to the DAT PNO, the mixer lists the scene and angle designation number of each recording. Generally, a mixer only enters the scene number once, then draws a line vertically alongside all the takes until the next angle. For example, the mixer lists scene 105 "A" in the scene box, then take 1. He or she lists take 2 below that and take 3 below that, all the while drawing a vertical line from 105 "A" until that angle is a

Sound Report

SHEET # _____ - OF - _____

TITLE _____ ROLL # _____

COMPANY _____ MACHINE _____ TAPE SPEED _____

PROD. NO # _____ HEAD TONES _____ _____ dB = _____ VU

MIXER _____ SYNC _____

BOOM OP _____ PRINT CIRCLED TAKES ONLY

SCENE #	TAKE	PNO	LEFT CHANNEL	RIGHT CHANNEL	COMMENTS	TIME CODE
						: : :
						: : :
						: : :
						: : :
						: : :
						: : :
						: : :
						: : :
						: : :
						: : :
						: : :
						: : :
						: : :
						: : :
						: : :

Figure 5.3 A typical 2-channel sound report form.

wrap. The next setup is 105 "B." Each take has its own line. Do not list all the takes together on one line. It is not only more convenient for the mixer to write, but it is much faster for an assistant editor or transfer tech to find material, as the writing will "eye-scan" much more easily and more efficiently.

A mixer may use a single microphone but have it split on two channels. The first channel (left) is recording at standard level; the second channel (right) is recording the exact same information only at a lower level (often −10 dB) in case of sudden bursts of sounds, such as gunshots, crashes, screams, and so forth. The mixer makes this notation accordingly.

In the middle of the roll, a mixer may decide to use two microphones and keep them on dedicated channels. He or she notes that actor one is on channel 1 (left), and that actor two is on channel 2 (right).

In the comments column, the mixer makes any pertinent comments that he or she feels the postproduction people may need. I personally love it when a mixer makes a comment such as "Great door slam" or "Neat machinery ka-thumps" or "Watch out for airplane in track." During interviews for this book, mixers confessed that if they

SCENE #	TAKE	PNO	LEFT CHANNEL	RIGHT CHANNEL	COMMENTS	TIME CODE
——	——	1	line-up tone	line-up tone −10	−20 dB = '0' VU	01 : 00 : 00 : 05
87	1	2	overhead boom	split −10 dB	watch for dolly creaks	01 : 01 : 22 : 12
	2	3			good door close!	01 : 03 : 43 : 20
87 "A"	1	4	actor ASHLEY	actor FRANK	watch overmodulations	01 : 05 : 55 : 03
	2	5			excellent -- no over mods	01 : 08 : 11 : 17
	3	6			nice variations	01 : 10 : 32 : 02
87 "B"	1	7	actor FRANK	overhead boom	watch off axis miking	01 : 13 : 16 : 19
	2	8			good -- some dolly creaks	01 : 15 : 52 : 01
	3	9			nice tool movt -- not overmodulated	01 : 18 : 07 : 12
	4	10			finally -- no wind buffet !!	01 : 20 : 32 : 18
87	W.L.	11			wild Lines -- scene 87 shouting	01 : 23 : 07 : 03
92	1	12	overhead boom	split −10 dB	watch wind buffet in places	01 : 26 : 20 : 14
	2	13			watch for airplane overhead	01 : 29 : 31 : 06
	3	14			decent -- lines in the clear	01 : 32 : 28 : 09

Figure 5.4 A closer view of the sound report data chart; lots of notes are the keystone for success.

really thought their notations were being read and used by anyone after the day's shoot, they would certainly make a bigger effort to write them. Sadly, many mixers do not feel that, in today's compressed postproduction schedules and budgets, anyone takes time to glean through their notes and/or ferret out wild tracks recorded for postproduction applications.

Many transfer departments use sophisticated calibrated vari-speed controllers. Many times, a director wants a set-up photographed off-speed, such as over-cranking the camera at 30 frames per second (fps) or higher for a slightly slowed-down effect, or under-cranking at 18 or 20 fps, which ultimately speeds up the shot when projected at a normal 24 fps. If the director does not want the harmonic pitch and timbre of the voice to sound pitched in relationship with the over- or under-cranking, then the vari-speed unit correctly pitch-shifts the audio up or down; this way, when it is played back at 24 fps, the visual action is slow-motion or accelerated, but the pitch and timbre of the soundtrack sound normal.

One particular underwater monster picture was entirely shot 2 fps slower than sound speed (22 fps) making the pace of the action faster. This not only allowed the producer to tell a 103-minute story in only 95 screen minutes (which also proved more desirable to the distribution company), but it also allowed a performance ediginess and tension to be instilled because the cast was speaking and moving slightly faster. If such notations are made in the comments column, the transfer department can effect the transfer accordingly, making daily transfers to match the picture.

Note that the last column is formatted for time code notations. In today's ever-increasing world of "smart" slates and time code dailies, the far right-hand column, which used to be reserved for transfer notations, is now being utilized by the production mixer to list time code starts for each take.

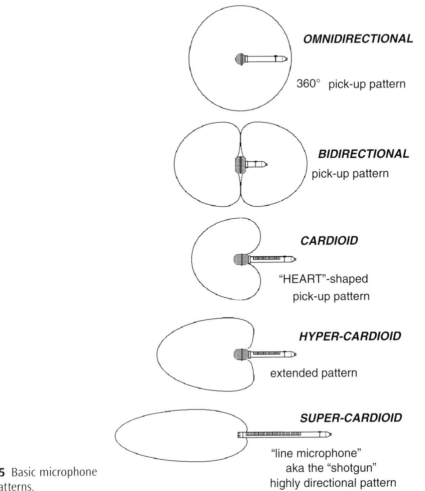

OMNIDIRECTIONAL

360° pick-up pattern

BIDIRECTIONAL

pick-up pattern

CARDIOID

"HEART"-shaped
pick-up pattern

HYPER-CARDIOID

extended pattern

SUPER-CARDIOID

"line microphone"
aka the "shotgun"
highly directional pattern

Figure 5.5 Basic microphone pick-up patterns.

MICROPHONES AND PICKUP PATTERNS

The primary tools in the arsenal of weapons at the mixer's disposal are the various kinds of microphones with their various types of pick-up patterns. Good mixers have carefully chosen kits they can mix and match, depending on the location and challenges of the sequence to record. Following is an explanation of the basic kinds of microphones generally used for production recording (Figure 5.5).

Microphone Pattern

Omnidirectional Microphone
This condenser microphone has an omnidirectional pick-up pattern, as illustrated in Figure 5.5. The good thing about the omnidirectional microphone is that it has a rela-

tively even pattern that picks up everything around it. The bad thing is that it has a relatively even pattern and that it picks up everything around it, including but not limited to camera noise, feet shuffling, crew downrange who are whispering, aircraft high overhead, the eighteen-wheeler truck making the grade 5 miles away, and so forth. As with the use of any microphone, though, you must choose the right microphone for the right job. In some situations you could not be better served than by using a good solid omnidirectional microphone.

Cardioid: A Directional Microphone

Both dynamic and condenser microphones can be cardioid. As indicated in the diagram, the cardioid microphone has a directional pattern of some degree, or what is called a "heart-shaped" pick-up response. That means it picks up more signal directly in front of it than to the sides and especially behind it. It is not just a matter of sound level that is affected. It is a matter of axis. As the actor moves off-axis, or to the side of the microphone, the character and richness of the voice thin and the frontal presence falls away. This is referred to as being "off-mike."

Dynamic microphones do not require phantom power and are known for being rugged and able to handle a wide dynamic range of sound-recording situations. Vents run alongside the microphone shaft, allowing sound to enter from behind, striking the diaphragm and canceling out some of the same ambient signal that enters from the front, which gives the directional microphone its unique function of cancellation. Signal cancellation is crucial for clear dialog recording, especially when working in exterior situations. Sound of identical character that enters the rear of the microphone as well as the front and that strikes the diaphragm equally is canceled out, thereby cutting down the amount of ambient noise in relationship to the unique sound being recorded directly in front of the microphone, such as the actor's voice. The more sound allowed in from behind the diaphragm, the more directional the pattern.

As you can easily see, this kind of microphone is more suited for precision miking of actors on a location set already filled with an abundance of unwanted ambient noise. The challenge is to keep the center of the pattern right on the origin of the desired sound; otherwise you suffer "off-mike" recordings.

Hypercardioid: Highly Directional or "Mini-Shotgun"

Like its directional cousin (the cardioid), this type of microphone is more than just somewhat directional, hence its nickname the "mini-shotgun." Actually, the term is sort of a misnomer, its origin unknown, though sales personnel probably concocted it; regardless, "shotgun" has come to designate microphones with a more forward pick-up pattern. The longer the microphone tube, the greater the number of vents (to allow for rear-pattern cancellation and frequency compensation), and the more directional the microphone.

Supercardioid: Ultra-Directional "Shotgun"

Early supercardioids were called line microphones or rifle microphones. The supercardioid is just that—super highly directional, and equally more difficult to keep directly on the desired spot of origin for the most pristine of recordings. This microphone is not a good choice if your actor is doing much moving or if you have to cover more than one actor on the set; however, for single setups or two-shots where you cannot get in close with a fish pole and a traditional microphone, the supercardioid can really reach out and grab the signal.

The biggest mistake in using any microphone is forgetting that it does not have a brain. In other words, it cannot tell the difference between your voice and noise. Every application has a requirement; a right microphone exists for the right job. Your job is to know which to choose. For music applications, certain microphones can handle the sound-pressure levels that a kick drum might give out, or the brash brass of a trombone or saxophone. Other microphones cannot handle the percussiveness as well but have a much better reproduction of the top end for use in recording violins and triangles.

Unfortunately in our industry, many craftspeople try to make one microphone do too many chores. The veteran mixer will have developed a taste and style of recording, either personally owning or insisting on the rental of a precise mixed assortment of quality microphones to fill his or her arsenal of recording tools.

The MKH 60 is a lightweight short gun microphone (Figure 5.6). It is versatile and easy to handle and its superb lateral sound muting makes it an excellent choice for film and reporting applications. Its high degree of directivity ensures high sound quality for distance applications.

Features

- Extremely low inherent self-noise
- High sensitivity
- High directivity throughout the whole frequency range
- Transformerless and fully floating balanced output
- Infrasonic, cut-off filter
- Symmetrical transducer technology ensures extremely low distortion
- Switchable pre-attenuation, switchable roll-off filter, and switchable treble emphasis
- Rugged and weatherproof
- Black, anodized light metal body

Technical Specs

- Pick-up pattern: super-cardioid/lobar
- Sensitivity in free field, no load (1 kHz) 40 (12.5) mV/Pa
- Nominal impedance: 150 Ohm
- Minimum terminating impedance: 1,000 Ohm
- Equivalent noise level: 6 (14) dB
- Equivalent noise level weighted as per CCIR 468–318 (25) dB
- Power supply: Phantom 48 ± 4 V

Profile Super-cardioid/lobar (short gun) interference tube microphone with infrasonic cut-off filter, switchable pre-attenuation, switchable roll-off filter, and switchable treble emphasis. Frequency response 50 to 20,000 Hz, sensitivity (free field, no load) 40 (12.5) mV/Pa at 1 kHz, nominal impedance 150 Ohm, minimum terminating imped-

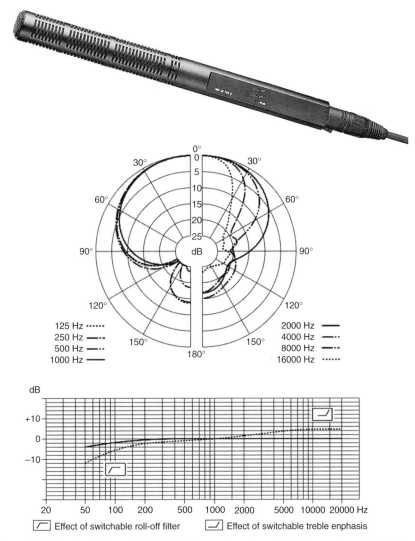

Figure 5.6 The Senheisser MKH 60 shotgun microphone. (Photo courtesy of Senheisser.)

ance 1 kOhm, equivalent noise level A-weighted 6 (14) dB, CCIR-weighted 18 (25) dB, maximum SPL 125 (134) dB at 1 kHz, phantom powering 48 ± 4 V, supply current 2 mA, dimensions Ø 25 × 280 mm, weight 150 g. Values in parentheses with attenuator switched on (−10 dB).

Here are some guidelines for the proper selection of the various microphone capsule options if you are using the Schoeps "Colette" system (Figure 5.7). Schoeps is often asked to recommend a microphone for a particular recording application, whether you are recording production dialog, custom sound effects, and especially if you are recording music. Some microphone manufacturers readily answer such requests. That might make sense if a microphone has a frequency response that is tailored to the

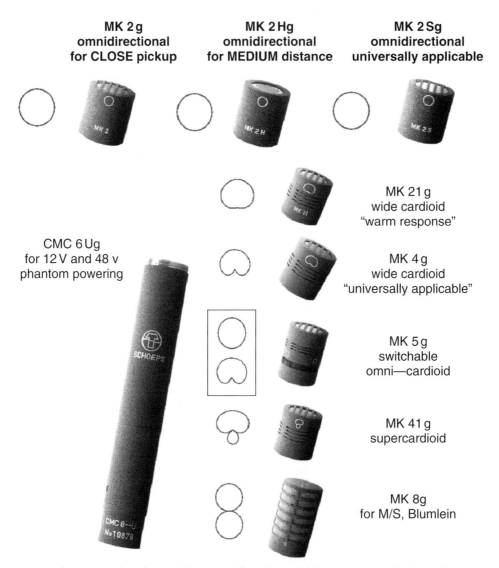

MK 2 g
omnidirectional
for CLOSE pickup

MK 2 Hg
omnidirectional
for MEDIUM distance

MK 2 Sg
omnidirectional
universally applicable

MK 21 g
wide cardioid
"warm response"

CMC 6 Ug
for 12 V and 48 v
phantom powering

MK 4 g
wide cardioid
"universally applicable"

MK 5 g
switchable
omni—cardioid

MK 41 g
supercardioid

MK 8g
for M/S, Blumlein

Figure 5.7 The Schoeps Colette, CMC "workhorse." (Photo courtesy of Schoeps.)

characteristic sound of a given instrument. But the possible applications for such microphones would then be restricted significantly.

Schoeps's opinion is that a good microphone ought to sound natural, just as one expects a good audio amplifier to sound; thus it should be suitable for any musical instrument or other production recording need. This requires flat frequency response and a directional characteristic independent of frequency. There will be no difference in sound quality whether the pickup is on- or off-axis. Obviously this ideal can be achieved only to a finite degree. With directional microphones, the proximity effect causes the low-frequency response to vary significantly while with nearly all microphones (especially omnidirectional microphones), the polar pattern is rarely ideal at the highest frequencies.

Only in rare cases can the correct microphone be chosen unequivocally, since, according to experience, one must also consider the aspects of taste, recording location, position of sound sources and the microphone, and the atmosphere of the music or other program material. Any absolute prescriptions would thus be of limited value at best. Schoeps offered the following text to help orient the choice(s) that the recording mixer must make before deciding which capsule(s) should be used for the recording challenge at hand.

The microphone type that comes closest to the theoretical ideal is the classic pressure transducer. It has an omnidirectional pickup pattern, reproduces even the lowest audio frequencies with full sensitivity, and has no proximity effect.

In practice some degree of directionality is generally considered desirable, and the most commonly used pattern for medium-distance pickup is the cardioid (MK 4/CCM 4 oder MK 4V/CCM 4V). In particular situations, however, there may be good reasons to make a different choice, including these observations from Schoeps:

- For increased directivity either for the sake of a "drier" recording or for the suppression of sound from adjacent instruments: supercardioid type "41" (= MK 41 or CCM 41), assuming that there is no nearby sound source or loudspeaker behind the microphone because it has a rear lobe.
- For decreased directivity or very natural sound quality even for sound arriving at the sides, or for improved low-frequency reproduction: the type "21" wide cardioid.
- For essentially perfect pick-up of low-frequency information and "room" sound: the omnidirectionals, type "2H" or "2S."
- For very close miking, with directional microphones it is necessary to compensate for the proximity effect by means of a corresponding bass roll-off. This is especially true when miking instruments; see our recommendations.
- For voice: the types "4S" or "4VXS."
- For instruments: the omnidirectional, type "2" may be of interest (no proximity effect, low sensitivity to "popping" or to solid-borne noise); for grand piano: the BLM 03 Cg.
- For very distant miking with essentially perfect bass response and/or as an "ambience" microphone: omni type "3."
- For outdoor recording if directivity is not required (at close miking distances): omni type "2S" + windscreen W 5 or W 5 D (advantage: low sensitivity to wind, "popping," and handling noise).
- For high directivity: type "41" with W 5 D, W 20 R1, or WSR MS ("basket"-type windscreen with built-in elastic suspension for mono or stereo).

As a starting recommendation, Schoeps suggests the switchable omni/cardioid capsule MK 5 + CMC 6 Ug microphone amplifier of the modular "Colette" series, or the corresponding Compact Microphone CCM 5.

One of the hottest high-quality shotgun microphones to come onto the market is the CMIT 5U (Figure 5.8). When you need to record dialog outdoors and the surrounding environment is very noisy and you find your current supercardioid pressed to the

Figure 5.8 The Schoeps CMIT 5U "Shotgun" mike. (Photo courtesy of Schoeps.)

limit and you are still not getting what you would like, you should look at the Schoeps CMIT 5U.

The Schoeps CMIT 5U has unusually low coloration of off-axis since the pick-up angles at low and high frequencies are kept reasonably similar to one another. At medium frequencies the directivity of the CMIT 5U is higher than one would expect from a microphone of this length, while at high frequencies the pick-up pattern is not narrow as with long shotgun microphones. This being the case, it is so much easier to cue the boom and keep actors "on mike" in very active scene scenarios.

This mike also has the audio quality that makes it extremely suitable for music recording as well as dialog. The directional pattern and sound quality are consistent in both the horizontal as well as the vertical planes, unlike some other shotgun microphones.

The CMIT 5U also enjoys a greater immunity to wind noise than the Schoeps supercardioid. It is very lightweight, utilizing a very sturdy all-metal housing. The capsule and amplifier of the CMIT 5U are built as a single unit, unlike the Schoeps "Colette" microphone series.

There are three pushbutton activated filters that allow the microphone to adapt to all kinds of recording situations—for high-frequency emphasis (+5 dB at 10 kHz) enhances speech intelligibility, and compensates the high-frequency loss caused by windscreens and "wooly" covers.

The steep low-cut filter (18 dB/oct. below 80 Hz) suppresses wind and boom noise nicely. A gentle low-frequency roll-off (6 dB/oct. below 300 Hz) compensates for the proximity effect.

Pairs of LEDs next to each pushbutton indicate the status of the filters, which is very handy when users need to know the status of their options on dark sound stages or night shoots.

In principle, Neumann shotgun microphones use a combination of a pressure gradient transducer and an interference tube. If the wavelength of the frequency is

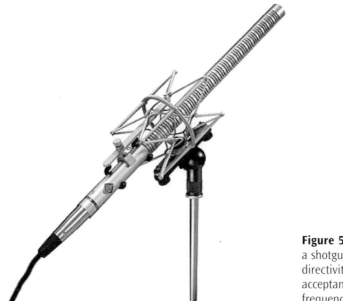

Figure 5.9 The Neuman KMR 82 is a shotgun microphone with a high directivity that remains within the acceptance angle independent of the frequency.

longer than the tube length, the microphones work as pressure gradient transducers. At higher frequencies they operate as interference transducers for lateral sound. Off-axis sound sources are picked up with reduced level, but without coloration.

The KMR 82 is less sensitive to wind and pop noise when compared to the KM 150 miniature microphone with a similar high directivity (Figure 5.9). The shotgun microphone features extremely low self-noise, good impulse response, and high output level.

The polar patterns of the KMR 82 shotgun microphone show it to have very directional characteristics. The microphone capsule is positioned inside a housing tube that is acoustically open but has a high flow resistance. The directional pattern of the microphone is lobe shaped. The attenuation of lateral sound is practically independent of the frequency. The KMR 82 has a frequency independent directivity within a pickup angle of 45° for audio signals that determine the tonal balance of the program material.

The "Smart" Slate

Figure 5.10 shows the Denecke "smart" slate. This time code lit display slate device is very handy, and especially used in music video work and fast location shooting scenarios. A wireless transmitter hooks up to the time code "out" connector of your audio recorder—which, of course, needs to have a time code generator (either built-in or outboard hook-up). The time code that is being embedded into your recording sync signal is exactly what will be transmitted to the smart slate.

As you can see in the photograph, there is a small wireless receiver (usually fitted with a patch of velcro on the back). *Note:* When you plug the connector wire into the

Figure 5.10 The smart slate.

receiver from the smart slate, the receiver's little red indicator light will come on, thereby powering it up automatically.

On the backside of the slate is a small toggle switch that is seated on a slim metal battery case. (The smart slate uses eight "C" cell batteries.) If you flip the toggle switch one way the time code numbers will illuminate on "low" intensity. If you flip the toggle switch "ON" the other direction, the time code numbers will illuminate on "HI" intensity. Obviously, high intensity will make the numbers easier to see in bright light situations; and of course, just as obviously, the "HI" intensity choice will wear out your "C" cell batteries a lot quicker as well.

The slate assistant will hold the smart slate up, after he or she has handwritten the Scene-Angle-Take information on the front, as with traditional slates. When the recording mixer rolls the audio deck, the time code will advance on the slate. When the slate assistant snaps the slate, the time code number will freeze on 00:00:00:00 a moment and then turn off. There are two small flush-mounted contact points near the end of the clapper arm, so when the two touch at the SNAP point, it activates the time code to cut off.

Even though this is a seemingly convenient and visually easy thing to see for picture editorial, the fact of the matter is that many mixers find that sync is not precise. You may experience as much as plus or minus two frames' accuracy. For those of us who come from the old school of precision, this is just not precise enough.

The Studio Microphone Boom

The studio microphone boom is a large wheeled perambulator with a small platform on which the boom operator stands while operating the traverse wheels that not only lengthen or shorten the boom extensions but also rotate and pivot the actual microphone position at the end of the boom arm. When properly operated, the boom functions silently and smoothly.

Studio microphone booms are used progressively less on feature films today because of complex and realistic set construction and the widespread use of practical locations being filmed under accelerated shooting schedules that don't allow the sound crew time and space to use the traditional perambulator boom. These silent microphone arms still have an important use in television production, though, especially when taping live-audience situations.

The techniques are considerably different from that of booming with a hand-held "fish-pole" style boom. Not only does a studio boom operator need coordination and dexterity to operate the traverse wheels accurately and smoothly, but he or she also must learn how to turn a microphone and extend the boom arm quickly (so as not to allow air buffeting to affect the delicate microphone diaphragm), and then rotate the microphone back into position once the boom arm has been thrust out into position. It is a technique wisely learned from the veteran boom operators who have worked the boom arms for many years, a technique that cannot be mastered overnight.

The Shock Mount and Wind Screen

Two of the biggest enemies of good exterior recordings are vibration and wind buffet. All microphones are mounted on something, whether a plastic friction clip or a cradle of a rubber band-mounted yoke. Budget constraints motivate you to new levels of inventiveness. Through experimentation and test recordings, you will develop a wide range of techniques to insulate the microphone from the vibrations of, say, a car as you hard-mount your microphone on the rear bumper to favor tailpipe exhaust. You will learn how to stuff foam around your mike and cram it into a crevice or lodge it between solid substances. You will learn how to detect wind direction and swirl patterns and how to effectively block them. You will learn to grab an assistant and physically place him or her between the source of unwanted breeze buffets and the microphone diaphragm.

Mount and Zeppelin

An effective way to control both vibration and wind buffet is a combination of the pistol-grip shock mount fitted with a windscreen tube called a Zeppelin. The microphone is fitted into the plastic ring clips, which hold it in place and protect it from undue vibration by the rubber-band trapeze.

Be careful to guide the microphone cable through the small round cutout at the bottom of the plastic ring, then snap the rear cap of the Zeppelin into place. Do not pull the microphone cable too tight, as the microphone shock mount works best if a little play of cable remains inside for movement. Depending on the breeze factor, you can either slip the gray "sock" over the Zeppelin or, if the breeze is fairly stiff, you might slip on the Ryocote "windjammer" (also referred to as a "wooly," "dead cat,"

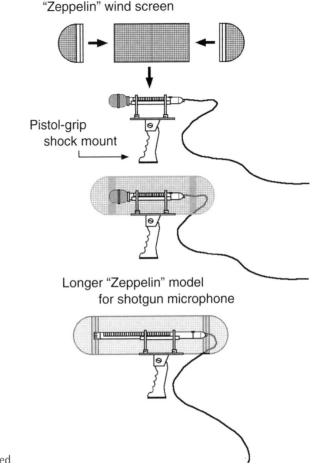

"Zeppelin" wind screen

Pistol-grip
shock mount

Longer "Zeppelin" model
for shotgun microphone

Figure 5.11 The pistol grip with the
Zeppelin wind protection tube attached.

"furry dog," or the "high wind cover") instead. These remarkable furry wonders have done much to knock down the kind of wind buffet that ruined many sound recordings in the past.

Fish-Pole Microphone Boom

As the name implies, the fish pole is a long pole with a microphone socket attachment to hold the microphone shock-mount. Most microphone fish poles are lightweight aluminum tubes that slide out and extend the length of the pole. Unlike with the studio microphone boom, do not extend the length of the fish pole during the recording process. You must either lengthen or shorten the desired length of the fish pole by unscrewing the friction locks and extending the second or third extension tube, then screwing it tight again before rolling sound.

Today, more and more production sound recording teams are taking advantage of wireless microphone booming techniques. This solves a multitude of issues, not the least of which is the length of cable that has to be constantly managed and monitored as the boom operator moves about as needed on the set. The wireless transmitter is located at the opposite end of the microphone boom from the microphone hanger. It does not take much to figure out that the collateral savings in costs and freedom of movement for the boom operator far outweighs the cost of having the microphone boom fitted out to be wireless.

GOOD MICROPHONE BOOM TECHNIQUES

Most microphone boom work is done by placing the microphone over the actors' heads, higher than the line of sight of the camera lens, pointing downward toward the spoken word.

Some mixers want the microphone to be pointing straight down, using an omni-directional pattern diaphragm mike, as it picks up a uniform ambient background recording, regardless of which way the performance comes at it. This view is not shared by all mixers and/or boom operators, just as all boom operators have their own favorite styles and techniques of how to record the best production tracks.

The unfortunate reality of having an omnidirectional microphone in a full-down position is that it tends to pick up many footstep sounds. Foot shuffling and movements will seem to dominate. Again, it depends on the circumstances and the surface of the floor.

Some boom operators cradle the fish pole downward, pointing the microphone up at the actor's voice, keeping the mike low enough to be out of camera view. Again, this lends itself to a less-than-desirable characterization of recording and does not always serve the project well. This technique is most often used for documentary or news work, where one is not concerned about the precise timbre or quality of the vocal recording or whether the microphone is seen in the frame. Many consider it a "lazy man's" cradle.

Truthfully, the best sound recording can be obtained by holding the fish pole high above your head and pointing the microphone at a downward, but slightly tilted, angle, aiming right at the throat of the actor. Some boom operators will tell you that the ideal target to aim the directional pattern at is the bridge of the nose. Others will tell you they aim at the upper chest, where the voice originates. They swear that the resonance of the chest is vital to the timbre of the recording. Still other boom operators aim right at the mouth, from where the voice issues.

These are all valid opinions that I have heard repeated many times. Each boom operator uses the technique that best serves the mixer and most successfully captures the desired vocal performance. Whatever technique you and/or your boom operator use, be consistent! Changing technique in the middle of recordings changes the timbre colorization from scene to scene.

Without a doubt, holding a fish pole above your head for takes is a grueling and punishing task (boom operators are perhaps the most physically fit craftspeople on the set). Because of this, it serves the recording team well for its members to look after each other. On one particular shoot, a boom operator held a big Sennheiser 815 super-cardioid microphone on a fully extended fish-pole boom to cover an extremely slow dolly shot that moved in closer and closer on Lloyd Bridges, who gave a four-and-a-half minute performance at a pulpit. At the height of the sequence, the cable man could see that the boom operator was fatiguing badly. He carefully brought his own boom in, which was equipped with the same kind of microphone, and cautiously lowered it down next to the boom operator's. At a slight pause in Lloyd Bridges' delivery, the mixer faded from the first microphone to the cable man's mike and whispered into the boom operator's headsets on his PL (communications term for "private line").

The boom operator raised his boom up and out of the way and stepped back silently. He lowered the fish pole and allowed himself a moment to rest, then raised his pole and reinserted his microphone alongside the cable man's. Again, as Lloyd Bridges paused to draw a breath, the mixer faded from the cable man's mike back to the boom operator's so that he could finish the take. Without that kind of teamwork, it just would not have been possible to sustain a fully extended, heavy mike recording for that length of time.

As a general rule, the master wide shot does not sound as good or pristine as the other close-up coverage angles. It is simple practicality: you have more set to cover, with more lights to watch out for and more potential noise to consider.

Boom Operator During Set-Up

One of the first things good boom operators do when starting on a show without a prior working relationship with other department heads is to find out who serve as the "keys." They also must identify the gaffer and key grip and introduce themselves, as these people decide how to fulfill the DP's (director of photography) lighting wishes. They decide exactly where a light is set and how the light is controlled, using flags, cutters, and scrims.

The importance of establishing a good relationship with fellow crew personnel is illustrated by the following example. A grip may "cut" (light control) a lamp by putting a "C"-stand on one side of the light. At the same time, the boom operator may really need that spot for maneuvering and properly booming the actors' movements. The grip could just as easily place the "C"-stand on the other side and use an elbow joint to put the scrim in the original position, thereby leaving the floor space available for the boom operator. However, if the boom operator has not made introductions and explained what is needed to fulfill the microphone-placement requirements, then he or she can blame no one else if the microphone cannot be placed in the necessary spot when the director is ready to roll camera and make a take.

The smart boom operator "babysits" the set. The boom operator gets the fish pole and stands by while the crew lights the set. The boom operator may wear headsets, slid down around the neck. This way everybody knows the boom operator is there, standing by to assist in the lighting collaboration; now he or she can follow the action without a boom shadow thrown somewhere on the set where the camera lens will pick it up. Boom shadows are the quickest way to fall into disfavor with the director and DP.

Being a good boom operator is also being a good gaffer or a good grip. One must know how to read the lights. One must know where to stand, where the camera will be, what size lens is used. Often a boom operator asks a simple question of the camera operator, such as, "What size lens are you using?" Sometimes a simple question like this causes the DP to be more attentive and to ensure that the crew cooperates more fully with the boom operator, allowing sound to get in and do its job effectively.

Director and cinematographer John LeBlanc has lensed and directed both feature films and commercials. "If the boom operator is not in there with us setting up the shot, I have no sympathy for the sound crew. I want good sound! I know that good sound will only help to make my work play better, but if the sound crew is not dedicated to getting in and showing us where the boom and microphones need to be while we're lighting the set, then it's their problem if they can't get in because they are suddenly making shadows."

As you can see, boom operators must know everyone's jobs in addition to their own to maximize the efficiency of the work. Unfortunately, although physical and technical demands on boom operators make theirs one of the most difficult jobs on the set, many production mixers will tell you they truly believe that boom operators are given the least respect—except, of course, from the production mixers themselves.

Checking with the Prop Department

The boom operator is responsible for talking to the prop department to discover pertinent information that will impact the sound recording, such as whether the firearms handler will use quarter-load, half-load, or full-load rounds in the guns to be fired on-screen. If full loads are used and a multitude of weapons are discharging, you will be deaf by the time you run through the sequence master and the various angles a few times. The microphones amplify the signal, and, with today's digital headsets for monitoring, the mixer and boom operator will have a bad time of it.

Many unfortunate situations occur when scenes using a practical weapon are rehearsed one way but actually performed differently. An example now gone to court is where an actor had rehearsed a scene during which he fires a pistol three or four times, then backs up and delivers his line. The mixer and boom operator compensated, covering the gunshots as rehearsed, then the actor lowered the pistol and began speaking. Right in the middle of his delivery, the actor whipped the pistol up and fired again. The mixer and boom operator flung their headsets off as they grabbed their ears in pain. They had already altered their record levels for the actor's voice, not his pistol shot, and they had been exposed and vulnerable.

USING THE WIRELESS MICROPHONE

Obviously many situations occur where the boom operator cannot take the microphone boom where traditional microphones may go. The obvious answer is to break out the RF (radio frequency) mikes. These wireless devices come in a multitude of models, but basically adhere to a simple and uniform configuration. A small microphone capsule can be either clipped or taped in a position somewhere on the upper part of the body, usually against the chest just above the heart. The capsule has a small wire that runs under the clothing to where the transmitter pack is attached. The transmitter pack is belted, taped, or otherwise affixed to the actor's body and has a short but critical transmission wire (antenna) taped in place to broadcast the signal to the mixer.

Batteries are consumed rapidly when using a radio microphone, so the boom operator should be prepared to change the batteries every couple of hours. It is not practical to turn the transmitter pack on and off between takes, so leave it turned on from the time you mike the actor to when you either wrap the actor or reach a point where the batteries, starting to show signal degradation, must be changed.

Before the boom operator approaches the actor, he or she goes to the wardrobe department to coordinate fabrics and textures as well as any special requirements, such as cutting holes inside the costume to allow wires of radio microphones to be connected to the transmitter worn somewhere on the talent's body.

Some fabrics, such as silk, wreak havoc with radio mikes, as they cause much noise. Another consideration may be whether an actress is wearing a brassiere. If so, the microphone wires can be hidden easily in the bra material, circling around the chest to the back. The wire can be taped as it descends down to the transmitter, which is often hidden in the small of the back. The absence of a bra necessitates carefully taping the wire to the body so that it does not move and show up as it pushes out against the fabric of the costume.

Due to delicate situations like the one above, boom operators must approach the task of placing radio microphones on acting talent in an extremely professional manner, concentrating on the primary mission: hiding the microphone where it will not be seen by the camera, where it captures the best recording of the actor's voice, while anticipating and solving potential problems with wardrobe fabrics and design.

Radio microphones are a fact of the entertainment world, and their use is increasing. A good boom operator not only understands the delicacies of the job but also is very sensitive to the feelings of all actors. The boom operator articulates clearly and succinctly what he or she requires of the performing talent in placing a radio mike on them. Humor and innuendoes are completely inappropriate and do not contribute to the professional trust factor that must be instilled and maintained. Every situation is different, and every actor responds differently. The boom operator adjusts the style of communication and demeanor to each, taking cues in comments or attitude. Again, the boom operator must never do or say anything to break the essential trust developed with the acting talent.

As Rusty Amodeo was handling the boom operator chores on an interview shoot with Barbara Walters and Jay Leno, the mixer warned Rusty to get it right the first time: "Get the microphone in the right place where it can't be seen and can't be heard, because Barbara won't let you get back in and adjust it." As soon as Walters entered the room, Rusty approached her to introduce himself, "Barbara, I'm Rusty Amodeo and I'm here to put a microphone on you."

"Well, give me the microphone and I'll put it on," she replied.

That's a tough situation for any boom operator. The microphone must go into an exact spot, and, more important, the place must be fabric-managed. The boom operator must run the wire so that the camera will not see it, and the transmitter must be situated properly with the transmission wire placed in a precise attitude for a clear signal.

"Fine, you want to put the mike on," Rusty answered as he held out the tiny microphone, pointing to a precise spot in the center of her chest, "then I need you to place the microphone right here, just under this flap of material, and then I need you to run the wire under and across to this side and tape it in place so that the connector will be—"

Barbara stopped him, "Well, maybe you should do it."

Rusty knew he had convinced her to allow him to do his job, but now he needed to win her confidence and trust. The two went upstairs, where her wardrobe department made the gown choice. Rusty opened his kit and removed the toupee tape (a clear durable tape sticky on both sides) to start affixing the microphone wire to her blouse.

"What are you doing?" she asked.

As Rusty continued to work he explained that he did not want to just put a mike on her. He wanted her to look her best, and using toupee tape would rigidly hold the microphone wire in place and prevent the button-down front from bulging open as she turned and flexed. It also would be in her best interest to protect the microphone from rubbing. In other words, Rusty was doing his job to make her look and sound as good as possible. Later, during the shoot, Barbara did not hesitate to allow Rusty to readjust, as now she was convinced that a truly dedicated professional was looking out for her and her image.

Because of wardrobe or camera coverage, boom operators constantly must consider new hiding places for the radio transmitter pack. Sometimes the small of the lower back is not an option, due to lack of clothing or a tightly fitting costume with the camera covering the back of the actor. Sometimes a boom operator hides the transmitter pack in the armpit. The toughest of all situations is when scanty clothing is worn, and all options above the waist are ruled out. More than once a boom operator had to revert to hiding the transmitter high on the inside of the thigh.

Although it is most desirable to place the microphone in the upper center position of the chest, you are not always able to do this. For instance, it is difficult to hide the microphone there if the actor is not wearing any shirt. Such was the case on a Paul Mazursky picture, *Moon over Parador*, starring Richard Dreyfuss. Jim Webb (not to be confused with the songwriter of the same name), the production mixer, and his boom operator struggled to figure out where to put the microphone.

As Mazursky rehearsed the actors, the boom operator noticed how the character that played Dreyfuss' valet followed him around like a shadow. The boom operator pointed it out to Jim, and the two of them hit upon the idea of literally making the valet character a traveling microphone stand. They placed a wireless microphone very carefully on the forward edge of the scalp of the valet, hidden just inside his hairline. In this manner, the valet, who spoke no lines of dialog during the scene, followed Dreyfuss back and forth in the bedroom of the manor, picking up Dreyfuss perfectly.

GETTING ROOM TONES AND WILD TRACKS

The production mixer must anticipate the audio trials and tribulations that will come during the postproduction sound-editorial phase. If the mixer works with the mind set that he or she is the one to make the material work, then the mixer is much more attentive to potential dialog lines or sequences, recommending recording pick-up wild lines with the actor after the camera has stopped rolling.

The mixer can either record such lines right then and there, while the crew holds still and the camera does not roll, or, what happens more often than not, the mixer takes the actor to a quiet area with a dead ambience and has the actor say the lines a number of times. These are usually short pieces of dialog spoken by a bit or minor character that were not clearly recorded during the actual on-camera shoot because of complex miking problems, practical equipment making noise that drowns out the line, or something like a door slam or a vehicle startup overpowering the dialog.

Aside from wild-track pick-up lines, ambient room tones are also needed. Many mixers try to record room-tone ambience whenever possible, but it is very difficult to get a full-scale camera crew to freeze in place and truly be silent while capturing a good 30 seconds of ambience. So many times we have gotten a room tone that has only a second or so of usable material. The mixer rolls tape, but the crew has not completely settled down, even to the sounds of feet shuffling. By the time the crew has actually come to an ideal audio texture, the director, extremely antsy to move on to the next setup, usually comments that that is enough, thinking the mixer has had a full 60 seconds, when in fact only 3 or 4 seconds of usable material can be salvaged.

People not sound aware often think that room tone is only needed for those little occasional holes or to patch over a director's voice cueing actors in the midst of a scene. They forget we may be required to patch-quilt entire scenes where one actor is looped but the other actors are not. Hence production dialog editors make a 3-second ambient piece fill a sequence lasting several minutes on-screen, as it must underline all the ADR dialog of the second actor that was looped. We often are stuck using a very loopy sounding ambience because the production crew did not religiously and seriously record room-tone ambience.

More times than not, the assistant director is responsible for helping the sound mixer get the necessary presence recordings. I have heard too many reports from mixers and boom operators alike about uncooperative assistant directors who do not care or understand the needs and requirements of anything but sync sound, which has inhibited presence recordings. The smart assistant director understands that by working with the sound mixer to record presence fill and wild-track pick-up lines, or even to arrange prop series sessions, such as recording a rare or unobtainable prop aside from the shoot, he or she is saving the production company literally thousands of future dollars that otherwise would be spent to recreate or fix something that hadn't been solved right then and there.

One of the most banal excuses I hear from those in positions to make decisions having collateral sound-cost consequences is that they are visual people. I have news for them: so am I, and so are my fellow craftspeople in the sound industry. Someone claiming to be "visually oriented" really is admitting to being sensory deprived. That person has immediately told me he or she knows very little about the storytelling process of making film. It is because we in sound are visually empowered that we can design and create spectacular audio events to make the visuality rise to new heights of production value, the whole becoming a more thrilling spectacle than visual-only thinking can produce.

SPLITTING OFF-SOURCE SOUND

Very often, the production mixer has a scene to record that has a practical television in the shot. The television audio should not play back and be heard by the actors' mikes, so the mixer takes an audio feed from the video source feeding the television and records it onto a dedicated channel.

In many cases a mixer records on a 2-track Nagra or DAT. The mixer line-feeds the video source onto channel 2 as he or she records the actors' dialog onto channel 1. This eliminates all the conversion speed-rate issues; it also creates ease in finding exact sync by having the live-feed material "transfer-recorded" in this fashion.

X-Y Microphone Configuration

The X-Y microphone configuration is important when you are recording a left-right stereo spread with two matching microphones. Recording stagnant ambiences with two matching microphones spread wide apart from one another is usually a problem, but whenever you have a situation where there is a sound-emanating source (such as a car, an airplane, or motorcycle) that is moving, ever changing the distance from itself and the two microphone diaphragms, you will experience phasing.

X-Y Pattern
As depicted in Figure 5.12, a sound source such as a car passing across the median axis of a bilaterally symmetrical pattern of both microphones experiences a phase wink-out.

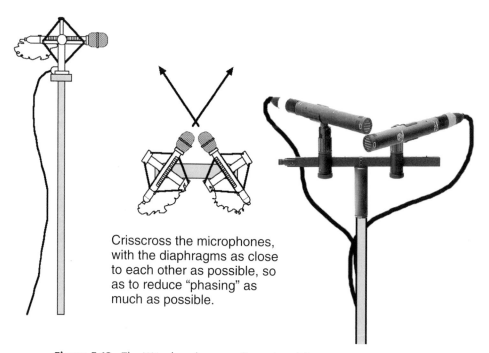

Crisscross the microphones, with the diaphragms as close to each other as possible, so as to reduce "phasing" as much as possible.

Figure 5.12 The X-Y microphone configuration. (Photo courtesy of Schoeps.)

As the car approaches, the sound of the engine takes ever so slightly longer to reach the far mike as it does the closer mike. As the car approaches, the time it takes to reach the far microphone decreases to the point that, as it hits the axis (center) point, the two microphones switch roles. Now it is taking increasingly longer for the sound to reach the far left mike. At this crossover point is a phase wink-out or drop-out of signal.

The severity of the phase wink-out is proportionate to how far apart the two microphone diaphragms are from each other. The closer they are to each other, the less the phase wink-out. That is why stereo microphones have the two diaphragms in the same capsule, either side by side or one on top of the other.

If you are using two monaural microphones to record stereo material and you have the potential for audio sources such as cars, trains, or aircraft, then you may wish to place the two mikes in what is called an X-Y pattern. In this configuration the left microphone is facing to the right, covering the right hemisphere, while the microphone on the right is pointing to the left, covering the left hemisphere. This places the microphone diaphragms physically as close as possible to each other to greatly reduce the time the audio source signal takes to reach one microphone diaphragm as to the other.

Figure 5.13 depicts a typical dual-capsule stereo microphone. Note how the diaphragms sit as closely as possible to each other, one on top of the other.

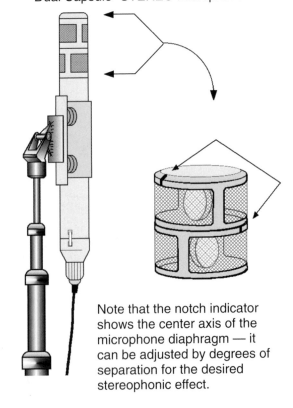

"Dual Capsule" STEREO microphone

Note that the notch indicator shows the center axis of the microphone diaphragm — it can be adjusted by degrees of separation for the desired stereophonic effect.

Figure 5.13 Stereo capsule microphone.

Stereo Capsule Microphone

The top diaphragm capsule rotates to increase or decrease the degrees of separation as desired. Be careful to maintain the correct up-and-down attitude of the stereo microphone, to keep the left and right coverage in correct aspect. The advantage of using a stereo "dual-capsule" microphone is that the left and right diaphragms are much closer together than by placing two monaural microphones in an X-Y pattern. The chances of experiencing phase cancellation and wink-outs are minimized greatly.

The USM 69i stereo microphone has two separate dual-diaphragm capsules. These are mounted vertically and rotate against each other. The directional polar patterns can be selected separately for each capsule. The capsules operate independently from each other. The USM 69i is a studio microphone for intensity stereo recording suitable for X-Y and MS recordings.

The microphone consists of the amplifier section and the capsule head. The amplifier section contains two microphone amplifiers operating independently from each

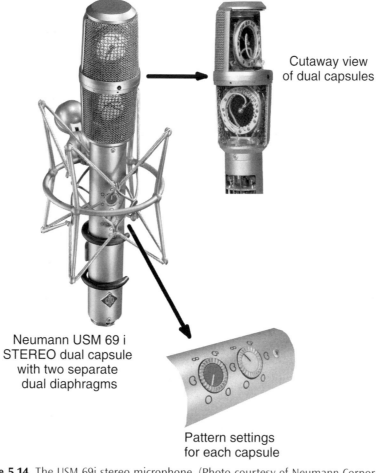

Cutaway view
of dual capsules

Neumann USM 69 i
STEREO dual capsule
with two separate
dual diaphragms

Pattern settings
for each capsule

Figure 5.14 The USM 69i stereo microphone. (Photo courtesy of Neumann Corporation.)

other. They have an extremely low self-noise. Two completely separate microphone capsules are positioned closely above each other within the capsule head. Their diaphragms are made out of gold-sputtered polyester film. The upper capsule rotates against the lower one over a range of 270°. Color markings on the lower capsule system help to identify the angle by which the upper capsule has been rotated.

When sound waves reach the microphone capsules from different directions they will generate audio signals with different intensity only, but not with time differences, since the capsules are in close proximity and the sound arrives at both capsules simultaneously. The result is an intensity stereo signal that can be summed together for excellent mono compatibility without causing interference.

The USM 69i has two built-in rotary switches. The five polar patterns of both capsules can be selected at the microphone itself. Therefore, no special AC power supply units or powering adapters are necessary. The two outputs attach directly to any 48-V phantom-powered connectors. In addition to the usual polar patterns (omnidirectional, cardioid, and figure-8), we have added a hypercardioid and a wide-angle cardioid pattern. A built-in DC converter generates the required capsule polarizing voltages.

THE ILLUSION OF MONITORING FIELD RECORDINGS

Eric Karson has been on many a shoot, both domestic and abroad, learning well the difference between what you think you've got and what you really have. Eric offers the following advice:

> We're on location, in the heat of battle, making the picture, and we are given headphones to monitor what we believe is actually being laid down on tape. Later when we wrap the shoot and settle into the picture editorial process, we discover that it does not really sound how we remembered it. Oh, it is what the actors had said, but the perceived quality value that we thought we had at the time was not really on tape. As a producer or director, you learn that lesson early on and sometimes in a very hard and brutal way.

In another case, John LeBlanc was asked to serve as director of photography on a low-budget western. The producer had made commercials successfully for several years but was inexperienced in the handling of feature projects. I received a call from John, asking if I would mind if he brought the producer, the director, the unit production manager, and the person the producer had hired to handle the production mixing chores.

The following day, we met and discussed the various aspects of the show as they related to sound. Unknown to me, John had heard the production mixer talk about how he would handle recording on the set during previous preproduction meetings, and, knowing a few things about feature sound, several mental red flags had gone up. John segued the conversation into having the young man convey his intentions for me to hear for myself.

With a great amount of eagerness, he explained how he would record on a DA-88 so he could use up to 8 channels at once, placing microphones all around the set. He wound up his dazzling litany with the warranty that the producer need not waste money on Foley, as his production soundtrack would make all that obsolete. John turned to me, "Well, Dave, whad'ya think?"

I did not know whether to laugh or cry. "I think that you are hurtling toward an apocalyptic collision with postproduction hell—that's what I think." The young man was offended by my comment, but I felt the need to make my point. "Tell me, son. How many feature films have you mixed sound for?"

He tried to change the subject. He started to detail all the big-name features he had mixed. I grabbed the previous year's edition of the Annual Index to Motion Picture Credits published by the Motion Picture Academy as I calmly began pointing out that one should not try to equate working on a postproduction re-recording stage in a totally controlled environment with the combat-zone-style rigors of recording in the field.

The young man finally admitted this was going to be his first time, but he had had more experience with digital sound than anyone else on the face of the earth. He actually extended his hand to me and said I could kiss his ring.

I returned to the Annual Index. "I don't see your name listed here under two of the titles you mentioned."

He explained that he did not mix on the actual soundtrack for those films but had handled mixing the sound for a making-of-a-film television program. John LeBlanc rose and shook my hand, as he knew nothing more was to be said.

Despite that afternoon's revelation, the producer decided to have the young man handle the production mixing job anyway, based on the digital sleight-of-hand that was offered—and I am sure a lot of it had to do with the temptation to save monies earmarked for the Foley process.

Several months later, John showed up with a video of the film. It was a work in progress, but clearly revealed the caliber of work of the mixer. John recounted how the production mixer became progressively more bogged down during the shoot, totally underestimating the reality of the work. It had gotten to the point that the crew was even making fun of him. Not only did the producer have to go ahead with the original plans to have the Foley performed, but much more work in sound effect development became necessary. Potential ADR requirements also had grown more and more, not less. Instead of trying to reinvent the wheel, the producer would have been far better off using veteran experts and following their advice. With extremely few exceptions, we do things the way we do for good reason—because we have practiced our craft enough that we have developed it into an art form.

MULTICHANNEL MIXING

When we speak about production recording in a multichannel format we refer to 2 channels, either a 2-track Nagra or a 2-channel DAT. Nagra's ¼" digital deck allows 4-channel field recording, and a very few individuals may from time to time record to a DA-88 8-channel.

When you think of the grandfather of multichannel production sound recording, you must be thinking of the renowned Jim Webb, who handled the production recording chores for the legendary film director Robert Altman on such pictures as *California Split*, *Buffalo Bill*, *Three Women*, *A Wedding*, and *Nashville*, the first Dolby 2-track matrixed stereo mix (this picture earned Jim the British Academy Award for Best Sound).

On *A Wedding*, Altman doubled the *Nashville* format. Jim Webb found himself recording on two 8-track machines simultaneously. Altman shot with two cameras amid 50 actors all interrelating with each other. Jim played musical microphones as he was mixing one group of actors holding a conversation, with camera setups moving from group to group. There was no real script, as Altman worked best with impromptu performances, so Jim had to be ready for anything.

For each setup, his cable man went out and made a character ID strip of tape with numbered assignments on each of the radio mikes affixed to the actors. When he came back to the sound cart, the cable man laid the assignment tape right across the bottom of Jim's fader pots on the mixing console so that he would know who was on which microphone.

"It was nuts. I had an assistant keeping the log on who was on what track just so that the script supervisor could keep all the material straight, as there was no time for me to keep an accurate log!" he remembers.

On *California Split*, Jim had the challenge of not only having to record 8-channel production dialog, but to do so while on a practical traveling location, a bus en route to Nevada. Keep in mind that, today, 8-channel mixing boards are commonplace, but in the 1970s Jim Webb's techniques were way ahead of mainstream production recording. The eight channels of signal had to be fed through two 4-channel audio mixers into the 1" 8-channel tape recorder located on the bottom shelf of the cart near the floor. A $\frac{1}{4}$" Nagra was fed a combined mix-down signal for protection back-up purposes. Jim Webb operated the first 4-channel mixer while his boom operator, Chris McLaughlin, operated the second 4-channel mixer.

RECORDING PRACTICAL PHONE CONVERSATIONS

For *All the President's Men*, director Alan Pakula told Jim Webb, "I don't want a throw-away soundtrack." (A throw-away soundtrack basically means a guide-track is being recorded so the actors can loop their lines later in an ADR session.) Jim could not agree more, so for every aspect of the production recording process Jim left no stone unturned.

Warner Brothers removed the wall between sound stages 4 and 11 to build the full-scale set of the *Washington Post* newsroom through the breadth of both stages. Jim recalls:

> We had one shot that was a 180-foot dolly shot inside the four walls of the set. In order to eliminate what would have been a nightmare of ballast hum due to the entire ceiling being filled with rows of fluorescent lamps, the construction crew rigged a huge rack for the ballast units just outside the sound stage and bundled the wiring in groups that fed back into the stage to the fluorescent tubes themselves.
>
> As you know, it seems that half the picture was performed on telephones. Well, they didn't want the traditional style of actors having to act out a telephone conversation with no one on the other end of the phone to play off on, so it was decided early on with the help of the special-effects crew to build a practical telephone system into the set. We had five lines that you could switch back and forth on as Redford might put one call on hold while he answered another or placed a second call while keeping one or two other lines

Academy Award winner
Best Sound

Figure 5.15 Production mixer Jim Webb won an Academy Award for his innovative techniques in recording complex multichannel production dialog on the political conspiracy thriller *All the President's Men.* (Photo courtesy of Warner Brothers.)

on hold. Each off-camera actor was on the other end of the phone conversation and was set up in an isolated area of the stage.

Jim warns that simultaneously recording an on-screen actor clean while also recording the telephone feed must be handled carefully:

> All the multiple phone calls are recorded in real time, which can be a problem if the on-screen actor's voice is in the phone feed. What you need to do is take the transmitter out of the handset of the on-camera actor's phone so that you don't experience 'double-up' of the live mike with the phone-line tap. You set up the actors on the other end of the phone with headsets so that they are hearing the on-camera lines from the production mike (prior to the record head) so that you do not get that delay as heard from playback. The nice thing about this technique is that the off-camera phone feed has total isolation because the on-camera actor has the receiver right to his ear, listening to the off-camera voice so there is no acoustic leakage. Dialog overlaps are never a problem as you have both actors in complete isolation, recording each actor on a dedicated channel. This allows dialog interplay in real time.

It was the first time Robert Redford had ever used this kind of telephone technique while shooting a picture. After the director sounded "cut" on the first rehearsal, Redford looked up and exclaimed his excitement over being able to act and react to a live actor on the other end of the line. Jim could not have been happier with the results. "It really sets the actor free to act rather than try to play to nothingness, or to carefully avoid overlaps of lines being read off-camera by the script person."

Was all this extra effort worth it? *All the President's Men* was awarded the Academy Award for Best Sound that year.

PERILS OF RECORDING IN SNOW

In the winter of 1989, digital production recording was anything but mainstream. Long before inclement-weather digital recording was being mastered, Paul Jyrälä had endured 105 days of production recording in freezing temperatures, handling the literal trench-warfare chores of mixing the war epic *Talvisota: The Winter War* in his homeland of Finland.

Moisture, hot and cold temperature extremes, dirt, and grit—all the sensitivity issues that inhibit DAT machines from working to their optimum potential plagued Paul during the grueling shooting schedule. His boom operator and cable man worked hard to wrap the equipment with cellophane and pad them with thermal blankets to keep moisture and cold at bay.

"There were times we thought we should be awarded, I think you Americans call it the Purple Heart," chuckled Matti Kuortti, boom operator. "No matter how careful the special-effect crew was, there is always the possibility of something going wrong. During one scene where we filmed birch trees being blown apart, a rather large sliver of wood flew past the camera and pierced the director of photography in his shoulder. All of us had to be on guard, as there was danger everywhere."

Paul used four Sennheiser 416 microphones, backed up by two Vega and two Micron wireless microphones. The team used Ryocote "woolies" to combat wind gusts

Figure 5.16 Production sound mixer Paul Jyrälä sits bundled against the freezing cold, his digital DAT and ¼" Nagra protected by thermal blankets and battery-operated heating units. The boom operators wear machinist face shields and padded jackets to protect them from flying rocks and debris during explosion effects while recording spoken dialog. (Photo by Ulla-Maija Parikka.)

and air concussion from explosion pots. Unlike American production recording techniques, Paul encoded the production recording on *Talvisota* with DBX II onto the original ¹/₄″. After the crew wrapped shooting for the day, Paul returned to the location barracks and carefully transferred the day's work himself. He decoded the DBX II signal and then re-encoded a noise reduction called Telecom (a European version of the Dolby noise-reduction system) as he transferred the dialog dailies onto 2-channel 17.5-mm fullcoat film. The first channel was a "flat" transfer with no Telecom encode, making it convenient for the picture editor. The second channel was the Telecom-encoded version Paul would work with later during the postproduction process.

Because of the meticulous attention to detail that Paul Jyrälä brought to the production mixing chores, the picture only had 5 percent of its dialog "looped" later in an ADR session—an astoundingly small percentage given the difficult recording circumstances of snow, mud, flying dirt, and debris. Paul earned his fifth Jussi (the Finnish version of the Academy Award) for Best Sound, and *Talvisota* was one of the seven finalists that made the American sound effect "bake-off" for consideration for an Academy Award nomination.

RECORDING STRAIGHT TO HARD DISK

Zaxcom Deva V—Digital Recorder

The Zaxcom Deva V is a direct-to-disk digital audio recorder. This production sound mixer brings a highly durable machine into any recording scenario. In the late 1990s, the first Deva series was really the first professional field direct-to-disk digital recorder that overcame the sensitivity factor of traditional computer disk recording systems.

1. **Faders 1, 2, 3, and 4:** There are four hardware faders. They can be assigned to any channel or combination of channels in your Deva. Software faders are available for channels not assigned to the hardware faders.
2. **Touch Screen Display:** The touch screen display is the main interface of the Deva. Most selections are made and displayed using it. You can use either a PDA stylus or your finger to make selections.
3. **Slate Mike**
4. **Function Buttons:** F1, F2, F3, F4, F5, F6, MENU, and ENTER. Many of the function buttons are used for multiple tasks. When the touch screen display shows the home screen, the function buttons perform the function written above them. In other menu modes, the function buttons can be programmed to perform additional tasks. The MENU and ENTER buttons always perform only those functions.

   • F1—CUE
   Displays the Cue or Playback Menu on the touch screen.

   • F2—C.TAKE
   Marks a take as a "Circled Take" in the metadata file. This button can be pushed either during record or after the take has been recorded but before the next take has started.

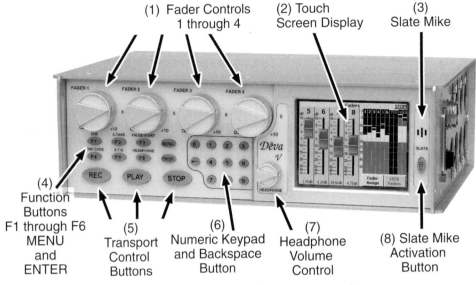

(1) Fader Controls 1 through 4

(2) Touch Screen Display

(3) Slate Mike

(4) Function Buttons F1 through F6 MENU and ENTER

(5) Transport Control Buttons

(6) Numeric Keypad and Backspace Button

(7) Headphone Volume Control

(8) Slate Mike Activation Button

Figure 5.17 Photo courtesy of Zaxcom Corporation.

- F3—FALSE START

Marks a take as a "False Start" in the metadata file. When this is done, the segment number does not increment when placed into the record mode the next time. This button can be pushed either during or right after the false start record.

- F4—TIME CODE

Displays the time code menu on the touch screen.

- F5—S.T.N.

Displays the SCENE TAKE NOTE menu.

- F6—HEADPHONE

Displays the HEADPHONE matrix menu.

- MENU

Advances the screen to the next menu. This is the same as touching the status button in any menu.

- ENTER

Confirms data entry.

5. **Transport Control Buttons:** These three buttons provide the Record, Play, and Stop functions.
6. **Numeric Keypad and Backspace Buttons:** These provide an alternative means of entering numeric data such as time code and metadata.
7. **Headphone Volume Control**
8. **Slate Mike Activation:** This button requires you to push and hold it to activate the slate mike. All routing for the slate mike is performed in the Disk Mix menu.

The Zaxcom Deva has enjoyed a robust and successful run of service for serious sound mixers. The Deva V is a high-quality 24-bit analog-to-digital converter with both microphone and line inputs that ensure a wide dynamic range. The Deva V can record a Sound Designer II audio file or either mono or polyphonic Broadcast Wave audio files. By utilizing a small keyboard, the production mixer enters pertinent data into the audio file directory. The Deva V is capable of recording at a 192-kHz sampling rate with 10 discrete channels. With a dynamic range of 120 dB, it can handle some really challenging recording assignments. One nice change from the original model was that it now uses FireWire as an I/O data access.

The Deva V uses a 100-gigabyte removable internal hard drive, or you can opt for an internal DVD drive option. Zaxcom claims these hermetically sealed drives can withstand as high as 150 Gs—certainly 30 times more than I intend ever to endure—but it does bring a lot of recording time for the mixer on the set. A separate DVD-RAM unit is easily hooked up so that the mixer can lay back protection copies to a recordable DVD, using the hard drives as a working medium only to record and file manage. Once the DVD is made and the material is safe in the hands of the postproduction transfer facility, the mixer can wipe the drive clean and use it again, or put it in the archive for safe keeping as a back-up protection for all the dailies.

The mixer may choose to put the Deva V into an "Intermittent" mode, which allows the unit to automatically make back-up recordings to the DVD when the Deva is not in "Record" mode. As soon as the Record mode is off, the Deva automatically continues recording back-up audio files to the DVD-RAM over the SCSI connector. If the mixer wants to record both to the Deva hard drive as well as to the DVD simultaneously, he or she switches to "Turbo" mode.

The Deva V always maintains a 15-second "pre-roll" in the RAM buffer, so if the mixer presses the Record button, the previous 10 seconds is automatically laid down to the hard drive, thereby doing away with waiting for the pre-roll. This feature is extremely helpful on a busy shoot, where the mixer must review previous recordings or where the director either does not understand pre-roll protocol or has not thought to warn sound that he or she is about to go for a "take" and roll cameras.

Rather than being caught right in the middle of playing back a previous cue and finding yourself totally incapable of spinning down to virgin tape to start recording again, simply hit the Record button, which automatically starts recording to the hard disk. You will not damage or record over the material you are reviewing, as it is impossible to accidentally record over a section of the hard disk that has already been used. Remember, computers do not work in a linear fashion. You can change from single-channel recording to multichannels for the next recording set-up by simply touching the proper buttons to tell the Deva how you want to record. In addition to industry standard XLR connectors, the Deva has a break-out cable with a multi-pin connector for line inputs.

Deva V—Left Panel

9. **Power Input Connector:** Standard 4-pin XLR connector for 9.5 V–18 VDC 1 Amp input
10. **Hard Drive Compartment**

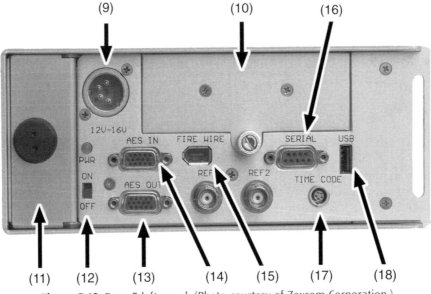

Figure 5.18 Deva 5 left panel. (Photo courtesy of Zaxcom Corporation.)

11. **Battery Compartment:** The black knob rotates to lock the battery compartment door. Li-ion and NiMH NP1 batteries can be used safely in the DEVA as long as they exceed 18 VDC.

12. **Power Switch**

13. **AES Digital Output Connector:** Connects the supplied AES. Digital output cable to this is a 15-pin mini which provides four pairs of AES digital outputs.

14. **AES Digital Input Connector:** Connects the supplied AES digital input cable to this 15-pin mini sub-four pairs of AES inputs.

15. **IEEE 1394 (FireWire) Connector:** This port can be used with FireWire hard drives, CD, and DVD-RAM device requires power, it can be turned on from the My DEVA menu.

16. **Serial/RS422 Connector:** This 9-pin connector is used for controlling the DEVA using an external Cameo or Deva-12 mixer.

17. **Time Code Connector:** This is the standard 5-pin Lemo connector used for time code I/O (Lemo EGG.OB.305.CLL).

18. **USB Port:** This port is designed for connecting Zaxcom-approved keyboards.

Deva V—Right Panel

19. **Camera Connector:** This is a standard 10-pin ENG-type camera connector. It outputs channels 5 and 6 to the camera and returns the monitor feed from the camera.
    Note: The two monitor feeds are summed to mono.

20. **Mike/Line Inputs 1, 3, 5, and 7:** Each input is electronically balanced and internally padded to handle either mike or line level signals (selected via the

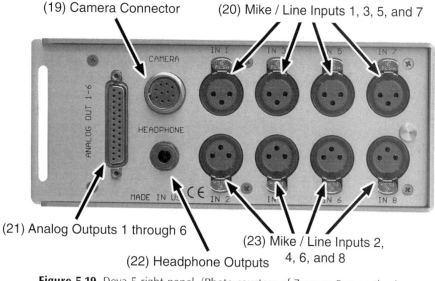

(19) Camera Connector

(20) Mike / Line Inputs 1, 3, 5, and 7

(21) Analog Outputs 1 through 6

(22) Headphone Outputs

(23) Mike / Line Inputs 2, 4, 6, and 8

Figure 5.19 Deva 5 right panel. (Photo courtesy of Zaxcom Corporation.)

INPUT CONTROL menu. (As of 8/28/04, Line Input Impedance has been increased to 4-K ohms).

21. **Analog Outputs:** 1–6–25-pin connector outputs 6 channels of line level audio. Menu selectable to output either channels 1–6 or 5–10.

22. **Headphone Output $^1\!/_4$":** Stereo jack, optimal 100-Ohm impedance. *Note:* Lower headphone impedances result in louder headphone output levels.

23. **Mike/Line Inputs 2, 4, 6, and 8:** Each input is electronically balanced and internally padded to handle either mike or line level signals (selected via the INPUT CONTROL menu.

Using a keyboard (not shown), off to the side of the unit, the recording mixer quickly enters the scene, angle, and take data that show up in the "slate" icon in the upper right-hand corner. This entry along with the time code is embedded in the directory of the audio file itself, thereby streamlining and removing possible errors by the assistant picture editor later in assimilating the material into the nonlinear editing system being used.

The Deva Mix-12 is a new concept in location mixing. It is a control surface for the embedded digital audio mixer of either the Deva IV or V location recorders. The Mix-12 is fully digital, only the microphone pre-amps, A-D, and D-A converts are used for analog connections to the outside world.

Mixing is performed in the digital domain via a floating DSP, ensuring the highest quality path to the recorder, unlike analog mixing consoles where distortion or channel-to-channel cross-talk and differences can occur over time or with temperature changes.

The microphone preamps are sound studio quality, ensuring no coloration of audio by transformers or other analog circuitry. The effects are superb with the ability

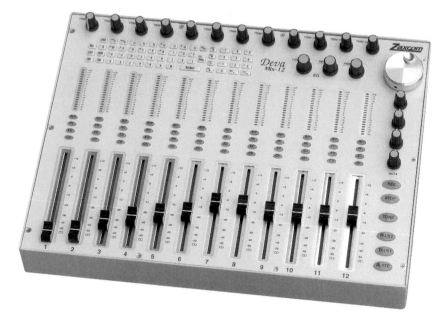

Figure 5.20 The Zaxcom Mix-12. (Photo courtesy of Zaxcom Corporation.)

to remove hum, buzzes, and even crickets by the two notch filters on each channel. There are 3-band shelving filters with individual control of level, Q, and frequency via the Devas graphic interface.

The Mix-12's soft knee compressor is one of the best available, chosen for its natural sound and transparency. Each of the 12 fader strips provides instant access to bus routing and effects for that channel. An LED input meter is provided on each channel strip to augment the Devas full-color output metering. Three separate talk-back busses can be routed to any combination of outputs and internal mix busses.

For further information, you can reach Zaxcom in Pompton Plains, New Jersey, at 973-835-5000 or on the Internet at www.zaxcom.com.

The ability to mirror duplicate back-up drives quickly to a cost-effective medium as well as the ability to build in data files to the directory of each audio file as they are created greatly enhances not only speed issues but also reduces the chances of error in data assignments later at the laboratory or at picture editorial.

Several other companies have brought some very impressive direct-to-hard-drive recording systems for the field.

Sound Devices—Digital Recorders

The introduction of Sound Devices 7-Series recorders in 2004 re-defined the category of file-based recorders for production sound. Their extremely compact size and high-feature content made them the first product capable of being a legitimate replacement for time code DAT. While file-based recorders for production sound have been available since 1998 (when the Zaxcom Deva was introduced) their use was limited to only the

Figure 5.21 Sound Devices 744t. (Photo courtesy of Sound Devices Corporation.)

largest feature films. Sound Devices 7-Series moved file-based recording into the hands of sound engineers recording effects, reality television, episodic television, commercial spots, documentary film and video, and feature film.

The 7-Series recorders were originally targeted to sound engineers working in over-the-shoulder environments. The unit's controls, size, and complement of connectors is more specific to "shoulder-bag" work versus cart work. Because the recorder is typically used alongside a field mixer, wireless systems, and power distribution in a single production bag, it needs to be as compact as possible. Additionally, only two sides can be used for connectors and only one control surface is practical in bag applications. Other portable products are available with controls on secondary surfaces, but these are less common in portable applications.

The transition to file-based recording opens numerous options and challenges to the engineer. The 7-Series has much depth in its choices of file type, sampling rate, time code rate, and file management that tape-based systems never offered.

The Sound Devices 744t is a hardy portable 4-track digital field recorder with time code capability. The super-compact 744t records and plays back audio to and from its internal hard drive or compact flash medium, making field recording simple and fast. It writes and reads uncompressed PCM audio at 16 or 24 bits with sample rates between 32 and 192 kHz. Compressed (MP3) audio playback and recording from 64 to 320 kbs are also supported. The time code implementation makes the 744t ready for any recording job from over-the-shoulder to cart-based production.

The 744t implements a no-compromise audio path that includes Sound Devices's next generation microphone preamplifiers. Designed specifically for high-bandwidth, high-bit-rate digital recording, these preamps set a new standard for frequency response linearity, low distortion performance, and low noise.

A 744t with microphone and headphones—no other recorder on the market matches its size or feature set. In addition, its learning curve is quite short—powerful does not mean complicated. While the 744t is a very capable recorder by itself, it truly excels when used in conjunction with an outboard audio mixer such as Sound Devices' own 442 or 302.

Its two recording media (hard drive and Compact Flash) are highly reliable, industry standard, and easily obtainable. The removable, rechargeable battery is a

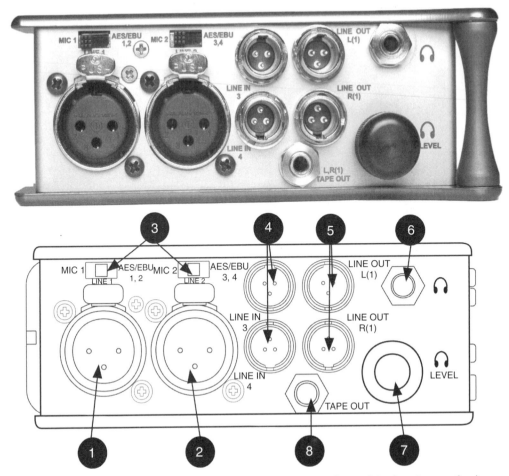

Figure 5.22 Sound Devices 744t, left side. (Photo courtesy of Sound Devices Corporation.)

standard Sony-compatible Li-ion camcorder cell. The 744t interconnects with Windows and Mac OS computers for convenient data transfer and backup.

1. **XLR Input 1/AES3 Input 1 and 2:** Dual function INPUT connection. Input type set with switch above. Active-balanced analog microphone, or line-level input for input 1. Transformer-balanced 2-channel AES3 input (1 and 2).
2. **XLR Input 2/AES3 Input 3 and 4:** Same as above only for 3 and 4.
3. **Mike-Line-AES3 Input Switch:** Selects the input level and mode of the associated XLR input connector.
4. **TA3 Channel 3 and 4 Line Inputs:** Active-balanced line-level input connectors. Pin-1 (GROUND), Pin-2 (+), Pin-3 (−).
5. **TA3 Master (L/R) Analog Outputs:** Active-balanced, line-level analog L/R Outputs for the Master Output Bus. Program source and attenuation level are user selectable. Pin-1 (GROUND), Pin-2 (+), Pin-3 (−).

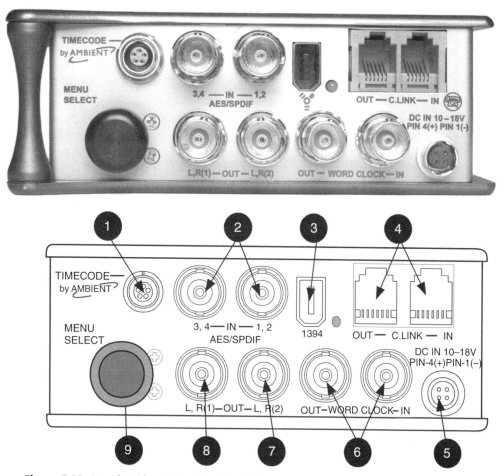

Figure 5.23 Sound Devices 744t, right side. (Photo courtesy of Sound Devices Corporation.)

6. **Headphone Output:** 3.5-mm TRS stereo headphone connector. Can drive headphones from 8 to 1,000-Ohm impedances to very high levels. TIP (left), RING (right), SLEEVE (ground).

7. **Headphone Volume:** Adjusts the headphone volume. *Note:* The 744t is capable of producing ear-damaging levels in headphones!

8. **Tape Output:** Unbalanced tape (–10 dBv nominal) OUTPUT on 3.5-mm TRS stereo connector. Signal source is identical to the Master OUTPUT Bus. TIP (left), RING (right), SLEEVE (ground).

1. **Time Code Multi-Pin:** Time code INPUT and OUTPUT on 5-pin LEMO connector.

2. **AES3id Inputs 1 & 2 and 3 & 4:** Unbalanced digital INPUT accepts two channel AES3 (or S/PDIF) on BNC connectors. Supports sample rates up to 200 kHz.

3. **FireWire (IEEE-1394) Port:** Connection to a computer to access the internal hard drive and compact flash volumes as mass storage devices. Direct connection to Mac OS (10.2 or higher) and Windows (XP and 2000 only) computers.

   FireWire Transfer Notice: Sound Devices STRONGLY recommends shutting down equipment before connecting TO or FROM any FireWire device with a connection that carries power (6-pin). There have been reports of isolated problems when "hot-plugging" IEEE 1394 (FireWire) devices. (Hot-plugging refers to making the connections when one or more of the devices is on, including the computer.) When hot plug-in, there are rare occurrences where either the FireWire device or the FireWire port on the host computer is rendered permanently inoperable. It is a common opinion that a FireWire connection which carries power is susceptible to this type of damage.

4. **C. Link In/Out:** RS-232 protocol interface on 6-pin modular ("RJ-22") connector for linking multiple 722 and 744t recorders together. Word clock, machine transport, and time code are carried on the C. Link connector.

5. **External DC In:** Accepts sources of 10–18 volts DC for unit powering and removable Li-ion battery charging. The Hirose 4-pin connector is wired PIN-1 (NEGATIVE –) PIN-4 (POSITIVE +) PIN-2 (–) and PIN-3 (+) are used to charge the removable Li-ion battery. DC ground at both PINS 2 and 3 is at the same potential as chassis and signal ground.

6. **Word Clock Input and Output:** Provides clock INPUT and OUTPUT for the 744t. Word input accepts sampling rates between 32 and 192 kHz. Word clock OUTPUT is the rate that the box is running. There is no sample rate conversion onboard the 744t.

7. **AES3id Output Bus 2:** Unbalanced digital OUTPUT, 2-channel, for OUTPUT Bus 2. Signal source is menu-selected.

8. **AES3id Master Output Bus:** Unbalanced digital OUTPUT, 2-channel, for the Master OUTPUT Bus. Signal source is menu-selected and is identical to the Analog Master OUTPUT Bus signal.

9. **Multi-Function Rotary Switch:** When in the set-up menu, the rotary switch moves between menu selections; push to enter selection or enter data. In RECORD and PLAYBACK modes, selects headphone monitor source; push action is user selectable.

Aaton Cantar-X—Digital Recorder

The Cantar-X Features the ability to record up to 8 discreet tracks of 96 kHz/24-bit audio to either an internal 60-gig hard drive or an external hard drive or optical drive via its built-in 6-pin FireWire connector, providing over 57 hours of 2-track 48 kHz/24-bit audio and more than 7 hours of 8-track 96 kHz/24-bit.

Any one of the Cantar's five transformer balanced mike-pres, four analog line-level or eight AES digital inputs can be routed to any track, or multiple tracks, quickly and easily in Cantar's intuitive routing input menu. Changes to routing or monitoring can be achieved "on-the-fly" by recalling custom presets that are stored in its nonvola-

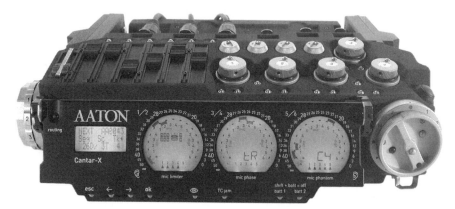

Figure 5.24 Aaton's Cantar, a lightweight, low-power mixer/recorder. Photo courtesy of Aaton.

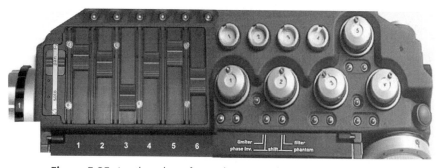

Figure 5.25 Another view of Aaton's Cantar. Photo courtesy of Aaton.

tile memory. Phantom power, limiters, phase reverse, and an adjustable hi-pass filter are switchable for each microphone input. A stereo mix-down of the discrete tracks can be recorded as a separate file and/or routed to any of the Cantar's two adjustable line-level analog outputs, AES digital output or headphone matrix.

A unique magnetic fader panel is provided for creating the stereo down-mix in the field and for controlling Pan and PFL SOLO checking for each track. The stereo mix-down file, the discrete tracks, or all can be burned at the end of the day to either an optional internal optical drive or an external FireWire drive, and the Cantar allows you to choose between CD-R/DVD+R/DVD-RAM formats so your resulting disks will realize a wide cross-platform compatibility in the postproduction environment.

The Cantar interface is the easiest to use in the most difficult missions. It offers the largest display surface of all portable recorders which simultaneously show every critical recording parameter. The custom-designed high-contrast LCD displays remain visible under bright sunlight, and at very low temperatures too; and because the swiveling front panel always offers the best viewing angle for both cart and over-the-shoulder work.

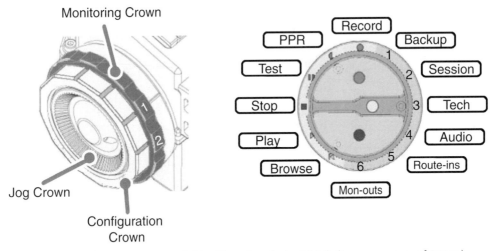

Figure 5.26 The 3-crown turret (left) with main selector (right). (Image courtesy of Aaton.)

The 3-Crown Turret (on left)
Monitoring Crown

1. **So:** 5 mike inputs, 4 line inputs, 6 digi inputs, and active tracks are sent to the headphones as Solos.
2. **Ph:** Mixer output and 17 user's grids to headphones.
3. **Lo:** Mixer and 9 user's grids to dual line-out.
4. **Fb:** Mixer and 9 user's grids to dual foldback.
5. **Di:** Mixer and 9 user's grids to dual Digi-out (AES). *Note:* the headphones receive the same signal as the one sent to the output being configured.

Configuration Crown   In TEST and PPR, push the Solo-Mix-Pan slider battery side, press the routing button (top left of the swiveling panel), and rotate the config crown to browse the 15 Input-to-Track configs and to activate the one showing while the routing button is released.

In REC, push the Solo-Mix-Pan slider battery side, press the routing button to verify the Input-to-Track configuration in use.

Note: To avoid finger errors, the current configuration cannot be modified in REC but there is a shortcut: by switching to PPR you have plenty of time (up to 35 seconds) to select another configuration and go back to REC. This operation creates another file and does not lose any audio sample between the two.

In REC, pull the Solo-Mix-Pan slider operator side, press the routing button to turn the three circular screens into a large Mon-Outs "Left-Center-Right" display. Since this doesn't affect the recording signals, you can on-the-fly listen to and select another monitoring pattern by rotating the config crown.

Jog Crown   The "one finger" jog is used to move the cursor in the message panel, to edit Scene&Take, to select high-pass filters, to modulate the backlight, to control the pan-pots, and to scrub the player in fast forward/reverse.

Note: [Shift•Jog] 10× accelerates the jog speed.

The Main Selector (on right)

The large 12-position Main Selector eliminates diving into subdirectories, and the unique three-crown turret gives instant access to all recording and monitoring configurations, even with gloves on.

> **Six "sound managing" positions:** •Rec •PPR •Test •Stop •Play •Browse, laid in the standard way.

> **Six "operand" positions:** •Mon-outs •Route-ins •Audio •Tech •Session •Backup, give access to all the possible settings of the machine. The black, white, and red buttons are made for the thumb; they work together with the large blue key [shift] activated by the index.

In test PPR Rec:
- [white] (reserved to insert prelocating marks)
- [shift•white] in PPR opens/closes the editing pane
- [black] sends slate mike to line-out and foldback
- [shift•black] sends slate mike to tracks too
- [red] in *PPR & REC* toggles the take gender: "p" (pickup), "w" (wild sound), "t" (sync), "n" (ignore)
- [shift•red] triggers the tone generator; tone stays "on" if SHIFT is released first

In Play
- [white] stops and starts the player from the marker
- [black] puts a start mark on the played position (to make a pause, press [white] then [black])
- [shift•black] resets the player to 00

In Inputs-to-tracks and Mon-outs
- [black] sets routing links, e.g., mike-in 3 to track 5
- [red] erases routing links

Nine rotary analog faders plus six linear digital faders—each entirely devoted to one specific task—give more possibilities and are faster to handle than four multifunction knobs.

All of Cantar's rotary knobs, faders, switches, and the enclosure itself are sealed against the elements to guard against damage caused by dust and moisture. Aaton's optional 12-volt rechargeable and re-cellable NiMH batteries connect to the Cantar via its dual 4-pin XLR DC inputs providing up to 15 hours of autonomous operation in the field.

Important note: When in Stop, internal Hdd sleeping, the current drain is a mere 270-mA. To keep the internal sync-clock running, do not switch off the Cantar during the working day. The sleep mode activation can start one second after Stop. (For more details, visit the Cantar web site and review the operational manual—see Tech chapter.

The Twin Battery Safety

The Cantar low-power high-efficiency electronics have the longest working time of all portable recorders. With a single set of on-board NiMH batteries, the 18 (15)-hour

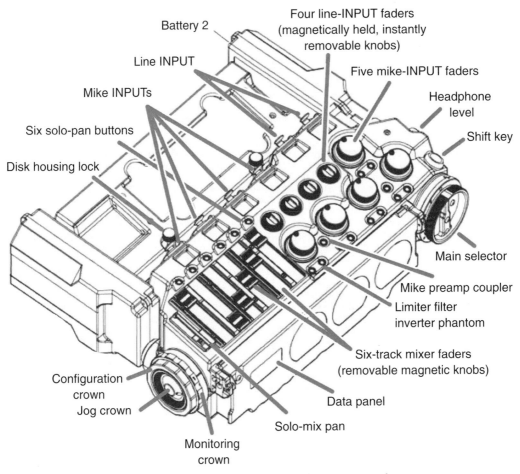

Figure 5.27 Aaton's Cantar mixer/recorder. Photo courtesy of Aaton.

Cantar beats all other recorders. And with the twin you will never be taken by surprise. While working on a mains-powered cart, keep a battery onboard. Activating both batteries will buffer the possible mains drops or cable bad contacts.

External 12 to 16 V DC can also be used, maintaining compatibility with most common DC packages. An optional Bluetooth module provides two-way communication between the Cantar and a Bluetooth-enabled PDA to vividly display all of the Cantar's settings at a glance. The Aaton Cantar records Broadcast Wave files which can be directly imported to most popular editing systems.

Routing 15 Inputs to 8 Tracks

Six primary tracks, T1 to T6, can receive any one of the 15 independent and permanently active inputs: lines 1 to 4, mike inputs 1 to 5, Digi (Aes) 1 to 6.

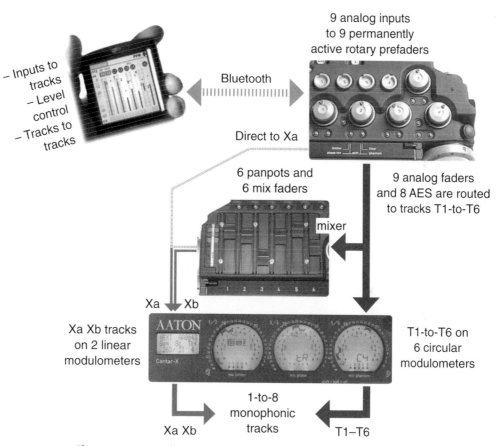

Figure 5.28 Aaton's Cantar mixer/recorder. Photo courtesy of Aaton.

Fifteen *inputs-to-tracks* configs can be stored. They are instantly recalled through the swiveling panel *routing* button and the config crown (a one-hand operation).

The primary tracks are monitored by pairs T1T2, T3T4, and T5T6 on the circular screens.

Two extra tracks (Xa Xb) receive the reference sounds out of the built-in digital mixer. These reference sounds are clearly separated from the T1 to T6 primary tracks: they are displayed on the rectangular display bar graphs. They also can be displayed on the rightmost circular modulometer by pressing the [EYE] button.

When the Xa Xb track pair is generated by the mixer, they are sent to tracks 7 and 8 and a "mix" icon shows on the circular displays.

When recording 8 tracks and no mix-down, tracks 1 to 6 are routed the standard way and the 7 and 8 tracks directly receive the signals selected in AUDIO-12;

Figure 5.29 Production sound mixer Petur Hliddal strapped into the truck as he tackles the grueling task of capturing a clean production track on location for *Syriana*. Carl Fischer, boom operator.

that is Line-in 3 and 4, or Mike 3 and 4, or Aes-in 7 and 8, or nothing (this latter position saves disk space).

See Cantar PostChain at *www.soft.aaton.com/swcantar*; Aaton, France +33 4 7642 9550; cantar-support@aaton.com

Petur Hliddal, veteran sound mixer for such diverse styles of productions as *Lucky You, The Aviator* (2004 version), *Big Fish, Divine Secrets of the Ya-Ya Sisterhood, Planet of the Apes* (2001 version), and *The Cider House Rules,* comments about using the Cantar X on the challenging shoot of *Syriana*:

I just finished work on *Syriana*, an ambitious globetrotting thriller involving five parallel stories, which intersect and diverge, all related to the international oil business. We shot dialogue scenes with two hand-held cameras, frequently with no lighting, in self-driven cars, boats, elevators, airplane cabins, and one 600-foot long supertanker. This was in addition to the usual assortment of inaccessible locations—rooftops, schoolrooms, desert hideaways, odiferous Moroccan kebab shops, Pakistani construction workers' shantytowns, desert power transmission line towers. Many of these locations were located far from the work trucks, on rough ground or sand, necessitating our using small departmental 4 × 4 pickups for equipment transport and storage.

At times the scenes we shot were loosely scripted or improvised and it was not unusual for us to be running four or five wireless mikes together with M-S ambience tracks to help with uncontrolled backgrounds. When you are shooting far from trucks or carts,

Figure 5.30 Production sound mixer, Stuart Wilson, using three Cantar X recorders simultaneously to cover all the wireless mikes and Ambience booms for the 2006 production of *Marie Antoinette.* Stephane Lioret, boom operator.

and the camera crews are hustling from moving car interiors to exterior drive-bys and back, shooting as fast as they can shoulder the camera and push the button, you have got to be light, fast, and flexible to keep up. The Cantar X could not have been more perfectly suited to the production problems I had to face and I could not have done nearly as good a job without it.

Our data traveled in two ways. When working on the cart, I mirrored the Cantar hard drive with a LaCie D2 DVD-RAM, which I shipped to the lab for warehousing. When over-the-shoulder, I used LaCie 60 GB pocket drives stuck in a carry case pocket. These were shuttled between the lab where DVD-RAM copies were struck for warehousing and our locations, where we reused them as needed. In addition, each weekend I loaded the Cantar drive to LaCie 120 GB hard drives on which I maintained a second file warehouse on location.

I have now completed two films with the Cantar X and I have to say for the first time since the "digital revolution" in film sound began, I feel I have stabilized my format decision-making. This machine is a beauty; your responsiveness, attention to the details of support, improvement, and modification are impeccable. Thank you so much for an excellent, elegant machine.

Stuart Wilson, production mixer for such projects as *Harry Potter and the Order of the Phoenix, The Constant Gardener, A Cock and Bull Story, Code 46, The Last Dreamers, The Intended, Room to Rent, Born Romantic,* and *The Last Yellow* to name just a few, shares his experience working with the Cantar X:

I'm just starting my next feature with the Cantar X and I think it's fantastic! From *The Constant Gardener* in the heat and dust of Northern Kenya and Sudan to the rain back in Europe, the faders and knobs are well sealed and have coped with a lot of rough treatment. It's definitely enabled me to do things I wouldn't have been able to do otherwise; mostly for those running-around shots where one has to be portable, I've been able to have a boom and up to five radios and mix on the shoulder.

The latitude one has is very good; the self-noise is very low and the headroom very high, so much so that I'm getting a bit lazy having left some of my old analogue gain riding technique to keep the signal within a healthy range as I know the recorder can cope with it.

On *The Cock and Bull Story*, the last Michael Winterbottom film, I was recording a scene with muskets and cannons and a crowd of extras: I set the levels so that the explosions wouldn't overload and recorded a couple of takes, but then you miss the value of having all those extras shouting in the heat of battle so I decided to do a take with levels set for the crowd and I would let the explosions go over (thinking it is easier to add a cannon shot in post than recreate 200 screaming soldiers in the studio!). The crowds were sounding good and then the explosions started and the Cantar wouldn't distort! There was a good 30-dB difference in the levels I'd set and it sounded great! The limiters are incredible."

On the issue of problem solving locations for good dialog recording, Stuart shared this situation:

I had this interview with Bertolucci. He said he didn't want to postsynch (loop) *anything*— and he said that he wanted to shoot it in a real Paris apartment. I immediately asked him, "How is the floor?" Because I knew that all the apartment buildings in Paris use these parquet floors.

Then he answered, "Well, the floors in these Paris apartments—they have their own voice." I replied, "But we don't want that voice to become a character in the film." So then I turned to the production manager and said, "I want to see the location." The production manager replied, "Well, you can't come. It's not finished yet and the art department is still doing stuff." I agreed, "Yeah, exactly that—when it's finished, it's too late!" After all, the art department has done their stuff, dressing and everything. I have to *be* there before and see if there is anything we can do about any problems, and if we can, can they be worked into the schedule.

The production manager tried to keep me away because he thought it was going to cause trouble or cost money. I wrote them an email and said that it was up to them. If I'd just arrive on the location site and it's already a fait accompli, then I cannot be held responsible for the sound. I will deal with what I could, and if that wasn't what they wanted, then that would be just fine! But, *if* they wanted me to take the responsibility for the sound, and that *is* the way I prefer to work, then I needed to see the place to see if there was any preparation that needed to be done or what *could* be done—what was *practical*. Obviously, they had to budget it, but I can give my proposals and then it's up to the producer and director.

Then they got nervous and said, "Okay, can you come tomorrow?" So I went to Paris from my home in London and recommended some things. I said that they should double glaze all the windows and they did it. In the main bedroom, where a lot of dialog was taking place, I talked to the production designer and he was thinking maybe he would have carpet on the wooden floor and eventually, I was not only able to persuade him to have carpet in this room, but to lift the carpet out and lay a new wooden floor on top of the old creaky one and then put the carpet on top of that. That *really* helped us a lot!

An argument used in the defense of leaving a location the way it is, is that when the actors move around and it's creaking, then it's like life and it's natural and it can be nice and atmospheric. But the problem is, if the camera moves like when we had a steadicam operator moving and the actors are still, then it's ridiculous and you can't use it because you just become aware of the camera and who's behind the camera.

The art department was very good. If they have two or three weeks to make some changes, screwing down floor boards, fixing door frames, that don't fit properly or window frames that don't close properly, then they can do it. They can get a carpenter in for one day. It's not really a big expense. They can do it as long as they have the time to do it. If they don't have much time (i.e., if I'm not brought in until the last minute) then it's stress for them and everybody is busy and then it's a problem.

In the end they were very happy and towards the end of the shoot the French production manager came to me and said that he was very impressed because I'd been very clear and that the director was very pleased with the sound—in fact they only looped one scene, so it was worth the gamble of making myself unpopular during pre-production so when it came to shoot the prep work was done and we all could concentrate on trying to get quality rather than just getting something just "*usable.*"

THE ULTIMATE GOAL AND CHALLENGE

The challenges of production sound recording make it a difficult and arduous job. The production mixers and their teams face the daunting and often disheartening struggle with the ignorance factor of the producer(s) and director and their lack of personal empowerment by not knowing what is possible and what preparations and techniques can most efficiently accomplish the mission. If they do not understand what is possible (and they will not understand that unless you have at least certain tools and procedural protocols), and if they do not understand the importance of what "quiet on the set" really means, then how can they hope to deliver what is truly possible? How can they dream to deliver the magic opportunities of production sound?

Nearly every director I have worked with in postproduction jumps up and down insisting on how much he or she wants the magic of production, but in reality so many of them do not do their part to assist the production mixers and their teams to bring that magic of performance to its fullest possible potential. So many times the opportunities are lost in the logistical heat of battle, in the sheer struggle of shooting the film, getting the shot before they lose the light. If ever a phase of the creation of the motion picture cried out for the discipline and regimentation of a military operation, it is the challenging battlefield of production.

Chapter 6
From the Set to the Laboratory

"That's a wrap for today!" shouts the assistant director. The camera crew breaks down the camera gear and carefully packs the cases into the camera truck. The second assistant camera person (known as the clapper loader in England) is responsible for the exposed negative. He or she sees to it that each roll of negative is carefully placed back in its opaque black plastic bag and secured inside the aluminum film can. The can is then taped so that it will not spill open accidentally. With a black Sharpie or a permanent felt marker, the second assistant labels each can, making sure the identification roll number matches what is on the camera report. The laboratory copy of the camera report is taped to the top of each can. When all the cans have been securely packed, taped, then labeled, and when they have their corresponding sound reports taped on properly, each film can is then packed in a moisture-proof bag. The second assistant camera person places all the film cans in a thermal box for delivery to the laboratory and gives the script supervisor a copy of each camera report to include with the paperwork. Another copy of each camera report is sent to picture editorial, and a third copy is sent to the production office.

The sound crew breaks down the mixer's sound cart, carefully packing the gear into the sound truck. The production mixer packs up the clone hard drive, back-up DATs or ¼" rolls to be shipped back to sound transfer or directly to picture editorial. The original copy of each sound report is folded up and placed into its corresponding box of ¼" tape, or wrapped around each DAT. As in the camera department, the sound mixer gives the script supervisor a copy of each sound report to include with the daily paperwork. A copy of each sound report is also sent to picture editorial and to the production office.

TRANSFER PROTOCOL

Before the film and sound rolls leave the set, the script supervisor reviews and confirms all circled takes with the picture and sound departments. If the location is within driving distance of the film laboratory and sound transfer, then a PA (production assistant) drives the rolls of film negative and sound rolls to their respective processing facilities each night.

Delivery Format

The negative has been developed, but what does the laboratory deliver to the client? Will the project be cut on film or cut digitally? These types of questions determine the protocol the production company follows to successfully carry the show through the various phases of postproduction to completion. Before the cameras even begin to roll, the director, producer(s), director of photography, and picture editor discuss the various ways to handle the picture editing process (described in more detail in Chapter 7). Once the picture editing process is determined, the technical parameters and spec sheet for delivery virtually dictate themselves.

Shot on Film—Cut on Film

If it is decided to cut on film, then the laboratory must print 1-light daily workprints of all the circled takes advertised on the camera report. Sound transfer must transfer a monaural 35-mm mag stripe of all circled takes on the sound report. On rare occasions, a project requires multichannel dailies, such as music events. In such a case, the production company may require that 2-, 4-, or even 6-channel 35-mm fullcoat transfers be made.

Early each morning, the picture editorial runner picks up the 1-light workprints at laboratory, then gets the rolls of single-stripe audio track from sound transfer. Once the picture assistant and apprentice sync all the dailies (discussed further in Chapter 7), they run the reels late in the afternoon or early evening when the director, producer, and picture editor convene to review the material. The first picture assistant must scrutinize the audio sync carefully during the projection of the dailies, as anything that may play back out of sync must be corrected before the reels of picture and their corresponding reels of mag stripe are edge-coded.

Once the dailies are screened, the first picture assistant and apprentice return the reels to their cutting rooms to make any last-minute adjustments to fix sync issues that may have been noticed during the screening. Once these adjustments are complete, the reels of picture and track either are sent out to an edge-code service or the picture editorial crew may have rented their own edge-code machine, such as the Acmade, so that they may do the work themselves. It is absolutely imperative that this edge-code process be done precisely with a focused attention to perforation accuracy as well as keeping the code number assignments straight. The edge-code number is printed onto both the picture and the mag stripe film. Note that the numbers must line up exactly parallel to each other.

Once editorial is satisfied that the daily rolls are in perfect sync and edge-coded, then they are sent to a telecine service where videotape transfers are made. A copy is sent back to the set for review when and if needed for a variety of reasons.

The picture and sound rolls are then returned to picture editorial where they are either broken down in a traditional "per scene/take" technique and carefully rolled up in individual rolls, or more commonly turned into what is known as KEM rolls. Each set of reels can be spun down at high speed on a flatbed editing machine to review alternate takes and extract the footage the editor wants to use in the final cut.

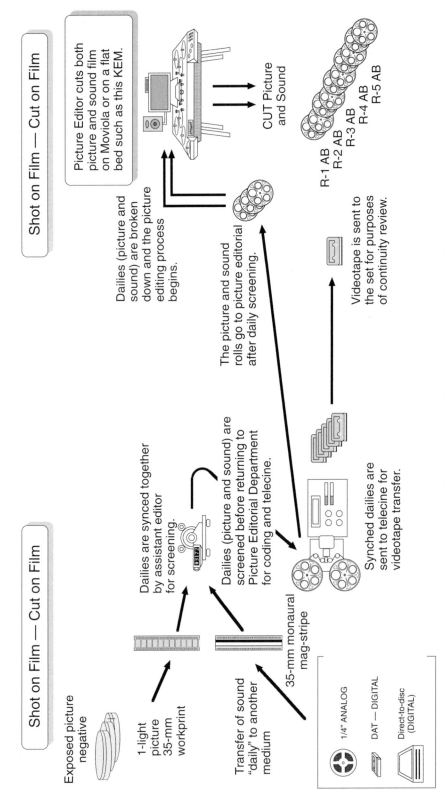

Shot on Film — Cut on Film

Shot on Film — Cut on Film

Picture Editor cuts both picture and sound film on Moviola or on a flat bed such as this KEM.

CUT Picture and Sound

R-1 AB
R-2 AB
R-3 AB
R-4 AB
R-5 AB

Dailies (picture and sound) are broken down and the picture editing process begins.

The picture and sound rolls go to picture editorial after daily screening.

Videotape is sent to the set for purposes of continuity review.

Dailies are synced together by assistant editor for screening.

Exposed picture negative

1-light picture 35-mm workprint

Dailies (picture and sound) are screened before returning to Picture Editorial Department for coding and telecine.

Transfer of sound "daily" to another medium

35-mm monaural mag-stripe

Synched dailies are sent to telecine for videotape transfer.

1/4" ANALOG

DAT — DIGITAL

Direct-to-disc (DIGITAL)

Figure 6.1 Editing flow protocol for Shot on Film—Cut on Film.

The picture editor is now ready to commence the editing process—cutting picture and soundtrack on separate rolls, in perfect sync with each other. This is the traditional "shot on film, cut on film" technique. When the picture is locked, the workprint is turned over to make duplicate copies (usually in a video format with time code) for sound editorial, then sent to the negative cutter to conform the negative to match the workprint.

This technique is virtually extinct in the form that has just been described, but it is important that one understands how things were done, especially if you find yourself working in film restoration or resurrecting vault footage from older films to construct new version cuts, new behind-the-scenes material for "bonus materials" on DVDs, and so on. It also helps one to understand why things are done the way they are—the roots of our art form.

To follow the four basic cutting protocols step-by-step, which may make it easier on the eyes than to look at one mass chart that seems a little overwhelming (wait until you see Cut-and-Conform) you can use the interactive DVD supplied with this book. On the main menu, choose button #1 SOUND—and OVERVIEW. A submenu will come up. Choose submenu button #6 PICTURE EDITORIAL PROTOCOLS and the next submenu will present you with the four protocols discussed in this chapter (reviewed for you step-by-step by a calm soothing narrator). Choose which "protocol" you wish to review and press the button. The exact chart, shown in this book, will unfold for you, panel-by-panel, in a process that should make it much easier to assimilate.

Edge Code and Key Codes on Film

While we are on the subject of working with film, now would be a good time to review what edge code numbers are and the difference between them and key code numbers.

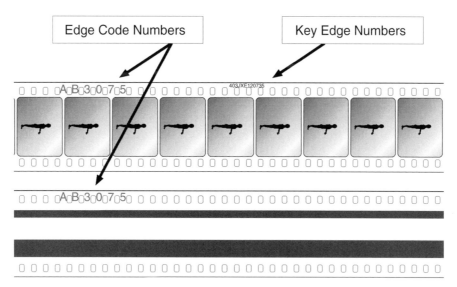

Figure 6.2 Edge codes and key codes, the two essential numbers on film for unique identification and sync.

On the 1-light workprint you see two sets of numbers. The first set is the edge code numbers. These numbers are latent images that have been photographically printed into the original negative by the manufacturer at the time of its creation. The colloquial term is "picture keys," or often just "keys." These numbers are printed identically into the 1-light workprint, if the laboratory's optical printer exposes the edges of the film at the same time as the picture image.

These numbers serve two functions. First, a piece of film can be picked out of the bottom of the trim bin or off the cutting-room floor, and, by reading the edge code number, you can look up the designation number in the code book (see Chapter 7). From there, you determine from exactly what scene, angle, and take number it is, as well as from what camera roll of negative it was printed.

Second, the negative cutter uses these numbers to not only find what negative roll to access but to visually match the exact frame to make the cut. I can vouch for the ease and necessity of this system, as I have had to match far too much footage by visual image alone. Many years ago, a project I worked on did not have the edge code numbers printed through on the workprint.

The edge code numbers are printed onto both the picture workprint and the mag stripe film in exact sync to each other. If they are not in exact parallel sync, then having the edge code number is obviously useless.

More than one numbering technique can be utilized when it comes to edge code. Some like to lock the start mark at the head of the roll and then reset the prefix code and footage counter, thus yielding the traditional letter and footage as follows: AA 1000. Some picture assistants like to set the number codes according to the day of the shoot; in this case, the first day of the shoot is AA, the second day is AB, the third AC, and so forth. Because a single day's shoot very rarely yields over 9,000 feet of dailies, it follows that no need would exist to move on to prefix AB until the second day's dailies.

Many first picture assistants who use the Acmade edge-coding machine to print their own edge code numbers onto the workprint like to print the edge code numbers in a sequence that lists the scene, angle, and take as the number prefix, followed by the footage count, such as 37A1000. This means that this is scene 37, set-up A, take 1. Custom coding each "angle" and "take" in this manner obviously takes much more time than simply setting the start mark at the beginning of the roll and letting the entire roll of film run from top to bottom. However, the organization and speed gained later by the incredible ease of being able to pick up a trim of picture and/or production audio track and instantaneously being able to know the scene/take are of inestimable value.

Shot on Film—Cut Nonlinear and Conform

If the film is to be cut electronically, digital systems such as Final Cut Pro and Avid are popular choices by professionals. A series of refined decisions must be made to structure a procedural protocol to deliver the picture and production sound into the digital nonlinear environment. These decisions must be made in preproduction, as they affect the entire postproduction process to come.

Many times, especially on larger budget pictures, the production company wants more latitude in screening work-in-progress, but prefer that it be done on film and not

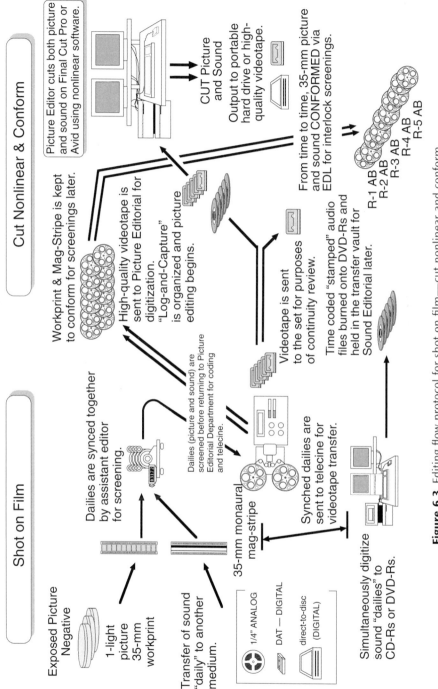

Shot on Film

Exposed Picture Negative

1-light picture 35-mm workprint

Transfer of sound "daily" to another medium.

35-mm monaural mag-stripe

Dailies are synced together by assistant editor for screening.

Dailies (picture and sound) are screened before returning to Picture Editorial Department for coding and telecine.

Synched dailies are sent to telecine for videotape transfer.

Simultaneously digitize sound "dailies" to CD-Rs or DVD-Rs.

1/4" ANALOG
DAT — DIGITAL
direct-to-disc (DIGITAL)

Cut Nonlinear & Conform

Workprint & Mag-Stripe is kept to conform for screenings later.

High-quality videotape is sent to Picture Editorial for digitization. "Log-and-Capture" is organized and picture editing begins.

Videotape is sent to the set for purposes of continuity review.

Time coded "stamped" audio files burned onto DVD-Rs and held in the transfer vault for Sound Editorial later.

Picture Editor cuts both picture and sound on Final Cut Pro or Avid using nonlinear software.

CUT Picture and Sound

Output to portable hard drive or high-quality videotape.

From time to time, 35-mm picture and sound CONFORMED via EDL for interlock screenings.

R-1 AB
R-2 AB
R-3 AB
R-4 AB
R-5 AB

Figure 6.3 Editing flow protocol for shot on film—cut nonlinear and conform.

video projected. In this scenario the negative is developed and a 1-light workprint is struck, as before. The sound daily takes are transferred both digitally to an audio file for nonlinear editing as well as a 35-mm mag stripe transfer made.

Workprint and mag stripe sound are synched together in the traditional fashion and screened for sync and edge coded as in the usual fashion. The difference is that in this case the workprint and mag stripe rolls are racked for future use and not cut in the traditional picture-editing process.

When the picture and track are sent to a telecine service a high-quality (DigiBeta) videotape is transferred and picked up by picture editorial. The videotape can either be contracted to an outside company to do a "log-and-capture" into QuickTime files in the specified format, or the assistant picture editor can do the work at picture editorial.

The digital audio files (usually AIFF, .WAV, or SDII) that were simultaneously transferred when the 35-mm mag-stripe daily was made, are burned onto a CD-R or usually a DVD-R. This is not only a medium to conveniently deliver the files to the client, but becomes a valuable vault back-up should picture editorial suffer a drive meltdown or media file corruption.

From time to time picture editorial will be called on to conform the workprint and 35-mm mag stripe to a particular cut version. The EDL (Edit Decision List) of the non-linear edit session will be printed out and the assistant editors will access the workprint and mag stripe and match the cuts, or what is commonly called "conforming."

This technique is becoming less and less popular as higher quality video projection venues become more available so that the production company may properly present their work-in-progress cuts and/or conduct test audience screenings. But as I have still found a few projects and filmmakers that embrace it to this day, it is included in this book for you to understand this particular option. With today's evolving laboratory techniques and digital intermediates, there is no longer any reason to actually "cut" the negative, in the traditional fashion.

When the locked picture is turned over to sound editorial, the supervising sound editor will probably want the original digitized audio files that were burned to CD-R/DVD-R and held for post-dialog editing, rather than use a generation-transferred video transfer audio from the telecine.

Later, when you make a QuickTime picture output for sound editorial, you should make a "video" and "audio" combo (self-contained file of course)—but you also want to ouput an audio OMF file to go with it.

Big Note: The use of OMF (open media framework) software to greatly accelerate and streamline the dialog editing process over the original discipline of phasing reprints against the work track, your picture editorial protocol *must* have imported and used the "professionally clean audio transfers" during the editorial process—as the soundtrack that is captured from a videotape transfer from the laboratory, even a DigiBeta, is going to have an inferior quality of audio than a digital-to-digital audio transfer, whether by FireWire download from the digital audio recorders drive or by high-quality A-to-D converter processors that professional audio transfer facilities use should the sound mixer opt to record in analog.

The sound editorial team will take this OMF file and decode it, which will extrapolate and create a Pro Tools session with all of the material that picture editorial cut, exactly in sync with where the picture editor cut it and in the layers of tracks that the picture editor created.

Note: When picture editorial outputs the audio OMF file, a menu will appear, asking what kind of "handles" you wish to build into the output. This is the sound material prior to when it was cut and after it was cut, which can be extended by the sound editor who may need to look for valuable fill presence or other audio needs.

In the early days of nonlinear editing (back when we thought a 9-gig drive was huge), it was a drive space issue as to how many pre- and post-handles we could afford to dedicate to an OMF output. With today's terabyte set-ups, storage space is far less a problem. I cannot think of any serious dialog editor who does not want as many of those audio file pre- and post-handles as he or she can have. It is therefore vital that picture editorial not ignore this menu option, but ask sound editorial how long the handles of the audio file should be factored into the output. Unless drive storage is an issue, picture editorial will always be told, "As long as we can have them!"

It is also at this critical output point that you have an experienced craftsperson set up the output settings; otherwise the OMF extrapolation of a Pro Tools session will not be in sync!

As with the "Cut on Film" protocol, you can access the "Shot on Film—Cut Non-linear and Conform" protocol on the interactive DVD with this book as explained earlier. This particular protocol *especially* lends itself to being better understood by reviewing the panel-by-panel narrative.

Shot on Film—Cut Nonlinear

The decision may be made that the laboratory will develop the negative and make a reverse (positive image from the negative) video transfer to a high-resolution video-tape such as the DigiBeta or even make full-resolution QuickTime video files (depending on the services the particular lab is capable of and offers). Circled takes are not necessary for the laboratory process with this style of delivery. All the footage is transferred to tape, thus giving picture editorial access to all the footage, rather than just the circled takes. This tape would come to picture editorial without sound, leaving the process of syncing the production audio track to the assistant picture editor and the apprentice.

Many laboratories offer services for handling the daily sound rolls as well, including syncing the slates. The producer decides either how much to pay out of pocket to an assembly-line style of delivery, or if the film's own crew will personally do the work, adding the care and passion that a project's own picture editorial team is bound to bring to the effort.

But here is the pivotal issue—precise log-and-capture digitizing chores should not be assigned to "get-start" interns and/or learning apprentices without the strict supervision of an experienced first picture assistant who is a seasoned veteran of how to properly import and prep picture and audio files for the picture editing process.

I said it again and I will harp on it again—junk-in, junk-out! Mistakes made at this critical point in the process are going to have astounding collateral cost ramifications down the line. All too often the producer will hire what appears to be a cost-

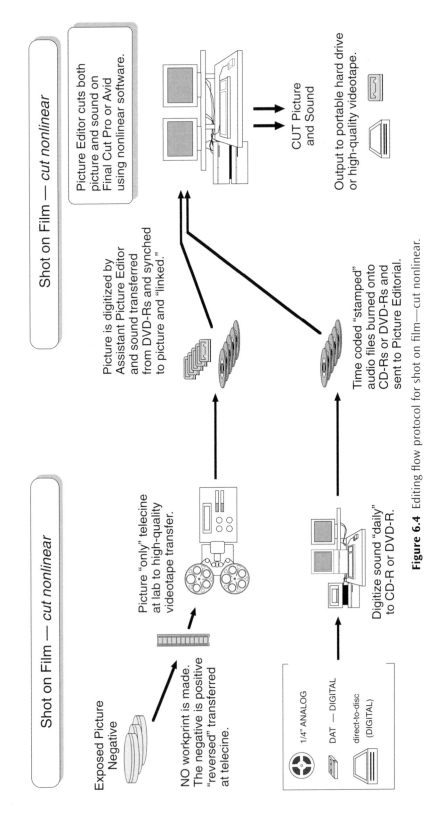

Figure 6.4 Editing flow protocol for shot on film—cut nonlinear.

effective way to get the picture from the lab and into the computer, so he or she will entrust such duties to an intern working for free or an apprentice just getting started. The ironic and sad part about this all too common mistake is that the producer does not realize that when these issues come up weeks or months later he or she is paying out far more money to fix problems that were created in a false decision of economy.

The world of file formats, innovations in laboratory delivery, and specific project demands dictate that you (or the editing team you employ) communicate closely with the laboratory service that you use. Before camera equipment and pictorial formats and audio recording decisions are made, you have to have your team members walk through the process from stem-to-stern so that everybody is on the same page. This will help eliminate, or at least reduce, the unseen surprises that always seem to rise up when this necessary collaboration is not practiced with a discipline.

That said, your picture editor will commence the assembly and editing process as your production shoot progresses. After production wraps and pick-up shots have been decided and completed along with all of the other visual special-effect inclusions, you will output your picture and sound at full resolution to either a hard drive (in digital file form) or videotape.

Please note that it is not a wise idea, if you are working on a serious project, to have picture editorial handle the strict discipline outputs of picture lock for postproduction sound editorial, especially with the increasing use of "digital intermediates."

In recent conversations with some of my colleagues who have already encountered working on films that are using digital intermediates, they have experienced serious sync issues—to the point that several post-sound firms require that they will not accept a picture output to prepare the sound elements for unless the output is handled by a reputable professional telecine service. Please take this last sentence of advice to heart. It is clearly obvious that digital intermediates are the way of the future in filmmaking, but in order to address new innovations in the filmmaking process, you must listen to those who have been on the frontlines of actually working with and having encountered the collateral issues that every new innovation invariably brings with it.

You can waste days, if not weeks, of precious schedule time and wrestle with the frustration and finger-pointing of why track drifts out of sync or who is to blame. The more technologically encumbered our craft becomes, the more the vital it is to rely on veteran craftspeople. A smart producer will quickly realize that a well-paid picture editor and assistant picture editor with the resumes of know-how and experience to accomplish the job are much more cost-effective than placing freebie interns and get-start apprentices in an effort to cut costs. Okay, soapbox lecture over.

Be careful how you output your final locked picture (as well as any temp-dub versions along the way) and you should find this protocol *very* satisfying.

As with the previous protocols, you can access the "Shot on Film—Cut Nonlinear" protocol on the interactive DVD with this book for review.

Shot on Video—Cut Nonlinear

Without question, the most activity in shooting productions, whether they be documentaries, student films, television (both short and long form), and more and more feature work, is various levels of high-quality video.

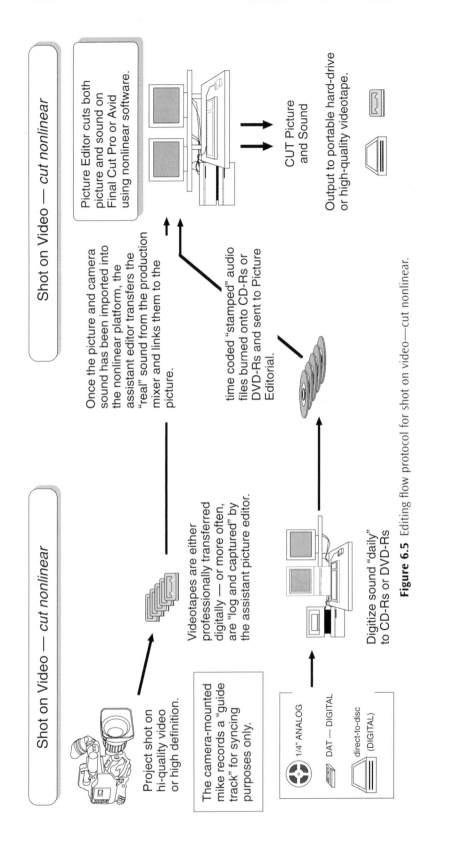

Shot on Video — *cut nonlinear*

Project shot on hi-quality video or high definition.

The camera-mounted mike records a "guide track" for syncing purposes only.

Videotapes are either professionally transferred digitally — or more often, are "log and captured" by the assistant picture editor.

🎞 1/4" ANALOG

📼 DAT — DIGITAL

💿 direct-to-disc (DIGITAL)

Digitize sound "daily" to CD-Rs or DVD-Rs

time coded "stamped" audio files burned onto CD-Rs or DVD-Rs and sent to Picture Editorial.

Shot on Video — *cut nonlinear*

Picture Editor cuts both picture and sound on Final Cut Pro or Avid using nonlinear software.

Once the picture and camera sound has been imported into the nonlinear platform, the assistant editor transfers the "real" sound from the production mixer and links them to the picture.

CUT Picture and Sound

Output to portable hard-drive or high-quality videotape.

Figure 6.5 Editing flow protocol for shot on video—cut nonlinear.

124

All video cameras have a built-in microphone, but any production coverage outside of personal home videos and/or news work insists on a traditional sound mixer and microphone boom operator to capture the expected audio quality that serious filmmakers cannot do without.

High-definition video brings a whole different set of media demands and disciplines than traditional video shoots. Fortunately, the learning curve on high-def is quickly taking hold and we are seeing fewer and fewer directors and producers poised with a razor blade on their wrists. But as I stated a few paragraphs before, once you decide if you are going to be filming in a more traditional video format or if you are going to shoot high-def, your cinematography, sound, and picture editorial department heads have to walk the path on paper before you start shoveling money out the door. Preproduction preparation is the cheapest and most cost-effective process in any production.

You will want to record a "guide track" on the built-in microphones on the video camera, and the assistant editor will want to capture this in the digitization process as a guide track to reference. Your sound mixer and boom operator will be capturing the "good stuff" with their own equipment, using the best audio recorders and microphones that the budget will allow. Whether you have a professional sound transfer service digitally import this audio or you have your picture editorial team handle these chores is your decision.

The "camera" soundtrack, upon "log-and-capture," will be linked to the picture, of course, and therefore becomes a very handy sync-checker-upper when the assistant imports the sound recording teams "good stuff" and syncs the dailies using the better audio files.

As with the previous protocol, when you make the QuickTime picture output for sound editorial, you should make a video *and* audio combo (self-contained as we discussed).

In the majority of instances, these projects are outputting the very material that they captured. In other words, you will not have to worry about the disciplines of video rate and film rate interpretations to resolve sync. It is, therefore, much more likely that picture editorial will generate the QuickTime and OMF files from the picture editorial workstation itself, rather than contract that work out to a telecine. This does not mean that you can make certain assumptions and not be careful to closely check the correct output settings to guarantee each video frame equals a video frame and that you are not altering the real time in any manner.

Even though more and more editorial software and user platforms are using computers with fast enough processors, high definition can still be sluggish at full resolution. I am sure by the time I write the fourth edition of this book, this comment will be obsolete, but for now, it is safer to check with sound editorial first and ask how they want the picture output (resolution wise).

As with the previous protocols, you can access the "Shot on Video—Cut Nonlinear" protocol on the interactive DVD for review.

Digital Food for Thought

Careful thought should be given to the choice of which nonlinear editing system to use. All systems are not created equal. All too often, I have seen a production company make a decision based on the appearance that a particular system was much cheaper to use and therefore should be more cost-effective, only to find out that the collateral ramifications of going cheap on the nonlinear system inflicted numerous extra costs on the postproduction budget when the sound-editorial process commenced.

Another mistake is believing the laboratories and sound facilities when they tell you they are equipped and qualified to do specific services you may require. I knew one laboratory that told the producer that the film was being developed right there on site, but in actuality it was being flown counter-to-counter to Los Angeles for processing by another laboratory subcontracting the work. The first laboratory did not want to take time away from the services and handling they did do. The problem then, and still, is that the more you subcontract and fragment the services, eliminating those craftspeople who could truly be handling the QC (quality control) of your lab work, the more mistakes, lost footage, misunderstandings in specifications, and general lack of personal involvement and commitment to excellence you will find.

Before you settle on a laboratory or sound facility, do yourself and your production budget a big favor and check out various possibilities. Talk to other producers and especially to postproduction supervisors who deal with numerous laboratories and sound facilities. Talk to those craftspeople who have had actual working experience with the laboratories or sound facilities you are considering. First-hand trench-warfare experience by those who work with these facilities is invaluable in guiding you through your production minefield.

DATA IS GOLDEN

Regardless of whether you decide to edit on film or digitally, regardless of what editing platform or protocol is chosen, the underlying constant to all procedures is that at this stage in the negative development through syncing of dailies, the precise and correct entry of data is crucial. Whether the key and edge code numbers are manually entered into the code book or into the information buffer of audio and picture files in the digital domain via the computer keyboard, this information is incredibly difficult to correct once entered incorrectly. Untold time and energy will be wasted trying to find a negative or sound roll because the code book data has either not been entered or the entries are sloppy and/or incorrect.

Unfortunately, this critical moment in the organizational structure of a project suffers the worst from fatigue and dyslexia. Many of us in postproduction have discovered that more craftspeople suffer from some form of dyslexia than one might think. Be careful to recognize such tendencies in yourself and either delegate certain critical responsibilities for data entry to someone else or be extremely cautious and thorough, double-checking numbers before you proceed. Incorrect data entry completely invalidates the ability to successfully utilize OMF functions later. In today's highly pressured schedules, losing the ability to use either the OMF or post-conform function severely slows down dialog editorial, potentially costing thousands of extra dollars to have dialog takes retransferred from source, not to mention having to endure the slow and painstaking process of phase matching (discussed in Chapter 14).

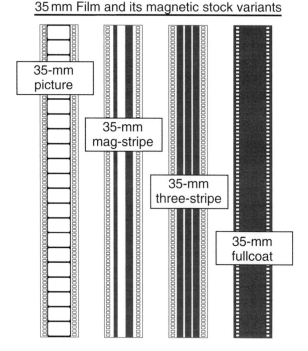

35 mm Film and its magnetic stock variants

35-mm
picture

35-mm
mag-stripe

35-mm
three-stripe

35-mm
fullcoat

Figure 6.6 The 35-mm magnetic stocks. There are the four kinds of 35-mm media used today, explained in detail in the text.

35-MM FILM STOCK VARIANTS

35-mm Picture

The 35-mm film stock on the far left of Figure 6.6 is photographic stock. Numerous types of photographic stocks exist, most of which are used to capture the visual action of a motion picture. Another reason for using photographic stock may be, for instance, to transfer the 2-track matrix stereo sound mix into the optical image that is combined photographically with the visual picture on the final release prints. The example shown has the classic four perforations per frame. Regardless of the incredible advancements in 24 P and high-definition digital projection, 35-mm film stock is still the most popular, and, to date, it renders the most cost-effective image resolution, which will carry the industry well into the next century. 35-mm film is also a global standard. Whether you take your film to Europe, Australia, China, the far reaches of Africa, or upper Siberia, the technical specifications of 35-mm are worldwide.

35-mm Mag Stripe

This 35-mm stock is used for monaural audio sound applications. The wide magnetic stripe on the right side of the film is for the sound. The thinner stripe on the left is called a "balance" stripe (also known as "guide" stripe) so that the film does not undulate as it tracks along in the Moviola, on the KEM, or especially on the re-recording stage playback machines. The balance stripe allows the film to roll up onto itself with an even thickness due to the emulsion layer.

35-mm Magnetic Three-Stripe

This 35-mm stock is also used for audio sound applications. A nearly obsolete variant of stripe formats, three-stripe has been recently revived at several major studio sound departments. Additionally, it is far easier to work with, as it uses an acetate base that tears, unlike fullcoat, which uses a polyester base that does not break. It is also far more economical than fullcoat for the preparation of stereo and/or multichannel sound work.

35-mm Magnetic Fullcoat

This 35-mm stock is also used for audio sound applications. Fullcoat is the most popular and dynamically the best sounding audio format for motion picture and television production. Because of the high rate of speed (90 feet/minute) with which the film passes over the head-stack array, and because of the breadth of the sound heads, the user can load up and saturate the magnetic properties of the film much more heavily than with other analog media, such as 24-track audiotape.

Most "digital" motion picture releases today are first mixed to 35-mm fullcoat in a 6-track configuration to take advantage of the full and rich dynamic range. Because fullcoat has a solid magnetic surface, the user can utilize one of a variety of configurations.

LINE-UP TONES

The disciplined use of line-up tones is the only basis of creating and later duplicating a precise and matching level of audio reproduction. Without it, we can only take our best blind guess, which even at its best never reproduces an exact duplication of the original. For this reason, the vast majority of audio craftspeople and sound facilities throughout the world have adopted and conformed their specifications and recording levels to uniformity by using SRTs (standard reference tapes). Equipment manufacturers design and build their products to operate to these standards. Facilities use SRTs to adjust their playback machines to properly reproduce the standard. This guarantees that a tape recorded halfway around the world will reproduce virtually identically in the studio environment so that 1:1 prints (the first one is identical to the copy made from it) can be transferred from the tape source as exact copies to the original.

In theory, if everyone used the identical reference tape and adjusted their machines correctly, recording a sample of the tones on the head end of recordings would be unnecessary. However, because a variety of reference levels can be used and all machines do not record perfectly and all operators do not set up their machines correctly, the recorded tones at the head of a tape ensure that the recording is reproduced correctly.

Line-up tones are usually sine (for sinusoidal) wave or pure tones, not square waves. Line-up tones are laid down on the magnetic stock prior to the start mark. If the audio transfer is analog, as with 35-mm magnetic film or analog magnetic tapes such as 2-inch 24-track analog tape, the line-up tones are recorded at "0" level on the VU (volume unit) meter, unless specified differently on the tape's content label.

Figure 6.7 The transfer facilities at Technicolor-Weddington never rest. In the foreground, Bruce Balestier is transferring dialog loads from the original production source for a dialog editor. Behind him, Rusty Amodeo supervises the layback session so that it is correctly done the first time. (Photo by David Yewdall.)

A 1-kHz (referred to as a "thousand-cycle tone") sine wave is the standard tone. If the transfer department is interested in very precise line-ups being made later, they follow the 1 kHz with a 10-kHz tone to adjust the high end, and a 125 Hz for adjusting the low end. Many who have been around awhile prefer to have a 40-Hz tone for the low end, but few sound facilities use it today.

If you are working with digital transfers, you do not have a VU meter, but a peak meter. In the digital world, "0" dB represents full scale or the absolute maximum recording level possible. Standard level then becomes some number of dB below full scale. Because digital and analog devices work together to accomplish recordings and re-recording jobs, an agreed-upon correspondence must exist between standard digital level and standard analog level. I have already discussed the standard analog level, but, in the absence of a precise digital standard, everyone has a different opinion on what the "0" VU is for them and their own recordings. The generally accepted standard digital level has been changing during the past few years.

VU and Digital Meters

When gray-market DAT machines were first available in the late 1980s, some sound facilities adopted –12 dB as "0" VU. Those of us who worked with, how should I say, high-concept, high-velocity sound effects projects discovered very quickly that –12 dB would not give us the sufficient headroom required for the thousands of vibrant and robust sound effects we were developing and delivering to the re-recording stages. Those who used –12 dB as "0" VU discovered clipping and a plethora of digital spiking.

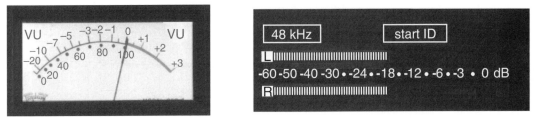

VU Meter   Peak Meter

Figure 6.8 The two basic audio signal meters: the volume meter (VU) and the peak meter.

The hardest lesson to teach the creative user was that the digital world has only so many 1s and 0s.

Let us pause for a moment to clarify something that probably puzzles many creative audio users who do not hail from an engineering background. In digital audio, the number of bits assigned to each sample (not the sampling rate) limits the dynamic range. If you are working in a 16-bit system, you have 65,636 possible volume levels to work with in each sample of the recording. If you try to drive the signal to 65,637, you will experience clipping and distortion because no more 1s and 0s are left to use. Of course, the volume-level saturation geometrically increases as you work at a higher bit rate. If you were working in a 20-bit system, you would have 1,048,576 choices, and working in 24-bit would give you 16,777,216 for each sample!

It did not take long to find out that all the hard work of analog sound effect recording of the past couple of decades was being squashed and spiked, especially when the mixer had recorded the material very hot, saturating the tape. Recordists and sound facilities alike quickly discovered that the dynamic characteristics of many of their recordings were just too powerful to be properly translated into the digital realm.

In 1990, through a series of collaborations between manufacturers, sound mixers, and engineers, the theatrical and television industries settled on –18 dB as the digital peak meter equivalent to "0" VU, even though many of the DAT developers were designing their equipment for –16 dB. For several years, –18 dB seemed to be settling in fairly well.

Obviously, the best way to control overloading (clipping) the maximum level of your digital recordings is to bring the volume of the sound down by adopting a lower decibel level as a "0" VU equivalent. Today, almost all of the high-concept sound mixers and editorial firms have moved to –20 dB, and a couple have gone so far as to adopt an extreme –22 or –24 dB as "0" VU. Their audio engineers tell me they have come to the point that they need those extra decibels of headroom. I personally do not agree with that extreme choice.

Pink Noise

Pink noise is an electronic signal that has equal energy levels at all frequencies across the range from 20 Hz to 20 kHz. Pink noise is often used to make measurements of electronic systems and acoustic spaces. It has an advantage over simple tones in

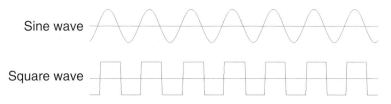

Figure 6.9 The same audio frequency played back first as a sign wave signal and then as a square wave signal.

that all frequencies are present simultaneously, allowing the user to make frequency response measurements quickly. Using an audio spectrum analyzer, a "flat" system or acoustic space is represented as a flat, easily interpreted line on the display. Users of pink noise must be careful to utilize analyzers that offer signal averaging over time due to the rapidly changing characteristics of pink noise; they must also be certain that the measurement microphone has a flat response as well.

Line-Up Tones for Your Own Use

Sound cues provided on the DVD that accompanies this book were carefully mastered so that you can use these line-up tones to check the performance and balance of your speakers.

The 1-kHz Sine Wave and Square Wave

The 1-kHz sine-wave line-up tone was mastered to read –18 dB on the digital peak meter ("0" VU). The 10-kHz sine-wave line-up tone was mastered to read –18 dB on the digital peak meter ("0" VU). 10-kHz tone is used to calibrate equipment to properly record and reproduce high-end frequencies.

The 40-Hz sine-wave line-up tone was mastered to read –18 dB on the digital peak meter ("0" VU). The 40-Hz tone is used to calibrate audio equipment to properly record and reproduce low-end frequencies, though many sound facilities use 100- or 120-Hz tone instead.

The pink noise was mastered to read –18 dB on the digital peak meter ("0" VU). You can place a spectrum analyzer in the ideal listening "apex" of the room and study your speaker reproduction characteristics. (Many consumer-level electronics stores offer excellent spectrum analyzer and audio pressure meters for amateur as well as professional use.) The 1-kHz square-wave line-up tone was mastered to read –18 dB on the digital peak meter ("0" VU).

TIME CODE: THE OBNOXIOUS ELECTRONIC CRICKET

What is time code? How is it used? Should we worry about more than one? Some of the most frightening postproduction war stories revolve around misunderstanding and misusing time code. I literally have seen craftspeople fall back against the wall and slump to a heap on the floor, holding their heads and crying with mental fatigue, because of mismatching time codes or because thousands of dollars of video and/or layback transfers were rendered useless after time code parameters were entered incorrectly. Time code is one of the most confusing and frustrating subjects to deal with in the postproduction process. It is important to get a good grasp on time code: what it does and how to use it as a valuable tool. Let us take a moment and appreciate its relationship to time and space.

In the beginning, before color television (and time code), there was black-and-white television, which operated at 30 fps (frames per second). Color television was introduced in 1953, and, to make color television compatible with the large number of black-and-white receivers, the engineers made a small adjustment to the television signal. They changed the frame rate from 30 fps to 29.97, which slowed it down by 1/10th of 1 percent.

No one noticed and no one cared—until time code came along. The first time code was used in videotape editing and counted 30 fps. If this time code was operated at exactly 30 fps, the time code generator and a normal clock agreed. After viewing an hour of program material, the time code and clock agreed that exactly 60 minutes and 0 seconds had passed.

However, because the television system operates slightly slower than 30 fps, the time code and the real-time clock do not agree. Imagine that you have two clocks, one with a slightly dead battery and one with a fresh battery. Because they are not both running at precisely the same rate, they do not stay in synchronization. Each counts hours, minutes, seconds, but their rates do not match.

When a television program assistant starts a stopwatch at the beginning of the program and then stops it at the end, time code and stopwatch will not agree. To make the slower-running time code address match the real time of day, the counting sequence was altered. It is important to remember that the time code rate was not changed; it still runs at 29.97, but the counting sequence was changed. The 0.1 percent speed change resulted in a difference of 108 frames per hour.

As we have discussed, American National Television System Committee (NTSC) systems run at 29.97 fps. Exceptions where video is run at 30 fps occur when special videotape machines are utilized during principal photography using motion picture cameras to film a television monitor screen. The television video feed is set to run at 30 fps to eliminate the black roll bar that would be visible on the television screen.

Keeping Film in Exact Sync

The most precise standard to maintain synchronization with film is the synchronizer, also known as a sync-block. When working with film, one can interlock the 16-mm or 35-mm picture and one or more 16-mm or 35-mm mag stripe rolls of sound together, side by side on sprocketed wheels (known as gangs) which are coupled to each other with a solid metal rod. When one wheel turns, the others turn exactly the same because they are physically coupled.

The synchronizer does two things. First, it keeps track of the position of the film by footage and frame number. Every frame has a unique identity. Second, it keeps the strands of film in exact synchronization. No matter how quickly or slowly the wheels are turned, the strands remain in perfect synchronization. This works because the film has sprocket holes (also known as perforation holes) that lace perfectly over the ever-

Figure 6.10 Editor with axe.

revolving teeth of the synchronizer wheel. The film is kept from jumping off of the sprocket teeth because a locking arm has been lowered and clicked into place. Each locking arm has two rollers with groove glides that allow the sprocket wheel teeth to pass through, yet the roller holds the film in place against the wheel, so the film does not slip and slide out of sync with the picture or other mag stripe strands.

Each rotation of the wheel equals one foot of film. Numbers 0 to 15, in the case of 35-mm film, on the front of the wheel identify each frame around the circumference. An analog or digital numerical footage counter keeps track of how many times the synchronizer wheel has been rotated. If the wheel is turned 152 times, that means 152 feet of picture and tracks have passed through together in exact sync.

Invisible Sprocket Holes

Think of time code as an electronic multi-gang film synchronizer. Time code provides the same two functions for nonsprocketed media such as audio and videotape. In the case of videotape, every frame of picture has a unique identity, and, while sound can be subdivided into units smaller than one frame, we also refer to it in terms of frames. Time code uses hours, minutes, seconds, and frames instead of film's feet and frames.

We call the time code identity the time code address. Time code also enables synchronization among two or more elements (equipment) by providing a means to measure and control the speed, or rate, of the material. If a videotape and an audiotape each has matching time codes, then we can use a computer to keep the two in sync by making sure that the time code address and speed (rate) match. It is important to think of these two different functions: address and rate. As long as the addresses and rate match, it does not matter at which absolute speed the material is played. The rates, however, must match exactly for the two elements to remain in sync.

The "Pull-Down" Effect

Film cameras are operated in the United States at 24 fps. If the film is never converted to television, it would always run at 24 fps from the camera to the theatre projector. When film is converted to a television format for broadcast, a change is required.

If NTSC television ran at 30 fps, the conversion from 24-frame film to 30-frame television would be fairly straightforward. As the telecine transfer is made, it pauses the film every fourth frame and duplicates the fourth frame; then it rolls four more frames and duplicates the eighth frame; then it rolls four more frames and duplicates the twelfth frame; and so on. By doing this six times every second, the extra 6 frames needed for 24-fps film to fit a 30-fps format is achieved. You can see this for yourself by sticking a videocassette of a movie into your machine at home, then taking the remote control and pausing the action. Now push the single-frame advance button. The action advances a single frame. Push the button a few more times with a slow and rhythmic pace, so that you can study the single-frame movements. You will see that every fourth frame has been duplicated. Aren't your eyes quick enough to see those duplications in real time? No, neither is mine.

This does not fully solve the problem of film-rate conversion to television, however. NTSC television operates at 29.97 fps, or 0.1 percent slower (i.e., 1/10th of 1 percent), so when film is transferred to television it is necessary to slow, or pull down, the film rate the same 0.1 percent to 23.976 fps. When sound editors use a system that has a 29.97-fps video source, they must make sure that the production recordings, which are made with 30-fps time code, are slowed down the same amount as the picture was slowed down when it was converted to television. If you convert 0.1 percent to decimal format, it would be 0.001 (since 1 percent is actually 1/100th or 0.01, 1/10th of that would be 0.001). To prove the point, multiply 30 fps by 0.001 = 0.03; now subtract 0.03 from 30 fps (30 − 0.03 = 29.97 fps). Take 24 fps and multiply it by .001 (24 × 0.001 = 0.024) and then subtract 0.024 from 24 (24 − 0.024 = 23.976 fps). 0.001 percent would be 0.00001 in decimal format. Are we good and confused yet?

Addresses and Rates

There are four different time code address types and four different time code rates. The addressing serves only to uniquely identify each frame, while the rate is essential to maintaining synchronization. As you review the various time codes below, remember that computers count from 0 and not from 1, like most humans do.

Addressing Modes

- 24-frame: each frame is numbered from "0" to "23"
- 25-frame: each frame is numbered from "0" to "24"
- 30-frame nondrop: each frame is numbered from "0" to "29"
- 30-frame drop-frame: each frame is numbered from "0" to "29" (but there is a unique counting sequence)

Frame Rates

- 24 fps: American film systems run at this rate
- 25 fps: European film and television systems run at this rate
- 29.97 fps: American (NTSC) television systems run at this rate
- 30 fps: American standard for non–television-based materials run at this rate

There are six normally encountered time code formats. The valid combinations of addressing modes and rates are as follows:

- 24-frame addresses and 24-frame rate
- 25-frame addresses and 25-frame rate
- 30-frame nondrop frame addresses and 30-frame rate
- 30-frame nondrop frame addresses and 29.97-frame rate
- 30-frame drop-frame addresses and 30-frame rate
- 30-frame drop-frame addresses and 29.97-frame rate

These combinations cover 99 percent of the normally encountered addresses and rates.

Audio Time Code Signal

Time code is recorded onto video- and audiotapes as a special audible signal. It sounds very raucous, much like a constipated electronic insect with a bad temper, but time code–reader electronics can interpret this sound and convert it into computer-readable addresses. The computer listens to the time code and notes when transitions occur in the recorded signal. A transition occurs when the recorded signal changes from a positive-going waveform to a negative-going waveform, and vice versa.

The transition is important to the time code reader. The easiest transition to detect is a rapidly changing one. If the transition is very gradual, it is difficult for the computer to detect it. Square waves have rapid transitions. As the time code signal is copied from one tape to another, it is possible for the shape of this square wave to become distorted and the transitions more difficult to detect. When the time code signal is rolled off, it means that the transitions are not rapid, and the time code reader is having difficulty detecting them.

Time Code Specifications for Video Transfers

When ordering video transfers of either cut film or from nonlinear picture editing platforms, you want the videotape to be transferred with certain information windows as well as a precise designation of time code rate. Remember: be very specific about which time code format you want.

1. Transfer at 29.97 nondrop frame
2. Monaural production audio on Channel 1 (left)
3. Audio time code on Channel 2 (right) with visual time code address burned into the upper left of screen
4. Film footage and frame numbers burned into the upper right of screen
5. VITC (vertical interval time code, explained later in the chapter) on lines 17 and 19

6. Academy picture starts at exactly 000 feet and 00 frames, and time code corresponds to exactly 00 minutes, 00 seconds, and 00 frames
7. Time code "hour" designation matches the film reel number. For example, Reel 3 shows up as 03:00:00:00
8. 30 seconds of time code preroll before the Academy picture start
9. If VHS videocassette tapes are being created, time code and production audio are recorded on the normal analog channels

Drop-Frame Time Code

Drop-frame time code is so named because the counting sequence skips, or drops 2 frames, every minute except at the 10s of minutes. The time code address increases from 59 seconds, 29 frames (00:59:29)—stepping past, or dropping, the 1 minute, 0 seconds, and 0 frames (01:00:00) to 1 minute, 0 seconds, and 0 frames (01:01:00.02). The same number of frames per second is still there; each frame is still uniquely identified; they are just labeled differently.

Check for Drop/Nondrop

You have picked up a videotape that does not have a properly completed transfer label: it does not designate whether the video transfer was made drop or nondrop. In concert with the previous section about the operation of drop frame, simply insert the videotape into a playback machine and spin the image down to the nearest one-minute address. By putting the controller into a flip-frame job mode and carefully flipping from frame 00:59:29 to the next frame, you will know instantly if the tape has been transferred drop or nondrop. If there is no 01:00:00 frame, and the next frame is 01:00:02, then the tape has been transferred drop-frame.

VITC

VITC (pronounced "Vit-See") stands for vertical interval time code. VITC is time code recorded in the television picture. It is not normally seen by viewers and is similar to the frame line that exists between frames of film. When projected, the film frame lines are not visible, and if one were to write numbers in the masked area between frames, these would not be seen during normal presentation. However, if the editor subsequently handles the film, the numbers are easily read. VITC operates in the same way. VITC is written into the television vertical interval. When the video machine is stopped, computers can read this time code very accurately.

Mixing Drop- and Nondrop-Frame Sessions

Most picture editors prefer to use nondrop-frame time code even though they are cutting on systems that are in fact running at 29.97 NTSC rate. The reasons vary, but perhaps it is related to the fact that some early editorial systems could not handle drop-frame time code and that the calculations involved in adding nondrop time codes were much easier than adding drop-frame time codes. Since the picture editors then were probably using nondrop, it made things easier when the sound and picture used the same addressing scheme.

With today's faster computers and much more sophisticated software utilities, however, it does not make much difference whether you use drop frame or nondrop frame, as long as you are consistent and all your people are using the same format. Even if they are not, the synchronization computers are capable of doing the math so that nondrop and drop-frame addresses can be easily synchronized.

Using Outboard A to D Encoders

If you are interested in having the best-quality digital sound transfers made from analog tapes or from 35-mm film, insist on having the material encoded or decoded through high-quality D-A/A-D (digital-to-analog/analog-to-digital) converters, such as the Apogee converters. Most people do not know that to make digital technologies such as the 8-track DA-88 recorders cost-effective and attractive, the manufacturers sacrificed high-end quality at the analog-to-digital and digital-to-analog conversion. Remember, there is no such thing as a free lunch. A really good deal is designed to appear as such because something, somewhere, was eliminated, sacrificed, or degraded to offset the expense.

Digital DA-88 recorders are fading away in favor of higher quality encoding platforms (such as the DigiDesign HD interface), not only because of the better sounding reproduction qualities, but also because of the limitation of only 8 channels per tape and the fact that digitizing 8 channels of a Foley session, for instance, required a transfer process.

Interlocking to time code meant "stem" type transfers, which would yield 8 audio files that would eat up a solid amount of disk space at the rate of 8×5 megabytes per minute (or 700–800 megabytes for a 20-minute reel). The net "performance" passages were usually 15 to 20 percent of that; or to look at it another way, you have 80 to 85 percent disk *waste*. This is why MR8 and MR16 technologies, which can quickly record a Pro Tools session straight to a removable hard drive, gained favor for a while. Straight to hard drive recording in ADR and Foley stage, re-recording predubing and final mixing is the standard, not the exception.

DA-88 technology served as a "bridging" intermedium, so to look to DAT technology as fading in popularity. With direct-to-disk recorders, such as the Deva, Aaton, Fostex, Sound Devices, and the Nagra V all utilizing high-quality straight-to-disk recording, the DAT is finding fewer users in the production and post-sound facility world. Keep this in mind as you plan the technical protocols for your project.

The fact of the matter is DA-88 needs to be *banished* from inventory requirements that are still in force at most studios. Because of the advance in digital sampling/bit rate and other DSP factors, requiring DA-88s as completed stem medium is actually degrading much of the work that so many audio craftspeople have labored hard to achieve in the first place.

I recently could not believe that my client came back to me and complained that payment on his delivery was held up because DA-88s had not been provided. With the ability to supply pristine audio file format stem outputs on CD-R/DVD-R cheaper, faster, and more accurately, why would anyone want to deliver a now-inferior medium!

Chapter 7
Picture Editorial and the Use of the Sound Medium

THE BASTION OF ABSOLUTES

You may wonder why I am going to first review the traditional "film" procedure of receiving, syncing, and preparing dailies for the picture editor to commence the creative process of editorial storytelling. The reason is twofold. First, it is important to understand the process, because, in a real sense the discipline of the process has not changed, only the technique and medium. The second reason is that sooner or later, much to your surprise you will find yourself in need of knowing how things were done, because there are millions of feet of film in vaults, and thousands of feet being sifted through on a daily basis for all kinds of reasons, everything from resurrecting a film to execute a director's cut, to film restoration, to assembling footage shot decades ago for developing valuable "behind-the-scenes" programs for the bonus materials options on today's DVD reissues.

When Terry Porter, over at Disney, handled the remixing challenge of the original *Fantasia*, elements that were nearly 50 years old had to be carefully brought out of film vaults, inventories checked, elements prepared, and old technology playback systems refreshed to be able to accomplish such a task.

Film restoration is a huge career opportunity for those who become infected with the love and devotion to not only saving classic film from being lost, but restore it back to its original glory. In order to even start to understand how to get your arms around such projects, you have to understand how they were structured and prepared in the first place.

Except for the fact that very few crews actually edit with film anymore, the technique and discipline of exacting attention to detail has not changed a bit. In fact, you have to be even more disciplined in that a computer only knows what you tell it. If you enter improper data, you cannot expect it to problem solve your mistake of input for you. So you need to pay attention to how and why we do things. It is as I keep harping at you—the tools will change every five minutes, but the Art Form does not.

FROM THE LAB TO THE BENCH

From the moment daily film and mag stripe transfers arrive from the laboratory and sound transfer, to the moment when the edge code number is applied to both picture and track after running the dailies with the director and picture editor, is the most critical time for the regimentation and precision that the film endures. It is during the daily chore of syncing up the previous day's workprint and corresponding soundtrack when the assistant picture editor and picture apprentice must practice their skills with the strictest regard to accuracy and correct data entry.

The film arrives, and the picture assistant and apprentice swing into action, racing to sync up all daily footage in time for that evening's screening. Errors made at this point in lining up the picture and soundtrack in exact sync are extremely difficult to correct later. Seldom have I seen sync errors corrected once they have passed through the edge-coding machine.

Odd as it may sound, the technique and discipline of syncing film dailies are not as straightforward as they may sound. For some reason, film schools allow students to learn to line up and sync their film dailies on flatbed editing machines. I do not care what any film school instructor tells you—a flatbed editing machine is not a precise machine. Veteran editors and especially prized professional picture assistants also will tell you that flatbed editing machines are inaccurate by as much as plus-or-minus 2 frames! (Most moviegoers notice when dialog is out of sync by 2 frames.)

This is not an opinion or one man's theory. This is a fact, without question; those who even try to debate this fact are showing the laziness and incompetence of their own techniques. The only way to sync film and mag track precisely is to use a multi-gang synchronizer. Because so much hinges on having picture and mag track placed in exact sync to one another, it never ceases to amaze me when someone knowingly uses anything but the most accurate film device to maintain rigid and precise sync.

Before you can actually sync the dailies, you must first break down all the footage, which I now describe in detail. As you wind through the rolls of workprint, you develop a rhythm for winding through the film very quickly. You watch the images blur by, and every so often you notice several frames that "flash-out." These were overexposed frames where the aperture of the camera was left open between takes and washed out the image. These flash-out frames are at the heads of each take. Pause when you come across these flash-out frames, pull slowly ahead and, with the help of a magnifying loop, determine precisely which frame the slate sticks meet as they are snapped together. That is where the clap is heard on the mag track.

Use a white grease pencil in marking the picture once you have identified the exact frame where the slate marker has impacted. Mark an "X" on that frame of film where the sticks meet, then write the scene number, angle, and take number (readable from the slate) across the frames just prior to the "X" frame. Find the scene and slate number on the lab report form included with the roll of workprint, and mark a check next to it.

Roll the workprint quickly down to the next group of flash-out frames, where you pause and repeat the process. After you have marked the slates on the entire roll of workprint, take a flange (a hub with a stiff side to it, or, if you like, a reel with only one side) and roll the workprint up. Watch for the flash-out frames, where you cut the workprint clean with a straight-edge Rivas butt splicer. Place these rolls of picture on the back rack of the film bench, taking time to organize the rolls in numerical order. You should probably practice how to wind film onto a flange without using a core. For the beginner, this is not as simple as you might think it is, but you will quickly master the technique.

After you have broken down all the picture, take a synchronizer with a magnetic head and commence breaking down the sound transfer. The sound transfer always come tails out. Take the flange and start rolling the mag track up until you come to the ID tag. This is an adhesive label, usually $^3/_4$" wide by a couple of inches long. The transfer engineer places these ID tags on the mag film just preceding rolling the scene and take the ID tag identifies. Break off the mag, keeping the ID tag. Then place the mag track into the synchronizer gang and lock it down; lower the mag head down to read the mag stripe. Roll the track forward. You hear the production mixer slate the scene and take, then you hear a pause, followed by off-mike words from the director. Within a few moments, you hear a slate clap. Continue to roll the mag track through until you hear the director call, "Action."

It is at this point that most sync errors are made, because not all head slates go down smoothly. During the course of the picture a host of audio misfires occur. Sometimes you hear a voice call to slate it again; sometimes you hear the assistant director pause the sound roll and then roll again. Also, you can mistake a slate clap for a hand slap or other similar audio distraction. If you are shooting multiple cameras, be careful which slate you mark for which workprint angle, unless all cameras are using a common marker, which is rare. Sometimes the slate clap is hardly audible; a loud, crisp crack often irritates the actors and takes them out of character.

Once you are satisfied that you have correctly identified the slate clap, use a black Sharpie marker to make a clean identification line across the frame exactly where the sound of the clap starts. *Do not* use a grease pencil in marking the slate impacts on the mag track. Once a grease mark has been placed on a magnetic track, it can never be completely rubbed off. The grease cakes up on the sound head and mars the soundtrack. Use a black Sharpie marker to mark the exact impact point on the mag track. Have no fear, the ink from the Sharpie does not harm or alter the sound on the mag track.

Remember that 35-mm film has four perforations to the frame, which means that you can be 1/96th of a second accurate in matching sync. The more dailies you sync up, the more you will study the visual slate arm as it blurs down to impact. You will get a sense of which perforation in the frame is the best choice. You are now changing the mechanical technique of syncing dailies into an art form of precision.

Using the black Sharpie, write the scene, angle, and take number just in front of the slate clap mark on the mag track in plain sight. Roll up the head end of the mag track back to the ID tag and place the roll of mag track on the back rack of the film bench alongside the corresponding roll of picture.

Once you have finished, you will have a back rack filled with rolls of picture and track. You will have rolls of WT (wild track) with no picture. You will have rolls of picture with no track. Check the labels on the rolls of picture that do not have any corresponding rolls of soundtrack. They should all have a designation of MOS (without sound) on the label.

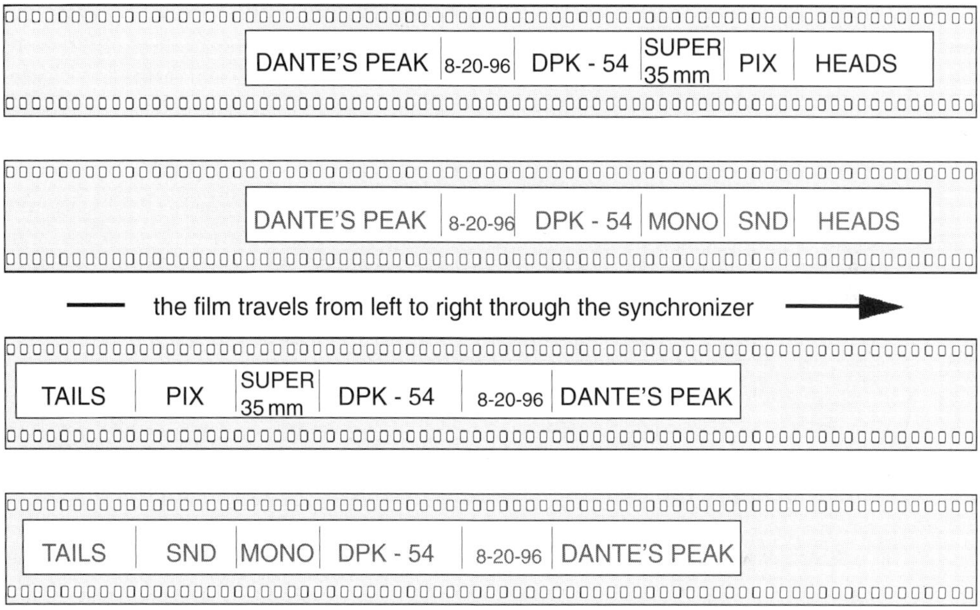

Figure 7.1 HEAD and TAIL leaders. This is standard labeling for daily rolls.

Check the lab reports and sound reports. All of the material inventory should have your check marks next to them. If not, call either the laboratory or the sound transfer facility to order the missing workprints or mag tracks.

You are now ready to start building your daily rolls. Professional picture editorial departments always build the daily rolls starting with the smallest scene number and building out to the largest. By doing this, the director and picture editor view an entire scene and its coverage starting with the master angle; then they review the Apple ("A") angle takes, then the Baker ("B") angle takes, then the Charley ("C") angle takes, and so on. You also review scenes in order; for instance, you would not screen 46 before you would screen 29. It helps to begin the process of continuity in the minds of the director and picture editor.

Once you have built a full reel of picture and track, put head and tail leaders on these rolls. It is traditional to use a black Sharpie marker for the picture label, and a red Sharpie for the sound label. With this kind of color coding, you can identify a picture or sound roll from clear across the room. Head and tail leaders should look much like the labels shown in Figure 7.1.

HEAD AND TAIL LEADERS FOR FILM

To the far right of the label, "HEADS" is listed first, then "PIX" (for workprint, abbreviated from "picture"), or "SND" (for mag track, abbreviated from "sound").

The next piece of information to add to the head label is the format in which the picture is to be viewed. This is rather helpful information for your projectionist, as he or she must know what lens and aperture matte to use. After all, it's not as easy as saying, "Oh, we shot the film in 35." Okay, 35 what? The picture could have been shot in 1:33, 1:85, 1:66; it could have been shot "Scope" or "Super-35" or any number of unusual configurations.

Do not write the format configuration on the sound roll, but list what head configuration the projectionist must have on the interlock mag machine. The vast majority of film projects have monaural single-stripe daily transfers, so list "MONO" for monaural. However, some projects have unusual multichannel configurations, such as those discussed in Chapter 5. When using fullcoat as a sound stock medium, picture editorial can use up to six channels on a piece of film.

The next label notation to make is the roll number. Each editorial team has its own style or method. Some list the roll number starting with the initials of the project, making roll "54" of the feature *Dante's Peak* list as "DP-54" or "DPK-54." Some do not list the initials of the show, just the roll number. Some editorial teams add a small notation on the label, showing which of that day's daily rolls that particular roll is. "DPK-54" could have been the third of five rolls of dailies shot that day, so it would be shown as "3-of-5."

Most editorial teams list the date. Last, but not least, list the title of the film. The tail leaders should have the same information, but written in the reverse order.

I always make my head leaders first on ³⁄₄" white paper tape, then I apply the labels onto color-coded 35-mm painted leader. Different picture assistants use their own combinations of color-coded painted leader, but the most common combinations are yellow-painted leader for picture and red-painted leader for sound. I run 5 or 6 feet of the painted leader, then I splice into picture fill, as picture fill is considerably cheaper per foot than painted leader.

Roll the picture fill down about 20 feet on both picture and sound rolls. At this point, cut in an Academy leader "HEADER" into the picture roll. The Academy leader roll has the frames well marked as to where to cut and splice.

The frame just prior to the first frame of the "8" second rotation is called "Picture Start." This frame could not be marked more clearly: it means just that—"PICTURE START." At this point, apply a 6" strip of ³⁄₄" white paper tape, covering 5 or 6 frames of the Academy leader with the "Picture Start" frame right in the middle. With a black Sharpie, draw a line across the film from edge to edge, on the top and bottom frame line of the "Picture Start" frame. Place another strip of ³⁄₄" white paper tape, covering 5 or 6 frames of the picture fill leader of the sound roll. Again, with a black Sharpie draw a line across the film from edge to edge somewhere in the middle of the tape, as if you are creating a frame line on the tape. Count four perforations (equaling 1 frame) and draw another line across the film from edge to edge. Draw an "X" from the corners of the lines you have drawn across the tape, so that this box has a thick "X" mark. With a hand paper-punch carefully punch a hole right in the center of this "X" on both rolls.

Pssst! The punched hole is for light to easily pass through, making it much easier for the projectionist to seat the frame accurately into the projector gate, which is traditionally a rather dimly lit area.

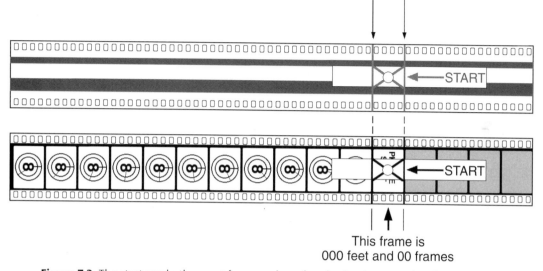

This frame is
000 feet and 00 frames

Figure 7.2 The start mark; the exact frame and synchronization between the picture and sound tracks are critical.

The Start Mark

Figure 7.2 illustrates the start marks. Snap open the synchronizer gangs and place the picture leader into the first gang, the one closest to you so that the "X," which covers the "Picture Start" frame, covers the sprocket teeth that encompass the "0" frame of the synchronizer. Close the gang until it locks shut. Place the sound leader into the second gang, the one with the magnetic sound head on top. Align it over the "0" frame in the same fashion as the picture roll. Close the gang on the sound roll until it locks shut.

From here on, these two pieces of film run in exact sync to one another. Anything you do to this film, you do to the *left* of the synchronizer. Do *nothing* to the right of the synchronizer; to do so would change sync to the two rolls of film and therefore cancel out the whole idea of using a synchronizer (sync block) in the first place.

The biggest mistake beginners make when they start syncing dailies is that they pop open the gangs for some reason. They think they must open them to roll down and find sync on the next shot. Not only is this not necessary, but it is a phenomenal screw-up to do so. Remember, once you have closed the synchronizer gangs when you have applied and aligned your start marks, *never ever* open them—even when you finish syncing the last shot of the roll. (Don't ask me why people open the synchronizer like that, I am just reporting common mistakes that I have often seen.)

After the last shot, attach an Academy leader "TAIL" on the end of the picture roll and fill leader on the end of the sound roll. When the Academy leader tail runs out, attach a length of fill leader and run the two rolls an additional 15 or 20 feet. Roll them through the synchronizer and break or cut the film off evenly on both rolls; then apply your tail leader identification tapes accordingly. You have just finished syncing dailies for the first roll of the day—great! Move on to the next roll. Time is running out, and you still have nearly 3,000 feet of film to go.

I am sure many of you are sloughing off this process of syncing dailies. Film is dead—nonlinear is where it is at, right? I would counsel caution for those who would love to sound the death knell of film. Years ago, when videotape came out, I read articles that predicted the demise of film—yet film is still with us. A few years later, David Wolper was shooting a miniseries of Abraham Lincoln in Super 16mm. I remember reading various professional publications of the time sounded the death knell for 35-mm film—yet, again, 35-mm film is still with us, and healthier than ever, even with the advent of "high-definition" and "24-P" technologies offered today.

When studios all shot their films on location, I read articles about the death of the traditional sound stages. Not only do we still have sound stages, but within the studios and independent arenas there is a resurgence of building sound stages throughout the world. Stages that had been converted for mass storage suddenly booted their storage clients out and reconverted back to being sound stages.

Not too long ago, I also read of the supposedly impending death of old-fashioned special-effects techniques, such as glass paintings and matte shots. These types of effects, it was claimed, were no longer necessary with the advent of computer-generated technologies. By the way, not only have we experienced a rebirth of glass paintings and matte shots, but a renaissance is also under way of the older "tape-and-bailing-wire" techniques.

Every so often I am still approached by various clients seeking shoot-on-film/cut-on-film options to produce their new projects. Several clients had worked in nonlinear and had decided it was preferable for them to return to film protocols.

Lately I have had the privilege to talk to many of my colleagues and other film artisans with whom I usually do not communicate on a daily basis. The broad base of film medium practitioners, in both editorial and sound re-recording applications, pleasantly surprised me. I would not sound the death knell for film-driven postproduction just yet.

"But We Are Nonlinear!"

One should be cautious not to slip into a factory-style mentality when it comes to the quality and technical disciplines that your dailies deserve. Just because a laboratory offers you a sweet deal for "all-in" processing, syncing, and telecine transfers does not guarantee technical excellence. More than one producer has found himself having to pay out considerable extra costs to have work done over again, rather than being done correctly to start with.

Precise attention to detail is most crucial at this exact point in the filmmaking process: the syncing of the dailies and the creation of the code book. It is shocking to witness the weeks of wasted work and the untold thousands of squandered dollars that result when the picture assistant and apprentice do not pay attention to detail and create a proper code book. I cannot overemphasize the importance of this moment in the process. The code book becomes the bible for the balance of the postproduction process. Any experienced supervising sound editor or dialog editor will confirm this.

Once you have performed a sloppy and inaccurate job of syncing the dailies, it is nearly impossible to correct.

With today's nonlinear technologies and the promise of faster assemblies from such advanced software applications as OMF and PostConform, these tasks become nearly automatic in nature. If you sync sloppily or enter misinformation in the directory buffer, you nullify the ability of OMF or PostConform to work correctly. Remember, a computer only knows what you tell it. If you tell it the wrong number, it only knows the *wrong number*. It's the cliche we always banter about, "junk in, junk out." You can be the hero, or you can be the junk man.

THE CODE BOOK ENTRY

For some reason, many inexperienced picture assistants and apprentices think that once they get the sound onto the mag film transfer for the KEM or into the computer for the picture editor, that is the end of it. What further need would anyone have to know about sound rolls and all that? It's in the computer now, right? Wrong. On more than one picture where the inventory was turned over to me for sound editorial, I was shocked to find that either no code book whatsoever existed or that the code book was only filled out regarding negative. After all, the crew did understand, at some point, that a negative cutter would be needed to assemble the original negative together for an answer print. However, when I looked to the sound rolls and all information regarding sound, nothing was filled in. The excuses for this ran the gamut, all of which were just that, excuses.

In our industry, things work the way they do for a reason. Entry spaces are under certain headings for a reason: *to be filled in*! Fill in all the entry spaces. Fill in all of the codes for negative, sound roll number as well as edge code numbers. If in doubt, ask. It is best to check with sound editorial to confirm what requirements are needed from picture editorial so that sound editorial will have a complete code book at turnover. After picture editorial has finished the director's cut and is locking the picture for sound editorial turnover, a team of sound craftspersons and negative cutters depends on your thorough and accurate code book log entries.

Figure 7.3 depicts a typical page from a code book generated by the picture editorial team. Note that the title of the film, number of day of shooting, followed by calendar date of the shoot, are listed at the top of the page. Note that the edge code series number is listed at the bottom of the page. When you three-hole-punch the page and start building up a thick binder, it is much easier to simply flip through the edges of the pages to search for the edge code number than if it were at the top.

The "Scene/Take" number is the first item listed on the far left. A "Description" entry is for the assistant editor to make important notes, such as "Tail slate," "2nd stix" (for "Sticks"), and, if the audio transfer comes from a different source on the "B" camera than from the "A" camera ("B cam sound"), notes make information quick and efficient to find.

The "C.R.#" is where the camera roll number is listed. Note that the picture assistant precedes the roll number with which camera. This greatly aids in such tasks as syncing dailies, where the assistants verbally call out their assigned camera slates:

scene/take	Description	C.R. #	acmade code	key number	S.R. #
64 "D"-1 (B)		B 44	054-1023-1269	K 125-7734-4474 -4711	8
-2 (B)	2nd stix		1270-1442	K 125-7734-4721 -4893	
64 "E"-2 (A)	A cam snd	A 57	1443-1515	K 139-8549-2222 -2294	
-3 (A)	Tail slate		1516-1573	K 139-8549-2305 -2362	
-4 (A)			1574-1667	K 139-8549-2376 -2469	
-2 (B)	B cam snd	B 45	1668-1745	K 125-8122-1126 -1193	
-3 (B)	Tail slate		1746-1810	K 125-8122-1203 -1267	
-4 (B)			1811-1892	K 125-8122-1278 -1359	

"Dante's Peak"   Day 7 shot: Tuesday 8-20-'

054-1000

Figure 7.3 The code book. This is the bible of data by which all production picture and soundtrack can be found.

- "Camera 'A' marker" (followed by a slate clap)
- "Camera 'B' marker" (followed by a slate clap)
- "Camera 'C' marker" (followed by a slate clap)

How are you, the picture assistant, going to know which slate clap on the mag roll syncs up with which workprint picture shot from three different cameras simultaneously? Of course, you could pick one, sync it, and lace it up on a Moviola to see if the actor's lips flap in sync. What if the action is far enough away that a 3 × 4 inch Moviola screen is not big enough for you to see sync clearly enough? What if the much larger KEM screen is not big enough either?

You would probably eventually figure it out, but it is good to know how, for those oddball shots that missed seeing the slate clap or for when there is not a slate at all. I promise that you eventually will cut sound in late because the assistant director did not give the sound mixer enough time to warm up or to follow production protocol in waiting until the mixer calls "speed" back to him before action proceeds. You will have several seconds of silence before sound comes up, but the entire visual action has been shot. And, of course, who can forget those occasions when they tell you they will "tail slate" the shot, and then, during the take, the negative runs out in the camera before the slate can be made? Like that's never happened before.

You must find some bit of sound. Do not look for anything soft. Look for sudden, instant ones that make a precise point. An actor claps his hands with glee in the middle of the sequence, and there is your sync point. I have often used the closing of a car door, even the passing footsteps of a woman walking in high heels (of course, figuring out which heel footfall to pick was interesting). Knowing how to sync when production protocol goes afoul is important, but you do not want to spend your time doing it unnecessarily. You must develop a fully thought-through methodology of how to handle dailies given any number of combinations, inclusive of weather, number of cameras, mixed camera formats, mixed audio formats, use of audio playback, splitting off of practical audio source, and so forth.

The next entry is for the edge code number, listed here in the figure as the "acmade code" (the numbers discussed in Chapter 6 that are applied to both the picture and sound precisely after your daily screening). In this case, the editorial team chose to code its picture by the camera roll method, rather than individual scene-and-take method. This method is commonly referred to as "KEM rolls."

For exhibition purposes, note that the first number always is 054 on this page, as this daily roll is #54. The second number is the last four digits that appear at the head of each shot, followed by a dash; the third set of numbers is the last four digits that appear at the end of each shot. Scene 64 "D" take 1 starts at 054-1023 and ends at 054-1269, plus or minus a foot for extra frames. You can instantly tell that this shot is 246 feet in length, which means that it is 2 minutes, 45.5 seconds long.

The next entry is the "Key number," the latent image number "burned" into the negative by the manufacturer. This is the number your negative cutter looks for to image-match the workprint and negative, or, if you cut nonlinear, from your EDL. Its from-and-to numbering entry is just like the edge code number entry, only the last four numbers are entered that appear at the end of the shot.

The last entry is the sound roll number ("S.R. #"). Unless you want to have your sound editorial crew burning you in effigy or throwing rocks at your cutting room, you are well advised not to forget to fill in this blank.

One of the biggest and most serious problems in code book assimilation occurs when the picture assistant and/or apprentice do not make entries clear and legible. I often have trouble telling the difference between "1" and "7" and distinguishing letters used for angle identifications.

With today's computerized field units (such as the Deva, Fostex, Aaton, or Sound Devices 744t), much more data entry is done right on the set, as the camera is rolling. In many respects, this is very good. Information is fresh in the minds of the production mixer and boom operator. The loss of precious code numbers is less likely, especially when the production is using time code smart slates. Conversely, all this can lull the editorial team into a false sense that they do not have to pay as strict attention to data entry and the code book. Again, a computer is only as good as what you tell it. If misinformation is put into it, unwinding it and getting it straight again is incredibly difficult and time consuming, often adding extra costs to the production. If for some reason the fancy time code and software "wink out" or "crash," you are dead in the water. When it works, a computer can be wonderful, but nothing replaces a trained professional's eyes and ears in knowing what must be done and doing it correctly and efficiently. The better your code book, the smoother the postproduction process that relies on it. It is just that simple.

THE DANGER OF ROMANTIC MYTHOLOGY

I have been both amazed and dismayed hearing film students talk about "cutting-in-the-camera" and other techniques and regarding cinematic history and mythology as if they were doctrine to adopt for themselves. These romantic remembrances really belong in the fireside chats of back-when stories; they are only interesting tales of famous (and sometimes infamous) filmmakers whose techniques and at times irresponsible daring dos that have no place in today's filmmaking industry. Mostly, critical studies professors who were neither there at the time nor have any knowledge of the real reasons, politics, and stresses that caused such things, retell these stories. Sure, it's fun to tell the story of John Ford on location in Monument Valley: upon being told he was seven pages behind schedule, he simply took the script, counted off seven pages, and ripped them out as he told the messenger to inform the executives back at the studio that he was now back on schedule. Do you think, though, that John Ford would dump seven pages of carefully written text that was a blueprint for his own movie? Some actually tell these mystical antidotes as if they had constructive qualities to contribute to young, impressionable film students, who often mistake these fond fables for methods they should adopt themselves.

THE POWER OF COVERAGE

The most important thing a director can do during the battlefield of production is to get plenty of coverage. William Wyler, legendary director of some of Hollywood's greatest pictures (*Big Country, Ben-Hur, The Best Years of Our Lives, Friendly Persuasion, Mrs. Miniver*) was known for his fastidious style of directing. It was not uncommon for him to shoot 20 or 30 takes, each time just telling the crew, "Let's do it again." The actors struggled take after take to dig deeper for that something extra, as Wyler usually would not give specific instructions, just the same nod of the head and, "Let's do it again."

Cast members tried to glean something from their director that might finally allow them to achieve whatever bit of nuance or detail Wyler had envisioned in the first place. As usual, though, precious little would be said except, "Let's do it again."

Not to diminish the fabulous pictures he made or his accomplishments as a director, but the truth of the matter is William Wyler shot so many takes because he was insecure on the set. He did not always know if he had the performance he was looking for when it unfolded. What he did know and understand was the postproduction editing process. He knew that if he shot enough coverage his picture editor could take any particular scene and cut it a dozen different ways. Wyler knew that the editing room was his sandbox to massage and create the picture he really envisioned.

After closer examination, it is easy to understand why the job of picture editor is so coveted and sought after. After the director, the picture editor is considered the most powerful position on a motion picture project. Some even argue that, in the case of a first-time director or a director possessing even the perception of having a tarnished or outdated resumé, the picture editor is at least equal to if not more powerful than the director.

I have been in strategy meetings where a heated argument arose among studio executives over who would handle the picture editorial chores. The picture editor does more than just assemble the hundreds of shots from over 100,000 feet of seemingly disorganized footage. For example, a sequence taking 1 minute of screen time and portraying action and dialog between two characters usually appears to occur in one location cinematically. In actuality, the sequence would have been broken down into individual angles and shot over the course of days, even months, due to appropriate location sites, availability of actors, and other considerations. Sometimes what seems to be one location in the movie is actually a composite of several location sites that are blocks, miles, or even continents apart. Some actors who appear to be in the same scene at the same time performing against one another actually may have never performed their roles in the presence of the other, even though the final edited sequence appears otherwise.

LEANDER SALES

"As an editor, you are deciphering performance, and being that I have this training as an actor just helps me that much more when I am looking at those various takes of film and deciding which performance feels better." Leander continued:

> It is all about the performance. To me, I think that it is what editing is about. Of course, there is a technical aspect to it, but it is about a gut-level response to what I see on screen when I analyze the dailies.
>
> So that's where it started, in drama. But that experience just led me into editing, and I love it. Because in editing you get a chance to work with everything—you get a chance to work with the work of the screenwriter, because often times you are cutting things out and adding things in—looping and ADR. You're working with the cinematographer's work, you're cutting things out and putting them back in. You're working with the production sound recordist's work—everything.
>
> A lot of times it gives you a chance to show the director things that he or she didn't see. Being an editor allows you to be objective. Because when the director is on set, often

Figure 7.4 Leander Sales, film editor and editing faculty at the North Carolina School of the Arts–School of Filmmaking. (Photo by David Yewdall.)

times he doesn't see certain things because he is so worried about other things. But as an editor, who is not on set, it allows me that objectivity.

Those are the moments that you look for. Those are the moments that actors look for, those true moments. You just feel it, and you can't repeat it—it just comes. That's the reason why Woody Allen says he never loops, or Martin Scorsese says he won't loop a certain scene because he says you can't recreate that emotion, because you don't have the other actor to bounce off of. It makes a huge difference.

Another important thing for a film editor, I feel, is just to live—life. You have to understand emotions, behavior—because basically that is what you are looking at when you are studying those performances. You are looking for the emotional context that you are trying to distill a truth and honesty. The more you live, the more it helps you to get to that truth. I lived in Italy for awhile, and I have traveled in Africa. Over there just helped me to understand life, and it opened so many doors for me as far as interest and just experimenting with things and trying to, I guess, see where I fit into the big picture of the world. That's important—how you fit into the big picture. That goes back to editing you see. You cut this little scene, but how does *it* fit into the big picture?

Editors are the only people who really get a chance to see the film from the first scene in dailies through to the release prints. I love that process. It's seeing the baby born, and then you put it out into the world.

MARK GOLDBLATT, A.C.E.

"Inappropriate editing can destroy a film," declares Mark Goldblatt, A.C.E. Like so many of today's top filmmaking talents, Goldblatt learned his craft while working for Roger Corman on B-films like *Piranha* and *Humanoids from the Deep*, learning how to creatively cut more into a film than the material itself supplied. Goldblatt went on to cut *Commando* and *The Howling*, then vaulted into mega-action spectacles such as *The Terminator* and *Terminator 2: Judgment Day*, *Rambo II*, *True Lies*, *Armageddon*, *Pearl Harbor*, and *X-Men: The Last Stand*, as well as the space epic *Starship Troopers*. He said:

> The picture editor must be sensitive to the material as well as the director's vision. On the other hand, the editor cannot be a "yes man" either. We should be able to look at the

Figure 7.5 Mark Goldblatt, A.C.E., picture editor.

dailies with a fresh eye, without preconception, allowing ourselves to interface with the director, challenging him or her to stretch—to be open to trying new ideas. Sometimes you have to work with a director who has an insecure ego, who can't handle trying something new, but the good ones understand the need for a robust and stimulating collaboration.

When the picture editorial process is completed properly, the audience should be unaware of cuts and transitions. It should be drawn into the story by design, the action unfolding in a precise, deliberate way. "Consistency is vital," comments Mark Goldblatt.

> The actor performs all of his scenes out of order over a period of weeks, sometimes months. It's very difficult to match and reduplicate something they shot six weeks apart that is then cut together and played on the screen in tandem. Sometimes you have to carve a consistent characterization out of the film, especially if the material isn't there to start with. You have to help build sympathy for the protagonist. If we don't care for or feel compassion for the protagonist, the film will always fail. If the audience doesn't care what happens to our hero, then all the special effects and action stuntwork money can buy will be rendered meaningless.

COST SAVINGS AND COSTLY BLUNDERS

Knowledgeable production companies bring in the picture editor well before the cameras start to roll. The picture editor's work starts with the screenplay itself, working with director, writer, producer, and cinematographer to determine final rewrite and to examine tactics of how to capture the vision of the project onto film. At this time, the decision of film-editing protocol is decided, and whether to shoot on film and cut on film (using a Moviola or KEM) or whether to shoot on film and digitize to cut on a nonlinear platform such as Final Cut Pro or Avid.

Close attention must be paid to the expectations for screening the film, either as a work-in-progress or as test screenings. Needs also are addressed for screening the film in various venues outside of the immediate cutting environment. Is the project a character-driven film without many visual effects, or is it filled with many visual special effects that require constant maintenance and attention?

These considerations should and do have a major impact on the protocol decision. The choice of whether to cut on film or nonlinear (and if nonlinear, on which platform) should not be left to the whim or personal preference of the picture editor. The decision should serve the exact needs and purposes of the film project. Not too long ago, I was involved in a feature film that wasted well over $50,000 because the project had left the choice of the nonlinear platform to the picture editor. The collateral costs required for its unique way of handling picture and audio files cost the production company thousands of dollars that would not have been spent if the appropriate nonlinear platform had been chosen for the project requirements.

Vast amounts of money also have been saved by not filming sequences that have been pre-edited from the screenplay itself, sequences deemed as unnecessary. Conversely, the opposite also is true. A number of years ago, I supervised the sound for a feature film that had a second-generation picture editor (his father had been a studio executive) and a first-time director. The film bristled with all kinds of high-tech gadgetry and had fun action sequences that cried out for a big stereo soundtrack. Halfway through principal photography, the director and picture editor deemed that a particular scene in the script was no longer relevant to the project, and, by cutting it, they would have the necessary money to secure a big, rich stereo track.

The producer was caught off-guard, especially as he had not been factored into the decision-making process, and threw a classic tantrum, demanding the scene be shot because he was the producer and his word was absolute law. The director was forced to shoot a scene everybody knew would never make it into the picture. The amount of money it took to shoot this scene was just over $100,000! Consequently the picture could not afford the stereo soundtrack the director and picture editor both had hoped it would have.

All who wondered why this film was mixed monaurally have now been given the answer. All who do not know to what film I am referring, just remember this horror story for a rainy day—it could happen to you. By authorizing the extra bit of stop-motion animation you really want or an instrumental group twice as big as your blown budget can now afford, you or those in decision-making capacities can wipe out what is best for the picture as a whole by thoughtless, politically motivated, or egotistical nonsense.

MILLIE MOORE, A.C.E.

Shoot the Master Angle at a Faster Pace

Millie Moore, A.C.E., once said:

> I love master shots, and I love to stay with them as long as possible, holding back the coverage for the more poignant moments of the scene. However, to be able to do that, the master must be well staged, and the dialog must be well paced. If the dialog is too slowly paced, you are limited to using the master only for establishing the geography of the actors and action. The editor is forced to go into the coverage sooner simply to speed up the action, rather than saving the closer coverage to capture more dramatic or emotional moments. At one time or another, every picture editor has been challenged to take poor acting material and try to cut a performance out of it that will work. A good picture editor can take an actor's good performance and cut it into a great performance.

"My work should appear seamless," remarks Millie Moore, picture editor of such projects as *Go Tell the Spartans*, *Those Lips, Those Eyes*, *Geronimo*, *Ironclads*, and Dalton Trumbo's *Johnny Got His Gun*. "If I make any cuts that reveal a jump in continuity or draw attention to the editing process, then I have failed in my job. An editor should never distract the audience by the editorial process—it yanks them right out of the movie and breaks the illusion."

Planning and executing a successful shoot is handled like a military operation, with many of the same disciplines. The producer(s) are the joint chiefs-of-staff back at production company headquarters. The director is the general, the field commander, articulating his or her subjective interpretation of the script as well as his ideas to

Figure 7.6 Millie Moore, A.C.E., picture editor.

manifest his vision on-screen. His or her lieutenant commanders—first assistant director, unit production manager, and production coordinator—hold productive and comprehensive staff meetings with the department heads, i.e., casting director, production designer, costume designer, art director, director of photography, sound mixer, picture editorial, grip and electrical, stunt coordinator, safety, transportation, craft services, and so forth.

From the first read-through to the completion of storyboards with shot-by-shot renderings for complex and potentially dangerous action sequences, literally thousands of forms, graphs, maps, breakdowns, and call sheets are planned and organized, along with alternate scenes that can be shot if inclement weather prohibits shooting the primary sequences.

Like a great military campaign, it takes the coordinated and carefully designed production plan of hundreds of highly experienced craftspeople to help bring the director's vision to reality.

Whether the film is a theatrical motion picture, television show, commercial, music video, documentary, or industrial training film, the basic principles don't change. Coverage should still be shot in masters, mediums, and close-ups with total regard for "crossing the line" and direction of action. Tracking (dolly) shots and crane shots must be carefully preplanned and used when appropriate. Many of today's movies suffer from the belief that the camera must be constantly moving. More often than not, this overuse of the camera-in-motion without regard to storytelling becomes weary and distracts the audience from the purpose of a film—*to tell the story*—or what I call the MTV mentality.

The editing style is dictated by the kind of film being made and the actual material the editor has. The picture editor knows which style is most appropriate after he or she has reviewed each day's footage and assimilated the director's concept and vision. Explains Mark Goldblatt:

> You can take the same material and cut it any number of styles, changing dramatically how you want the audience to respond. You can build suspense—or dissipate it, setting the audience up for a shock or keep them on the edge of their seat. It's all in how you cut

it. I can get the audience on the edge of their seat, realizing danger is about to befall the hero, because the audience sees the danger, and all that they can do is grip their seats and encourage the hero to get the hell outta there—or I can lull them into thinking everything is fine, then shock them with the unexpected. It's the same footage—it's just the way I cut it.

The picture editor's job is to determine which style is appropriate to that particular scene in that particular film. The picture editor may cut it completely differently for some other kind of film. The experienced picture editor will study the raw material and, after due consideration, allow it to tell him or her how it should be cut; then the editor just does it.

THE NONLINEAR ISSUE

Goldblatt continues:

> There's a mythology to electronic editing. Don't misunderstand me, digital technology is here to stay—there's no going back—but there is a common misperception of the advantages. The technology makes it much easier to try more things. Let's face it, when you can do more things, you try more things. This way the editor can have his cut, the director can have his cut version, the producer can have their cut version, the studio can have their cut version(s) (often more than one), and, of course, they want the audience test screenings the *very next* day!
>
> The problem is that working in digital doesn't give you as much time to think about what you're doing. When we used to cut with film on Moviolas and splice the film together with tape, we had more time to think through the sequence—you know, problem solving. In digital, we can work much faster, so we sometimes don't get the chance to think the process through as thoroughly. Nowadays, you see a number of movies that obviously look as if they had not been given the opportunity to completely explore the potentials and possibilities of the material, often without respect of postproduction schedules being totally out of control.

Many editors regard this problem as "digital thinking"—conceptualizing driven by the executive perception that digital is cheaper. Unfortunately, most studio executives who currently make these kinds of creative decisions are not trained in the very craft they impact.

"I think that the editorial process is given short shrift since the coming of electronic editing," comments Millie Moore.

> Because it is faster to cut electronically, less time is being scheduled for the editorial process. That could be fine if all else stayed the same; however, such is not the case. While postproduction schedules are shrinking, many directors are shooting considerably more footage per scene—the more the footage, the more time it takes the editor to view and select.
>
> Also, because it is so fast to cut electronically, the editor is being asked to cut many more versions of each scene, which is also time-consuming. Compressing postproduction schedules while increasing the workload defeats the advantage of electronic editing. Although it may be faster, it does not create the "art form" of editing that takes know-how and time. The more you compress the time schedule, the more you crush the creative process.

There is no doubt that digital is here to stay. However, there needs to be a greater awareness of what we have lost in the transition. Only when the time-tested values of film editing are honored will digital technology fulfill its potential. This starts at the grass roots level—film students who understand that digital manipulation is not the art form. It is a tool, just like the Moviola—it just works differently.

Years ago sound editors didn't have magnetic stripe to cut sound; they cut optical track, having to paint their splices with an opaque fluid to remove pops and ticks that would otherwise be read by the exciter lamp in the sound head. When magnetic-stripe technology came along in the early fifties, it didn't change technique and principles of creative sound editing or sound design. It was a new tool to make the job easier. Now digital has come along to accelerate the process of cutting picture as well as sound. The technique and principles of how you cut a scene or design sound have not changed—we're just using a new kind of tool to do the job.

SOUND AND THE PICTURE EDITOR

Millie Moore, A.C.E., at one time contemplated her career:

> Prior to pursuing a career in the picture editing arena, I was a postproduction supervisor and an associate producer making documentary films for Jack Douglas. We were the first people to use portable $1/4''$ tape. Ryder Sound had always handled our sound facility transfer and mixing requirements. Loren Ryder had brought in the Perfectone, which was the forerunner of the Nagra, which was manufactured in Switzerland. Ryder Sound used to come up to Jack Douglas's office where we would shoot the introductions to the show.

Millie was head of all postproduction for Jack, turning out 52 shows a year as well as a pilot. Eventually, Millie was sent down to Ryder Sound to learn how to use the Perfectone herself so that Jack did not have to always hire a Ryder Sound team for every need. For some time, Millie was the only woman sound recordist in Hollywood, using this new $1/4''$ technology from Europe.

On more than one occasion, when Millie would go to Ryder Sound to pick up recording equipment, Loren would ask her what kind of situation she was heading to shoot that day. Moore said:

> He would often suggest taking along a new microphone that they had just acquired or some other pieces of equipment that they thought might be of value. In short order, I became experienced in various kinds of microphones and amplifiers—of course, I spent half my time on the telephone, asking questions of the guys back at Ryder.
>
> I ended up teaching other people to use the equipment for Jack, especially when we went global in our shooting venues. Jack wanted me to move up to a full-fledged producer, but I turned him down. Frankly, I didn't want to live out of a suitcase.
>
> It was then I decided that I wanted to move over to picture editing. It became very satisfying. I was working on several projects at once, either hands-on or as a supervising consultant for Jack. If there was anything really special that needed care, he and I would go into a cutting room and close the door and go over the material together.

It was very challenging for us, as we shot on both 16-mm and 35-mm film. On-location material was shot in 16-mm, and interviews were shot in 35-mm, so we had to combine these two formats. For a long time, I was the person who had to do the optical counts.

It was time to move on. Millie wanted to move into features, but in those days it was extremely hard for women to get lead position jobs, especially under union jurisdictions.

The independently produced *Johnny Got His Gun* was Millie's first feature film. The producer, who had worked at Jack Douglas's, wanted Millie to handle the Dalton Trumbo picture, an extremely powerful antiwar film:

> Every director with whom I worked was a new learning experience. However, I feel that I learned the most from working with Michael Pressman. He and I were still young when we first paired up on *The Great Texas Dynamite Chase*. Although it was not my first feature film as an editor, it was his first film as a director. Since then, we have collaborated on various projects, which have given me the opportunity to watch him develop his craft and grow. I have learned a great deal about the editing process from him. Aside from directing films, he has wisely spent a great deal of time directing theatre productions. I feel that his work in the theatre has allowed him to gain a greater understanding of staging and blocking, as well as an expertise in working with actors. His background in theatre has broadened him, enabling him to get more textured and full performances as well as more interesting visual shots. When I look at dailies, I can frequently tell when the director has had theatrical training. Whenever I talk to young people getting started, I always encourage them to get involved in local theatre so that they can gain skill in staging and blocking, as well as working with actors.

Millie is very discerning with her craft:

> The best editing is invisible. You should walk away from seeing a picture without being aware of the cuts that were made, unless they were made for a specific effect.
>
> For the most part, I do not believe in using multiple editors. It's a very rare case that you don't feel the difference of each editor's sense of timing. I mean, what is editing, but an inner sense of timing—setting the pace of a film? In fact, one of the most important jobs of the picture editor is to control the tempo and the pace of the story. Through the cutting art of the picture editor, sequences can be sped up or slowed down, performances can be vastly improved, intent and inflections of dialog radically redesigned, giving an entirely new slant on a scene and how it plays out. When you keep switching from one editor to another through the course of the film, it lacks synchronic integrity. Even if you don't see it, you will feel a difference. It takes a rare director to herd over a project that utilizes multiple picture editors and end up with a fluid and seamless effort.
>
> Whenever I had to have a second picture editor on the team, I always tried to have the choice of that editor. Very simply, I wanted that editor to have a pace and timing as close to my own as possible—so the picture would not suffer. Most often, I turned my own picture assistants, whom I had trained to have a taste and feel for the cutting to be similar to my own, into the second picture editor.

Millie has cut several projects on an Avid, but she does not allow the technology to dominate her. "Nonlinear editing is just another tool, but God bless it when cutting battle scenes, action sequences, or scenes with visual special effects. For me, this is where the nonlinear technology makes a substantial contribution."

Millie has altogether different feelings if she is working on a project that does not require special visual effects:

> I don't need all the electronic bells and whistles if I am working on a character-driven film. It is much more satisfying, and frankly, you will be surprised to learn, a lot cheaper. Once all of the collateral costs are shaken out of the money tree, working on film with either a Moviola or a KEM is more cost-effective. Additionally, you will discover that you are not as restrained by screening venues as when you are working in digital.
>
> I miss the Moviola. Cutting on an Avid is much easier physically, but it is much quicker to become brain-dead. Working on the Moviola is a kinesthetic experience—the brain and body working together, preventing dullness and brain fatigue. I could work many more hours on the Moviola than I can on an Avid, and stay in better physical shape as well. Working on a digital machine, there is too much interference between you and the film—it fractures and dissipates your concentration. The wonderful thing about the Moviola is that there is absolutely nothing between you and film. You touch it, you handle it, you place the film into the picture head gate and snap it shut, and you are off and running.
>
> To me, editing is as much a visceral as it is a mental act. Consequently, I love being able to touch film and have it running through my fingers as it goes through the Moviola. Even though working directly on film has a number of drawbacks, such as the noise of a Moviola, broken sprocket holes, splices, and much more, working on a keyboard gives one very little of the tactile experience of film. The young people today who are becoming editors have been deprived of this experience, and I think that it is very sad.
>
> Young editors today are not learning to develop a visual memory. When you cut on film, you sit and you look and you look and you look. You memorize the film. You figure out in your head where you are going, because you do not want to go back and tear those first splices apart and do them over. On film, you know why you put the pieces of film together the way that you did. You've spent time thinking about it. While you were doing other chores or running down a KEM roll to review and out-take, your subconscious was massaging your visual memory through the process—problem solving. On a computer, you can start hacking away at anything that you want to throw together. If it doesn't look good, so what—you hit another button and start over. There is no motivation to develop visual memory.

The use of visual memory is critical, for both picture editor and sound editor.

There is as much to do in sound as in picture editing. At a running, someone might say, "Oh, Millie, that shot is too long," and I would answer, "No, wait. Sound is going to fill that in." Love scenes that seem to drag on forever in a progress screening, play totally differently when the music is added. When I cut the sequence, I can hear music in my head, so I cut the rhythm and the pace of the love scene against that.

Young editors are not developing this ability because it is too easy to put in an audio CD and transfer temp music cues into the computer to cut against. This works when they have CDs on hand, but what about if they need to cut a sequence without them? Ask them to cut film on a KEM or a Moviola in the change room of a dubbing stage, and watch the panic set in! The training is just not there. Some new editors panic if they don't have a time code reference to which they can pin their work.

Master picture editors will tell you that if you want to learn how to construct a film, watch it without sound. Sound tricks you—it carries you and points you, unawares, in many directions. By the same token, for many films if you only listen to the soundtrack you do not have the director's entire vision. The visual image and the audio track are organically and chemically bound together.

Sound effects and music are as important a voice in films as the spoken dialog; the audience uses them to define the characters' physical being and action. Sound effects go right in at the audience; they bypass the dialog track in that they are proverbial—like music, they hit you right where you live. They also are extremely powerful in the storytelling process. In the performance of a single note, music sets the tone for what you are about to see and probably how you are about to feel. Good picture editors know this, and, as they sculpt and shape the pace and tempo of the film, they keep the power of the coming soundtrack well in mind.

HOWARD SMITH, A.C.E.

Howard Smith, A.C.E., veteran picture editor of both big-action and character-driven pictures (*Snakes on a Plane, City of Ghosts, The Weight of Water, The Abyss, Near Dark, Dante's Peak, Twilight Zone: The Motion Picture*), made the transition from cutting picture on film with a Moviola and a KEM to cutting nonlinear via the Avid:

> As the picture editor, my primary task is to work with the director to try to shape the material so that it is the most expressive of what the film is intended to be. You try to tell a story, and tell that story as effectively as it can be told.
>
> It has been said that the editing process is essentially the last scripting of the movie. It's been scripted by a writer, the project goes into production, where it is written as images, and then it goes into the editing process—we do the final shaping. Obviously, we are trying

Figure 7.7 Howard Smith, A.C.E., picture editor.

to achieve the intent of the original written piece. Things will and do happen in production through performance, through art direction, through camera—that happen through stylistic elements that can nudge the storytelling a little that way, or this way. One has to be very responsive and sensitive to the material—I think that is the first line that an editor works at.

They look at the dailies, preferably with the director so the director can convey any input as to his intentions of the material. There may be variations in performance, and without the input from the director it will be more difficult to know his or her intentions versus happenstance, in terms of the choice of performance.

Early takes of a scene may be very straight and dramatic. As the filming continues, it may loosen up—variations could bring countless approaches to how you may cut the sequence. Which way does the editor take it? The material will give all kinds of paths that the editor can follow.

Years ago, there was a movement for editors to go on location, to be near the director and crew during production. This can often be a good thing, as a good editor can lend guidance and assistance in continuity and coverage to the shoot.

As we have moved into electronic editing and the ability to send footage and video transfers overnight via air couriers or even interlocking digital telephonic feeds, the pressure for editors to be on location with the director has lessened. Personally, I do not think that this is necessarily better. At the very least, we lose something when we do not have that daily interaction as the director and editor do when they share the process of reviewing the dailies together.

During production, the editor is cutting together the picture based on the intention of the script, and the intention as expressed by the director. By the time the production has wrapped, within a week or two the editor has put together the first cut of the movie.

The director has traditionally gotten some rest and recuperation during those first couple of weeks before he returns to the editing process. For approximately 10 weeks, as per the DGA contract, the director and editor work together to put the film together in its best light for the director's cut.

What editing will do is focus—moment to moment, the most telling aspects of the scene. When you do this shaping, it is such an exciting experience, the mixing of creative chemistry. Most directors find that the most exciting and often satisfying process of the filmmaking experience is the film editing process. It is during these critical weeks that everything really comes to life. Sure, it is alive on the page of the script, it is alive on the set during principal photography, but when you are cutting the picture together, the film takes an elevated step that transcends all the processes up until that point—it really becomes a movie.

Obviously the addition of sound effects and music, which will come later after we have locked the picture, will greatly elevate the creative impact of the film, taking it to new heights—but that is only to take the film to a higher level from a known quantity that we have achieved through picture editorial. Great sound will make the movie appear to look better and be more visually exciting; a great music score will sweep the audience into the emotional directions that the director hopes to achieve, but the greatest soundtrack in the world is not going to save or camouflage bad picture cuts.

With the advent of nonlinear technology we are now able to add in temp music and sound effects in a far more complex way than we ever could with a Moviola or KEM, we are able to work with sound and music even as we are cutting the picture—as we go along. We now see editors spending more time, themselves, dealing with those elements. I don't know if that is a bad thing, especially if you have the time to do it.

I remember when I was working on *The Abyss*. We were not working digitally yet. There were many, many action sequences. Jim [Cameron, the director] expressed to me that you can't really know if the cut is working until the sound effects are in. I thought that was very interesting. It was the first time that that way of thinking had ever been put to me— and you know Jim and sound!

On a visual level, if you are working on a big special effects picture with a lot of visual effects, and they are not finished, what have we always done? We used to put in a partially finished version along with one or more slugs of SCENE MISSING to show that there is a missing shot, or we shoot the storyboard panels that represent the shots.

Before, when I cut an action piece, I always cut it anticipating what I know the sound designers could do with the action. I have a car chase sequence, and the vehicles are roaring by the camera. I will hold a beat after the last car has passed by, giving sound effects time to pan a big "whoosh" off-screen and into the surround speakers. If I do not give that beat, the editor is not going to have the moment to play out the whoosh-by sound effect, and the re-recording mixer is not going to be able to pan the whoosh off-screen and into the surround speakers.

That was part of my editing construct, based on my editing experience previously. It would leave a little bit of air for the composer, knowing that music would have to make a comment, and music needs a few seconds to do that, and then sound effects would take over.

I remember Jerry Goldsmith [film composer] saying, "They always want me to write music for the car chase, and I know that you are not going to be able to hear it—but I write it anyway." We know that even if the sound effects are very loud, if you did not have the music there, you would feel its absence. The emotional drive is gone. Through experience, these are things that you learn over a period of years.

Because of the Avid and the Final Cut Pro, I am now cutting sound effects into the sequences almost as soon as I make my visual cuts. I layer in visual type sounds, temp music, etc. Now, when I am playing the newly cut sequence for the director for the first time, I have a rich tapestry of picture and audio for him to evaluate, rather than the way we did it before nonlinear days. When we would watch the cut sequence with only a production track and mentally factor in sounds to come, sounds that definitely have an effect and influence on the pace—the rhythm and the voice of the scene. This tells the director if the film is working on an emotional level. It adds this emotional component immediately, so you can feel the effectiveness of the sequence, in terms of the storytelling overall.

These sounds are not cut in to be used as final pieces. Do not misunderstand. I am not doing the sound editor's job, nor do I pretend to be able to, nor do I want to. I know full well that when we turn the picture over to sound editorial, my sound effects and temp music are going to be used only as a guide for intent, then they will be stripped out and replaced by better material.

Working with Cameron was a real concept for me. He would bark, "Let's get some sound effects in here right now! Let's see if this scene is kicking butt—right now!" So we would.

This puts the supervising sound editor and his or her sound designer to work problem solving these questions and needs early on. Traditional scheduling and budgeting fail dismally to fulfill the Camerons of the filmmaking industry (who already understand this audio equation to picture editing) and an ever-growing number of filmmakers inspired and empowered by understanding *what* is possible. Trying to

Figure 7.8 Joe Shugart, picture editor.

function with outdated budget philosophies and time schedules is sure to make future cinematic achievements even *more* rare.

A SERIES OF BREAKS

Picture editor, and future director, Joe Shugart contributed the following reflections:

During my 18-year career in film and television editing, I've often been asked by assistants, friends and family how I got to where I am now. I usually throw out something funny like "You mean how did I get to the middle?"

Living in Los Angeles can make you jaded. You always hear about the overnight sensation. Actors, artists, and producers all can be heard saying, "If I could just catch a break, my career would explode." But that's not how breaks usually happen. Breaks in the film business are small and often imperceptible, and it takes a lot of them.

My first break came in the late spring of 1988. Having finished film school, I was a producer/director currently working as a waiter. I heard about an action movie called *Cyborg* which was coming to film in my home state of North Carolina. Since they already had a producer and director, I decided to go for a more realistic job, apprentice editor. I somehow talked the production coordinator into giving me the address of the film editor and so I sent her a copy of my student film with a letter explaining that I was a hard worker and would like to be considered for the position of apprentice editor.

She called me and asked if I would work for free for the summer. Now unless waiting tables has blossomed into some lucrative high-paying job I'm not aware of, you can understand my nervousness over embarking into the movie business—could it actually pay *less* than waiting tables? Yes, it can. Despite a molehill of savings, I decided to go for it.

The days were long, filled with marking the sound and picture, syncing the dailies, coding the edges of the film and track with numbers so they could always be matched up, and logging everything into a book since they didn't furnish a computer. The director and editor were fantastic to work for, and they allowed me to watch the dailies projected every day, a real thrill which is unfortunately not done so often now, especially on the small films.

The job was going well, and after eight weeks of filming the crew was ready to wrap and move back to Los Angeles, where editing would resume. I was talking with the picture editor one day near the end and asked her if they would be hiring someone in Los Angeles to replace me. She said yes. "Can I replace me?" I joked.

She told me if I wanted to stay on they would love to have me. The icing on the cake came the next day when she told me that they would pay me $350 a week. That's a *six*-day week, usually from 9 a.m. to about 9 p.m. The math worked out to about $5 an hour, not including overtime, since they wouldn't be including any of that either. I took it in a heartbeat and made a temporary move to Los Angeles for three more months of postproduction.

Cyborg opened to moderate success, but when it was done, the phone was not ringing with calls from agents and producers with high-paying offers, so I returned home and got a job while I tried to catch that next break. The break came in the form of a call from the first assistant editor of *Cyborg*, the guy who had been in charge of running the editing room and teaching me all those skills. He was getting a chance to move up and cut a small horror movie. He said he needed a first assistant and he thought I was the one for the job. That was all I needed to hear. I packed up my old VW with what it could hold and made the four-day journey west.

The job as the first assistant was much more demanding. It not only included the syncing, logging and coding of dailies, but lots of work lining up optical and visual effects. Let's say a creature has to explode in a burst of light. Well, the point where this effect must occur is translated to the visual FX creators by referencing the film's key number, or edge number, where the burst must start and end. The sheets used to convey this information are called "count sheets," and it takes careful notation to ensure accuracy. If the director wants to reverse the motion of the film, speed it up or slow it down—those too are optical effects and must have a new piece of film negative generated so the shot can appear in the film (this is not necessary for films which are finished on video or hi-definition). All of this work—and *more* fell under my domain.

Anyway, that was a tough job and the movie ended up going to that great video store in the sky without a release. But it led to the next break, working on *Jacob's Ladder*—a great film where my skills in visual effects were severely tested. That break led to the next, and the next after that. Within a few years I was given the chance to cut a scene or two alongside the first-assistant-turned-editor from the horror movie.

Then I began co-editing episodes of Zalman King's *Red Shoe Diaries*. Zalman liked my work and enjoyed my company so much he gave me a chance to cut my first half-hour episode on my own. This time it wasn't going to be on film—this time it was cut on the Avid system. I ended up editing or co-editing 16 of these episodes, which led to getting my first feature. They loved my work, so that led to more.

Nine small features and countless episodes of television later, I found myself needing another break. This was in 2002. The independent film market had severely dried up, and there was worry throughout the industry of a possible actors strike. The small budget films simply were not paying much of a salary to editors (they still aren't) and the big films were impossible to get. After years of being a full-fledged editor, I was stuck and went back to work as an assistant editor. It was heartbreaking.

A shift in programming was occurring then with this relatively new thing called "reality" television. My dramatic editing background looked good to producers of these shows and another break occurred when I was hired to co-edit the first "reality feature" by the makers of *The Real World*. This film was called *The Real Cancun*, and though it was not well received, I *was*.

The company, Bunim-Murray Productions, loved me and continued to hire me. This relationship led me to receiving the daytime Emmy award in 2006 for single camera editing on their show called *Starting Over*. Its title carries profound implications into my career. This business has a way of changing the rules as soon as you get comfortable.

Along the way, I wrote and directed my first half-hour 35-mm film, *Bad to Worse*—which the author of this book, David Yewdall, so graciously agreed to design and cut the dialog and sound effects for. He worked for free, as I had done so many years ago, because he loves the creative process. I can never repay him for the countless hours and creative genius he brought to my film. I will be forever in his debt.

The film went on to show at two film festivals, the Los Angeles International Short Film Festival and the Marco Island Film Festival. I hope someday to direct a feature, if I can only *catch a break*, or maybe a series of them.

TOUCH IT—LIVE IT

Leander Sales helms the picture editorial discipline at the North Carolina School of the Arts–School of Filmmaking. Leander knows the vital importance of the synchronizer and flat-bed editing machines.

If you are going to be in film school, then *touch* film. Get to know film and the whole process. If you can get a chance to cut on a Steenbeck, you will get a true sense of history. If the kids would just work with the film on the flatbed, I think they would understand the history of film a lot better, because they are living it. Of course, that's where I came from, I learned cutting on film, but now everybody is cutting on the Avid or the Final Cut Pro, including me. I appreciate those formats as well. When I used to work on film, it is amazing how you can manipulate it, how you can look at every frame, just hold it up to the light and you can look at every frame. We are living in a digital world and will never go back to cutting on film, but I still think people should understand that history.

I remember working with an editor by the name of Sam Pollard. He would just hold the film up and looking at where he made his marks and how he made his cuts and, wow—you look at it and it is like life is just frozen in that frame. Now you run them all together through the machine, at twenty-four frames a second, and you create something new.

I remember the first scene I was cutting. Sam Pollard [picture editor] gave me an opportunity to cut a scene in *Clockers*. He gave me the footage and he said, "Here it is, go cut it."

That was it—go *cut* it. I remember it was the scene of the guys crushing up the car, pretty much two-camera coverage with all these jump cuts in it. And I was like, wow, this is my first scene. It was so exciting to put it together and at the end of the day, have Sam come up and look at it and say, "Okay."

Then another scene came and another scene came. So, I was very happy to finally get a credit as an editor.

What's interesting is that Sam doesn't like assistants who are working with him who do *not* want to cut, because the next growth step should be to cut. As an assistant you should want to move up to be an editor. I feel the same way. When I hire somebody as an apprentice, your desire should be to move up to be an assistant, and then to editor. And if your heart isn't there, I'm thinking that I could have hired somebody whose heart *would* be—who would really have a strong hunger to edit—not someone who just wants to hang out in the editing room—but someone who wants to *do* it. It's really important to have that hunger, because once you have that hunger, nothing else can stop you, *nothing*! And with the accessibility of editing equipment right now with Final Cut Pro, there is absolutely no excuse. Go and get a little mini-DV camera and shoot—there is no reason why you shouldn't be making a film—especially if you *want* to do it.

FINDING A WAY TO BREAK INTO AN EDITING JOB

Going to a film school is one thing, but how do you go out and actually secure your first job, to start building a resumé of experience, let alone learning your craft by the historic tried and true method of on-the-job training? When I ran my postproduction companies in Los Angeles, we had adopted the Roger Corman approach to training and bringing new blood into the industry's work force. Personal introductions were vital to us. Flashing a diploma from USC or UCLA did not mean squat. In fact, we had one graduate from USC who we first had to break from the misinformation that he had learned there and retrain him in the real world. Today he is a very successful sound editor who is supervising his own product—and we are extremely proud of him as well as the other 34 apprentices that we brought in and trained.

I would give each apprentice one month to figure out if they were in love with the *idea* of working in postproduction or if they were in love with *working* in postproduction. Therein lies the first major hurdle. If they worked hard and showed initiative and responsibility they were advanced to become a second sound assistant within a few months. Before too long they would start cutting practice sessions (Foley was always a great starting place to learn the art of synchronization and using the equipment) or by cutting background effects. If they showed the right growth in technique and creative philosophical style they would be entrusted with a real cutting assignment as they evolved into an editor's role. When the time came we would write letters to accompany their paycheck stubs to verify days of employment if and when they wished to join the union.

These kinds of opportunities are not as available as one might think, and even when they are there is great competition for the precious few apprentice starting positions open. How then do you "break in"?

For some it is creative fiction, along with a lot of self-confidence and the ability to be a quick study. For Leander Sales it started with an introduction from his uncle, who is a successful character actor.

> After I spent two years in Italy it was my uncle, Ron Dortch, who said that he knew a guy who was a sound editor—go and talk with him. So I went to see Rudolph Gaskins, who was working out of a sound facility by the name of Sound One in New York at that time. I sat with Rudy and I said that I was looking for a job and that I would really like to get into editing. He said, "Well, I don't know of anything that is happening right now."
>
> So I told him that if he found anything to let me know—and that I would do it for *free*! During the day I was selling sofa beds and at night I can come and do whatever this editorial job would be. "You don't have to pay me." I told him. "I just want to *learn* what happens in the editing room." He said, "Alright, I'll keep that in mind. No one has ever offered to work for free."

Two weeks later he called back, "There's this guy coming back from Atlanta and he's going to start sound editing and he is looking for an apprentice sound editor for a film entitled *School Daze*. The director is Spike Lee."

Oh, wow! Spike Lee! He gave me his number and told me to give him a call. I gave him a call. Spike came to the phone and said, "Yeah, this is Spike." I said, "This is Leander Sales and I would like to apply for that job as apprentice sound editor." He said, "Talk with Maurice Schell, the supervising sound editor."

I went to interview with Maurice and he said, "This is only a four-month job." I replied, "Yo, man, please, please, I really want this job." And Maurice asked if I had ever worked on a film before. No, I hadn't. He asked if I had ever gone to film school—no. He asked if I had a resumé—no, nothing. I just have a desire to do this. He said, "Well, we'll think about it." That was his reaction—we'll think about it. He called me up on a Monday and he said that I would start working on Wednesday. And I said, "I'm there!!"

I had four months to learn what I could—four months! That's how I saw it. They would say, "Go and get this or go and get that." And I would *run* to get it! And I would *run* back, because I didn't want to miss *anything*. Syncing dailies, marking up track, threading up the Moviola—all of that. So I would run to get their breakfast or coffee and run back, and they kept saying "Boy, that guy is fast!"

Leander also helped a few new talents along the way:

Determination and desire is where it is at. I remember there was this guy who wanted to get into editing. He was with craft services for one of Spike's films where he would set up the food for dailies. You know, people would come and have dinner while they watched dailies. And then one day he said to me, "Man, I'm really interested in editing. Do you think I could hang out in the editing room after I finish craft services to watch you guys put these dailies back together to get ready for the next day?" I said, "Sure, come on."

And every day he would break down the craft services very quickly after dailies. It was my turn to say, "Wow! That guy is fast!" He would come back to the editing room with us to watch and learn—and now he's editing, he is a sound editor.

Disabled people are only handicapped if they allow it to become a stumbling block issue. Steve Rice, who you will read about in Chapter 14, was missing his left foot due to a Viet Cong rocket during his service in the Vietnam War. Nobody wanted to hire him at first, until I offered him his first job as a combination grip/gaffer for a documentary I shot on a Navajo reservation. To my surprise he overcompensated (as many handicapped people do) and worked as hard as three men.

A few months after that I asked if he wanted to learn postproduction editorial, so I asked him to show up at the studio two hours before the boss would arrive—and in two hours I taught him how to sync dailies and log them in properly. With just that two-hour instruction and his desire and passion to do the work, the head of the studio hired him on the spot. Steve went on to become one of the most amazing dialog editors that I have ever known.

Conscious or subconscious prejudices and negative perceptions are probably the single most inhibiting obstacle that you will have to overcome—and not only physical handicaps.

Leander had a similar occasion to give a disabled person a chance.

We had a guy come in who had a condition with his leg, so he was hobbling along with a cane. He could not walk without this cane, but he said, "I want to be the apprentice." I looked at him and said, "I don't know, because you've got to run to the city and get these heavy dailies, these sound rolls and film from the lab. Do you think you can do this, are you up for this?" He said, "I really want to do this, man, I really want this." I asked, "What about your leg?"

He told me that he was in physical therapy but he knew he could do it if he was just given the opportunity to try. So I told him that I would try him for a week. Oh man, he worked *so* hard. He went and did his physical therapy on the weekends. He would hobble, but he always got those dailies to us.

MORE CRAFTSPERSONS OF COLOR

Leander had these comments about getting more women of color into filmmaking:

I think I was fortunate—no, I was *lucky* to have worked with Spike Lee. Spike is one of the most prolific filmmakers in our time. Here is a filmmaker who said he wanted to set out to make a certain number of films, and he is doing just that. I worked on *nine* of his films, back-to-back—starting out as an apprentice and worked my way up to editor—with *one* filmmaker. Oh, I worked on other films in between and after that, but I have been so fortunate to have that opportunity to work with someone who works year after year—and not just as a filmmaker, but just trying to get more people of *color* into the unions. Because it is lily white out there. For example, you go to a set with an all white crew and all white cast, and most people think, okay, that's just normal, that's the way it is. But as soon as you get a black crew, or a mostly black or half black, people start thinking "What's wrong? What's wrong with this picture?" What's wrong with this picture is that many white people think people of color should never be in positions of power.

Now may be a good time to review Chapter 4 before you start shooting your film; this way, as you press on into the postproduction phases described in Chapters 8 through 20, you will develop a conscious predetermination to *plan for success*.

Chapter 8
Temp Dubs and Test Screenings
A Critical Objective View

"We've just had a test screening, and the upshot is that we are throwing out the first reel and starting the picture with reel two."

– John Carpenter, director, after a last-minute test screening during the predubbing of Escape from New York

Okay, so you think you have a surefire hit—the most important picture of the year. Of course, every other producer and director believe their film is the one, but that's only to be expected. You lived with the project for months, perhaps even years. You know every word, every moment, every cut. Actually, all this places you at a tremendous disadvantage. You lost your objectivity, especially if you were in the throes of the love–hate evolution that so often grips intensively involved craftspeople who are completely immersed in their project.

TEST SCREENING

The time comes to arrange a test screening. No, don't screen the picture for your friends and colleagues. They are not the audience that buys the millions of tickets you hope to sell. You made the film with a particular audience in mind, one that buys the tickets for the genre you are carefully nurturing. You kept a keen eye on your audience from the beginning during the writing of the script; you kept your audience in mind as you set up the shots; you kept your audience in mind as you started cutting the sequences together, or maybe you didn't.

If you took the popular and myth-ridden stance that you made a film to suit your own taste, a movie you would like to see, without considering the ticket-buying audience, then you really must have a test audience screening, and quick! Of course you made a movie you would like to see, but that does not mean you throw away the collaborative and advisory powers of a carefully planned test audience screening.

Keep in mind the words "carefully planned" in preparing a test screening. The last thing you want is to have a test screening for just your friends. They often do not give an accurate and critically objective judgment of how your film will be received. Oddly enough, this is one area many filmmakers fail to handle correctly, often getting distorted results.

Several years ago, my team and I handled the sound design and editorial chores for a first-time director's feature film. The producer contracted a firm to recruit a test audience to attend a quiet test screening on a studio lot. We sat in the back row with the producer and the nervous director as the opening scenes rolled. Within 10 minutes, audience members got up and walked out. In the middle of the third reel, the action on the screen portrayed the roving vampires as they entered a quiet country bar and had just begun feeding on the patrons. Bill Paxton rose up from sucking the blood from a victim's neck with great delight, "Finger lickin' good!"

Test audience viewers suddenly rose in groups and left the theatre en masse. From an audience of just over 300, we counted 152 people who had walked out by the middle of the film. The director, Katherine Bigelow, was hiding in the back row, tears rolling down her cheeks. The fault was not hers, but those who had been contracted to run the test screening. I would say that Katherine has done just fine since then, going on to direct pictures such as *Blue Steel*, *Point Break*, and *K-19: The Widowmaker*.

Many producers would have been sharpening the razor and drawing the warm bath water by this time, but the veteran producer of this picture had been here before. He knew what had happened. The test screening firm recruited the wrong audience by telling them that the picture was a country-western version of *Raiders of the Lost Ark*—and so the wrong audience came to view the film. They expected a PG-rated, fun-filled action picture, but got an R-rated blood-and-guts vampire story with a very dark and graphic edge.

Instead of panicking, the producer knew to schedule another test screening, only this time made sure the right kind of target market audience was recruited. Frankly, *Near Dark* has become a cult classic in its own right.

Jim Troutman, supervising sound editor for such films as *Duel*, *Sugarland Express*, *Jaws*, *Charlie Varrick*, and *Midway*, to name a few, recalls how a test audience screening saved a very important and legendary moment in *Jaws*:

> We thought the picture was ready to try out on a Midwestern audience, so we took it to Dallas, Texas, for a test screening preview. Verna Fields [vice president of production at Universal] and I sat in the middle of the theatre with an audiocassette recorder. We recorded the audience's vocal reactions against the film's audio track as it played on the screen. It was the scene where Roy Scheider is chumming off the back of the boat, trying to attract the great white shark. He turns to look back at the cabin—the shark lunges up full-screen behind him. It's an enormous shock scare. The audience went nuts! We thought we had allowed plenty of time for the audience to settle down as Roy backed up into the cabin where he delivers his line to Robert Shaw, "You're gonna need a bigger boat."
>
> Well, when we played back the audio cassette tape to listen to the audience reactions, we discovered that the pop-scare was so big that it took far longer than we had anticipated

for the audience screams and chatter to settle down—they never heard Roy's punch line. So we went back to the cutting room, found the trim boxes of that scene, and pulled the 'out' trims of the sequence. We reconstructed an additional 35 feet of action showing Roy's shocked reaction and a more deliberate pace in backing up into the cabin. This gave enough time for the audience to settle down and hear Roy's delivery, giving the audience a much-needed moment of comic relief.

All through the post-editorial process of *Escape from New York*, Debra Hill and John Carpenter had not test screened the picture for an objective test audience. We were deep into the sound mixing process, so deep in fact that we were nearly finished with the predubbing process on Stage D at Goldwyn Studios and about to commence with the final mix. Just as we were wrapping a predub pass, John Carpenter and his picture editor, Todd Ramsay, came onto the stage, looking a little pale and unable to hide the fact that their confidence was shaken. They informed us that they had just had a test screening, and much to their surprise a number of comments motivated them to rethink the final cut. They were going into an emergency tactical meeting with producers Debra Hill and Larry Franco.

When the dust settled, it was decided to scrap the entire first reel of the picture. In essence, the film would now start with reel 2. So the heist scene at Denver's Federal Reserve was cut, the subterranean subway flight from Denver to Barstow was cut, as was the subsequent ambush by a federal police SWAT team and the takedown of Snake Plisken. Was it the right decision? According to preview cards of the test screening, it was.

With the advent of the Internet, producers and studio execs are having a difficult time having test screenings without finding their film posted all over the Internet within hours of the test, even though they are weeks if not months away from actually finishing the film. This is making it extremely hard to trust a film to an intimate "test" group and feeling confident about keeping the warts and unfinished misperceptions out of instant global chat rooms. Many producers are reacting by saying that they will dispense with the practice of test screenings, but we all know that is not a realistic option either. Somehow you have to get the ultrasound image of the mother's womb to see if you are going to have a healthy bouncing baby or if you are about to hatch a fungus-amungus. Somehow you have to deal with test screenings!

USE OF TEMP DUBS

As the cost of making motion pictures has increased, so too has the use of test screenings. Having to expose their work-in-progress films to studio executives and/or potential distributors, let alone test audience reactions, directors, and producers are reticent to show their projects with only the raw production track.

As a result, the barroom brawl looks real dumb with the actors flying wildly from Sunday hay makers with no chin sock impacts and body falls. What will the audience think of this long dolly shot that moves at a snail's pace and does not seem to progress the action? Arnold Schwarzenegger jumps the fence, swings his big powerful 45-caliber pistol up, and shoots. The production track sounds like a kid's cap gun! The new computer-generated image of the *Tyrannosaurus rex* rises over the actors and spreads its jaws in a menacing roar, but no sound emanates because the beast is nothing but a CGI (computer-generated image) composited against live actors filmed months earlier against a green screen or blue screen.

The producer calls in the supervising sound editor and reviews the list of needs. We require punches, body falls, furniture breaking, and vocal "args" and efforts for the barroom brawl.

The director chose music from a CD of another, previously released movie for temp music during the long, slow dolly shot to manipulate the audience's emotions and make it appreciate the moment's grandeur and magnificence. We must have high-velocity, bigger-than-life, Hollywood-type pistol shots with bullet zip-bys for Arnold's pistol. We need a sound designer to immediately develop some T-rex vocals—something no one has ever heard before. The producer wants the hair on the back of the audience's necks to stand on end with anticipation and terror. And—we need this all for a temp dub tomorrow afternoon!

Do not laugh. This kind of unreasonable request happens all the time. For some reason, directors and producers think that sound editorial can throw any kind of sound at any sort of visual problem instantaneously—after all, isn't that why the motion picture industry turned digital?

Granted, a sound editorial team can make many things happen very quickly. Standard fare such as fist fight sound effects and weaponry are easy enough to whistle up. Most of us keep a large array of animals, both real and fantasy from previous projects, at our beck and call via DVD-R storage or on large terabyte servers. These can be transferred into a nonlinear digital workstation quickly and efficiently enough. However, new conceptual sound effects, such as noises no one has ever heard before, take a little preparation.

Unexpected temp dubs are the worst. Here a producer is very wise to decide on and set the supervising sound editor and sound editorial team early on; also at this time the smart producer has empowered the sound editorial unit to begin developing conceptual sounds.

I like to have access to review special effects work as early as models are being made or even when concept drawings are approved. On John Carpenter's *The Thing*, key members of my crew and I attended not only daily screenings of the first unit from Alaska, but also dailies from the visual effects studio. John wanted us to have every moment of creative thinking and experimentation at our disposal so we could make no excuses like, "If we only had enough time, we could have . . . ."

When a temp dub is set on the schedule, the supervising sound editor sits down with the producer, director, and picture editor to finitely outline what sound effects and dialog work must be covered. (For example, "Do we need to bring in one or more actors for temp ADR or additional wild lines that do not exist in the production track?") Defining the scope of work that must be done for the temp dub is extremely important; without that, the work goes wildly and scatterbrain mentality goes on, focusing on very little and spinning everybody's wheels to no avail. What sound effects, dialog, and music are needed to tell the story?

Many low-budget pictures do not have the financial luxury of bringing in cast members for temp ADR; they often must resort to using members of the immediate production company as temporary voices for a star actor. Later, during the final sound editorial preparations, the star actor is brought in to replace the temporary ADR with his or her own voice.

Swimming in the swift waters of theatrical postproduction and not colliding with the temp dub syndrome is very difficult. By wanting conceptual material too fast, too soon, producer and director are exposed to truly temp sound effects, material that we have only stuck in for test screening purposes, and do not intend to use in the final mix.

Temp dubs are a good-news/bad-news thing. The good news is that we get to try out different concepts ahead of time to see how the material works; the bad news is that the director and producer listen to the stuff back and forth all day long in the editing room for weeks and it gets etched in their brains like a tattoo. Temp dubs often close down their thinking to new concepts. Even when we make the real-thing sound effects the way we intend for the final mix, the client has become so ingrained that it is very difficult to break through and germinate new concepts.

Temp dubs can suck the creative lifeblood right out of a crew. On Andrew Davis's *Chain Reaction*, co-supervising sound editors John Larson and David Stone were faced with a daunting series of temp dubs and test screenings that literally marched week by week right down the schedule to the week prior to commencing the predubbing process for the final mix itself.

I was brought onto *Chain Reaction* with a very focused mission—design and cut all the major action sequences throughout the picture, passing any sound editorial chores that I did not want to be bothered with off to the two sound editors on either side of my room. However, I was not to concern myself with or be distracted by any of the temp dubs. If I had any material that was cut and ready that could be added to the temp dub process, that was great. But I was not to divert design and cutting energies from the final mix. If it happened to help the temp dub process along the way, that was great, but always keep focused on the only soundtrack that really counts—the FINAL MIX!

It is exactly this kind of supervisory philosophy that separates a great soundtrack from one hardly more than a compilation and revision of one temp dub after another. I have heard many a sound editorial crew who has completed major motion pictures agonize over the fact that there was never a chance to design and cut the final mix. The postproduction schedules and test screenings were so compressed and intensive that they could barely make the first temp dub. From then on, it was not an issue of being able to design and cut new material, it was only about updating the picture changes between test screenings quickly enough to make the next temp dub update and subsequent studio or test screening.

In the "old days" (early and mid-1980s), a temp dub was a couple of units of temp music transferred from CDs and two or three units of sound effects. The dialog track was usually a 1:1 of the editor's cut production track that the dialog editor had run through, flipping out various unwanted sounds and adding some temporary additional lines. Today, temp dubs are gargantuan preparation events, even requiring predubbing. Commonly, motion pictures have four-to-seven-day temp dub schedules. After two or three of these temp dubs, your postproduction budget is exhausted. A temp dub used to be a simple monaural 35-mm single-stripe mix, suitable for interlock just about anywhere in southern California for test screenings. On larger projects temp dubs are elaborate stereo mixes, complete with surround channel. If they are being interlocked to a silent answer print, they will most likely be 35-mm fullcoat mixes with 4-to-6-track head configurations. Today, most test screenings are handled with a high-quality video projector that has an encoded AC3 file of the 5.1 temp mix synched to the picture, in most cases using high-end digital tape; sometimes, on lower budget films, one of the assistant editors is qualified and experienced to make a viewing version DVD from a QuickTime output and the AC3 audio track.

One does not dispute the actual need of producing a temp dub and of having test screenings. Producer and director, though, must embrace the counsel and advice of the supervising sound editor and structure a schedule and battle plan to achieve the mission, rather than just throw mud at the wall and see what sticks.

Chapter 9
Spotting the Picture for Sound and Music

> "The studio jet is waiting for me, so we're gonna have to run through the picture changes as we spot the music, the dialog, and sound effects all at once—okay?"
>
> *– Steven Spielberg, announcing his combined spotting-session intentions as he sat down behind the flatbed machine to run his segment of* Twilight Zone: The Motion Picture

Spotting sessions are extremely important in the ongoing quest to produce the requisite desired final soundtrack. They present an opportunity for the director to mind-meld with the music composer and the supervising sound editor(s) on the desired style and scope of work in a precise sequence-by-sequence, often cue-by-cue, discussion. The various functions (music, sound effects, and dialog/ADR) have their own separate spotting sessions with the director, allowing concentration on each process without thinking of or dealing with all other processes at the same time.

During this time, the music composer and supervising sound editor(s) run through reels in a leisurely and thoughtful manner, discussing each music cue, each sound effect concept, each line of dialog and ADR possibility. This is when the director clearly articulates his or her vision and desires, at least theoretically. Very often, the vision and desires concepts are very different from the style and scope-of-work concepts—these often are completely different from each other from the start and probably will be so even at the final outcome—for practical or political reasons.

The spotting process also is an opportunity for the music composer and supervising sound editor(s) to share thoughts and ideas collaboratively, so their separate contributions to the soundtrack blend together as one, keeping conflict and acoustic disharmony to a minimum. Sadly, the truth is that often very little meaningful collaboration occurs between the music and sound editorial departments. This lack of communication is due to a number of unreasonable excuses, not the least of which is the continuing practice of compressing postproduction schedules to a point that music and sound editorial do not have time to share ideas and collaborate even if desired. (I briefly discuss the swift political waters of competition between sound effects and music in Chapter 19.)

SIZING UP THE PRODUCTION TRACK

Before the spotting session, the condition of the production dialog track must be determined. To make any warranties on the work's scope and budgetary ramifications, the supervising sound editor must first screen the picture, even if it is only a rough assemblage of sequences. This way, the supervisor obtains a better feel for both audio content and picture editorial style, which will definitely impact how much and what type of labor the dialog editors need to devote to re-cutting and smoothing the dialog tracks. Reading the script does not provide this kind of assessment. The audio mine field is not revealed in written pages; only by listening to the raw and naked production track itself through the theatrical speaker system will the supervisor be able to identify potential problems and areas of concern.

Two vital thoughts on production track assessment are as follows: first, clients almost always want you to hear a "temp-mixed" track, especially with today's nonlinear technologies. Picture editors and directors do not even give it a passing thought. They use multitrack layering as part of their creative presentation for both producers and studio, but it does not do a lick of good to try to assess the true nature of their production dialog tracks by listening to a composite "temp mix." Clients usually do not understand this. They often want to show you their "work of art" as they intend it, not as you need to listen to it.

This is likely to lead to unhappy producers who complain when you return their work-in-progress tape or QuickTime video output file, to supply a new transfer with *nothing* but the raw production dialog, which means that they have just wasted money and time having the videotape or QuickTime video output made for you in the first place. However, if you had supplied them with a "spec sheet" (precise specifications), they would not have made the video output the way they did, and you would not be rejecting them now and insisting on a new transfer. Or, if they still supplied you with an improperly transferred video output, you have a paper trail they was ignored, taking you off the hook as a "trouble maker" because *they* did not read the spec sheet in the first place.

Second, to assess the quality of raw production track properly, listen to it in a venue that best replicates the way it will sound on the re-recording stage. This dispels any unwanted surprises when you get on the re-recording dub stage and hear things you never heard before. The picture editor, director, and producers are always shocked and amazed at what they never heard in their audio track before.

Never try to assess track quality on a Moviola, on a flatbed editing machine (such as a KEM or Steinbeck), or even on a nonlinear picture editorial system such as an Avid or Final Cut Pro. All picture editorial systems are built for picture editors to play tracks as a guide for audio content. I have never found a picture editorial system that faithfully replicates the soundtrack. Many times picture editors must use equipment on which the speaker had been abused by overloading to the point that the speaker cone was warped or damaged. Few picture editors set the volume and equalization settings properly, so track analysis is very difficult, with very few picture editors setting up their systems to reproduce the soundtrack with a true "flat" response.

For these reasons, I always insist on listening to the cut production track on a re-recording stage, and, if the sound facility has been selected by this time, I want to run the picture on the very re-recording stage with the head mixer who will be handling the mixing chores. This is the best way to reveal all warts and shortcomings of the production track. You will then know what you are dealing with, what your head mixer can do with the material, and how it can be most effectively prepared for the re-recording process (see Chapters 12 and 13).

The screening also gives the director and producer(s), along with the picture editor(s), an opportunity to hear the actual, and often crude, condition of their production track—transparent to the ears through the theatrical speaker system without the benefit of audio camouflage that temp music and temp sound effects often render. I guarantee you that you will hear sounds you have never heard before, usually unpleasant ones.

TEMP MUSIC AND TEMP SOUND EFFECTS FIRST

The picture editorial department must understand the necessity of going back through its cut soundtrack and removing any "mixed" track (where the dialog track has been temp-mixed with either music and/or sound effects), replacing it with the original raw sync dialog track; hearing the dialog with mixed music or sound effects negates any ability to properly evaluate it.

The smart picture editor who cuts on a nonlinear platform will do himself or herself a great favor by keeping any temp sound effects, temp crash-downs, temp music, or any other non-pure production sound cues on separate audio channels. The first two or three audio channels should be devoted to production dialog *only*. Any re-voicing, added wild lines, even WT (production wild track) must be kept in the next group of channels. In this way the picture editor will have a very easy time of muting anything and everything that is not production sound. I have had to sit and wait for over an hour while a rookie picture editor, faced with the fact that we are not there to listen to his total cut vision, has to take time to go in and first find and mute each cue at a time because he or she has them all mixed together without disciplined track assignments.

The dialog mixer is the one who mixes it, the one who fixes it, to create the seamless track you desire; this is your opportunity to get the mixer's thoughts and comments on what he or she can and cannot fix. The mixer runs the worktrack through the very console that ultimately will be used to accomplish the dialog predubbing. During this run, the mixer determines what he or she can accomplish, often pausing and making equalization or filtering tests on problematic areas, thereby making an instant decision and warranty on what dialog lines most likely will be saved or manipulated. What dialog cannot be saved obviously must be fixed, using alternate takes and/or cueing material for ADR. If temp music and temp sound effects are still left in the cut production track (as a mixed combine), your head mixer cannot discern what is production and what is an additive.

AFTER THE "RUNNING"

You had your interlock running with your head mixer on the re-recording stage—and had to call the paramedics to revive the clients after they discovered their production track was not in the clean and pristine shape they had always thought. The preliminary comments stating that the production track was in such good shape and that only a handful of ADR lines were anticipated fell apart in the reality run-through, which yielded a plethora of notes for ADR. Suddenly, you cue this line and that line for reasons ranging from airplane noise to microphone diaphragm popping, from distortion, off-miked perspectives to off-screen crew voices. The next step is for everybody to go home, take two Alka-Seltzers, and reconvene in the morning to address the issues afresh.

The supervising sound editor is wise to bifurcate the upcoming spotting session. Clients often try to make one spotting session cover all needs. Unfortunately, as one facet of the sound requirements is being discussed, other audio problems and considerations tend to be shut out.

It is much smarter to set up a spotting session where the supervising sound editor(s) and both the dialog editor and the ADR supervisor sit with the director, producer(s), and picture editor to do nothing but focus on and address the dialog, ADR, and Group Walla needs. The supervising sound editor(s), along with the sound designer, then schedule a spotting session specifically to talk about and spot the picture for sound effects and backgrounds. The supervising sound editor(s) may have one or more of his or her sound effects editors sit in on these spotting sessions as well, for nothing is better or clearer than hearing the director personally articulate his or her vision and expectations as you scroll through the picture.

CRITICAL NEED FOR PRECISE NOTES: A LEGAL PAPER TRAIL

During a spotting session, both the supervising sound editor(s) as well as the attending department heads take copious notes. If the sound editorial team does not understand something, they must pause and thoroughly discuss it. It is very dangerous just to gloss over concepts, assuming you know what the director wants or intends. If you assume incorrectly, you waste many valuable hours of development and preparation that yield worthless efforts. In addition, you lose irretrievably precious time, which certainly erodes the confidence level of the clients.

As obvious and apparently simple as this advice is, the failure to take and keep proper spotting notes can cause calamitous collisions later. On many occasions, a producer relied on either my own notes or the notes of one of my department heads to rectify an argument or misconception that simmered and suddenly boiled over. Consequently, your spotting notes also act as a paper trail and can protect you in court should the rare occasion of legal action arise. Remember, sound creation is not an exact industry. It is an art form, not a manufacturing assembly line. Boundaries of interpretation can run very wide, leading you into potentially dangerous and libelous territory if you have not kept accurate and precise spotting notes. The purpose is to accurately map and follow the wishes of the director and producer, and to achieve the same outcome and creative desires.

Some supervising sound editor(s) go so far as to place an audiocassette recorder or small DAT recorder with an omnidirectional mike in plain view to record the spotting proceedings; the tape then can be reviewed to ascertain the precise words of the director or producer when they articulated their creative desires and asked for specifics.

THE SUPERVISOR'S BIBLE

Because spotting sessions often move at a rate considerably faster than most people can push a pencil, most of us resort to a series of shorthand-like abbreviations or hieroglyphics to jog our memories later. Therefore, you must take time soon after the spotting session to go back through your notes and type a much more formal narrative with appropriate footnotes and directions for others going through the sound editorial adventure with you. Using a personal computer notebook in a spotting session is not a good idea. You cannot write or manipulate where you want the information on the document quickly enough. Write your notes by hand during the spotting session, then transcribe them to your computer later.

The supervising sound editor dedicates a binder (sometimes more than one) to amass the steady flow of notes, logs, EDLs, schedules and all revisions, and copies of faxes and memos from the producer's office, from the director as well as the picture editor. In short, this binder contains all the pertinent data and paper trail backups that guide the development of the soundtrack to successful fruition and protect you from future misunderstanding.

As a result of all the care taken, you will develop an awareness and observational focus that is extremely important in the spotting session process. You will notice that which the picture editor and director have not seen, and they have lived with their film for months, in some cases even a year or more before you have been called in to

Figure 9.1 Supervising sound editor George Simpson reviews sound effect cues as he builds his "cut-list bible," having handled such projects as *16 Blocks*, *Freedomland*, *The Ring Two*, *Paparazzi*, *Tears of the Sun*, and *Training Day* to name a few. (Photo by David Yewdall.)

"spot" the picture with them. One such case occurred during a sequence where the actor came to his car, opened the door, got in, and closed the door. I put my hand up for a question. The editor stopped the film. I asked on which side of the cut did they want the door to close. The editor and director looked at me like I had just passed wind at the dinner table. "When the door closes, you match the door close. What could be easier?" asked the picture editor. I pointed out that as the actor got into the car, the door closed on the outside cut, and, when they cut inside the car with the actor, the door closed again. "The hell you say," replied the editor.

I asked them to run the sequence again, only very slowly so we could study the cut. Sure enough, actor David Carradine got into the car and the door just closed; as the angle cut to the inside, you clearly could see the door close again. The editor, who had been working on the picture for just over a solid year, sighed and grabbed his grease pencil to make a change mark. All this time he, the director, and the producer had never seen the double door close.

SPOTTING SESSION PROTOCOL

Very early on, one learns that often insecure sensitivity in the first spotting session requires certain delicacy when discussing problematic topics thereafter. On one of my earlier pictures, I spotted the picture with a picture editor I had known for a number of years, dating back to Corman days. I had not worked with the director before; in fact it was his first feature directing job. We finished running through a particular scene where actor Donald Pleasance was discussing a crime scene with a woman. I commented to the picture editor that the actress could not act her way out of a paper bag. The picture editor's brow furrowed as he gave me a disapproving glance. At the end of the reel, the director, noticeably fatigued, left the room for a smoke break. The picture editor grabbed the next reel off the rack, leaned over, and informed me that the actress was the director's wife. After that colossal faux pas, I learned to research diligently who was who in the production team and in front of the camera.

Other sensitive situations can arise when you have a tendency to count things and are spotting the film with a picture editor who thinks his or her work is beyond reproach. Such was the case when we held our spotting session on the sci-fi horror film *The Thing*. I brought my core team with me, as was my custom. I had already handled two pictures for John Carpenter, so I was not concerned about unfamiliar ground. I knew he was very comfortable and secure with himself.

The problem arose because I tend to count things, almost subconsciously. I developed this habit while supervising soundtracks and having to think on my feet during spotting sessions. In the case in question, a scene in the film depicted Kurt Russell checking out the helicopter outside when he hears a gunshot from within a nearby laboratory building. He jumps off the chopper and runs into the building and down the hallway, hearing more pistol shots. He reaches the lab, where Wilford Brimley was warning the rest of the staff to stay away. In a matter of moments, the team outmaneuvers and subdues the scientist after he empties the last two bullets from his pistol.

Once again, I raised my hand with a question. The picture editor paused the film. I glanced around to my team members and then to the director. "Do you really want us to cut eight gunshots?" I was taken aback by the picture editor's response. "You can't count! There are only six gun shots!"

I was willing to let it go. I knew full well that the editor had only meant to have six, so I would just drop two from the guide track. But John Carpenter loved to have fun. He grinned like a Cheshire cat at the opportunity. "Let's go back and count 'em."

The picture editor spun the reel back to the exterior with the helicopter. He rolled the film. The first off-stage gunshot sounded, and everyone counted. "One." Kurt jumped off the chopper skid and dashed into the building, past boxes of supplies as another shot rang out. "Two." Kurt reached the doorway to the lab. He was warned that Brimley had a gun. Wilford turned from swinging his axe at the communication equipment and fired a warning shot at Kurt. "Three." Kurt told the guy next to him to maneuver around to the doorway of the map room. As the other actor reached the doorway, the crazed scientist fired another warning shot at him. "Four." The actor ducked back as the bullet ricocheted off the door frame. The scientist stepped into the center of the room as he fired two more on-screen shots. The image cut to the door frame, where we saw three bullets hit and ricochet away. Everyone counted. "Six and . . . ." Nobody dared continue counting. The picture editor stopped the film and growled at me. "So you'll cut two of them out."

As it turned out, we could only drop the one as the hero was running down the hallway because it was off-stage. The way the picture editor had cut the sequence as Brimley emptied his pistol, we couldn't trim any additional pistol shots without the picture editor first making a fix in the picture, which he was unwilling to do.

WHAT REVELATIONS MAY COME

Other, more costly ramifications, constructive or not, certainly can come out of a spotting session. I was spotting the sound requirements on a superhero-type action picture when the director and I reached the point in the film of a climactic hand-to-hand battle confrontation between the hero and the mobster villain. At the very point where the villain literally had the upper hand and was about to vanquish his vigilante nemesis, a door at the back of the room opened. The mobster villain's young son entered to see his father in mortal combat at the same time the villain turned to see his son. Taking full advantage of the distraction, the hero plunged his huge bowie knife into the villain's back.

The director noticed my reaction and stopped the film, asking me what the matter was. I politely apologized: I guess I missed something somewhere in the picture, but who was the hero? The director was shocked at my apparent lack of attentiveness. If I had been paying attention I would have known that the whole picture revolved around this guy on the floor, our superhero, and how he was taking revenge against the forces of the underworld for the loss of his family.

Yes, I did notice that. I also pointed out that in a blink of the eye the director had changed the hero from a sympathetic hero to a moralistically despicable villain. Not only had he stabbed the mobster villain in the back, but he performed this cowardly act in front of the villain's son.

A steel curtain of realization dropped on the director. This elementary rule of storytelling had just blown its tires while hurtling down the highway of filmmaking. The director told me to commence work only on the first nine reels of the picture, as he was going to meet with studio executives to decide what to do about the ending.

A few weeks later, the set, which had been torn down in Australia, was being rebuilt in Culver City, California (where they shot *Gone with the Wind*) precisely as it had been in Australia, *precisely*. Frames from the master angle of the film were used to meticulously replace broken shards of glass that lay on the floor so that the two filmed segments would match. Actors were recalled from all over the world. Lou Gossett, who played the police lieutenant, had crossed through the carnage at the end of the action sequence when it was first shot in Australia, was not available, so the director had to employ the industry's top rotoscope artist to painstakingly rotoscope a moving dolly shot to carefully mask out the telltale knife protruding from the mobster's back from the original Australian shoot footage that had Lou Gossett crossing through.

Other audio challenges resulted from the re-shoot when we discovered that the boy portraying the mobster's son had grown since the original shoot, and his voice was changing. This meant pitch-shifting the boy's dialog tracks upward by degrees until we could accurately match the pitch and timbre of the original material shot months before in Australia.

The observant problem-solving approach to spotting sessions is invaluable. Learn to glance at a building, then turn away. Now ask yourself how many floors comprise the construction of the building. How many windows are in a row on each floor? Are they tinted or clear? Develop your observation skills to accurately recall and describe what you see, and it will serve you extremely well.

Also learn to *listen* to what people say. People often repeat what they *thought* someone said, or their own perception of *what* they said, but not what was *actually* said. These kinds of skills stem from dialog editing and transcribing muffled or garbled words from a guide track to cue for ADR. You do not transcribe the gist of what they said, or an interpretation—you must write down *precisely* what they said. Even if you intend to change the line later in ADR, you first must know exactly where you are before you can continue forward.

Chapter 10
Custom Recording Sound Effects
The Real Fun and Adventure

> "Why do you have to go clear out to Oklahoma to custom record a
> Steerman for? Save the money—use our crop-duster sound effects
> from *North by Northwest*. Nobody will ever know the difference!"
>
> *– MGM/UA executive, dissuading the producer*
> *from custom recording sound effects for*
> The Aviator *(1985 version).*

I laid behind the low wall of rocks hastily piled together as an impromptu bullet-resistant shield to protect myself from the spray of lead I knew would be flying toward me at any moment. Having just signed a release of responsibility should I accidentally be wounded or killed, my partner, Ken Sweet, and my first assistant, Peter Cole, still tried vigorously to talk me out of placing myself in such a dangerous position. "Why can't you just leave the tape recorder and microphones there and clear out of the line of fire?" Ken asked.

I gazed up at my concerned partner as I slipped on my headsets. "Have you ever recorded bullet zing-bys before—let alone stereophonically?" Ken sighed. "No."

"Well, neither have I." I powered up the Nagra recorder. "I don't have the slightest idea what to expect, so I wouldn't have a ghost of a chance of making a qualified preset. The only way I know how to do this is to stay here and monitor the tape as we are recording, then make quick adjustments between volley fire."

"It's a bad idea," growled Ken. "We're wasting time. Get back to the firing line and keep accurate notes," I insisted.

Ken and Peter gave up and went back the 400 yards to the firing line, where the two contractors and clip loaders were finishing preparations. Over the past three days, we had recorded 27 different machine guns. We had recorded in a variety of acoustically different locations west of Las Vegas, chewing up over 9,000 rounds of ammunition.

I rolled over to check the equipment again. The microphones were live; the batteries were strong. In a few minutes the shooting team would be ready. I tried to relax. How did I ever get myself into this position in the first place?

I had been on Stage "D" at Goldwyn Studios in the midst of a temp dub on *Twilight Zone: The Motion Picture* when Don Rogers, head of the sound department, asked if I could step outside a second. Out in the hallway, Don briefed me that they had an awkward situation. A Chuck Norris picture was temp dubbing over on Stage "C" and the director was throwing quite a tantrum. It seemed that the sound editing crew had cut inappropriate weapon sounds, and, to make matters worse, the supervisor was calling every firearm on the screen an Uzi. Don wondered if I would mind coming back to Stage "C" and try to inject some damage control.

As soon as I walked on stage, I was introduced to Steve Carver, the director of the film *Lone Wolf McQuade*. He ordered the reel to be run. As the workprint flickered on the screen, Steve would point and demand, "What kind of gun is that?!"

I felt like I was being flashed silhouette identification cards in a precombat briefing. "That's a Mac-10."

On screen, another stuntman jumped into view, brandishing another kind of weapon. Carver pointed again. "And that?!"

"That's an M-16." Another stuntman kicked in the door of the cabin. Carver grinned as he pointed once more. "What about that one?"

I smiled as I recognized the weapon. "Oh my, I've never seen a Ruger Tri-Automatic before."

Carver signaled the mixer to halt the projection as he turned to me with a curious expression. "Then how do you know it is one?"

"I meant I've never seen one in action, just in last month's issue of *Guns and Ammo*."

Steve smiled. "Then you have the sounds of these weapons in your library."

"Not yet, but I will soon." That was how I came to lie there, waiting for the first machine-gun burst. The radio crackled, and my assistant asked if I was ready. I turned on the Nagra and radioed back that I had speed.

I heard a faint distant burst, and a beat later I could barely hear the bullets flying high overhead just prior to impacting the far cliff wall. I lifted the radio. "No, no guys. You're way too high. You have to bring it down lower."

A few moments passed, and then another burst was heard, followed by a flight of projectiles passing somewhat lower, but still not low enough. I lifted the radio. "Still too high. You have to come lower still."

A short time passed before I felt a series of impacts and disorienting debris. I had been struck in the back of the head, and, since I knew being struck by a bullet probably would not feel like what you think, I experienced a moment of disbelief and shock. Instantaneously, another 9-mm slug somehow flew between the crevice of two rocks, came under my head, and struck the ground 2 inches from my left eye. It then flew forward, striking a river rock and flipping back in front of my face on the ground as a mangled lead lump.

I moved my hand cautiously behind my head and gingerly felt my scalp for blood or an open wound. Fortunately, I only was struck by a rock that had been struck by a bullet. I suddenly felt immense relief that I was not mortally wounded, more than happy to endure a nasty lump rather than a hole in the head. My eyes focused on the still-hot lump of lead in front of my face. I was instantaneously aware that this piece of metal had flown under my head. I picked it up and set it in the palm of my hand to look at it.

I suppose several awkward moments had passed and the firing line crew had not heard from me. The radio crackled. It was Peter calling, "David . . . David?"

Snapping back into reality, I picked up the radio. Unfortunately, however, I did not pay strict attention to my exact choice of words. "I'm okay Peter; I have a bullet in my hand."

Peter's voice wailed away, "Oh, my gawd!! We've shot David!!"

If you are interested in hearing some of these recordings, especially the bullets whizzing past my head (which you hear in a lot of movies now) put the interactive DVD on and look under the Custom Recording FX Button and find Recording Guns on the submenu. Note how each succeeding flight of bullets get closer and closer.

I am the first to encourage you not to record weapons like this. I was lucky—but stupid and irresponsible. Although we captured some of the most remarkable bullet flights in a you-are-there perspective, far better ways are available today to record such effects without putting yourself in harm's way. If that bullet had grazed one of the rocks as it passed through the stone barrier, it could easily have changed course and struck me in the head, instead of passing just underneath my eye. It is better to plan the process with a safe and sane philosophical agenda. Problem solve how you could monitor your tape recorder and make adjustments in another way instead of placing yourself in a dangerous and compromising position. Be smart and survive. This does not diminish the excitement or thrill of recording live action sound effects. After all, you will be able to enjoy practicing your art form for a much longer period of time.

Most sound editors do not know one weapon from another. Since we were serving a director who was fanatical about the audio signature of weapons used in the film, we had to find some way to help the sound editor identify and use the correct sound effects with on-screen gunfire. We took a page from classic World War II aircraft identification posters, the ones with a series of aircraft silhouettes. If you see this silhouette, then it is this kind of enemy aircraft. I cut out photographs from numerous periodicals and books that showed the weapon profiles and carefully listed the applicable recordings.

I called it "see-a-gun/cut-a-gun." If you see an actor using a weapon that visually matches one seen in any of these sound effects catalog pages, then one or more sound effects cues listed under each picture are the appropriate ones to cut.

In Figure 10.2, John Fasal, Charles Maynes, and Alan Murray are custom recording both American and Japanese World War II weapons for *Flags of Our Fathers*. This action war epic was directed by Clint Eastwood, produced by Eastwood and Steven Spielberg, and picture edited by Joel Cox, who has worked with Clint on numerous projects, starting with the 1976 *The Enforcer*.

Figure 10.1 "See-a-gun/cut-a-gun." We incorporated photographs of the exact weapons we recorded, then grouped sound cues that pertained to each weapon together. In this fashion, the sound editor need only flip through the pages of the catalog until he or she recognizes the weapon being used in the film—a different spin on the police "mug-shot" idea. (Photo by David Yewdall.)

Figure 10.2 Custom recording World War II weapons for *Flag of Our Fathers*.

The particular weapon shown at the bottom of figure 10.2 is a Japanese Type 92 medium machine-gun, firing 7.7-mm rounds, fed by 30 round stripper clips, much like the Italian Breda.

The photo on the right shows the supervising sound editor, Alan Robert Murray, discussing some of the weapons that armorer Dave Fensil has brought on for that day's work. This is the fourteenth picture that Alan has helmed the sound supervisor chores for Clint, starting back with *Firefox* in 1982, and on which he has served as a sound editor on seven others, starting with the 1980 film *Bronco Billy*. Alan knows what Clint likes, he knows what Clint wants—but more importantly, he knows what Clint *needs.*

The photo on the left is of John Fasal setting up his gear in preparation for multiple recorders to capture multiple perspective recording. In this case, John recorded with two Sound Devices 744t recorders as well as a Fostex FR2 and an analog Nagra IV.

Alan Murray wandered around in various distant postions with a Fostex FR2 to capture perspective character recordings. Charles Maynes was also recording with a Sound Devices 744t as well as two Fostex FR-2s and his PowerBook with a Denecke AD20 preamp attached.

Charles, sound recordist, and sound designer/editor, remembers the session:

> I am not certain of all the mics that John had running, but I was using a Crown SASS mk2, two Shure SM-57, two MXL 990, two Oktava MK012, a Sanken CSS-5, and a Heil PR-40.
>
> John and I kind of worked independently as far as setups and such. As sound crafts-people are well aware, everyone has their own way of going about doing this kind of high-impact dynamic recording—and there is no sense in trying to change one person's work methods. You just hire people who you trust to get good sounds and be done with it. Alan had worked with John Fasal for an awfully long time, so I think he was the insurance policy in the shoot. I had not worked with Alan before, so I think he was a little concerned about what I might get, but to not go into too much detail, we came back with great tracks from each of us.

Charles shakes his head with satisfaction.

> As to setting up the mics—we basically had mics all over the place. We recorded the impact area which was about 150 meters away—(too close frankly) close-ups on the weapons and then medium close. This the fifth gunshoot of the year for me, so I was pretty confident that I could get at least a few good tracks from the set, but we ended up with few clunkers.
>
> As to the value of analog—I think it is done for weapons—Recording at 96 k gives amazingly lifelike quality, and the right mics being used can give you every bit of compression you might have been used to with the Nagra-IV. Though the Nagra can sound quite rich, its signal to noise ratio is dismal compared to high def digital.

THE ADVENTURE OF CUSTOM RECORDING

Custom recording sound effects is probably my favorite phase of the soundtrack creation process. Maybe it is because of my memories of venturing out to capture the exact kinds of sounds needed to successfully mount a project. Maybe it was the freedom I felt as I packed my car with recording gear and any special props I might need and simply got out of town. You cannot help but feel a bit like Indiana Jones as you set out to capture new sounds.

A wonderful side benefit from custom recording is the incredible learning experience that goes with it. If you truly are dedicated to the sound job, you cannot help but immerse yourself totally into the subject, learning the mechanics of how things work by studying sounds that emanate from whatever you are recording.

Sometimes the adventures were short and poignant; sometimes they became multiteam military-style operations involving thousands of dollars and careful planning. No matter how small or large the custom recording undertaking, my commitment to new recordings had a great deal to do with my growing reputation as a supervising sound editor and my marketability in the industry in the early 1980s.

Hopefully, the supervising sound editor is set for the project early enough so that he or she can screen dailies, or at least view significant event sequences long before picture editorial is ready to lock picture and turn it over for sound editorial work. Early on, you will discover that the screenplay, the scripted roadmap of how the movie is intended to be made, is not the last word in the actual outcome of the visual adventure ultimately turned over to sound editorial. The smart supervising sound editor only uses this as a guide of expectations and challenging promises. Once he or she actually sees footage, then the precise audio needs make themselves crystal clear.

After an overview of the sound effects material either in the sound library or in any wild track (WT) recordings the production mixer may have gotten on the set during principal photography, the supervising sound editor starts to list needs for custom sound effects recording. The supervising sound editor usually has one or more favorite locations that historically have been successful sites to record exterior sound effects. From prior experience, he or she knows air traffic patterns and temperature inversions that affect wind currents. In addition, the supervising sound editor has probably developed a relationship with local authorities or with individuals who occasionally enjoy developing sound effects and are willing to lend a hand.

More often than not, the supervising sound editor personally goes out and custom records the sound or teams up with other sound effects recordists in larger sessions that require multiple microphones and a team effort.

Increasingly more custom sound effects recording is done by specialists who devote much of their careers to custom sound recording. These men and women all have various reputations for specialties. A supervising sound editor may hire one individual because he or she is known for quadraphonic background recordings. On the other hand, a different sound effects recordist may have a reputation for eerie organic sounds, while another is known for being good with vehicles. The supervising sound editor considers who is best suited for each job and checks for schedule availability. Once the recordist has been set, the supervising sound editor usually runs sequences of action with the sound effects recordist, reviewing certain details of action and the concept of the performances. For instance, it is vital to articulate precisely how an engine should sound: Should it be cherried up? Should they unbolt the muffler and shift it back a little? Should it have a couple of spark plug wires removed? Should they even physically remove a spark plug? How heavy-handed does the sound recordist get? By the time the supervising sound editor completes the briefing, the scope of work is well defined, and the sound recordist has a clear picture of the mission to accomplish.

Steven Spielberg's *Jaws* required a great deal of attention and creative forethought. Contrary to what one might think in light of its history, *Jaws* was not intended to be a big picture. In fact, it was the little "horror" picture for Universal that year, a small project to add to the package of big films that the studio was offering. Box office history has shown that the year's other big pictures were comparative failures, and that *Jaws* saved the financial future of the studio.

No one could make that kind of prediction during the principal photography phase of the picture. The postproduction budget was not only unremarkable, but low budget and bare boned in design. Jim Troutman, the picture's supervising sound editor, had to make do with what little he had, and to do it quickly. One of the better decisions was allowing him to custom record the Orca, the sharking boat used to search for the dreaded great white.

"The Orca played throughout a good third of the picture. We had to record it doing all kinds of things to match the action in the movie," Troutman remembers. "They had been very smart and had brought the Orca out to Los Angeles along with the Swedish captain that maintained and operated the boat for the studio."

Jim and his recording team set up early in the morning. The captain took the small boat beyond the breakwaters of the Los Angeles harbor, out where Jim could get good, clean recordings.

"We recorded the flapper on the exhaust bouncing and spitting; we recorded the engine cruising along, under strain, with trap door open, with trap door closed—and then I happened to glance over the gunnels of the boat, and I began to pay closer attention to what was going on."

Jim stepped over to the captain. "Excuse me for asking, but this is a very interesting optical illusion. We seem to be riding lower in the water than we were a couple of hours ago." The captain calmly replied in his heavily accented English, "Ja, vee are sinking."

Jim's eyebrows shot up as he immediately announced that he had recorded enough material of the Orca heading west, and now he thought they should record the more important "flank speed" segment as they headed back to port.

One of the more interesting underwater recordings made earlier in the day utilized an underwater hydrophone. Jim and his team had tried to make underwater point-of-view recordings of the Orca, with mixed results. At one particular point, the mixer had Jim listen to a very strange emanation through his headsets. After a moment, Jim asked the captain if he knew what was making the peculiar sound. After listening to it, the captain nodded that he indeed had some experience with this back in Scandinavian waters—they were listening to the sound of shrimp eating. This is the strange and almost alien sound you hear as the movie begins. The Universal logo has just faded to black, and before the underwater title shot fades up, all we hear is Jim's recording of shrimp eating. From before the first frame of visual picture, Jim had set a weird and unearthly mood for things to come. *Jaws* won an Academy Award for Best Sound that year.

Figure 10.3 Eric Potter and Charles Maynes recording a Metro Rail train at 80 mph.

WHY A CUSTOM RECORDING SPECIALIST?

Why have special custom sound effects recordists record sound effects when you have the production mixer and all his or her gear out on location anyway? I have met very few production mixers who understand how to record sound effects. A production mixer's prime directive is to capture the spoken word on the set. When the actors speak, the production mixer does everything to record the actors' performances as cleanly and vibrantly as possible. As discussed in Chapter 5, the production mixer must overcome incredible ambience adversities to do this. He or she knows where the microphone must be placed to capture the best timbre of the human voice.

Good mixers know the necessity in doing everything to keep extraneous noises out of the production track. Audio intrusions such as generators, airplanes overhead, footsteps, cloth rustlings, and close proximity camera noise are some of their daily nemesis. The valuable experience of the seasoned production mixer is a precious commodity indeed. Despite all this, I would not hire a production mixer to record custom sound effects, especially vehicle series. They just do not understand the dynamics and intricacies of required performance cues and, more important, where to put the microphones.

When I was working on a period picture (circa 1919) entitled *Moonbeam Riders*, the authentic motorcycle engines of this action-adventure racing story challenged us. I was told the production mixer had exactly custom recorded what I would need for the Aero Indian motorcycle in the final reel of the film. Of course, I was more naive back in 1978. Our reels were due to start predubbing first thing in the morning, and, as often happened, we found ourselves cutting late into the night to finish the work on time.

By 3 a.m. I finally completed the old Harley and turned my attention to the Aero Indian. I pulled the 400-foot roll of 35-mm WT from the back rack of my table, laced the film over the sound head of the Moviola, and started to audition it. With every foot that passed over the sound head, I became more and more dismayed. If the sound recording was not suffering from vibration distortions, then it was the mixer talking during the performance or drastic changes in level as the bike performed. As the roll grew smaller in my hand, my blood pressure rose correspondingly higher. The recording was worthless! I knew the material needed was not there.

This was only one of many instances where a production company has had a perfect opportunity to custom record historically rare or one-of-a-kind props—only to squander the opportunity.

It is one of the most important lessons to learn as a producer or director: rather than dictate how you think the quickest and most cost-effective method of producing a great soundtrack, listen to your supervising sound editor's advice—he or she has a hundred times more experience than you do by virtue of his or her resumé of experience. Been there, done that—learn from their experience. In the end they will save you precious thousands of dollars as well as getting the job done correctly the first time. Do not find yourself being a victim of the old postproduction adage, "They can't find enough money or time to do it right, but somehow they find more money and extra time to do it *over*!"

Making a Career Out of Recording Sound Effects

By far, Eric Potter is one of the most respected specialists who has developed an extremely successful career recording sound effects to problem solve some of the most challenging motion pictures produced today. Such pictures as *War of the Worlds*, *Master and Commander*, *Spider Man*, *The Time Machine*, *Ocean's Eleven*, *Ronin*, *The Peacemaker*, *Independence Day*, and *Twister* are just a handful of the projects that have benefited from a very impassioned young man who has traveled to the far reaches of the earth to record anything and everything.

"We recorded this LAV (light armored vehicle) at Camp Pendelton Marine Base for *War of the Worlds*. Both Eric and I were recording four-channel sound at 96 kHz/24-bit using the Sound Devices 744t recorders," recalls John Fasal. "At the time, the 744t had just been introduced."

Fear of Being Stereotyped

By the end of the 1960s, legendary director Robert Wise was afraid of being typecast as a director of period costume pictures. While looking for a project that would completely change his image, he got a call from an associate at Universal who talked up a wacky science-fiction thriller written by a young kid named Michael Crichton (*The Andromeda Strain*). Wise jumped at the opportunity. What a change from *Helen of Troy*! It had the potential to rival his other science-fiction classic, *The Day the Earth Stood Still*.

Joe Sikorski studied the *Andromeda* script and reviewed the sound effects material on hand at the studio. Very little lived up to the level of both story hardware and visual art direction that Wise was capturing on film. Sikorski met with Wise to discuss the

Figure 10.4 Sound effects recording specialists John Fasal (left) and Eric Potter take a break from recording custom sound effects for the epic Spielberg remake of H. G. Wells's science-fiction classic *War of the Worlds*.

concerns of having the new and modern sounds the picture needed. Although Joe Sikorski and fellow sound editor Bob Bratton had tackled a similar style high-tech computer film the year before (*Colossus: The Forbin Project*), *The Andromeda Strain* went way beyond anything they had done in *Colossus*.

Sikorski proposed custom recording all new types of stuff to make the underground bio-tech lab come to life. But where could they do it? Wise told Sikorski he would get back to him. Three days later, Wise called Sikorski to let him know that he had secured the cooperative assistance from the Jet Propulsion Laboratory in Pasadena.

For two full days, Sikorski had a sound mixer, boom operator, cable man, and access to all the high-tech "toys" he would want to record. Nitrogen fill tanks, a vacuum pump on an electron microscope, centrifuges, laboratory ambience backgrounds, clean room doors, hydraulics, air compressions, transformers, switches, air vents, mechanical hand movements, sterilization processes, cutting-edge telecommunication gear—Sikorski not only had access to the real sounds, but also to the best technical advisors to guide him in their use.

At the time, Robert Wise did not consider *The Andromeda Strain* a big sound job, as we think of big soundtracks in today's acoustical barrages, but *Andromeda* was. Each moment of the picture had a precise and focused audio event that underlined and supported the visuals. It did not blast you out of your seat with a wall of sound; instead, it reached out with a special singularity in the storytelling process. The unique custom-recorded sound effects added a fresh spin that really captured your attention.

SOUND EDITORS RECORD THEIR OWN MATERIAL

Some of the best sound effects recordists have come from the ranks of sound editors. They are driven to record out of frustration because they need specific characterization in their sound effects to make their edit sessions really come alive. Others record because they love the challenge and freedom of using the world as their sound stage. Either way, sound editors bring editorial experience with them that dramatically affects

Figure 10.5 John Fasal leans out over the starboard railing with a long microphone boom so he can get the microphone down as close as possible to record the bow wash against the wooden hull in *Master and Commander: The Far Side of the World*.

how the material is performed and consequently recorded. Some of the best sound effects I have ever heard have been recorded by sound editors who learned how to record their own material.

Before I draw up battle plans to custom record a whole series of sound effects, I always sift through the production sound reports first, noting the WT recordings and listening to them before I make commitments on what to record. Needless to say, the more that sound editors become frustrated by lack of material in the studio's sound library, coupled with increased frustrations of improperly recorded WTs from production, the more they venture out to custom record their own sounds.

In the old days, by strict union definition of job functions, sound editors were not permitted to record their own sound effects. I knew of several editors who got slapped with $500 fines by the union for doing the work of a Local mixer. Like a shark that has tasted the blood in the water, though, once we had recorded sounds for our precise and unique applications and had cut them into sync to the picture, we had to have more. We liked the results and refused to turn back. Many of us decided to have dual unionship.

If we were 38 miles from the intersection of Hollywood Boulevard and Vine Street in Hollywood, we were legally outside union jurisdiction. This is the main reason why I started returning to my hometown of Coalinga to custom record my sound needs in the late 1970s. A secondary reason for recording away from the Los Angeles area should be painfully obvious. In terms of controlling ambient sound, a city is one of the worst places to record; unless, of course, you need busy streets and noisy neighborhoods with police helicopters patrolling overhead.

At the beginning of my sound editing career, I did some limited custom recording for one picture or another, especially while contracting Roger Corman films (*Humanoids from the Deep, Battle beyond the Stars*). *Escape from New York* was the film that swept me into serious field recording and made me understand the unique styles, challenges, and disciplines of stereo. Suddenly, I was no longer thinking monophonically. Now I thought in three dimensions—left-to-right, right-to-left, and in the surround channels. At first, though, trying to problem solve the stereo requirements for the many audio challenges of a motion picture can be mind-boggling.

Custom Recording Vehicles

With *Escape From New York* we staged our first serious sterephonic car-recording expedition. The Coalinga morning air was cold and still; a light fog lingered through the early afternoon. I soon learned that such conditions are perfect for sound effects. The best recording trips have been during the late fall and winter. Sound carries very well through cold air, and crickets and other pesky insects are frozen and silent.

I have developed a special background for recording vehicles—born out of the frustration of trying to make an old library car effect series work on a sequence without the proper components of recorded material to make the action come alive. I had recorded many vehicle series over the previous five years with mixed results, but it was John Carpenter's *Christine* that focused and galvanized the style and standards by which I would record vehicles in the future.

With *Christine* we had a vehicle that, during some sequences of the film, had to sound sad and beat-up; in other sequences, though, the car needed to sound tough and beefy. This would require a mechanic and whatever assistance he or she would need for the car to sound a variety of ways.

When recording vehicles, you must be very sensitive to the local authorities. Not all roads fall under local jurisdiction. If you are not careful, you can find yourself in deep trouble if you record car stunts on the wrong stretch of highway. Personally, though, I have yet to find one highway patrolman or county sheriff who does not like to assist and be involved in recording hot cars for the movies, but you must *involve* them in your early planning and listen carefully to their recommendations.

Figure 10.6 shows us custom recording the out-of-tune character vehicle (an LTD) for the 1989 production *Cohen and Tate*, starring Roy Scheider and Adam Baldwin. It was much easier for us on this picture for two reasons. First, the production company gave us the actual car to do with as we pleased. We ran it into the ground, we sideswiped it; Gonzo even got up on the roof and threw himself down as bodyfalls—still some of the best body-to-car material available! Second, we had already established the ground work on how to really custom record cars on John Carpenter's horror possessed-car picture *Christine*; and ever since then, the sound effects editor always had the audio coverage to make the vehicles really sound like what they needed to sound like—it is all about understanding making the bits and pieces of cues that you will weave together later to create the reality of the sequence.

For *Christine*, the highway patrol suggested that it would be much easier, with much less "maintenance observation" required on their part, if we hired a security officer to be with us as we worked. This benefited both parties. A uniformed

Figure 10.6 The author and his recording team out in the San Joaquin Valley just outside his home town of Coalinga to record an out-of-tune LTD for *Cohen and Tate*.

officer with experience in traffic management and radio communication with the local authorities gave us instant access should a troublesome situation arise. He also lent a visual symbol of authority and legitimacy to people driving through the recording zone.

We quickly discovered, however, that we could not use the road we first had in mind because it fell under state jurisdiction, making necessary a mountain of complex paperwork and approvals from the state capital to use a state highway. Local authorities noted several alternate roads that fell under county jurisdiction, making it vastly easier to receive permission and clearances so that we could perform various stunt driving for the express purpose of recording sound effects.

We did not choose a location at which to record simply by fingering the map and picking a place at random. We drove out (at the same time of day the recording was planned) and stopped on each road, got out, and walked the length, listening to the ambience, considering potential audio problems posed from a nearby factory, airport, field pumps, and so forth, not the least of which was daily wind shift patterns. On some locations, we discovered that if we had not gotten our recordings by noon we were doomed to winds that kicked up for the remainder of the day.

I secured the assistance of Tim Jordan, a school friend who owned his own automotive shop in my hometown. Tim served as head mechanic and vehicle liaison officer, knowing who in town owned what kind of car. I briefed him on the sound effects requirements and the range of automotive changes and challenges he would make on the performing vehicles while we were out in the field. In a matter of moments Tim and his assistant could remove spark plug wires, in some cases removing a spark plug completely for a real raspy clatter. The two men would detach the muffler and move it back slightly, causing a gap, or they would change the timing. All of these alterations had to be done quickly, and often with the audition result that the desired effect was not realized. In a matter of minutes, though, the car was ready to make awful (but necessary) noises.

Christine was the first picture on which I used two recording teams. The first recording unit, or "close-up" perspective team, would always set up on the road itself, close to the car. The second recording unit was the "semi-background" perspective team, set off the road 20 or 30 yards to get a softer performance. Approach recording a car series with the material needs of the sound editor in mind. You seldom record a single performance with all the elements of that recording working together in their proper balanced volumes. The undercarriage may overwhelm tire hum; engine dynamics disappear under tire skids. A perfectly balanced mixture of elements in one recording almost never happens. Therefore, do not approach recording cars with the idea that each recording is an end unto itself. Every recording is but one piece of the puzzle of sound effects that must be cut and blended together to make a slick car sequence work. With this understanding deeply rooted, the intelligent custom sound recordist breaks the action into traditional parts. Smart supervising sound editors always record cars in the same groupings, from which a sound editor can create any movement.

A typical vehicle performance series is broken down into single cues, as follows. Of course, your own needs for vehicle recordings may vary, but this is a good guide.

Vehicle Mechanicals

- Trunk open and close
- Hood up and down
- Hood and/or trunk release mechanism
- Driver door open and close
- Passenger door open and close
- Into car movement/out of car movement
- Seat belts movement and buckling up
- Window cranked (or motor) up and down
- Emergency brake set and release
- Shifter movement into gear/reverse movement
- Glove compartment open and close
- Cigarette lighter movement
- Radio switch on and off

- CD player movement—disk in and out (or cassette player)
- Rummage through glove compartment
- Gas flap release (on newer vehicles)
- Gas cap key and off and on movement (especially older vehicles)
- Various dashboard clicks, knobs, and lever settings
- Keys into ignition movement (be careful not to use a keychain)
- Turn-signal relay clicking
- Windshield wipers—recorded dry (various speeds)
- Windshield wipers—recorded wet (various speeds)
- Brake squeaks (with squeaky brakes, roll car down slope with engine off, brake to stop—various)
- Roll car over light gritty asphalt
- Roll car off asphalt onto shoulder of road
- Pry off and put on hubcaps
- Overhead light
- Convertible room open/close mechanism (if applicable)
- Moon/sun roof mechanicals
- Pedal movement
- Mirrors (if motorized)

Now you must record the performance of the car engine itself. Contrary to those who would assume they know how car sound effects are recorded, let me assure you that the best series are recorded in a very methodical, often boring manner. Note that the perspective of the recording from the tailpipe area sounds completely different from that made before the front bumper. Likewise, a recording made from the side of the car sounds different from that from either front or back. These positions become extremely handy and critical later in sound editorial when the actual demands of the visual picture may require the car to start, have a short idle, then pull past the camera and away. Another shot may require a rear perspective view, where a front-end microphone does not sound appropriate. It all boils down to common sense.

Recording a Car—Start and Idle

Following is a list of idles and revs required in a static position. Note that "jump" revs are recorded in a static position; the car does not actually leave the ground and fly by.

- Start, idle, and off (close front perspective)
- Start, idle, and off (close tailpipe perspective)
- Start, idle, and off (mid-side perspective)
- Start, light revs, and off (close front perspective)
- Start, light revs, and off (close tailpipe perspective)
- Start, light revs, and off (mid-side perspective)
- Start, medium revs, and off (close front perspective)
- Start, medium revs, and off (close tailpipe perspective)
- Start, medium revs, and off (mid-side perspective)
- Start, big angry revs, and off (close front perspective)
- Start, big angry revs, and off (close tailpipe perspective)

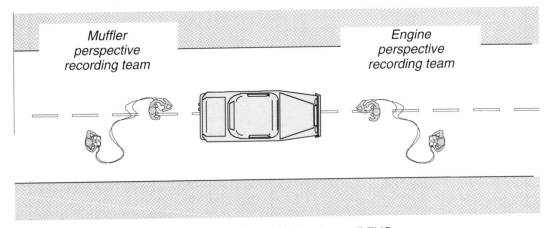

Recording car START and IDLES—car REVS
(from two perspectives simultaneously)

Figure 10.7 Recording the static position start and idles as well as the static rev cues.

- Start, big angry revs, and off (mid-side perspective)
- Start, "jump" revs, and off (close front perspective)
- Start, "jump" revs, and off (close tailpipe perspective)
- Start, "jump" revs, and off (mid-side perspective)

I have met few car owners who take kindly to having their vehicles "jumped." Actually, vehicles seldom make such a sound when they leave the ground. It has become one of those Hollywood audio clichés, a metaphor we expect or even feel satisfaction from because we believe in the way it benefits the action on screen. To add to the sensation of flight, move the microphones away from the engine as the engine peaks in its "freewheeling" rev, duplicating the sensation that the vehicle is passing by in flight.

Recording a Car—Start and Aways
Following is a list of variations on the start and aways.

- Start, short idle, and away—various speeds (close front and by perspective)
- Start, short idle, and away—various speeds (close tailpipe away perspective)
- Start, short idle, and away—various speeds (mid-side away perspective)

In addition to the three basic perspectives, you also need the driver to perform each take with a different emphasis. One start-and-away should be slow and lethargic. Another should be at normal speed, with yet another a little faster, building to a fast and hard away, throttling downrange.

Recording a Car—In to Stop
Using the same philosophy as the start and aways, now you must deal with variations of where the car actually stops. One of the most overlooked approach-and-stop cues is

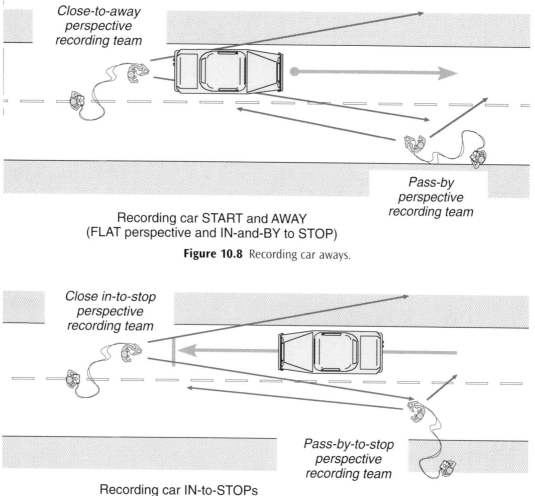

Recording car START and AWAY
(FLAT perspective and IN-and-BY to STOP)

Figure 10.8 Recording car aways.

Recording car IN-to-STOPs
(FLAT perspective and IN-and-BY to STOP)

Figure 10.9 Recording car stops.

having the vehicle approach and pull up into a driveway. This cue sounds so much different from simply pulling up to a stop on the street. Refer to the following list.

- Long in approach and stop, engine off—various speeds (stop close front perspective)
- Long in approach and stop, engine off—various speeds (close by and stop tailpipe perspective)
- Long in approach and stop, engine off—various speeds (mid-side away perspective)

The car should not always stop directly in front of or to the side of the microphones. Performances that have the car pass to a stop a bit past the microphones are

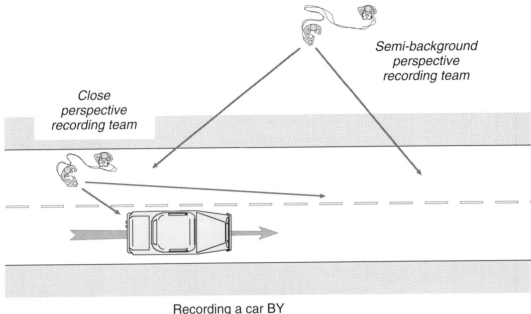

Recording a car BY
(from two perspectives simultaneously)

Figure 10.10 Recording car bys.

not only a good idea but vital for perspective placement. You might also have the driver approach, slow as he or she nears, then pass by 8 to 15 yards from the microphone and U-turn back in to stop. These types of in-to-stops are excellent for estate driveways.

Recording a Car—Bys

I have never encountered a sound effects library that has too many approach and bys for any given vehicle series. Remember, don't record for only the film you are working on, but for any future uses. Refer to the list below for guidelines.

- Approach, by, and away—various speeds (stop close front perspective)
- Approach, by, and away—various speeds (close by and stop tailpipe perspective)
- Approach, by, and away—various speeds (mid-side away perspective)

You should not only record numerous variations such as sneak by, slow by, normal by, medium by, fast by, race by; you also must think about accelerating or decelerating on the by, shifting gears as in upshifting or downshifting just prior to or just after the by itself. You should also not record all your approach and bys from the same location. If a seam or a tiny piece of debris is in the road, you will discover later that you got a rhythmic click or thump in the same spot in the performance, quickly making the vehicle bys predictable and uninteresting.

Start and aways, in and stops, approach and bys are all very obvious. They are the "getting there" cues, but vehicles do not drive *only* like that, they need transitions

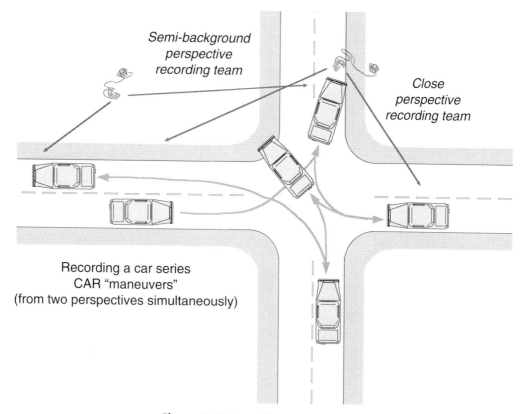

Figure 10.11 Recording car maneuvers.

and dipsy-doodles to tie the "getting there" cues together into a single ribbon of reality.

Recording a Car—Maneuvers

Maneuvers are one of the most vital, yet greatly overlooked, performances a vehicle can do. As a sound editor, I can cut bits and pieces of vehicle maneuvers and weave them into the transitional moments of screen action in a way that not only bridges one "getting there" effect to another, but also inject a variety of interesting moments that bring the vehicle to life and create a character, a performing actor made of metal and rubber.

You should most certainly record several sets of maneuvers, moving from one location to another, as the surface on which the tires bear down is revealed to the microphone more dramatically than any of the other "getting there" cues. Remember that the sound of a tire on asphalt is totally different from how it sounds on cement, let alone how it sounds on a dirt road. Refer to the list below for the ranges of maneuvers.

- In and maneuver about—slow and deliberate (perspective #1)
- In and maneuver about—slow and deliberate (perspective #2)

- In and maneuver about—normal (perspective #1)
- In and maneuver about—normal (perspective #2)
- In and maneuver about—fast and aggressive (perspective #1)
- In and maneuver about—fast and aggressive (perspective #2)

Last but not least, record a variety of onboard constants. I usually set a pair of microphones on the back bumper, pointing downward toward the road and being influenced by the tailpipe. The second pair of microphones is inside the vehicle in a wide separation with the windows up. Later, in sound editorial, I cut the tailpipe constant alongside the interior constant to develop the right blend.

One of the most vital and important points about onboard recordings is the illusion of speed. Many vehicle onboard recordings I have heard from other sound libraries are flat and lifeless, a dead giveaway they had been recorded literally. When you record onboards, find a road with a very long gradual grade so that the performing vehicle engine always "works" and does not freewheel. Very often we must drive at slower speeds in lower gears to simulate higher speeds, an audio illusion wise to learn early. Recording reality is not always the most desirable. If you are interested in hearing some of these recordings, put the interactive DVD on and look under the CUSTOM RECORDING FX button and find RECORDING A CAR SERIES on the submenu.

To add to the recording challenge, *Christine* had been filmed during both rainy and dry weather. I did not want to cheat the wet tire sound effects under a dry car recording any more than I had to, so we decided to record the vehicles both dry and wet. This required hiring a water truck and driver. It was a hot August day when we custom recorded the wet car series. The water truck operator surely thought we were out of our minds when he arrived. He glanced about for a dirt road or construction site to wet down as he asked me where I wanted the water. I gestured down the hot broiling asphalt of the highway.

"Are you nuts? The water will evaporate in a matter of minutes!" he snapped.

I assured him I understood that, but the work order did specify a mile-and-a-half stretch of county road. He asked me if I knew how much this load of water cost. Again I assured him I did, especially since I was paying for it. I asked him if he was getting paid for doing the job, and, if so, why should he care where and how the water was being utilized?

He shrugged. "Whad'ya want me to do when I finish dumpin' it?"

Smiling, I stated, "I guess you had better go back and get another load. At the rate of evaporation, you're gonna be busy all day."

For the next six hours, the water truck shuttled back and forth, laying down a fresh surface of water on the stretch of road.

Christine had another unique problem. After the car was beat up and hurt, "she" limped back to the garage to heal. The re-recording mixer was capable of adding echo to the sound effects as the car rolled into the garage, but I wanted to customize a really unique audio event into the recording when *Christine* gets back to her "nest" in the garage. A somewhat surprising location presented itself. Regrettably, my California hometown had been decimated in the 1983 earthquake destroying 360 buildings and 11 square blocks of downtown. The powerful quake had also rendered the Sunset School buildings unusable for several years. Originally, the school had been designed with a unique open hallway, and concrete corridors between buildings that had a roof but no walls between the wing groupings of classrooms. I knew recording a vehicle in a real garage with enclosed walls would add so much reverb to an engine recording it would be unacceptable. At Sunset School, the semi-open corridor provided a taste of enclosed reverb, but still allowed the major echo build-up usually accompanying interior recordings to escape into the open grassy breezeways. It was perfect. We just had to maneuver the performing vehicles up concrete steps into the hallway corridors.

Once we experienced the subdued reverberation, I knew we must customize several exact shots, as I just loved the sound of *Christine*'s puffing engine, achieved by having four spark-plug wires removed and the exhaust pipe unbolted. This procedure worked well for the sequence in the movie where *Christine* blows up the gas station and returns to the garage. She enters the shelter with her entire chassis sizzling from the fire, turning past Robert Prosky as he watches her in disbelief. We had recorded very slow pass-bys in the corridor, allowing the performing car to basically idle as she passed. The Doppler effect of the tailpipe was perfect, and the entire effect built toward the crowning moment when she backed into her stall and switched off.

A signature effect of *Christine* in the movie was a complete accident of chance. While out on the county road recording start and idles, we discovered that the hydraulic system of the car wheezed and whined as it relaxed. At first, Tim Jordan was apologetic about it, jumping out of the car to cure the unwanted sound. I asked him to leave it alone for a moment, as we should specifically record the comical little wheeze with the pathetic metallic edge. Later during sound editorial, we decided to factor the sound into the sequence where *Christine* backs into her stall and turns off. The wheeze/ whine became her pitiful exhalation. When John Carpenter (director) heard it on the re-recording stage, he asked if we could also use it in the last shot of the movie when the camera moves in close on the compressed block remains of *Christine* in the wrecking yard, and a little piece of her grill flexes.

Do not record vehicles in the same way as production dialog. For recording dialog you put your microphone out on a fish pole and hold it up in the air just above the actors as the ideal placement to record their voices. Dialog recording mixers follow the

Figure 10.12 *Sometimes you just really have to "get into" your work!!* John Fasal gets into an M1 Abrams Main Battle Tank to do some serious custom recording for Steven Spielberg's *War of the Worlds*.

Figure 10.13 Charles Maynes recording a metal press.

same philosophy for recording sound effects—but that does not (and actually seldom does) yield the most vibrant and exciting performance for sound effects. Oddly enough I have my microphones very low to the ground, especially when recording the tailpipe perspectives. Also pay very close attention to what comes out of the tailpipe, should you choose to take up position there, as I discovered with *Christine* on the "angry revs." You need to try various placements until you find what pleases you the most.

Rule of thumb: "If it sounds good, it is correct." The placement of the microphone is an illusion of the reality you are creating for the screen.

Because sound travels better in colder air and fewer people and vehicles are out at night, so, too, less ambient gray noise clutters the atmosphere. Some of my best vehicle recordings were done during the late fall through early spring, around or after midnight. The only allusion we have to nighttime is the sound of crickets, but crickets are also heard during the day, even though they are not as lively.

Recording Multiple Points of View Simultaneously

With the advent of digital nonlinear editing technology, it has been much easier to record and develop complex multichannel "points-of-view" performance recordings. During an action chase sequence, such as in the movie, *Road Warrior*, the audience's point of view is all over the big tractor-trailer rig. One moment you are up in the cab with Mel Gibson; the next moment you are back on the rear of the tanker with the rear gunner; and the next moment you are on the front bumper of the tractor with Vernon Wells. Each one of these angles is going to sound, and should sound, totally different. With the decelerations and the accelerations as the big rig maneuvers about, the powerful engine is going to be the foundation character. The rpm rate, whether it is rising or falling as well as what gear the tractor is in cannot and should not suddenly be different from shot to shot. The ever-changing dynamics of the truck should have continuity, linking the series of shots together in a binding motion.

To cut a vehicle series together from individual cues that were recorded separately has always been a very challenging and arduous task. With today's technology we can easily record and re-master multiple points of view in synchronous stereo pairs that if we cut from one angle to the other, the dynamics of the engine will always be exactly at the correct rpm, whether decelerating or accelerating, making the sound editorial task vastly easier.

For a similar assignment, Eric Potter and his team had gone out to custom record the big Kaiser 5-ton Army truck with the turbo charger for an action chase sequence. After studying the sequence in the picture with the supervising sound editor, the two had worked out the various kinds of actions that needed to be covered. In addition to a standard series of recordings, a list of specialized moves and road surfaces were noted.

Eric had decided that the best way to tackle the problem was to hire several other recording colleagues to join the team, bringing not only their own expertise but also their own equipment to use. In all, Eric had a 12-man recording crew. Some of the recorders were digital DAT machines; some were $\frac{1}{4}''$ stereo Nagras. After evaluating the microphones in their arsenal, the recording teams agreed on what type of microphones and recording formats would work best in the various positions chosen.

Each recording team had a 5-watt communication radio. Three recording teams were positioned in a huge triangle configuration out on the desert salt flats. The stunt driver would perform the vehicle in its "chase" sequence action by driving around in a huge 1-mile circle, allowing each of the three "ground" recordists to have a close drive-by point of view followed by a long away and a long approach.

The fourth and fifth recorders were in the cab of the truck, recording action as miked from the front bumper and from inside the cab angled toward the driver's feet. The sixth recording team had their microphones positioned between the tractor and the box, able to get bright and "ballsy" exhaust raps. The seventh recording team was positioned on the rear of the truck, with microphones attached on shock mounts to the rear underside, favoring suspension and rattles.

Eric used a toy clicker as a sync slate, which he held up to his 5-watt communication radio when he clicked it. Each recordist had his own radio receiver held near his own slate mikes of their field mixer so that each recording would have a very short click point to be used later by the sound librarian to edit and align the material for mastering (as described in Chapter 11).

As with recording car series, it is very important not to allow tire skids or screeches into the performance. The primary task is to record a wide and full range of engine revs, accelerations, and decelerations that can be cut clean. If tire skidding is heard in the recording, it is very difficult to cut out later, denying the sound editor the use of clean engine sounds where the tire skid has been heard. A sound editor will invariably not want the skids that are in the recording for the sequence he or she is cutting, but would rather add tracks of skids and surface reactions separately so that they can be properly controlled and balanced later in the mix.

As with recording car series, do not allow tire skids or screeches into the performance. The primary task is to record a full range of engine revs, accelerations, and decelerations that can be cut clean. If tire skidding is heard in the recording, it is very difficult to cut out later, denying the sound editor use of clean engine sounds where the tire skid can be heard. A sound editor invariably does not want the skids in the recording for the sequence being cut, but would rather add separate tracks of skids and surface reactions so they can be properly controlled and balanced later in the mix.

Recording Animals

Recording animals can be extremely challenging. Many movements or vocals that must be recorded are so subtle that you must record the animals under very strict audio controllable conditions. Many choose to record animals on a Foley stage, which can work for various kinds of animal recordings, but some animals do not respond naturally in an alien environment. The biggest problem in recording real animal vocals and movement performances is that the vast majority of animal trainers who contract with entertainment industries train their animals to react to vocal or signal commands. This makes it impossible when working with a trainer who is constantly blowing his or her whistle or snapping a clicker or shouting vocal cues, most of the time either on top of or intruding into the desired part of the animal's vocal.

One animal trainer that does not rely on making unwanted noises or speaking to his performing animal during sound recordings is Karl Lewis Miller of Animal Action. Karl trains his dogs to perform on cue or make desired reactions or vocals by use of visual signals. Only once or twice during the recordings of his dogs did he actually have to speak. Daddy, the big Saint Bernard that played the title character in *Cujo*, ambled up to the stone Karl had set on the ground as Daddy's "marks." I had advised my boom operator, Chuck Smith, to extend the microphone pole to give some distance between himself and the big dog.

Chuck waved me off, thinking Daddy was about the most docile canine he had ever come across, and therefore stood far too close to the mark. I rolled the Nagra and announced "speed." Karl silently got Daddy's attention, then stuck his finger out, pointing at Daddy's nose, then made a wide sudden gesture. The dog lunged forward, stopping within inches of the microphone, his giant jowls snapping, reminding us how he had made *Cujo* so terrifying. He growled, barked, and lunge-snapped. After a full minute of canine viciousness, the trainer made another motion. The massive dog stopped his performance, backed up on the stone mark, and returned to his docile and friendly self as if nothing happened. Chuck turned pale with fear. Perspiration streamed down his forehead as he immediately began to loosen the microphone pole tube locks and extend the pole to its maximum 18-foot reach.

An interesting trick the trainer used to keep his dogs from barking, while still allowing the animal to perform vicious growls and vocal gutturals when desired, was to insert a tennis ball into the dog's mouth. The ball was a toy, so the dog was having fun, but it inhibited the animal from barking.

As animal trainers strive to be in demand, more and more are learning to train their animals to perform to visual, rather than audio cues. Such noise cues end up on production tracks over the dialog when the animals perform on screen, spoiling many a soundtrack and making preparations in sound editorial much more difficult.

Check out the interactive DVD under button 5—CUSTOM RECORDING FX and choose the sixth button on the submenu to watch Mark Mangini custom recording tigers in Seoul, Korea.

Recording Airplanes

Recording airplanes is similar to recording vehicles. After all, you still want to record engine start, idle, and offs. You still want to record engine start and rev ups and downs.

You still want to record engine start, taxi, and aways as well as taxi in toward mike, stop rev, and offs. The major difference is where you position the microphones for maximum yield, and, especially with propeller craft, not be subject to massive wind buffeting.

Several unique positions are necessary to get the power of the propeller aircraft engine on tape. I took up position just out in front of the Steerman with the assistants holding onto the tail section of the plane while the pilot would rev up the engine to a very high rpm. The amazing harmonic rise and fall from these recordings became vital for power dives, in-flight maneuvers, strained pull-outs, and so forth. We also had the aircraft perform a figure-8 around us doing variations: some with engine revving up, some with engine decelerating.

While recording the 1920s-era biplane aircraft for *The Aviator*, we were challenged not only to find the precise and authentic aircraft with the correct engine, but to find them in a part of the country remote enough to safely record without jet aircraft interference or distant traffic noise. After calling Oshkosh, Wisconsin, the home of aviation, we were quickly referred to Hurley Boehler, an aviation expert and liaison out of Tulsa, Oklahoma. Hurley was able to put together not only the correct and exact engine combinations called for by the producer, but was able to locate an excellent area to record the aircraft where we would be unfettered by unwanted audio intrusion.

We had two recording teams, each recording with a Nagra IV-S at 15 ips (inches per second) for maximum saturation. Our two-week recording expedition took in three biplanes and six period automobiles from the second largest private car collection in the world, out of Muskogee, Oklahoma. Each day, we wrapped the recording session between 2 and 3 o'clock in the afternoon, then shipped all the $1/4$″ tapes back to my studio in North Hollywood, where they were edited and logged by the sound librarian. That recording adventure taught us some very important lessons.

First, always tell the recordist who will be inside the aircraft recording onboard perspectives that you have asked the pilot to simulate engine failure as the plane is diving and swooping. As the Steerman went roaring past us, the pilot flipped the magneto off and on to simulate major engine trouble.

All we could see was our recordist, his eyes big as saucers, fingers embedded in the fabric of the cockpit lining with an abiding certainty that he was about to meet his maker.

Second, try to find a high position to record the aircraft fly-bys and especially the long lazy turns that work well for exterior in-flight constants. If you record these cues too close to the ground, you run the risk of picking up ground reflection as well as bird chirps and creature noises.

The ultimate recording is made from a unique "third-position" aerial platform. Such platforms do not exist naturally, unless you have a very tall tower in a recording environment with *no* wind—try to find that! The serious aviation recordist will have a special, all-welded metal, hot-air balloon "basket" rig made. The reason for this is to eliminate every conceivable noise-generating source that conventional hot-air balloon baskets are notorious for. This multi-tier platform is made of lightweight aircraft metal and has two levels. The top position is the pilot/safety officer platform. His job is to turn the burner off during the actual time of recording and back on when the recorders are turned off. As the safety officer, he also maintains radio communication with all recording mixers, boom operators—both just below him, on the ground and/or in the performing aircraft as well as the performing pilot. He is, therefore, responsible for the overall control of action and subsequent safety precautions.

The recording mixer sits with the boom operator in side-by-side seats with body harnesses on the lower level of the metallic rig. The multitrack recorders are strapped into a foam-insulated roll-bar type of welded rack in front of and alongside the recording mixer. The boom operator is strapped into his seat next to the recording mixer. The boom operator has control of the "hot-head" type pillow block pylon that runs through the center of the dual-level basket. This absolutely silent pillow-block mechanism allows the boom operator to rotate the lower deck from side to side or completely around in a 360-degree movement as required to keep the fixed angle multi-microphone set-ups in perfect spatial positioning as desired.

With this unique recording position, the usual audio clutter associated with point-of-view microphones that are confined to being on the ground is eliminated. The hot-air balloon will drift with the prevailing wind, so breeze buffet, which often plagues recordings (especially after 11:00 a.m.) is cut down tremendously. The trick is for the performing pilot to understand that she needs to use the hot-air balloon as the center of performance—keeping her bys and maneuvers to large circular arcs around the hot-air balloon in addition to hard bys. Just think of it as recording a car for "estate" driving and the creative possibilities will all become clear to you. If you are interested in hearing some of these recordings, on the DVD look under the CUSTOM RECORDING FX button and find RECORDING AN AIRPLANE on the submenu. This will take you step by step, very much like recording the car. I only wished I had prewarned Steve Rice on the last cue, as he was in the plane at the time that it had, um, *engine troubles.*

This is also where multi-recorder points-of-view-style philosophy pays off. Careful breakdown and mastering of these audio cues back in the studio by the librarian will be crucial. (This is explained in detail in Chapter 11.)

Recording Explosions

As a precaution, I made arrangements for the Westside Fire Department to stand by one Sunday morning at the Federal Pit as we detonated a custom-made explosive device for the helicopter explosion in John Carpenter's *The Thing*. The nine firemen watched with interest as a 1-foot hole was dug in the ground. I then poured 5 pounds of black powder into a steel pipe. On either side of the pipe, we strapped two small 1-inch pipes filled with black powder. I placed the bottom end of the pipe bundle into the hole, then placed an upside-down trash can on top, knocking a hole through which the top of the pipe would fit. My assistant then shoveled gravel into the trash can in and around the pipes. We set a second trash can, right-side up, on top of the base can and filled it with high-octane gasoline.

The two smaller pipes would actually make the "bang"; the main pipe was to launch a short steel sleeve up through the bottom of the second trash can, igniting the fuel and blasting it up and out.

To simulate helicopter debris for the explosion, my assistant, Peter Cole, had absconded with all kinds of metal siding and scrap found alongside the road, including

Figure 10.14 Too big a blast.

some old signs still being used by the county. (Fortunately, the fire captain had a good sense of humor about the roadside markers.) We ran the detonator wires back about 200 feet, where Peter had the battery and ignition switch. I had taken up a position about 50 feet back from the device with my microphones spread wide left and right, where I hoped to catch an acoustical concussionary slap off the far wall of the pit.

The fire crews and their trucks pulled back 200 yards to safety. All were instructed not to verbally react or say anything until well after the event. I told Peter I would yell "rolling" and he should silently count to three, then hit the switch. After being satisfied that the tape recorder was rolling properly, I yelled "rolling" and waited for the detonation. Almost 10 seconds passed without an event. I peered out of my foxhole to see Peter struggling with the battery. It was not strong enough to set off the detonator through that much wire. I quickly called out for him to stop trying.

I jumped up and ran over to check the device. Gasoline was starting to leach from the upper can. We had to do something quickly, before fuel drenched the pipes below. I yelled to the top of the pit for someone to drive my car down. Within moments someone delivered my Dodge Diplomat down into the Federal Pit to Peter's position. I lifted the hood and pulled the detonation wire over to the car battery. Grabbing a hold of Peter to get his undivided attention, I yelled, "Whatever you do, when you touch these two wires, do not hesitate or wait for the explosion. Touch the second wire and instantly drop to the ground, as fast as you can. Do you understand?"

Peter nervously nodded. As he took the detonation wire, his hands were shaking. I repeated my previous instructions. "I will say 'rolling'—then you count silently to three and touch it off. Got it?"

I ran back to my foxhole and turned on the tape recorder. "Rolling!" Three silent moments passed, and then the air was split by the explosion. Peter was actually starting to drop for the ground when the second wire touched the car battery terminal. The main pipe split open and flattened out, flying over Peter's head like a Frisbee, landing 200 yards away, only 3 feet from a fireman.

The fireball mushroomed out like a miniature atomic explosion, blowing over my foxhole, then rising skyward. Metal debris flew everywhere. Most of the Federal Pit was ablaze when the fire trucks headed down to douse the flames. Satisfied that I had captured the audio event I stood up from listening to the playback of the recording to find the fire captain standing next to me, watching his men mop up the aftermath. He turned to me and winked. "Well son, that was about as good as sex." Then he continued on down the hill. I was not quite sure what to say to a comment like that, except I doubt Roger Ebert ever gave a thumbs-up rating with a quote like that.

As it turned out, I learned some very valuable lessons about recording explosions. First, always work with a professional explosive's contractor who knows what he or she is doing.

Second, unlike the auto bullet flights discussed at the beginning of this chapter, explosions are definitely recordable without your having to be with the equipment. The most important part of the explosion is the first fraction of a second after the initial blast ignition. If you are not set to properly record that, then the rest of the recording is meaningless. I usually use the horn of a big car at semi-close proximity, such as a Cadillac, to act as a pseudo on-site recording-level test. It is only a guess, but it gets you close to a safe recording level. As with recording gunfire, your first few shots are either overmodulated or underrecorded, until you find the ideal record setting. Do not depend on one explosion. That is one of the primary reasons we like to record these types of high-maintenance, high-cost-per-performance events with multiple tape recorders. On the first explosion, if one recorder overmodulated, there is a good chance that one of the others did not.

After the first explosion, each recorder should be carefully rewound and reviewed for you to hear the playback of the blast. The sound effects recordist should pay strict attention to the VU meter, as a quality speaker monitoring system cannot be on-site to audibly analyze the recording. Headsets should only be used as confirmation that the recording was successfully made; they should not be depended on to render a quality analysis of the frequency breadth of the recording.

Third, do not rely on record limiters to keep from overmodulating. If your first explosion is overmodulated, then make a new level adjustment. By using record limiters, you invite unwanted signal compression that can ruin the desired effect.

Fourth, record gunfire and explosions at the fastest tape speed you can. At the very minimum, record with an analog tape recorder at 15 ips. If can get your hands on an analog tape recorder capable of field recording at speeds of 30 ips, you truly will be ecstatic with the results. (Review cue #22 on this book's audio CD for a comparison of how the same rifle-shot sounds recorded by an audiocassette at 1-5/8 ips, an analog Nagra recording at 7-1/2 ips, an analog Nagra recording at 15 ips, by a digital DAT, and a direct-to-disk digital recording on the Deva. Each recorder is using Electro-Voice RE-16 microphones in an X-Y configuration. Absolutely no equalization or signal manipulation occurs prior to the audio CD mastering. Each rifle-shot cue is presented absolutely raw for better quality comparison.)

Fifth, and most important, do not try to integrate debris into the recording of the explosion. As explained in Chapter 12, debris such as the metal signs and junk should not be used in a staged explosion. Debris should be recorded as separate audio cues and cut together with the explosion blasts later during the editorial process.

To achieve a unique explosion sound, try taking several recordings of the same explosion, recorded on different tape recorders using different microphone configurations, and then blend them together. Often, one set of microphones delivers a more "crackly" character to the explosion, with little low end. Another stereo pair has a rich bottom-end boom, with little high-end. A third stereo pair may have more mid-range with a near overtone tail to it. Putting all three stereo pairs together during the sound-editorial process delivers a combination that none of the stereo pairs alone could capture.

The Cannons of *Master and Commander*

Supervising sound editor/sound designer Richard King won an Academy Award for Best Sound Editing for *Master and Commander: The Far Side of the World*. Like all the work that Richard tackles, his emphasis is always on developing a "palette" of sound that is unique and interesting for each project. *Master and Commander* was certainly no exception. Figure 10.15 shows Richard recording a Hotchkiss gun as part of the sound design recording process. Richard shares his experience with the cannon challenges.

> This weapon was recorded for *Master and Commander*. John Fasal, Eric Potter, and I were the sound effect recordists. We needed something for the ship's volley guns, which were positioned high up the masts or along the rail. These fired a small projectile about 1–1½" in dia or, more often, grapeshot. Although it's a more modern weapon (late 19th/early 20th century) we chose the Hotchkiss gun as it is approximately the correct caliber, and the amorers were able to convert it from a breech loading gun to a muzzle loader.
>
> We were also able to use black powder, which produces a different sound when fired than smokeless powder. We fired *round* shot made of lead. We recorded this in a rather

Figure 10.15 Richard King records a Hotchkiss gun with special vintage black powder shells.

Figure 10.16 Richard King and his custom effects recording crew recording Civil War vintage cannons with various types of naval shot in the snow-covered National Guard base in northern Michigan.

small box canyon north of Los Angeles, a shooting range which we rented for the day, and found that the small canyon made the retort of the gun "hang" in the air for a moment, giving us a satisfying and dramatic audio effect.

We had a large array of mics close around the gun, going to several different recorders—a Deva, a DAT machine, and a Nagra IV-S to give us that analogue crunch. We also had several mics downfield, aimed both *at* and *away* from the gun—to get more of the decay and low end, and several mics on the hilltop over which the projectiles were fired to get the missile pass-by whirrs.

The large guns recorded for *Master and Commander* were 12-lb. and 24-lb. field pieces of Civil War vintage. Over a period of several months, the dimensions and construction of the various types of shot had to be researched and then cast from scratch, round shot, bar shot, chain shot, and grape shot, and the armorers made up the black powder charges in linen sacks.

In January 2003, we all convened at a National Guard base in Northern Michigan, which has a very large howitzer range, to do our recording over a three-day period. John Fasal set up close to the gun with his array of mics and recorders. We vaporized a pair of SM-57s which were placed too close to the muzzle of the gun, but before they got fried we got some great sounds from them! Eric Potter was about a quarter mile downrange behind a concrete berm recording shot pass-bys and impacts into a wooden target we had constructed out of oak to simulate a ship's hull.

I was driving around on a snowmobile with a DAT machine and a Neumann 191 recording from as much as a half-mile away. The cold air and especially the open space of the large range definitely affected the sound, but I found that when we put all the channels into Pro Tools and played everything together, the sum was much more dramatic then any of the individual parts. And great fun was had by all.

Smaller Is Often Bigger

Just as you record vehicles in slower low gears to create the illusion of speed, you must look to other, smaller props to sell the illusion of size. Glass and metal chains illustrate this point.

Big chains do not make big chain noise; they make very disappointing clunky sounds. Accurately judging how chains will sound is extremely difficult when you go to the hardware store to pick the correct size and grade of chain for your recording. I take along my tape recorder and listen to the chains through the very microphone I intend to use. How does the microphone hear the chain metal? Small links, as well as brass or brass alloy metal, work best, but you must test them by listening to their movement and clanks through the recorder's microphone, as not all chain links are created equal.

Concerning glass, say you have a sequence in which a huge storefront window is smashed. Do not buy thick sheets of storefront glass. They only sound dull and "thunky." Single-thickness glass sheets make the biggest sounds. We discovered that holding the glass sheet horizontally in the air, then swinging a solid steel bar upward from underneath just as you let go of the glass, produces the best results with longer air-flight time for glass shard ring off.

Remember, you must wear goggles. It is also advisable to wear thick motorcycle gauntlets and wrap your body in packing blankets for protection. However, be aware of unwanted cloth and leather glove movements with all this protective armor.

One of the best glass-breaking sequences I recorded was performed outdoors. My father and I went to an old concrete bridge that crossed a dry streambed. I placed one set of microphones near the glass sheets to break, and the other set down near the bottom. My father then dropped one sheet of glass at a time, making sure it clipped the edge of the bridge railing. The glass burst into shards, cascading a wonderful shower of glass down to the concrete slope below, where I got a very nice impact and shard slide.

An amazing glass recording I made 15 years ago still is being used around town today: the exploding light bulb smash for *The Philadelphia Experiment*. We took an 8-foot 2 × 12 and drilled five rows of 20 holes, the exact width to screw in a light bulb. Into these 100 holes we screwed 100 6-inch fish-tank bulbs. Taking the prop to the Foley stage, I had an assistant hold the bottom of the board so it would stand upright. The assistant wore heavy gloves and goggles; several thick packing blankets were also draped over him. Slipping on my goggles, I took an iron bar to the light bulbs in one smooth swing. The result was an astounding explosion of glass.

The largest wood rips and tears are not recorded with huge logs or thick lumber, but with thin plywood sheets exposed to the weather. The lamination on the plywood comes apart because of being soaked in water and baked in the sun for several years. Stand back a couple of feet from the microphone and pry the layers apart with various intensities. These recordings produce amazing results when combined with the wrenching whine a tree makes as it begins to fall from being chopped through. Veneer and plywood "separation" rips truly sell the desired moment.

IMPORTANCE OF SCRIPT BREAKDOWN

Every producer, director, unit production manager, production coordinator, director of photography, and anyone aspiring to these jobs should read this section very carefully. The described incident is not unique to the film discussed herein, but is one of many. Setting your supervising sound editor before you commence principal photography is an excellent and advisable idea. After reading the script, the supervising sound editor apprises you on a number of sound editorial requirements that lie ahead. Don't just listen to their advice—follow it! They save you tens of thousands, if not hundreds of thousands, of dollars.

Producer Ross Hunter was looking for a full, exciting sound job for his 1970 smash hit, *Airport*. Hunter sent a copy of the screenplay to Joe Sikorski at Universal Studios. Sikorski carefully read through the script, making numerous notes and underlining areas of concern. A few days later he sat down with Hunter and reviewed his notes. He had made a precise list of approximately 120 sound events that concerned him deeply. The producer must guarantee that these recordings would be made during the principal photography process, as all the equipment and labor necessary to create these sounds would be available at that time.

The production company secured the St. Paul Airport in Minnesota, with exterior runway and tarmac filming to occur when the airport was shut down in the evenings. Months passed. The production company had wrapped the shoot and returned to Los Angeles. Several weeks later, Hunter called Sikorski about doing a temp dub for the sequence where George Kennedy tries to get a stuck Boeing 707 out of the soft ground between two runways. The congo line of snow plows and scrapers lines up, awaiting Burt Lancaster's order to move forward and plow the distressed airliner off the airfield, making room to open up runway Two-Niner for the inbound bomb-damaged Trans Global airliner to land. Hunter wanted to have a temp sound effects job underline the visual excitement of the sequence to show it to a test audience and see how it played.

Sikorski said they would be happy to oblige. "You need to send over the sound effects recordings that we asked you to make while you were up there filming." After an awkward pause, Hunter replied, "We forgot. We didn't get any."

Sikorski explained that the studio's sound library did not have the sounds the sequence required. Hence he had given the painstakingly precise "sound-event" notes to the producer in the first place. Hunter understood, then asked Sikorski to work up a budget of what it would take to custom record the sounds he needed. Several days later, Sikorski received a call from Hunter, who had just reviewed the custom recording budget. "Are you out of your mind? This is half the budget of the picture! Couldn't we just go down to LAX [Los Angeles International Airport] and record this stuff?"

Sikorski explained to the producer that, even if they could get permission and cooperation from the FAA to record at Los Angeles International, his team certainly would not be able to get the clean, isolated recordings that sound editors need. He suggested they might try putting together some odds and ends, mixing them together to get through the temp. This ray of hope delighted Hunter. "Anything, try anything!"

In addition to a multitude of other sound effects requirements for the temp dub, Sikorski pulled numerous sounds of jets, motor whines, turbine start-ups, and other noises and cut them into elements to remix as new sound effects masters for the jet revs. A couple of weeks later, Sikorski was on the dubbing stage, supervising the temp mix with Hunter.

An exciting sequence grew to a climax. Burt Lancaster orders the line of snow plows forward. The flight assistant glances at George Kennedy in the pilot's seat, while the aircraft shudders from the engines, straining to pull itself out and says: "Petroni, she won't take much more!" The furrows on Kennedy's brow deepen with determination as he chomps on his cigar. "Well, she's gonna get it!"

Kennedy shoves the engine controls forward with a resolution to either get her out of the mud or tear themselves apart in the effort. Sikorski's newly created jet revs scream out, adding to Alfred Newman's exciting musical score. The angle cuts to a close-up on the landing gear as the tires mash down on wood plankings. Sounds of wood moaning and twisting tell of the incredible weight bearing down. Suddenly the 707 wallows up from the soft ground and lunges out onto the taxiway; the engine revs peak and settle down into a reverse to slow. To be sure, it was an exciting audio moment and a memorable sequence in theatrical film history.

Joe Sikorski soon found himself manufacturing various sound events from other sounds to make do. It is not what he wanted. Customized sound recording undoubtedly would have brought the picture to an even higher level of achievement. It is, however, a tribute to what a creative sound editorial team can do when faced with having to make do with what's at hand.

Sound editors often must work with what they have even when the producer went to the trouble of recording WTs. I was working on a helicopter action movie that involved several very stylish-looking choppers. To add delight to the project, the cinematography was fairly good, especially the aerial action footage. The picture editor had thought through the material most succinctly and had cut it with an eye for action stereophonic sound. I had been informed that the production mixer went to great lengths to record all kinds of helicopter action sounds. Eagerly gleaning the ¼" production tapes, I tried to find the golden recordings that would jump to the forefront and make the show come to life. To my dismay, only a handful of cues were usable. As during the recordings, crew members were constantly talking.

Later, on the re-recording stage, we were mixing the sound effects predubs when one of the producers (also an owner of one of the helicopters) got up. "That's not a Hughes 500! Why didn't you use the wild tracks of the helicopters we recorded?!"

I had had it!! I spun around on him with fed-up looks to kill. "I would have *loved* to have used your wild track recordings! But your crew couldn't keep their mouths shut. If they had kept quiet while your mixer was trying to record your helicopters, then I could have used your wild track recordings! Maybe next time you'll teach your crew how to keep their #$ percent*ing mouths shut when your production mixer is trying to get a priceless recording!"

Suffice to say, I didn't hear another word out of him during the rest of the mix. It is infuriating to spend hours pouring over what should have been fabulous production recordings only to find them filled with voices and other noises. I just could not contain my anger.

FIELD RECORDING IN 5.1

Recording 5.1 ambience "fields" can yield some very exciting results. But one must not be deluded into thinking that 5.1 "imaging" is just what you want for production sound. Believe me, I have been around this block with numerous highly talented, highly qualified sound mixers. The basic issue is that unless you are perfectly aligned with the camera's exact point of view, so that the spatial positioning matches precisely with what the camera lens sees—it will never work.

Take that one step further. When production shoots have multiple camera angles, three, four, five, or more cameras on a common marker, each with its own distinct point of view, you would have to have a 5.1 rig for each camera in precise alignment and movement with each camera. The one problem with this scenario is really twofold. First, you have the problem of close proximity to a camera that makes noise. I am sorry—all cameras make some noise and digital recording has only sharpened the ability to hear it. Second, the crew itself. People, by and large, are totally unaware how noisy they are. Even when they think they are being perfectly silent, they make noise. We have talked about this problem in a previous chapter, so I will not rehash it.

Talk about a postproduction headache! The worst I ever had to handle was 48 channels of production simultaneously. That is expected if you are shooting 70-mm concert performance projects, not for straightforward film shoots; and what about when the director and cinematographer (and rightfully so) want to move the camera, fast and fluidly?

Now, of course, the veteran supervising sound editors know that 5.1 "imaging" recording is great—for postproduction purposes. For this application (at least in terms of feature and television work) the postproduction custom recording game is exactly what this kind of recording is well suited for.

Now, let us say you are shooting a three-camera (fixed position) project, such as a stage play shot on video or film or live concert shoots. These are applications that readily jump to mind that 5.1 "imaging" recordings could really make a difference and give a very live and present image.

If you decide that you want to utilize the 5.1 "imaging" technique, whether it be for postproduction custom recording or if you have a production application that makes sense and it would really yield an exciting difference, then you might want to consider the Schoeps MDMS U Matrix for Double M/S system, as shown in Figure 10.17.

The Double M/S matrix is a supplement for the Double M/S Set. This set is a surround microphone set-up tailored for recording situations in which a small, lightweight, and easy-to-use arrangement is needed. Here are the main properties:

- Only three microphones and channels are required for 5.0 surround.
- It is very small and lightweight.
- It can be protected well against wind (with windscreen and "fur" Windjammer).
- It allows postproduction processing.

The Schoeps Double M/S matrix (type designation DMS Matrix) offers a complete 5.0 surround signal directly. It is a small, sturdy box containing high-quality transformers which form a passive decoder matrix. As can be seen in Figure 10.17, the microphone signals are converted directly into the 5.0 surround signals L/R/C/LS/RS. The directivity functions of the resulting channels are adjusted for optimal sound quality and localization.

An additional switch enables a second setting, which is a 4.0 four-channel L/R/LS/RS set-up without the center channel, optimized for ambience recording. Phantom powering is required on only three of the output channels: L, R, and LS.

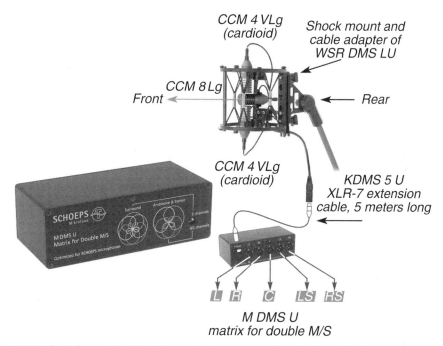

CCM 4 VLg
(cardioid)

Shock mount and
cable adapter of
WSR DMS LU

CCM 8 Lg
Front

Rear

CCM 4 VLg
(cardioid)

KDMS 5 U
XLR-7 extension
cable, 5 meters long

L   R   C   LS   RS

M DMS U
matrix for double M/S

Figure 10.17 The Schoeps Double M/S matrix (type designation DMS Matrix) offers a complete 5.0 surround signal directly. Photo courtesy of the Schoeps Corporation.

PREPARING FOR SUCCESSFUL RECORDINGS

Put together a kit of supplies and tools to take along on location recording sessions. The one thing you can count on is that unforeseen problems and "whoopsies" are parts of your recording adventure. The larger the crew and the more complex the scope of work, the more Murphy's Law ("Whatever can go wrong, will") rises up to try and frustrate you.

Probably the most common shortcoming in field recording is lack of an adequate and dependable power supply. You do not find an abundance of AC wall outlets built into the rocks in the field. Therefore, pay attention to the inventory of batteries necessary to sustain your equipment during your session. Not all batteries are created equal, especially battery packs unique to certain recording devices and custom designed to be used only with those units. This is where the analog Nagra ¼" machines show they are such great workhorses. The internal battery cavity holds 12 D-cell batteries, which, when the recorder is properly used, easily sustain the machine all day long, and longer. Have a full set of back-up batteries securely packed and sealed should your battery meter test suddenly plunge.

The other great thing about D-cell power is that if you do break down in the middle of nowhere with battery shortcomings, just go to the nearest convenience store and you are back in business. I shy away from using any tape recorder, whether analog or digital, that has custom-designed batteries unique to that unit. Where do I find emergency battery supplies if I am up in the High Sierras? I doubt the local trading post has any custom batteries in the stockroom, let alone the JMV-3871/X88 rectangular power cells required by a particular portable digital machine.

Towels are extremely useful, in covering and insulating equipment, in drying things that get wet, or even in helping isolate wind buffets in emergencies. I usually keep a couple of bath towels and several hand towels in the trunk of the car for such use. In addition to traditional towels, towelette packets with pre-moistened wipes are extremely handy.

Keep several plastic clothes bags from the dry cleaner in a separate paper bag. Plastic clothes bags make excellent microphone and equipment wraps when recording in damp, drizzle, or even a full-fledged downpour. Use $^3/_4''$ paper tape to wrap the plastic clothes bag tightly around the recorder or microphone(s) so that loose plastic does not flap about, making unwanted noise.

Adhesive tape is very handy. You should use a wide but gentle paper tape if you need to tape microphone cable firmly against the side of a vehicle to keep cable vibration from spoiling the recording. You do not want to pull the tape up and have the paint job come with it. I like to have a roll of $^1/_2''$ Scotch Magic Tape for paperwork or lightweight applications, as well as a roll of gaffer's tape or at least duct tape for heavy-duty needs. I also keep several colors of $^3/_4''$ paper tape for color-code labeling. You will also need several Sharpie markers of different colors.

Always keep a tool kit, including both full-sized Phillips and flat-head screwdrivers (in addition to a fine instrument size of each). You should have a claw hammer, a 1-inch paintbrush never used for painting, a pair of needle-nosed pliers, and a standard set of pliers. Include large and small sets of Allen wrenches.

Stock a separate head cleaner kit, with a can of compressed air to blow dust and debris out of the equipment, along with head cleaner and head cleaning swabs secured in heavy-duty zipper-lock freezer bags. Include a steno or small notepad so that you or your assistant can jot down recording information to assist in the sound library work that soon follows.

Pack a set of flares in the car for both emergency use and traffic control. Also pack a fire extinguisher, just in case. Purchase at least two heavy-duty flashlights for your kit. Many recording sessions are done in the night. You can also use flashlights as microphone reference points for the shooter to see. As your recording experience increases, you will develop a system of signaling with flashlights rather than risking audio intrusion on a recording by speaking.

Always have a personal safety kit. This should include a standard first-aid kit with the basic bandages, gauzes, iodine, medical tape, and snake bite kit. Fortify the first-aid kit with good eye wash, petroleum jelly, calamine lotion, strong sun block, and insect repellent.

Include several pairs of ear plugs to protect the eardrums from the sound of close proximity gunfire.

The personal safety kit should also include several pairs of goggles and heavy construction gloves. You should have a little accessories bag to keep in the safety kit that has safety pins, a good pair of scissors, and a box of industrial single-edged razor blades or an Exacto knife.

When recording sound effects outdoors, especially in desert regions, dehydration and sunstroke are real dangers. Many technicians get deeply involved and forget that

Figure 10.18 The lonely recordist.

the sun is beating down on the top of their uncovered head, or they forget to use sunscreen SPF 35 on their face and arms. Three hours later, they wonder why they feel funny and their skin feels tight and crispy. You should also include a water spray-bottle. Being able to spray water onto the body or onto a prop you are recording is also very useful.

Take along a change of comfy and warm clothes, especially socks and shoes. I have lost count of recording trips where, for one reason or another, I either fell into or found it necessary to get into water, such as a mountain stream, pounding surf, flooded fields, swimming pools, or other liquid masses that will spoil your attire. I especially remember what the sloppy mud and clay of Oklahoma can do, not only to your clothing but also to your equipment and vehicle mats.

When you know you must put yourself into the wet and muck to properly achieve an audio performance, do what is necessary, no matter what you are wearing. Hence, you should record in junk clothes, taking a change of clothing with you. Remember, wear cotton clothing, not nylon or plastic, as synthetic fibers make "shushy" noises when you move, obviously spoiling your recording.

Proper planning and preparation of equipment and supplies go a long way to help you achieve supremely recorded sound effects. The rest is limited only by your own imagination. But I guarantee you, some of the fondest times you will remember for years to come are the custom-recording adventures that you made to capture new and exciting sound effects!

Chapter 11
The Sound Librarian
The Curator of an Audio Empire

"The best chefs collect the best ingredients before they start cooking—and the best sound editors approach sound effects the same way. Recording fresh sounds and building a library of them is more important than the latest digital "gizmo" or plug-in. You don't need an atomic eggbeater to make a cake. It might make it faster—but not always *better*."

– Steve Lee, Weddington Productions

Custom recording new sound is vital! It is what keeps our work fresh and exciting. But recording the new sound dues is not enough. If you ever hope to efficiently work with the recordings you spent so much time making, adopt a sound library system that not only assimilates the data but offers swift and easy access to it. A dedicated sound librarian developing and maintaining the sound library helps. Because few of us can afford such a luxury, we must do it ourselves. In my particular case, I am too protective of my material not to do it myself. This is not necessarily bad. Being your own librarian gives you an incredible edge because you have an intimate knowledge of not only each cue's labels, but you also know exactly how you entered and "cleaned" the material.

THE EVOLUTION OF "FINDING IT"

Supervising sound editors know they must work quickly and be extremely flexible in custom recording and gathering precise sound cues from the sound effects library to mount their film or audio project. Before the advent of digital sound technology, the most common media in which to store sound effects were 35-mm magnetic film (both monaural stripe and fullcoat for multichannel stereo), $\frac{1}{4}$" tape, and audio cassette tape. A few unique libraries transferred sounds to 4-channel $\frac{1}{2}$" tape or 24-track 2" tape (using time code as a reference), but they were not really part of the mainstream theatrical sound editorial community.

Figure 11.1 At Weddington Productions, thousands of ¼″ tapes are kept in a temperature- and humidity-controlled environment, even after they have been digitally transferred to DAT cassettes. These tapes await retransfer as soon as technology significantly improves analog-to-digital converters or geometrically higher sampling rates and bit depth. At that point, it is worthwhile to return to the original ¼″ tapes to take advantage of the analog source. (Photo by David Yewdall.)

For sound effects, most of us started custom recording our sound effects on ¼″ tape in the 1970s and early 1980s. Back then we carefully edited and "leadered-out" the individual sound cues by splicing in white ¼″ leader. Most of the time we physically wrote the cue number on each white section of white tape. In this manner, the transfer operator could easily count the white leaders that would spin across the sound head at high speed. Some used a red Sharpie to edge every tenth sound cue leader, making it even easier for a transfer operator to identify and spin down to cue 46, for instance. He or she simply counted as four red-edged leaders flew by and then paid closer attention to counting the last six white leaders.

OPTICAL SOUND TO MAGNETIC FILM

Thousands of priceless sound effects have filtered down to us from previous years on magnetic 35-mm film; many were carefully remastered from 35-mm optical track. These first sound effects were originally recorded in a device known as a sound camera. The equipment was so bulky it had to be mounted inside a vehicle called the sound truck to move it quickly from one location to another. The sound mixer recorded

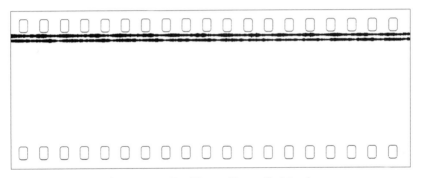

Figure 11.2 The 35-mm film optical track.

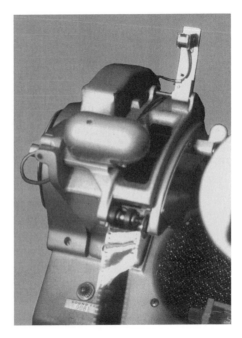

Figure 11.3 This Moviola is equipped to read both magnetic and optical sound. The editor has flipped up the magnetic sound head (single track) out of position to check the optical soundtrack from a section of release print. Note the thick cylindrical unit protruding from the film. An exciter lamp inside shines a narrow beam of light through the optical track. The light is read and translated into modulations.

directly into the sound camera, which "photographed" an image of the sound onto the area just inside the perforation holes of 35-mm film.

This continual undulating area of "photographed" sound is known as an optical track. Optical track technology still is used today in theatrical presentations of features presented in theatres with no digital technology. Also, optical track still is used in the audio presentation of 16-mm prints. The sound is created through an exciter lamp in the sound camera that creates one of many types of optical track formats. The film is then sent to the laboratory and developed. The optical soundtrack can then be played on a synchronizer, Moviola, or projector also equipped with a playback exciter lamp optical head. Light passes through the optical soundtrack image of the film and strikes a photoelectric cell, causing current fluctuations that accurately reproduce the analog audio signal for playback.

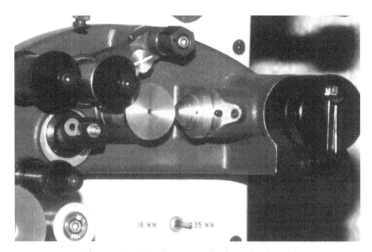

Figure 11.4 Projector optical reader head.

During the first three decades of motion picture sound, sound editors had to work with their tracks very carefully. An editor would take much greater care in ordering the needed sound effects, especially the number of repetitions. If cutting a gun battle, you ordered enough repetitions of a particular gun to cut the sequence. If you suddenly came up short or ruined the material with which you were working, the remedy was not as easy as it is today with digital technology. Now we simply highlight the needed sound and duplicate it with a computer keystroke. An editor back then, though, would have to order the desired sound cue from the sound librarian, who would build the master effect into a roll with other 35-mm optical masters, which would then be shipped with a work order to be loaded onto an optical camera and shot over and over again onto a fresh roll of 35-mm film. The magazine of film would then be shipped to the laboratory to be developed. Depending on how busy the sound department and laboratory were, a day or two could easily pass before a sound editor would receive reprints of the necessary gunshot effect to complete the work.

Not only did the sound editor need to be careful about the amount of material ordered, but also with handling the film. Most sound editors wore at least one white cotton glove so that fingerprints or skin oils would not be left inadvertently on the track. The emulsion of the track could easily be scratched, causing pops and crackles. The sound editor laced up the optical track on the sound head of the Moviola. After adjusting the sync point of the sound effect, the sound editor carefully noted on the film the exact foot and frame point for the sound assistant to build the cue into individual reels of sound called "sound units." These units held numerous individual sound cues, spaced precisely apart by "fill leader" (35-mm film that was usually recycled newsreel or release prints).

The sound editor assembled sound cues with the "fill leader" together with Mercer clips. This roll was then sent to assembly, where the assistant hot spliced the sections of film together; and, using "blooping ink," the assistant made sure the splice points did not have any exposed scraped emulsion areas that would cause loud pops due to a bright burst of light leaking into the optical reader.

With the advent of magnetic film in the early 1950s, the cut-and-assembly technique changed dramatically. Although the sound librarian still had to send assembled masters of sound effects to the transfer department for quantities of reprints to be made for sound editors, 35-mm magnetic film was not developed at a lab. Once it had been removed from the 35-mm magnetic film recorder, it was instantly ready to be broken down and used by the sound editor.

The sound editor still threaded the 35-mm magnetic film under the sound head of the Moviola or synchronizer and still made precise sync notations, but instead of preassembling the sound cues with sections of filler using mercer clips for hot splicing, the sound editor merely hung the cut sections of magnetic sound effects on a series of hooks in a trim bin.

After the sound editor completed cutting the reel, the trim bin was rolled into the assistant's room, where an apprentice assembled the individual sound cues into the sound units. As before, the empty distance between sound cues was spaced out with "fill leader," but instead of hot splicing the cuts and painting the splices with blooping ink, the apprentice used a Rivas tape splicer and taped the backside of the film.

Whether the sound editor cuts with optical sound, magnetic film, or modern digital technologies, the basic techniques and demands on the sound librarian have changed very little. As this book has repeated over and over—only the tools change; technical disciplines, artistic techniques, strategies, and philosophy of sound always have remained the same—and always will.

ORGANIZING A SYSTEM TO FIND STUFF

At the heart of the sound editorial world is the sound library—a vast wealth of sounds, both historical and designed. The sound library must be a highly organized and protected shelter, safe from the ravages of heat and moisture, safe from destruction or loss, yet available at a moment's notice as demands may require. The sound librarian is the gatekeeper, shepherd of the flock, audio accountant, charged with the responsibility of organizing and protecting the limitless frontier of sound bites.

The sound library is never complete—ever growing, ever expanding. Challenges to the sound librarian not only include the management and care of hundreds of thousands of sounds, but also involve keeping track of the continually evolving technology by which the library is archived, cataloged, accessed, and protected.

I find sound library work both relaxing and enriching. I have learned much about our world through listening to and working with my own sound library. Some of the most enjoyable times in my audio work have been dealing with historical sound effects, especially recordings of that which does not exist today, or of museum pieces no longer utilized. When was the last time you heard a Daimler-Benz engine or a Messerschmitt 109 approach and rip by at emergency war speed? What distinguished the sound of a P-38 Lightning with its turbo-charged engines from all other aircraft? One can almost catch the acrid smell of burned oil in the nostrils after a long day of processing and remastering these fabulous historic recordings. It can be very stimulating, especially knowing your work goes toward preserving and archiving these vanishing wonders.

Assigning Sound Cues Part Numbers

No industry standard exists by which one builds and maintains a sound library. Sure, techniques abound, some designed to serve and expedite the sound editor, others designed only to serve the supervisor/owner, shrouding the contents of the library from outside influences.

The first and foremost starting point for precise identification and accessibility of an audio cue is carefully assigning a "part number" to each sound cue entered in the library. Regardless of whether a computer database is utilized, nothing is more accurate in recognition than a dedicated part number.

"Topic-Roll-Cue" System

Some sound libraries are set up with initials to designate the topic, prior to the actual part number, such as CR6-87. "CR" stands for crashes, "6" stands for sound roll number, and "87" stands for cue #87. The transfer operator reads the sound effect numbers from the transfer order form, seeing the need to print CR6-87 for a sound effects editor. From the tape rolls stored on the library shelf, the transfer operator withdraws tape CR6, loads it into the playback machine (usually an analog $\frac{1}{4}''$ or $\frac{1}{2}''$ tape, but sometimes a digital DAT), and spins down to cue #87. If the material is archived on $\frac{1}{4}''$ tape, the transfer operator listens to the 40-cycle tone voice slates, which at high speed "beep" as they fly by the playback head. If the material is archived on $\frac{1}{2}''$ tape, the transfer operator enters the time code reference, which spins the tape down to the precise point on the tape. The transfer operator decides on which of the three available channels the desired sound cue can be found.

If the material is archived on digital DAT, the transfer operator simply enters the PNO (program number) on the keypad of the machine or remote on the unit's keypad and then presses the play button. The machine spins at 200 times speed to find the precise PNO requested.

As library part numbering systems go, the "topic-roll-cue" system at least allows for an ongoing growth of the sound library, in a linear fashion, while keeping common topic sound effects together. Instead of sound rolls numbering from 1 and progressing numerically, sound rolls have initials for topic designations and any number of rolls in that category. This is not a common system.

"Linear Numbering" System

Many sound libraries use a linear style of numbering rolls and sound effects, making for an easy and universally understood way to cross-verify material. This system works especially well when mastering sound cues to consecutive digital DATs. This system can be applied whether you are sending a transfer order to have analog transfers made (i.e., 35-mm fullcoat or 35-mm single stripe) or you are sending an order to have the sound cues downloaded into a nonlinear computer editing system, such as Pro Tools. Say the transfer order notes that DAT 0120-73 must be transferred stereophonically.

The transfer operator knows it is the 120th DAT in the sound library, puts the DAT into the machine, and punches in 73 as the PNO.

ARCHIVING STABILITY

In today's computer audio file environment, many an editor has suddenly lost giga-bytes of audio files when a drive corrupted, was accidentally dropped, or died in some other rather uncreative fashion. I have heard too many horror stories of "I didn't have any back-up" or "I should have burned the stuff to disk before I started work!" or some other wrist-cutting statement.

Most of us have crossed over from the days when we cut the sound for our proj-ects on 35-mm fullcoat and 35-mm single stripe. Many of us adapted to the changing technology and growing success of our businesses and scope of work. Very few of us working today remember recording sound effects from a sound truck with the optical camera—no, I am not one of them. Most of us remember venturing out from our editing rooms to record with Sony TCD-5 audio cassette recorders, then graduating to Nagra ¼", along with higher quality microphones as budgets allowed. With early experimen-tations in digital recordings, many of us tried the clumsy and cumbersome Sony F-1, while others ventured into true experimenting with incredibly expensive digital tape decks that were only teases of things to come.

Then, in the late 1980s, the first gray-market digital DAT decks were adopted by those who wanted digital technology in the field. As you can see, this gave us a sound effects library compilation filled with a frightening intermixture of technologies and formats.

As a sound library tool, digital DAT was the answer to many technological and organizational problems, not the least of which is the ability to defeat print-through of overmodulated sound effects such as gunshots, explosions, crashes, metal, and so forth. Sound librarians jumped with joy as they were able to record a digitized program code number with each sound effect recorded on the DAT. During search-and-seize time to make transfers of these sound effects, nothing was faster in the tape format world.

DAT technology presented a great opportunity to retransfer our multi-format sound libraries into digital-based realms, a medium that would solve a host of prob-lems that had plagued sound artists for decades. By 1987 the race was on to convert to a DAT master system. Naturally, a new set of problems and disagreements arose, not the least of which was understanding the differences between the standard VU meter, which sound craftspeople had been using for decades, and digital peak meters that digital DAT machines used. This misunderstanding caused thousands of overmodulated transfers to DAT among many linear thinking sound facilities throughout the industry. This costly mistake is felt even today, as many libraries had to return to their 35-mm mag and ¼" originals vaulted away in cold storage and remaster them all over again.

Even the manufacturers of the digital DAT machines disagreed on what "0" VU equaled on their DAT meters. Many claimed it was at –12 dB on the peak meter; most thought it was –16 dB. Still others who did not understand the calibration differences at all simply thought that, like Nagra machines, they should set their "0" dB reference

Figure 11.5 As the sound librarian at Weddington Productions, Steve Lee carefully edited original ¼" tapes before having them digitally transferred to DAT master tapes. Eventually these DATs will be retransferred to CD-ROMs and DVDs as carefully prepared audio files (such as AIFF, WAV, or SDII).

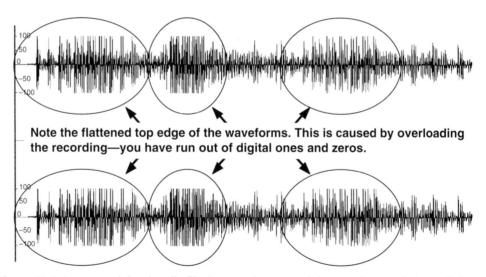

Figure 11.6 An overmodulated audio file, improperly mastered due to using −12 dB instead of −18 dB or more = "0" VU.

tone at −8 dB on the digital peak meter. All these choices resulted in overmodulation, and, depending on the degree of error, you can easily see the degree of the disaster.

After several years of disagreement and trial and error, most of us now generally accepted and understood that the "0" VU level equaled −18 dB on the digital DAT peak meter. Since many action sound effects, such as gunshots, explosions, crashes, and impacts, were recorded in the "saturation" style (see Chapter 10), that extra headroom certainly would be needed to properly remaster the analog recording. Many sound editorial facilities, especially those with a reputation for high-concept sound effects, started using –20 dB as equaling "0" on the VU meter.

Mastering to CD-Rs—and Then DVD-Rs

The CD-ROM was a great and cost-effective per megabyte rate for drag-and-drop storage medium for several years. With a maximum capacity of 700 megabytes, the cost hovered at around a penny per 15 megabytes of storage. As the cost of DVD-R recorders and disks dropped, the cost per megabyte for storage became extremely beneficial. A DVD-R holds approximately 6 times as much data as a CD-R; and with the introduction of Blu-Ray technology the storage protection capacities are astounding.

Even so, the traditional DVD-R is assured considerable life as a cheap, high-capacity, and affordable way to record to a medium that, if properly stored and maintained, has the ability to sustain a very long shelf life. Unlike a digital DAT, or other analog media, DVD-Rs can be scanned by computer archival software, and, in a very short time, you can build an extremely complex and thorough database in which to find the material you need.

Following are three important things you must be aware of in handling CD-R/DVD-R.

1. Do not touch the data surface of a disk. Do not set a disk on a tabletop, and of course never slide the disk's data surface across anything. Doing so will cause scratches and damage that does not allow the CD-R/DVD-R player's laser to properly read bytes of data, causing error and the danger of permanent loss of audio files.
2. Do not store CD-Rs or DVD-Rs in an environment that is too hot, or atop equipment that radiates heat. If the disk warps, you cannot get it to read correctly in a player, resulting in the loss of material on it.
3. Do not store these disks in bright light for any length of time. Whenever I transport my disks from one facility to another, I either pack them in black leather carrying cases with zip flaps, or, if I am moving full racks of CD-Rs or DVD-Rs, I spread heavy towels over them to avoid exposure to direct sunlight in transit.

Several of us in the sound community ran fade tests on various brands of disks, placing them in direct sunlight as it shone through an open window for various lengths of time to test the stability of the disks after bright light. We discovered that not all CD and DVD brands are created equal. Two of the brands tested faded, resulting in a permanent loss of data after only 15 minutes of direct exposure to sunlight. Others lasted for several hours; still two others took 2 weeks of day-in and day-out exposure to show fade damage. Regardless of the rate of fade damage, such a test should motivate you always to keep your CD-Rs and DVD-Rs stored in a dimly lit and temperature-stable environment.

To prepare audio files for disk mastering, the sound librarian first "cleans up" (explained later in this chapter) each audio sound file until he or she is satisfied it is ready to be committed to be "burned" to a CD-R or DVD-R disk.

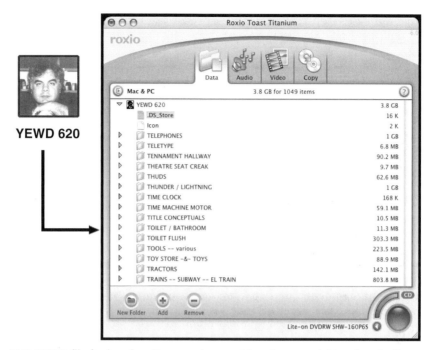

YEWD 620

Figure 11.7 DVD-R file for burning. Once you have put together your folder of audio files, you must run Norton Utilities software on it, as well as computer "virus" and "worm" checks so that you do not include dangerous anomalies onto your CD-R and DVD-R masters.

The sound librarian creates a folder and names it; in the case of my own sound library, and the example being shown, the disk name is YEWD 620. YEWD 620 is the DVD-R "disk address." If you desire a custom icon on your DVD-R you must highlight a file icon that has the desired image on it. I always leave an empty file folder with my library icon image on the desktop of the computer. Then you will Apple keystroke/"i" to open the information window. The icon image will be shown in the upper left corner of the information window. Move the cursor over and highlight the icon image; then copy the icon by using Apple keystroke/"C." Move the cursor up to the upper left-hand corner and tap on the little gray box to put the window away. Next, you will highlight the new DVD-R file folder that you just created and open its information window. Highlight the file icon in the information window and paste the custom icon (Apple keystroke/"V") that you have just copied from your master icon image.

With the assistance of color-coding and the infinite variations of custom icons available, your DVD-Rs are easily recognized as a workstation copy from a vault master, or a work-in-progress back-up from a finished DVD-R master. I use unique icons to distinguish Foley back-up DVD-Rs or dialog back-up DVD-Rs from anything else I am using. You create additional topic folders that reside inside the DVD-R master folder. You place audio files to be mastered inside these topic folders.

After the DVD-R master folder is filled (not to exceed 4.3 gigabytes), you are very wise to run Norton Utilities' Disk Doctor and at least one anti-virus software to ensure that the data directories and resource forks are not damaged or missing. It does not do any good to master an audio file and not to be able to use it later because it is damaged or does not open and function.

Close the DVD-R master folder and click on it twice. The folder menu will pop up, displaying the inner topic folders. Now is the time for you to reposition the folder window on the computer monitor screen *exactly* the way you want it to appear whenever the disk is used later, for this is exactly the position and configuration that the DVD-R will permanently format it, in the manner in which it will always open.

Once these processes are complete, you boot up the DVD-R recording software, such as Adaptec's "Toast." You must select the DATA option on the software window to burn a DVD-R for data storage. You drag-and-drop the folder, in this case "YEWD 620" of the master file to be burned onto blank DVD-R. The software scans it and shows it to you in its own menu window.

The drawer of the recorder opens as a prompt asks for a blank DVD-R to be loaded. Place a fresh disk in the tray and close it, commencing the recording of data called "burning." A menu will appear, asking at what speed you wish to burn the disk. Even with today's ultra high-speed burners that can burn at incredible speeds, I still burn my master DVD-Rs at "BEST QUALITY" (slower) speed. You will suffer fewer artifacts later.

Note the open folder to the left. This is only to show you what the folders inside the computer disk drive looks like. Note that the software window shows YEWD 620 as a disk icon (the custom icon is shown as the first item as a document). The audio files inside the first folder show exactly as they did in the original drive.

Burning a duplicate master back-up copy is always wise, as it can be stored in a dark temperate place so that, if necessary, it can generate additional copies in the future. A work copy is made, one used for the day-to-day workstation environment.

Even if you are working in a big editorial environment with terabyte servers, you still need to burn DISK vault DVD-Rs as protection. Drives will fry, files can corrupt—accidental deletions will always happen. Without a dependable disk vault archive, you are playing Russian Roulette.

BASIC "CLEANING UP" OF AUDIO FILES

The sound cue rarely comes directly from the microphone into the recording device in a pristine configuration. Though many of us personally learned and taught our colleagues and recording assistants to speak as little as possible when recording sounds in the field, unwanted vocals always need to be removed. In addition, the audio action does not always start on cue or play out as planned.

We always try to record everything during a session. Even if it goes wrong, the sound event that follows has value and a use sometime, somewhere. While recording sound effects for *Christine*, I had briefed the dual recording team not to speak or react, even if disaster struck. If an accident should occur, I wanted the sound of it to be clean. As it turned out, the stunt driver lost control of the car during a power reverse on a section of highway just wet down by the water truck. He spun off the road and slid right for my brand new Cadillac El Dorado. In my heart, I knew he could not avoid a collision, yet I held the stereo microphones steady as I watched. Fortunately, the stunt driver narrowly missed my car, after slamming the transmission into first gear and gunning the engine so hard that it threw a rooster tail of mud and dust across not only my own car but two others. Of course one unplanned bonus to this near catastrophe was that we got a great clean recording of a high whine gear box with tires spinning in mud, swerving up onto the pavement and a great wet spin-out skid as the car throttled down the road. And no, not one person on my team let out a vocal reaction, not even a heavy breath *until* I yelled, "and CUT!!" Then of course everybody came unglued.

The point was that I was prepared and disciplined to keep the mouths of my team and my own *shut*. My recording crews did the same. However, many recording crews often talk and react, making all kinds of unnecessary movements and extraneous noise, such as eating, gum chewing, or jingling coins in their pockets while recording. I do not like editing out these voices every time I need to use the audio cue. If a sound editor is pressed for time and has to cut the sound cue for an edit session hurriedly, he or she is more likely to overlook vocals and extraneous noises and movement, which only show up on the re-recording stage later. Therefore, make sure that all nonperformance vocals are edited out of the master, and that you have carefully gone through the sound cue to ferret out other problems, which must only be edited out and fixed repeatedly during sound editorial sessions. Cutting and cleaning the sound cue once prior to CD-R or DVD-R mastering prevents all this unnecessary work.

Listen for digital ticks, zits, or glitches, and be prepared to remove them. Using the digital pencil, you can "draw" out a digital tick simply by zooming in very close, so that you can clearly and easily connect the waveform from the exact point at which it suddenly shoots straight up to the point (usually only a few samples in length) to where the tick returns to the normal waveform. By drawing across it in this manner, the digital tick itself disappears, and you probably will not hear any residual aftereffect. (Listen to cue #14 on the accompanying CD to better understand the sounds of digital ticks, zits, and glitches.)

Drawing out the digital tick is not always possible, especially when working with a very active sound with a very busy frequency field. Sometimes with harmonic sounds it is impossible to completely purge the audio file without hearing a bump. Two other options of removing ticks is to cut them out, being careful to select cut points where the audio wave is at a curve point that matches smoothly and does not cause yet another tick or snap.

When all else fails, you should import the audio file into a Pro Tools edit session, cut out the offending problem using the "shuttle" option, then build in cross-fades until you are happy with the resulting playback.

Sometimes neither one of these options solves the problem. In such cases, it is necessary to create a Pro Tools edit session, import the audio file into the session, find the offending problem(s), and then cut and cross-fade to blend away the bump that a direct cut cannot solve. Once I have cut, cross-faded, and reviewed the audio file, I then create a new copy by using the Bounce-to-Disk option. (The mechanics of digital editing and manipulation is discussed in Chapter 18.)

Once the new audio file has been re-recorded using Bounce-to-Disk, I then throw the original file into the computer trash can and flush it away. The new bounced file

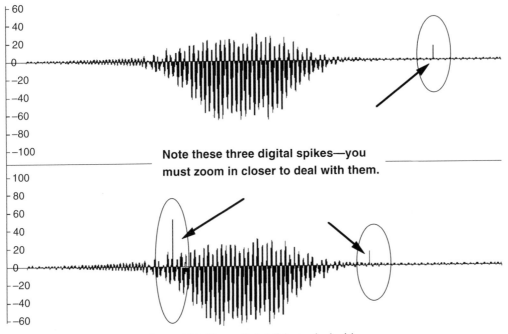

Note these three digital spikes—you
must zoom in closer to deal with them.

Figure 11.8 Three digital ticks to deal with.

becomes the audio file to master the CD-R or DVD-R—free of those bedeviling ticks and snaps.

COMPLEX SOUND EFFECT MASTERING

When I transfer my sound effects into the digital realm of my workstation, I utilize the strengths of both digital and analog technologies in what I refer to as a grass roots, common sense approach. I do not like to overprocess the sound cue or cut raw material. My goal is to deliver to the re-recording console a cut session of sounds not requiring the mixer to signal process and noise gate to the degree it does when material comes completely raw.

Depending on the rawness and dirtiness of the original recording, the effort devoted by the mixer to each cue can take a staggering amount of stage time. As the hourly rate ticks by, the mixer can be stuck with the time-consuming task of trimming equalization on each cue or feeding some cues through noise gates.

On the other hand, prepolished sound mastering is not a task for beginners. The most common mistake made by sound editors who start working with signal processing is that they lay on excessive amounts, using the various DSP (digital signal processing) functions with the finesse of a rhinoceros suffering from diarrhea. They try to make the sound effect as pristine as if it were a final mix. You can overprocess the sound effect to a point that the mixer cannot unwind or use it for the project. The beginner does not understand that the dynamics and character of sound change when

Figure 11.9 A simple but extremely effective signal path for entering sound into the digital domain. The DAT sends the analog signal from the Sony deck, up to the 30-band Klark-Teknik equalizer, down to the Night Technologies EQ3, down to the Eventide Harmonizer, then into the Pro Tools interface.

cues are layered together. What may sound good when played by itself may be completely lost and overwhelmed when layered in against other sound cues. If you remove or manipulate the audio file's frequency and dynamic qualities too much before mastering, you may emasculate its potential use later during sound editorial.

If I am transferring sound effects cues into the computer, I use a Night Technologies EQ3 equalizer in tandem with the Klark-Teknik DN 30/30, a 30-band graphic equalizer. The signal path of the sound goes from the DAT machine (analog outs), through the two equalizers, then into the Pro Tools interface, where it is digitized into the computer. The Night Technologies EQ3 equalizer allows tremendous flexibility in a virtual nonphase shift environment to manipulate the range of frequencies to emphasize, especially in the high end, referred to as the "air" bands. I experience tremendous success with all kinds of sounds that need extra help with high-end clarity. Adding such high-end emphasis with any other equalizer always brings a rush of bias hiss or unwanted "shushy"-type anomalies.

Although nonlinear editing is wonderful and convenient, DSP functions, especially regarding equalization options, are still a bit "edgy" for my ears, lending an undesirable sterility and a noticeable footprint of signal processing to the sound. There

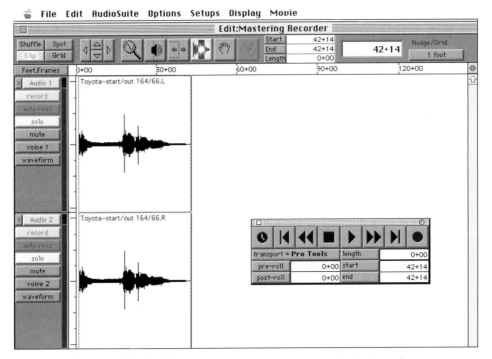

Figure 11.10 Digitizing (recording) audio data into a Pro Tools session.

are those who can make magic with these plug-ins, but not many. It is kind of like the adage that anybody can pick up a bow and draw it across the stings of a violin, but how many really make music? And then there are those who can play a Stradivarius.

I digitize my sound into the computers two different ways. I will either transfer an entire sound effect DAT or ¼" tape into a Pro Tools session. Then I will break the transfer audio file down into the desired individual cues. As I make each cut I will tap twice on the cue (which will pop up the NAME AS option) and rename the segment as I wish the new audio cues to be named. If the audio files are stereo, I name the left channel (always ending the name with .L). Then I highlight the name and copy the name (Apple + "C" key) so that every letter and space will be exact. I then tap twice on the right channel of the cut clip. The NAME AS option window will appear. I highlight the name that is there and paste in the copied name from left channel (Apple + "V" key). I then back up two spaces (to erase .L) and type in .R. I move on to the next cut audio cue and rename it.

After I have cut up and renamed all of the cue clips that I want and eliminated the unwanted audio material, I highlight all of the cut audio segments; then I go up to the upper right-hand side of the Pro Tools session window to the AUDIO bar and open that menu up, come three-fourths of the way down the list of options to "Export Selected as Files," and release. Up comes the OUTPUT OPTIONS menu.

You must make a series of choices to make sure that your final audio files are exactly as you want them and exactly where you want them.

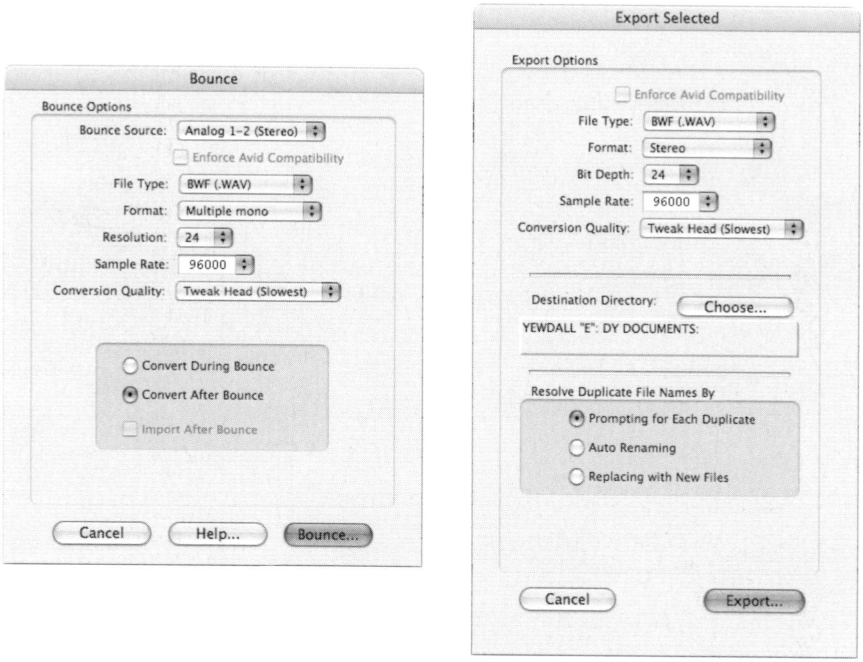

Figure 11.11 The Output Options Window to "Export Selected as Files."

FILE FORMAT: You may choose to output your new audio files in Sound Designer II (SDII), AIFF, or .WAV.

RESOLUTION: You can output your new audio files in either 16 or 24 bit.

CHANNELS: You can output your audio files in either mono (1), or stereo from .L/.R (interleaved). If you have stereo audio files and intend to work with them in nonlinear environments then you will want your stereo .L and .R files to be output as mono (1). The stereo output option is when you are making audio files that you wish to burn later as audio CD disks—which means that they will be at a sampling rate of 44.1 kHz and interleaved as stereo from your .L/.R source.

SAMPLE RATE: You can output your files at the following sample rates: 96 kHz, 48 kHz, or 44.1 kHz (if you are using Pro Tools HD).

CONVERSION QUALITY: You can choose how good the quality of the output will be. Like most things, higher quality means trading out speed. You can output it: LOW (fastest); GOOD; BETTER; BEST; TWEAK HEAD (slowest). Obviously I never opt for anything but the "Tweak Head" speed. With today's gigahertz speed CPUs, there is no reason to opt for anything of less quality.

DESTINATION DIRECTORY: You push "CHOOSE" and a window will come up for you to guide a path for the computer to place your new audio file outputs into a particular target folder.

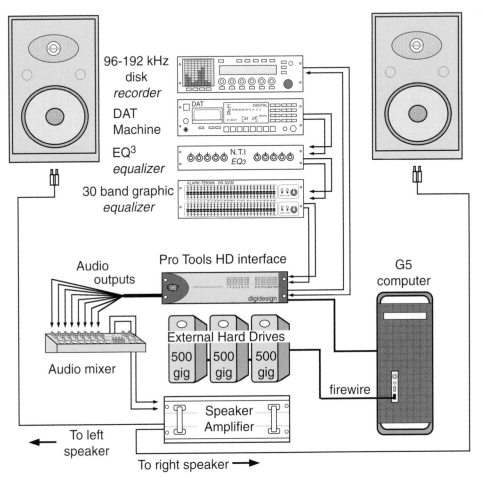

Figure 11.12 A typical workstation SIGNAL PATH.

RESOLVE DUPLICATE FILENAMES BY: You will choose how you wish the computer to deal with any accidental duplicates. This will not become an issue if you are targeting a file folder simply to hold your new files for later disbursement.

Today's hard-drive storage space capacities are light years beyond where they were just a few years ago. Believe it or not, when I worked on *Starship Troopers*, a 9-gig drive was as big as we could get. Now, we think nothing of hooking up multiple 500-gig drives or 1- to 2-terabyte drives. Every editor will have his or her own way of using drives. Some companies will work from a server; some editors will dedicate entire 350-gig drives to each project. It all depends on the project and the budget that the editor (or company) has to work with.

When loading a drive with audio files or cutting sessions, do not invade the storage capacity of the drive beyond the recommended 10 percent margin. On a 300-gigabyte drive, this would leave you with a relatively safe working storage volume of 30 gigs. That may be a lot of computer memory to some, but those of us who cut theatrical-style sound know we need much more drive space, as disk memory gets chewed up in a hurry. This is primarily why I spend seemingly immense, yet appropriate, preparation time before cutting. Recognize the need to prepare and polish sound effects before you cut them, a seemingly obvious concept often overlooked in the heat of battle when cutting complex sequences.

My primary thought in prepping audio sound files is to distill them down to a reasonable and workable size, cutting out unnecessary and wasteful parts that gobble up valuable disk-storage space. Once the sound is trimmed to a realistic size, I decide whether I should spend the time and effort to polish it even further, such as building in fade-ins/fade-outs. Be very careful in making fade decisions in the audio file master, as they cannot be removed from the editorial session later. Conversely, as you become proficient in the art of complex audio cleaning and preprep, you will discover that sounds with logical permanent fade-ins or fade-outs built into them save much time for the editor later.

Listen to "CLEANING A SOUND CUE" example on the DVD included with this book. This depicts a before-and-after comparison of identical sounds. The "before" version is the raw recording as played back from the DAT master. The "polished" version is the same sound, but after I muted the space between performances, being very careful not to clip the overtones on the end too tightly, and then added short but effective fade-ins and fade-outs.

I prefer to have front-end sync sound effects, such as door-opens and closes, gunshots, impacts, face punches, telemetry beeps, and other precise cues prepared whenever possible for drag-and-drop or spot-mode sync cutting. These obviously benefit the sound editor when frame flipping across countless visual special-effects computer graphic scans for the purpose of cutting precise, frame accurate bursts and trills.

When the clock is ticking and you are cutting a complex gun battle with multiple shooters wielding various weapons, nothing speeds the ability to assemble a full and dynamic impact firefight more than having the weapons mastered with spot mode preparation. Thorough preparation of audio file masters to better achieve this editing style is time-consuming, but the untold hours of future schedule time it saves is well worth the investment.

Now is an appropriate moment to comment on the monitoring system used when you are working on complex mastering of your audio files. Do not attempt this by only listening to your material through headphones. In 1988 the Hollywood sound editing community got a fabulous boost by the advent of Sony's MDR-series dynamic stereo headphones. Editors stood aghast as they heard sounds in their own material that had been inaudible through conventional headphones. Many editors adopted these headsets as the new standard. At my own shop, we insisted everyone use them, as we did not want disparity between what editors heard.

Regardless of the new technological breakthrough, we discovered the hard way that a sound editor does not hear the full and complete frequency range needed when determining cut points during editing. We got the material to the re-recording stage only to discover that editors were clipping off the long low-frequency overtones of metal rubs, explosions, and gunshots because they could not hear the low-end frequencies in their headsets.

The ideal way to work, of course, is to invest in a superior set of monitor speakers for your workstation. Even with expensive digital headsets, you are not going to be able to hear a lot of low-frequency signal.

To properly monitor the full frequency and dynamic value of audio, pay close attention to your speakers. Be very picky about choosing a good close proximity speaker. It should perform with a transparency that allows you to properly evaluate the material and not worry that the speaker is adding any "color." Nothing is worse for a sound editor than to hear the session play as desired at the workstation, only to take the material onto the re-recording stage and discover that the realities of the material do not translate.

This is another reason why I do not bulk up my room with artificial amounts of subwoofer toys. I have listened to numerous editors having a great time playing with sounds in their rooms, cutting massive helicopter chases or moving the framework of the walls with concussive explosion effects—but the truth is that they are only fooling themselves. The material never sounds like it did in their editing suite on the re-recording stage. The editor will be in for one big sickening surprise.

Audio file preparation is not simply a case of distilling the effect to a workable size to make more disk storage space for other sound effects. This is not about just cutting out unnecessary audio within the effect (e.g., recordist voices, unnecessary bumps, and movements as the recordist repositions or prepares for another performance). This is about internal signal integrity and gleaning the maximum richness each sound effect cue can yield. For lack of a better term, I call it dynamic expansion.

Listen to MOVING A GRAND PIANO sound cue on the DVD included with this book. The recording is of two men pushing a grand piano on a hollow wood floor. The first task was to distill the 2:30 minutes of raw sound recording down to a workable 30 seconds. Another task was remedying the fact that the maximum volume peaks of the wheels striking either grit or hardwood floor seams were suppressing the wonderful low-end richness of the piano's wood frame, which was reverberating from the vibration of its internal strings. Using the DSP function "normalize" as a global parameter would not achieve any further richness.

Sure, I could have used a dynamic envelope algorithm that would act like a noise gate and a gain brain expander, but such tools are only good for quick bandage-type work, often yielding disappointing flat and sterile results. (I use the zoom-in function to get extremely close so I can study each waveform, often enlarging the waveform image to single samples, ferreting out digital ticks and zits. I study and remove distortion patterns and often redraw the waveform itself to repair and salvage, rather than cut and remove, the offending material.)

It took me 4 hours to bring the rolling piano effect to a full richness, bringing out the resounding piano chords and the rumble and weight of the instrument, rather than the lifeless original rolling about with massive distortion spikes.

Most sound designers and sound editors choose to use one or more software functions to accomplish DSP tools in Audio Suite. Of course, I use DSP parameters as well, but not as an end-all and certainly not as a defining formula to accomplish a desired result. I listen to each sound, not just what it sounds like, but what it tells my instincts about how to maximize its potential. At this level, I audition and understand the dynamic possibilities that lie within the overall performance. I then highlight

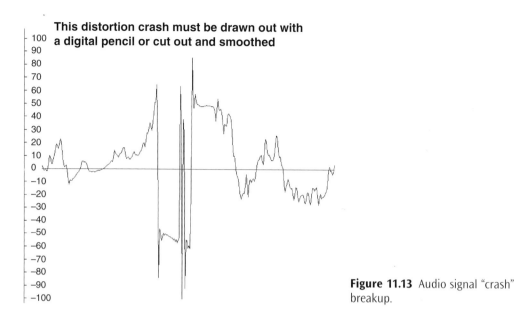

This distortion crash must be drawn out with a digital pencil or cut out and smoothed

Figure 11.13 Audio signal "crash" breakup.

precise regions, even within a fluid action, and lay on DSP functions ranging from normalization to pitch shift to parametric equalization. This kind of decision making can only come from years of experience supervising pictures, cutting and combining millions of sound effects, and working on the re-recording stage with the mixer to learn what one should and should *not* do to an audio file prior to the re-recording mixer for the predubbing process.

Listen to the NORMALIZATION EXAMPLE sound cue on the DVD provided with this book to listen to two examples of using the Normalization DSP function as well as simple equalization.

AUDIO FILE PROTOCOL

It is very frustrating to find audio files that have been mastered onto a CD-R or DVD-R with incorrect stereo designations. This is a direct result of ignorance on the part of inexperienced librarians importing audio files from ¼", DAT, or any other outside audio source into the Pro Tools nonlinear workstation.

Pro Tools works with stereo files in single split left and right monaural files, which, when laced precisely together, make a stereophonic image. The file designations contain an L for left channel, and an R for right channel. When entry recordists import audio directly into a Pro Tools session as the recording platform, Pro Tools automatically names the incoming file according to the channel into which it was imported, and it assigns a sequence designation. If you import a stereo pair into a Pro Tools session on the first two audio channels, the resulting designation assigned to the recording by the Pro Tools software is as follows:

- Audio 1-01
- Audio 2-01

Rename Audio 1-01 by double-clicking on the file waveform of Audio 1-01. A name window will appear. It will ask you to name the region. As an example, you may rename it "078/02 Peckerwood Canyon." To designate the stereo left/right position, you must add a period (.) immediately followed by an L. You want the option "name region and disk file" highlighted so that the file name is altered. Before you choose "okay," you should highlight the window with the new designation and copy it with the Command/C keystroke.

Audio 1-01 now reads "078/02 Peckerwood Canyon.L". Now double-click on Audio 2-01. The name window will appear. Paste in the copied name so that the exact duplication of the name and use of characters and spacing is assured. Back up one space to erase the L and replace it with R. It now appears as follows:

- 078/02 Peckerwood Canyon.L
- 078/02 Peckerwood Canyon.R

This gives you a proper stereo pair. The point to this whole left/right designation issue is that only one way exists to properly prepare a Sound Designer II audio file so that it will be acknowledged as a stereo cue and show up as such in the region list. The period (.) and L or R must appear as shown above; otherwise it will not boot up correctly as stereo.

Following are several examples of files seen at other sound facilities where inexperienced craftspeople did not understand audio file protocol. These designations are noted incorrectly, and Sound Designer II software does not allow them to boot up into its stand-alone platform.

The left/right designation does not come before the description; it does not have the period (.) come after the L or R; it does not appear in parentheses or brackets. The stereo left/right designation only works at the *end* of the file name and only with the *period* (.) immediately *preceding* it.

I am making a big deal of this because I have wasted countless hours retransferring and re-labeling sound files from other sound libraries. The lack of disci-

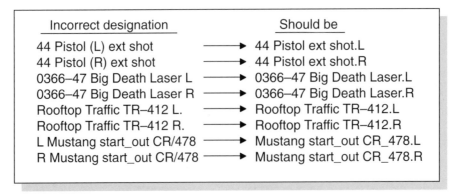

Figure 11.14 Left-Right audio file designations.

plined library procedure throughout the industry is staggering. Editing talent gets bogged down with file management work that should have been done correctly in the first place. The cost of wasted CD-Rs and DVD-Rs with improperly labeled audio files is compounded by the additional time and financial expense of downloading the material to a work drive, re-addressing the mastering and labeling chores, and then remastering to CD-R or DVD-R.

Contrary to the opinion of some librarians, it is not necessary to put a period (.) and an M at the end of a monaural sound file. If there is no designation, it is de facto a monaural sound file without a mate. Many librarians put this on the end of a monaural file so that it will not be confused with an interleaved stereo file, which has no dot (.) designation at the end of the audio name.

MULTICHANNEL MASTERING TECHNIQUES

You can only record single or stereo pair channels into Sound Designer II software. With a limitation of two inputs, you must record wider formats directly into a Pro Tools session, where you are limited by the number of inputs of the I/O interface. For instance, if you are recording into a Digidesign 888 I/O, 8 discrete channels can be recorded simultaneously. Be careful to make sure that you have your XLR inputs plugged correctly. XLR #1 goes into input channel one, XLR #2 goes into input channel 2, and so forth. Before opening the Pro Tools recording session, check your inputs to ensure proper calibration. (You can learn how to check your equipment and recalibrate your system interface in Chapter 6, Line-Up Tones. Also, a step-by-step demonstration of how to properly tone and calibrate BIAS on magnetic stock can be viewed on the DVD included in this book; under button #1 SOUND—an OVERVIEW—submenu WE USED TO DO IT ON FILM.)

Once satisfied that your inputs are calibrated correctly, you can either open or create a Pro Tools session to record multiple channels. If you are recording 8 channels simultaneously, you need to create 8 audio tracks, under File in the menu bar.

Open the mix window under Display in the menu bar and verify that the inputs are coming in accordingly. Make sure that each audio track has its own voice and will not be in conflict with another track, either because of voice assignment or duplicated input channel assignments.

Turn off the record safeties on each audio track, which illuminate white with red lettering. Hit the return bar on the computer keyboard, returning the digital sound head to the 000+00. Open the transport window under Display in the menu bar. Press the round Record button on the far right in the transport window control bar. Roll your source tape and press the Forward button on the transport window (the single triangular button just to the right of the black, square Stop button). If you have followed these steps correctly, all 8 channels will start laying down a red band path, in which you will see waveforms drawn in each channel shortly after you hear sound.

When you reach the end of the material you wish to record, press the black square Stop button in the transport window control bar. The recorded red bands will suddenly turn white showing their automated name designations.

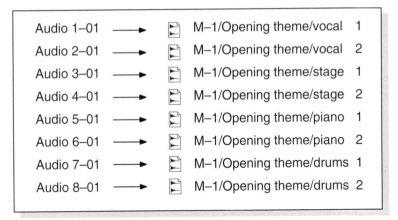

Figure 11.15 Eight-channel music transfer.

Say this is a live concert multi-track recording. The production mixer would have completed a track assignment sheet (review Chapter 5 on multi-track recording). Rename the audio files so they are easier to work with later in an edit session. After studying the production mixer's track assignment sheet, you may rename the audio files as described earlier and as shown in Figure 11.15.

After I have recorded in a number of synchronous 8-channel cues and renamed them, my preference is to color code the groups of 8 with alternating color designations. This helps distinguish each set of 8 audio files from each other. I color code the first set red, the second set pale blue, the third set red, the fourth set pale blue, and so forth. This checkerboarding effect makes the hundreds of audio files easily stand out in their 8 groups as they are listed in the drive partition window.

MIXED MEDIUM SYNCHRONOUS MASTERING

An interesting technique in today's action-oriented sound effects world is using multiple recorders during custom recording sessions to record the same action from various points of view (see Chapter 10). Any time multiple points of view are desired, especially when the dynamics and action are constantly changing, this technique of recording and subsequent mastering is of supreme value.

A sound librarian received seven sets of raw recorded audio rolls from Eric Potter, who had been contracted to put together and cover the recording session of a 5-ton Kaiser truck. These rolls had not been recorded in interlock or time code. The stereo Nagras had their crystal sync modules in during recording, so the material was resolved to sync during transfer by the sound librarian. Recording with a digital DAT using absolute time is extremely accurate, causing no concern about speed drift. The material had been recorded with different types of tape recorders in different formats, yet each recording was of the same audio performance event recorded at the same time by different recordists in different points of view.

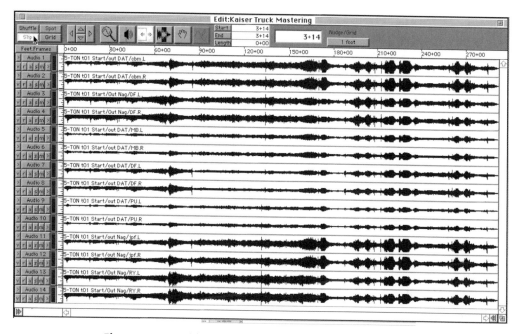

Figure 11.16 Multi-angle recording of a Kaiser truck maneuver.

The sound librarian first loaded each version of the recordings into the computer. Following the sound reports very carefully, the sound librarian was careful to account for each matching set of cues for each of the seven recorders.

After entering the hundreds of cues, the sound librarian created a Pro Tools edit session just to align, trim, and remaster each recorded event in its seven discrete angles. He then dragged in the first 7 stereo pairs. Finding the "clicker" sound at the head of each cue, the librarian zoomed in extremely close to align the click sync point of each stereo pair exactly together.

That was the easy and obvious part. From then on, the librarian had to watch out for and correct the drift of the recordings, finding occasional points easily aligned and matched, such as a gear box clunk, sudden burst revs from the exhausts, and so forth. (An experienced sound editor who understands this type of waveform matching and editing usually performs this task.) At each cut or move, the librarian used an appropriate cross-fade to heal the cut, avoiding the potential for digital ticks due to mismatching waveforms at the cut point or a difference in the rise and fall of the engine's performance.

A series of recordings like this is incalculably valuable for the sound editor throughout the sound editorial process. The editor can either choose one angle over another according to the visual on the screen, or can use one or more angles played together to further dramatize the action, knowing that the rise and fall of the engine and the dynamics of the performance will always match.

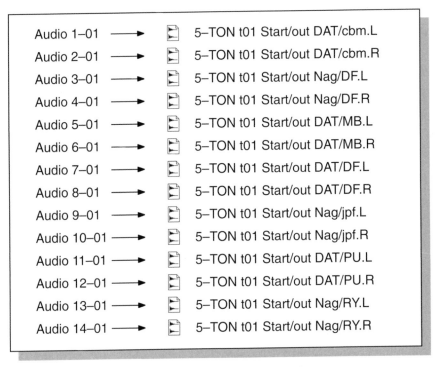

Audio 1–01 ⟶ 📄 5–TON t01 Start/out DAT/cbm.L

Audio 2–01 ⟶ 📄 5–TON t01 Start/out DAT/cbm.R

Audio 3–01 ⟶ 📄 5–TON t01 Start/out Nag/DF.L

Audio 4–01 ⟶ 📄 5–TON t01 Start/out Nag/DF.R

Audio 5–01 ⟶ 📄 5–TON t01 Start/out DAT/MB.L

Audio 6–01 ⟶ 📄 5–TON t01 Start/out DAT/MB.R

Audio 7–01 ⟶ 📄 5–TON t01 Start/out DAT/DF.L

Audio 8–01 ⟶ 📄 5–TON t01 Start/out DAT/DF.R

Audio 9–01 ⟶ 📄 5–TON t01 Start/out Nag/jpf.L

Audio 10–01 ⟶ 📄 5–TON t01 Start/out Nag/jpf.R

Audio 11–01 ⟶ 📄 5–TON t01 Start/out DAT/PU.L

Audio 12–01 ⟶ 📄 5–TON t01 Start/out DAT/PU.R

Audio 13–01 ⟶ 📄 5–TON t01 Start/out Nag/RY.L

Audio 14–01 ⟶ 📄 5–TON t01 Start/out Nag/RY.R

Figure 11.17 Five-ton truck rename files.

After the raw recordings had been aligned and cut to match each other, the sound librarian opened the mix window under Display in the menu bar. He checked that each stereo pair was set for output channels one and two. Then the librarian performed a Bounce-to-Disk of each stereo pair by highlighting the entire sound cut, making sure that all the cuts and fades had been included. Bounce-to-Disk is found under File in the Pro Tools menu bar. A Bounce window will appear.

Under Bounce Type, the librarian chose the split stereo (two mono files, best for Pro Tools) option. Then the librarian chose Bounce, which brought up a window for naming the new files and designating where to store the new material. Some librarians like to store a shorthand of information that helps the sound editor know what kind of recording medium was used (in some cases, the initials of the recordist), which helps track style patterns throughout the entire recorded series. Using this technique, the performance cue shown in Figure 11.17 may be retitled.

These 14 audio cues (7 stereo pairs) represent the simultaneous recording of a single audio event. You can see how easy it would be for a sound editor to recognize the desired files. "5-TON" denotes the vehicle. The take (or cue) of the audio file is listed as "t01." The take number is placed in this precise order of the name, as the take number automatically lines the groupings of recordings together in their stereophonic pairs. All of "t01" line up, then "t02," and so forth. If the take number were placed at the end of the audio file name, the computer would look at the alphabetically first word used in the description. In this case it would be an S.

A very short description of action is listed next. (A complete description can be entered into each audio file by opening the information window and leaving the entire text there.)

The recording medium is listed next, noted as DAT or Nag, for Nagra. The recordist's initials are listed after the recording medium, followed by the appropriate stereophonic designation (.) .L or .R.

THE SOUND EFFECTS INVENTORY DATABASE

As you amass an audio empire, it is very difficult to recall material. The thousands of audio files become a blur as you struggle to remember where you put the "inverted numb-knuckle lock screw metal squeak." The number one weapon in the arsenal of organization for the sound librarian is a good computer database. You can acquire database software that has been specifically designed and written for sound library work, such as Leonardo or Metropolis, or you can use one of the numerous off-the-shelf software programs, such as FileMaker Pro or ClarisWorks, and structure your own. Regardless of whether you purchase sound librarian software or tailor your own from preexisting software, you must have a structured regimen whereby the entered data can be retrieved in various ways.

DiskTracker

If you are on a very tight budget—and believe me, the vast majority of us are—you will get a lot of service and firepower from a program called DiskTracker. (You can find DiskTracker on the Web at DiskTracker.com.) The fee is amazingly reasonable, especially in light of what you can do with it.

Once you have installed your DiskTracker software, you will want to find the application icon program in the DiskTracker folder and highlight it. Open the information window (Apple/keystroke i) and increase the memory allowance. Because of the size of the scanned data I keep I have had to increase the memory allocation ten times the original size.

Boot up the software and make a new library file. Scan a few disks and then quit. Go back into the DiskTracker folder to find the document that you have just made. Highlight it and make an alias (Apple/keystroke M). Drag this alias out onto the desktop of your computer. Personally, I place my library alias in the lower center of my screen. From now on, if you need to access it to search for audio files or scan in new CD-R or DVD-R disks, all you have to do is tap twice on the alias icon on the desktop.

Once you have burned a sound effects library on CD-R or DVD-R, put it back in the disk tray and boot up your software from the desktop file icon. When your CD-R or DVD-R appears on the desktop, open the SCAN MOUNTED VOLUME option under the SCAN window in the menu bar. The window will open and show you all of the data volumes that your computer is seeing. Your internal and external drives will show up as drive icons. Your CD-R or DVD-R will show up as a disk icon with its assigned name next to it. Highlight the CD-R or DVD-R icon and press the SCAN button on the lower right of the window. The DiskTracker software will scan the disk.

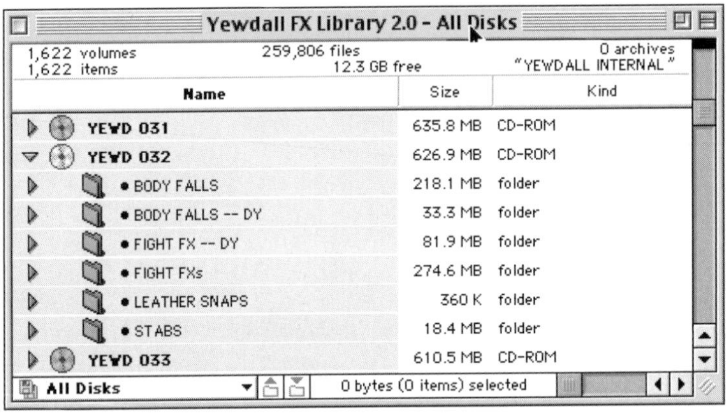

Figure 11.18 DiskTracker scanned data file.

Once the scan is complete, put the CD-R or DVD-R in the computer trash can to EJECT.

It is a good idea to SAVE after each disk scan. The software has a tendency to crash if you scan too many disks without saving, and you can save yourself the angry moment of having to face doing it all over again by simply getting into the rhythm of this habit.

Notice in Figure 11.18 that the CD or DVD icons match your original files exactly. You can open up the folders and physically look through the ranks of audio file data. By going up to the menu bar to VIEW and selecting LIST VIEWS . . . you may select exactly what kind of data you wish to be shown: Name, Size, Kind, Type, Creator, Created Date, Modified Date, Free Space, Scanned Date, Items, Serial Number, and so on.

I keep my viewing data extremely simple: Name, Size, Kind. I can always change it later, but I really do not need to wade through a lot of visual text on a day-to-day basis.

Printouts

If I should wish to print a hard copy of disk data (I do not personally use the printing option in the software; I find the material too difficult to read), I will open up what disk icons and folders in the DiskTracker software window that I wish to reveal; then I go up to VIEW and open the LIST VIEWS . . . option and turn off all but the NAME option.

I then select all (Apple/keystroke A), which will highlight the entire data scan; or, if I want to print data on only one or just a few CD-R or DVD-R disks, I will simply highlight with the cursor those disks I wish to capture.

I then move over to the word processing software (such as AppleWorks or Word) and paste (Apple/keystroke V) the selected data in. Now I can quickly tidy up the data document, such as highlighting and changing font selections for disk titles so that they will stand separate from audio files. I also keep an icon art palette in my word processing folder from which I can highlight CD disk icons or folder icons. By quickly scrolling down the page and pasting (Apple/keystroke V) in disk icons or folder icons I can make a very easy document for the eye to scan. For permanent hard copy outputs I even go back and color code all of the audio file names just as they appear in the original data field.

Duplicate Files

At one time it was a huge problem to grapple with duplicate files. Especially if you are your own librarian as well as handling the chores of supervising projects and cutting reels for the stage, when would you have time to physically research the duplicate audio file issues? DiskTracker can do that for you. When you are in between projects and want to do some library maintenance, open up the software and go up to the menu bar to SEARCH. Come down and highlight the DUPLICATE ITEM CRITERIA option. The menu will offer you a number of choices to choose from. You can create a filtering combination by cross referencing files by duplicate Name, Size, Kind, Label, Creation Date, Modification Date, Depth, Item Note, Finder Comment or File Type, Creator or Version, etc.

I simply choose NAME. I then press the OK button and go back up to SEARCH and draw down to FIND DUPLICATE ITEMS. That window will come up and you will need to make sure that the upper box is checked—CHECK ONLY ITEMS WHICH MATCH THE FILTER.

You will need to select the kinds of folders or applications or icon files that you either wish to ignore or wish to see. Then select that you want to look at your entire scanned list and engage. The software will scan through its data and present you with a detailed list of any and all things that have duplicate names (or by whatever filter you opted to utilize). You can print this out to a hard copy if you wish; or, if your audio files reside on drives within your server, such as the 2.5-terabyte resources I use, you can actually sit and carefully weed out your duplicates. By that I mean that when you highlight a name in the scan and eliminate it (Apple/keystroke X), the software will not only remove the audio file data from the software but will remove the audio file itself from the hard drive *if* the hard drives are connected to the CPU you are using— that is why you must be careful when eliminating data from the scan file.

As you learn to use this option with skill you will be able to use it like a surgeon's scalpel, but until you master the technique I highly suggest you use caution. I have found myself having to go back to cold storage CD-R or DVD-R back-ups and restoring several files that I had accidentally eliminated from the data scan, only to find that it had also eliminated them from the computer hard drive I was using.

Looking for Audio Files

Now you have an up-to-date data scan of your sound effects CD-R or DVD-R library. You suddenly are given a cutting task and find that you need to pull dozens of sound effects, many of which you cannot remember where they reside. Boot up your alias icon and go up to the SEARCH option in the menu bar. Select FIND . . . and a window will appear (see Figure 11.19).

First rule of the DiskTracker search technique: do not attempt to enter the exact name of what you are looking for. Chances are you will not get it right and you will

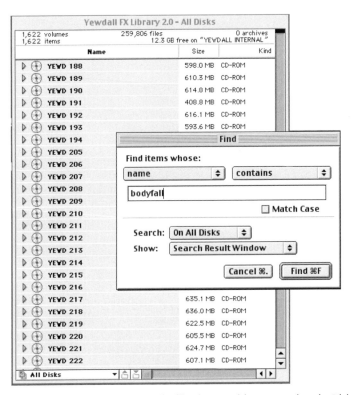

Figure 11.19 SEARCH menu to FIND audio files by matching name data in DiskTracker.

just be frustrated. Remember that a computer only knows what you tell it. It only knows what has been entered and it does not read your mind. By the way, here is a major reason why I do not like unrelated nicknames given to sound files. An audio file that has been named "Joe's Magic Whirly" has *nothing* in the name that you can grab onto in a subject-style search. In reality this effect may be a powerful wind-up and constant motor that you recorded at a local car wash. In the sound project that you used it in, you may have used it for a prop or scene that was a magical machine wind-up that belonged to Joe or the recordist's name was Joe. So what?! Years later, you are trying to find this sound that you know is perfect for your needs and you cannot remember the exact name and you cannot even use something like "machine" or "car whoosh" or something else that should have been part of the name.

That lecture over, let us move on to searching for things that *do* have something in the name that we can find easily. Think in terms of topic names or a piece of a name that you would most likely have used. There is a favorite New York traffic sound that I love to use, but I can never remember where I put it. All I can remember is that a good colleague friend of mine from New York gave it to me and she had used the name "Bronx" in the title, so whenever I want it I simply enter "Bronx" and up it comes.

Sure, that works fine when you remember a word in the name, but what if you can't remember that? What if it isn't just one audio file, but a series or genre of sound? That is when "topic" works best. I want to pull some bulkhead wrenching sounds for a deep pressure dive on a submarine. I don't look under "submarine." That sound is made by metal, and I know that I would have put it in with metal. Enter "metal" in the FIND window. Up may come several hundred audio files (and folders) that have the word "metal" in them. Believe me, it takes only a minute or two to scroll through several hundred audio names rather than search through a quarter of a million audio files in the entire data scan.

The truth of the matter is, once you are visually scanning the genre or type of sounds, looking for the one you remembered, you will come across dozens that will trigger your imagination and give you ideas that you did not previously think of. That is another reason why I like to take a little time and just wade through the files, reminding my subconscious about material that can be utilized to fulfill some audio event design.

As you practice doing this, you will develop little tricks and short-cuts on how to get to your desired destination. I know, for instance that a favorite "pfft!" effect I like to use resides in a folder I named "magic." I just need to enter "magic" and find which CD-R or DVD-R disk has the "magic" folder and I know I will find the desired sound effect.

Perhaps you need a variety of bodyfalls. Instead of listing "bodyfalls" as a plural, list it as a singular "bodyfall" as the scan may disregard a plural word because the "s" is not in the text. However, the singular text is part of the plural spelling, and therefore will show up.

After you enter the name to search for, hit the Return key and the software will scroll out a SEARCH RESULTS window (Figure 11.20). Notice the bi-directional arrow near the upper right-hand side, just to the right of Modified. If you touch the bi-directional arrow with your cursor the *Size/Kind/Created/Modified* data field will change to *Path*. This field will show you exactly where your desired audio file can be found. It will list the CD-ROM designation name and then the Folder name that the audio file resides in.

THE TRADITIONAL CATALOG DATABASE

The data itself and how it is entered into the computer will determine the ease with which you find specific material and the amount of customized filtration you need to search for information. By entering data with a slant toward accessibility, you will quickly discover that adding terms or abbreviations will increase the ease of finding material later. As you build a sound library, regardless of whether the root master is on digital DAT or analog tape, you need to compile a linear log.

Figure 11.21 is an example of a root master log. This is ¼" tape AFS 1909 from the Weddington Sound Effects Library. When Steve Flick and Richard Anderson worked on *The Final Countdown*, they had a sound recording team on the aircraft carrier *USS Nimitz*, recording anything and everything they could, from interior ambiences

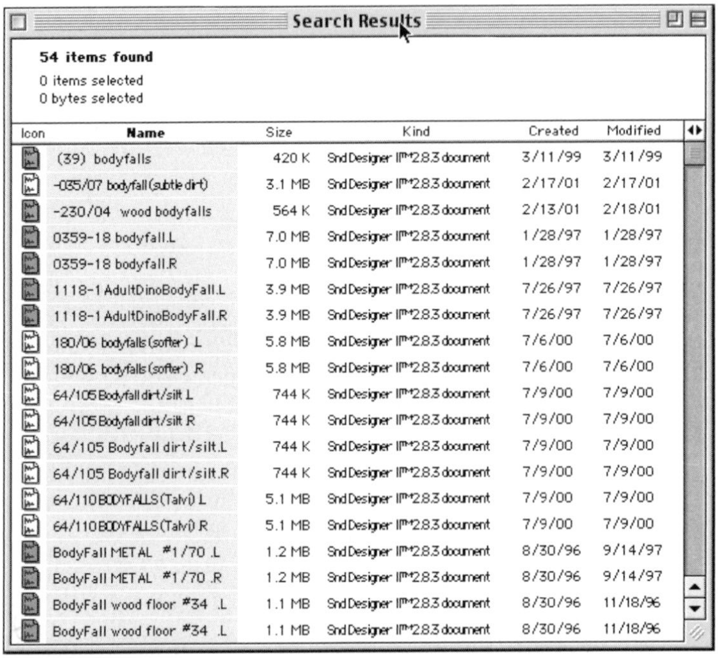

Search Results

54 items found
0 items selected
0 bytes selected

Icon	Name	Size	Kind	Created	Modified
	(39) bodyfalls	420 K	SndDesigner II™2.8.3 document	3/11/99	3/11/99
	-035/07 bodyfall (subtle dirt)	3.1 MB	SndDesigner II™2.8.3 document	2/17/01	2/17/01
	-230/04 wood bodyfalls	564 K	SndDesigner II™2.8.3 document	2/13/01	2/18/01
	0359-18 bodyfall.L	7.0 MB	SndDesigner II™2.8.3 document	1/28/97	1/28/97
	0359-18 bodyfall.R	7.0 MB	SndDesigner II™2.8.3 document	1/28/97	1/28/97
	1118-1 AdultDinoBodyFall.L	3.9 MB	SndDesigner II™2.8.3 document	7/26/97	7/26/97
	1118-1 AdultDinoBodyFall.R	3.9 MB	SndDesigner II™2.8.3 document	7/26/97	7/26/97
	180/06 bodyfalls (softer) .L	5.8 MB	SndDesigner II™2.8.3 document	7/6/00	7/6/00
	180/06 bodyfalls (softer) .R	5.8 MB	SndDesigner II™2.8.3 document	7/6/00	7/6/00
	64/105 Bodyfall dirt/silt .L	744 K	SndDesigner II™2.8.3 document	7/9/00	7/9/00
	64/105 Bodyfall dirt/silt .R	744 K	SndDesigner II™2.8.3 document	7/9/00	7/9/00
	64/105 Bodyfall dirt/silt.L	744 K	SndDesigner II™2.8.3 document	7/9/00	7/9/00
	64/105 Bodyfall dirt/silt.R	744 K	SndDesigner II™2.8.3 document	7/9/00	7/9/00
	64/110 BODYFALLS (Talvi) .L	5.1 MB	SndDesigner II™2.8.3 document	7/9/00	7/9/00
	64/110 BODYFALLS (Talvi) .R	5.1 MB	SndDesigner II™2.8.3 document	7/9/00	7/9/00
	BodyFall METAL #1/70 .L	1.2 MB	SndDesigner II™2.8.3 document	8/30/96	9/14/97
	BodyFall METAL #1/70 .R	1.2 MB	SndDesigner II™2.8.3 document	8/30/96	9/14/97
	BodyFall wood floor #34 .L	1.1 MB	SndDesigner II™2.8.3 document	8/30/96	11/18/96
	BodyFall wood floor #34 .L	1.1 MB	SndDesigner II™2.8.3 document	8/30/96	11/18/96

Figure 11.20 The matching audio file names to "bodyfall."

<<<<<< **AFS1909** >>>>>>

THE FINAL COUNTDOWN

SPEED: 7.5 ips   **FORMAT:** 1/4-inch Fulltrack Mono
TONE: 1kHz   **FLUX:** '0' VU = 120 nWb/m
NR: None   **DATE:** 07/31/'79
NOTES: Formerly MX-11

Jets on USS Nimitz

Cue	Description	Fmt	Time
01	F-8 JET LAUNCH: on aircraft carrier. With burners	M	00:40 MX11-1 DAT 1266-35
02	16 JETS PASS BY: aircraft carrier. PA vox over beginning. You can't really count the number, but it sounds pretty good. Good trail off	M	01:09 MX11-2 DAT 1266-36
03	JETS IDLING: on aircraft carrier	M	01:25 MX11-3 DAT 1266-37
04	F-8 JET IDLE: ECU on aircraft carrier. RLA's note sez "good for constant." still sound like white noise	M	00:42 MX11-4 DAT 1266-38
05	A-6 JET IDLE: ECU on aircraft carrier.	M	00:25 MX11-5 DAT 1266-39
06	F-14 JET WARM UP/IDLE: on aircraft carrier. White noisey. A-6 in B.G.	M	01:30 MX11-6 DAT 1266-40

Figure 11.21 Root master log.

of Combat Information Center to the explosive shriek of steam catapults hurtling F-14 Tomcats into flight.

Every audio file mastered into a sound library comes from another source, whether recorded on a Foley stage, a scoring stage, on location during production, or from a custom sound effects recordist. These sources have different formats and are on different original media. Part of the data entered into a library should also be a notation of its source.

In the case of the example shown, note in the header data of the catalog under "Notes" that AFS 1909 used to be known as MX-11. The librarian has also notated what recording speed the analog tape had been recorded at, that the format of tape was ¼", and that it was recorded on a full track monaural head stack. Listed as well is the date on which the material was recorded. Most logs today also denote the recordist's name. The header relates to the project that the effect was specifically recorded for, in this case for *The Final Countdown*. The tone is 1 kHz (1,000 cycles), and the flux notation signifies the strength of the recording and the amount of magnetic influence.

Each cue is listed in numerical order. The sound librarian enters the "Description" information in a manner making cross-referencing easy. In the case of the first cue, a sound editor can ask the computer to find all the jets; if the sound editor is interested in a strong engine/afterburner sound, "launch" or "launching" can be requested. Maybe the editor is interested in aircraft carrier material. The filter parameters the editor sets in the search request narrow the material displayed for review. If the sound librarian does not enter a detailed enough description into the catalog entries, the computer cannot accurately search and retrieve the material that is being sought. Hence it is unwise to list only cute nicknames that add no meaningful information to the content.

The sound librarian will want to keep track of the monaural or stereo FORMAT (Fmt). The length, or TIME duration, of the sound cue is helpful. In the case of this catalog data entry, the original ¼" roll and cue number are listed, as well as the subsequent digital DAT master roll number and PNO. In this case AFS 1909 was digitized to DAT 1266. Most of us have digitized our ¼" and 35-mm mag masters to digital DAT masters. Do not discard the ¼" originals! Many of us realized the advantages in being able to return to the original ¼" source and re-digitize after better technologies and techniques have been developed. Among other things, many of us learned that the analog-to-digital encoders on many digital systems were not as good as they could have been, and, for the sake of our libraries' integrity, we decided to start using outboard analog-to-digital encoders as outboard augmentations to the mastering system.

With data carefully entered in such a thorough manner, the sound librarian can ask the computer to print out catalog pages so that he or she can have a linear compilation of the library's root masters in sequential order.

Now the editor is interested in jets and enters "jet" into the search parameter. He or she scrolls through all the sound entries that have "jet" listed. Note that each of the F-14s is listed together in a group because the sound librarian had listed the make of jet first. If it hadn't been done that way, the computer would have looked at the first word of the description and listed all sound cues of jets in alphabetical order, based on the first letter of the first word, making it much harder to group the types together.

Cue	Description	Fmt	Time
1266-31	F-14 JET TAXI: on aircraft carrier.	M	00:20
1266-34	F-14 JET LAUNCH: on aircraft carrier. Very good. "Double cat shot." Very flamey, phasey sound. Launched w/double catapult.	M	01:15
1266-40	F-14 JET WARM UP/IDLE: on aircraft carrier. White-noisey. A-6 in B.G.	M	01:30
1266-52	F-14 JET TOUCH & GO: two of them	M	01:00
1266-54	F-14 JET TAKE-OFF: burners very long. Good!	M	01:10
1266-59	F-14 JET PASS BY: low and slow. Good, clean recording	M	01:10
1266-60	F-14 JET PASS BY: low and slow. Same as 1266-59 but better. Then F-4 PASS BY, around which time the tape gets mysteriously hissy. I dunno	M	02:15
1266-62	F-14 JET PASS BY: low and slow.	M	00:40
1266-63	F-14 JET PASS BY: low and slow.	M	00:50
1266-33	F-8 JET TAXI: on aircraft carrier.	M	00:20
1266-35	F-8 JET LAUNCH: on aircraft carrier. With burners	M	00:40
1266-46	F-8 JET TAKE-OFF: w/burners, Very long and good Crisp, w/some overmod, though quite useable	M	01:35
1266-78	F-8 JET TOUCH & GO: nice whistle on approach, wheels touch and engines throttle up and out	M	00:55

Figure 11.22 Index: "jets."

Inputting a specific jet type, such as F-14 or 737, makes locating the effects you desire easier to retrieve.

Note that the Cue numbers are not sequential. In this case, the computer is alphabetically lining up to F first, then the number. Although an F-8 is a lower designation than an F-14, the computer is looking at the first number after the F. The number 1 is lower than 8; therefore the F-14 comes up on the computer before the F-8. To perform good data entry as a sound librarian, think of sound with the cold logic of a computer. Only then will you produce a database with the greatest flexibility and information access.

UPGRADING OUR LIBRARIES TO 96 kHz/24-BIT

As we are now evolving up to a 96 kHz/24-bit audio file standard format, we will have no choice but to go back to our original ¼" and 35-mm mag source to recapture the deeper bit rate and geometric breadth of the audio that is there, but had not been captured when we worked at 48 kHz/16-bit starting back in the late 1980s.

Converting your 48 kHz/16-bit audio files to 96 kHz/24-bit files is a total waste of time. Why convert a 48/16 to 96/24 when you will not experience any additional gain in signal fullness?

To achieve the desired broader richness, you must go back to the root source. It is for this reason that those who started building our sound libraries back in the days of 35-mm mag and recording ¼″ analog never threw original analog recordings away. We put them into cold storage, waiting patiently for the next upgrade of technology to pull them out of the vault and re-digitize them with the new digital possibilities. It is kind of like the old adage of building a home. The builder's saying goes, when you build your house, you will actually do it three times because, as you go, you will rethink and redesign changes. The same is true with the early digitization of analog libraries to digital.

The really ironic thing about this is that those of us who recorded analog when we custom recorded our sound effects, especially those of us who understood the superior performance of 15 ips, will benefit completely from retransferring to a 96 kHz/24-bit standard. Those who custom recorded the material in the early days of DAT that, for the majority, was 48 kHz/16-bit will not benefit any additional depth or fullness because the 1s and 0s are just not there.

Chapter 12
Sound Design
Myths and Realities

As my partner Ken Sweet and I seriously immersed ourselves into sound effects development chores for John Carpenter's *The Thing*, we decided to try using a sound designer for the first time. The term had hardly been born, and few pictures presented the sound crew with the time and budget to allow experimentation. We called some colleagues to get recommendations for sound design talent.

The first place we contracted used a 24-track machine, something we did not use much in feature film sound work. The concept of layering sounds over themselves for design purposes appeared promising. The film-based Moviola assembly at sound editorial facilities like ours just could not layer and combine prior to the predub re-recording phase. Ken and I sat patiently for half the day as the multi-track operator ran the machine back and forth, repeatedly layering up the same cicada shimmer wave. The owner of the facility and the operator kept telling us how "cool" it would sound, but when they played their compilation back for us, we knew the emperor had no clothes on, at least at this facility.

We called around again and someone recommended a young man who used something called a Fairlight. We arranged for a design session and arrived with our ¼" source material. We told the eager young man exactly what kinds of sounds we needed to develop. Ken and I could hear the concepts in our heads, but we did not know how to run the fancy gear to expose the sounds within us. We explained the shots we wanted, along with the specially designed cues of sound desired at those particular moments. The young man turned to his computer and keyboard in a room stacked with various equipment rented for the session and dozens of wire feeds spread all over the floor.

Once again, Ken and I sat patiently. An hour passed as the young man dabbled at this and fiddled with that. A second hour passed. By the end of the third hour, I had not heard one thing anywhere near the concepts we had articulated. Finally, I asked the "sound designer" if he had an inkling of how to make the particular sound we so clearly had defined.

He said that he actually did not know how to make it, that his technique was just to play around and adjust things until he made something that sounded kind of cool, and then he would lay it down on sound tape. His previous clients would just pick whatever cues they wanted to use from his "creations."

Deciding it was going to be a long day, I turned to our assistant and asked him to run to the nearest convenience store and pick up some snacks and soft drinks. While I was digging in my pocket for some money, a quarter slipped out, falling onto the Vocorder unit. Suddenly, a magnificent metal shring-shimmer ripped through the speakers. Ken and I looked up with a renewed hope. "Wow!! Now *that* would be great for the opening title ripping effect! What did you do?"

The young man lifted his hands from the keyboard. "I didn't do anything."

I glanced down at the Vocorder, seeing the quarter. It was then that I understood what happened. I dropped another quarter, and again an eerie metal ripping shring resounded. "That's it! Lace up some tape; we're going to record this."

Ken and I began dropping coins as our sound designer sat helpless, just rolling tape to record. Ken started banging on the Vocorder, delivering whole new variants of shimmer rips. "Don't do that!" barked the young man. "You'll break it!"

"The studio will buy you a new one!" Ken snapped back. "At least we're finally *designing* some sound!"

Ken and I knew that to successfully extract the sounds we could hear within our own heads, we would have to learn and master the use of the new signal-processing equipment. It was one of the most important lessons we learned.

I always have had a love-hate relationship with the term "sound designer." While it suggests someone with a serious mind set for the development of a soundtrack, it also rubs me the wrong way because so many misunderstand and misuse what "sound design" truly is, cheapening what it has been, what it should be, and what it could be. This abuse and ignorance led the Academy of Motion Picture Arts and Sciences to decide that the job title "sound designer" would not be eligible for any Academy Award nominations or subsequent awards.

I have worked on mega-million-dollar features that have had a sound designer contractually listed in the credits whose work was not used. One project was captured by a sound editorial company only because it promised to contract the services of a particular sound designer, yet during the critical period of developing the concept sound effects for the crucial sequences, the contracted sound designer was on a beach in Tahiti. (Contrary to what you might think, he was not neglecting his work. Actually, he had made an agreement with the supervising sound editor, who knew he had been burned out from the previous picture. They both knew that, to the client, sound design was a perceived concept—a concept nonetheless that would make the difference between contracting the sound job or losing the picture to another sound editorial firm.)

By the time the sound designer returned from vacation, the crucial temp dub had just been mixed, with the critical sound design already completed. Remember, they were not sound designing for a final mix. They were designing for the temp dub, which in this case was more important politically than the final mix, because it instilled confidence and comfort for the director and studio. Because of the politics, the temp dub would indelibly set the design concept, with little room for change.

Regardless of what you may think, the contracted sound designer is one of the best in the business. At that moment in time and schedule, the supervising sound editor only needed to use his name and title to secure the show; he knew that several of us on his editorial staff were more than capable of accomplishing the sound design chores for the picture.

THE "BIG SOUND"

In July 1989 two men from Finland came to my studio: Antti Hytti was a music composer, and Paul Jyrälä was a sound supervisor/mixer. They were interested in a tour of my facility and transfer bay, in particular. I proudly showed them through the sound editorial rooms as I brought them to the heart of our studio—transfer. I thought it odd that Paul simply glanced over the Magna-Tech and Stellavox, only giving a passing acknowledgment to the rack of processing gear. He turned his attention to studying the room's wraparound shelves of tapes and odds and ends.

Paul spoke only broken English, so I turned to the composer with curiosity. "Antti, what is he looking for?"

Antti shrugged, then asked Paul. After a short interchange Antti turned back to me. "He says that he is looking for the device that makes the *Big Sound.*"

I was amused. "There is no device that makes the Big Sound. It's a philosophy, an art—an understanding of what sounds good together to make a bigger sound."

Antti interpreted to Paul, who in turn nodded with understanding as he approached me. "You must come to Finland so we make this Big Sound."

I resisted the desire to chuckle, as I was up to my hips in three motion pictures simultaneously. I shook their hands as I wished the two men well, assuming I would not see them again. Several weeks later, I received a work-in-progress video of the picture on which Paul had asked me to take part. Still in the throes of picture editorial, it was falling increasingly further behind schedule. My wife and I watched the NTSC (National Television System Committee) transfer of the PAL (phase alternating line) video as we sat down to dinner. I became transfixed as I watched images of thousands of troops in this 1930s-era epic, with T-26 Russian armor charging across snow-covered battlefields.

The production recordings were extremely good but, like most production tracks, focused on spoken dialog. In a picture filled with men, tanks, airplanes, steam trains, and weaponry, much sound effects work still had to be done. The potential sound design grew within my head—my imagination started filling the gaps and action sequences. If any picture cried out for the Big Sound, this was the one—*Talvisota: The Winter War*, was the true-life story of the war between Finland and the Soviet Union in 1939. It proved one of the most important audio involvements of my professional career. It was not a question of money. It was an issue of passion—the heart and soul of a nation beckoned from the rough work-in-progress video.

I made arrangements to go to Helsinki and work with Paul Jyrälä to co-supervise this awesome challenge. I put together a bag filled with sound effect DAT tapes and a catalog printout to add to the sound design lexicon that Paul and I would have to use.

This project was especially challenging, as this was pre-nonlinear workstation. The film was shot 35-mm with a 1:66 aspect. They don't use 35-mm stripe or fullcoat for sound editing. But they did use 17.5-mm fullcoat and had one of the best 2-track stereo transfer bays I had the privilege to work in. To add to the challenge, we only had nine 17.5-mm Perfectone playback machines on the re-recording stage, which meant that we had to be extremely frugal about how wide our "A," "B," "C" predub groups could be built out. We had no Moviolas, no synchronizers, no Acmade coding machines, no cutting tables with rewinds, and no Rivas splicers. We did have two flatbed Steinbecks, a lot of veteran know-how, and a sauna.

AMERICAN SOUND DESIGN

Properly designed sound has a timbre all its own. Timbre is the violin—the vibration resonating emotionally with the audience. Timbre sets good sound apart from a pedestrian soundtrack.

Sound as we have seen it grow in the United States has distinguished American pictures on a worldwide market. Style, content, slickness of production, rapidity of storytelling—all made the sound of movies produced in the United States a benchmark and inspiration for sound craftspersonship throughout the rest of the world. For a long time, many foreign crews considered sound only a background behind the actors. They have only in recent years developed a Big Sound concept of their own.

For those clients understanding that they need a theatrical soundtrack for their pictures, the first hurdle is not understanding what a theatrical soundtrack sounds like, but how to achieve it. When you say "soundtrack," the vast majority of people think *only* of the music score. The general audience believes that almost all nonmusical sounds are actually recorded on the set when the film is shot. It does not occur to them that far more time and effort were put into the nonmusical portion of the audio experience of the storytelling as was put into composing and orchestrating the theme of the music score itself.

Some producers and filmmakers fail to realize that theatrical sound is not a format; it is not a commitment to spend giga-dollars or hire a crew the size of a combat battalion. It is a philosophy, an art form that only years of experience can help you understand.

The keys to a great soundtrack are its dynamics and variation, with occasional introductions of subtle, unexpected things: the hint of hot gasses on a close-up of a recently fired gun barrel, or an unusual spatial inversion, such as a delicate sucking-up sound juxtaposed against a well-oiled metallic movement for a shot of a high-tech device being snapped open.

The Sound Design Legacy

When you ask a film enthusiast about sound design, the tendency is to recall legendary pictures with memorable sound, such as *Apocalypse Now* and the *Star Wars* series. I could not agree more. Many of us were greatly influenced by the work of Walter Murch and Ben Burtt (who worked on the above films, respectively). They not only had great product opportunities to practice their art form, but they also had producer-directors who provided the latitude and financial means to achieve exceptional accomplishments.

Without taking any praise away from Walter or Ben, let us remember that sound design did not begin in the 1970s. Did you ever study the soundtracks to George Pal's

War of the Worlds or *The Naked Jungle*? Have you considered the low-budget constrictions that director Robert Wise faced while making *The Day the Earth Stood Still*, or the challenges confronting his sound editorial team in creating both the flying saucer and alien ray weapons? Who dreamed up using soda fizz as the base sound effect for the Maribunta, the army ants that terrorized Charlton Heston's South American plantation in *The Naked Jungle*? Speaking of ants, imagine thinking up the brilliant idea of looping a squeaky pickup truck fan belt for the shrieks of giant ants in *Them*. Kids in the theatre wanted to hide for safety when that incredible sound came off the screen.

When these fine craftspeople labored to make such memorable sound events for your entertainment pleasure, they made them without the help of today's high-tech digital tools, without harmonizers or vocorders, without a Synclavier or a Fairlight. They designed these sounds with their own imaginations of working with the tools they had at hand and being extraordinarily innovative, understanding what sounds to put together to create new sound events—how to play them backward, slow them down, cut, clip, and scrape them with a razor blade (when magnetic soundtrack became available in 1953), or paint them with blooping ink (when they still cut sound effects on optical track 35-mm film).

DO YOU DO SPECIAL EFFECTS TOO?

In the late summer of 1980 I had completed Roger Corman's *Battle Beyond the Stars*. I was enthusiastic about the picture, mainly because I had survived the film's frugal sound editorial budget as well as all the daily changes due to the myriad of special-effects shots that came in extremely late in the process.

I had to come up with seven different sounding spacecrafts with unique results, such as the Nestar ship which we created from human voices. It is the community choir from my hometown college of Coalinga, California. Choral director Bernice Isham had conducted her sopranos, altos, tenors, and basses through a whole maze of interesting vocal gymnastics, which were later processed to turn 40 voices into million-pound thrust engines for the Nestar ship, manned by clone humanoids. You can listen to several examples of the sound effects creations developed from the choral voices, which continue to be used in many films to this day.

We had developed Robert Vaughn's ship from the root recordings of a dragster car, then processed it heavily to give it a menacing and powerful "magnetic-flux" force, just the kind of quick-draw space chariot a space-opera gunslinger would drive.

The day after the cast and crew screening, I showed up at Roger's office to discuss another project. As was the custom, I was met by his personal secretary. I could not help but beam with pride regarding my work on *Battle*, so I asked her if she had attending the screening, and if so, what did she think of the sound effects?

She had gone to the screening, but she struggled to remember the soundtrack. "The sound effects were okay, for what few you had."

"The few I had?"

The secretary shrugged. "Well, you know, there were so many special effects in the picture."

"Special effects! Where do you think the sound for all of those special effects came from?" I snapped back.

She brightened up. "Oh, do you do that too?"

"Do that *too*?" I was dumbfounded. "Who do you think makes those little plastic models with the twinky-lights sound like powerful juggernauts? Sound editors do, not model builders!"

It became obvious to me that the viewing audience can either not separate visual special effects from sound effects or has a hard time understanding where one ends and the other begins.

A good friend of mine got into hot water once with the Special Effects Committee when, in a heated argument he had the temerity to suggest that to have a truly fair appraisal of their work in award evaluation competition they need to turn the soundtrack off. After all, the work of the sound designer and the sound editors were vastly affecting the perception of visual special effects. The committee did not appreciate, nor heed my friend's suggestion, even though my friend had more than 30 years and 400 feature credits of experience behind his statement.

I have had instances where visual special effects artists would drop by to hear what I was doing with their work-in-progress "animatic" special effect shots, only to be inspired by something that we were doing that they had not thought of. In turn, they would go back to continue work on these shots, factoring in new thinking that had been born out of our informal get-together.

SOUND DESIGN MISINFORMATION

A couple of years ago I read an article in a popular audio periodical in which a new, "flavor-of-the-month" sound designer had been interviewed. He proudly boasted something no one else supposedly had done: he had synthesized Clint Eastwood's famous .44 magnum gunshot from *Dirty Harry* into a laser shot. I sighed. We had done the same thing nearly 20 years *before* for the Roger Corman space opera, *Battle Beyond the Stars*. For nearly two decades Robert Vaughn's futuristic hand weapon had boldly fired the sharpest, most penetrating laser shot imaginable, which we developed from none other than Clint Eastwood's famous pistol.

During the mid-1980s I had hired a young enthusiastic graduate from a prestigious southern California university film school. He told me he felt very honored to start his film career at my facility, as one of his professors had lectured about my sound design techniques for Carpenter's *The Thing*.

Momentarily venerated, I felt a rush of pride, which was swiftly displaced by curious suspicion. I asked the young man what his professor had said. He joyously recounted his professor's explanation about how I had deliberately and painstakingly designed the heartbeat throughout the blood test sequence in reel 10, which subconsciously got into a rhythmic pulse, bringing the audience to a moment of terror.

I stood staring at my new employee with bewilderment. What heartbeat? My partner, Ken Sweet, and I had discussed the sound design for the project very thoroughly, and one sound we absolutely had stayed away from because it had screamed of cliché was any kind of heartbeat.

I could not take it any longer. "Heartbeat?! Horse hockey!! The studio was too cheap to buy fresh fullcoat stock for the stereo sound effect transfers! They used reclaim which had been sitting on a steel film rack that sat in the hallway across from the entrance to dubbing 3. Nobody knew it at the time, but the steel rack was magnetized, which caused a spike throughout the stock. A magnetized spike can't be removed by bulk degaussing. Every time the roll of magnetic stock turns 360 degrees there is a very low frequency 'whomp.' You can't hear it on a Moviola. We didn't discover it until we were on the dubbing stage—by then it was too late!!"

The young man shrugged. "It still sounded pretty neat."

Pretty neat? I guess I'm not as upset about the perceived sound design where none was intended as I am about the fact that the professor had not researched the subject on which he lectured. He certainly never had called to ask about the truth, let alone to inquire about anything of consequence that would have empowered his classroom teachings. He just made up a fiction, harming the impressionable minds of students with misinformation.

In that same sequence of *The Thing* I can point out real sound design. As John Carpenter headed north to Alaska to shoot the Antarctica base-camp sequences, he announced that one could not go too far in designing the voice of *The Thing*. To that end, I tried several ideas, with mixed results. Then one morning I was taking a shower when I ran my fingers over the soap-encrusted fiberglass wall. It made the strangest unearthly sound. I was inspired. Turning off the shower, I grabbed my tape recorder, and dangled microphones from a broomstick taped in place from wall to wall at the top of the shower enclosure.

I carefully performed various "vocalities" with my fingertips on the fiberglass—moans, cries, attack shrieks, painful yelps, and other creature movements. When John Carpenter returned from Alaska, I could hardly wait to play the new concept for him. I set the tape recorder on the desk in front of him and depressed the "Play" button.

I learned a valuable lesson that day. What a client requests is not necessarily what he or she really wants, or particularly what he or she means. Rather than developing a vocal characterization for a creature never truly heard before, both director and studio executives actually meant, "We want the same old thing everyone expects to hear and what has worked in the past—only give it a little different spin, you know." The only place I could sneak a hint of my original concept for *The Thing*'s vocal chords was in the blood test scene where Kurt Russell stuck the hot wire into the petri dish and the blood leaped out in agony onto the floor.

At the point the blood turned and scurried away was where I cut those sound cues of my fingertips on the shower wall, called "Tentacles tk-2." I wonder what eerie and horrifying moments we could have conjured up instead of the traditional cliché lion roars and bear growls we were compelled to use in the final confrontation between Kurt Russell and the mutant Thing.

DAS BOOT: MIKE LE-MARE

I believe "legendary" is the only word to properly describe the audio storytelling achievement that Mike Le-Mare (*Blow-Up, Ronin, Without a Clue, Bloodsport, New Jack City, Reindeer Games, The Terminator, Enemy Mine*, and *The Neverending Story*) and Karola Storr along with their British-German team, accomplished in 1981 with *Das Boot*, a film directed by Wolfgang Peterson.

Never before had anyone been nominated *twice* for an Academy Award in the sound arts on the same picture. Mike Le-Mare was nominated for Best Sound as well as Best Sound Effect Editing.

Many attribute the successful experience of *Das Boot* to the careful and thoughtful sounds Mike gave to the film. The sound effects, by design and intent, were profoundly responsible for the psychological, claustrophobic terror during such sequences such as the depth charge attack, which left the audience with sweaty palms, gripping the armrests. Who could not be affected by stress and creaks of the metal hull of the U-boat enduring the pressures of the North Atlantic? Mike's broad palette of audio textures—unsettling air expulsions, pit-of-the-stomach ronks, and low-end growls—seized the audience, making real to them the vulnerability and mortality of the submarine crew in a way that transcended the visual picture.

Such a track did not magically happen because Le-Mare could hear the potential sound design in his head. Nor did it happen because he willed it. Granted, such beginnings are vital, the will to strive for excellence is essential, but without rolling up his sleeves and attending to the countless details and processes, without challenging himself and his crew to take the extra effort to achieve more, such sound experiences are not possible.

Le-Mare had been brought onto the project early enough to be able to do a significant amount of custom recording. The production company had access to a World War II-era German U-boat. To record the authentic diesel (for surface) and electric (for underwater maneuvering) engines, Le-Mare was allowed access to a permanently moored U-boat at Wasserburg where he made carefully controlled recordings of the submarine engines. Many variations were required for the various sequences; precise notes kept; strict attention paid to microphone aspect; engine gears and revolutions per minute (rpm) were written down, such as U-boat: CLOSE—diesel engine startup and CONSTANT—nice tappets, then engine shuts down (in 2nd gear at 202 rpm). Recordings were made of the engine in all gears, under strain, cruising, at flank speed, reversing—recorded close up, medium perspective, down the companionway, or as heard from the conning tower.

Le-Mare made most of his recordings with a ¼" Uher 4200 Report Monitor and Nagra III tape machines, using both Sennheiser and Neumann microphones. He obtained some authentic German hydrophone recordings that had extremely detailed notations, such as HYDROPHONE: destroyer approaches and passes overhead, 250 rpm slows to 160 rpm (2 shaft—4 blade) then slows to stop TK-1.

From his own extensive sound effect library back in London, Le-Mare pulled a variety of ship horns, bilge water slops, tanks flooding with sea water, tanks blowing with air, vents, safety pressure valves, ASDIC pings, and all the metal and metal-related groans and rubs he could put together.

To help focus and define the authenticity of his sound design, Le-Mare brought in numerous German naval veterans who had served on U-boats during the war. He would tell them the use of each sound cue grouping, and then he would play it.

"No, it did not sound like that," the submariner would say. "It sounds more like the bulkheads crying out in agony."

Sometimes Le-Mare would get emotional reactions from the men as the sounds evoked still-present realities from their memories.

Figure 12.1 Mike Le-Mare and Karola Storr (*Das Boot*) tackle the challenge of John Frankenheimer's action-thriller *Ronin*.

"There were times that I would have conflicting opinions," Le-Mare explained. "I resorted to acquiring World War II-era recordings, unsuitable for theatrical use, but I would listen to the texture and timbre of them and do an A-B comparison to see that our audio recreations were on the right track. This and the U-boat servicemen really helped me out a lot."

Unlike most submarine movie crews that build the practical set open on the side so that the cameras can get the shots easier, U-96 was built in two sections, front and rear. To this day, the two halves (now joined together) are still on display at Bavaria Studios in Munich. Le-Mare recalled:

> After wrapping principal photography, they took the two sections out to mount together for the tourist display. We were fortunate to get 12 of the actors to come back later to custom record them running through the companionway from back-to-front and back. This kind of action would be just about impossible to duplicate correctly on a Foley stage. We laid down a series of Neumann microphones alongside the floor's metal plates so that we could properly hear the texture of the footsteps and body movement as the men ran forward. They would grab grip bars above the hatchways as they frantically swung through and continued on. This kind of sound lent an incredible realism for the audience and really helped to draw the viewer in as part of the crew, rather than just watching the film at arm's length.

Le-Mare brought onto the Foley stage all kinds of electric motors for the sounds of the echo range finder, compass, depth gauge, generator, and other equipment for controlled isolated recordings. He brought in switches and various mechanisms for periscope handle movements and fine adjustments, ballast tank operations, rudder controls, hydroplane wheel turns, and so forth. Each item was carefully recorded, making numerous variations for the future sound editorial process.

Le-Mare had Moviolas and Acmade's Pic-Sync Competitors shipped in from London to supply his British sound editorial crew with the equipment it felt most comfortable and confident using, while the German crew used flatbed Steinbecks. With *Das Boot*, German re-recording stages were challenged by the number of tracks it took to mount the required sound. With a limited number of soundtracks generally used in film production, picture editors ran the mixing sessions. Not with *Das Boot*. Aside from Klaus Doldinger's haunting music score, Mike Le-Mare came onto the dubbing stage with as many as a 110 hard-effect tracks and an average of 20 Foley tracks in addition to the dialog, ADR, and backgrounds. In fact Le-Mare was asked to get behind the console and help in the mixing at some busy moments, because he was the only one who had a grasp of the material and how it all would work together. For all this, Le-Mare was nominated not only for Best Sound Effects Editing as the supervising sound editor, but also for Best Sound as one of the re-recording mixers.

It was one of the most complex soundtracks ever to be mixed on Stage "A" at Bavaria Studios. So thorough was the feature's preparation and the attention to detail given it, a month after Le-Mare and his sound crew had finished the two-and-a-half-hour feature version, the director and producers decided that Le-Mare and his team should prepare the television version. They went back to the drawing board to prepare the new five-and-a-half-hour version. Of course, the conventional method would have been to cut down the feature version, but, in this case, new scenes were actually added and existing materials were extended to generate a longer picture.

More producers should consider hiring quality theatrical editors to handle foreign language conversions, but it comes down to money. Remember this—you get what you pay for. So many foreign language remixes seem comical and often slipshod. The producers must be willing to pay for fine craftspersonship to achieve a high-quality standard.

THE DIFFERENCE BETWEEN DESIGN AND MUD

David Stone

Supervising sound editor David Stone, winner of the Academy Award for Best Sound Effects Editing for 1992's *Bram Stoker's Dracula*, is a quiet and reserved audio artist. As sound design field commanders go, he is not flamboyant nor does he use showmanship as a crutch. What he does is quietly and systematically deliver the magic of his craft—his firm grasp of storytelling through sound. Though he loves to work on animated films, having helmed projects such as *Beauty and the Beast*, *A Goofy Movie*, *Cats Don't Dance*, as well as *Pooh's Grand Adventure: The Search for Christopher Robin*, and *The Lion King II*, one should never try to typecast him.

Stone has time and again shown his various creative facets and the ability to mix his pallet of sounds in different ways to suit the projects at hand. He leaves the slick illusionary double-talk to others. For himself, he stands back and studies the situation for awhile. He makes no pretense that he is not an expert in all the fancy audio software or that he was up half the night trying to learn how to perform a new DSP (digital signal processing) function. Stone offered the following insight:

> We're all becoming isolated by using so many computerized devices. Music and movies that used to play to an audience are now playing to an individual. This makes us think

Figure 12.2 David Stone, supervising sound editor and Academy Award winner for Best Sound Effect Editing for *Bram Stocker's Dracula* (1992).

we can rely on tech as a magic genie, to make a good soundtrack for us. But what a great piece of film really needs is the work of a social group. Our best student filmmakers are the ones with more highly developed social skills, because film is the great collaborative art.

There was a time when Hollywood soundtracks kept getting better because freelance sound people were circulating and integrating into different groups for each film. So skills and strategies were always growing in a fertile environment. It's the social power that makes great films extraordinary . . . the same thing that audiences enjoy in films that have more ensemble acting, where the art is more than the sum of its parts.

I think if film students could study the history of the soundtracks they admire, they'd see this pattern of expert collaboration, and that's quite the opposite of what happens when too few people rely on too much tech to make movie sound.

Being a computer vidiot is not what creates good sound design—understanding what sounds go together and when to use them does.

Many times I have watched young sound editors simply try to put together two or more sound effects to achieve a larger audio event, often without satisfaction. A common mistake is to simply lay one pistol shot on top of another. They do not necessarily get a bigger pistol shot; in fact, they often only diminish the clarity and character of the weapon because they are putting together two sounds that have too many common frequency dynamics to compliment one another—instead the result is what we call *mud*.

A good example of this is the Oliver Stone film *On Any Sunday*. The sound designer did not pay much attention to the frequency characteristics of his audio elements, or, for that matter, to overmodulation. As I listened to the presentation at the Academy theatre (just so you will not think that a lesser theatre with a sub-standard speaker system was the performance venue) I was completely taken out of the film itself by the badly designed football effects. The lack of clarity and "roundness" of the sound was, instead, replaced by overdriven effects with an emphasis in the upper mid-range that cannot be described as anything other than distortion.

A newly initiated audio jockey may naively refer to such sound as befitting the type of film, the "war" of sports needing a "war" of sound. Frankly, such an answer is horse dung. Listen to the sound design of *Road to Perdition* or *Saving Private Ryan*. These are also sounds of violence and war in the extreme, and yet they are designed with full "roundness" and clarity, with each audio event having a very tactile linkage with its visual counterpart.

I have harped on this throughout this book and will continue to do so, because it is the keystone of the sound design philosophy: if you take the audience *out* of the film because of bad sound design, then you have failed as a sound designer. It's just that simple.

I hope you will be patient with me for a few pages as I am going to introduce you (if you do not already know these sound artists) to several individuals who you may want to use as role models as you develop your own style of work and professional excellence. As you read about them, you will see a common thread—a common factor is all of them. They do not just grind out their projects like so much sausage in a meat grinder. They structure their projects as realistically as they can within the budgetary and schedule restraints; they know how to shift gears and cut corners when and if they have to without sacrificing the ultimate quality of the soundtrack that they are entrusted with. They custom record—they try new things—they know how to put together an efficient team to accomplish the mission.

Gary Rydstrom

Sound designer/sound re-recording mixer Gary Rydstrom has developed a stellar career with credits such as *Backdraft, Terminator 2: Judgment Day,* both *Jurassic Parks, Strange Days, The Haunting, Artificial Intelligence, Minority Report,* and the stunning sound design and mixing efforts of *Saving Private Ryan.*

Richard King

This supervising sound editor/sound designer is no stranger to challenging and complex sound design. Winning the Academy Award for Best Sound Editing for *Master and Commander: The Far Side of the World,* Richard has also helmed such diverse feature films as *Rob Roy, GATTACA, The Jackal, Unbreakable, Signs, Lemony Snicket's: A Series of Unfortunate Events,* Steven Spielberg's epic version of *War of the Worlds,* and *Firewall,* to name but a few. King says:

> One of the requirements of the job is to place myself within the world of the picture, and think about sound as dictated by the style of the film. This can range from "Hollywood" (where you really don't hear any sounds not specifically relating to the scene at hand—I try not to work on these—boring!), to hyper-real, where, as in life, one is set up to accept the odd, off-the-wall sound, though of course carefully selected to support/counterpoint or in some way support and contribute to the moment.

Figure 12.3 Supervising sound editor/sound designer Richard King. On the left, Richard and his team are custom recording canvas sail movement for *Master and Commander: The Far Side of the World*, which earned Richard an Academy Award for Best Sound Editing (2004).

Figure 12.4 Supervising sound editor/sound designer Jon Johnson. Academy Award winner for Best Sound Editing in 2000 for the WWII sea action-thriller *U-571*.

Jon Johnson

Supervising sound editor Jon Johnson first learned his craft on numerous television projects in the early 1980s and then designed and audio processed sound effects for *Stargate* and later for *Independence Day*. Taking the helm as supervising sound editor, Jon has successfully overseen the sound design and editorial projects such as *The Patriot, A Knight's Tale, Joy Ride, The Rookie, The Alamo, The Great Raid,* and *Amazing Grace,* to name a few. In 2000, Jon won the Academy Award for Best Sound Editing for the World War II submarine action-thriller *U-571*.

John A. Larsen

Supervising sound editor John Larsen is one of the few sound craftspeople-artists who is also a smart and successful businessman. His sound editorial department on the

Figure 12.5 John Larsen reviewing material with assistant sound editor Smokey Cloud.

20th Century Fox lot continually takes on and successfully takes extremely difficult and challenging projects through the postproduction process.

One of his first important sound editing jobs came when he worked on the 1980 *Popeye*, starring Robin Williams. He continued to practice his craft on *Personal Best*, *Table for Five*, *Brainstorm*, and *Meatballs II*. In 1984 he served as the supervising sound editor for the television series *Miami Vice*, where he really learned the often hard lessons of problem solving compressed schedules and tight crews.

After sound editing on Fandango and *Back to the Future*, John picked up the gauntlet to supervise feature films in 1985. Since then he has handled a wide breadth of style and demands from pictures like *Lord of Illusions*, *Down Periscope*, *Chain Reaction*, and *Jingle All the Way* to high-design projects such as *Alien 4: Resurrection*, *The X Files* feature film, *The Siege*, the 2001 version of *Planet of the Apes*, *I-Robot*, *Daredevil*, *Elektra*, *Fantastic 4*, and all three *X-Men* features. He has literally become the sound voice of Marvel Comics for 20th Century Fox.

"How can anyone who loves sound *not* be excited about the potential creation of unknown and other worldly characters? It is a dream come true! We should all strive to be so lucky," he said.

John understands exactly how to tailor difficult, and often highly politically "hot-to-handle" projects through the ever-changing, never-locked picture realm of high-budget, fast schedules with high expectation demands. John adds:

> As a sound supervisor you must be prepared, you must be a step ahead, you must know your crews strengths as well as their weaknesses. With talent comes character but out of these character trains comes extreme and fantastic talent. People with real skills sometimes come with the baggage you must learn how to recognize and deal with. None of us are perfect—we are human beings—not G5s!

Richard Anderson

Supervising sound editor/sound designer Richard Anderson actually started his career as a picture editor, but in the late 1970s became the supervising sound editor at

Figure 12.6 Richard Anderson sitting in front of the giant server that feeds all of the workstations with instant access to one of the most powerful sound libraries in the business.

Gomillion Sound, overseeing numerous projects of all sorts and helming several Roger Corman classics, such as Ron Howard's first directorial effort, *Grand Theft Auto*. A couple of years later Richard won the Academy Award, along with Ben Burtt, as co-supervising sound editors for Best Sound Effect Editing for *Raiders of the Lost Ark*.

Richard teamed up with Stephen Hunter Flick as they worked together on projects such as *Star Trek: The Motion Picture*, *Final Countdown*, Oliver Stone's *The Hand*, *Poltergeist*, *48 Hours*, *Under Fire*, and many others.

As one of the best role models that I could think of for those who would aspire to enter the field of entertainment sound, Richard Anderson's personal work habits, ethics, and superb style of stage etiquette and leadership are extraordinarily evident as he supervised such projects as *2010*, *Predator*, *Beetle Juice*, *Edward Scissorhands*, *The Lion King*, *Being John Malkovich*, *Dante's Peak*, and more recently *Madagascar*, *Shark Tale*, and *Over the Hedge*. But perhaps one of Richard's more satisfying efforts was in the field of audio restoration for the director's cut version of David Lean's *Lawrence of Arabia*.

Audio restoration, whether it be resurrecting and expanding a film to a version that a director had originally intended, which has become a very popular process in recent years, or whether it be to clean up and bring back an existing historic soundtrack to the way it sounded when it was first mixed—removing optical crackle, hiss, transfer ticks, and anomalies that include, but are not limited to, nasty hiss presence due to sloppy copies, made from copies, made from copies, rather than going back to the original source.

Stephen Hunter Flick

Supervising sound editor Stephen Hunter Flick started his career in the late 1970s, a veteran of Roger Corman's *Deathsport*, which happened to be my first supervising sound editor's job and when I first met Stephen. He soon teamed up with Richard Anderson and helped tackle numerous robustly sound designed projects, serving as supervising sound editor on no less than *Pulp Fiction*, *Apollo 13*, *Twister*, *Predator 2*, *Starship Troopers*, *Spider-Man*, *Terminator 3: Rise of the Machines*, *Arthura: A Space Adventure*, and many others. In addition Stephen has won two Academy Awards for Best Sound Effect Editing for two action-driven features, *Robocop* and *Speed*.

Figure 12.7 Stephen Hunter Flick taking a break from organizing a project in his cutting rooms on the Sony Lot in Culver City.

Having worked with Stephen from time to time on numerous projects, I would also entice the reader to learn from the leadership techniques of Stephen. Many supervising sound editors, when faced with conflict or the giant finger-pointing-of-fault that often arises during the postproduction process, will sacrifice their editors to save their own skin as they are first and foremost afraid of losing a client, or worse, having a picture pulled from their hands.

Stephen has, time and time again, demonstrated his leadership character to protect his talent. He is the supervising sound editor—he is responsible, which means *he* is responsible. If his team members make mistakes or have problems, he does not sacrifice them up to protect his own skin. He will deal with the problem within "the family," adopting a more basic and mature wisdom that comes from years of veteran know-how, rather than finding the guilty or throwing a scapegoat to the clients—just *fix* and *solve* the problem. He has earned great respect and loyalty from hundreds of craftspeople who have worked with him and for him over the past 30 years.

I was in between pictures at my own editorial shop when Stephen asked if I would come over to Weddington to help cut sound effects on *Predator 2* for him. Several days later, John Dunn, another sound effects editor, asked if I could bring some of my weapon effects to the opening shootout in reel 1. I brought a compilation DAT the following day with several gun effects I thought would contribute toward the effort.

Just after lunch, Flick burst into my room (as is his habit, garnishing him the affectionate nickname of "Tsunami") and demanded to know, "How come your guns are bigger than mine?!"

"I never said my guns are bigger than yours, Steve."

Steve shrugged. "I mean, I know I have big guns, but yours are—dangerous!"

With that, he whirled and disappeared down the hall just as suddenly as he had appeared. I sat in stunned aftermath, pondering his description of "dangerous." After due consideration, I agreed. The style by which I set my microphones up when I record weapon fire, and the combinations of elements if I editorially manufacture weapon fire to create audio events that are supposed to scare and frighten, have a "bite" to them.

Gunfire is an in-your-face crack! Big guns are not made by pouring tons of low-end frequency into the audio event. Low-end does not have any punch or bite. Low-end

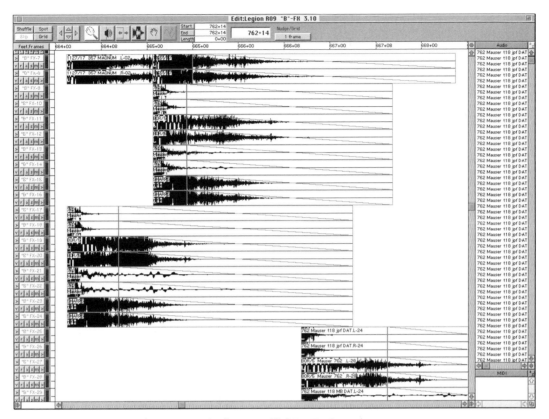

Figure 12.8 The "Mauser rifle" Pro Tools session.

is fun, when used appropriately, but the upper mid-range and high-end bite with a low-end under bed will bring the weapon to life. Dangerous sounds are not heard at arm's length where it is *safe*, but *in your face*. They are almost close enough to reach out and touch you. Distance, what we call "proximity," triggers your subconscious emotional responses to determine the danger.

I approach blending multiple sound cues together in a new design to being a choir director. Designing a sound event is exactly like mixing and moving the various voices of the choir to create a new vocal event with richness and body. I think of each sound as being soprano, alto, tenor, or bass. Putting basses together will not deliver a cutting punch and a gutsy depth of low end. All I will get is muddy low-end with no cutting *punch*!

The Pro Tools session shown in Figure 12.8 is a rifle combination I put together for the 1998 action-adventure film *Legionnaire*, a circa 1925 period film. We had several thousand rifle shots in the battle scenes; for each, I painstakingly cut 4 stereo pairs of sounds that made up the basic signature of a single 7.62 Mauser rifle shot. The reason is simple. Recording a gunshot with all the spectrum characteristics envisioned in a single recording by the supervising sound editor is impossible. Choice of microphone, placement of microphone, selection of recording medium—all these factors determine the voice of the rifle report.

Listen to the individual cues and the combination mix of the "designed" 7.62 Mauser rifle shot on the DVD provided with this book.

As an experienced sound designer, I review recordings at my disposal and choose those cues that comprise the soprano, alto, tenor, and bass of the performance. I may slow down or speed up one or more of the cues. I may pitch-shift or alter the equalization, as I deem necessary. I then put them together, very carefully lining up the leading edge of each discharge as accurately as I can (well within 1/100th of a second accurate), then I play them together as one new voice. I may need to lower the tenor or raise the alto, or I may discover that the soprano is not working and that I must choose a new soprano element.

If possible, I will not commit the mixing of these elements at the sound editorial stage. After consulting with the head re-recording mixer and considering the predubbing schedule, I will decide whether we can afford cutting the elements abreast and leaving the actual mixing to the sound effects mixer during predubbing. If the budget of the postproduction sound job is too small and the sound effects predubbing too short (or nonexistent), I will mix the elements together prior to the sound editorial phase, thereby throwing the die of commitment to how the individual elements are balanced together in a new single stereo pair.

The same goes for rifle bolt actions. I may have the exact recordings of the weapon used in the action sequence in the movie. When I cut them to sync, I play them against the rest of the tracks. The bolt actions played by themselves sound great, but now they are mixed with the multitude of other sounds present. They just do not have the same punch or characterization as when they stood alone. As a sound designer, I must pull other material, creating the illusion and perception of historical audio accuracy, but I must do it by factoring in the involvement of the other sounds of the battle. Their own character and frequency signatures will have a profound influence on the sound I am trying to create.

This issue was demonstrated on *Escape from New York*. During sound effect predubs, the picture editor nearly dumped the helicopter skid impacts I had made for the Hueys upon descent and landing in the streets of New York. Played by themselves, they sounded extremely loud and sharp. The experienced, veteran sound effect mixer, Gregg Landaker, advised the picture editor that it was not necessary or wise to dump the effects at that time; let them stay as they were in a separate set of channels because they could be easily dumped later if not wanted.

Later, as we rehearsed the sequence for the final mix, it became apparent that Gregg's advice not to make a hasty decision paid off. Now that the heavy pounding of the Huey helicopter blades filled the theatre along with the haunting siren-like score, what had sounded like huge and ungainly metal impacts in the individual predub now became a gentle, even subtle, helicopter skid touchdown on asphalt.

WHAT MAKES EXPLOSIONS BIG

For years following *Christine*, people constantly asked about the magic I used to bring such huge explosions to the screen. Remember, *Christine* was mixed before digital technology, when we still worked to an 85-dB maximum. The simple answer should transcend your design thinking into areas aside from just explosions. I see sound editors laying on all kinds of low-end or adding shotgun blasts into the explosion combination, and certainly a nice low-end wallop is cool and necessary, but it isn't dangerous. All it does is muddy it up. What makes an explosion big and dangerous is not the boom, but the *debris* thrown around.

I first realized this while watching footage of military C4 explosives igniting. Smokeless and seemingly nothing as a visual entity unto themselves, they wreak havoc, tearing apart trees, vehicles, masonry—the debris makes C4 so visually awesome. The same is true with sound. Go back and listen to the sequence in reel 7 of *Christine*, the sequence where the gas station blows up. Listen to the glass debris flying out the window, the variations of metal, oil cans, crowbars, tires, tools that come flying out of the service bay. Listen to the metal sidings of the gas pumps flying up and impacting the light overhang atop the fueling areas. Debris is the key to danger. Prepare tracks so that the re-recording mixer can pan debris cues into the surround channels, bringing the audience into the action, rather than allowing it to watch the scene at a safe distance.

THE SATISFACTION OF SUBTLETY

Sound design often calls to mind the big, high-profile audio events that serve as landmarks in a film. For every stand-out moment, however, dozens of other equally important moments designate sound design as part of the figurative chorus line. These moments are not solo events, but supportive and transparent performances that enhance the storytelling continuity of the film.

Undoubtedly, my reputation is one of action sound effects. I freely admit that I enjoy designing the hardware and firepower and wrath of nature; yet some of my most satisfying creations have been the little things that hardly are noticed: the special gust of wind through the hair of the hero in the night desert, the special seat compression with a taste of spring action as a passenger swings into a car seat and settles in, the delicacy of a slow door latch as a child timidly enters the master bedroom—little golden touches that fortify and sweetly satisfy the idea of design.

REALITY VS. ENTERTAINMENT

One of the first requirements for the successful achievement of a soundtrack is becoming audio educated with the world. I know that advice sounds naive and obvious, but it is not. Listen and observe life around you. Listen to the components of sound and come to understand how things work. Learn the difference between a Rolls Royce Merlin engine of a P-51 and the Pratt-Whitney of an AT-6, the difference between a hammer being cocked on a .38 service revolver and a hammer being cocked on a .357 Smith & Wesson. What precise audio movements separate the actions of a hundred-ton metal press? What is the audio difference between a grass fire and an oil fire? Between pine burning and oak? What is the difference between a rope swish and a wire or dowel swish? How can one distinguish blade impacts of a fencing foil from a cutlass or a saber? What kind of metallic ring-off would go with each?

A supervising sound editor I knew was thrown off a picture because he did not know what a Ford Cobra was, and insisted that his effect editors cut sound cues from an English sports car series. It is not necessary to be a walking encyclopedia that can regurgitate information about the South American Kerrington mating call or the rate of fire of a BAR (that is, if you even know what a BAR is). What is important is that you diligently do research so that you can walk onto the re-recording stage with the proper material.

I remember predubbing a helicopter warming up on stage. Suddenly the engine wind-up bumped hard with a burst from the turbine. The sound effects mixer quickly tried to duck it out, as he thought it was a bad sound cut on my part. The director immediately corrected him; indeed that was absolutely the right sound at exactly the right spot. The mixer asked how I knew where to cut the turbine burst. I told him that, in studying the shot frame by frame, I had noticed two frames of the exhaust that were a shade lighter than the rest. It seemed to me that that was where the turbo had kicked in.

Reality, however, is not necessarily the focus of sound design. There is reality, and there is the perception of reality. We were rehearsing for the final mix of reel 3 of *Escape from New York*, where the Huey helicopters descend and land in an attempt to find the president. I had been working very long hours and was exhausted. After I had dozed off and fallen out of my chair several nights before, Don Rogers had supplied a roll-around couch for me to sleep on during the mixing process. The picture editor paced behind the mixers as they rehearsed the reel. He raised his hand for them to stop and announced that he was missing a "descending" sound.

Gregg Landaker and Bill Varney tried to determine to what element of sound the picture editor was referring. The exact components of the helicopters were all there. From an authenticity point of view, nothing was missing.

I rolled over and raised my hand. "Roll back to 80 feet, take effects 14 off the line. Take the feed and the take-up reels off the machine and switch them; then put on a 3-track head stack. Leaving effects 14 off the line, roll back to this shot, then place effects 14 on the line. I think you will get the desired effect."

Everybody turned to look at me with disbelief, certain I was simply talking in my sleep. Bill Varney pressed the talkback button on the mixing console so that the recordist in the machine room could hear. "Would you please repeat that, Mr. Yewdall?"

I repeated the instructions. The picture editor had heard enough. "What is that supposed to accomplish?"

I explained. "At 80 feet is where Lee Van Cleef announces he is 'going in.' The next shot is the fleet of Hueys warming up and taking off. If you check the cue sheets, I think that you will see that effects 14 has a wind-up from a cold start. Played forward, it is a jet whine ascending with no blade rotation. If we play that track over the third channel position of a 3-channel head stack, which means the track is really playing backward while we are rolling forward, I think we will achieve a jet whine descending." Listen to the sound cue of "Huey helicopter descending" on the DVD provided with this book.

From then on, more movies used helicopter jet whine warm-ups (prior to blade rotation) both forward and reversed to sell the action of helicopters rising or descending, as the visual action dictated. It is not reality, but it is the entertaining perception of reality.

In today's postproduction evolution, the tasks of equalization and signal processing, once considered sacred ground for the re-recording mixers, increasingly have become the working domain of sound designers and supervising sound editors. Accepting those chores, however, also brings about certain responsibilities and ramifications should your work be inappropriate and cost the client additional budget dollars to unravel what you have done.

If you twist those signal-processing knobs, then know the accompanying burden of responsibility. Experienced supervising sound editors have years of "combat" on the re-recording mix stage to know what they and their team members should do, and what should be left for re-recording mixers. I liken my work to getting the rough diamond into shape. If I overpolish the material, I risk trapping the mixer with an audio cue that he or she may not be able to manipulate and appropriately use. Do not polish sound to a point that a mixer has no maneuvering room. You will thwart a collaborative relationship with the mixer.

The best sound design is done with a sable brush, not with a 10-pound sledgehammer. If your sound design distracts the audience from the story, you have failed. If your sound design works in concert with and elevates the action to a new level, you have succeeded. It is just that simple.

Sound design does not mean that you have to have a workstation stuffed full of fancy gear and complex software. One of the best signal process devices that I like to use is the simple Klark-Teknik DN 30/30, a 30-band graphic equalizer (see Figure 12.9). Taking a common but carefully chosen wood flame steady, I used the equalizer in real time, undulating the individual sliders wildly in waves to cause the "mushrooming" fireball sensation.

Listen to audio cue on the DVD provided with this book to listen to the before and after of "mushrooming flames."

"WORLDIZING" SOUND

Charles Maynes wrote a perfect article on the subject of "worldizing" of sound and so with permission from Charles Maynes and the *Editors Guild Magazine* (in which it appeared in April 2004), we are proud to share it with you here.

> "WORLDIZING: Take Studio Recordings into the Field to Make Them Sound Organic"
> By Charles Maynes
>
> For some of us in sound and music circles, "worldizing" has long held a special sense of the exotic. Worldizing is the act of playing back a recording in a real-world environment, allowing the sound to react to that environment, and then re-recording it so that the properties of the environment become part of the newly recorded material. The concept is simple, but its execution can be remarkably complex.

In Walter Murch's superb essay on the reconstruction of the Orson Welles film *A Touch of Evil*, he quotes from a 58-page memo that Welles wrote to Universal to lay

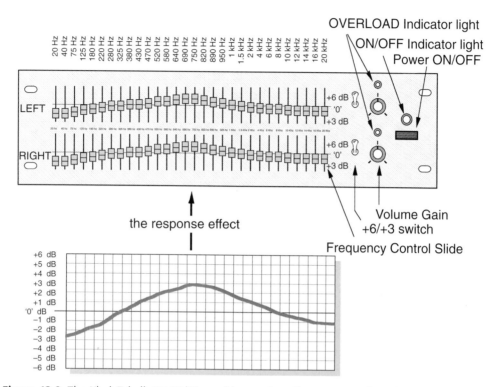

the response effect

Figure 12.9 The Klark-Teknik DN 30/30 graphic equalizer. If you turn up the volume gain full to the right (which equals +6 dB level) and flipped the +6/+3 dB switch up into the +6 position, then this would give you a total of +12 dB or –12 dB "gain" or "cut." Note how the settings of the frequency faders affect the response curve.

Figure 12.10 Re-recording pre-recorded sounds under freeway overpasses in the "concrete jungle" of the city. (Photo by Alec Boehm.)

out his vision for the movie. At one point, Welles describes how he wants to treat the music during a scene between Janet Leigh and Akim Tamiroff, and he offers as elegant a description of worldizing as I can think of:

> The music itself should be skillfully played but it will not be enough, in doing the final sound mixing, to run this track through an echo chamber with a certain amount of filter. To get the effect we're looking for, it is absolutely vital that this music be played back through a cheap horn in the alley outside the sound building. After this is recorded, it can then be loused up even further in the process of re-recording. But a tiny exterior horn is absolutely necessary, and since it does not represent very much in the way of money, I feel justified in insisting upon this, as the result will be really worth it.

At the time, Universal did not revise *Touch of Evil*, according to these notes, but the movie's recent reconstruction incorporates these ideas. Worldizing is now a technique that has been with us for some time and will likely be used and refined for years to come.

WALTER MURCH AND WORLDIZING

The practice of worldizing—and, I believe, the term itself—started with Walter Murch, who has used the technique masterfully in many films. However, it has received most of its notoriety from his use of it in *American Graffiti* and in the granddaddy of the modern war film, *Apocalypse Now*.

In *American Graffiti*, recordings of the Wolfman Jack radio show were played through practical car radios and re-recorded with both stationary and moving microphones to recreate the ever-changing quality of the multiple moving speaker sources the cars were providing. On the dub stage, certain channels were mechanically delayed to simulate echoes of the sound bouncing off the buildings. All of these channels, in addition to a dry track of the source, were manipulated in the mix to provide the compelling street-cruising ambience of the film.

In *Apocalypse Now*, the most obvious use of this technique was on the helicopter communications ADR, which was re-recorded through actual military radios in a special isolation box. The ground-breaking result has been copied on many occasions.

SOUND EFFECTS

In the previous examples, worldizing was used for dialogue or music, but it has also been used very effectively for sound effects. One of my personal favorite applications of the technique was on the film *GATTACA*, which required dramatically convincing electric car sounds. Supervising sound editor Richard King and his crew devised a novel method to realize these sounds by installing a speaker system on the roof of a car, so that they could play back various sounds created for the vehicles.

According to King, the sounds were made up of recordings that ranged from mechanical sources such as surgical saws and electric motors to propane blasts and animal and human screams. In the studio, King created pads of these sounds, which were then used for playback.

Richard and Patricio Libenson recorded a variety of vehicle maneuvers, with the prepared sounds being played through the car-mounted speakers and re-recorded by microphones. They recorded drive-bys, turns, and other moves to give the sounds a natural acoustic perspective. As King points out, one of the most attractive aspects of worldizing is the way built-in sonic anomalies happen as sound travels through the atmosphere.

King also used worldizing to create a believable sound for a literal rain of frogs in the film *Magnolia*. To simulate the sound of frogs' bodies falling from the sky, King and recordist Eric Potter began by taking pieces of chicken and ham into an abandoned house and recording their impacts on a variety of surfaces, including windows, walls and roofs. Using this source material, King created a continuous bed of impacts that could then be played back and re-recorded. For the recording environment, King chose a canyon, where he and Potter set up some distant mics to provide a somewhat "softened" focus to the source material. A loudspeaker system projected the recordings across the canyon to impact acoustic movement.

In addition to this, King and Potter moved the speakers during the recordings to make the signal go on and off axis. This provided an additional degree of acoustic variation. King and Potter created other tracks by mounting the speakers on a truck and driving around, which provided believable Doppler effects for the shifting perspectives of the sequence.

Another interesting application was Gary Rydstrom's treatment of the ocean sounds during the D-Day landing sequence in *Saving Private Ryan*, where he used tubes and other acoustic devices to treat the waves during the disorienting Omaha Beach sequence.

MYSTERY MEN

Charles Maynes contributed the following thoughts:

> I used worldizing in the film *Mystery Men*, a superhero comedy that required a distinctive sound for a doomsday device called the "psycho-defraculator." The device could render time and space in particularly unpleasant ways, yet it was home-made and had to have a

Figure 12.11 Charles Maynes found that a squawk box in a trim bin creates a distinctive sound for the doomsday machine in *Mystery Men*. (Photo by Steven Cohen.)

somewhat rickety character. I was after a sound like the famous "Inertia Starter" (the Tasmanian Devil's Sound) from Warner Bros. cartoons, but I also wanted to give the sense that the machine was always on the verge of self-destruction.

We started by generating a number of synthesized tones, which conveyed the machine's ever-accelerating character. After finding a satisfying basic sound, we needed to find a suitable way to give the impression of impending collapse. By exhaustively trolling through the sound library, I found various recordings of junky cars and broken machines, and I began to combine them with the synthetic tones. I spent a considerable amount of time vari-speeding the elements but was never really satisfied with the result.

Since this was in 1999, we still had a film bench nearby, with a sync block and squawk box. I remembered how gnarly that squawk box speaker sounded and thought, worldize the synth, that's the answer! So I took the squawk box into my editing room, plugged the synthesizer into it and was quickly satisfied with the distortion it provided.

Then I realized that using the squawk box inside a trim bin might be even better. So in came the trim bin, which became home to the speaker. As I listened, I noticed that the bin was vibrating at certain pitches and immediately tried to find which were the best ones to work with. After some trial and error, I started to put various bits of metal and split reels into the bin and noticed that it started really making a racket when the volume was turned up. I had arrived at my sound design destination. The compelling thing about this rig was that I changed the frequency of the synthesizer so that different objects would vibrate and bang against one another, creating a symphony of destruction. The sound was simultaneously organic and synthetic and gave the feeling that the machine was about to vibrate itself to pieces, like a washing machine during the spin cycle, with all the fasteners holding it together removed.

IN THE FUTURE

Charles continued:

Traditionally, it has been difficult to impart the acoustic qualities of real-world locations to our sound recordings using signal processors and electronic tone shaping, but this may well be changing. A new wave of processors now appearing on the market use a digital process called "convolution" to precisely simulate natural reverb and ambience. Using an actual recording made in a particular space, they separate out the reverb and other acoustic attributes of the sound, then apply those to a new recording.

The source recordings are generally created with a sine wave sweep or an impulse, typically from a starter's pistol, which is fired in the space being sampled. Hardwave devices incorporating this technology are available from both Yamaha and Sony; software convolution reverb for Apple-based digital audio workstations (including Digidesign Pro Tools, Steinberg Nuendo and Cubase, Apple Logic Audio and Mark of the Unicorn Digital Performer) is available from the Dutch company AudioEase.

While it seems as though this might be a Rosetta stone that could be used for matching ADR to production dialogue, there are still limitations to the technology. The main one is that the reverb impulse is being modeled on a single recorded moment in time, so the same reverb is applied to each sound being processed with the particular sample. However, the acoustic character of this process is significantly more natural than the digital reverbs we are accustomed to. This tool was used very effectively to process some of the ADR on *Lord of the Rings* to make it sound as though it had been recorded inside a metal helmet.

One of our goals as *sound designers* is to imbue our recordings with the physical imperfection of the real world, so that they will fit seamlessly into the world of our film. We want the control that the studio offers us, but we aim to create a sound that feels as natural as a location recording. Worldizing is one way to do this, and so are the new digital tools that help to simulate it. But sound editors are infinitely inventive. The fun of our job is to combine natural and artificial sounds in new ways to create things that no one has ever heard before!

Charles Maynes is a sound designer and supervising sound editor. His credits include Spider-Man, Twister, *and* U-571. *Special thanks to Richard King, John Morris, Walter Murch, and Gary Rydstrom for their patient help with this article.*

WORLDIZING *DAYLIGHT*

I think one of more interesting applications of worldizing was the work done by David Whittaker, M.P.S.E., on the Sylvester Stallone action-adventure film *Daylight*. In the last part of the film, when the traffic tunnel started to fill up with water, the sound designing chores beckoned for a radical solution. After the sound editing process and premixing was complete on the scenes to be treated "underwater," all the channels of the premixes were transferred to a DA-88 with time code. Whittaker tells about it:

> We purchased a special underwater speaker, made by Electro-Voice. We took a portable mixing console, an amplifier, a water-proofable microphone, a microphone preamp, and two DA-88 machines—one to play back the edited material and the other one to re-record the new material onto. We did the work in my backyard where I have a large swimming pool—it's thirty-eight feet long by eighteen feet wide.
>
> We chose a Countryman lavalier production mike, because it tends to be amazingly resistant to moisture. To waterproof it we slipped it into an unlubricated condom, sealing the open end with thin stiff wire twisted tight around the lavalier's cable. After some experimentation we settled on submerging the speaker about three feet down in the corner of one end, with the mike dropped into the water about the same distance down at the opposite corner of the pool, thus giving us 42 feet of water between the speaker and the microphone. We found we needed as much water as possible between the speaker and the microphone to get a strong effect. We literally hung the mike off a fishing pole—it looked pretty hilarious.
>
> We then played back and re-recorded each channel one at a time, using the time code to keep the DA-88 machines in exact sync phase. The worldizing radically modified the original sounds. The low frequencies tended to disappear, and the high frequencies took on a very squirrely character, nothing like the way one hears in air.
>
> The result became a predub pass onto itself; when we ran it at the re-recording mixing stage, we could play it against the "dry" original sound channels and control how "wet" and "murky" we wanted the end result. Actually, I think it was very effective—and it certainly always made me smile when I would go swimming in my pool after that.

SOME FINAL ADVICE TO CONSIDER

I learned more than one valuable lesson on *Escape from New York*. As with magicians, never tell the client how you made the magic.

Escape from New York's budget was strained to the limit and the job was not done yet. The special effect shots had not been completed, and the budget could not bear the weight of being made at a traditional feature special effect shop. They decided to contract the work to Roger Corman's company, as he had acquired the original computer-tracking special effect camera rig that George Lucas had used on *Star Wars*. Corman was making a slew of special effect movies to amortize the cost of acquiring the equipment, in addition to offering special effect work to outside production companies, *Escape from New York* being one.

The first shots were delivered. John Carpenter (director), Debra Hill (producer), Todd Ramsay (picture editor), Dean Cundey (director of photography), Bob Kizer (special effects supervisor), and several members of the visual special effects team sat down in Projection "A" at Goldwyn to view the footage. It has been suggested that the quality expectation from the production team was not very high. After all, this was only Corman stuff, how good could it be?

The first shot flickered onto the screen—the point of view of Air Force One streaking over New York harbor at night, heading into the city just prior to impact. Carpenter, Hill, and Cundey were amazed by the high quality of the shot. After the lights came up, John asked the visual special effects team how it was done. The team members, proud and happy that Carpenter liked their work, blurted out, "Well, first we dumped black paint on the concrete floor, then we let it dry halfway. Then we took paint rollers and roughed it up, to give it the 'wave' effect of water at night. Then we made dozens of cardboard cut-outs of the buildings and cut out windows. . . ."

Carpenter's brow furrowed as he halted their explanation. He pressed the talkback button to projection. "Roll it again, please."

Now they viewed the footage again, only with the discerning eye of foreknowledge of the illusion's creation. Now they could see the imperfections, could see how it was done. The reel ran out and the lights came up.

Carpenter thought a moment, and then turned to the visual special effects team. "No—I am going with what I saw the first time. You fooled me. If I ever ask you how you did something again, don't tell me."

The lesson of that afternoon was burned indelibly into my brain and I have referred to it time and time again in dealing with clients who want to know how something was made. Do not destroy the illusion and magic of your creation by revealing the secrets of how you did them, especially to your clients.

Here endeth the lesson. Now go forth ye inspired and create great audio masterpieces so that the world may dream.

Chapter 13
Sound Editorial
Sync-Sync, Chop-Chop

"Think about sound effects as though they are music—find the
right 'note' for every sound event, then build a 'chord' around
it, choosing sounds in higher and lower registers that
will support that key 'note'."

– *Dave Whittaker*, M.P.S.E.

All through a film's evolution, sound endures uneven recordings, mismatching formats, missed opportunities, temp voices, temp music, and temp sound effects. It suffers clipped lines, radio interference, line static, digital zits, dramatic level shifts, noisy backgrounds, fluorescent ballast, power hums, and just about every other insult and shortcoming a sound engineer can imagine—not to mention ignorance, carelessness, and mindlessness. The project experiences noncommunication, miscommunication, misinformation, improperly entered data in the code book, improperly transferred material, lack of notations in the production sound report, let alone physical misplacement or total loss of materials. Just because the negative and original sound rolls are vaulted at the laboratories and sound transfer facilities does not mean something unexpected cannot happen to them. Murphy's Law is ever-present and devilish in thwarting creative and idealistic expectations. All during this time, one person or another inevitably will say, "Oh, don't worry about it; we'll fix it later in post."

Guess what. Post is here! The production sound and locked picture will be turned over to sound editorial. You can have no "fix-it-later" attitude here. Sound editorial must gather the various broken pieces of the production sound process and put them back together again, in addition to creating the sound effects and ambiences that creatively bind the entire soundtrack together.

The head of the sound editorial team is the supervising sound editor; in the case of a big, complex feature project, two editors team up as co-supervising sound editors. Like a field commander carefully deploying forces, the supervising sound editor divides the work, assigning a specialist to each aspect of the sound tasks.

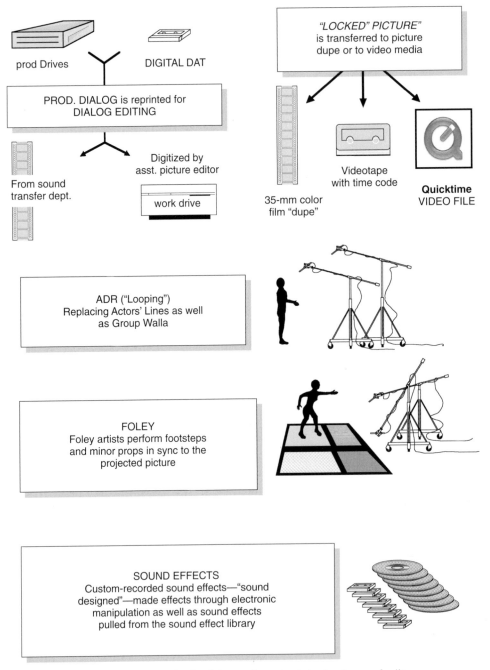

prod Drives

DIGITAL DAT

PROD. DIALOG is reprinted for
DIALOG EDITING

From sound
transfer dept.

Digitized by
asst. picture editor

work drive

"LOCKED" PICTURE"
is transferred to picture
dupe or to video media

35-mm color
film "dupe"

Videotape
with time code

Quicktime
VIDEO FILE

ADR ("Looping")
Replacing Actors' Lines as well
as Group Walla

FOLEY
Foley artists perform footsteps
and minor props in sync to the
projected picture

SOUND EFFECTS
Custom-recorded sound effects—"sound
designed"—made effects through electronic
manipulation as well as sound effects
pulled from the sound effect library

Figure 13.1 Sound editorial crew flow chart: basic phases of edit.

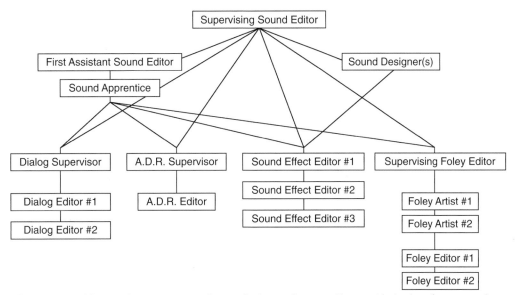

Figure 13.2 This sound crew structure is a typical crew for a medium-to-big-budget feature project with an average schedule and temp dub requirements.

The supervisor organizes and coordinates each editor's efforts, focusing the creative work so that when various components of the sound elements are brought together in the re-recording process, the result is a seamless audio experience performing with a transparency of reality.

WHO'S WHO IN SOUND EDITORIAL

Figure 13.2 illustrates the sound editorial structure of a typical medium-budget action picture. (This same sample crew was outlined in the budget breakdown in Chapter 4.)

Sound Editorial Crew Tree

Supervising Sound Editor
The supervising sound editor is the creative authority of the sound preparation process, working hand-in-hand with the director, picture editor, and producer(s) in realizing the audio potential of the film. The supervisor's shoulders bear far more than the recognition limelight of the title. His or her taste in sound and choice in sound crew—sound editors, sound designer(s), Foley artists, transfer department crew, ADR and Foley stage mixers, as well as choice of final re-recording stage and mixing team—are pivotal factors that focus the combined efforts of all toward an artistically successful soundtrack. Such expert guidance vastly increases the production value of the film.

Conversely, inappropriate taste in sound or choices of team members can lead headlong to disaster, plunging the project into a budgetary hemorrhage and irreparably destroying the chances of a quality sound experience. Directors and producers are well aware of this.

The supervising sound editor enters into a series of meetings with the director, picture editor, and producer(s), covering a wide range of audio concepts and concerns. As discussed in Chapter 4, unwise clients decide what mixing facility to use without including the input and professional experience of the supervising sound editor.

As today's postproduction schedules become increasingly complicated and more outrageous, the supervising sound editor literally is becoming a tactical field commander whose talent assignment and schedule problem-solving skills are often considered more important than the ability to sound design or cut sound. After all, these chores can be assigned to specialists hired as needed. In simplistic terms, the supervising sound editor's job is to hold the hands of the director and producers through an often arduous and anxiety-filled postproduction process.

The supervising sound editor holds the promise of a wonderful and inspiring soundtrack to come, all the while scrambling to deliver these promises without budget overruns. On top of all of this, the supervising sound editor must deliver these promised audio ingredients to the re-recording stage on time, while enduring the inevitable hail of changes, both in the film and the director's heart and mind.

From the outset of consideration, the supervising sound editor receives a script from the production company considering him or her to head the project. The supervisor reads it carefully, breaking out all the audio events and potential challenges to be addressed. Budgeting and bidding on a project based solely on reading the script is extremely difficult, however.

As soon as the supervising sound editor is asked to consider a show, research must be done. The supervisor first should determine who the director and producer(s) are, and then look them up in the Annual Index to Motion Picture Credits published by the Academy of Motion Picture Arts and Sciences, gleaning any information about screen credits and earlier work. Sometimes the supervisor charts the projects, especially for someone unknown, showing the evolution of a first-time director who rose through the ranks of cinematographer, picture editor, or producer. This kind of information lends a feel for a director's expectations with regard to sound. If the director has previous projects listed, the supervisor takes time to review them on various video media to determine the style of sound exhibited in other work. Likewise, the supervisor does the same in regard to the producers, especially noting if and on what project(s) the director and producer(s) have worked together before.

The supervising sound editor may want to trace the present project back to either commencement of principal photography or announcement in the trades (*Hollywood Reporter* and *Variety*), where back issues can yield any publicity information on creative or political footnotes. The Internet has also become a valuable resource, providing nearly instantaneous information. All of this lends the necessary information for developing a philosophy and tactical strategy that helps the supervisor better serve the project at hand.

Next, the supervisor insists on personally listening to raw daily recordings in a playback environment that accurately reveals any problems impacting the scope of work to be done. Experience has taught me that a picture editor's opinion on the quality of the dialog track is not always an accurate determination, though it can be a weather

Sound Editorial Crew Flow Chart

	week #1	week #2	week #3	week #4	week #5	week #6	week #7	week #8	week #9	week #10	week #11	Re-recording MIX schedule week #12	week #13	week #14	week #15	week #16	total weeks
Supervising Sound Editor	x	x	x	x	x	x	x	x	x	x	x	x	x	x	x	x	16
First Asst. Sound Editor	x	x	x	x	x	x	x	x	x	x	x	x	x	x	x	x	16
Sound Apprentice	x	x	x	x	x	x	x	x	x	x	x	x	x	x	x	x	16
Dialog Supervisor		X	X	X	X	X	X	X	X	X	X	X	X	X			13
Dialog Editor #1		X	X	X	X	X	X	X	X	X	X						10
Dialog Editor #2				X	X	X	X	X	X	X	X	X					9
A.D.R. Supervisor		X	X	X	X	X	X	X	X	X	X	X	X	X	X	X	15
A.D.R. Editor						X	X	X	X	X	X	X	X				8
Sound FX Recordist				X	X												2
Sound Designer		X	X	X	X	X	X	X	X	X	X	X	X				12
Sound Effects Editor #1			X	X	X	X	X	X	X	X	X	X	X				11
Sound Effects Editor #2			X	X	X	X	X	X	X	X	X	X					10
Sound Effects Editor #3				X	X	X	X	X	X	X	X	X					9
Supervising Foley Editor		X	X	X	X	X	X	X	X	X	X	X					11
Foley Artist #1							X	X	X								3
Foley Artist #2							X	X	X								3
Foley Editor #1							X	X	X	X							4
Foley Editor #2							X	X	X	X							4

Figure 13.3 The supervising sound editor carefully charts out the use of labor requirements for the most efficient use of budget dollars.

vane of expectations to come. The supervisor immediately gets a feel for not only how difficult the dialog preparation is liable to be, but how much ADR is needed, how much Group Walla is necessary, how broad and detailed the sound effect editing will be, and how much Foley should be scheduled. The supervisor then makes up an asset plot chart, mapping out in a timeline what labor should be hired at which point and for how long. In a relatively short period of time, with much experience from previous projects to help assess the new project, the supervisor arrives at a cost-to-complete.

Sound Editorial Crew Flow Chart

Once the supervisor is chosen by the client for the project, he or she must carry out the tasks of developing, cutting, and overseeing the mixing of the project soundtrack, while staying within the boundaries of the contracted budget and schedule. Schedules and budgets, as well as changes and renegotiations, are an entire science unto themselves, and this book is not designed to address those issues.

First Assistant Sound Editor

The first assistant sound editor is the supervising sound editor's secret weapon in the war of organization and technical discipline. The first assistant is the direct conduit

Figure 13.4 First sound assistant Peter Cole rewinds a 1,000-foot transfer onto a projection reel for the Foley editor. The first assistant is the first to be hired by the supervising sound editor and the last to be laid off. His or her work literally makes or breaks the ability of the sound editorial team to successfully mount and complete a project, in addition to helping keep editorial costs from rising unnecessarily.

from the picture editorial department. Picture dupes, videotapes, change notes, code books, sound reports, EDLs, and all transferred materials pass through the first assistant's domain and control before the editors receive them. If they do not, the first assistant cannot vouch for the material being current, correct, and viable. The first assistant is the organizational foundation on which the entire sound editorial project rests.

Sound Apprentice
Shortly after the first assistant sound editor commences work, the sound apprentice is hired. This position is not to be confused with the second sound assistant. The term "sound apprentice" is being used less in the industry, replaced by the term "intern," as more editorial facilities try to sidestep a potential union position. In past years the apprentice was the break-in position, but as union domination slowly ebbed, so has the structured ways of entering the industry's work force.

Regardless of this position's name, the apprentice is an assistant to the assistant, and, working at the job, he or she will begin to learn and understand the process—why we perform tasks a certain way. What is one of the most important factors in building a strong base of technical and procedural discipline? Unless you understand why, you will never appreciate the procedures to achieve the desired result.

Sound Designer
Depending on the postproduction schedule restrictions as well as the complexity of the project, the supervising sound editor may want to contract a sound designer to

create sound effects, ensuring the continuity and efficiency that will satisfy the director's taste and vision. This is especially true for high-concept projects. This work used to be done by the supervising sound editor, but since the late 1980s the supervising sound editor has shifted the ever-growing sound development needs to sound designing talent on a full-time basis. (Review Chapter 12 for more detailed information on the role of sound designer.)

Dialog Supervisor

On some projects, the dialog supervisor is called the co-supervising sound editor; on others, the ADR supervisor. Regardless of the title, the task is of primary importance. Music and sound effects may be used or discarded in the mix, but dialog almost never is discarded. When the actors' lips flap, vocal utterances must surely be heard. Hence strict attention must be given to the preparation of dialog tracks; whether original production recordings or ADR "looped" lines, they must be seamlessly edited so that the audience is unaware of the editing process. (See Chapter 14 for an in-depth review of the importance and editorial philosophy of the dialog editor.)

ADR Supervisor

For weeks prior to turnover, the picture editor, director, and producer(s) become increasingly aware of the quality shortcomings of their production track. On some pictures, the ADR supervisor is hired separately from the supervising sound editor and sound editorial crew. Often the ADR supervisor is the political trade-off to secure a project. The ADR supervisor, more than any other postproduction craftsperson, interfaces and works with the acting talent. When temperamental or difficult talent is involved, the producer's first concern is who is going to handle the ADR politics and responsibilities.

A special talent exists for cutting ADR lines. Most of the time, an ADR line never just lays into the actor's mouth. The actor or director has signed off on the line because of the performance, more than anything, so it falls to the ADR editor to massage (cut) the actor's words in such a way as to lend a seamless and natural delivery, yet still fit the lip movements. This is not so easy a task! (Review Chapter 15 for more detailed information on the role of ADR supervisor/editor.)

Sound Effects Editors

The experienced supervising sound editor will know the editing style and talent of the sound effects editors with whom he or she works. Almost all sound effects editors tend to lean toward their own favorite tasks or specialties. Some are more talented in cutting animal vocals; others are better versed in cutting vehicles and mechanical devices. Few sound editors can truly say they are proficient at cutting all sounds. Understanding how to sync up sound and make it work is one thing; it is far and away another to know how to massage the material and make a special audio event from a handful of common audio cues.

With today's digital nonlinear systems, a supervisor can assign a particular type of sound to a single sound effects editor to cut throughout an entire picture. Some supervisors call this "horizontal editing." This lends a greater precision in continuity to a picture. The sound effects editor who cuts the windshield wipers on the car in reel

Figure 13.5 Wendy Hedin, a New York-based supervising sound editor working at her nonlinear workstation. She has helmed such projects as *Purity*, *Chinese Coffee*, *You Can Count On Me*, and *The Autumn Heart*, to name just a few.

2 is the same editor who cuts the windshield wipers in reel 9, thereby guaranteeing a matched particular style and rhythm.

This mishap befell *Raiders of the Lost Ark* during the track chase sequence. As the truck barreled through the water duct, the driver turned the wipers on. The sound effects editor interpreted the material one way and cut the windshield wipers "swish-thunk, swish-thunk, swish-thunk." The chase crossed over into the next reel, and the sound effects editor who cut his portion of the chase had certainly checked with the other sound effects editor to make sure he was using the same windshield wiper sound effect, only he had neglected to ask the interpretation. He cut it "thunk-swish, thunk-swish, thunk-swish." This certainly was not the end of the audio world, but a little humorous "oops," recounted as a valid example of techniques and thinking that must be addressed.

Foley Supervisor
Some pictures do not have a Foley supervisor. Each sound effects editor (or sometimes the supervising sound editor) marks up the Foley cue sheets, noting cues to be performed in each reel. The advantage of having a dedicated Foley supervisor, especially on a picture where thorough and complete coverage is expected, is that the style and design of the layout are consistent from reel to reel.

The best intentions of the supervising sound editor to mark up the Foley sheets and oversee the Foley walking are often distracted by other demands, such as future client meetings, having to sit on another stage for the previous project's M&E or airplane version, or unscheduled emergencies seemingly always arising.

Some Foley supervisors not only mark up the Foley cues, but also serve as lead Foley artists on the stage. This is an added bonus, as they lay out the cue assignments in the most logical ways, develop a working relationship with their Foley mixers, knowing how the two of them like to work, and help make the flow of work most efficient.

Foley Artists

The term "Foley artist" has become the preferred designation of the Foley walker, which even earlier was known simply as the "stepper." These people perform the foot-steps, cloth movement, and prop work as requested on the Foley cue sheets. Foley artists work on a Foley stage, performing footsteps and props while they watch the action in real time as projected on a screen or television monitor in front of them. (See Chapter 16 for a thorough overview of Foley.)

Foley artists are often hired for their strengths and specialties. If the supervising sound editor is working on an important feature project, he or she may hire a Foley artist known more for the ability to give texture and characterization to the footsteps, rather than just providing common footfalls. The trade-off, however, is usually that the footsteps are not walked precisely in sync. If the footsteps are performed to frame-accurate sync, then texture and character are sacrificed, and vice versa. A good supervisor always opts for texture and character, knowing full well the sync issue can be fixed by good, disciplined Foley editing. The last thing the supervisor wants is common, clunky Foley.

I do not endorse the hang-and-pray technique. I have heard many producers say they would prefer to have their Foley walked-to-sync and hung-in-the-mix. They really are saying that they do not want to incur the costs involved in transfer and precision sync editorial. When you get on the mixing stage, all the practical trade-offs are quickly forgotten when they grumble that the sync is rubbery and the performance does not seem to be what it should be, a performance always helped out by the Foley editor.

Other Foley artists are known more for creative prop work and not so much for good footsteps, just as others are not skilled at prop work but specialize in footsteps. Of course, one should have a relationship with a number of Foley artists, with a thorough knowledge of their strengths and weaknesses, so that appropriate Foley artists for a project can be contracted.

THE STRATEGY BREWS

The director engages the supervising sound editor in sweeping concepts for the soundtrack rolling around in his or her brain for months, now bursting at the seams to manifest itself into dramatic and bold audio events. The producer meets with the supervising sound editor in private and bemoans the fact that the picture is over-budget, overschedule, and teeters on the edge of disaster. Of course, they are counting on sound to save it.

Large calendar pages are taped to the wall in monthly progression, with dozens of yellow sticky notes showing the turnover date of latched reels, various progress screenings, spotting sessions, ADR and Foley stage bookings, temp dub(s), test audience screenings, commencement of predubs, and when finals start. This is the battle map upon which the supervising sound editor will deploy forces. Start talent too soon, and no money will remain to maintain the crew through to the predubs; hold back too long, and the supervisor risks delivering to the stage late or compressing necessary creative time for properly producing the work.

The biggest danger is from the director and producer themselves. In their zeal to develop a temp soundtrack to commence test screenings, they all too often deplete and exhaust precious time and financial assets. Although one or more temp dubs are scheduled and budgeted, invariably the project is sapped by the little "nickel-and-dime" needs that irreparably detract from the final product. The experience of veteran supervising sound editors pays off here, for they have been in this situation numerous times, dealing with the same old requests that weaken the sound editorial assets inch by inch.

To cut corners and save costs, both client and inexperienced postproduction supervisor will hire cheaper labor. Experienced veteran talent does not work for a union rate card minimum. For good work, you must hire good talent with experience, which costs more than the skills of the aspiring apprentice. Producers and production accountants with bean-counter mentalities look at the higher paid, experienced craftsperson as just a more expensive craftsperson. However, those who have been around the block a few times themselves understand how the industry works and realize that the extra cost for veterans actually saves money because of their ability to do the job better and faster than apprentices.

This is not to say that get-start apprentices should never be used. On the contrary, as an industry, we have a responsibility to train and build a work force to fortify the veteran ranks. The best way that new talent learns their craft is from the veteran craftspeople.

The Turnover

When picture editorial begins to turn over material to sound editorial, it turns over a fairly standard set of materials, which is received by the first assistant sound editor. Nothing should be picked up and used by the supervising sound editor or other department sound editors until the first assistant has logged it in and prepared it for use.

A binder should be kept to record materials received. The day and the exact time it was received should be recorded. You will be surprised how many times you need to prove what time something was received to avert misunderstandings, untrue warranties by third parties, and even court action. Keep a binder also tracking materials that leave sound editorial. The listing should show what materials were removed from the premises and who ordered the removal of said materials. This person usually is responsible for the materials while they are off-site, but, if not, the person who is responsible for the materials also should be listed. The log should also show what date and time said materials left the premises and where the materials were destined. As with the receipt binder, this tracking binder also proves invaluable in keeping the sound editorial firm legally safe.

Dupe Picture and Video Dupes

In the old days we received 35-mm black-and-white dupes of the editor's color work-print. Oh, you missed a lot of fun! Many dupe prints were brittle and would break easily or you would find yourself standing on the end of a loose piece of film that was being fed into your Moviola and suddenly it would rip perforations! I think I learned some of the most creative and bizarre curse words; even editors who could not bring themselves to use a classic four-letter word would blurt out, "You fornicating harlot!!" By the late 1980s, 35-mm color dupes were becoming more affordable—we could see the image better, but it was only a passing phase as videotape editing, first using analog 24-track machines before giving way to the approaching nonlinear technologies.

Even when we were still cutting much of our material on 35-mm mag film with Moviolas, we still required videotape transfers for many other reasons—everything from running reels with your editors, spotting sound effects at home after hours, and especially when you would go to the traditional sound facilities to conduct ADR and Foley sessions.

When we stepped up to videotape transfers and cut with digital workstations, instead of 35-mm dupes on Moviolas, a supervising sound editor almost always would ask for two formats of videotape transfers. Most sound editors worked on $1/2$" VHS tape (usually VHS), but many sound facilities (where ADR and Foley stage work was done) preferred to use $3/4$" Umatic tapes.

With today's nonlinear technology, virtually all postproduction sound work is now done on QuickTime video files (usually output at 720×480). Before our computers really became accelerated, if an editor wanted to work in QuickTime, he or she almost always had to have the image output in a low-res level, so that the computer would have less digital information to process in real time. Today, high-speed Mac G4s and especially G5s and the Mac Pro computer systems run so fast that we are working with full resolution with no problem at all, even if the project was shot in hi-def.

Most editors understand that to make their computers work more smoothly and not hang up as much, we always put our QuickTime picture files on a dedicated external hard drive. For myself, I prefer using an Avastor HDX-800 Portable Hard Disk Drive with triple output capability (USB, FireWire 400 and 800), using the FireWire 800 port for the fastest data transfer possible from the drive, which is great for high-resolution, high-edit density, and high-track count Pro Tools HD sessions. I keep my audio library and edit sessions on separate external drives using FireWire 400s chained together.

Because picture editorial can easily make their own picture and guide track outputs from their nonlinear systems (such as Final Cut Pro or Avid), tremendous savings in telecine costs are obviously being realized in the postproduction budgets. You have to be careful, though. If you are making videotape outputs, for whatever reason, the disciplines of input, file management, and EDLs are not strictly adhered to, and the assistant editors do not understand frame rates and other quirky anomalies that sometimes arise; a videotape transfer from a nonlinear system can suffer all kinds of inaccurate sync issues.

Think of them as a pool of constantly undulating tide. They lose and gain time, drifting along on the average. Nonlinear systems do not sync to time code, contrary to general perception. They are run by time stamp, a completely different discipline. The only absolutely *accurate* way to make videotape copies from the nonlinear editor's cut is to take the system drives to a video telecine equipped to read these drives and precisely resolve the time stamp to the time code equivalent.

From the outset, establish a very clear understanding with picture editorial that *if you are using or in need of videotape outputs*, you will accept video transfers made directly from a nonlinear system for spotting and temp effect development *only*. When hard sync cutting is being done for final work, however, let picture editorial know you will only accept video transfers done by a legitimate telecine facility that will resolve their drives.

When working with QuickTime video outputs, we do not suffer so many sync issues. Clearly, there can always be something that can ambush you, if the before-mentioned disciplines have not been properly exercised. Actually, in order to protect myself from having to suffer financial loss from the sloppy (and often ignorant) part of both inexperienced picture assistants and editors, I would call up Wade Coonfer (at the time he was head of postproduction at UCLA), a practical and experienced authority in how to oversee and handle outputting the picture and OMF files correctly the first time. I would make a time that we could take our portable drives over to picture editorial to extract the final-cut reels so we could commence our sound work.

Once, in fact, I had to tell the picture assistant to remove his hands from the keyboard and place them on the wall and patiently stand by while Wade sat down and sifted through his horribly disorganized hard drive structure and saw to it that the session settings were correct and that our OMF outputs would be properly made with the correct information that was vital to our editorial success. I cannot tell you how valuable and comforting it is to have a consultant at the ready to step in and keep both the project and yourself from going off the budget cliff of wasted efforts.

Traditional cutting reels are approximately 900 feet long. We refer to them as "thousand footers." When we say reel 1, reel 2, reel 3, we are referring to the traditional configuration. These reels are mixed in thousand-foot configurations; then the supervising sound editor and assistant sound editor join them to make the 2,000-foot AB configurations that are ultimately sent to movie houses around the world for theatrical presentation.

With nonlinear technology, most work is turned over to sound editorial in pre-built theatrical presentation. These are known as reel 1AB, reel 2AB, reel 3AB, and so on. Traditional 1,000-foot reels 1 and 2 are combined to make a 2,000-foot projection reel known as reel 1AB. This means that the cut reels combine as follows: reel 1 and reel 2 become reel 1AB; reel 3 and reel 4 become reel 2AB; reel 5 and reel 6 become reel 3AB; reel 7 and reel 8 become reel 4AB; reel 9 and reel 10 become reel 5AB. You can always tell the difference between theatrical film and television postproduction craftspeople. Television editors rarely refer to the cut reels as "reels"; instead, they refer to them as "acts."

Never have more than one reel transferred onto a single videotape cassette. Because of the logistics of sound editor specialists who need access to different reels simultaneously and because changes are made to some reels and not others, it is wise to have each reel of the film transferred to its own dedicated videotape. In addition, ask for more than one copy of each tape. The number of copies you request depends on budget and needs, but it always seems like never enough copies are around when you need them.

Production Audio Source

You must take possession of the original production sound tapes, whether they be DATs, ¼" tapes, or audio files generated by the digital field recorder that the production mixer used on the set. Prepare the dialog by utilizing the OMF option (see Chapter 14). Regardless of whether you can successfully use OMF, you still need to access the original audio source at some point, if for no other reason than to run an "A-B" comparison between the OMF audio file as resurrected into a Pro Tools session and the original recording to be sure that the dailies had not been "quashed" or equalized in the Log and Capture originally done by the assistant editor.

Make certain that the client has a precise inventory accounting when the material is delivered to you. This information is listed into the receipt binder. Rarely does a film have every roll accounted for when the material is delivered to you. If you sign for the material blind to any shortcomings, you are the responsible party; and the last thing you want is to find yourself in some legal action for whatever reason and you have signed for something you do not have.

If you use the OMF option, make special arrangements with picture editorial to develop a precise EDL along with copies of the audio files to build the dialog editor's Pro Tools session. (This process and protocol are discussed in detail in Chapter 15.)

Code Book

As discussed in Chapter 7, the bible of where to find this information is the code book. Picture editorial will supply a photocopy of the code book, which spends most of its time in the dialog editing department. Sometimes an extra copy of the code book is made, so that the first assistant sound editor has a dedicated copy in the assistant's room.

Lined Script

Photocopies of the lined script, including opposing pages of notes, are supplied by picture editorial. The ADR supervisor needs a copy for reviewing and cuing the picture for loop lines. The dialog editor needs one at the workstation, and the first assistant sound editor needs a dedicated copy in the assistant's room.

Cast List

The production office supplies you with a cast list, identifying who is playing which character. This list is vital to the ADR supervisor.

Continuity

Picture editorial supplies continuity, an outline form breakdown of each reel with the scene numbers included, along with a very short description of action. Each member of the sound editorial team receives a copy of the continuity, which makes it much easier to find their way around the picture, knowing the sequences included in each reel.

LFOP Chart

The LFOP (last frame of picture) chart, also known as the LFOA (last frame of action) chart, is supplied by picture editorial to rectify and compare notes with the first assistant sound editor. Every first assistant sound editor double-checks and verifies the validity of these charts and usually makes his or her own for accuracy.

As discussed in Chapter 7, in sound we must count Picture Start on the Academy leader as 000 feet and 00 frames, not frame 1. Most LFOP charts start out wrong because picture editorial often ignores the practical disciplines of postproduction and insists on counting Picture Start as frame 1; this can cause delays of time and wasted money because of sound editorial's delay in redoing these charts.

Another strange phenomenon is getting picture dupes or video transfers (whether videotapes or video QuickTime files) with either no tail pops at all, or tail pops that are not precisely 3 feet 0 frames from the last frame of picture. I am constantly puzzled that some picture editorial teams simply put one arbitrarily wherever they want one.

In 35-mm film, the head pop is precisely 9 feet 00 frames from the Academy leader Picture Start frame. That is represented by a single frame of 2 on the picture. Precisely 3 feet 00 frames from the head pop is the first frame of picture. The same is true for the tail pop, only in reverse, precisely 3 feet 00 frames from the last frame of picture. Experienced picture assistants often punch a hole through this frame so that it visually blips when you hear the one frame of pop and shows up clearly in the video transfer. Some picture assistants use a black Sharpie to draw a frame line around this tail pop frame and then draw an X from corner to corner, or they write tail pop in the frame itself.

Those who do not know what to use for audio pop for both head and tail pops should take a single frame from a 1,000-cycle tone (1 kHz). All kinds of line-up tones can be cannibalized on the head end of your 35-mm mag stripe dailies. If you are working entirely in the digital nonlinear domain, simply ask a sound editorial service to supply you with a tone folder of audio files. Any reputable sound service will be more than happy to supply you with the correct material, or you can access the line-up tones off the interactive DVD inside the back cover of this book.

Also remember that an important difference exists between video pop and film pop. If you are working on television material that has been shot at 30 frames and no drop frame is used, you use a video pop. Editors that work in time code reference rather than feet and frames in their nonlinear software forget this fact. For them, one frame is 1/30th of a second. Therefore when the sound is mixed together and transferred to film, the sound assistant rolls down the mixed fullcoat master on a synchronizer to find the head pop, only to discover that its duration does not quite reach the next frame line. Hence, it is important when working on a nonlinear editing system to develop your pop frame while working in the foot-and-frame mode, and not in time code.

A quick way to check the pop audio file in your tone folder is to simply drag it in and spot it precisely to a frame line, making sure that your session is in foot-and-frame mode. Zoom in extremely close so that you can see the end of the pop very clearly. If it does not precisely reach the next frame line, then it is not a film pop.

Developing the Cut List

The show is turned over for sound editorial work. The supervising sound editor delegates the production dialog editing chores to the dialog supervisor (as described in detail in Chapter 15). The ADR chores are turned over to the ADR supervisor (as described in Chapter 16). The Foley tasks are turned over to the Foley supervisor, or the supervising sound editor may opt to do them (as described in detail in Chapter 17).

Most supervising sound editors develop their own cut lists, rather than leaving the sound effect creative decisions up to the individual sound effects editors. Much of the time, they do this because they have a more thorough knowledge of the sound effects library; on a few occasions, they may be exercising fanatical control over each and every sound tidbit cut. Mostly, the cut list is meant as a creative guide. It helps the sound effects editor cutting sound for a particular reel or sequence establish continuity with the supervisor's vision for the sound as well as with other sound effects editors who may be cutting the same kind of action in other reels.

In the old days of cutting sound on magnetic film, supervisors assigned entire reels to a sound effects editor. With today's nonlinear technology, we are moving into what we call a "horizontal" style of cutting. Because we literally can be anywhere in the picture in a matter of seconds, the weight and physicality of winding down 35-mm film do not limit us. Therefore, we now assign types of sound to individual sound effects editors. One sound effects editor, known for a mechanical hardware style of sound editing, may be asked to handle the robotic sounds throughout the entire film and nothing else. Another sound effects editor may be asked to handle only animal vocals throughout the film and nothing else. Predub these horizontal layers separately, then play them back together to make the full soundtrack.

The supervising sound editor uses one or more computers to audition sound effects as he or she writes a cut list on a second computer. Because we are experiencing so many near-daily changes, we seldom list the foot and frame of the sound cue to which we are referring. We use the continuity, which was supplied by picture editorial, to list the scene number with a one-line description. Below that, we list the various sound event moments that need attention. Under these subheadings, we list the sound effect number and file name. For those sound editorial firms that have their libraries completely computerized, the description data, even if it does not apply to the picture at hand, is also printed.

We depend on the hired sound effects editors to know what we talk about within the context of a scene. If they are puzzled and do not understand, then we depend on them to ask specific questions, which can be easily answered. Most supervising sound editors allow their sound effects editors to be creative and add material into the mix as well, but first they must cut and fulfill the cut list.

```
Date : 01/08/97                Editor's Cut List        Page 10
                        THE 5TH ELEMENT

MOTOR -- LOWER FRIDGE

      CWK0003-91          AIRCRAFT: Flaps, electric, Cessna 172, buzzy.
      SPT

      CWK0003-92          INDUSTRIAL: Forklift, electric

HUM -- GUN IDLE

      DAX0034-03          CREDIT CARD SCANNER: touch phone beeps followed
                          by electronic information beeps.  RESTRICTED!!

      DAZ0034-14          MOTOR: small CU pool motor, steady constant
                          idle -- no on or off.  Watch perspective.

ELEVATOR DOORS OPEN

      DAT1126-28          LEONOV POD DOOR:  sweetener for R-7.
      MPT

      DAT1473-020         SPACE SHIP DOORS:  "Star Trek" like space
      MPT                 doors, hissey hi-end slide w/small click
                          impact.  GREM2 NOTE:  Clamp elevator doors

PANEL SLIDE

      CWK0005-29          TRIPOD LEGS, SMALL: Smooth, metallic sliding
      SPT

      CWK0005-32          TRIPOD: Slide telescoping leg in.
      SPT

      CWK0005-36          TRIPOD: Slide telescoping legs, single stage
      SPT

      CWK0005-42          COPY MACHINE:  Slide table tray
      SPT

      DAT1365-001         PNEUMATICS/SERVOS:  a variety of wheezy
                          metallic slides -- much like hatch closures.
```

Figure 13.6 A single page of the "cut list" from R-2 of *The Fifth Element*.

WHICH PREPARATION TECHNIQUE?

No absolute exists as to how to approach the cutting and predub breakdown of any given film. Every project dictates its own spin, demands its own style, challenging you to overcome the various hurdles of budget shortcomings and unrealistic schedule demands. Two basic kinds of approaches can be adopted: all in and mix and A-B-C.

All In and Mix Approach

The "all in and mix" approach is used when the budget is so small and the dubbing schedule is short, loosely referred to as the hang-and-bang, a euphemism for put-it-up-and-just-mix-it-without-the-frills. This style of preparation is contingent on the film not being a heavy sound effects design show, not having events such as big car chases, gun battles, flying spaceships, or medieval warfare. If the show consists of simple vehicle work, such as door opens and closes, or phones ringing with pick-ups and hang-ups, then this kind of film can be done as an all in and mix.

Cut your most important sound cues in the first few soundtracks, moving out toward the last few reserved for backgrounds. The total number of soundtracks you are able to cut, to mix all at once, is contingent on how many inputs the dubbing console can handle and how many channels can be exported from the machine room. The other factor that must be dealt with is the number of channels required by production dialog, ADR, and Foley—as they must come along at the same time to achieve the concept of all in and mix.

It will behoove you to make a field trip to the dubbing stage contracted to mix the film, even if you have worked there in the past, as the sound facility may have upgraded the stage since last you mixed there.

A drawback to the all in and mix approach is that little margin exists for adding sound effects, especially ones that must be designed and cannot be thrown easily into the mix on a Pro Tools unit hooked into the console. Your delivered tracks must be as polished and final as you can make them.

The advantage to all in and mix is that nothing sits by itself naked to the client during predubbing. Rather than predubbing only the backgrounds, and having the client fuss and nitpick little flaws or choices, all the tracks are running at once, helping each other camouflage the inevitable imperfections each may have in its singularity.

A-B-C Approach

Soundtracks that are taken seriously are almost always mixed in the "A-B-C" approach. Essentially, all the basic elements are predubbed by themselves, then polished and refined exactly as intended. This approach also gives tremendously more control over the basic elements when you reach the final mix.

"A-B-C" refers to A-FX, B-FX, C-FX. The supervising sound editor tells the sound effects editor which approach to take for preparation. If the A-B-C approach is chosen, then the sound effects editor knows to break out the basic sound effect groups. On complex sound effect shows, the supervising sound editor often does this. He or she makes a chart and lists A-FX, B-FX, C-FX, and so forth.

STARSHIP TROOPERS   editor: Yewdall   **R-5**   v.14 -- Final turnover

"A"-FX	"B"-FX	"C"-FX	"D"-FX
Spaceship Engine: DRONE	Servos & Motors	Bulkhead door Impacts	System "whine"
	Hydraulics	"POD" Rotation	Telemetry Beeps
Spaceship Engine: back-out of space dock			
		Pier Coupler Release	"Collision" Alarm
Spaceship Engine: Rev up and warp drive		Metal Ronks & Movt. -- moving out --	Warp Drive Targeting
Laser Rifle "Power-Ups"			
Laser Rifle "SHOTS" (Blue rifles)	Laser Rifle "SHOTS" (Red rifles)	Laser METAL impacts	Laser "SIZZLES"
		Laser "FLIGHTS"	Laser "ELECTRICAL"
	Laser Rifle "MOTOR" (recharges)	Laser "BODY IMPACTS"	

Figure 13.7 Predub group strategy assignments for A-FX, B-FX, C-FX, etc. for R-5 of *Starship Troopers*.

A-FX, B-FX, C-FX

Beneath each heading, the supervisor lists what kinds of sound groups are desired in each designation. Often the supervisor uses a felt marker, giving each group a color code, and then marking the cut list printouts of each color code by each sound effect listed, to avoid any error.

For example, take the sequence of reel 7 in John Carpenter's *Christine* where Christine slams into and destroys the gas station. I cut the car engine sound effects on A-FX. Nothing else was in this predub pass except the car engine. I could cut other sounds in this A-FX group only if they occurred before or after the car engine, but never during the car engine material, which had to be completely by itself.

In the B-FX pass, I cut the tire skids and the wet-road effects. I could cut other sound effects in this pass prior to or after the gas station scene, but never during tire skids or wet road cues.

In C-FX I cut metal-oriented sounds: suspension movement, collision impacts, bumper tears, gas pump metal impacts and falls, debris for explosions, and so forth.

In D-FX I cut the various layers of the explosions.

Predub these by themselves, and when you play them back together you have much better control over the individual concepts. If the director asks to favor the skids more, you have not married them to the engines, or vice versa. This technique is basically simple, in principal, but oddly enough falls apart in the heat of battle for beginners. Only after enduring the dubbing stage and gaining the logical and methodical style of a re-recording mixer does a sound editor truly learn how to break down sound effect sequences to maximum efficiencies.

This is another problem that nonlinear technology has brought to the learning process. In the old days of working on mag film, all my editors came to the dubbing stage. We would call back to the shop at a certain point in the dubbing process of a reel so that everyone could come watch the playback. The sound editors definitely were on stage for their reels.

With nonlinear technology allowing horizontal editing, as many as eight or ten editors may have worked on a single reel of sound on big action pictures. Having eight or ten sound editors sitting on the stage while part of the reel with their own work is being mixed is just not practical or economical. Therefore, we are losing whole groups of new sound editing talent who have not experienced the intimate techniques, styles, and tricks of interaction with re-recording mixers.

Marking Sync on Film

I describe this process to you, even though we work in the nonlinear world now, because many of you will, sooner or later, find yourself going through film vaults or old inventories of film productions made before digital technologies. You may find yourself working in restoration or developing a prior cut version than needs to be reconstructed. Therefore, it is valuable for you to understand *how* we did it and how it works. When we worked on film, as we have discussed, we used a Moviola and a synchronizer. After we had cut the sound cues in the desired fashion, we marked the closest even foot inside the sound cue.

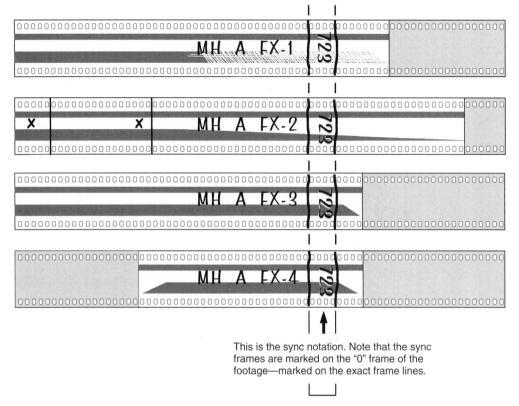

This is the sync notation. Note that the sync frames are marked on the "0" frame of the footage—marked on the exact frame lines.

Figure 13.8 Marking sync on film with a black Sharpie.

Marking Film Sync

In Figure 13.8, the footage marked is "723." Using a black Sharpie, box either side of the frame, then write the footage in the frame itself. The ink of the Sharpie does not harm the soundtrack. Behind it, mark an abbreviation for the show, especially when you have more than one show in the shop at a time. In this case "MH" is the abbreviation for *Moscow on the Hudson*, which was in the shop with two other projects. Mark the A-B-C pass designation and then the FX channel number. In this way, anyone picking up a piece of film lying on the floor that had been carelessly knocked aside knows exactly where it belongs because of these abbreviations.

The sound assistant rolls fill leader through the synchronizer and marks the frame (723) where the four cues land. The assistant backs out the fill leader strands, to the left of the synchronizer. Each sound cue then is taken off its respective trim bin hooks, one by one. The assistant carefully lays the boxed footage mark over the marks on the fill leader, then carefully guides the front end of the sound cue to the leading edge. At this point, the assistant turns both fill leader and mag film over and splices white 35-mm splicing tape on the backside to bind them. In the course of a single motion picture, it is not unusual to chew up half a million feet of fill leader, nearly a million feet of 35-mm mag stripe, and a hundred thousand feet of 35-mm fullcoat.

Figure 13.9 A four-gang synchronizer. The cut picture is in the first gang, closest to the front. Sound cues are built into the fill leader, with sync footage notations bracketed around the even foot frame.

Each roll of built sound cues is known as a unit. If you have cut 60 tracks of sound for B-FX, then you have 60,000-foot rolls of sound units built and delivered to the stage for predubbing. These racks of film units hold as many sound units as I cut for reel 9 of *Leviathan*, which had over 450 tracks at the height of the destructive climax. By the time the sea floor laboratory was destroyed by the monster, Mike Le-Mare and I had broken the sound action into A-through-W predubs.

Imagine the sheer weight of film stock that had to be carried around by the editorial team. I always felt sorry for the assistant sound editor and apprentice when they delivered units to a dubbing stage that had a machine room upstairs with no elevator or dumbwaiter to raise the tons of film. Hauling around a motion picture keeps you in better physical shape than working nonlinear.

If I remember correctly, when Universal sent their truck up the street to my editorial shop to pick up our unit inventory for John Carpenter's *The Thing*, the thousands of units of film weighed close to 5 tons!

Today, we can carry around thousands of sound effects, all the mix stems from all the reels of a major motion picture, all the cut sessions, final mixed stems, encoded AC3 files, and all the paperwork on a handful of DVD-Rs in a small black leather carrying case.

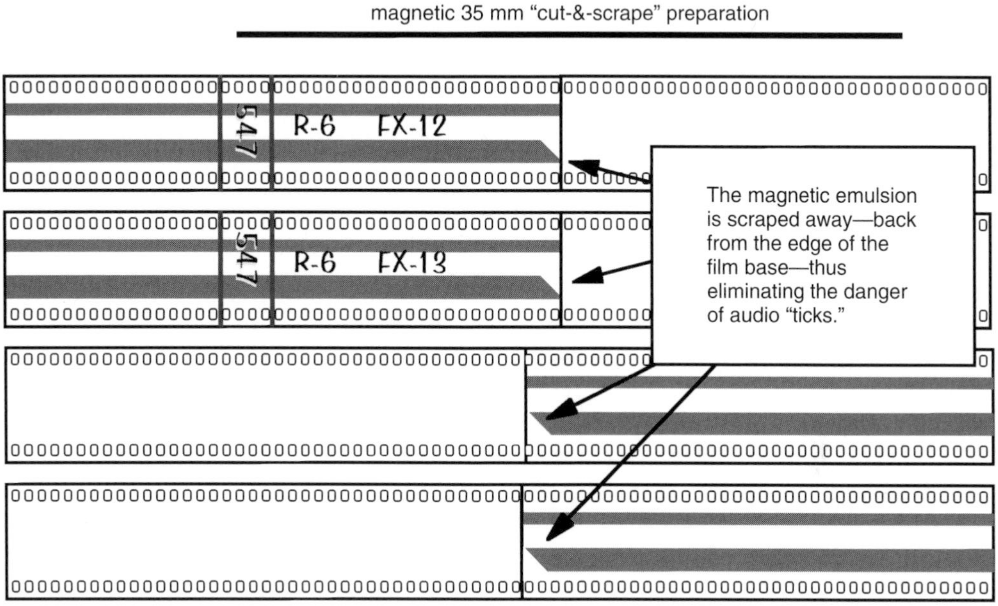

magnetic 35 mm "cut-&-scrape" preparation

The magnetic emulsion is scraped away—back from the edge of the film base—thus eliminating the danger of audio "ticks."

Figure 13.10 Cut sound cues showing several types of scraping or wiping techniques used on 35-mm mag stripe. Note the "thatching" technique in the upper track.

Separation of Sound Cues

No matter if we cut on film or cut on nonlinear systems, the wisdom of custom recording sound effect cues in single-cue actions becomes crystal clear. It is nearly impossible, and only a fluke of luck when it does occur, that you can record a single piece of action that covers everything. First, aside from being impossible, you would not have control over the levels of individual components. That is why you do not want your tire action sounds to be married to the engine. While you are recording, it is fun and thrilling. Now, however, at your workstation, you are cursing yourself for being foolish and allowing the stunt driver to do spinouts and skidding noises over the precious engine maneuvers. Yes, you want the tire skids and road texture, but you want to control them, putting them where you want, not where your recording dictates.

Leading Edges

Study the chart of the four tracks of sound cues from *Moscow on the Hudson* in Figure 13.10. Note that no leading edge of mag track actually touches the leading edge of the splice. We had to scrape the mag track away from the leading edge, just prior to the actual sound cue itself. This inhibited any ticks that may occur from a magnetic signal striking the sound head as the splice passed over it. The most common technique was to scrape across two perforations (half a frame) at a 45° angle.

Other techniques can also be used, such as a gentle fade-in (as in FX-2). This kind of fade was especially useful in the fade-out configuration, instead of enduring sudden cut-offs of overtones or unwanted ambience presences.

We use the exact techniques today in nonlinear digital editing, except, of course, we aren't using a single-edged razor blade or acetone to dissolve magnetic coating. Our nonlinear software is equipped with a whole selection of fade options to perform what we used to do on film—*to a point.*

The thatched fade-in technique as depicted in FX-1 is the only kind of track manipulation that nonlinear digital has not mastered yet, contrary to what any digital software writer tells you (they probably do not understand what it is). We frequently used to use this technique to break up and thin out vocal tracks, such as vocals over a radio that were coming and going in clarity as the operator rotated the frequency dial. We also used it, in the fine-thatched form depicted here, to thin out the volume of something that banged in too hard. Digital software writers state that this technique could be achieved by using the volume control, but it is not the same.

Whenever I need the thatched track effect for vocal break-up, I transfer the sound to a 35-mm mag track, break out the single-edged razor blade, and go at it. Then I transfer it back in a Pro Tools edit session.

Other little techniques demonstrate what degaussed single-edge razor blades are good for, such as crescent notches. I have tried to duplicate the effect with counter-digital cross-fades to varying degrees of success, but it was never as precise as what mag stock and a razor blade could do with a veteran editor who really knew what he or she was doing.

These comparisons are not meant to negate nonlinear. On the contrary, as a sound editor who has worked nearly 20 years on mag stripe and made a fruitful transition to nonlinear digital, I love it. I write about it to challenge and explain to digital software writers that the editorial tasks to emulate are not completely mastered yet. Thatching would be a fabulous ability to have in digital mode.

Crescent notching would be another. To master these techniques, however, you must sit down with the film veterans who used them in order to understand why they are used and why they are still needed. Then you will be able to write the software equivalents.

Fade techniques are obviously not reserved for magnetic film editing alone. The same technique is used in digital nonlinear preparation. The experienced editor knows to add a fade-in or fade-out to a cue, however short or long, as shown in Figure 13.11, and also use them to cross-fade as shown in Figure 13.12.

Digital Fade Choices

For veteran sound editors who cut on 35-mm mag film, the greatest joy about working with nonlinear digital is not having to scrape fade-ins and fade-outs as in the past, wearing out a 100-count box of single-edged razor blades. Many used the foul-smelling and finger-staining Track Wipe for years, which became a known carcinogen, thought to have been responsible for more than one death among the sound editor work force. (Track Wipe was a mixture of 50 percent acetone and 50 percent film cleaner. The percentages would differ depending on the strength and cutting desire of the editor using it.)

The real advantage of working with nonlinear digital is the ease with which undesirable fade-ins and fade-outs can be erased. In addition, unlike with magnetic

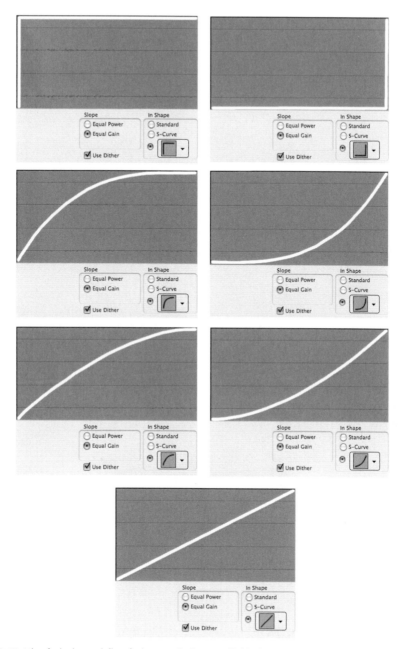

Figure 13.11 The fade-in and five fade-out choices available in a nonlinear Digidesign Pro Tools session.

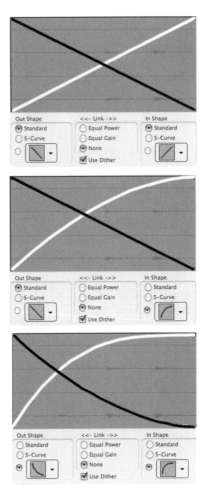

Figure 13.12 Using fades to cross-fade and blend in various combinations make for seamless transitions.

film cutting, cross-fading between tracks is possible. This is a great boon to cutting and compositing sounds.

Cutting Backgrounds

I absolutely love backgrounds. When I started *Escape from New York,* I knew that rich stereo backgrounds were not only nice to have, but vital. The stereo background predub is the stereophonic canvas upon which the entire motion picture soundtrack sits. Music will not play all the time. Hard effects do not play all of the time. Foley, dialog, and ADR are monaural in nature. Group Walla can, and ought to, be recorded and cut stereophonically whenever appropriate and possible, but crowd scenes do not occur all the time. What does play all the time are the backgrounds, always present, so don't slough them off.

Unfortunately, most pictures do not have stereo backgrounds prepared thoroughly. A common tendency is to hold them down during predubbing, rather than letting their full potential thrive during the predubbing, adding yet another dimension to the film. How does the client know what wonderful textures are available if they are not heard during predubbing? If you choose to hold down the backgrounds during the final mix, fine, but do not squash them during predub. In more than one final mix I have had to stop the dub to have the machine room recall a background unit because a client was requesting something that had been held down and out during predubbing.

Another problematic area is the mastering process of the material itself. Not all sound effects libraries are created equal, as discussed in Chapter 11. Not all sound librarians see to it that the material is carefully cleaned and gleaned before the audio file is mastered to a permanent storage medium such as CD-R or DVD-R. Many effects, even at big sound editing facilities, have scads of sound cues with distortion, glitches, digital zits, drop-outs, and other blemishes. Unfortunately, many forget that sound editing means playing through and editing the material.

Having premastered material that has been carefully cleaned and polished is fabulous, and, as you become familiar with the material, you will gain confidence in each sound cue, remembering where its peculiar peccadilloes are located. However, if you expect the re-recording mixer to use your background material with trust, not only must you listen to it carefully and make sure it is smooth and polished, you also must "dramatically" listen to it against the action on the screen. Although it sounds extremely basic, you would be surprised how often this is not done. Most sound editors think of backgrounds as generic, nonsync audio texturing. I cut backgrounds to help tell the story of the action, often finding little bits of action that I can sync up to something in the background to give it a belonging.

The real magic of backgrounds does not happen when you cut one stereo pair. It happens when you lace up two or more stereo pairs. Two sounds played together are not 1 + 1 = 2. They become 1 + 1 = 3 or 4. They become a whole new sound. Listen to the background carefully as it plays against the production dialog track. If it distracts instead of adding, then change it.

Sometimes the most wonderful thing about a background is its magnificent power (e.g., the omnipresence of spaceship engines throughout entire scenes within a battle cruiser), and sometimes it is its delicacy and intimate subtlety (e.g., the quiet and musty basement of an old house before dawn). Backgrounds set a mood, like choral inversion airs or tonal presences. Two of the most requested backgrounds I have used in films are "Pipe Test" and "Peckerwood Canyon."

"Pipe Test" was developed from only two frames of a "1" metal deck rustic grind, sampled and processed, then manipulated over a 2.5 growth—an unearthly presence that often fit the producer's request for "something we have never heard before."

My wife, Lisa, and I recorded "Peckerwood Canyon" just south of Yosemite Valley in the Sierra Nevada Mountains. It is the slow movement of air through the pine trees, with no bird calls, no movement, no insects—about every minute and a half is the most wonderful echo of a woodpecker as heard about a hundred yards away. Producers and directors have wanted audio cassette transfers of this background to play in their cars while commuting. Listen to the examples of backgrounds on the DVD provided with this book for a series of examples on layering stereo backgrounds to create an environmental envelope for the audience. Each series background example will add one

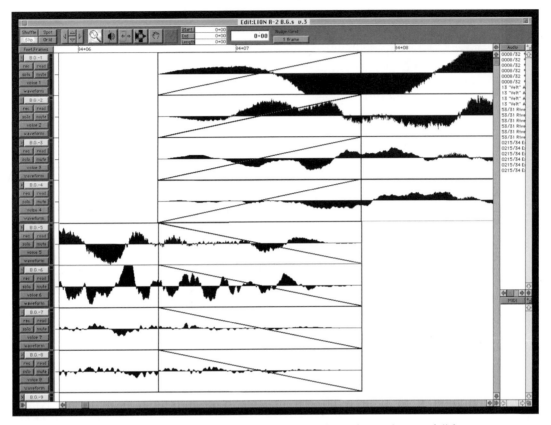

Figure 13.13 Note the outgoing audio tracks and incoming audio tracks overlap one full frame during the fade-in/fade-out cross-over.

additional layer to itself every 4 seconds, giving you the opportunity to study and evaluate the effect of layering.

To keep the re-recording mixer from taking the backgrounds casually, I often work on rather important sound cues, which can be justified to be in the background pass. By doing this, the mixer must listen to them and address their valuable addition, as they cannot be ignored.

Pro Tools One-Frame Overlaps

Note the extreme close-up of the backgrounds in the Pro Tools session graph in Figure 13.13. At a scene change or a perspective split, I overlap the material by at least one full frame—sometimes as many as four frames, depending on how the transition sounds. Every cut situation will tell you how many frame overlaps work best. This same technique is used whether cutting on mag film or cutting nonlinear. This overlap, with a one-frame fade-in on the incoming background tracks and a one-frame fade-out on the outgoing background tracks, lends a smooth transition. By not using this technique,

Figure 13.14 Charles Maynes, working at his studio set-up at home. Because of today's ability to send entire sessions via DigiDelivery, Charles finds that he is doing more and more work at home, instead of wasting valuable time commuting to and from the various studios.

you risk a digital tick at the scene change, or at the very least you will experience a strange edginess to the cut, something not quite settled.

When stuck for a stereo background and all you have of the material is a monaural recording, make a "pseudo stereo" background version by following this simple procedure. After importing your monaural background into the Pro Tools session, drag it over into channel #1. Now highlight the background with the "hand," hold down the Control and Option keys and drag down a duplicate copy of the background into channel #2. Now cut the background right in the center. If the background is 100 feet, cut it at the 50-foot mark. Now drag the second half of the background forward in front of the first half, allowing them to overlap about 6 to 8 feet. Now blend the two ends with at least a 5-foot cross-fade. Move both sections of the cut background so that the cross-fade is in the middle of the background on channel #1. Now, using the Cut/Reveal tool, open both ends of the cut background so that the lengths of the backgrounds of channel #1 and channel #2 are identical. Highlight and play the background. Most monaural backgrounds can be given a startling stereophonic illusion by using this process. The trick is, you must cut out any obvious impacts or sounds that show up a bit later in the other channel, thus giving away what you have done. (Listen to the audio examples of pseudostereo backgrounds on the DVD provided with this book from monaural material without using electronic delay techniques. Each example will play the original material monaurally for 4 seconds, then it will suddenly open up into its pseudostereo potential.)

Layering Techniques

Figure 13.15 shows a moment of an artillery barrage of a French Foreign Legion fortress in North Africa in the feature film *Legionnaire*. It is nearly impossible to find the perfect single sound effect for almost anything. By now it is probably apparent that layering sounds is how sound editors develop these rich and vibrant audio events that are so

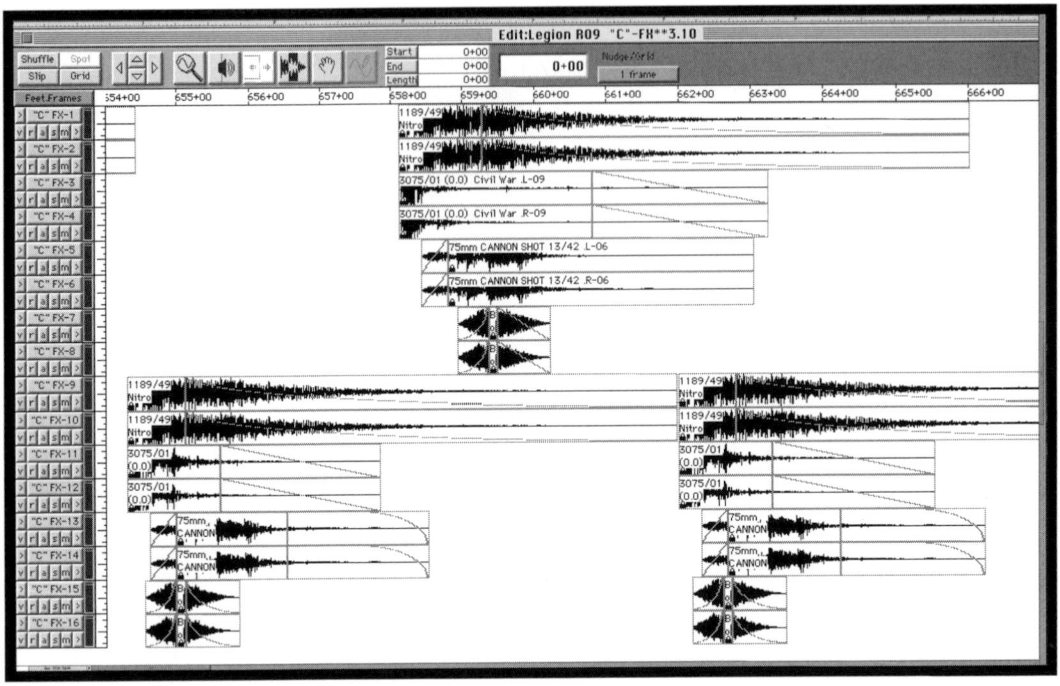

Figure 13.15 Pro Tools session—cannon barrage predub from *Legionnaire*.

enjoyed. Listen to sound cue of layering *Cannon Fire* on the DVD provided with this book to hear the component cues and final combustions.

Pro Tools—Cannon Fire

The layering technique made the artillery field piece feel truly dangerous. From studying the C-FX session shown in Figure 13.15, you can see that I made the field piece by layering four stereo pairs of effects. These effects are only for the actual firing of the cannon, not for shell impact or any collateral debris effect.

The first effect is a rich black-powderish, low-end whomp explosion called "Nitroglycerine Blast." The second layer gives the cannon a dangerous bite, achieved by using a Civil War cannon shot, which surprisingly does not have much low-end fullness, but does have a wonderful cutting edge that will cut through almost anything. I made several vari-speed versions of this effect, adding a speed recognition addendum to the audio file name—(0.0) meaning normal speed, (2.0) meaning half-speed, (4.0) meaning quarter-speed, and so on. The third layer is the shell flight of an M-4 Sherman tank's 75-mm cannon firing downrange. This gives the overall sound a historic period feel. I cut off the actual shot of the 75-mm cannon, using a quick fade-in of the projectile whirring away toward the target.

Although the final designed cannon shot sounds as if it had been recorded today with modern digital technology, it also sounds exactly correct for the period of the picture, which is 1925. I had exactly the concussionary shot I wanted with

Nitroglycerine Blast and the Civil War (0.0) recoil. I wanted the effective shell whir as the 75-mm projectile flew downrange. Adding the discharge shot of the Sherman tank to both Nitroglycerine Blast and Civil War (0.0) recoil would only muddy the combination of sounds and detract from the fullness already achieved. The fourth layer is a short, high-end shell flight of an incoming mortar shell. This shrill high-end sweetener works much like the Civil War cannon bite, giving danger and menace to the flying shell projectile.

Refer to the three cannon shots shown in Figure 13.15. The second one shows the shell flight happening a little later than the first or third. This goes back to picture editorial issues discussed in Chapter 7. The picture editor did not make a thorough study of the material. Physics tells us that if the target is in the same place, and the cannons have not moved from their primary location, then the shell should take the same number of frames to travel from cannon discharge to shell impact. The biggest challenge I had in the cannon fire was to make each shell flight sound natural and believable; some flew for a long time, and others were instantly on target.

Whip Pan Techniques

The example shown in Figure 13.16 is a moment in the B-FX predub of *Starship Troopers* when infantry trainees are working out with tag laser rifles. This session is 18

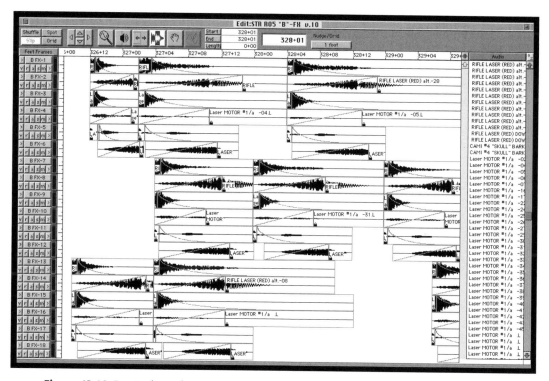

Figure 13.16 Pro Tools session—Laser Tag firefight elements from R-5 of *Starship Troopers*. Note the carefully sculpted fade-outs for fast left-to-right and right-to-left fly-bys.

channels wide. It contains three groups of three stereo pairs of sounds. (Listen to Laser Fire audio cues on the DVD provided with the book to hear this cue.)

Pro Tools—Laser Fire

Three stereo pairs work together to create the laser fire from one rifle. I did something here that I very rarely do and almost never recommend. If you look closely (you may need a magnifying glass), you will note that the fade-in and fade-out configurations on each stereo pair do not match. The reason for this is actually quite simple: no mixer on earth could have panned these laser shots quickly or accurately enough from left to right and right to left, so I decided to prepare the material with prepanned laser fire by virtue of radical inverted fade combinations. This must be undertaken very carefully; if prepared improperly, the mixer mostly likely will not be able to unwind it, requiring rework.

I started using this technique of prebuilding pans into the material by using fade-ins and fade-outs for the Wesley Snipes picture *Boiling Point*. The re-recording mixing schedule was woefully inadequate, especially considering that the sound effects mixer would have to devote several days to pan-potting all the car-bys needed for street traffic. By using this technique, though, the sound effects mixer needed to make only minor adjustments in balance and volume, leaving him free to pay closer attention to far more important sound effects. The fade panned car-bys simply performed as designed, crossing left to right or right to left as planned.

This places much responsibility on the sound editor and especially on the supervising sound editor should these prebuilds not perform as anticipated. What sounds like a piece of heaven at your workstation in the cutting rooms can easily degenerate into an ugly finger-pointing disaster when a producer watches the clock ticking off hundred-dollar bills because your designed pan-bys are not working correctly. However, situations such as the two described above frankly point to this technique as time and money savers. The best way to rally support from your mixing colleagues for using this method is to consult with them first, well in advance of predubbing. No re-recording mixer will be your ally and support you if it blows up in your face because it does not perform as you expected if you had not consulted him or her ahead of time. Mixers most likely will bounce the reel to save their own skin, sending you back to the editing room with egg on your face as you recut it.

Using an Off-the-Shelf Audio CD Sound Library

An advantage to buying ready-made sound effects from commercial CD sound libraries is the ability to amass thousands of sound effects in your audio arsenal very quickly as a beginning sound editor who has not had the benefit of years of custom recording. By the mid-1990s, audio CDs were finally starting to offer theatrical-style sound effects, which gained a wider acceptance among those accustomed to custom recording their own material.

Not all sound CD offerings are created equally. Many have that flat documentary-type sound, of little value to theatrical sound editors. Others are developed through synthesized means, which also offer little. Some sound libraries offer a few good sound effects on CD, with the rest of the material pure junk. Before spending money, try to listen to the product first.

One sound publication firm that has truly excelled in serving the feature-film market is Sound Ideas, based in Toronto. Starting with their 6000 General series, Sound Ideas began to develop a rich theatrical feel for its product. Subsequent library series have been as good, if not better.

Regardless of what audio CD series you use, the most disappointing flaw is the lack of sufficient variations. For instance, when cutting an action car sequence, you require numerous variations in the car-bys or maneuvers so you don't repeat the same cue. When it comes to complete vehicle series (aircraft, boats, cars, trucks, motorcycles, etc.), you will be extremely hard pressed to find any CD that gives you all the nuts and bolts you require. Here comes that same speed with that same road texture and that same little bump in the pavement thump at the same place in the car-by. When you think through your road texture and performance variations, you are looking at 25 to 40 variations, not the three or four usually offered on CD libraries.

Having good sound effect CDs in your library for secondary and miscellaneous sounds is absolutely necessary, but, for key action vehicles, consider custom recording. Review Chapter 10 for further details on custom recording a complete vehicle series.

Techniques in Cutting Vehicles

Almost everybody thinks cutting cars is easy, until they get in and try cutting anything but the standard ins and stops and start and aways, let alone complex maneuvers and car chases. Before getting into understanding complicated cutting, let me start by saying that the usual first mistake of a learning-to-cut sound editor involves how a car starts and stops. In many a film sequence, the sound editor does not take the time to observe the physics and mechanics of how a car actually works. The sound editor cuts the sound of the engine so that the rpm rises as the car visually moves forward, and I have watched many a scene where the engine sounds completely out of touch with the car coming to a stop. Observe the real thing before you try to duplicate it on film. Note that a car engine starts to accelerate before you see the vehicle move. Obviously you must play with it. If you allow the acceleration to begin too soon, it sounds odd; if you accelerate with the visual, it feels equally odd. Move the acceleration against the picture and play it against action until it feels connected.

Other things almost magically fall into place. Little bits of noises and nuances you heard before but did not make any sense suddenly fall where they should, such as the engagement of a transmission, little clunks that, when massaged for sync, bring the action to life. (Listen to sound cue of the Cut Car Sequence from the DVD provided to hear this cue and its components from the movie *Jackie Brown*.) For demonstration purposes, I have not cut this in an A-FX, B-FX, C-FX style, but in an all in and mix style, so that you can hear all the separate elements as well as how they work together.

Pro Tools—Car Sequence

The sequence cut in Figure 13.17 was when Robert Forster left the shopping center, got into a Cadillac, started it up, backed up, and drove away. Listening to the single combine, you may think it unremarkable, until you realize that the movements in the sequence are a careful weave of single audio events. Stop thinking of finding one sound cue that does it all, and start thinking of the component parts from the palette of sounds at your disposal, so that you may paint your own reality.

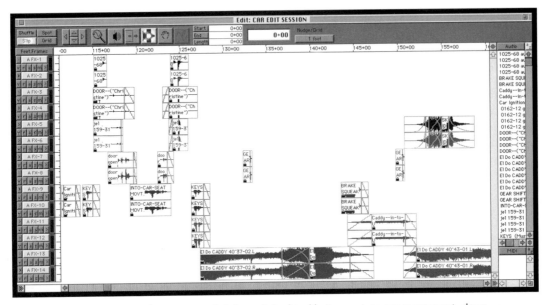

Figure 13.17 Pro Tools session—car predub from R-6 of *Jackie Brown*. Into car movement, door, keys, Cadillac start, back up, and away with tire grit and swerves.

I audition my file of various keys into door locks, looking for the more solid metal sedan key, not the CJ-5, which has a more hollow metal lock over-ring, and not the Honda, which sounds too small. I lengthen the unlocking movement as the man on film fiddles with the door longer than my sound effect lingers, and I shorten the part of the key extraction to speed up the urgency the actor displays.

I always cut two stereo pairs of car door opens and closes. Move in tight and match the latch movements on both effects exactly, or they do not sound as *one* door. No two are ever identical, nor should they be. If you do not match the latch movements, the two door effects only sound like one door cut on top of another, with no relationship to each other. Once you match the latch movements, the *two* doors will sound as *one* door—*one-plus-one equals a new one!* You can create an unlimited variety of doors and textures by mixing and matching doors. Experience and technique help develop your own favorite combinations.

(Car warning alerts, such as door open dinging or seat belt jingles, are optional. I usually do not cut them in unless the client specifically asks for them, and when I custom record vehicles I always try to defeat the warning alerts on the car prior to recording. On the screen, they are often distracting.)

I cut an into-car movement track. When I custom recorded the cars for *Christine*, I captured what has become one of the most used into-car seat movements in the business, better than Foley and with an interesting character of seat springs and cushion movement. Just sync up the seat spring point where the actor's weight has bottomed out (excuse the pun), then shorten or extend the ins and outs.

I usually cut two different key movements into the key ignition, depending on key ring and desirability of jingle. It is important to pay attention to the make of the car series you are using to cut. Many discerning ears, whether of the re-recording mixer, the producer, or the general viewer, are quick to point out when the cut sound effects are of a Dodge instead of the Ford depicted on-screen. The two vehicles sound different, so pay attention. That is not to say you do not use creative license, but certain signature elements, such as the throat of the engine that can take a viewer out of the story, are so wrong they are distracting.

I have the entire car series residing in a file folder on an external drive, where I can access it. I cut an engine start-up, and probably have to shorten the duration of the engine settling down into an idle. I cross to another track for the acceleration of the engine as the car backs up. I sweeten a little brake squeal on another track if it fits the character of the car. I cut in a little transmission clunk movement as the driver changes from reverse to drive. In this particular case, the driver is anxious and pulls out quickly, turning hard left, then accelerates down the street. On a separate track I cut in a little tire sweetener to sell the tire turn, as it grinds down on the pavement with the strong acceleration away.

Splitting off Tracks

Pay attention to preparing the sounds so that it is as easy as possible for the re-recording mixer to work with your material. This is especially true for fast action sequences, where perspective shifts change quickly. Sure, a re-recording mixer can make the perspective shifts on the console; sometimes it is necessary, for technical reasons, such as harmonic sounds that must not be split. However, most sounds can be split for perspective. If you do not prepare the material so that all the mixer does is set perspective volume levels or equalization shifts on one set of channels over another, you quickly will find your mixing counterpart becoming more perturbed with you, eventually bouncing reels back to the cutting room for more thorough preparation.

Say I am using 5 channels of sounds playing together to make the flying reality of an Apache helicopter. I cut the cues into FX-1, 2, 3, 4, and 5. Those 5 channels will be my close-up group. The action is working fine, and then I come to a cut where we favor the enemy tank as it barrels along on the ground with the Apache maneuvering in the background. I split off the material from FX-1, 2, 3, 4, and 5 and move the cues over to FX-6, 7, 8, 9, and 10 as a background group. As with the one-frame overlap technique shown in the cutting of backgrounds, I extend the leading edges of this perspective split, fade-out the outgoing channels, and fade-in the incoming channels.

The action holds on the enemy tank for a few moments, then cuts back to the close angle of the helicopter. Again, I split the five channels of sound back to FX-1, 2, 3, 4, and 5. This process goes on throughout the entire sequence of action. Analyze each shot, deciding where the perspective splits should be placed. Often I need an additional 5 channels for more complex coverage, as I may need a medium-angle group. In that case, I reserve 15 channels in a row to handle the perspective preparations for 5 channels of sound, split into three basic angle perspectives.

The next time you watch a car chase, such as the chase through Paris in John Frankenheimer's *Ronin*, note how many layers of material must have gone into the preparation for the two key vehicles. Engines, gear-box whines, tires on cobblestone and asphalt, suspension, skids—all need perspective splits made to control the two cars as they race through city streets.

To best way to understand the concept of when to split, how to split, and where to place the split-off material is to put yourself in the shoes of the re-recording mixer. If you had to mix this insane tidal wave of sound coming at you in real time, when do you want the material split-off, how would you like it split, and where do you want the material? Study the action—the film will tell you where it wants to be split—if you only pay attention and think it through.

The danger is that you can oversplit the material as well, called the "ping-pong" effect. As you develop a resumé of experience, you learn when you are running the danger of oversplitting. Sometimes you work it with the sable brush, and sometimes the most effective way is clubbing with a sledge hammer for sensation and dramatic effect.

The best advice I can give you is this, offered twofold.

First, if your mixer is hindered, you are not splitting it well. Remember, part of your job is to make that task as easy as possible so that time is not wasted in track management, but creatively spent mixing the material to a higher level of entertainment.

Second, if the audience is disrupted or distracted from the story, you have failed. Anything that draws attention away from the continual stream of storytelling to the fact you are making a movie is wrong.

Building in Volume Graphing and Equalization

With nonlinear workstations, it is easy to build in volume graphing, as well as equalization and other signal-processing additives. Today's editors exchange and talk about their plug-ins like kids trading their baseball cards on the playground. Play all you want, be as creative as you want, pump your signal-processing gear until you are blue in the face. Just remember this: when you have had your fun and think you're only decibels from an Academy Award nomination, walk onto the dubbing stage, turn your cue sheets over to the re-recording mixer, and face the responsibility of what you have done.

Very few sound craftspeople working today can signal process successfully prior to the dub stage. Many do it; many think their work goes to the stage and is mixed just fine. Many do not know their work is dumped and others are brought in to re-cut and re-prepare the material because their processed work is unmixable. With every signal-processing adjustment made, you progressively are inching out on the limb a little further. After a while, the breeze starts to kick up a bit; the branch becomes a bit more unstable. Decide how far out on that limb you are willing to go. Your next job may depend on the reputation of how much time and trouble you caused by having to have material re-prepared or remixed because you went too far.

We will discuss the reverse philosophy of what I have just preached in the next chapter (Chapter 14)—I am sure you cannot wait to hear how and why I will tell you one thing on this page and the flip side in the next chapter.

Volume graphing is not nearly so crucial an issue; in fact, many mixers do not mind a little volume graphing to help them understand the intent of the sound editor and facilitate the mix. It is not a good idea, however, to be finite about your levels, especially when you attempt to lower them too far.

Cueing the Picture

As made very clear, the vast majority of postproduction sound editorial work today is done in the nonlinear realm with videotape transfers of either the cut workprint or the Final Cut Pro or Avid picture edit sessions. However, many would prefer to mix, or at the very least, check predubs or final mix in a playback mode against the final 35-mm picture. Most picture editorial teams try and get the silent first trial answer print on the dubbing stage for the re-recording mixers to use during the re-recording session for at least final playback if not the final mixing process itself.

When the 35-mm first trial (often called the "black track" because there is a black mask where the optical soundtrack eventually goes when the final mix is complete) is made available, the first sound assistant cues the picture. The sound assistant calls the dubbing stage and asks the head mixer what kinds of picture cues the mixer prefers.

The Ten-Ten Cue Technique

Some mixers prefer what are called "ten-tens." The sound assistant has a template, usually a strip of tape on the bench between the two rewinds. A line has been drawn on the left end of the tape. Ten frames of 35-mm film from that line cross from left to right. There is a bold cross drawn on frames 11, 12, and 13. The frame count continues to the right. Three more bold crosses are drawn on frames 24, 25, and 26. As the sound assistant winds the picture slowly from the left rewind to the take-up rewind on the right, he or she watches for the changes in shots. By this time, the assistant has the film virtually memorized. Where perspective and/or scene change cues need to be made, the assistant brings the film down to the tape template, placing the frame line at the line on the left side of the template. He or she takes a grease pencil (some mixers even dictate what color grease pencil, so ask) and boldly marks the two sets of three crosses where the template crosses are set.

As the film runs through the projector at 90 feet a minute, these crosses appear as a mere one-two beat prior to the perspective split or scene change. Where the third set of crosses would have occurred is where the change takes place.

The Wipe Cue Technique

Other mixers prefer the "wipe" cue, which is often not quite as precise in nature. The wipe cue is accomplished by drawing a diagonal straight-edged line with a grease pencil from left to right across the film, usually 1 foot prior to the perspective split or scene change. At the frame line of the wipe, the assistant uses the grease pencil to draw a thick line across the film, emphasizing the frame line itself. As the film runs through the projector, the wipe suddenly travels across the screen, ending in a blip-type frame line.

Presentation

A most vital concept to keep in mind is presentation. Dozens of sound effects must work together to make a reality. Very often, however, either confidence or doubt is set with the very first effect played by the effects mixer as the track is auditioned in a solo mode to determine what is truly there.

If you do not lead off with your strongest cue, you are inviting doubt, from the effects mixer back to producer and director. Make a good first impression. You do not want to give a perception of weak material, so why put your sweetener or support material in the first tracks the mixer auditions? Nobody cares if your support effects are not as strong, just as long as they are not your foundation sound pieces.

Cue Sheets: Hand-Made or Computer-Generated?

Cue sheets are not only the blueprint of the soundtrack you have spent weeks and months preparing. They are also the first turn key to the philosophy of presentation. I have seen many fine sound editors who could cut up a storm, who knew how to make magic of sound, but who also neglected the presentation of their cue sheets. Their cue sheets were sloppy, often with words misspelled. Before the first sound cues hit the screen, the producer and director had glanced at them and cringed, wondering what kind of soundtrack they were getting. Even if the work itself was superb, already the atmosphere of doubt was set.

Some editors still prefer to hand make cue sheets, citing the personal touch and their last authorship of the design. It gives them the opportunity to make side notes and draw flow lines, to add color-coded underlines.

Most, however, use a computer program that extrapolates an exact map of what was cut. The smart sound editor takes the time to ripple through the computerized columns to erase unnecessary number information, or to rename files from the sound master file according to the action on-screen.

The information header should have specific information of what show, who cut it, what kind of session it is, and what version date the cut represents.

An Example of an Information Header

Think about the comfort and the visual flow of the cue sheet so that the mixer is not wasting effort and time trying to figure out the cue sheet, taking away time from turning the dials and equalizing the material.

Show Title   Believe it or not, I have seen re-recording mixers trying to figure out how to mix a reel with cue sheets that actually belonged to the same reel of an entirely different project. (No wonder nothing was in sync!)

Editor   The editor's name should always be on the cue sheet. Not only is this an indictment of the guilty party to throw rocks at if everything blows up, but more importantly,

show: **"Starship Troopers"**   editor: **David Yewdall**   reel #: **5**   group: **"D"-FX**   version: **v.18**

Figure 13.18 The top of your cue sheet should have clear, neat, and pertinent information so that the re-recording mixer knows what show, what reel, who cut it, what predub group, and which version.

it tells anybody working on the mixing console who should know the content of the reel most intimately should questions arise that need swift and accurate answers.

Reel No. (#)   The re-recording mixer should be able to see in large, clear print what reel he or she is working with.

Predub Group   The cue sheet needs to clearly show what predub group the cue sheets represent. Remember, the cue sheets are a blueprint, a road map to most efficiently guide the re-recording mixer through the contents to be dealt with.

Version   Do not forget the *version* number. If the sound effects are not working in sync, the first thing the re-recording mixer is going to do is first check the version number on the cue sheets and the version number on the picture (or videotape). If they do not match, well, get it off the stage until sound and/or picture editorial can bring the most current versions that have both a matching picture and cut audio elements. Some crews use the date rather than a version number. Both techniques work fine. It is not a good idea to interchange these techniques. Decide to use either version or date as a protocol for charting picture changes and updates and stick to that protocol.

The "Dubbing" Cue Sheet

Study the cue sheet pictured in Figure 13.19. This is a computer-generated cue sheet that has been "cleaned-up" for the dubbing stage. What that means is that any computer cue sheet program is going to display the data of the audio cut with all of the precise computeresque exactitudes. By that, I mean that the actual cue "Oil Fire" is actually listed in my library as: **097-42_Oil_Fire_w/low+6**.

When the computer software displays it in the cut region the data may shoot up as: **097/42_Oil_Fire_w/low+6-18.R**.

That means that it is showing you the entire name, the eighteenth cut in that session, then the right channel is displayed to you. I really do not want all that in each data window; it is just too much data clutter. So I will eliminate everything except what I want the mixer to see; and in this case, I will add a perspective description like "close" or "distant." I will then highlight this new name and copy the text "Oil Fire close," then scroll down and paste it into each cut region that the entire name shows up in, thereby giving me a name: **Oil Fire close**.

I will repeat this technique in each displayed channel and change any cut region field data that I wish to simplify.

If you look up at the channel data window, you will see that you can combine left and right channels into a single track. The reason that .R will show up at the end of the clip name is because I have combined all the stereo channels into one track. So the computer shows only the one track name that represents both the left and right sides. The data window tells you this by showing you this information expressed as **Stereo.1/2**.

This means that this single represented channel of sound is actually 2 channels of sound, because it takes a left and a right channel. As you can see, this will save on an awful lot of cue sheet paper by condensing stereo cues, as well as saving on the wear and tear of dubbing mixers' eyes in studying the cue sheet. An additional help

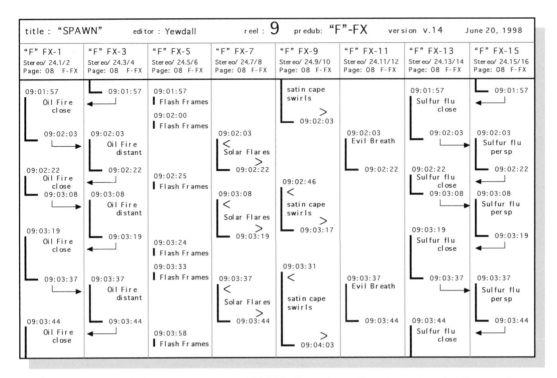

Figure 13.19 A typical computer-generated "dubbing" cue sheet. Note the regimented line-up of time counts and the "cleaned-up" audio file names for ease of use on the re-recording stage.

to the mixer is not to read the entire audio cue as "097/42 Oil Fire w/low+6-18.R"; therefore, I will go into the computer program and cleanup the cues, removing unnecessary data that will mean nothing to the re-recording mixer.

In addition, computer programs do not make split arrows such as you see in FX-1, FX-3, FX-13, and FX-15. I make an arrow template and put these in manually, because when an audio track is split for perspective and/or volume shift issues, a re-recording mixer is really thankful to see where the event is going.

You might want to check out computer cue sheet programs before you buy them. I really stay away from one program in particular, in that it makes you change the names of your audio files so that it will read them a certain way in the cue sheet. This is like the tail wagging the body of the dog: it is engineered backwards. Other computer cue sheet programs are designed to be much more friendly to editors, who usually have to make their cue sheets in the middle of the night or minutes before the actual mix commences and do not have time to put up with a lot of backward computer program engineering.

The sideways V's in FX-7 and FX-9 tell the mixer that the effect has built-in fade-ins or fade-outs. These symbols are built into the computer program and will show up automatically; although, once again they are canard, because if you are a precise editor who builds in one-frame fade-ins and fade-outs to guard against digital ticks, the computer will not know this any differently from a 30-frame fade-in or fade-out, but will show the fade-in and fade-out symbols regardless. So here again, I remove any fade-in or fade-out symbols that do not truly represent an important fade that the mixer may be interested in knowing about.

Packed and Ready to Go

The sound assistant has gone over the flow chart of the material advertised from the various departments. He or she has seen to it that the editors have cut to the proper versions. The assistant also has seen to it that the sessions have been backed up and protected. Finally he or she has seen to it that the cue sheets have been properly made and that the various editors are speaking with one style and voice, as far as presentation is concerned.

Since 1978 I have taken an organizational chart template to an economy copy center and have special 10″ × 13″ white envelopes printed up. Each envelope holds a reel of dialog cue sheets (including ADR and Group Walla), or a reel of Foley cue sheets, or a reel of hard effects cue sheets, or a reel of stereo background cue sheets. As each group of cue sheets is completed, the sound assistant check marks the appropriate box on the front of the envelope, along with the show title, editor's name, type of cue sheet group, completion of predubbing on the material, etc. On the bottom is a large box for the supervising sound editor to write notes while he is on the dubbing stage with the mixers. He or she can pencil in update notes to be made before the final mix.

This is not only a good organizational help to keep the flood of paperwork straight and easily accessible, but it is also good presentation to your client. They see how you work with clean and neat envelopes with precise notes that are easy to find. It instills their confidence in you and your ability to handle the complex job of developing their soundtrack, and they are more willing to listen to your advice when the chips are down because they have seen your neatness and orderly procedure.

Chapter 14
Sound Editorial
Ultra Low-Budget Strategies

"I know what I said—but now we're dealing with reality!"

– *Steve Carver, director of* Lone Wolf McQuade

You just finished reading about the structured, more traditional techniques and disciplines for recording, editorial preparation, and delivery of the myriad sound cues necessary to create the theatrical film experience known as the soundtrack—and you think all this book talks about is big-budget features with big teams of craftspeople to get the job done. Well, before we discuss the dialog editing, ADR and looping techniques, the world of Foley, music, and the re-recording process, I think we should pause and discuss the fact that a great deal of the work you will do will *not* and *cannot* afford the budget requirements to mount the type of sound job that you will find yourself faced with.

I assumed that as you have been reading this book you understood one extremely important axiom—the *art form* of sound does not change, no matter the budget and schedule on the table. All of the audio recording techniques, the science, and the pure physics of the soundtrack of a film *do not change*—only the strategies of how you are going to get your arms around the project and solve it.

The upcoming chapters regarding the dialog, ADR, Foley, music collaboration, and edit preparation in concert with the strategies of the re-recording mix process apply to the development of the final soundtrack the *same* way, whether you are working on a gigantic $180 million space opera or if you are working on an extra-features behind-the-scenes documentary for a DVD release or a student film. The *only* differences is the dollars allocated in the budget and the schedule demands that will, if you have been paying attention to what you have read thus far (and will continue to read about in the following chapters), dictate to you exactly *how* you are going to develop and deliver a final soundtrack that will render the fullness of the sound design texture and clarity of a sound budget with 10 times the dollars to spend, to as much as 100 times the budget that the blockbuster films command.

I could not have supervised the sound for 11 Roger Corman films if I did not understand how to shift gears and restructure the strategies of ultra low-budget projects. That does not mean that all sound craftspeople know how to shift back and forth between big-budget to ultra low-budget projects and maintain the *perception* of quality standard that we have come to expect from the work we do.

There are many who can practice their art form (whatever specific part of the soundtrack that he or she is responsible for) in the arena of mega-budget films, where they can get approval to do custom recording halfway around the world, have unlimited ADR stage access, and be able to spend two or more days to perform the desired Foley cues per reel.

Conversely, there are craftspeople who can tackle and successfully develop and deliver a final soundtrack for ultra low-budget projects but who cannot structure, strategize, and oversee the sound supervisory responsibilities of mega-budget pictures.

Then there are those of us who move back and forth between huge budget jobs and tiny budget jobs at will. Over the years I have observed that those sound craftspeople who started their careers in a sound facility that was known for and specialized in big budget pictures usually had an extremely difficult time handling the "I ain't got no money, *but* we need a great soundtrack regardless" budget.

This is the realm of disciplined preplanning, knowing that it is vital to bring on a supervising sound editor *before* you even commence principal photography. This is where the triangle law we discussed in Chapter 4 regarding the rule of "you can either have it *cheap*, you can have it *good*, or you can have it *fast*," really rises up and demands which two choices that all can live with.

Even if the producer is empowered by how important the soundtrack is to his or her project, the majority of first-time producers almost never understand *how* to achieve a powerful soundtrack for the audience, but they especially do not know or understand how to structure the postproduction budget and realistically schedule the post schedule.

This has given rise to the position commonly known as the postproduction supervisor, who, if you think about it, are really adjunct producers. Many of the postproduction supervisors that I have had the misfortune to work with do *not* know their gluteus maxim from a depression in the turf. With few exceptions, postproduction supervisors almost always just copied and pasted postproduction budgets and schedules from other projects that he or she *thinks* is about the same kind of film that he or she is presently working on. Virtually, without fail, these projects always have budget/schedule issues because every film project is different and every project needs to have its own needs customized accordingly. I have been called into more meetings where the completion bond company was about to decide whether or not to either shut the project down or take it over, and on more than one occasion their decision pivoted on what I warranted that I could or could not do in the postproduction process. By the way, this is an excellent example of why it is vital to always keep your word clean—do what you say you will do, and if you have trouble or extenuating circumstances to deal with do not try to hide it or evade it. Professionals can always handle the truth. I tell my people, "Never lie to me, tell me *good* news, tell me *bad* news—just tell me the truth. Professionals can problem solve how to deal with the issues at hand."

YOU SUFFER FROM "YOU DON'T KNOW WHAT YOU DON'T KNOW!"

Every film project will *tell* you what it needs—if you know how to listen and do some basic research. You can really suffer from what I call, "You don't know what you don't know." It can either make you or break you. Think about the following items to consider before you dare bid or structure a soundtrack on the ultra low-budget projects.

> What **genre** is the film? Obviously a concept-heavy, science-fiction sound project is going to be more expensive to develop a soundtrack for than a film that is an intimate comedy-romance.

> Read the **script**, highlighting all pieces of action, location, and other red flags that an experienced supervising sound editor has learned to identify, what will surely cost hard dollars.

> Look up other projects that the **producer** has produced, noting the budget size that he or she seems to work in.

> Look up other projects that the **director** has directed, and talk with the head re-recording mixer who ultimately mixed the sound and knows (better than any other person on that project) about the quality and expertise of preparation of the prior project.

> Look up other projects that the **picture editor** has handled for the picture editing process. Look him or her up on IMDb (Internet Movie Database) and pick several pictures that are credited to them. Scroll down to the "Sound Department" heading. Jot down the names of the supervising sound editor(s), especially the dialog editor. Without revealing the current project you are considering, ask these individuals about the picture editor; you will learn a wealth of knowledge, both pro and con, which is going to impact the tactical and political ground that you will be working with.

Case in point: When Wolfgang Petersen expanded his 1981 version of *Das Boot* into his "director's cut," why did he not have Mike Le-Mare (who was nominated for two Academy Awards on the original 1981 version) and his team handle the sound editorial process? For those who understand the politics of the bloody battlefield of picture editorial, understand the potential of being undermined by the picture editor. You need to find out as much as you can about him or her, so you can navigate the land mines that you might inadvertently step on.

SOUND ADVICE

As the producer, you really need to engage the supervising sound editor and have him or her involved from the beginning if you are working on a fixed budget. A supervising sound editor will always have a list of recommended production sound mixers, not just name production sound mixers, but mixers who have a dependable track record of delivering good production sound on tough ultra low-budget projects.

If you think about it, that makes perfect sense. The supervising sound editor is going to inherit sound files from the very person he or she has recommended to the producer. When it comes to protecting your own reputation and an industry buzz that your word is your bond, then friendship or no friendship, when it comes to protecting your reputation *and* losing money on the project, then the supervising sound editor is going to want the best talent who understands what to get and what not to bother with under budgetary challenges.

I will not rehash what we have already discussed in Chapter 5—because the art form of what the production mixer will do does not change—only the choice of tools and knowing how to slim down the equipment costs and set protocols in order to save money.

When the supervising sound editor advises the producer on specific production sound mixers to consider, he or she will also go over the precise strategies of the production sound path—everything from the production sound recording on the set through picture editorial to locking the picture and the proper output of the EDL and OMF files, and of course, how to structure the post-sound editorial procedure. On ultra low-budget projects, it is vital that the producer understand the caveats of a fixed budget, so that the supervising sound editor can guarantee staying on budget and on schedule, as long as the "If . . ." clauses do not rise up to change the deal.

The "If" disclaimers can, and should, include everything from recording production sound a particular way, that proper back-ups are made of each day's shoot prior to leaving the hands of the production sound mixer. All format issues must be thoroughly discussed and agreed on, through the usage of sound (including temp FX or temp music) during the picture editorial process, then locking picture and handing it over to the supervising sound editor. The producer must be aware of what can and what cannot be done within the confines of the budget available.

With very few exceptions, projects that run into postproduction issues can be traced back to the fact that they did not have the expert advice of a veteran supervising sound editor from the beginning.

PRODUCTION SOUND

It is very rare to come across an ultra low-budget project that has the luxury of recording to a 4-track (or higher) recorder. You usually handle these types of production recordings in two ways.

1. You record to a sound recorder, whether the project is shot on film or shot on video, the production track is recorded on a 2-track recorder such as a DAT recorder or a 2-track direct-to-disk.
2. If the project is being shot on video, especially if in hi-def, the production sound mixer may opt to use only an audio mixer, such as the Shure mixer shown below. The output from the audio mixer is then recorded onto the video-tape, using the camera as the sound recorder, which also streamlines the log-and-capture process at picture editorial.

One decision you will have to think about if you are shooting video and you wish to opt for the production sound being recorded to the videotape, is whether the project set-ups are simple or highly complex. If the camera needs to move, enjoying more freedom will mean that you do not want a couple of 25-foot axle audio cables going from the sound mixer outputs into the back of the video camera's axle inputs. At the very least, this will distract the camera operator any time the camera needs to be as free as possible.

The best way to solve the cable issue is to connect the sound mixer outputs to a wireless transmitter. A wireless receiver is strapped to the camera rig with short pig-tail axle connectors going into the rear of the camera.

Double Phantoming—The Audio Nightmare

Whether you opt for a cable connection from the sound mixer to the camera or if you opt to have a wireless system to the camera, the first most important thing to look out for is the nightmare of "double phantoming" the production recording.

Video cameras have built-in microphones. Any professional or semiprofessional video camera has XLR audio imports so that a higher degree of quality can be achieved. Because a lot of this work is done without the benefit of a separate audio mixer, these cameras can supply phantom power to the microphones.

When the crew does have a dedicated production sound mixer, using an audio mixer, you *must* turn the phantom power option off in the video camera. The audio mixer, shown in Figure 14.1, has a LINE/MIC select switch under each XLR input. The audio mixer needs to send the phantom power to microphones—not the video camera, as the output becomes a LINE (not a microphone) issue.

If the video phantom power select *is* turned on, the camera will send phantom power in addition to the audio mixer, automatically causing a "double phantom" recording which will yield a distorted track. No matter how much you turn the volume down, the track will always sound distorted. The next law of audio physics is that sound once recorded "double phantomed" cannot be corrected, is useless, and can only serve as a guide track for massive amounts of ADR.

Using the Tone Generator

Different manufacturers have different means of generating a known line-up tone for the user. In the case of the Shure mixer (Figure 14.1), the first microphone input volume fader (on the far left) controls the tone generator. You simply pull the knob toward you, turning on the generator, creating a 1-kHz tone. Leaving the PAN setting straight up (in the 12 o'clock position) will send the 1-kHz signal equally to both channel 1 (left) and channel 2 (right). The center master fader can then be used to calibrate the outputs accordingly. Notice the icon just above the master fader that indicates that the inside volume control knob is used for channel 1 (left) and the outside volume control ring is used for channel 2 (right).

If you line up both channels together you will send the line-up tone out to the external recording device, e.g., the video camera or a 2-channel recorder such as a DAT.

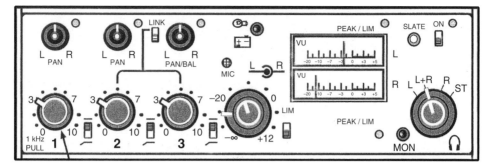

Figure 14.1 The Shure FP33 3-Channel Stereo Mixer. This particular model is powered by two 9-volt batteries.

The production sound mixer coordinates with the camera operator to make sure that the signal is reaching the camera properly, that both channels read whatever –dB peak meter level equals "0" VU, such as –18 dB to as much as –24 dB, and that the recording device (whether it be an audio recorder or the video camera) has its phantom power option turned OFF. Once the recording device (audio recorder or video camera) has been set, only the production sound mixer will make volume changes.

The Pan Pot Controllers

If you are using a single microphone, and wish to have both channels receiving the signal, then you should leave the Pan Pot Controller (above the microphone input volume fader being used) in the straight-up (12 o'clock) position, as shown in Figure 14.2 in configuration A.

If you are using two microphones and wish to have each channel kept in its own dedicated channel, then push in on the Pan Pot Controller knob. It will then spring out so you can turn it to either hard left or hard right. This will send microphone input 1 to channel 1 (left) *only* and microphone input 2 to channel 2 (right) *only*, as shown in configuration B. This does not necessarily make a stereophonic recording. Unless you set the microphones up properly in an X-Y pattern, or if using a stereo dual-capsule microphone, you will face potential phasing issues and no real disciplined stereophonic image. This configuration is best used if you have your boom operator using a boom mike and a wireless mike attached to an actor or two wireless mikes, one on each actor, or two boomed mikes that by necessity need to have the mikes placed far enough apart wherein one microphone could not properly capture the scene.

Also note in Figure 14.2 that there is a Flat/Hi-Pass setting option just to the right of each microphone input volume fader. Standard procedure is to record Flat, which means the selector would be pushed up to the flat line position.

If you really feel like you need to roll off some low end during the original recording, then you would push the selector down to the hi-pass icon position. Just remember, if you decide to make this equalization decision at this time, you will not have it later in postproduction. You may be denying some wonderful low-end whomps, thuds, or fullness of production sound effects. You must always record with the idea that we can

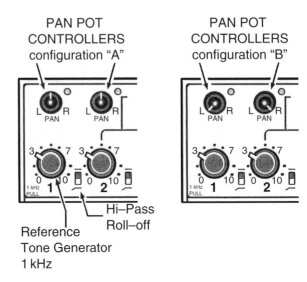

Figure 14.2 The Pan Pot Controllers.

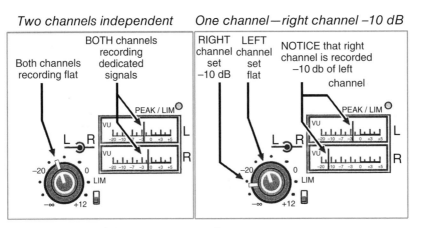

Figure 14.3 Two recording strategy set-ups.

always roll off any unwanted low-end rumbles later during the re-recording process, but you cannot restore it once you have chosen to roll it off.

Two Recording Strategies

In Figure 14.3, "two channels independent" requires that the Pan Pot Controller above each microphone input volume fader be set to either hard left or hard right, depending on which channel the production sound mixer wants the signal to be sent. This is also the set-up setting you would want if you are recording stereophonically.

In Figure 14.3, "one channel—right channel –10 dB" requires that the Pan Pot Controllers above each microphone input volume fader be set to the straight-up (12 o'clock) position. This will send a single microphone input equally to the Master

Fader—only you will note that *after* you have used the 1-kHz tone generator to calibrate the desired recording level coming out of the audio mixer to either the camera or to a recording device, you will then hold the inside volume control knob in place (so that the left channel will not change) while you turn the outside volume control ring counterclockwise, watching the VU meter closely until you have diminished the signal 10 dB less than channel 1. In the case of Figure 14.3, the left channel is reading −3 dB (VU), so you would set the left channel to −13 dB (VU). This is known as "right channel −10 dB," which is used as a volume "insurance policy," so to speak.

During the recording of a scene there may be some unexpected outburst, slam of a door, a scream following normal recording of dialog—anything that could over-modulate your primary channel (left). This becomes a priceless insurance policy during the postproduction editing process, where the dialog editor will only be using channel 1 (left), except when he or she comes upon such a dynamic moment that overloaded channel 1. The editor will then access that moment out of channel 2 (right) which should be all right due to being recorded −10 dB lower than the primary channel. Believe me, there have been countless examples where this technique has saved whole passages of a film from having to be stripped out and replaced with ADR. As you can see, this is a valuable technique on ultra low-budget projects.

Single Monaural Channel—Flat

Figure 14.4 shows a single microphone with both channels recording the same signal at the same volume. The Pan Pot Controller above the microphone input volume fader is set straight up to send the audio signal evenly to both left and right channels.

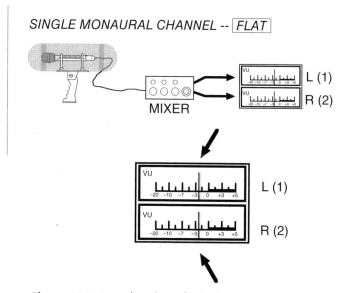

Figure 14.4 One microphone for both channels—FLAT.

Single Monaural Channel—Right −10 dB

Figure 14.5 shows a single microphone. The Pan Pot Controller above the microphone input volume fader is set straight up to send the audio signal evenly to both left and right channels; however, the Master Audio Fader is set right channel −10 dB less than left channel.

Two Discrete Monaural Channels—Recorded Separately

Figure 14.6 shows two microphones with the Pan Pot configurations set to hard left and hard right, thus being able to use two different kinds of mikes. The production

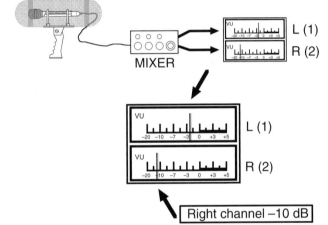

Figure 14.5 One microphone for both channels—channel 2 (*right*) set −10 dB from channel 1 (*left*).

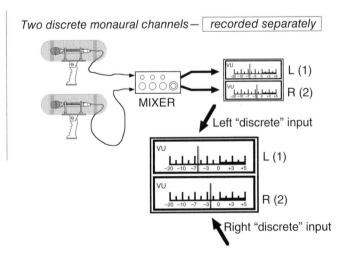

Figure 14.6 Two discrete monaural channels.

sound mixer must make precise notes on the sound report of what each channel is capturing, i.e., channel 1: boom mike, channel 2: wireless. The microphones do *not* have to be the same make and model, as this configuration is not for stereo use, but simply isolates two audio signals. The set-up could be that you have a boom operator favoring one side of the set where actor A is and a cable man, now acting as a boom operator, using a pistol-grip-mounted shotgun mike, hidden behind a couch deep in the set where he or she can better mike actor B, and so forth.

Two Discrete Channels—Recording Stereo

Figure 14.7 shows two microphones in an X-Y configuration, which greatly reduces phasing issues. The pan pot configurations are set to hard left and hard right. To record a correct stereophonic image both microphones must be identical.

The most dramatic phasing problems take place when an audio event, such as a car-by (as discussed in Chapter 10), causes a cancellation wink-out as the car (or performing item) crosses the center point, whereby the audio signal, which was reaching the closer microphone diaphragm a slight millisecond quicker than the far microphone, is now going to reach the second microphone diaphragm before it reaches the first one. This center point area of crossing over is where the phasing cancellation wink-out area comes into play. If the two channels are folded together, which often happens somewhere in the postproduction process and certainly will be noticed if it is televised and the stereo channels are combined in a mono playback option, there will be a drop-out at the center point. This is why you want the two diaphragms as close together as possible.

Notice in the Schoeps X-Y configuration, the microphone capsules are actually over/under, getting the two diaphragms as close as possible to zero point.

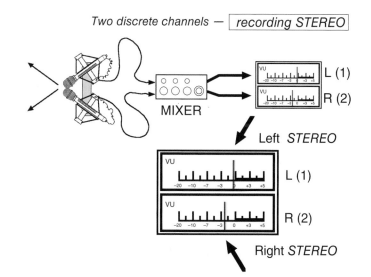

Figure 14.7 Stereophonic recording using X-Y microphone configuration.

SOUND EDITING STRATEGIES

Budget restrictions should only compel you to rethink *how* you will get your arms around the soundtrack. I have heard too many editors slough it off as, "I'm not going to give them what they're not paying for." I suppose that kind of attitude makes one feel better about not having a budget to work with—but it backfires on you, because when all is said and done nobody will (A) remember, (B) have knowledge of, or (C) give a damn what the budget and schedule restrictions were. *Your* work is up there on the screen—and that is *all* that matters.

You must know how to cut corners without compromising the ultimate quality of the final soundtrack. This is where veteran experience pays off. Some of the best supervising sound editors in features today learned their craft by working in television, a medium that always was tight and fast. It is far more difficult for an editor who only knows how to edit big feature style to shift gears into a tight and lean working style.

You have to learn how to work within the confines of the budget and redesign your strategies accordingly. The first thing you have to decide is how to do the work with a very tight crew. Personally, I really learned how to cut dialog by working on the last season of *Hawaii 5-O*, where they would not allow us to ADR anything. We *had* to make the production track work and we did a show every week!

I have developed a personal relationship with several colleagues, each with his or her own specialty. When we contract for a low-budget project, we automatically know that it is a three-person key crew. I handle the sound effect design/editing as well as stereo backgrounds for the entire project; Dwayne Avery handles all the dialog editing, including ADR and Group Walla editing; and our third crewmember is the re-recording mixer Zach Seivers in North Hollywood. The only additional talent will be the Foley artist(s), and the extent of the Foley work will be directly linked to how low an ultra low-budget project can afford. Vanessa Ament, a lead Foley artist/supervisor, put it this way:

> Sometimes I think Foley artists and Foley editors lose sight of what Foley is best used for. There is a tendency to "fall in love" with all the fun and challenge of doing the work, and forgetting that edited sound effects are going to be in the track also. Thus, artists and editors put in sounds already covered by effects. The problem with this is three-fold. First, the sound effects editor can pull certain effects faster out of the library or cut in recorded field effects that are more appropriate without the limitations of the stage. Second, the Foley stage is a more expensive place to create effects than the editing room, and third, the final dubbing mixer is stuck with too many sounds to sort through. I remember a story about a very well respected dubbing mixer who was confronted with 48 tracks of Foley for a film and in front of the editor, tore up the pages with tracks 25 through 48, tossed them behind him and requested that tracks 1 through 24 of Foley be put up for pre-dubbing. The lesson here is: think of the people who come after you in the chain of filmmaking after you have finished your part.

On Carl Franklin's *One False Move*, Vanessa Ament only had two days to perform the Foley, because that was all the budget could afford. It was absolutely vital that Vanessa and I discuss what she absolutely had to get for us and what cues she should not even worry about, because I knew that I could make them myself in wild record-

Figure 14.8 Vanessa Ament, lead Foley artist, performing props for *Chain Reaction*. The Foley artist assisting her is Rick Partlow. (Photo by David Yewdall.)

ings or I had something I could pull from the sound effect library. And *that* is really the key issue—Foley what you *absolutely* have to have done. If your Foley artist has covered the project of all the have-to-get cues and there is any time left over, then go back and start to do the B list cues until your available time is up. You have to look at it as how full the glass is, not how empty it is.

For the dialog editor, it becomes a *must* to work with OMF, which means that the assistant picture editor(s) had to do their work correctly and cleanly. As I have said before, "junk-in, junk-out." If the dialog editor finds that a reprint does not A-B compare with the OMF output audio file identically, then you are in deep trouble. If you cannot rely on the quality of the picture editorial digitizing process, then you are going to have to confront the producer with one of the "If" disclaimers that has to affect your editorial costs. "If" you cannot use the OMF, and the dialog editor has to reprint and phase match, there is no way you can do the editing job on the same low-cost budget track that you are being asked to work with.

I have seen this "If" rise up so many times that I really wish that producers *have* to be required to hire professional experts who really know the pitfalls and disciplines of digitizing the log-and-capture phase of picture editorial. So many times, producers hire cheap learn-on-the-job interns to do this work because they save a lot of money— only to be confronted in postproduction with the fact that they will be spending many times as much to fix it as it would have cost to do it right the first time.

It is also at this stage of the project that you really understand how valuable a good production sound mixer who understands the needs and requirements of post-production is to an ultra low-budget project. He or she will understand to grab an actor who has just a few lines as bit parts, and on the side, record wild tracks of them saying the same lines with different inflections, making sure that their performance is free and clear of the noise that constantly plagues a location shoot.

I cannot tell you how much the production sound mixer Lee Howell has saved his producer clients by understanding this seemingly simple concept of wild tracks of location ambiences and sound reports with lots of notations about content. Precise notes showing the wild tracks of bit players will save a producer from flying in actors

Figure 14.9 Clancy Troutman oversees the progress of his sound designer, Scott Westley, at Digital Dreams in Burbank, CA. (Photo by John LeBlanc.)

for ADR sessions just to redo a handful of lines. It becomes the fast track road map to where the good stuff is.

Good production track is pure gold—literally worth gold when you do not have a budget to do a lot of ADR or weeks and weeks of dialog editors to fix tracks.

I can always tell the amateur dialog editor. His or her tracks are all over the place, with umpteen tracks. You must prepare your dialog with ambience fills that make smooth transitions across three or four primary tracks, not including P-FX and X-tracks (you will read about dialog strategy in Chapter 15).

Have your director review a ready-to-mix dialog session, not during the mix, but with the dialog editor, making his or her choices of alternate performances then and there, rather than wasting valuable mixing time deciding which alternate readings he or she would prefer.

Not all supervising sound editors, or for that matter, sound editors who support the supervisor's strategies can shift from meg-budget projects to ultra low-budget projects with a clear understanding of the art form and the necessary strategies to tackle either extreme without waste or confusion. Clancy Troutman, the chief sound supervisor for Digital Dreams Sound Studios located in Burbank, California, has worked on projects that challenge such an understanding.

Clancy is a second-generation sound supervisor, learning his craft and the disciplines of the art form first as an apprentice to and then as a collaborator with his father, Jim Troutman, veteran of several hundred feature films. Jim's vast experience, knowledge of sound, creativity, and expertise have teamed him over the years with some of Hollywood's legendary directors, including Steven Spielberg, Mel Brooks, Peter Bogdanovich, and Sam Peckinpah. Clancy worked under his father on sound designing and sound editing for *Osterman Weekend*, *Life Stinks*, *The Bad Lieutenant*, *Fast Times at Ridgemont High*, and *Urban Cowboy*.

Clancy came into his own, stepping into the supervising sound editor position with such projects as *Beastmaster*, *Cop* with James Woods, *Cohen & Tate* with Roy Scheider. Other challenging projects include supervising the sound for *Police Academy:*

Mission to Moscow, Hatchet, Pentagon Papers, and the *Toolbox Murders,* to name just a few.

His work on *Murder She Wrote, China Beach,* and *Thirtysomething* honed his skills in the world of television demands and challenges, earning him the supervising sound editor chores for the popular cult television series *The Adventures of Brisco County Jr.,* starring Bruce Campbell.

This eclectic mix of product has given Clancy the understanding how to shift back and forth between traditional budgets and schedules to ultra low-budget strategies. Even though Clancy has amassed one of the largest sound effect libraries in the business, he really believes in the magic and value of the production sound recordings captured on location.

Collaborating with clients to yield as much bang for the buck as possible has been both Clancy's challenge and ultimate satisfaction with problem solving the project at hand. He loves to design and create a unique sound experience for the film that, for the present, only lives in the client's imagination.

THE EVOLUTION BLENDING OF EDITOR AND RE-RECORDING MIXER

Those of you who have not been part of the film and television sound industry for at least the last 25 years cannot truly understand why the things have worked the way they have and why there is so much resistance to the evolution of the sound editor and the re-recording mixer moving closer together and becoming one and the same.

The traditional re-recording community struggles to remain a closed "boys club"—this is no secret. Since the days when the head re-recording mixer (usually handling the center chair or dialog chores) literally reigned as king on the re-recording stage, he could throw out anything he wanted to. Many a reel got "bounced" off the stage because the head mixer did not like how it was prepared or did not care for the sound effect choices. Mixers often dictated what sounds were to be used, not the sound editor.

Even when I started supervising sound shows in the late 1970s, we would see and sometimes be a part of butting heads with the head mixer who ruled the stage and held court. The major studios were not the battleground where change was going to take place. It took independent talents such as Walter Murch and Ben Burtt, who had the directorial/producerial leadership to give them their freedom.

I remember how stunned I was when I was supervising the sound for John Carpenter's *The Thing.* We were making a temp mix for a test audience screening. The Universal sound department was already upset that one of their pictures was not going to be left to Universal sound editors and that ADR and Foley chores would not use Universal sound facilities, but worst of all, the final re-recording mix was going to be across town at Goldwyn.

I could write an entire book on postproduction politics and the invisible mine field of who controls what, and when you should check that stinging sensation in your back that might be something more than just a bad itch.

We no sooner got through the first 200 feet of reel 1 when I put my hand up to stop. The head re-recording mixer did not stop the film. I stood up, with my hand up—"Hold it!" The film did not stop. I had to walk around the end of the console, step up on the raised platform, and as I paced toward the head mixer, he hit the STOP button, stood up, and faced me square on. "What seems to be the problem?"

Then I made one of the greatest verbal goofs, the worst thing that I could possibly have said to a studio sound mixer: "You're not mixing the sound the way I *designed* it."

Snickers crossed the console, as the head mixer stood face-to-face with me, holding back laughter. "Oh, boys—we are not mixing the film the way Mister Yewdall has *designed* it."

He started to tell me that he was the head mixer and by god he would mix the film the way *he* saw fit, not the way I so-called *designed* it.

Naturally, I had a problem with that. We stood inches apart and I knew that this was not just a passing disagreement. This was going to be a defining moment. I knew that the Universal crews were upset that they were not doing the final mix; I knew that the temp mix was a bone thrown to them so they were not completely shut out of the process. John Carpenter had mixed all his films with Bill Varney, Gregg Landaker, and Steve Maslow over at Goldwyn Studios in Dolby stereo, and he certainly intended that *The Thing* was also going to be mixed by his favorite crew—the political battle was rumbling like a cauldron.

I informed the head mixer that he *was* going to mix the film exactly as I had conceived it, because I had been hired by John Carpenter a year before principal photography had even started developing the strategies and tactics of how to successfully achieve the soundtrack that I knew John wanted. John wanted my kind of sound for his picture, and I owed my talent and industry to John Carpenter, not to studio political game playing. To make matters worse, Universal Studios did not want the film to be mixed in Dolby stereo, saying that they did not trust the matrixing. They said it was too undependable, and boy, that took an amazing knockdown, drag-out battle royal late one night in the "black tower" with all sides coming to final blows.

So, now I stood there, eyeball-to-eyeball with the head mixer, knowing I did not dare flinch. He then made a mistake of his own, when he said, "Maybe we should get Verna Fields involved in this decision." (Verna Fields was, at that time, president of production for Universal Studios.)

I agreed. And before he could speak I told the music mixer her telephone extension. I could tell from the head mixer's eyes that he was caught off guard that I even knew her number. But, we literally stood there like statues, staring at each other with total resolve while Verna Fields left the Producers Building, paced past the commissary, and into the sound facility.

I didn't even have to look; I recognized the sound of her dress as she stormed into the room. Those of you who have had the honor of knowing Verna know *exactly* what I am talking about; those of you who don't missed out on arguably the most powerful woman Hollywood has ever known, certainly one of the most respected.

"What seems to be the problem here?!" she demanded.

The head mixer thought he was going to have a lot of fun watching Verna Fields rip a young whippersnapper to ribbons. With a sly smirk he replied, "I don't have a problem, but it seems Mister Yewdall does."

Verna was in no mood for games. "And that *is*?"

I kept my eyes locked onto the head mixer, for to look away now would be a fatal mistake. "I told your head mixer that he is not mixing this film the way I *designed* the sound."

The head mixer was doing everything to contain himself. He just knew that the "design" word was going to really end up ripping me to pieces, and with any luck, I would get fired from the picture.

Instead, Verna's stern and commanding voice spoke with absolute authority. "We are paying Mister Yewdall a great deal of money to supervise and design the sound for this motion picture—and you *will* mix it *exactly* as he tells you."

If I had hit the head mixer with a baseball bat, it would not have had as profound an effect. It was as if a needle had popped a balloon, or you had just discovered your lover in bed with somebody else! I still did not turn to her. I actually felt sorry for the head mixer for how hard it had hit him.

"Are there any other issues we need to discuss?!" demanded Verna.

The head mixer shook his head weakly and turned back to his chair. I turned to see Verna; her thick Coke-bottle glasses magnified the look in her eyes. I nodded my thanks to her as she turned to leave.

Independent sound mixing had gone on for some time, but not on the major studio lots. By noon it was all around town. The knife had cleanly severed the cord that the head mixer ruled as king. The role of the supervising sound editor suddenly took a huge step forward. The unions tried to fight this evolution, for as long as we were working on 35-mm stripe and fullcoat, they could keep somewhat of a grip on it. But when editors started to work on 24-track 2" tape, interlocking videotape to time code, the cracks were starting to widen. It was clear that the technological evolution was going to rewrite who was going to design and cut and re-record the soundtrack. Union 695 actually walked into my shop a few months later with chains and a padlock, citing that I was in violation of union regs by having a transfer operation, which clearly fell under Union 695 jurisdiction.

I asked them what made them think so. They marched back to my transfer bay (Figure 14.10) and recited union regs that Union 700 editors could not do this kind of work. I corrected them by pointing to John Evans, who was my Union 695 transfer operator.

The first union man pointed to the left part of the array, where the various signal processing gear was racked. "His union status doesn't allow him to use that gear."

"He doesn't," I replied.

"Then who DOES?!" he snapped back.

"I do."

The union guy really thought he had me. "Ah-Ha! You're an editor, not a Y-1 mixer!" He started to lift his chains.

"Excuse me," I interrupted. "I know something about the law, gentlemen. Corporate law transcends union law in this case. I am the corporate owner, and as a corporate owner I can do any damn thing I want to. If I want to be a director of cinematography on a show I might produce, I can do that—and the union cannot do one thing to stop me." I pointed to John Evans. "You see, only *he* uses his side of the rack; when the signal processing gear is utilized, I am the one who does that."

Figure 14.10 David Yewdall's transfer bay, designed and built by John Mosley.

I noticed that the second union man had drifted back and grabbed the phone; I supposed to call the main office. He came back and tapped his buddy on the arm—they needed to leave.

A couple of days later the two men returned (without chains and a padlock) and asked if I would like a Y-1 union card. "Gee, why didn't you ask me that before?"

More and more of my colleagues were going through this process, carrying dual union cards. Alan Splet is a perfect example. Alan was David Lynch's favorite sound designer, having helmed *Eraserhead*, *The Elephant Man*, *Dune*, and *Blue Velvet*. On *Dune*, Alan even served as the fourth re-recording mixer on the console with Bill Varney, Gregg Landaker, and Steve Maslow on Stage D at Goldwyn. Alan's work was truly an art form. His eyesight was very poor (I often had to drive him home late at night when the bus route stopped running), but what a pair of ears he had and what an imagination. His work was wonderfully eclectic, supervising and sound designing films such as *The Mosquito Coast*, *The Unbearable Lightness of Being*, *Dirty Rotten Scoundrels*, *Dead Poets Society*, *Mountains of the Moon*, *Wind*, and of course, the film he won the Academy Award for, *Black Stallion*.

I remember him literally having a 35-mm transfer machine to his left; he would play his ¼" sound masters through an array of sound signal equipment to custom transfer each piece of mag film as he needed it. He would break it off, turn to his Moviola, lace it up, and sync it to picture. This was an extremely rare technique (and often a luxury)—but it was the key to his designing the kind of audio events he wanted. But this kind of trust takes a director and/or producer to back your play.

Then nonlinear editing became the new promise of lower budgets, faster schedules, and better sound. We have already spoken about the philosophy and collateral cost issues, so I will not rehash that. It scared the bejesus out of hundreds of veteran sound editors, many who felt that they could not make the transition and dropped out of the industry.

For a while it was really only an issue for editors, but it soon became apparent to the re-recording mixers that it was going to affect them in a huge way. Even today, many mixers are scrambling to compete with, learn, and embrace Pro Tools as an end-all. Those who only thought Pro Tools was only for editing were not understanding the entire process—and now it is here. More and more projects are no longer being mixed at the traditional houses, because these projects are being completely edited, re-recorded, and print-mastered with Pro Tools.

Is it as good as mixing at the traditional stages? I didn't say that. What I think philosophically does not mean a thing. It is a reality of the evolutionary process that big multi-million-dollar re-recording mix stages will only be used for the big pictures, and virtually everything else is going to be done, at least in part, if not totally through the computer, using software and a control mix surface by one- or two-man mixing crews, often by those who supervised and prepared the tracks in the first place.

THINK BIG—CUT TIGHT

One of the first things you are going to do, in order to capture the Big Sound on a tiny budget, are crash-downs, pre-predubs, all kinds of little maneuvers to streamline how you can cut faster.

In the traditional world I had 10 stereo pairs of sound effects just for a hydraulic door opening for *Starship Troopers*. When I handled the sound effects for *Fortress II*, they could not afford a big budget, but they wanted my kind of sound. I agreed to design and cut all the sound effects and backgrounds for the film on a flat fixed fee. The deal was that you could not hang over my shoulder every day. You can come Friday afternoons after lunch and I will review what I have done. You make your notes and suggestions and then you leave and I will see you a week later.

The other odd request I made in order to close the deal, since I knew how bad they wanted my kind of sound, was that I could use some wine, you know, to help soften the long hours. I had meant it as a joke. But, sure enough, every so often I had deliveries of plenty of Zinfandel delivered to my cutting room. Actually, in retrospect, the afternoons were quite—creative.

One of the requests that they did ask of me was that they really wanted space doors that had not been heard before. So I designed all the space doors from scratch, but I couldn't end up with dozens of tracks with umpteen elements for these doors every time they would open and close, not on an ultra low-budget job. So I created a concept session. Anything and everything that the client may want to audition as concept sound that was going to have an ongoing influence in the film—from background concepts, to hard effects, laser fire, telemetry, etc. I designed the doors in their umpteen elements, played them for the client on Friday for approval. Then I mixed each door down to one stereo pair, which became part of my *sound palette*—a term I use to mean the sound kit for that particular show.

I will use the same procedure in creating my palette for anything and every-thing that repeats itself. Gunshot combos, fist punch combos, falls—mechanicals, a myriad of audio events that I used to lay out dozens of tracks for the sound effect re-recording mixer to meticulously rehearse and mix together in the traditional process—was being done now in sound effect palettes or what some editors call "show kits," especially if they are working on television shows that repeat the basic stuff week after week. Don't reinvent the wheel, build your kit and make it easier to blaze through the material.

It might take me a week or two to design and build my sound palette, but once built, I could cut through heavy action reels very quickly, with a narrow use of tracks. Instead of needing as many as 200 or 300 tracks for a heavy space opera sequence, I could deliver two at the most three 24-track sessions, carefully dividing up the audio concepts in the proper groups. This made the final mixing much smoother. This style of planning also allows you to cut the entire show, not just a few reels of it, as we used to do on major projects with large sound editorial teams.

I have even gotten to the point that I back up every show in its show kit form. I have a whole series of disks of just the *Starship Troopers* effects palette, which is also why I can retrieve a Pro Tools session icon from a storage disk, load up the *Starship Troopers* disks, and resurrect any session I made. This sort of thing can come in extremely handy down the road when a studio wants to do some kind of variation edit, director's cut, or what have you. More than once I have been called by a desperate producer who has prayed that I archived my work on his film, as the studio cannot find the elements.

Strange as it might sound, but I have had more fun and freedom in sound design working on smaller budget pictures than huge budget films that are often burdened with political pressure issues and crunched schedule demands.

KEEP IT TIGHT—KEEP IT LEAN

The reality of your team is that you will find yourself doing most if not all your own assistant work. Jobs that were originally assigned to the first assistant sound editor are now done by the dialog editor or the sound effects editor or the Foley editor (if you can afford to have a Foley editor).

I very quickly found that hiring an expert consultant on a daily basis was a valu-able procedure. Ultra low-budget jobs are almost always structured on a fixed flat fee, not including "If" factors. This means that you cannot afford to make a financial mistake by doing work on a bad EDL or wasting time going back to have the OMF re-outputted because picture editorial did not do it right the first time.

In the last few years I have been working rather successfully with the 3- to 4-man crew system. A client will talk to us about a project, and if we like it and feel we can do it within the tight parameters, we will sit down and discuss exactly what kind of time frame the client will allow, as more time makes it more realistic to be

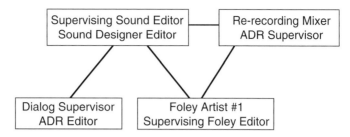

Figure 14.11 Typical ultra low-budget crew.

accomplished. If the client insists on too tight a schedule, the client either needs to come up with more money, because they have chosen the other set of the triangle (want it *good* and want it *fast*, therefore it cannot be *cheap*).

If they have to have it cheap, then they have to give you more time, because we already know they want to have it good. Besides, I am interested in turning out only good work, so that option is always on the table.

Several projects that I have done lately have been structured as depicted in Figure 14.11. It is vital to have a veteran dialog editor, a master on how to structure and smooth the tracks. Though I have cut my share of dialog, I am known for my sound effect design, especially action and concept, so I take on the sound design and sound editing chores for the backgrounds and hard FX. We use a lead Foley artist who also embraces the job of cueing the show as well as performing the action. The budget is a direct reflection of how many days of Foley walking the project can afford. I go over the show notes and make it very clear to the Foley artist exactly what cues we absolutely have to have performed and what cues I can either pull from my library or custom record on our own. This keeps the Foley stage time to the leanest minimum with as little waste as possible.

You notice that I have the re-recording mixer to my side, an equal in the collaboration of developing and carrying out the ultimate re-recording process. On several projects, the re-recording mixer doubled as the ADR supervisor, scheduling the actors to come in and be recorded. The ADR cues, however, are sent back with the stage notes for the dialog editor to include in a separate set of tracks, but part of the dialog session. This will yield a dialog session with probably 3 to 4 primary dialog tracks, with 4 to 5 ADR tracks (depending on density) and then the P-FX and X-Track. This means the dialog session that will be turned over to the re-recording mixer should be 10 to no more than 14 tracks.

The key to really being able to give big bang for the buck is if you have a powerful customized library. This is where most starting editors have a hard time. Off-the-shelf libraries are, for the most part, extremely inferior to those of us who have customized our sound libraries over the last 30 years. I always get a tickle when my graduate editors, who have frankly gotten spoiled with using my sound effects during their third and fourth year films, go out into the world and sooner or later get back to me and tell me how awful the sound libraries are that are out there. Well, it's part of why I push them, as well as you, the reader, to custom record your own sound as much as possible.

Even if you manage to get your hands on a sizeable library from somewhere, there is the physicality of knowing it. Having a library does not mean anything if you have not auditioned every cue, know every possibility, every strength, every weakness. It takes years to get to know a library, whether you build it yourself or work with a library at another sound house.

You need to spend untold hours and hours, going through material, really listening. You see, most people do not know how to *really* listen. You have to train your ear, you have to be able to discern the slightest differences, detect the edgy fuzziness of oncoming distortion.

I will cut one A session; this will be "Hard FX." Unlike traditional editing when I break events out into A-FX and B-FX and C-FX and so forth, I will group the controlled event groups together, but they are still in the same session. After all, we do not have all the time in the world to re-record this soundtrack. Remember, we are making the *perception* of the Big Sound, not the physical reality of it.

I will cut a second B session. This will be my stereo background pass. Remember my philosophy about backgrounds: dialog will come and go, music cues will come and go, Hard FX will come and go, but *backgrounds* are heard all the time, even if extremely subtle. The stereophonic envelope of the ambience is crucial, and I give it the utmost attention.

On an ultra low-budget project like this, I expect 8 Foley tracks will be about as much as we can expect, unless we have to suddenly go to extra tracks for mass activity on the screen. Even then, I do not want to spread too wide.

The best rule of thumb is to prepare the tracks in a way that you yourself could re-record them the easiest.

RETHINKING THE CREATIVE CONTINUITY

Speaking of intelligently approaching soundtrack design, here is another important consideration—what if you are not preparing it for the re-recording mixer(s) to get their arms around? What if, on small budget or bigger budget projects, the supervising sound editor/sound designer is *also* serving as the re-recording mixer?

Actually, it makes sense in a big way, if you stop to think about it. Since the advent of the soundtrack for film in 1927, the approach has been a team of sound craftspeople, each doing his or her part of the process. When it reached the re-recording mixing stage, the re-recording mixer had no intimate knowledge of either the preparation or the tactical layout and the whys of how certain tracks were going to work with other tracks or what the editors had prepared that was yet to come to the stage in the form of backgrounds that would serve both as creative ambient statements and/or audio bandages that were there to serve camouflaging poor production recording issues. That process occurred because working on optical sound technology made it impossible for one sound craftsperson to record production dialog (on optical sound cameras)—and then follow the process through the various disciplines of sound editing, and then ultimately be the re-recording mixer. Even in 1953, when we moved to magnetic stripe/fullcoat film technology, the process still required a platoon of expert audio crafts-

Figure 14.12 Mark Mangini, sound designer/supervising sound editor/ re-recording mixer.

people to properly record, transfer dailies and reprints, design, and edit sound in strategic groupings before it could be brought to the re-recording stage for the head re-recording mixer to bring it all together.

However, with today's digital software tools and ever-expanding capacities of storage drive space and faster CPUs, a single sound craftsperson can do the same work that it took 10 or 12 craftspeople to do a decade ago.

Who better would know the material? Not the re-recording mixer who was not involved in the sound designing process, the editing of that material, or structuring the predub strategies. So, you see it really makes sense that we are starting to see and are going to see a major move to very tight teams, and in some cases single sound designer/re-recording mixer artists.

One such advocate of this move is Mark Mangini, truly a supervising sound editor/sound designer and re-recording mixer. As a supervising sound editor/sound designer he has helmed such feature projects as *Aladdin, Beauty and the Beast, Star Trek IV: The Voyage Home, Gremlins, Lethal Weapon 4, The Fifth Element, The Green Mile, The Time Machine*, and *16 Blocks*.

Recently he was troubled by the decision of a producer who shunned the idea of the sound supervisor/sound designer also being the re-recording mixer, as it is the exception and certainly not the norm. Here, then, are the words of Mark Mangini when he decided he needed to write the producer and put his thoughts down for the record, thoughts that make a lot of sense—the logic of an inevitable evolution.

On the Importance of Designing *and* Mixing a Film

A letter from sound designer Mark Mangini to the director of a big-budget studio film:

> It is my desire to design, edit, *and* mix your film. Though the Producer and the editor are very well intentioned in wanting to use the Studio's mix facilities with existing mixers there, they do have some very fine people. I believe that I can bring so much more to the film as the Sound Designer *and* Mixer, as I have done on your previous projects.

I must state at the outset that, for a studio film, this style of working is non-traditional and, as such, will encounter some amount of resistance from your fellow filmmakers accustomed to working in traditional ways (designers only design, editors only edit, and mixers only mix).

This way of working is non-traditional because of the natural and historical compartmentalization of job responsibilities in every aspect of filmmaking, not just sound. As such, very few individuals have taken the time or had the incentive, like myself, to develop natural outgrowths of their skill-set and be proficient in multiple disciplines.

I am certainly not the first to work this way. Walter Murch, Gary Rydstrom, Ben Burtt, to name a few, come to mind and have all been championing the benefits of the *sound designer* in its broadest interpretation and what that person can bring creatively to a soundtrack. These men have truly been the authors of their respective soundtracks and they are successful at it by virtue of being responsible for and creatively active in all aspects of sound for their films. This does not simply include being the sound editor *and* the re-recording mixer but encompasses every aspect of sound production including Production sound, ADR, Foley, Score recording, sound design and editing, *and* mixing.

As you have seen in our past work relationship, I have performed in exactly this fashion and I hope that you have recognized the benefits of having *one* individual whom you can turn to creatively and technically to insure the highest quality soundtrack possible in all the disciplines. This is the way I work and want to continue to work with you.

Though it may appear that this workflow was necessitated by budget (or lack thereof) on our previous films, it was and is, in fact, a premeditated approach that I believe is the most creative and efficient way of working. Just imagine how far we can take this concept with the resources that the Studio is offering.

Unfortunately, Hollywood has not "cottoned" to this approach in the way that Bay Area filmmakers have. We still want to pigeonhole sound people by an antiquated set of job descriptions that fly in the face of modern technology and advancement. It is certainly not rare or unheard of in the production community to see hyphenate "creatives" that *write* and *direct*, that *act* and *produce*, etc.—it is no different in sound. I am simply one of a small group of sound fanatics that wants to work in multiple disciplines and have spent a good deal of time developing the technical acumen in each one.

As such, regarding making "all the super-cool decisions that will give me the most creative and technically etc. . . .

I have no doubts that this is the way to do it. There are decided creative, technical and financial advantages to working this way. This work method is not, in fact, all that unusual for the Studio or the mix room we anticipate using. There have been numerous films that have mixed there that are working in this exact same fashion. New yes, but not unheard of.

As we spoke of on the phone, I will be working side by side with you, building the track together in a design/mix room adjacent to picture editorial. In the work flow that I am proposing this is a very natural and efficient process of refinement all the way through to the final mix that is predicated on my ability to mix the track we have been building together and on doing it in at the Studio's dub stage, which uses state of the art technology NOT found in any of the other mix rooms on the lot (and with traditional mixers that are not versed in how to use it).

The value of having the Sound Design team behind the console cannot be overestimated. It seems to me almost self-evident that having the individuals who designed and edited the material at the console will bring the most informed approach by virtue of an intimate knowledge of every perforation of sound present at the console and the reasons *why* those sounds are there. This is a natural outgrowth of the collaboration process that we will share in during our exploratory phase of work as we build the track together prior to the mix.

There will be the obvious and natural objections from less forward thinking individuals who will state that having the sound editors mix their own material is asking for trouble. "They'll mix the sound effects too loud" or "They won't play the score" are many of the uninformed refrains that you might hear as objections to working in this fashion.

I would like to think that, based on our previous work together, you might immediately dispel these concerns having seen, first-hand, how I work but there is also an issue of professionalism involved that is never considered: This is what I do for a living. I cannot afford to alienate any filmmaker with ham-fisted or self-interest driven mixing.

I consider you a good friend and colleague. As such, I think you know that I am saying this from a desire to make your film sound as great as I possibly can. It's the ones that think outside the box that do re-invent the wheel.

Sincerely,

– Mark Mangini, sound designer/supervising sound editor/re-recording mixer
(*Note:* This is a letter I wrote to a director, regarding a big-budget studio film I was keen on doing. I have modified the original text to make the ideas and comments not project specific and more universal. MM)

DON'T FORGET THE M&E

Just because you are tackling an ultra low-budget project does not mean that you do not have to worry about the inventory that has to be turned over just as in any film, multi-million dollar or fifty thousand dollars. The truth of the matter is, passing QC (quality control) and an approved M&E (music and effects) is, in many ways, more difficult to accomplish on ultra low-budget films than on big budget films, for the simple fact that you do not have extra money and manpower to throw at the problem. It therefore behooves you to have a veteran dialog editor who is a master of preparing P-FX tracks as he or she goes along. (We will talk about this more in Chapter 15.)

You are really going to have to watch how much coverage you have in Foley today. For some reason, the studios and distributors have gone crazy, demanding over-Foley performing of material. I mean stupid cues like footsteps across the street that you would never hear; the track can be written up for missing footsteps. I have heard some pretty interesting horror stories, and frankly, I do not know why. I assume it is an ignorance factor somewhere up the line. When in doubt—cover it.

AN EXAMPLE OF ULTRA LOW-BUDGET PROBLEM SOLVING

Just because you do not have a budget does not mean that you cannot problem solve how to achieve superior results. I recently received an e-mail from a young man, Tom Knight, who was just finishing an ultra low-budget film that was shot in and around London. I was impressed that the lack of a budget did not inhibit the team's dedication to achieve the best audio track that they could record during a challenging production environment as well as the postproduction process. Tom submitted the following details on the project and their approach to problem solve some of the audio hurdles:

Figure 14.13 This set-up was for recording an impulse response for a convolution reverb (London). Equipment: Mac iBook running Pro Tools LE, M-Box, Technics Amp, Alesis Monitor One MKII, AKG 414. (Photo by Tom Knight.)

The film's title is *Car-Jack*, an original production, written, produced, and directed by George Swift. I was responsible for all the audio production within the film including original music, location recording, postproduction and mixing.

George approached me about the film because I had worked for him on a short animation the previous year. We were both studying for BAs at the time in our respective subjects and stayed on to study for master's degrees.

The 40-minute film about a gang of car-jackers was produced for virtually no budget (less than £1,000), even though there was a cast and crew of over 50 people. Everyone worked on the project for free because they believed in the film, which ensured a great spirit on set. We were fortunate enough to have access to the equipment we needed without hire charges from the university (Thames Valley University in Ealing, London).

The film was predominantly shot on a Sony Z1 Hi-Def camera and cut digitally using Adobe Premiere. The production audio was recorded onto DAT and cut at my home studio with Pro Tools before being mixed in the pro studios at Uni.

When we filmed indoor locations, I made sure that I went equipped with a laptop (including M-Box), amp, and speaker so that I could record impulse responses. This process involves playing a sine sweep that covers every frequency from 20 Hz to 20 kHz through a speaker, and recording the outputted signal back onto disk through a microphone.

The original sweep can then be removed from the recorded signal, which leaves the sound of the room or space that the recording was made in. Convolution reverbs like Logic's Space Designer can take an impulse recording and then make a fairly accurate representation of the acoustical space back in the studio. This is ideal if you intend to mix lines of production dialogue with lines of ADR, because you need the sounds to have similar acoustic properties, so that they blend together and create the impression that they were recorded at the same time.

Figure 14.15 shows us setting up the shot before we go for a take. If you look closely under the actress's left hand you can see some tape on the wall. This is where the DPA mike is positioned. The reason it is positioned there is because Heathrow Airport is only 2 miles

Figure 14.14 Set-up for recording the impulse response for a convolution reverb, same process as above but from the reverse. This part of the room was where the main gang boss character conducted his meetings so it made sense to take the impulse from here. (Photo by Tom Knight.)

Figure 14.15 Rooftop scene from the film (London). Equipment: Sony Z1 Camera shooting in hi-def, Audio-Technica AT897 Shotgun + DPA Condenser mikes running through a Mackie 1202-VLZ Mixer onto DAT. Cast and crew (left to right): Annabelle Munro (lead actress), Tony Streeter (lead actor), David Scott (cinematographer), George Swift (director), Tom Knight (boom operator/sound mixer). (Photo by Julia Kristofik, make-up artist.)

away and that particular day the planes were taking off straight towards us, and then alternately banking either left or right as you see this picture. Placing it there (rather than on the jacket of the actor) meant that the wall shielded it to some extent from planes that banked left which were heavily picked up by the shotgun.

If the planes banked right then the DPA was wiped out but the shotgun survived due to its directivity. The planes literally take off every 30 seconds from Heathrow so there was no chance of any clean production audio. It was just a case of gathering the best production audio possible to facilitate ADR later on.

To me, this is a classic example of how understanding the disciplines of the *art form*, and, as we discussed in Chapter 4, "Success or Failure: Before the Camera Even Rolls," this clearly demonstrates the issue of planning for success, rather than what we see all too often of fixing in post what was not properly thought out and prepared for *before the cameras even rolled*. Thank you, Ted, for contacting me and submitting this excellent example just in time to be included in this chapter.

THE BOTTOM LINE

The bottom line is this: No matter if you are working on a multi-million-dollar block-buster or you are cutting a wonderful little romantic comedy that was shot for a few thousand dollars on HD, the art form of what we do does not change. The strategies of how we achieve that art form within the bounds of the budget and schedule change of course, but not the art form—the *art form* is the same.

Chapter 15
Dialog Editors
Hollywood's Unsung Heroes

"Good dialog editing is like a form of magic—you carefully weave
the tracks like a sleight-of-hand to create an illusion transparency.
If you do your job right—nobody notices what you've done."

– Dwayne Avery, M.P.S.E.
Dialog editor

How many times have you sat in the theatre, enjoying the movie, and sighed with
admiration for the dialog editor's skill and handiwork? "Wow, that was great cross-
filled presence. It's so transparent, you can't even tell the difference between those two
angles."

Of course you don't. If you did notice, it was not because the dialog editor did a
good job; it would be because the dialog editor did a poor one. Dialog editing is an
invisible art form. If the work is good, the audience never notices. This is a good news/
bad news thing to dialog editors. The good news is the great satisfaction that the
transparency of their work does not reveal the fact that the dialog track is a patchwork
of hundreds of cuts and pieces of presence so expertly prepared that the bits of production audio fit together seamlessly, smoothed by the dialog editor's handiwork. The bad
news is that the dialog editor's efforts are usually so good that nobody notices. Only
editorial colleagues know the work's excellence and the contribution of dialog editing
to a motion picture.

How big of a contribution is it really? Sound effect design may be used or discarded, backgrounds may be used or discarded, music cues may be used or discarded—but the dialog track always plays, always! The dialog track is the most
important audio element in the film, and as discussed in Chapter 5, one of the more
neglected aspects of the production shoot.

QUALITY CONTROL BEFORE POSTPRODUCTION

On *Frank & Jesse*, a picture starring Bill Paxton and Rob Lowe, which I served as supervising sound editor, the production team had been working on a flatbed KEM and had never listened to the raw production track in a quality-controlled environment. To make a precise assessment of the ADR requirements, I insisted on running the picture with the contracted re-recording mixer, Bob Glass, Jr., on his stage. We barely got into the second reel when I called over to the editing room and told the producer we would wait until they came over to hear it for themselves.

Unbeknownst to them during the production shoot, the production mixer had been experiencing condensation popping on the microphone diaphragm. The cold morning air warmed up, and, as the sun rose toward noon, condensation was affecting the track with periodic popping noises. The producer and director listened in disbelief. Surely it must be something in the sound transfer. Could it have been introduced on the KEM? It couldn't have been that way on the set!

My first assistant pulled arbitrary $\frac{1}{4}$" tapes from the boxes that had arrived from the lab. We laced them up one at a time and spun down and stopped randomly to listen. The popping noises were in the original $\frac{1}{4}$" recordings. Vast sections of scenes filmed outdoors were affected. Glass and I advised the producer and director that as much as 80 percent of the picture had to be looped to fix the problem. Panic seized the studio executives. Nobody had budgeted or anticipated the tens of thousands of dollars in ADR costs to fix a problem that should have been discovered, flagged, and problem-solved during the production shoot.

As it turned out, we saved the studio vast sums of money by spending just a few thousand dollars in a cleverly prepared series of dialog tracks that were then carefully scrubbed and processed with an audio software known as Sonic Solutions.

The key was not processing raw dailies. Dwayne Avery, the dialog editor, prepared the flawed dialog tracks in edited form, then downloaded the separate cut dialog tracks into the Sonic Solutions system to be fixed. This process is known as "de-clicking." While we were at it, we had the Sonic Solutions subcontractor do selective surgical processing on several problematic dialog angles that would have been virtually impossible for our re-recording mixer, Bob Glass, Jr., to accomplish with a traditional analog mixing console.

DIALOG EDITING STRATEGY

The supervising sound editor hires a key dialog editor, often referred to as the dialog supervisor. Depending on the size of the project, the length of the schedule, and other monetary factors, the dialog supervisor may decide that one or more other dialog editors are needed to assist in the work to be done.

During the course of sound editorial, the supervising sound editor may go over the work expectations from the client, including one or more temp dubs, as well as the calendar timeframe within which the work must be accomplished. The two also discuss what degree of polish and preparation are needed for the temp dub. The lead dialog editor should always be part of the "spotting session(s)" described in Chapter 9. He or she is there during those critical discussions with the director, picture editor, and producer that evolve into a finite battle plan to accomplish any temp dub wishes and to define the final expectations for a polished dialog track.

In turn, these discussions also focus the budget demands accordingly. If the director and producer expect a more polished dialog edit for the temp dub, more dialog editors are hired to get the work done quicker to better serve the temp dub needs. Conversely, if the director and producer are using their editor's cut track (also known as the editor's work track) as the dialog portion of the temp dub, with perhaps a few fixes for clarification or correction of a particularly bad passage of production sound, then that requires a much lighter dialog team on the temp dub and allows the dialog editor to properly cut the dialog over the sound edit schedule.

DIALOG SEQUENCE SHEETS AND THE EDL

When the turnover materials discussed in Chapter 13 arrive to the first sound assistant's bench, he or she immediately starts preparing material for the dialog editor. Back when we cut on film, before any cut editor's tracks may be handled by anyone in sound editorial, they were first sent to sound transfer where 1:1 copies (exact duplicates) are made, not only for protection, but because other departments (ADR, Foley, sound effects) needed a copy—not the original—of the editor's cut track. The dialog editor must have the original.

Today, cutting dialog on Pro Tools, we get the picture editor's guide track from the QuickTime video output. When picture editorial makes the QuickTime file, they will choose that both picture and sound be included. The smart way to make a guide track output is for the assistant picture editor to assign only the production (and temp dialog inserts) track on channel 1 (left). Channel 2 (right) can be the combined dialog, temp sound effects and temp music combined, especially if the picture editor and director have things that they want the sound team to match or to reference. But it is *vital* that channel 1 (left) be the production track *only*—no temp sound effects or temp music should be in this track as it will only hinder the progress of the dialog and ADR supervisor and their editing team to their job correctly.

Back when we worked on film, the assistant sound editor would roll the picture dupe and cut production track, which had the invaluable edge code numbers printed on the edge every 16 frames (one 35-mm foot). The assistant sound editor would carefully construct a dialog sequence sheet.

Dialog Sequence Sheet

The sound assistant laced up the picture dupe and the editor's cut track into a synchronizer, placing the start marks on the 0 and zeroing out the footage counter. The assistant lowered the sound head of the synchronizer onto the mag track and plugged the headsets into the workbench mixer. As the assistant rolled through the track, he or she would carefully watch for splices in the soundtrack. When one arose, the assistant paid close attention to the edge code numbers (described in Chapter 6).

In my shop, our technique was not to list every splice cut, as some did. We were more interested about listing the cuts when the edge code number changed. This title: **"SALVADOR"** Editor: Steve Rice Reel: 4 page: 1-of-14

footage	Edge Code #	Scene/Angle & Take #	Sound Roll	Notes:	# of Reprints
9		"POP"			
12	023-1033	36 - 3	21	master	x 1
27	024-1216	36 "C"- 2	22	close of Woods	x 1
42	023-1896	36 "B"- 2	21	close of Savage	x 2
56	024-1475	36 "C"- 4	22	close of Woods	x 1
59	023-1660	36 "A"- 2	21	medium two shot	x 2
78	023-1033	36 - 2	21	master	x 1

Figure 15.1 The dialog sequence sheet.

represented a change in the sound roll. If splices occurred within a sequence where the edge code numbers did not change in sequential order, or changed very little, we knew that the picture editor had simply tried a cut, did not like it, and put it back together, or had made an internal cut, which we knew our own dialog editor would be able to sequentially match. We did not want to clog the dialog sequence sheet with hundreds of repetitious notations that we knew full well the dialog editor did not need. The dialog editor needed to know what rolls of reprints were necessary to commence cutting chores.

The assistant entered the first even-foot number that landed within the dialog cue to be listed. He or she then listed the first edge code number that appears on the edge of the film. He or she kept rolling through the roll, entering new edge code numbers as the scene/take/angle changed. After the assistant finished with that task, each edge code number listed in the codebook was looked up. The assistant listed the scene, angle, and take next to the edge code number entry.

In the sound roll column, the original source tape number was entered. The assistant made a photocopy of the sheets completed, three-hole punched them, and placed them in the supervisor's "bible." Once this was done, the assistant turned over a picture dupe, the editor's cut track, and the dialog sequence sheets to the dialog editor.

The dialog editor then laced up the picture dupe and editor's cut track in the Moviola and ran the reel, pausing every so often to enter any notations in the "note" column. After the dialog editor had run through the entire reel, he or she decided how many dialog reprints were going to be required from the original ¼" or DAT source. The dialog editor photocopied the completed dialog sequence sheets and gave a copy to the first assistant, who put together a transfer order so that sound transfer could complete the reprint work as quickly as possible.

	Footage	Duration	First/Last Key	Lab Roll	Cam Roll	Sc/Tk	Clip Name
			Project: *FOOLS GOLD*				
			Bin: *REEL 2AB*				
			Sequence: *REEL 2AB*				

Project: *FOOLS GOLD*   Pull List for REEL 2AB (Picture 2) – page 2 of 18
Bin: *REEL 2AB*   Tue. July 14, 1998 5:25 PM
Sequence: *REEL 2AB*

REEL 2AB: 284 entries   handles = 0
Pull List   1 dupe
     30 opticals

	Footage	Duration	First/Last Key	Lab Roll	Cam Roll	Sc/Tk	Clip Name
21.	156+15 163+04	6+06	KC 11 8267–5060+08 5066+13	062	123	14/2	14/2.omf
22.	163+05 172+11	9+06	KC 27 8267–5060+08 5069+14	063	124	17C/1	17C/1.omf
23.	172+12 174+01	1+05	KC 45 5140–3218+12 3220+01	054	103	21H/3	21H/3.omf
24.	174+02 189+07	15+05	KC 45 5140–3377+06 3393+11	054	103	21H/4	21H/4.omf
	189+07		3393+11				J/6.omf
25.	189+08 212+02	22+10	KC 45 5140–3752+01 3772+11	054	103	21J/6	21J/6.omf
26.	212+03 219+14	7+11	KC 45 5140–4137+14 4145+09	054	103	21K/2	21K/2.omf
27.	219+15 226+05	6+06	KI 01 8078–1790+02 1796+08	056	105	21M/1	21M/1.omf

Figure 15.2 The EDL (edit decision list).

The EDL

Today, working in the digital nonlinear realm, the first sound assistant receives an EDL (edit decision list) from picture editorial when they generate the OMF (Open Media Framework). The EDL is cleaned up and made easier to read, as it is always a computer document that can lend itself to quick restructuring. It takes a little extra time to do this, as the picture department originally sent over is a tidal wave mass of numerical data. (Not the picture assistant's fault, that is just how computers work.) For some reason, some picture departments become confused about what data should be requested when they generate an EDL, so they are often not properly generated in the first place. That is why I would call in Wade Coonfer, an expert in postproduction procedures and nonlinear protocols, and have him output their EDLs and OMFs for us correctly in the first place.

Most of the time, sound editorial receives an EDL perfect for negative assembly, but that does not do sound editorial much good unless you request the scene/take as well as the sound roll entry. The lab roll is the sound roll. Most of the time the picture EDL is sent to us; this is significantly different from the sound EDL. All picture editors will overlap soundtracks, steal alternate readings, put in a bit of off-screen dialog that was not there before. A picture EDL will not reflect these cuts, but picture assistants forget to think about that when they choose the EDL menu options. Picture editorial must call sound editorial prior to making the EDLs to double-check the necessary items.

The EDL handles much the same chores as the dialog sequence sheet. It shows at what footage (or in time code if you prefer) each cut takes place. It shows the duration of the clip until the next cut, it shows the first and last of the key edge numbers. Remember, we do not have edge code numbers in the digital realm; only if we sync our dailies on film and edge code them prior to telecine and digitization do we have edge code numbers. The picture digital workstation does not have those edge code numbers, but it does have the negative key edge numbers. Sometimes these numbers are helpful to the dialog editor trying to find something in the codebook.

The EDL also lists scene/take and clip name. The computer is extremely literal. If you make a cut, it acknowledges it. We often get 50 to 60 pages of an EDL for a single reel, with the computer listing every single cut, even if it is the same scene and take, over and over. The smart supervising sound editor makes a copy of the EDL and cleans it up, so as to make the mass of data much easier to read by the dialog editor. Choose a clear typeface and large point size. Sound editors usually work in dimly lit rooms. Small font sizes squashed together are extremely hard to read, causing eye fatigue and burning out the dialog editor in a short time.

The supervisor sees that Scene 21"J"-3 is listed five times in a row, which is unnecessary. If an internal cut has been made, the dialog editor can figure that out in two seconds. The supervisor erases four of the repetitive listings, thus saving the dialog editor from scanning unnecessary lines. The next line reflects the next true change in a scene, angle, and take that the dialog editor must know.

Once the supervisor has finished cleaning up the reel, a copy is made and collapsed even further. All but the scene, angle, takes, and sound roll notations (or lab roll) may be eliminated. Finally, all redundancies are eliminated. Only one of any scene, angle, and take remains. The supervisor then rearranges the data according to sound roll numbers. Upon completion, this is printed out and forwarded to the first assistant to make up a transfer order so that sound transfer can complete the dialog reprint work as quickly as possible. You may find that what would have been 60 pages of massive number printouts that were hard to read is now reduced to some 12 to 20 pages that are much easier read and move the editorial work move along more efficiently.

AUTO ASSEMBLY: OMF OR PHASE MATCHING SYNC

Most EDLs denote the clip name showing ".omf" after the scene/take designation. It is important to transfer the dialog from the original source to use OMF software to extrapolate a Pro Tools session of exact cuts from the editor's work track. Unfortunately, many projects have to be completely reprinted from the original production tapes because the original digitization by the picture assistant was very poorly done. A tremendous loss in clarity had occurred, and noise had been introduced to the dialog recordings because of poor line connections prior to the workstation's digital interface or the use of cheap digital-to-analog encode equipment.

Open Media Framework

When it works, it is wonderful. It saves the extra step and cost of retransferring the source dialog material into the digital domain for dialog editing. It saves precious time in preparing for temp dubs as well as for finals. The key is in how well the picture department did its job when first entering the dailies into the digital picture worksta-tion, such as Final Cut Pro or Avid.

Here is demonstrated the classic example of the adage, "Garbage in, garbage out." If it is not put in clean, with attention to exact signal path disciplines, the result is a tainted and dirty dialog track from the OMF file that is not as good as that from the original source. If you do not pay attention to the exact disciplines of syncing dailies, the OMF audio file will never line up in precise sync. Your only hope for gaining true sync rests on how good the eyes and ears are and how many years of battle-line experi-ence the dialog editor has.

I was finishing a temp dub on a film when the picture editor started ranting and raving about our out-of-sync cutting. I quietly slipped behind the stage Pro Tools unit, booted up the dialog session, and zoomed in extremely close on the very passage in question. The reprint was laid precisely in sync to his work track, and when he realized that, he stepped back and asked, "I don't get it. How is that possible?"

Everybody on stage knew how it was possible. His department was anything but the poster child for procedure and discipline. I allowed him to save face by telling him that this was just a temp dub and that we had not had the time to prepare the material fully, but that it would be in sync by the final mix, which we did. My dialog editors spent agonizing wasted days visually re-syncing material that should have been able to match-sync to a picture editor's 1:1 guide track.

To Trust or Not to Trust OMF Media Files

The first question a supervising sound editor must answer is whether the audio integ-rity of OMF media files are good enough to use for final sound editorial. My first assistant makes a Pro Tools edit session by using the OMF software to extrapolate a reel of dialog. The transfer engineer then pulls several tapes advertised on the EDL and makes half a dozen cues from various part of the reel, choosing one for intimate dialog, another for exterior ambience, and so forth. I drag the new dialog transfers into the Pro Tools edit session, phase-matching them against the OMF audio file that already exists in the session. I then pull the drive and take it onto the dubbing stage, where we can listen to and assess the quality of the material through the stage speaker system where the film is dubbed.

We boot up the session on the stage Pro Tools unit and make an A-B comparison, first listening to the OMF file, then flipping back to the new transfer from the original tape source. If we do not hear a difference in the two, we feel confident enough to use the OMF media files for dialog editing and final re-recording. If we do hear a differ-ence, we know that picture editorial did not enter the original audio into the worksta-tion properly.

We have resorted to reprinting more often than being able to use the OMF files as supplied by picture editorial. If you must transfer it over again, you will spend several thousand dollars unnecessarily because picture editorial did not do its job correctly the first time. This is part of what I keep talking about when I refer to collateral costs.

Hence, the experienced producer or postproduction supervisor always must ask who is handling transfer chores. The client makes a deal with a sound facility for handling the dailies and having a guaranteed individual handling the work because they know and understand that that particular transfer engineer doesn't just roll the stock and push the record button. They know that that particular individual handles the job like an artist, knowing how important it is to maintain the magic of the production track.

It is extremely rare to get this kind of service at the major laboratories or factory-style sound facilities. It is a specialty service found virtually at the independent boutique sound houses that specialize in theatrical craftspersonship. Entire feature projects are pulled away from facilities when the client discovers that the specific individual promised or contracted to do the work is not actually doing it.

A very important sound house was trying to cut costs on a project because they had other financial issues in the facility. They were handling the dailies on a rather important picture; they had gotten the contract to do the job with the understanding that a particular transfer man was going to handle the work. The picture editor knew, from a previous picture, that this transfer man handled the daily chores of transfer to 35-mm stripe with a simultaneous mastering to a Pro Tools session so that the digital dialog audio files were already mastered. The picture editor knew this person's work, he knew the kind of sound transfer notes this person made, including a separate list of interesting WT (wild track) and important audio notes to pay attention to. This kind of work is not done by 99 percent of transfer personnel.

The sound house needed to save money, so they replaced this transfer man with a less costly person. Within 24 hours the picture editor called up screaming, followed by the producer who called up screaming. Because the sound house was caught trying to shortchange the project, the daily transfer job was pulled from the facility. The collateral damage was that the word spread around to other producers. This sound house suddenly lost transfer work right and left and they were suddenly dropped from being considered to handle the postproduction editorial chores.

Sounds like an isolated case? You would be shocked to know how much this goes on all the time. Just know that this kind of game playing goes on, and remember this one important fact—*studios do not make motion pictures,* people *make motion pictures.*

REPRINTING DIALOG CUES FROM ORIGINAL SOURCE ON FILM

The transfer engineer opens the $^1\!/_4''$ tape box and pulls out the sound report (if the original sound is on digital DAT, it is usually folded and wrapped around the DAT cassette like a hot dog bun). (Flip back to Chapter 5 to refresh your memory on the sound report and to study the information at the top of the form. The information listed is key to how the transfer engineer is able to make a perfect duplicate of the original source.)

Quarter-inch ($^1\!/_4''$) tape usually syncs to a Pilotone or to 60 cycles, which resolves via a crystal controller, known as "crystal sync." The 35-mm film recorder has a precision stepping motor that has been engineered to resolve to 60 cycles at precisely 24 frames per second or 25 fps, depending on whether the transfer engineer chooses the American 24 fps or the European 25 fps, by the simple press of a button.

The transfer engineer threads up the $^1\!/_4''$ tape (stored tails out) or the DAT cassette, which should always be stored rewound back to heads when not in use. The engineer spins the $\frac{1}{4}''$ tape at high speed. The tape should not be dragged over the sound head, but should glide just off the head. Even though it is not touching the playback head, the engineer can count the takes as they spin by. Clicks are heard, which at normal speed are the tail tones the production mixer enters. This makes it much easier for the transfer engineer to locate a precise cue quickly. Once the engineer finds it, he or she stops the tape machine, and then plays the verbal slate the production mixer recorded prior to rolling action to verify that the correct take is identified. The engineer rewinds the tape to just before the slate and stops.

The transfer engineer writes a scene/angle/take designation on a label placed prior to the actual material to be transferred. The engineer rolls the 35-mm film recorder; when it obtains speed, the engineer pushes the Record button. The engineer rolls the $\frac{1}{4}''$ or DAT machine. The production mixer is heard slating the desired take. Slate sticks are heard, and the scene plays out. These transfers are broken down by the first assistant or apprentice and forwarded to the dialog editor.

Nonlinear Reprinting

There are two ways to transfer production dialog into the computer for editing purposes. The first technique is very basic and grass roots in nature. When the scene is originally shot, a smart slate with a time code generator is *not* used. It basically runs on a tape recorder using crystal sync. The scene is slated, making a sync mark, either by using a clapper slate or by an actor verbally slating the take and clapping hands in plain view of the camera. Experienced dialog editors know how to drag this kind of transfer into an edit session and phase match the sync against the editor's work track.

Some picture budgets are so low that they cannot afford to rent the more expensive sound equipment to have the basic necessity of time code transfers or crystal sync resolution. We actually transferred the $\frac{1}{4}''$ tapes and/or the DAT cassettes into the computer without the benefit of a sync resolver. The transfers inevitably would drift slowly out of sync, but my dialog editors were from the old school of editing disciplines, and as long as they knew what they had, they could sync anything. Fortunately for us, our equipment would drift longer rather than shorter, thereby making it easier for the dialog editor to simply pull the material up, back into sync, rather than having to lengthen it, which makes the entire process much more difficult.

The second technique is taking advantage of the time code signal and using PostConform to accurately extrapolate a Pro Tools session with all the cuts in place, ready for the dialog editor to separate and massage. The transfer engineer carefully transfers the material into the computer using Lynx to precisely guarantee sync resolution. Once the transfer is recorded into the Pro Tools session, the engineer double-clicks on the audio file waveform, which allows renaming the file with the exact scene/angle/take designation. The engineer then pulls down the menu option to time stamp the transfer, placing a precise time code address in the audio file's directory. This procedure is critical to linking and extrapolating a Pro Tools edit session with all the cuts and edit decisions the picture editor had made in exact sync.

PostConform gives you the benefit of using the power of the computer to extrapolate an editing session where the exact cuts have already been brought into sync to the editor's work track, saving the time of phase matching, traditionally part of the dialog editor's job. This allows the dialog editor to spend more time massaging the material to make it cleaner, work out the presence fill problems, split out the production effects, and so forth.

The advantage of PostConform over using OMF is that transfers are made from the original audio source, whereas OMF gives the dialog editor the audio file that the picture assistant or apprentice entered into the picture workstation. You are stuck with whatever the quality and technical discipline he or she had when executing input digitization. You are at the mercy of the technique and experience of the picture department, or lack of it.

First Assistant Becomes a Transfer Engineer

In today's ever-evolving industry, the tasks of sound transfer into the digital domain have changed dramatically. Sound transfer used to be the sacred task of sound transfer departments, and, for many kinds of transfer requirements, it still is. However, most audio transfer is now being handled by sound editors themselves as well as assistant sound editors and even apprentices. This book does not dwell on the union jurisdiction and philosophical arguments, but must acknowledge the evolution of those handling these transfer tasks, recognizing that each is very important. Whether these tasks are handled in the traditional way through the sound transfer department or whether more of these tasks are being handled by non-sound personnel, the audio disciplines detailed in this book still must be addressed.

Today, assistant sound editors take the responsibility of transferring back ADR from recording sessions as part of the editorial preparation. They usually receive the cues already in audio file form and name designated as they were burned onto a CD-R or DVD-R by the ADR stage where the recording session was conducted. This is a simple computer transfer. If, however, the session was conducted at a facility that has not been equipped with nonlinear recording gear, they will most likely turn over some kind of digital tape medium such as DATs or if you are unlucky, DA-88s. Assistants must learn the signal path disciplines as well as time stamping techniques when transferring such material into Pro Tools and preparing the proper audio files for the editors, always making sure to make a back-up copy of everything before turning it over to the editors for work.

LAYING OUT THE DIALOG TRACK STRATEGY

Dialog editors must be predictable. They must always prepare their sessions in the same methodical manner, always laying out the tracks the same way. This makes it much easier on the dialog mixer when predubbing commences. Mixers do not like to reinvent how they mix material from one reel to the next. They want each reel to match in style and technique; this not only allows them to get into and maintain a rhythm and a flow, but adds continuity to the track. Whether dialog editors cut on a Moviola and build sync on a sync block (synchronizer) or whether they cut nonlinear in a Pro Tools session, the technique and art form are absolutely identical.

The first track is the editor's work track, or guide track. After I import my QuickTime picture into my Pro Tools session, I will go back up to the Movie menu and select IMPORT AUDIO FROM CURRENT MOVIE. A menu will pop up, showing me whether or not there is an audio track embedded in the QuickTime video file; I choose it, and a menu will come up asking me if I want it in the AUDIO FOLDER of my present Pro Tools session, which I do.

Pro Tools will extrapolate a sound file transfer from the QuickTime movie and it will show up in the region list of my Pro Tools session (see Chapter 18). I then drag only channel 1 (left channel) across into the first audio track at the top, all the way over until it will go no further. This is the guide track to which either my OMF session will line up, or I use to phase match reprints or use as a waveform guide in cutting ADR lines.

If you have to use a videotape transfer and work with Pro Tools by locking to audio time code from the right channel of the tape, then you must transfer the left channel from the videotape, locked to time code to guarantee sync with the video picture. Most videotape machine audio outputs are 10 dB lower than 0 level. Hence, most dialog editors have a difficult time matching waveforms; the editor's work track transferred in from the videotape is 10 dB lower than the levels of their dialog reprints. If I have to use a videotape transfer, I will highlight the entire GUIDE TRACK, then go up to the AudioSuite menu and draw down to GAIN CHANGE and increase the volume by +10 dB.

Another way to raise the level is to have a "4-10" box, which converts –10 dB signal upward as needed. This allows the entering of material into the Pro Tools recording already elevated where desired. Panasonic DAT machines, such as the 3500 and 3700, formerly had a 4-10 switch on the back panel of their rack-mounted machines, but more recent models have done away with them.

Once the dialog editor has the editor's work track in, he or she checks that the head pop is precisely on the 9+00 foot and frame (exactly 6 seconds, zero frames in time code.) If the dialog editor is making a dialog editor from scratch, without the use of OMF or PostConform, then he or she will make several more audio tracks to the Pro Tools session. Most dialog editors who work nonlinear try to keep the number of dialog tracks to 8. The editor clicks on the audio track designation twice so that he or she can rename it. The tracks are retitled (DIA-A, DIA-B, DIA-C, DIA-D), as many DIA channels as the editor thinks are needed for the actual recut dialog. Then several other audio tracks are added and renamed X-DIA and P-FX. Some dialog editors have more than one X-DIA and often more than one P-FX track.

Pro Tools DIA Session

The X-DIA track holds any bits of sound used by the picture editor that the dialog editor is not using in the primary A, B, C tracks. These are the bits not meant to be used in the dialog predub; however, never throw away any production track a picture editor has cut—never! There will come a time, and rather often it seems, when the picture editor is pacing behind the re-recording mixers, wondering what happened to his or her track and must be able to account for it. In the X-DIA, track(s) are usually

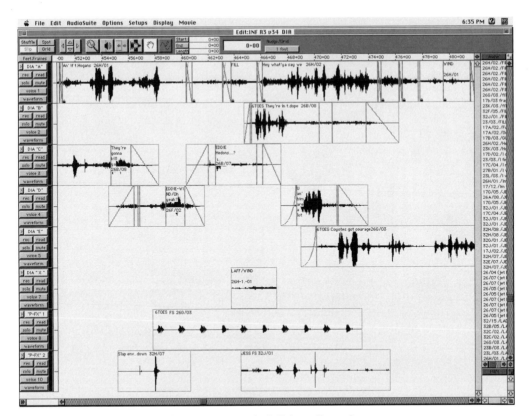

Figure 15.3 A typical dialog edit session.

lines that cannot be used for the final soundtrack and must be looped, or they can be bits of noise and junk you do not want in the predub.

The P-FX is where valuable sound effects that occurred during the production recording are split off, sounds you absolutely want to protect for the M&E version (foreign soundtrack). Often these little tidbits of sound are mastered up into a sound editorial library as magic tracks for future shows.

Different dialog editors approach the posturing of sync dialog cues on the A, B, C tracks differently. Some dialog editors working on character-driven projects that often have intimate controlled-dialog recordings find it preferable to favor a particular character to be on DIA-A and another character to be on DIA-B. This can be done on films shot in controlled-ambience environments, such as a sound stage.

Films shot in a mixed bag of locations (e.g., cars in traffic, city streets or practical interiors, office locals) prohibit assigning the character-per-track approach. Instead, the dialog editor keeps the same-recorded material in the same dialog track. Take, for instance, a scene shot on the loading dock of a shipyard. The scene is covered in a master angle, a medium shot, two over-the-shoulder opposing shots, and two close-ups.

Unavoidably, each angle has a slightly different colorization in the ambience of the background. Every time that microphone changes position, the background ambience is going to sound differently—that's pure acoustical physics. The dialog re-recording mixer reaches up on the console and twists the parametric equalizers to adjust and match each angle to another to make them sound as flawlessly the same as possible. The mixer may even send the signal out of the console to an outboard rack to the right, where the favorite signal processing equipment is kept, such as a universal dip filter. The mixer may pause and play the angle back and forth several times until satisfied with the equalization and/or compression and/or noise reduction that the track must be run through to achieve what is necessary.

The scene cuts to the opposing angle, and the dialog editor puts that cut on the next dialog track down, the DIA-B. The mixer goes through a similar procedure to balance that angle. The next picture cut, or several picture cuts into the scene, the picture editor returns to the same scene, angle and takes as the earlier cut where the dialog re-recording mixer had run through the signal-processing gear—but the editor did not remember to put it in DIA-A!

This is a mistake, and one of many reasons why dialog editors tactically must think carefully about their cuts. In these instances, the dialog sequence sheet or the EDL aids the dialog editor in thinking through the placement of the cuts. If scene 36"A"-2 was cut into DIA-A, and several cuts downrange in the sequence the picture editor used 36"A"-2 again to continue the action, then make sure all cuts of 36"A"-2 always show up in DIA-A. This makes it much easier for the dialog mixer to predub, as he or she does not need to stop and repatch the signal path to chase 36"A"-2 to a different channel.

The dialog editor's success depends on always laying out the dialog tracks in the same style and technique, keeping identical material in the same dialog tracks, splitting out throwaway material to the X-DIA, and separating all production sound effects to be kept for the M&E version (foreign) to the P-FX track(s).

Lip Smacks, Tisks, and Other Unwanted Noises

Most people who do not work with raw production sound recordings are amused when they hear them for the first time. These are very rough and unpolished, and one is amazed to hear a favorite actor smacking his lips, "tisking," or clacking dentures! What is all this lip smacking? Many distracting and odd sounds emanate from the human face.

One job of the dialog editor is to decide what "lip" business is really acting, and what is nervousness, loose dentures, or a "ham-in-the-rye," which is what most big lip smacks are.

Dialog editor craftspeople who cut on 35-mm film often have a special "diamond" punch for quickly eliminating "smacks" and "tisks." This stainless steel punch has a sharp diamond pattern that is placed, pointing end-to-end, on the mag track. The playback head does not detect a dropout, not at 90 feet a minute, and the procedure is faster than physically cutting in a frame of fill track or taking a degaussed razor blade to it.

The dialog editor must be careful, however. Some lip smacks are part of the performance and must be left intact. When we start a new show, we often discuss the philosophy of lip smacks and tisks with the director, picture editor, and producer

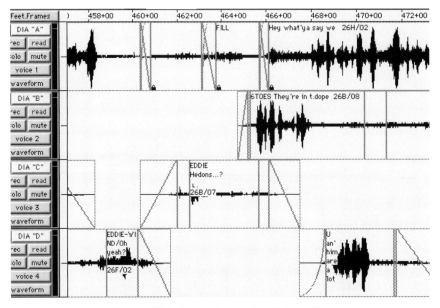

Figure 15.4 Closer view of the dialog edit.

during the spotting session. Include the client in the decision-making process whenever possible; this way the sound editorial team does not go out on a limb, making an erroneous decision.

Fixing denture "clacks" is not as easy. These either must be carefully scraped down with a razor blade or surgically filled. This is where the ability to cross-fade material in the digital domain of Pro Tools really pays off, for you cannot do this with 35-mm mag film.

P-FX Preparation

Not all production sound effects must be split out and protected for the foreign M&E. You may want the Foley to reduplicate the production sounds, so splitting them out for protection is not necessary. Sound effects may be developed that are better than what was recorded on the set. However, you may absolutely want to keep many little production-recorded jewels. Make sure these sounds do not have any dialog over them, as this defeats the whole purpose of saving them for the M&E.

Sometimes I like a particular prop that makes a specific sound, but the sync dialog take has an actor speaking while that prop makes its peculiar noise. If I am very interested in salvaging it, I listen to the alternate readings of the scene to see if the prop performs its unique sound between actors' lines, and then I steal that sound cue, just for the prop noise.

On many occasions I review the reel with my dialog editor, pointing out particular production sounds I do not want left in the dialog tracks. Sounds that would muddy up and diffuse the precision of a sound effect specifically developed for that moment must be dropped and filled. In such cases, the dialog editor extracts the production sound effect, moves it down to the X-DIA, and then fills the hole in the dialog track with matching ambience to prevent a dropout.

I remember cutting dialog on the opening reels of *The Punisher*, starring Dolph Lundgren. I was the supervising sound editor and knew exactly what kind of sound effects I was going to lay into the various sequences. In reel 3, Lou Gossett, Jr., drives to a blown-up mansion in his unmarked police car. He greets his partner, opens the car door, gets out, and closes the door as he carries on a conversation. I did not like the edgy sounding production car or its distorted doors, so I cautiously extracted them, making sure not to encroach on Gossett's lines or those of his partner. I took another reprint of the same angle and take to pull pieces of production presence, which did not have car noise or dialog, but did have the production movement of the disaster team digging out the rubble, as this movement was the underlying presence of the shot.

After I cut in the pieces of ambience fill and feathered the splice with a degaussed single-edged razor blade, no one could tell I ever touched it; of course, you heard Gossett and his partner talking, and the background activity—you just did not hear the car come in to stop or the car door open and close.

When we predubbed the reel on dubbing 3 at Warner Brothers, the head mixer, Wayne Artman, noticed the delicately cut stealth vehicle with absolutely no anomalies to the dialog being spoken. He glanced over at me and smiled, knowing we would have a really good mix, realizing he would not need to grapple with having to control unnecessary production effects, which often get in the way of a well-designed sound effect track.

It is not always that easy for dialog editors to make precise decisions on extracting production effects. Most dialog editors are not involved in the sound design process and must review the reel with the supervising sound editor for specific instructions on what to move into the X-DIA and what to move to the P-FX. A thin line exists between a supervisory judgment call and a dialog editor's responsible preparation.

Creating Great Fill

Probably one of the most demanding chores that a dialog editor has to grapple with is the need to glean out of the production recordings good "fill" presence. It is vital to have smooth fill, the presence of the dialog performance where no one is actually talking, the ambience of the scene. This is really important if you have major differences between the various angles of the microphone in the "Apple," "Baker," "Charlie" angles and the colorization of the sound or the emphasis of some audio source (such as an air conditioning vent, traffic, or fluorescent ballast) changes so dramatically from cut to cut that you have to extend and fill it to smooth out the dialog. This is exactly what Dwayne Avery was referring to as the "sleight of hand magic"—if you can develop smooth fill that does not sound loopy then you are well on your way to being able to assemble a sequence that the re-recording mixer can weave together on the dubbing stage into a seamless work of art.

Sometimes you have some really challenging situations where finding fill is just impossible. Probably the biggest lament I hear from production mixers is being able to shut the crew up long enough to get 30 seconds of good clean ambience that will be pure gold in the postproduction edit process.

Probably the biggest challenge of room tone ambient fill is a large hard surfaced environment, one in which the overtones of any noise at all becomes a wave; this and harmonic tones are the deadliest challenges that face the dialog craftsperson.

To prove my point, if you have (or can rent) the DVD of *Sister Act*—run down to 53:00 and listen. This is a scene where Whoopi Goldberg has just conducted her choir of nuns for the first time in a song, performing it in a traditional manner. Then, there is a pause, a moment when you think the performance is over, but she then conducts the nuns in a more jazzed-up hip version. Listen carefully to the ambience of the cathedral during that moment of "silence" at exactly 55:19 seconds. There is a very bad bump where either the dialog editor made a sloppy cut or something happened in the re-recording process, where the mixer may have had to slide a track to extend to cover a hole (perhaps caused by the editor cutting out unwanted production noise or someone talking, or even the director calling "Cut" on the previous angle); and when the dialog re-recording mixer slid the track and tried to punch in, it bumped because the presence was not flat, there were descending overtones by some pew movement or something in the background, and at exactly 55:19 it was repeated.

The reason this is so important is because that bump yanks the audience right out of the movie. You are enjoying the film, you are into what is going on, and then a flaw in the track calls attention to a bad piece of editing or mixing and your attention and suspension of belief are broken. This is exactly what you do *not* want. It takes a dialog editor years to really master the various techniques and gimmicks of how to use the sleights-of-hand to camouflage the warts and rough edges that are inherent in all production dialog because of intercutting between the differences of microphone set-ups and of course the challenge of a quiet enough location in the first place.

I cannot think of a better example of a noisy location that had one of the worst dialog editing I have ever listened to than in Paul Mazursky's 1982 film *Tempest* with John Cassavetes. There is a scene shot at an exterior cafe with car-bys and busses with absolutely no extensions or attempt to make fill handles to smooth out the incredible bumps in the production traffic from cut to cut. I do not buy into the excuses from filmmakers when I call attention to bad dialog editing and they say, "It's real—it's documentary style . . . ," or the best one, "I meant it like that."

Bad filmmaking is bad filmmaking; even documentary films take great care in their production track. If you audibly yank the audience out of their fluid viewing of your film, then you are a bad filmmaker. There is no excuse for bad dialog editing, and unfortunately, too many directors and producers do not know who to hire to handle their production track like the precious lifeblood of the performance that it is.

With today's nonlinear digital editing platforms, the art of creating film is much easier than it was on 35-mm mag. If you run up against a piece of presence that will not loop end to end because it is different at the heads and tails, and if it does not have any kind of signature that will betray itself if run backwards, you can simply highlight, duplicate (Apple-D), and then go up to AudioSuite and draw down the menu to Reverse. In this fashion the duplication *has* to match, because the join will be exactly the same ending and starting. Every once in awhile you will run up against a cue that defies that approach, and you cannot use this technique on any fill that has internal audio events in the background, as they will instantly be recognized as reversed track.

What kills you is an actor who never shuts up and a director who is so paranoid about stock that he or she doesn't let the scene breathe so the dialog editor has any material to work with. I always sighed when I had to cut dialog tracks of actors who talk fast and never allow any places for fill. Of course, it could be worse. There are those actors who always seem to talk out of sync; even though the tracks phased perfectly, they always seem to look rubbery.

Magic and Transparency of Great Dialog Editing

There are dialog editors—and then there are dialog editors. Cutting dialog is not just the mechanical procedure of phase-matching reprints, filling holes, or extracting lip smacks and unwanted noise; it is the massaging and evolutionary improvement of an actor's performance. Master dialog editors take the time to review alternate takes, looking for a better reading, a clearer articulation, whatever brings the polish of a diamond to the spoken word. Remember, the dialog track always plays, truly the star of the soundtrack, and so a tremendous amount of attention must be paid to making it as clear and pristine as possible.

On *Twilight Zone: The Motion Picture*, my partner, Ken Sweet, handled the dialog editorial chores throughout the entire picture. Two challenging sequences were in the first episode when Vic Morrow is dragged to the train in the rain and, in the Spielberg episode, with Scatman Crothers.

Morrow tragically was killed during the filming, so we did not have access to him for ADR. The train sequence had been filmed the night before the accident. The artificial rain deluge was extremely heavy, thwarting any attempt by the boom operator to keep water from popping the microphone diaphragm without a rain bonnet. The director dismissed the need, saying they would ADR the scene later in post. We were not allowed to use a sound-a-like for looping the few lines obliterated by rain pelting, so Ken Sweet rolled up his sleeves and scrounged the production track like I have never seen a dialog editor do before.

He spent days cutting bits and pieces, sometimes as wide as one-fourth of a frame (a single perforation) from alternate takes to reconstruct a fluid piece of dialog that worked, without hearing the giant impacts to the microphone from the rain machine. Remember, *Twilight Zone: The Motion Picture* was cut years before digital nonlinear editing. Ken did not have the luxury of cross-blending two pieces of audio files with a digital cross-fade. Everything he cut was on 35-mm mag stripe.

In Spielberg's episode, Scatman Crothers offers the elder members of a retirement home a second chance at youth. Scatman was 81 years old when he filmed this magical segment, and understandably had trouble with precision in diction and enunciation. Ken Sweet tackled the dialog editing with a labor of love because of his admiration for Scatman and went the extra distance to pore over alternate takes, stealing "D"s, "T"s, and "R"s from outtakes where the actor had properly enunciated the consonant or vowel. Often Ken would steal such pieces from words or phrases entirely different from the word or phrase on which he was working. He would lift wherever he found a matching piece that could work, for he could not run the risk of making a single noticeable cut. Not one insert could be made that would give away the fact that Ken was re-sculpting the delivery of Scatman's speech. This was truly a work of editorial art.

Steve Rice faced a similar dilemma on *The Aviator*. When we spotted the picture with director George Miller, we were informed that Christopher Reeve was halfway around the world on another shoot and unavailable for any looping whatsoever. Somehow Steve would have to save all the production lines that dealt with the actor's voice. This was no small task, as Christopher Reeve wore a thick aviator's leather jacket throughout most of the picture. Naturally, the wireless microphone was positioned in such a way that the jacket was constantly rubbing the microphone any time Reeve moved.

I glanced over at Steve and we grimaced together, as we knew full well what challenges lay ahead. However, Steve Rice had been trained in the art of dialog editing by Ken Sweet just a few years before and he had learned his art well. As far as tenacious work habits, I have never seen better. Steve never came to me with a problem; he came to me with a solution to a problem. He had launched his dialog editing career with me on *Battle Beyond the Stars* and *Escape from New York* and, with Ken Sweet's tutelage, he became a master dialog artist.

Creating That Which Is Not There

When we started *Moscow on the Hudson*, we were faced with a potentially costly situation that Paul Mazursky already conceded would need to be done. In the sequence where Robin Williams is standing in a long cold line at night, waiting to buy shoes, he pauses to talk to Leonid, an old friend (Alexander Narodetzky), also waiting in line. When the scene was shot, Robin's close-up angle was fine, but, on Alexander's angle, the sound of the wind machine that gently blew snowfall dominated the audio track, making his close-up sync dialog completely unusable.

Les Fresholtz, the head dialog mixer on Warner Brothers Dubbing Stage 5, had earlier advised Mazursky to loop the actor. The picture editor, Richard Halsey, agreed with the director that it was a definite redo. To ADR this actor would require flight costs as well as daily expenses for at least the director and picture editor to fly to Munich to loop the actor's lines. Including the cost of an ADR stage, the funds needed to bring the actor back, and other stock expenses, Mazursky was facing at least a $10,000 black eye to the budget.

I suggested to Paul that he hold off making that kind of commitment until my dialog editor dug through alternate readings in an attempt to rebuild the original performance. Halsey scoffed at the idea, saying that Fresholtz had written it off as unsalvageable. I asked Paul if waiting another week would make that much of a difference on the schedule, after all, it was $10,000. Paul shrugged and gave us permission to at least try it. I told Steve Rice to work on that sequence first to see what could be done.

Late the following week, Mazursky asked me what the verdict was on the Alexander Narodetzky dialog. I turned to Steve who gave me the "high" sign that it worked just fine. I told Paul that the $10,000 did not need to be spent. Halsey was doubtful of the quality of the recut and asked Fresholtz to listen to it on the big screen in Dubbing 5. We assembled behind the sprawling console in Dubbing 5 the next day to run the sequence. Where the harsh and intrusive wind machine had marred the dialog track Steve had masterfully recut it from alternate angles where the wind machine had been. The trick had not been just using alternate takes, this is done all the time. The trick was finding usable alternate takes and making them fit in the full face-front close-up angles ruined by the wind machine, making the mouth movement precise, and especially not changing or altering the inflection of the actor's performance.

This last point is the key to the entire art form of dialog editing. It is not enough to understand and master the ability to sync lip-flapping movements with words. You carefully must guard and protect the performance and inflections so vital and cherished by the client.

Richard Halsey was so stricken with disbelief from the flawless and seamless work of Steve Rice that his knees literally gave out and he fell down in front of the credenza on his butt right next to me.

When to Equalize and Set Volume Graphing

The basic rule is never use signal processing on any cut dialog. You want interesting sounding vocals for monsters and ghouls? Prepare the material "flat"—signal processing is done by the re-recording dialog mixer on the stage. You do not have the proper acoustical environment to make such a decision in the editing room on a nonlinear workstation. The result would be something that cannot be unwound and reprocessed at the mixing stage; a smart dialog editor does not pre-equalize or preprocess the cut material in any way.

Prepare the elements of the material so that no matter how you wish to use it in processing the vocal, it is easier work for the mixer. For example, cut the voice on channel 1 and cut any additives, such as animal growls or inorganic pieces, on channel 2 in exact parallel to the cut dialog. In this way, the re-recording mixer can assign the two tracks into a Vocorder or Harmonizer and play with it while the director and producer attend. This way, it is their taste and creative desires you ultimately serve, not your own.

Many dialog editors use volume graphing more and more, building in volume shifts. A few years ago this practice was seen as an absolute editorial sin, but today it is done to a greater degree, with better results as dialog editors learn how to use the software.

As the evolution of nonlinear workstations and re-recording mix stages move and meld more and more into one and the same, there will be a greater need for dialog editors to work in rooms that truly do emulate the acoustical representation of a dubbing stage, as they will be asked to not only cut and prepare but to be responsible for the signal processing function, even unto mixing and delivering a dialog predub stem to the stage for a final mix.

Eventually, of course, more and more product will be prepared and mixed completely on mini-stages and not on full-scale dubbing theatres. More of this work is being done today than you might think, which is why we are seeing a lot of disparity between important feature film soundtracks and everything else.

View the interactive DVD with this book under button #4, Dialog Editing, for more organizational charts and an A-B comparison audio demo for EQing tracks. There is also a video demo of *Bad to Worse*, a film where you can view each stem of the soundtrack one at a time: the CUT EDITOR'S TRACK/my CUT DIALOG SESSION/my BACKGROUND session/my HARD FX session/the FINAL MIX.

Chapter 16
ADR and Looping
Getting the Lips to Flap in Sync

"The actors were whispering ... whenever they weren't yelling."

– Jeffrey Haupt

I believe in the magic of the production track. If the director and producer want less ADR in their films and more of that magic production, then they must work more closely with the production mixer. They must put a lot more effort and patience into getting the magic of the production track at the time of principal photography, or they ultimately pay extra budget dollars and time to revoice the actors later on the ADR stage. All right, best effort or not in trying to capture a great production track, the fact is, here you are with a certain amount of need for revoicing dialog.

Before we proceed, the first thing we need to do is clarify the difference between ADR and looping. Today we so often use the term *loop* or *looping* when we talk about an ADR session. We say, "We need to loop these lines" or "She does not loop well," when we are really referring to the process of vocal replacement and not the actual technique itself.

The technique of looping goes back to the beginnings of motion picture sound. In order to re-perform dialog over an existing visual performance, a "looping editor" would have to roll both picture and optical track through a synchronizer, listening for the lines using the optical head mounted over the second gang of the sync block. Once the editor found the line to be looped, he or she would cut both picture and track out, precisely in sync, making a mark with a grease pencil of the matching frame lines. The editor would add a little extra on either side of the line so that the actor would have a lead-in. Both picture and sound were then spliced head-to-tail, making a film loop, with the start frame clearly marked and punched in the center.

The loop editor would then take a grease pencil and make an angular one-foot-long cue on the picture. This was a visual reference for the actor to see when the first frame of modulation of the line to be re-performed actually started.

The punched hole in the film was to assist the projectionist when he or she would slide the looped picture into the gate of the projector. It was often extremely difficult in the dim light of the projection booth to see the grease pencil marks once the film was inside the gate area, but there was no mistaking the bright illumination coming through the punched hole, even when the douser of the projector was closed.

Once the picture film loop was loaded into the projector and the audio film loop was loaded into an optical playback dummy (term used for a play-only machine that slaves to other machines), the projector and playback dummy were put on the line (interlocked together by a distributor drive unit) so that when the projector ran forward, the playback dummy would run forward exactly in sync.

The looping mixer was given a green light and the mixer would tell the looping editor and actor on the stage that the next cue was ready. With that the mixer would roll the projector, which of course rolled the playback dummy. The cue to be re-performed would be seen on the screen, along with the grease pencil cue that would cross the screen (usually left to right), ending with the beginning of modulation of the line to be replaced. The original recording was also being heard as the actor would spend a few moments rehearsing it.

When the actor was confident that he or she was ready, the loop editor would tell the mixer that they were ready to make a take. The mixer would have the recordist put the optical film recorder on the line with the projector and playback dummy. Once the mixer rolled the projector and got up to speed, the actor would perform the line. The loop would continue to go around and around, allowing the actor to re-perform the line several times, sometimes giving variations and different reflections to the performance.

Once the actor and looping editor were satisfied, the mixer would stop the projector and the crew would take down the picture and audio loops and put up the next cue loops. This is the way it was done for many years. The basic difference being that in the early 1950s optical sound recording was replaced by 35-mm magnetic film recording.

Understand that there was no way to stop and back up and listen to these recordings. The projector, reproducer dummies, and recorder were incapable of operating in reverse, as we know today. What became known as rock-and-roll technology, which allowed projector and playback equipment to stop and reverse in sync, did not come into existence until the mid-1970s. As late as 1978 I worked on a picture that was mixing at the Warner Brothers sound department where we still could not stop and back up.

A variation of this style of looping was done at a few studios, such as Universal, who specialized in a heavy amount of looping, especially as they were handling vast numbers of television shows. These looping rooms used the same technique of using physical film loops, but with an important variation difference. At the end of each day's shoot two copies of the circled takes were transferred to 35-mm mag stripe by the sound department. These copies were made on two interlocked mag stripe recorders, making them simultaneously. The picture editorial apprentice would pick up one set and the show's loop editor would pick up the other set. The loop editor would break down all of the lines that each actor said, carefully making notes of scene/angle/take. Each actor's lines were then made into a loop, but a slightly different kind of loop. They did not bother with picture, which was too costly and took too much time for the process to run the cycle through the laboratory and back to sound editorial.

The loop editor would make each loop the length of the performance and again as long with two extra beats of fill. This would allow room for the actor to comfortably repeat the line during the blank period of the loop after he or she had just heard the original portion of the track played back in their headsets.

These loops were carefully marked with show code number, actor name, scene, angle, take, and then each actor's loops were placed in 2,000-foot film cans and stored on a rack. The following day, after the actor had completed that day's shoot, he or she would report to a looping room where the actors would re-loop all the lines that they had performed the day before. This gave incredible latitude to picture editorial and subsequently sound editorial during the sound editorial phase after picture lock, greatly speeding up the postproduction phase as they rarely had to call actors back in, except to change performances with different dialog than originally written.

These looping rooms did not project picture. The machine room loader threaded the loop onto a sprocketed 35-mm playback machine. As the loop played, it traveled around and around over the playback head, first playing the actor's original performance, then falling silent as the blank 35-mm fill passed over. This allowed the actor in the booth to repeat the line he or she just heard. As the loop continued around, the actor would hear the loop again and then, during the blank spot, would repeat the line, only this time altering the performance, giving a different inflection or emphasis. This process continued until the actor delivered 10 or 15 variations, enough from which the loop editor and director could choose.

Once the cue was finished, the machine room loader removed the first loop and loaded the next, continuing the same process through the listed cues. The recordist placed a hand written note of the next loop's code number on a piece of tape and placed the tape on the 35-mm mag stripe (*after* the record head) for ease in breaking down the recordings later by the loop editor assistant. Once ready the green light would come in, notifying the room that the loop was mounted and ready to roll. The looping mixer would roll the loop for the actor to listen to and get comfortable with. Once the actor signaled that he or she was ready, the recordist would place the 35-mm mag stripe film recorder on the line, interlocking it to the reproducer dummy.

The actor stood next to a music stand that held the looping editor's notes and printouts of the actor's lines. This gave the actor a tremendous advantage. The actor could close his or her eyes and *concentrate* on *listening* to the performance and then re-performing his or her performance, either as an exact match or with variations. It gave the actor the freedom to *act*, rather than be overwhelmed with having to watch picture, take notice of cue stripes or hear beeps in the headset, or try to match lip flapping to the visual. All of these non-acting demands distracted and pulled the actor out of the realm of delivering an audio performance.

That said, we will review this philosophy and present style of how to recapture this almost lost art form in the last part of this chapter.

This technique will also serve you well when it is extremely difficult to access actors who are literally unavailable to an ADR stage or looping room. You must be very creative in working with these actors, even when they are shooting a film in the jungles of Africa or Antarctica, definitely nowhere near an ADR stage until long after your postproduction schedule and the 2-track print master has already been delivered to the laboratory. I will discuss the mechanics of this location looping technique later in the chapter under "Remote Location Looping."

ADR

In the mid-1970s, with the advent of the rock-and-roll system, where projectors, reproducers, and recorders could stop, reverse, and roll forward again in absolute sync, the system of ADR came into being.

Contrary to some beliefs, ADR does not stand for "All Dialog Is Ruined," though some directors would certainly argue that with me. The initials ADR are quoted two ways: "Automatic Dialog Recording" and "Automatic Dialog Replacement." Personally I do not understand why some refer to it as "Automatic Dialog Replacement" because it does not replace anything—it takes an ADR editor to do that. Where the term really stems from is the fact that for the first time an ADR mixer could program into the stage automation equipment a precise foot and frame that he or she wished the film recorder to record and what foot and frame the mixer wished the film recorder to cease recording.

Based on these numbers that were physically entered into the automation using analog pushbutton switches, the equipment would react to preset parameters to roll at high speed (in those days six times speed was high speed) down to the desired line, sense the proximity of the foot and frame and automatically slow down and park itself so many feet before the line. As computer programs started to drive the automation equipment, programming became even more complex and more detailed—entering a digital reality.

Time code was used when the video was on a magnetic tape medium and the video machine needed to be slaved in perfect sync with the rest of the equipment, and so ADR stages became automated set-ups so that the ADR mixer could choose whether to work and enter in and out cues in either feet and frames or in time code.

The mixer would roll back and forth through the line for the actor to get a sense of the performance. Precisely 3 feet before the foot and frame entered by the mixer, the automation triggered the ADR beeps (single-frame 1-kHz tone), so that the actor would hear three very short rhythmic beats just prior to the actual line to be replaced. These are known as the "beeps" (or "pips" to many English editors), spaced every 16 35-mm frames apart, equal to one beep every foot. Where the fourth beep would have landed is silent (known as the fourth silent beep)—*this* is the exact frame where the actor must begin to speak the line being replaced, otherwise referred to as "first frame of modulation."

The idea was that the actors also watched their physical performance projected up on the screen. There was no need for laborious grease pencil cues to be marked on the film, as the three beeps prior to action provided them with an accurate rhythmic cueing. The actors had a chance to watch themselves and became quite aware of things about them in the movie realm that they might want to react to and that might influence their new performance.

436 Louie IN > 04:09:45:10 OUT > 04:09:48:00	(catch breath) "I think you are fooling yourself." scene 53 ext ⌐ HEAVY NIGHT INSECTS ⌐
437 Marla IN > 04:09:48:25 OUT > 04:09:52:00	"Please don't make this any harder than it is." scene 53 ext ⌐ HEAVY NIGHT INSECTS ⌐
438 Marla IN > 04:10:01:16 OUT > 04:10:09:00	(ADDED – muffled reaction of Marla in her car – frustrated) scene 53 ext ⌐ HEAVY NIGHT INSECTS ⌐

Figure 16.1 Here are three ADR cues that you can use to practice your technique and develop an understanding of the process. (The practice session can be found on the interactive DVD that is included with this book.)

This was a great toy. The studio that I was working at in 1977 was installing this kind of automated technology on Stage C, and I became very involved in this new process. But we very quickly discovered that some actors are perfect for ADR-style re-performing and others are totally intimidated by it, some to the point that they would devise all kinds of strange personal techniques in order to face the microphone.

Many who supervise performing talent on an ADR stage often notice how many actors are distracted by the beeps that precede the dialog cue to be re-performed. They are not used to hearing the beeps and especially not used to the rhythmic timing. I have therefore decided to include a kind of rehearsal exercise for those who would like to be better prepared before stepping onto an ADR stage costing many dollars by the minute.

For those of you who are interested in a little practice exercise before you attempt doing it on the real ADR stage, I suggest you use the practice session provided below as you listen to and emulate the three cues on the DVD provided with this book; you will find it under the DVD menu button ADR Practice.

The Practice ADR Lines

Just as you will experience on a professional ADR stage, you will hear three rhythmic beeps, then a piece of production dialog, the line intended to be re-voiced. The beeps and dialog cues are repeated four times, to assist you in getting used to the rhythm of the beep cues and the silent fourth count which is the cue to lip-sync your voice against the production dialog. The Colin-Broad streamer is also incredibly useful for Foley cues. But we will talk about that later when we discuss Foley in Chapter 17.

To assist you in understanding the use of automated Colin-Broad streamers, all of the ADR practice cues have Colin-Broad streamers animated into the visual picture. This terrific automated system really helps the actor as the visual line moves across the screen from left to right in addition to hearing the three preceding one-frame beeps.

To further the practical realism of line replacement, the practice cues have noisy ambiences, making it difficult to hear the original dialog at times. As you listen to the DVD cue with the beeps and production cue repeated six times, try to repeat the line in perfect sync. As you master the ability to match sync, change the inflection and performance, while still keeping the temp and rhythm in perfect sync. This should help any aspiring actor overcome the fear of working with the beeps and better understand what is expected in working on today's ADR/looping stage.

Aspiring actors, in both film and especially theatre, who want to be trained and prepared in the technical needs and expectations of ADR, will want to acquire the separate ADR/looping exercise DVD, which is available separately from this book. It has over a hundred ADR cues, along with cue sheet visuals that provide a boot-camp training to properly prepare you to go to the ADR stage and do it for real—in front of the director and producer!

The ADR Supervisor

The ADR supervisor, more than any other postproduction craftsperson, interfaces and works with performing acting talent. When temperamental or difficult talent is involved, the producer's and director's first concern is who handles the ADR responsibilities—and politics.

Some actors love to ADR. They see it as a chance to get back on stage and improve their own performance, to massage it, fine-tuning it in a way not possible on location. On the other hand, many other actors dislike ADR immensely. They are intimidated or inhibited by the ADR stage process. To them, the on-screen sync track was the magic performance they provided while filming the scene on location. Many actors do not listen to the production track with a discerning ear. They only hear their own performance and, once satisfied, often refuse to loop a requested cue. Many are not audio aware. These actors do not always notice the intrusive airplane flying overhead marring the recording; neither do they hear the distorted brittleness in the track where they shouted or suddenly burst forth in a dynamic shift, catching the production mixer off-guard causing the voice to be overmodulated.

This is where strong and politically smart ADR supervisors really earn their salaries. If a supervisor gains an actor's confidence that he or she is sincerely interested in improving and magnifying the performance, the actor almost always defers to the opinions and recommendations of the ADR supervisor.

An ADR supervisor does not always have to be the best ADR editor in the world (one can always hire ADR editors with reputations for cutting good sync), but the ADR supervisor must appear on stage neatly dressed with a professional bearing of calm self-confidence. The supervisor also must be extremely well organized, able to locate the right paperwork at any moment. If the supervisor does not have the answer literally at the fingertips, he or she must know where and how to get it in a timely manner without fuss.

The ADR supervisor must articulate clearly, to the actors as well as the director and producer(s) as needed, why certain cues are added and how they will improve the outcome of the final soundtrack. The ADR supervisor should not give the perception of being just the bearer of bad news or a presenter of problems, but rather of a professional presenting solutions. The ADR supervisor works hard, surgically gleaning out problematic dialog lines (for both performance and technical issues). He or she compiles a complete list of lines to be looped and devises tactical solutions for gaining access to remote actors not available for formal looping sessions.

Nothing is worse than being on an ADR stage or, even worse, on the re-recording stage and having a director or producer notice that lines were missed. It is bad enough when a director or producer decides on additional dialog needs after the fact; it is altogether a most undesirable situation to overlook lines that either clearly were requested in the initial spotting session(s) or were not gleaned out by common sense by the ADR supervisor while cueing the ADR lines at the workstation.

Listen Carefully to the Production Track

One pitfall that the director, picture editor, and producer(s) constantly encounter is losing touch with their production track. Remember, they have lived with the picture and their production track for weeks, often months, and on occasion even years. They know every word, every production sound effect, every dropout, every flaw. They have grown so close to it, however, they have lost the ability to hear it anew, as heard by an audience for the first time. It is often very difficult to convince directors and producers that a dialog line must be looped when the repetitious playback of that line is indelibly etched in their minds.

In a spotting session, I hear a problematic line. The director, picture editor, and producer are not flagging it. I hold up my hand. "What did they say?" Invariably, the director or picture editor will tell me what the actor said instead of realizing that my not understanding the line was related to its lack of clarity.

The best ally a supervising sound editor and ADR supervisor can have is the dialog mixer who helms the ultimate re-recording of the project. Many times a director or producer disagree with or try to badger the ADR supervisor, claiming nothing is wrong with a particular line. "You can make that work." However, when the dialog mixer says to loop it, nobody questions it. After all, the dialog mixer is the ultimate authority through whom all dialog tracks must flow. He or she has the power to bounce the reel off the stage and refuse to mix it if the material cannot be made to work because of the way it has been prepared. It is for this reason that, as supervising sound editor, I always insist on having the sound facility set in place and the mixing crew contracted at the outset of commencing the postproduction sound editorial chores. The first thing I want is an interlock running of the picture with the dialog mixer, who usually helms the stage.

Naturally, I have my dialog editor (responsible for cutting original production tracks) as well as my ADR supervisor on stage for the running. More important, I want the director, picture editor, and producer(s) in attendance to hear exactly what the dialog mixer says about one cue or another. The dialog mixer runs the production track through the very mixing console used during the predubbing process. Often, the picture editor, director, and producer(s) hear the track truly for the first time, through quality theatrical speakers that are extremely transparent; they do not color or hide the flaws or warts of the recordings—*all* is revealed.

Many veteran dialog mixers explain that they have a three-point rating system as the team discusses the various dialog lines. If they rate it a "one" that means they have no problems with the technical characteristics of the line and can make it work; however, if they want to loop it for performance reasons, that is the call of the director and/or producer(s). A "two" means they do not like what they hear. Either there is a fringy edge (usually the threshold of distortion) or some kind of hum or noise, such as overhead aircraft, offstage traffic, or other intrusive sounds. The dialog mixer feels that he or she can work with the line if necessary, but would rather have it looped. If the mixer rates the line a "three" that means there is no choice but to loop the line, as the dialog mixer cannot equalize it or work with it to make it sound right. Do not even argue with the dialog mixer about his "three" count; even actors who have died can and do have line replacement done by soundalikes.

From time to time the dialog mixer pauses and lays on a few equalization moves or runs the sound through a universal dip filter to make sure that some offending noise can be notched out without encroaching on the characteristics of the voice. By the time the running is over, there is usually no question as to the scope of work to be done. The mental alignment of the sound editorial team and picture editor, directors, and producer(s) becomes fairly well set. With a short conversation regarding tactics of dialog preparation and perhaps other options to save certain critical lines, such as using Sonic Solutions or renting specialized signal-processing gear for the dialog predub process, everyone leaves the running focused on the job ahead.

Having an interlock running with the dialog mixer at the beginning also relieves the mixer of responsibility with you. It is one thing to show up on the re-recording stage for dialog predubs and have the dialog mixer zinging the sound editors because something was not done, but, when the dialog mixer is part of the decision-making process from the beginning, he or she is bound to the sound editorial team as well as the director and producer(s) by what was counseled before work began.

Crushed Schedule Trends of Mega-Monsters

Several ADR supervisors have shared the nightmare trend, especially on huge accelerated schedule mega-budget pictures, that they rarely even get a chance to have an actual and realistic ADR running as described in detail above.

Nonlinear technology with Final Cut Pro and Avid makes it easier and easier for picture editors and directors to put in visual special effects (as work in progress) and have a sound team (either for temp work only or the eventual actual sound editing contractors) start developing and make crash-down temp sound mixes long before the picture even gets to a point of being considered ready to turn over to sound editorial.

R.J. (Bob) Kizer is one of the industry's more respected ADR supervisors (Steven Spielberg's version of *War of the Worlds, The Terminal, Master and Commander: The Far Side of the World, Catch Me If You Can,* the 2000 version of *Planet of the Apes, X-Men* and *X-Men: The Last Stand, Anna and the King, The Siege, Alien Resurrection,* to name a few). He confesses that he often only gets his first real interaction with the picture editor and director about what lines to set up and cue for an ADR session during the first temp dub.

I personally find this appalling—certainly not Bob's choice—but it is important to take notice of the inevitable evolution of how things are being done: not for art form's sake, but for schedule and business considerations. Often, these decisions are made by those who do not understand the collateral costs that are incurred by what might seem like expedient practices, but, in fact cost untold wasted dollars due to ignorance of the process.

Figure 16.2 On an ADR stage, R.J. Kizer clarifies a point for David Kulczycki before he replaces a dialog cue. "One thing you have to master right away as an ADR editor is when to speak up and when to keep your mouth shut. You won't always know when you failed to do the former, but you will quickly know when you failed to do the latter." (Photo by John LeBlanc.)

Tighter budget films cannot afford that kind of technique, and are better served by the ADR running technique as we talked about earlier in this chapter. But, it is vital to understand how and why certain techniques and trends are constantly evolving and the professional ADR supervisor will know how to shift gears from one technique to another, depending on the client and the studio involved.

Kizer has a few thoughts to share on the opportunities and discipline of ADR (and/or looping):

ADR has changed a lot from how it was done 15 years ago, and it is on the verge of changing yet again. The transistor revolution of the 1950s brought about the introduction of "Automated Dialog Replacement" in the late 60s and early 70s. The computer revolution of the mid-80s brought about the use of personal computers in the compiling of cueing information for ADR sessions. There must be at least eight different cueing softwares out there. (And who knows how many are floating around Europe and Asia?)

Cutting movies on the Avid and Lightworks has made re-cutting much easier and less labor intensive. Consequently, ADR editors *must* do their cueing on some kind of computer system just to keep up with all the changes. On *Master and Commander*, for example, I had a new version of the picture turned over to me every Friday. It would take me 8 days to conform my programming. As you can see, I quickly fell behind. I then had to conform my programming to every other version and gamble that I wouldn't be called to the ADR stage during a version that I had skipped.

Back in the days of shooting ADR on film and mag, I used to allow 10 minutes per cue. Today, I allow 4 minutes per cue. These days it is extremely rare to encounter a location mixer who only uses a reel-to-reel Nagra to record the production track. Thankfully the days of using a DA-88 are behind us. Nowadays, more and more location mixers are using hard-drive recorders (like the Deva). Production dialog is now routinely coming to us as 48 kHz/24-bit, broadcast Wave files.

Likewise, ADR is being recorded at 48 kHz/24-bit. Many ADR stages in Los Angeles and New York use Pro Tools as either the primary or secondary recording device. (Todd-A-O is still holding on to the Fairlight, but that will soon change.)

On the set, location mixers are using combinations of radio mikes and boom mikes to record the track. On multichannel recorders, they will assign individual actors to specific channels and place the boom on a separate channel.

For the 2005 remake of *War of the Worlds*, the production dialog was recorded across 8 channels. Channels 1–5 were individual radio mikes, channel 6 was the boom mike, and channels 7–8 were combines (bumped up by 8 dB) to be given to sound transfer for transfer to mag stripe—Spielberg likes working with film and mag, and so he has his editor cut his movies on a Moviola.

Some location mixers are very lazy and they take the radio mikes and the boom mike and combine all the signals into one channel and leave the other channels blank. It's true!

As a result of this multi-mike recording situation, many ADR editors are having their ADR recorded with two mikes: a traditional boom mike (either a short shotgun like the Sennheiser MKH 416 or MKH 60 or the Neumann KMR 81) and a lavalier microphone. So the ADR editor ends up with two channels recorded per cue. Both channels are cut and presented for predubbing. The dialog re-recording mixer will then decide which channel to use or use a combination of the two, whichever way matches the production track the best.

As you can guess from the above, if production dialog has 8 channels per "line," then the edited Pro Tools session could easily be 64 channels wide. Usually the dialog goes through and strips out the channels that are not needed. So the edited session comes in around 12–16 channels wide.

The edited ADR session can be extremely wide; two channels per cue, plus however many alternates the director asked for, split for on-stage/off-stage treatment, and phone and TV speaker treatment—you can end up with 72 channels of ADR being presented for predubbing. (Personally, in ADR I have found only two specific instances where I was glad I had the lavalier mike recording. All the other times, we have only used the boom channel.)

More directors today do not know their craft nor do they know anything about any of the other crafts. Their sense of hearing is severely skewed to listening to extreme rock-and-roll music. Some show up to the final mix after having inhaled several lines of cocaine. Drugs like cocaine increase the heart rate, which will increase blood pressure. That sends more blood to the head, and the increased pressure affects your hearing. Things tend to sound more muddy. It's like having water in your ear. So directors start complaining that the dialog sounds too muddy. And the mixer is forced to EQ everything higher, so that dialog starts to become shrill.

Richard Portman always used to say, "Sound is round." By that he meant sound is a medium that should not be cut jaggedly like picture. Sound has an approach, a by, and an away. If you chop it all up, it becomes hard to listen to, and eventually the brain will tune it all out. Film editors like to cut sound as discrete blocks of events, just as they cut their picture.

They want to hear the car when they see the car. If they don't see the car, they don't want to hear it.

ADR Cueing   R.J. Kizer, supervising ADR editor on ADR cueing:

In England, a device was created by Colin Broad called the Video Streamer. It had a software that allowed the operator to enter all the event addresses (cues) for a character, then it would trigger an electronic streamer or wipe for each event without having to stop in between. This allowed an actor to ADR an entire scene as a single take, if he so desired. So far, Disney and Fox have installed this box and software on their feature ADR stages. I have used it successfully (it can be a bit buggy) on three features, most tellingly on *War of the Worlds*.

Meanwhile, an outfit down in New Zealand has come with something they call *VoiceQ*. This uses a QuickTime movie and track. The operator loads in the QuickTime movie and sets the starts and stops for all the cues by marking the guide track in a timeline. You type in the dialog for the cues in a special window. Now, the software analyzes the track for each cue and then displays the dialog on a running subtitle banner on the picture. The letters of the words are squeezed together or stretched out according to how fast or slow the word was said on the track. This eliminates the need for the Actor to look down at his script as he is speaking his lines. All the dialog is up on the screen.

Each cue will be triggered automatically as the film is running, allowing the actor to do as many cues in a run as he wants. And like the Colin Broad Video Streamer, the software allows for the importing of cue data from other software via a tab-delimited text file. I have been lobbying Fox to get VoiceQ. I believe the software was originally developed to accommodate foreign language dubbing, but they have used it on *Lord of the Rings* and *King Kong* for principal ADR.

APPROPRIATE USE OF LANGUAGE

Language is a very delicate and extremely important part of the soundtrack. So few producers, directors, or writers truly understand the ramifications and broad audience enthusiasm for their film because of judicious and careful use of profanity in the dialog track. This is not about what previously was known as the Television Network Standards and Practices Board. This is a question of common sense and a calculated decision on the part of the producer of defining the audience for the film.

In an industry immersed in an assault on the senses, where we are exposed to extremes of cinematic content, most of the new generation of filmmakers unfortunately is desensitized and perhaps suffers from ignorance of this controversial and delicate subject. Seriously ponder for what audience you have been making the picture, and then rethink the use of profanity or slang used in the script. I have witnessed several projects that could have done much better commercially but were banished to a harsher MPAA rating because of the careless use of blasphemy and profane dialog.

Not an issue of Victorian prudishness, this is the experience of being associated with over 100 theatrical motion pictures, watching their creative evolutions through to box-office success or failure, and witnessing elements that made them successful and those that weakened them, turning off audiences. The topic is broached here because it is during the looping process that you may wish to rethink your dialog track through one more time with a critical eye toward this cause and effect; you still can make changes and improve the film's commercial worth.

Aside from primary content consideration, you must address television coverage. After you finish the M&E (foreign) mix, you will need to prepare a television version. You will not find an official no-no wordlist anywhere. Probably out of fear of violating the First Amendment, nobody wants to dictate and formally publish such a no-no list, nor will I. However, many sound editorial firms, especially those dealing with network television, have lists compiled from meetings and verbal edit strategies. Of course, the list is constantly changing. At one time, certain words could not be said on television or even in movies, and now they are heard on a regular desensitizing basis. Each network and cable channel has its own threshold of acceptance.

Determining what is profane or what will trigger a harsher MPAA rating is not as obvious as you might think. The word *hell* is a good example, an extremely common and virtually everyday word that has lost much of its impact. If an actor says, "Oh, what the hell," this is not a problem. If an actor turns to another actor and says, "You go to hell!", this *is* a problem, for now it is used in a damning way against another human being. Therein lies the difference.

The most powerful and surefire trigger to not only doom your film to a harsher MPAA rating but also to turn off a huge cross-section of the audience is the use of blasphemy. Should an actor place the word *god* in front of the word *damn*, the most profane word has been uttered; yes, it is even worse than the *f* word.

It is just amazing to me how warped the cable censorship community has become. American Movie Classics and other popular so-called family channels will bleep out the *s* word, yet they will leave in the harshest of all obscenities by leaving the *god* words in. This is not an indictment based only on Christian ethics. *God* is a global term that applies to the specific names that define the pinnacle deity of almost all religions; therefore using it in a derogatory way is worse than hearing Al Pacino say the *f* word so many times in *Scarface*. If you do not understand what I'm talking about, then I suggest you check out the Ten Commandments that Moses brought down from the mountain top.

The body count, bullets, and blood mentality that desensitizes the audience will (and is) eroding the viewing tolerance. I should know. I have worked on many films that I would not, by choice, go to see. I have been bombarded by images and language that for long periods of time has desensitized me. It took months to return to a mental state where I could act and react to things in a normal way (whatever that is supposed to be). But you are never really the same.

Hollywood argues that their studies tell them the kinds of movies that the public wants to see. Statistical studies will yield information in exactly how you present the question. We did not believe Hollywood's box-office studies of the public taste and demand, and after making our own study it quickly revealed why. Fewer and fewer middle age and older moviegoers were going to the theatre because of the product, not because of a lack of desire to go see a movie in a theatre. It becomes kind of a chicken-and-egg argument, doesn't it?

After conducting a study of moviegoers, as well as patrons who rented from local video shops, we discovered that language, without a doubt, was the number-one reason why a significant number of potential patrons stopped going to the movie theatres. At the very least they had become far pickier about which films they wanted to see. Many of their comments surprised us, especially in regard to the specificity of objectionable words. For instance, many viewers reacted very badly to the word *crap* or *crappy* in film dialog, saying they actually would prefer to have heard that other overused defecation *s* word cliché.

While it is true that some of these comments came from areas many refer to as the Midwest or the Bible Belt audience, filmmakers forget that that audience accounts for a giant share of income and can certainly wield powerful critical acclaim or disapproval. Have you ever considered the collateral loss of dollars that you do not know about, because you did not know what was possible to begin with? I think the movie *The Rookie*, starring Dennis Quaid, is an excellent example of a picture that has heart, passion, emotion, action, interesting photography, good sound, and music score and yet does not have one curse word in the picture. By the way, it was rated *G* for all you Hollywood-hype executives that spout that *G*-rated films are poison at the box office.

This is not just a lesson in ethics or morals, but a good business lesson in possibilities. Just remember for which audience your film is targeted for and analyze your visual image and dialog track with a critical eye and ear. It will tell you what must be done. You may also find it interesting that since, as we have discussed in this book, foreign sales stream income now dominates the domestic market, you should pause and think through the tastes and tolerances of foreign markets. Each overseas audience market has their own thoughts and reactions to film language. Sometimes it may be translated out, but certain words are universally recognized. This is not to say that you cannot or should not make *R*-rated films. They definitely have their market. This is about recognizing what market your film is really speaking to and make sure that the content speaks the presentation to match.

A few years ago I was supervising the sound on what should have been a cute little *PG*-rated robotic film. We had just sat down to commence the spotting session when the lead actor turned and used the *god* word, not once, but several times. I raised my hand for the editor to stop. I turned with a puzzled expression to the producer, "So you're making an *R*-rated film?"

He recoiled at my comment. "What gives you the idea that we're making an *R*-rated film? This will be rated *PG*!"

I shrugged, "That's what I thought your market was going to be. But you sure have an *R*-rated film now."

The producer asked how I came to assume that. I explained that after working on more than a hundred theatrical motion pictures, on many of which I am privy to the interactions of the producer and the MPAA, I have come to know what will trigger certain ratings, and using the *god* word will get you an *R* rating.

The producer scoffed at me. What did I know? I was just a sound editor! Several months later, when we commenced the final re-recording process the producer burst onto the dubbing stage with a deluge of profanity. How could the MPAA have given them an *R* rating? I glanced knowingly at the head mixer who smiled with an unspoken I-told-you-so acknowledgement.

Rather than take the time to go back in and loop the offending lines and resubmit the film for a new MPAA rating, the producer did not understand that it was this simple language issue that garnished the *R* rating, so the lines were never replaced. Consequently the picture was released as an *R*-rated film which was not the audience for which it was designed for. The film failed miserably, all because of a dozen *god* outbursts in the dialog track.

Finally, if you do not want your film to play on a well-known cable channel and have muted dropouts in the soundtrack because you did not supply a television version, accept the advice from the ADR supervisor regarding getting television coverage while you have the acting talent on stage for the primary ADR session.

CUEING ADR LINES

After a thorough run-through and discussion with the director and producer on actor performances and availabilities, the ADR supervisor goes through the film to cue the dialog, noting both replacement and added lines to be recorded.

Before computer programs, ADR cue sheets were always typed. A real professional never took handwritten ADR cue sheets to the stage. Never give an actor a handwritten ADR cue sheet, unless you are adding or collaborating on new dialog on stage with the actor. The neatness and precise look of the ADR cue sheet are your ambassador of professionalism and trust. Watch for misspelled words or crossed-out lines with handwritten corrections. Many actors are intimidated by the ADR stage already. If you give the actor handwritten cue sheets, you do not instill confidence and inspire the actor; you may find yourself soon replaced and it may not be up to your supervising sound editor; he or she may be compelled by the director's or producer's office to do it.

The Traditional ADR Form

Note that each ADR line in Figure 16.3 has a cue number. Almost all ADR supervisors use the reel number as the first designation, so all cues in reel 4 are the 400 series (401, 402, and so on). Many supervisors leave a blank box in between each cue, allowing space to add lines on the spur of the moment, but also making it much more comfortable for the actor to find and read the lines in the dim light of the ADR stage. The actor must concentrate on the image projected on the screen to match sync, and not waste time to find the written cue on the page.

List each part by the character name, not the actor's real name. Every ADR supervisor has a specific technique and preference as to how to prepare ADR sheets. Many supervisors list ADR cues just as the ADR form is displayed in Figure 16.3. In other words, ADR cues are listed in a linear order, in sequence of performance, listing each character. Other ADR supervisors choose instead to put all the lines for each character on a separate page. Their contention is that this is not as confusing to the actor on the ADR stage. I simply take a yellow highlighter to all of actor 1's lines, and on another copy I highlight all of actor 2's lines, thereby making it immensely easier for the actors to focus on their own dialog requirements.

As supervising sound editor, I prefer ADR sheets in linear order. With today's computer software, it is so easy to extract per-character variants from the master cue list and print them for the actor on stage, but I do not want to fumble through a dozen separate sheets looking and accounting for lines of dialog.

Each line has a "start" and "to" designation. This designation either is listed in feet and frames or in time code. Many veteran theatrical editors still like to work in feet and frames, but video outputs from the cut picture are offering fewer and fewer opportunities to use feet and frames. Aside from personal preference, a few ADR stages cannot even display feet and frames anymore, and so time code is the only choice in those instances. (Always check with the stage before starting this task.)

When cueing the line to be ADR'ed, list the exact frame in which the first audible modulation can be heard—exactly! At the end of the line, add 1 foot extra for overtones

A.D.R. show title: _____"Island Mist"_____ pg. _1_ -of- _5_

EDITOR: _Boguski_   REEL : **4**

MIXER / RECORDIST _Schwartz / Porter_   TAKE PREFS   NOTES:

CUE / Character		TAKE PREFS		
401 Jeanie START: 01:10:02 TO: 01:15:00	"You tell me where all the animals have gone!"			
CUE Character START: TO:				
402 Jeanie START: 01:15:10 TO: 01:21:00	"Two weeks ago this entire archipelago was crawling with exotic creatures."			
CUE Character START: TO:				
403 Richard START: 01:22:07 TO: 01:32:00	"Maybe they're just timid -- wrong time of day to come or something."			
CUE Character START: TO:				
404 Jeanie START: 01:31:20 TO: 01:38:00	"I hardly think so, besides the air itself -- it lacks that certain aroma."			
CUE Character START: TO:				
405 Richard START: 01:40:12 TO: 01:48:00	"Aroma? -- Aroma of what?" (beat) "You mean their stink?"			
CUE Character START: TO:				
406 Captain START: 01:48:15 TO: 01:57:00	"She's right, my boy. The air was full of life."			

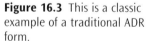

Figure 16.3 This is a classic example of a traditional ADR form.

to die off. Not all ADR mixers like their start cues the same way. Some want it 2 frames prior; others want it as many as 8 frames prior; still others want it right on the frame of modulation. You will probably use more than one ADR stage to complete all ADR work for the picture. Each stage may want the start cues slightly different. Either tell the mixer that all your cues are right on the frame so that specific preferences can be utilized, or print out new sheets with the preferred frame specifications already listed for each recording venue.

The ADR supervisor soon has a list of the stages, both local and around the world, that will be dealt with to accomplish the looping chores of the picture. The ADR supervisor discusses preparation preferences as well as media requirements from the ADR mixer and/or audio engineer of each facility. It often is necessary to prepare separate ADR sheets for individual ADR facilities, customizing the data to best accommodate that facility's own capabilities or limitations.

Most good ADR supervisors have an added line of notations for each cue. They list a reason why the line is to be re-performed (e.g., noise, distortion, performance, television coverage, and so on). This has developed out of frustration from ADR supervisors, supervising sound editors, producers, directors, and re-recording mixers who, in the final analysis, have to make it all work. Initially, the producer or director perceives that the dialog for the film is basically in good shape and does not require much looping. Then the ADR supervisor and supervising sound editor run the reels with the re-recording mixer on a dubbing stage to analyze the true quality and nature of the production sound. It never fails to shock the producer and director, who have never truly heard their production track in this theatrical environment, just how bad and brittle their soundtrack is.

Now come the lines added because of unwanted vocal overlaps that went unnoticed before, for instance, airplane noise not detected on the little speakers of a picture editorial workstation. The rhythmic ticking was not noticed because of early morning condensation impacting the microphone diaphragm. If you loop the passenger character in the front seat of the car talking, you either must loop the driver or cross-fill all the noise from the driver's dialog under the passenger character to avoid a series of checkerboarded dropouts, which ultimately accomplishes nothing if you were intent on getting all that noisy background out from behind the passenger character's lines in the first place.

Now the ADR lines start adding up. At an average of 10 minutes per line to successfully record, the producer and director get nervous. Their good-shape dialog track is now escalating into several hundred, even a thousand-plus ADR cues. Then you send an ADR kit to South Africa to an actor on location but with access to an ADR stage in Johannesburg for an afternoon. The budget cannot afford for the ADR supervisor to fly down there to oversee the session. What comes back is a marked-up ADR sheet with only a fraction of the ADR lines done. The actor either does not understand or does not care about the technical problems of the scenes. The actor considers his or her performance fine.

I received a $1/4$" back-up master from an ADR stage in Florida, where a name actor had performed his ADR session unsupervised. Without due consideration of why the ADR cues had been written up and without calling the editor in Los Angeles to ask why he was expected to loop certain lines, he arbitrarily decided not to loop some lines and to loop others. As I ran the $1/4$" back-up master, I could hear the actor scoff as the film rolled. He demanded to know what idiot had cued the lines. He crossed out a line and wrote "omit." Of course, he did not pay attention to the background noise, which the ADR supervisor knew would give the dialog re-recording mixer absolute grief later. Guess who caught the criticism from the re-recording mixer when he heaved a sigh and said, "I can't make this work! Why didn't you loop this line?!"

By making notes as to why the particular ADR line has been cued, the ADR supervisor not only informs and educates the actor to gain cooperation but also makes a paper trail record that may be necessary to prevent later blame and to show the producer and studio executives that the ADR supervisor had prepared the job correctly in the first place.

Note in Figure 16.3 the six squares to the right of the ADR line. The ADR supervisor keeps a close record of which takes are most desired, kind of like the circled takes on a production sound report. Before direct-to-disk digital recording systems, such as Pro Tools, ADR was recorded to multichannel magnetic stock. At first it was 3-channel

35-mm fullcoat, and when the 4-channel 35-mm head stack came out in the late 1970s, we were thrilled to have one extra channel. Then stages started adapting 24-track 2″ magnetic tape, especially when Dolby Laboratories made the Dolby A 24-channel noise reduction encoder/decoders. This became even more popular with the Dolby SR (Spectral Recording) encoder/decoder. Cue sheets during these years had 24 square boxes for the ADR editor to keep notes in, especially in keeping what take was on which channel.

With today's direct-to-disk nonlinear recording systems, "what *channel*" is irrelevant. It becomes a matter of "what *take*," as it all resides on the hard drive unless otherwise thrown away by the user. It really falls to the ADR mixer assistant to help the mixer keep the take numbers straight, as after recording a line, the mixer would need to tap twice on the recorded audio track to rename it. That renaming would become critical for future reference. It becomes very easy to record numerous takes before the director chooses one or more to "print," which is an old term that meant that the sound transfer department should make a transfer copy (in whatever medium was required) for the ADR editor to cut. With today's digital technology we do not "print" anymore, though the term still sticks, it just means that the ADR editor will want to pay strict attention to the director's choices. The ADR supervisor also makes notes as to how to cut the line. The director may ask for the first part of the line from take 3 with the second part from take 9.

ADR Software to Further Automate the Process

Figure 16.4 is from the ADR cue sheet for the character Ashley from the romantic comedy *Just My Luck*. Note that as in the traditional ADR form, the information disciplines are the same with a few important variations.

The header lists the name of the film, the name of the actress (not the character she plays) who will be replacing the lines cued, the name of the supervising sound editor (R.J. Kizer). Note the piece of information on the far left hand side of the header. This is very important information—Cued: First/Last Mod. This tells the ADR mixer exactly how the ADR was cued, that there were no pre-frames built into the cue, as was the practice a few years ago.

The next line of information tells us the count (what cue number the line is). As in the traditional ADR form technique, the first number denotes what reel of the project is being cued. The last three numbers refer to each cue in numerical order.

The next item of information is the In/Out, referring, of course, to the first frame of modulation of the line to be replaced and the last frame. Before automation ADR software that will actually drive the recorders, we usually built in one extra foot after the last detected frame of modulation. This allowed for overtones so they would not sound clipped. *Note*: The In/Out counts have *both* 35-mm feet and frames as well as time code.

The next item of information is the name of the character that Lindsay Lohan plays in the film *Ashley*.

The next very important piece of information is the version identification. On *Starship Troopers* I had to keep 18 version cuts straight, so you really need to know to what version the cue feet and frame/time code numbers sync with.

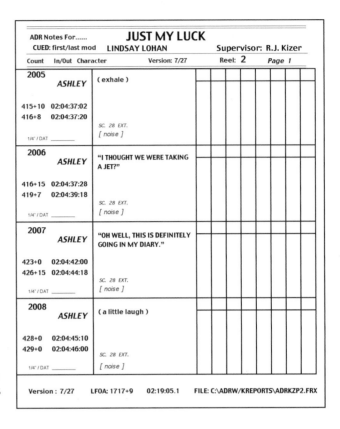

ADR Notes For......	**JUST MY LUCK**		
CUED: first/last mod	**LINDSAY LOHAN**		Supervisor: R.J. Kizer
Count In/Out Character	Version: 7/27	Reel: **2**	*Page 1*

2005 ASHLEY	(exhale)
415+10 02:04:37:02 416+8 02:04:37:20	
1/4" / DAT _____	SC. 28 EXT. [noise]
2006 ASHLEY	"I THOUGHT WE WERE TAKING A JET?"
416+15 02:04:37:28 419+7 02:04:39:18	
1/4" / DAT _____	SC. 28 EXT. [noise]
2007 ASHLEY	"OH WELL, THIS IS DEFINITELY GOING IN MY DIARY."
423+0 02:04:42:00 426+15 02:04:44:18	
1/4" / DAT _____	SC. 28 EXT. [noise]
2008 ASHLEY	(a little laugh)
428+0 02:04:45:10 429+0 02:04:46:00	
1/4" / DAT _____	SC. 28 EXT. [noise]

Version : 7/27   LFOA: 1717+9   02:19:05.1   FILE: C:\ADRW/KREPORTS\ADRKZP2.FRX

Figure 16.4 A computer program printout for the first few ADR lines for R-2 of *Just My Luck*.

In this case the date (July 27) is used as the identifying version number.

The next item of information tells us what reel has been cued (in this case reel 2).

The last item of information on this line is the page number.

Note the fine print under the In/Out footage/time code numbers. $^1/_4$" / DAT roll designation. The ADR mixer will tell the supervising ADR editor in what $^1/_4$" or DAT roll he or she can find the back-up protection.

There are three pieces of information in the next box to the right of each cue number. The first bold type is obviously the cue itself. If it is not actually dialog, but breaths, grunts, sights, exhales, or other vocal peculiarities, they are listed as such in parentheses. Dialog is listed in quotes.

The second piece of information in this box is in fine type near the bottom of each box—Scene Number, Int. or Ext.

The third piece of information in this box is also in fine brackets under the scene number—the explanation of why the line is being replaced. In this case, because of [Noise].

At the bottom of each page, the software will repeat the version date (or number). It also lists the LFOA (also known as LFOP; the last frame of action). In this case it is 1,717 feet plus 9 frames. This tells us instantly that this is an A-B reel, and not the traditional 1,000-foot reels that were described in Chapter 7. The next number is the time code frame of the LFOA (02:19:05.1; this tells us that it is reel 2, 19 minutes, 5 seconds, and 1 frame).

The next piece of information tells us the exact file that Kizer produced to make this cued report.

All that said and done, there are many ways to approach producing ADR cue sheets with software. You can spend a great deal of money (on average $2,000) or you can use much more cost-effective variations.

One of the reasons why you really want to use properly authored software for cueing your ADR is that the supervising ADR editor can show up on the stage, hand a disk of the file that he or she has produced (a TAB delimited text file).

The mixer will take this disk and enter the file into the computer system in the stage's recording booth equipment system. One popular system is the Colin-Broad VS-P2, which allows direct entry of cues from a remote keyboard, downloading an ADR list to both SR/MR Controller and the Video Streamer (CBServer Software). It requires the Video Streamer with RS422 processor board and EPROM update. Set the SR/MR system to Auto/ADR—the list will be entered on both the SR/MR and the Video Streamer. Many major ADR stages today are set with this system to read the time code numbers and automatically set up each cue.

The Video Streamer is a wipe-streaming projection device that will automatically project a white traveling wipe or streamer across the screen, just like we used to make by hand in the old days with a grease pencil and ruler, drawing them right onto the 35-mm picture dupes. For further information, you can check out this and other devices by Colin-Broad at their website, colinbroad.com.

VoiceQ—for ADR, Foley, and Dubbing

We all know that dialog replacement is an integral part of filmmaking, and depending on your director, it can be a nightmare experience. We who have had to endure the instant preparation expectations of clients and suffered the promises of so many software products have gotten tired of the big-If syndrome. If you rename your audio tracks with certain key letter inclusions so that the software will understand what to do with it. . . . If you have enough money to afford the huge expense that certain packages entail. . . . If, If, If!

KIWA International Ltd., out of Auckland, New Zealand, has developed a system that really does seem to fit the supervising ADR's dreams and fantasies, VoiceQ. After extensive chats with R.J. Kizer, and looking into the product myself, I contacted David Kite of KIWA and invited him to formally present his product in this chapter where it is a welcome consideration:

> It is common practice to re-record and synchronize the majority of dialog and sound effects after filming is complete. In addition, do not forget all the work that accompanies the translation of most movies into alternate languages for release in foreign markets.

The two most common forms of queing actors in an ADR session are streamers and 3 beeps just prior to the cue to be re-performed. A streamer works by cueing in the actor through the use of a vertical line that moves in succession across each frame until the event is reached, which is the cue to start. We just spoke of this technique by using the Colin-Broad cue projection device.

The 3-beep method aligns a loop with the movement on screen and cues the actor using a series of three audio beeps. On the fourth "silent" beep the actor reads the loop and attempts to match the voiceover aligned with the voice movements and performance on screen.

While these methods can be considered industry standards for expediting the ADR process, they are both highly inefficient. Multiple repetitions may be required to ensure accurate synchronization with the footage, time wastage often occurs in setting up and waiting for the cue event, and any dialog changes are made manually in the recording studio. The result is a significant loss of time, and thus reduced productivity and efficiency.

VoiceQ expedites the dialog replacement process during audio postproduction through visual on-screen cues. The Apple Mac digital software products and VoiceQ ADR and VoiceQ DUB can be standalone or integrated seamlessly with any Pro Tools and any other recording systems via MIDI time code. VoiceQ ADR was conceived for automated dialog replacement, which is the practice of re-recording parts of the dialog in the original language to obtain optimal sound quality. VoiceQ DUB has been designed for dubbing, the replacement of one language with another.

The principal function of both VoiceQ ADR and VoiceQ DUB is to scroll the dialog across the screen in sync with the film. This is achieved with such a level of accuracy that actors can literally see when to start each individual word that they need to speak, which makes their task considerably easier enabling them to give a better performance in considerably less time. Preparation of ADR sessions outside the recording studio further reduces cost and valuable recording time.

A VoiceQ session consists of the live video stream with the lines to be spoken by the actor scrolling across the bottom of the screen from right to left. At the left-hand side of the screen is a vertical line. When a word hits the line, it is time for that word to be spoken. Lines for different actors are distinguished by color and vertical alignment, allowing for multiple actors to be recorded simultaneously. Symbols and characters can be added to facilitate interpretation and expression of the dialog as well as for Foley and sound editing. A line may be previewed on screen upon request and a host of other features are available for all key production personnel. Although a multitude of reports for scheduling and other purposes are provided VoiceQ advocates paperless processes.

The VoiceQ Screen consists of three distinct sections. The Script Editor section enables input and editing of dialog, scenes, comments, time code parameters, character assignment, and progress tracking of each line.

The Timeline Editor section includes synchronization of lines, words and symbols, scrolling speed, zoom in/out, toggle text, time code, and preview line on/off. Selection of the language to be displayed and the FPS rate and Offset as appropriate. Play control deck for standalone mode. The Character Editor section can add and edit Foley category and characters, select dialog by character(s), filter by character, and change colors and altitude of dialog displayed on screen by character.

When a word hits the yellow vertical line it is time for the actor to speak that word. Synchronizing each word allows for gasps, breaths, and silence within a line.

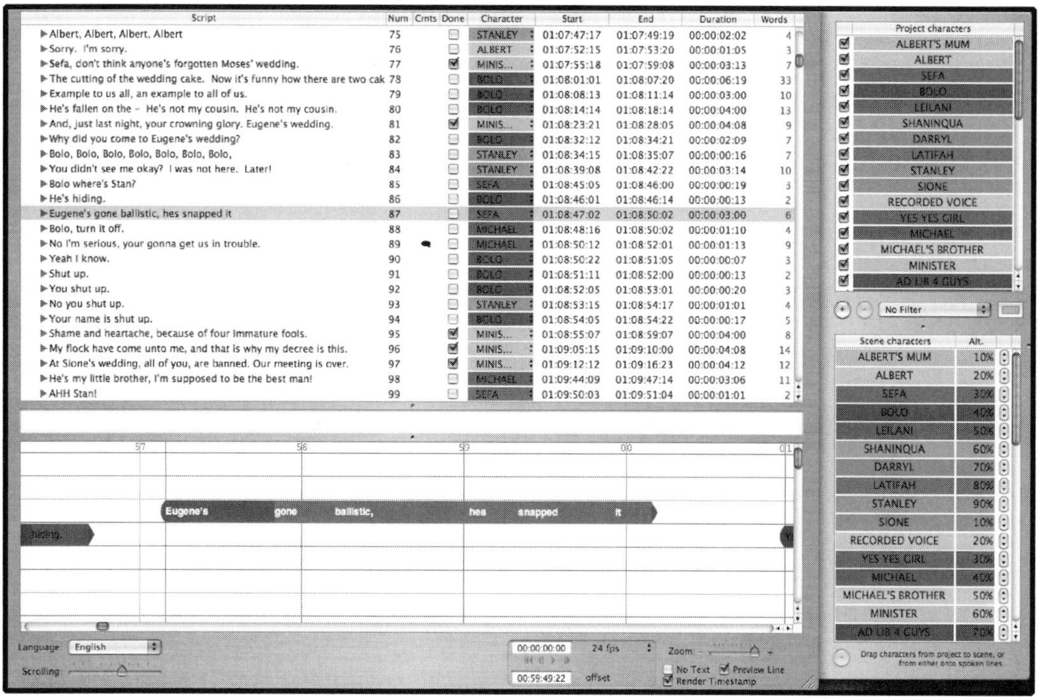

Figure 16.5 The main VoiceQ screen.

Text is overlayed live onto a QuickTime format of the film and can be output to an external monitor, TV, or projector. Overlaying of text enables changes to be made on the fly and immediately displayed on screen. Note that each character is color coded to allow for multiple actor recording.

Dragging lines and words using the audio waveform makes the synchronization process easy and updates all other areas of the application automatically.

VoiceQ provides a host of preferences to suit the user, actor, ADR supervisor as well as the audio engineer and mixer.

VoiceQ is Unicode, enabling the selection of any language for translation and dubbing for foreign markets. Some of the features of VoiceQ are:

- Scrolling synchronized dialog over video
- Simple drag and drop features
- Multi-language capability
- Manual and automated script input
- Spotting, detection, and adaptation functionality
- Frame-accurate cueing
- Feature-rich reporting and character filter functionality
- Real time on-the-fly script editing
- Works as standalone or in conjunction with Pro Tools LE and Pro Tools TDM systems

Figure 16.6 VoiceQ on screen output.

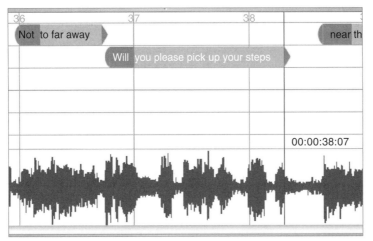

Figure 16.7 Synchronization of dialog.

- Includes MIDI time code generator
- Output through DVI- or S-Video to external monitor, TV, or projector
- Configurable on-screen presentations
- Automated file saving
- FPS or feet and frames
- Choice of scrolling or static script cue
- Automated line referencing, notes, and progress tracking
- Jog wheel option with user-definable key mapping
- Abundance of quick keys for common functions

  Some of the VoiceQ benefits:

- Better for actors
  - No more paper; read the script directly off the screen
  - Record with other cast members for improved dramatic interplay
  - Improved dramatic interpretation and comedic timing

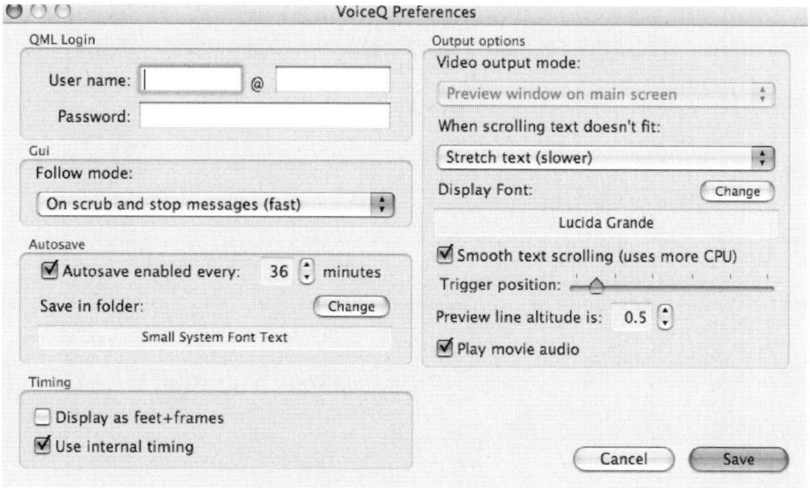

Figure 16.8 VoiceQ Preferences.

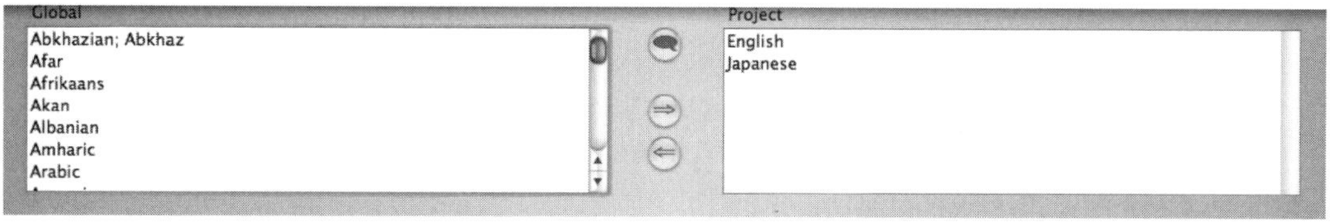

Figure 16.9 VoiceQ Project Languages.

- Better for directors/ADR supervisors
  - Reduced recording time leaves more time for creative play
  - Make your script changes and display on-screen instantaneously
  - Reference the original script against other iterations and languages
- Better for engineers
  - Greater accuracy means halving the time spent in editing
  - Perfectly timed streaming Foley symbols and notes give you greater accuracy and control
  - Completing projects in half the time means quicker throughput of projects
- Better for producers
  - Streamlined processes means less time and costs in actors
  - Improved production standards mean lower costs in postproduction
  - Greater accuracy gives you a better sounding and synchronized product
- Better for your business
  - Simplicity of VoiceQ means you can diversify your business
  - Financial and qualitative advantages of VoiceQ may make gains in margin and turnover
  - Keeping your film secure on an external drive means you only need to plug it into VoiceQ when needed

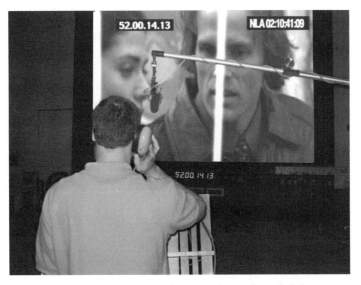

Figure 16.10 Actor preparing to replace a line of dialog.

ADR STAGE: THE CREW

ADR Mixer

The ADR mixer must be highly experienced in the use and placement of various microphones and must know how to listen to the production track and match the colorization and timbre of the ADR stage microphone so that the actor's voice blends into the production track as seamlessly as possible. In addition, the ADR mixer must be a politician, knowing when to guide and handhold and when to remain quiet and step back.

The ADR stage is known for everything from making magic to provoking bouts of fisticuffs. Tempers flare and feelings get trampled. The ADR mixer de facto becomes both host and problem solver, but the mixer almost always has the last word. Most ADR mixers whom I have met are slightly reserved, politically smart individuals who know how to focus on the good of the show and how to guide the temperaments of all concerned toward a constructive end.

The great ADR mixers are extremely comfortable and smooth with their equipment. With what seems like effortless magic, the mixer rolls the tape, presses the in-line mike, and slates the multi-track and DAT back-up recorder. "Cue four-oh-three take five, channel six."

A beat later the three rhythmic ADR beeps sound, and, on the silent fourth, the actor performs the line. Without being asked, the mixer quickly rewinds the tape and hits the talk-back button so all on the stage can hear. "Playback."

The tape rolls, and everybody hears the production track. At exactly the right moment, the mixer mutes the production dialog as take 5/channel 6 plays back the new performance. The mixer smoothly slips out the production track exactly at the end of the cue so those on stage can get a sense of how the new line sounds.

Figure 16.11 ADR recording engineer Derek Casari prepares to record for an ADR on the ADR stage at 20th Century Fox. (Photo by John LeBlanc.)

We wait for a response from the director. Is it a circled take, and we go on to the next cue, or do we try another take of this cue? It is a circled take, and yes the director wants to try another one. The mixer calmly switches off channel 6. "Save channel 6, moving on to channel 7." The recordist makes the appropriate note on the ADR protection report, and they roll the videotape to try it again. The instant feedback may help ease the actor into relaxing about the process and help toward a successful and rewarding completion.

ADR Recordist

The ADR recordist supports the ADR mixer. The recordist is responsible for receiving either the film dupes or the videotapes of the picture prior to the ADR session. If the session is being synced to videotape, the recordist spins down to the 1-minute time code designation and checks if the tape really is drop or nondrop time code as advertised on the label. Many times people just assume the label is filled out correctly, and even more frequently, the video transfer facility fails to list the technical specifications at all.

If the videotape is drop frame, the visual time code numbers (note the semicolon for the frame count) jump from 01:00:59;29 to 01:01:00;02, skipping over 2 frames. Obviously, if the tape is nondrop, the visual time code numbers (note that it is a colon and not a semicolon for the frame count) simply flip from 01:00:59:29 to 01:01:00:00.

Once the time code rate has been determined and verified, the recordist makes sure that the proper number of multi-track audiotapes (such as 2″ 24-track analog or 1″ 48-track digital) have been properly degaussed and time code striped for the upcoming work. The recordist prepares all labels for the multi-track masters as well as the ¼″ or digital DAT back-ups. The recordist also lays down line-up tones on all tapes, making sure that all channels are recording properly and that the stock is stable and reproducing properly. The recordist further confirms that the signal path from the mixer's console is patched through the noise-reduction encoders and that the right console fader assignments indeed go to the correct input channel on the recorder.

The recordist also does a shakedown run of the videotapes supplied by the ADR supervisor, making sure that the time code is reading correctly and that the production track on channel 1 is playing clearly. Videotapes are not all transferred with equal attention to quality or time code. The last thing you want is to run an ADR session and discover that your videotape has dropouts in the time code. If you do not have a good back-up tape at your disposal, the entire session can come to a screeching halt, or at least to a short-tempered delay.

At the start of the ADR session, the recordist takes the ADR sheets from the ADR supervisor and sets them up so that the mixer is only concerned with the business at hand. The recordist keeps all paperwork and organizational chores out of the mixer's way so that the mixer can focus on balancing the microphones and capturing the actors' performances clearly without distortion or unwanted noise.

As the ADR session progresses, the recordist methodically and carefully maintains the back-up digital DAT, checking that each cue has its own program number (PNO) and determining which takes are requested by the director as "circled" takes. The recordist monitors the playback head of the multichannel, vigilantly listening for any breakup, distortion, or other anomalies that inhibit a successful audio conclusion.

Up to this point, another option to fix it existed all the way down the line from the first day of principal photography, but not anymore. Nobody else can fix it. You either get the recording clean or you fail. At the first sign of clicks, pops, distortion, or other unwanted noise, including squeaks from the actor pivoting around on a stool too much, the recordist flags the mixer (who may not be hearing it from the pre-record head position), who then asks for a retake or diplomatically informs the talent that they are making unwanted noise.

The recordist ultimately is responsible for seeing that the master multi-track is either delivered to the client, goes to the transfer department to transfer the circled takes to whatever medium the editor dictates, or downloaded into a digital workstation format such as Pro Tools.

Microphone Choice and Placement

A most important factor in good ADR recording is the choice of microphone. As discussed earlier, not all microphones have the same colorization or character. The ADR mixer needs to know exactly what microphones the production mixer used on the set, so that the same model of microphone is used to record the ADR.

Often I pick up a production roll and find no mention of the microphones on the sound report, not even the model or head stack configuration of the sound recorder itself is listed. Although many production mixers do recite an audio checklist at the head of each production roll before they roll their line-up tone, it must be assumed, as often is the case, that the production roll is not in easy access to the ADR mixer; if the production mixer had listed the recorder and microphone information on the sound report, it would be instantly available.

At any rate, the ADR mixer needs to know the model of microphone used in order to duplicate the audio texture and colorization, so that the new ADR lines flow as

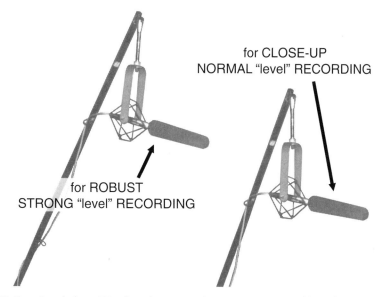

for CLOSE-UP
NORMAL "level" RECORDING

for ROBUST
STRONG "level" RECORDING

Figure 16.12 Two Sennheiser 416 microphones used on an ADR stage. Although there is no need to use windscreens indoors, the mixer leaves on the windscreens because they were used on the microphone during exterior filming. The mixer tries to recreate the exact colorization of the microphones so that the ADR lines better match the production performance.

seamlessly as possible with the original production material against which they are cut. Otherwise, the audience will be mentally yanked out of the performance of the scene because the ADR lines glaringly stand out from production.

Most ADR stages have two matching microphones set up for the session. The first microphone is approximately 2 feet from the actor, slightly higher than the forehead and angled downward toward the mouth. At this distance, a de-popper screen in not needed, but some actors have a well-trained stage voice that requires protection from their powerful "P"s (as Christopher Lee apologized to me once, "Ah yes, I have vented many a theatre.")

The second microphone is placed farther back from the first, between 4 and 6 feet, depending on the perspective required. This microphone is also slightly higher than the closer mike. With this configuration, the ADR mixer can switch from one microphone to the next to achieve a more desirable perspective in matching the original production track. Without the two-microphone set-up, the ADR mixer constantly must get up, go out into the stage, and readjust the microphone position from cue to cue, wasting precious time and accelerating the fatigue and irritability factors. The only time to move the close-up microphone any nearer the actor is on those rare occasions when recording intimate whispering and extremely subtle vocals that require the microphone ultra close. Be very careful about the popping "P"s and hard consonants with this in-your-face proximity.

ADR Protection Report

The ADR supervisor sits on the ADR stage near the acting talent, interacting with them and the director. The recordist maintains the multi-track recorder and digital back-up DAT. The recordist keeps track of the ADR cue number and lists each take and its channel. If the back-up is made to ¼″ tape, the recordist notes the time code start. If the back-up is being made to a digital DAT, the recordist notes the PNO that the DAT machine assigns to the tape each time it rolls.

The recordist also circles those takes the director and/or ADR supervisor want to keep. These takes are protected on the multi-track recorder. The mixer does not record over those channels if additional attempts at the performance of that cue are requested.

Note that the protection report also lists microphones used, tape speed, whether noise reduction was used and what kind, and so forth. Always prepare these forms as if someone with absolutely no knowledge of your procedures and protocol is working with the material and cannot converse with you on the phone if they have questions.

A.D.R. PROTECTION REPORT page: ____ -of- ____

TITLE: ________ TAPE #: ____ DATE: ____ STAGE: ____

PROD. CO.: ________ ☐ 1/4" ☐ NAB ☐ DOLBY A ☐ DOLBY SR

MIXER: ________ ☐ DAT ☐ CCIR ☐ NON-DOLBY

RECORDIST: ________ ☐ FULLTRACK ☐ OTHER SYNC on channel ____

☐ -10dB Right ☐ COPY

HEAD TONES: ________

MICROPHONES: ________ ☐ 59.97 ☐ 60 Hz ☐ TIME CODE ____

CUE #	TAKES	ch	timecode	DAT PNO	NOTES

Figure 16.13 An ADR protection report.

Additionally, a copy of the ADR protection report is kept in the multi-track tape box. A copy is also given to the ADR supervisor, especially valuable because of the DAT PNOs.

Several years ago a mixer shipped out a good amount of material in great haste without filling out the necessary information. He simply told the messenger that the transfer man should call with any questions the next day. Sad but true, the mixer had a fatal heart attack that evening. Also sadly, the transfer man was left with many unanswered questions.

ISDN Telecommunications Interlock

Sometimes it is not possible for economic or scheduling reasons that directors and actors can be in the same place at the same time. Increasingly, telecommunication ADR sessions are necessary. Say three actors in a film live in New York. The director must oversee their ADR session but also must remain in Los Angeles for another postproduction task. Do not fear, many ADR stages now offer digital interlockable sessions. Book an ADR stage in New York and schedule the three actors to show up for their lines. At the same time, book a small ADR or viewing stage in Los Angeles. Both stages hook up and interlock using an ISDN line. Logically, these kinds of sessions are simply referred to as "ISDN session"—that was a real stretch. One line handles the time code feed, while a second line handles the digital audio feed of the actors' performance as heard through the mixer's console. A third line handles the communication feed for the director and/or ADR supervisor to communicate with the actors just as if they were on stage with them.

The New York and Los Angeles stages both have identical picture (film prints, videotapes or QuickTime video files) with matching production track. The third line with time code interlocks the Los Angeles videotape machine and slaves it to the mechanism of the New York machine. The digital audio feed is decoded through a quality digital-to-analog decoder on the Los Angeles stage and played through a good speaker system. The price of the hours of phone lines is a fraction of the cost of flying the actors to Los Angeles, paying per diem and expenses, or for the director and/or ADR supervisor to fly back to New York.

THE RETURN OF THE LOOPING TECHNIQUE

As frustration mounts over the issue that the director cannot get the actor to recapture the magic of the production track, one starts to look for alternatives. Naturally, if the production track just did not have that jet noise over the dialog, or if the actor had not been so far off-mike—the what-if's mount up like dead insects in a bug-zapper.

Forget the what-if's—you will just have to place more emphasis on giving the production mixer what he or she needs to record better production tracks for your next project. You have to overcome the frustration of the here and now. When you have acting talent that is not classically trained, you are almost always going to have to replace more dialog during the postproduction phase.

Almost all first-time actors are inhibited and intimidated by the beeps in the ears and concentrating on a poorly projected image of themselves on a screen or on a monitor as they try to match the lips in sync. As they have to pay attention to doing all of this, they cannot possibly concentrate on acting the performance. Isn't that what all of this is about?

The actress just could not make it happen. The stage clock was clicking off the hourly rate, the director was frustrated that he wasn't getting the performance, the actress could not walk and chew gum as the producer's thermometer was rising, foreshadowing an oncoming stroke.

I turned to the ADR mixer and signaled him to shut it down. He was recording straight to a Pro Tools session. I asked him to cut away the production track on either side of the actress's line, highlight the line as much after it and a couple of seconds more. "Go up to Options and select Record Loop," I told him.

I went onto the stage where the actress was about to pull her hair out. The director was literally pacing. I gestured to my ears for her. I told her that she would hear her line in her headsets, then there would be a silent space and then she would hear her line again. Forget looking at the screen, forget trying to sync your lips to what you see. "Close your eyes and listen to your line, and then during the silence that follows, perform your line—all I want you to do is focus on being an actress and bring forth your character. You will hear it again, and you will perform it again, with a different inflection maybe. Forget the technical bull#%!* and just act!"

The director looked at me suspiciously as I turned. I winked at him and gave the ADR mixer the signal to roll. The actress held her headsets close to her ear and closed her eyes. After a couple of times just listening to her line, she started to repeat it, re-performing it—and the difference was night and day. Suddenly we were getting a performance—the character that was on the screen started to come to life.

Sounds just like the technique we talked about at the top of the chapter, at the studio that had all the actors loop all of their lines every day, no matter what. Well it works. And using the Record Loop option in the Pro Tools menu makes it easy.

It is also amazing how much material you can do in an hour using this method. Instead of six to eight lines an hour using the ADR method, we were easily doing 10 to 15. You sacrifice the toy playback machine for the director to roll back and forth after each take and review the ADR line in sync, which is not in sync most of the time anyway. What you gain is an actor who can become an actor again. Which method you choose to employ is up to you.

Though the Loop Record mode works extremely well with digital video QuickTime files (so you can loop your visual picture in sync with your audio loop), the method of not using a picture reference transcends the technical prowess of technology and allows the actor to concentrate on his or her acting.

Remember, we are servants to the performance on the screen. All the rest of this technical minutiae is just that, techno-wizardry mumbo-jumbo. Personally, I believe in the KISS principle, "keep it short and simple"; and when it comes to the art form on the screen and the need to serve the actor in his or her ability to capture that performance, then I am about making it as simple and streamlined as possible.

Recording Dialog Using the Looping Technique

The technique is the same no matter what nonlinear system you use. Figure 16.14 shows a Pro Tools session with a line of dialog that has been isolated and highlighted so that

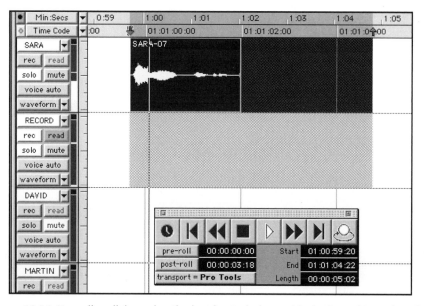

Figure 16.14 Recording dialog using the looping technique with the Record Loop function.

the line will play back for the actor, and then the same amount plus a couple of extra seconds during the silent phase so the actor can re-perform the line that he or she just heard. Once the recording head (the line that crosses from left to right) reaches the end of the highlighted area it will immediately loop back and repeat again.

The key is to get set up properly. First of all, whether you were going to hold an ADR session or a loop session, you would have transferred the cut work track from the locked picture into your work session. Refer to the section in Chapter 18, "Importing."

Prior to the looping session, the ADR editor (who has now, technically, become a loop editor) would have built a session for each reel of film. In this case the actress's character name is Sara. The loop editor would break out and isolate each character's lines to be looped and place them in their own channels. Rename each audio channel with the actor's character name. Refer to the section in Chapter 18, "Renaming Audio Channels."

This makes it much easier and efficient during the actual looping session to jump to the next line to be done, thereby not wasting the actor's time, waiting for the looping mixer to scroll down and find each line and prepare it during the looping stage time, which is one thing you want to avoid.

Move the track that has the character lines that you are going to be looping to the top of the session. Name the second audio channel "Record." This is the channel that you will actually record the new looped lines that the actor on the stage will re-perform.

Activate the solo buttons on the character channel (in this case, Sara) that you wish to hear as well as the Record channel that you are going to record to. This will mute all other channels in your session.

Open the Show Mix Window under Display in the menu bar. You need to assign all your character channels, those channels that have the cut-up production track and are meant for the actor to listen to, to output 1. Refer to Chapter 18.

Some actors wish to be able to hear their own voice as they are re-performing the line during the silent space; some would rather not hear it, as it may be distracting. If the actor wants to hear his or her voice, then you need to also assign the output of the Record channel to output 1. If not, simply assign it to output 2 so that only the looping mixer can hear in the booth and the director and loop editor can hear through their own headsets. This means that you need to have a headset signal path that can bifurcate the playback signal from the actor and the director and loop editor. The loop editor will control who will be able to hear what from the outboard mixing console.

While you are in the Show Mix Window mode, make sure that your input channel assignment for the Record channel is the same channel that the line input feed that carries the signal from the stage microphone(s) are plugged into. Refer to the section in Chapter 18, "The Interface I/O."

Make sure you engage the rec button on the Record channel. This is an arming safety. You will not record anything if this button is not on.

Now select Show Transport Window under Display in the menu bar. The Transport Window will appear. This is your tape recorder, complete with all the controls to interlock, record, play, stop, etc.

Using the Line tool, highlight from the front edge of the cue to be looped and continue on again for as long as and a couple of seconds longer. This allows a comfortable amount of time for the actor to re-perform the cue in between the playback phases. If the actor is a little slow in responding to re-perform, you may have to open the distance up a little wider. With a cue or two you will immediately sense how much extra time you should allow for each actor's style and ability.

Take the cursor and press the button on the far right-hand side of the Transport Window. This is the Record Arming switch. Once you have armed the Transport Window you are ready to roll. When you press the Play button (the triangle button that points to the right), the record head (line) will start scrolling across the highlighted area. You will hear the dialog line from the channel above and then during the following blank area, and the actor will re-perform the line, which will be recorded in the Record channel.

Once the actor has re-performed the line (as many times as the actor and/or loop editor and director may want), then press the black square button in the center of the Transport Window. This is the Stop button. A bold file name will appear in the region list; it will read "RECORD 01"; refer to Chapter 17. You can tap twice on this file name of the cue you just recorded. A window will pop up for you to rename this cue. Simply enter the character name and cue number that is advertised on the loop editor's ADR sheet.

Note: Remember that if you end a file name with a number, it is a good idea to put a slash after it. Take the cue above as an example. The time code hour tells us that this is reel 1. The loop editor's cue sheet shows this line as cue 107. You tapped twice on the file and named it "SARA 107/". This will avert disk management confusion when the cue is cut. Pro Tools automatically renames a cut clip with a dash and sequential number assignment (i.e., -01, -02, -03). If you named the audio cue "SARA 107," a cut clip name may read "SARA 107-07." A visual scan may become confusing to the human eye. If, on the other hand, you named it "SARA 107/"—a clip name will read "SARA 107/-07," a much easier number to visually scan.

It will also prevent you from relying on Pro Tools to automatically name your audio clips, which presented us with a disaster when we had inherited a show that had been started by another sound editorial facility. Their protocols were not anywhere near professional and experienced and they had allowed Pro Tools to auto-name based on the name of the audio channel. During the course of the ADR sessions, they had a particular actress come in over seven sessions. Each session started with a new session. When we got the show we discovered that we had seven identical names for seven different performances. "JANICE-09" was being seen by the computer seven different times and of course did not know which "JANICE-09" was the correct one to select to boot up the Pro Tools cut session. In such a case it defaults to the first one it sees, which most of the time is the wrong one. So you can see that there is more than one reason to be particular about your audio cue name protocol.

Remember what we talked about in Chapter 11; this is the part number for this series of performances for this line.

Once you have completed recording the loops for this reel, simply Save and Close this reel session and open up the next reel session and continue the process.

Once you have finished with this actor, simply move the track which holds the original lines (in this case SARA) down from the top position, somewhere below the Record channel, then move the next character channel up to the top to more easily work with the next actor. You will find that you can move along very swiftly and the difference in the performance material will amaze you.

If the director wishes to see a line in sync with the picture, you can easily pull the line in from the region list, align the waveform against the original line, place the session in interlock by Apple keystroke J, and play the videotape back.

The director should not be encouraged to do this too often as this will slow the session down to a snail's pace. The director should get used to reviewing the scene prior to looping the sequence, and then listen to the actor re-performing. Remember what we said about the importance of developing a visual memory in Chapter 7? The same is true for directors.

Remote Location Looping

By now the ADR supervisor has all but two of the film's actors accounted for; those two are on other projects. One is on location in Lapland in the northern part of Finland, the other is shooting in Kenya, both remote locations with no ADR facilities nearby. The ADR supervisor has talked to the production companies of both projects, and both are willing to collaborate in getting the dialog looped. Great, but how do we actually do it?

Using a variation of looping, you take a page from that technique manual and give it a little different spin. The ADR supervisor scrolls through the picture editor's cut track (also known as a DIA 1:1, PIX DIA track) on the digital workstation, ferreting out all the lines the two actors must re-perform. The ADR supervisor (or assistant) digitally copies each line and groups them together, one after the other.

You can do this one of two ways: Check with either the sound facility or the production mixer on location where the distant location talent is located and see what they are capable of doing. If they have a nonlinear editing platform, you can simply send a CD-R or DVD-R with the audio files to be replaced along with a Pro Tools session that the ADR supervisor had prepareded to make the job easier for the distant location recording them.

If they do not have a nonlinear editing platform, they most certainly will have a digital DAT recorder, so make a DAT copy from your workstation's DAT machine and feed in 30 seconds of –18-dB line-up tone. Then highlight the first line, and again as much blank with an extra couple of beats as blank space. Go up the Options menu and drag down and choose Loop Playback.

Roll your DAT tape and play the line and subsequent blank space. It will play, then loop and play again, loop and play, loop and play again. Let it record at least 12 to 15 repetitions. Then stop the playback. Do not stop the DAT machine immediately. If you press the Rec Mute button, the DAT machine will record 5 seconds of silence before it stops and parks itself in a record stand-by pause mode. This also allows the actor on location to know you are moving on to the next cue.

Highlight the next dialog cue the same way you did the first one, then repeat the recording process. Take clear and accurate notes of which dialog cues are at which DAT PNO. Put each of the two actors on his or her own separate DAT tapes, as they are heading off to two different parts of the globe.

When the digital DAT and a copy of your ADR notes arrives in Lapland, the actor and production mixer get together after their day's shoot or on their off-day. The production mixer in Finland should know where to find a good acoustically flat-sounding environment to record. It is helpful if the ADR supervisor adds any interior or exterior notes. Such indications guide the production mixer in deciding the kind of environmental deadening necessary. He or she may string up a couple of packing blankets or angled cardboard sheets to trap and flatten reflection or slap.

The production mixer sets up a DAT machine to play back the source DAT you sent. The mixer then plugs in a set of headphones for the actor so that the actor can hear the dialog lines as they repeat themselves loop style.

The production mixer sets up a second DAT machine or a 1/4" deck. The note that the ADR supervisor sent along also specifies the kinds of microphones used on the original shoot. If the production mixer does not use the exact kind of microphone, one is chosen from the mixer's own set that comes as close as possible to the texture and colorization.

The production mixer lays down line-up tones, then rolls the playback DAT machine as the recorder is rolled. In the headsets, the actor hears the line to be looped; then he or she repeats the line during the silent part of the recording, just like traditional looping procedures. This technique works extremely well when you have no method of getting your acting talent to a real ADR stage.

Inhuman Vocalities

On many occasions you may want to use a human voice to perform character grunts, whines, growls and barks of dogs, monkeys, cats, pigs, horses, rhinos—all kinds of creatures. Vocal specialists can emulate huge nostril snorts of bulls, for example; other specialists create unearthly creatures that defy description. As you can imagine, these talented individuals cost more for a day's work than a standard Group Walla vocalist. If you think their price too high, try going out in the pasture with your DAT machine and recording an angry bull snorting. Some cinematic creatures need an entire team of vocal specialists just to create the wide range of vocals, breaths, snorts, and gutturals—no one person can do it all.

Group Walla

The director is filming two actors sitting in a lounge, talking over drinks in the intimate setting of a booth. A couple can be seen sitting in a booth behind the main characters. Occasionally someone walking by or a waitress delivering drinks can be seen. The rest of the bar is brought to life by cutting sound effects of, say, a bartender making drinks off-camera, maybe an occasional cigarette machine movement. Depending on the kind of bar scene, the editor might cut in occasional billiard sounds. The sound effects editor pulls some cocktail lounge Crowd Walla, everything from intimate conversational murmur to three guys chuckling at the bar to occasional chatter from the back billiard room. This is a classic situation for Group Walla. The sound effects editor lays some library Walla tracks, but the unique specificity of the scene is developed and borne out of the recording of custom Group Walla.

Organized groups specialize in hiring out Walla groups as needed. The supervising sound editor or ADR supervisor chooses a group and has the group leader look at a videotape of the film, along with some initial conceptual thoughts of their goals. After the group leader looks at the videotape, he or she meets with the supervising sound editor and ADR supervisor to go over notes. Working within the confines of budget restraints, they work together to structure how many voices the budget can afford and how much time will be allocated on an ADR stage. They discuss the need for specialized ethnic or dialect requirements. There may be a need for a session where vocal talent is auditioned for inclusion in the Group Walla session.

The more languages and/or different vocal inflections a vocal talent can bring to a session, the more apt that individual is to work consistently. Sounding different on demand throughout a film is very cost-effective. In big crowd sequences, every vocal performer in the group should field numerous voices, as the ADR mixer records the group several times in the same scene, layering each recording until the Walla Group of 12 to 15 men and women sounds like hundreds.

There is an important footnote to atmospheric foreign language Group Walla. Unless you personally speak the language, either ask the actors what they are saying or brief them with a strict set of performance parameters regarding slang. On one such picture, we were surprised to hear Vietnamese theatre goers laughing hysterically during a serious sequence where the hero is hiding in the reeds of a Vietnamese jungle while a North Vietnamese ambush patrol passes by. It turned out that the Walla Group performers had made up a bit of impromptu dialog where the on-screen North Vietnamese are talking about their command officer. They groused that their leader was probably lost and did not know where the hell they were. Another performer commented that they were sure that *they* were going to be ambushed by a roving American patrol. The idea was not really bad—the humor was nice—except the vocalists peppered the dialog with Vietnamese profanity.

A good supervising sound editor works with both the director and ADR supervisor to write specific off-stage vocal dialog, scripting a more accurate and refined finish to a period picture or a film with much technical hardware. Research a period film, studying news events of the day as well as indigenous nomenclature and slang. Well-thought-out Group Walla scripting and texturing for specific sequences adds an immeasurable spin on the atmospheric hubbub.

For *Moscow on the Hudson*, I secured the services of a group of recently immigrated Russians, who would bring with them the latest and freshest of street terms and translation variations that would best fit the picture. I also used them to check over the dialog editing sessions before they went to the re-recording stage to make certain that there were no mistakes, as my English-only speaking dialog editor did not speak a word of Russian. However, as I pointed out to Paul Mazursky, sound is sound—the phasing of dialog tracks (as we discussed in Chapter 14) would make it unimportant that my dialog editor could speak Russian. He would be able to check alternate takes by audio relationships and I would have a Russian translator, Anastasia, check his work to verify that everything was just right, and it all was.

Recording Group Walla

In the past, most Group Walla sessions were recorded monophonically. The new trend is recording Group Walla stereophonically, especially in big crowd scenes. The Group Walla actors are placed strategically around the ADR stage for a feeling of depth and separation. The ADR mixer records the entire scene with the Group Walla actors standing in a particular position on channels 1 and 2; then the mixer rewinds to the top of the sequence as the actors move to change the spatial placement of their voices. They not only change their physical position in the room but utilize a different colorization and texture to their voices for the next recording pass.

The ADR mixer safeties the first two channels (so they cannot be accidentally recorded over) and then records the next stereophonic pass on channels 3 and 4. The actors move again. The mixer records on the next stereo pair and so on and so forth until they build up a layered crowd that captures the size and energy required.

All these recordings must be recorded flat. No echo or equalization beyond the removal of line or system hums is built into these recordings. It is vital to deliver this material to the mixing stage during predubbing as flat recordings for the re-recording mixer to echo and manipulate as desired. To add echo or other graphic or parametric equalization, especially noise gates or expansion dynamics, prior to the dialog predubbing only traps the dialog mixer into signal processing that cannot be undone if inappropriate.

TECHNIQUES OF CUTTING ADR

Cutting ADR is not like phase-matching production dialog. Although the words are the same (most of the time), the precise rhythm and timing are almost always a little different. Some actors are so good at ADR that the editor just imports the ADR line into the edit session and lines it up against the waveform of the production dialog track. When the editor plays it back against the video picture, it lays in precisely.

Sometimes, it seems that no matter how the editor syncs it up, too much vowel or word squirts out in the middle or at the end. The editor must learn how to study the human mouth when people talk. See how the lips move when they form consonants and vowels. The editor learns all too quickly that when the human mouth closes, extra modulations cannot spill over.

Start by finding a hard consonant in the word you are trying to sync. Good consonant choices are "D"s, "B"s, or "T"s, as they are executed in one frame. Vowels are drawn out over several frames and, as a result, are not good choices to sync to. "S"s and "R"s are equally poor choices, as they begin modulation without a dramatic and precise movement of sync.

Some ADR editors use computer software that assists in sculpting the loop line in to sync to match the waveform from the production track. Like all technological tools, the software is only as good as those using it, and like most digital processing devices must be used like a fine sable brush rather like than a paint roller. The ADR editor probably will have more satisfying results by learning how to edit, rather than by relying on algorithmic shortcuts. With a little practice, the ADR editor learns to sync the hard consonants that dictate precision of visual sync, and then to adjust the vowels and blend them with various combinations and lengths of cross-fades.

With more practice and confidence, the ADR editor learns how to steal consonants and vowels from other readings and words and to massage them into the problematic loop line. This kind of work is only advisable to the master craftsperson, the ADR editor who knows the actor's voice and inflections as well as his own. To misuse this technology and have the reel bounce on the re-recording mix stage can have disastrous effects and erode confidence in the eyes of the director and producer.

The other side of the coin is pure magic. There is an art form of being able to take the actor's voice and, through the skilled hands of the ADR editor, bring forth a better performance than the actor originally gave.

During the ADR session, the director or producer may request that the ADR supervisor cut alternate readings, as they wish to see which performances work best. Tactically, it is not wise to go to the dubbing stage with numerous alternate readings. The re-recording stage costs anywhere from $400 to $800 per hour, and is not to be used as a very expensive audition session.

The smart ADR supervisor has the director and/or producer come to the sound editorial room where the loop lines are prepared. The director and/or producer must listen to the cut material and make selective choices. If it turns out that the director simply cannot decide on a few lines until heard on the dubbing stage, the ADR editor prepares those lines as stage alternates, but at least dozens of other alternate preparations are decided on in advance of the dialog predubbing in a much less expensive environment.

Chapter 17
Foley
The Art of Footsteps, Props, and Cloth Movement

"They had to blame the failure of the picture on something.
So they blamed it on Foley."

– Gary Larsen, from a Far Side *cartoon*

In the early days of sound when the silver screen developed a set of lungs, relatively few sound effects were cut to picture. With rare exceptions, and only on major motion pictures, sound effects were cut when nothing was in the production dialog track. With each picture the studios turned out, fresh ideas of sound methods pushed steadily forward. Both audience enthusiasm and studio competition fueled the furnace of innovative approaches in sound recording and editorial, along with new inventions in theatrical presentation.

Artisans such as William Hitchcock, Sr. (*All Quiet on the Western Front*), Robert Wise (a director who started as a sound editor before he rose to become a picture editor for Orson Welles on *Citizen Kane* and *The Magnificent Ambersons*), Ronald Pierce, Jack Bolger, Gordon Sawyer (Sam Goldwyn's legendary sound director), Roger Heman, and Clem Portman overcame more than just new creative challenges—all also overcame the problems presented by the new technology of sound, dealing with constant changes in new equipment variations and nonstandardization.

JACK FOLEY

Even though the Warner Brothers had been producing several synchronized sound films and shorts as experimentations with Vitaphone's sound-on-disk system, it was John Barrymore's *Don Juan*, which premiered October 26, 1926, at Grauman's Egyptian

Theatre, that thrilled the audience and positively pointed the way for audience acceptance and appeal of sound. These early films synchronized musical scores and some sound effects as they could, but the following year it was Warner Brothers' production of *The Jazz Singer* that sent other studios scrambling to license, adapt, or develop systems of their own. Starting out as a stunt double in the silent era of the mid-1920s at Universal, Jack Foley soon found himself working as assistant director on several pictures filmed on location in the Owens Valley, then shooting inserts and shorts back at the Universal lot. When *The Jazz Singer* opened at the Warner's Theatre on October 6, 1927, with synchronized singing, segments of lip-sync dialog, and a story narrative, it was evident that tremendous opportunities to overcome the new challenges would present themselves.

Universal had finished making *Show Boat* as a silent picture prior to the premiere of *The Jazz Singer* when the studio realized its picture instantly was rendered obsolete. Universal would have to find a way to retrofit it with sound before they released it.

Like so many breakthroughs in technology or procedure, the mother of invention is usually forced into a dedicated ingenuity by individuals with little choice but to do something never done before—not because they want to, but because they have to. Such was the case with people like Jack Foley. Engineers set up a rented Fox-Case sound unit interlocking the recording equipment to the projector so that the picture would be thrown onto a large screen on Stage 10. A 40-piece orchestra, under the direction of Joe Cherniavsky, would perform the music visually to the picture. In an isolated area to the side, Jack Foley and the rest of the sound effect performers also watched the projected picture as they made various sound effects, performing crowd vocals such as laughing and cheering, as well as clapping while the orchestra performed—a technique that became known as "direct-to-picture." The retrofitted soundtrack worked remarkably well, and soon other silent pictures that needed sound were brought to Universal to utilize Stage 10 for similar treatment.

During the first few years of the talkies, sound effects almost always were recorded on the set along with the actors' voices. Many scenes were not filmed using sound equipment and required direct-to-picture effects to augment them. Soon, the advent of optical sound allowed editors to cut an ever-increasing amount of sound effects, including footsteps in precise sync to the picture. Such cutting was considered a sweetening process, adding something that did not already exist in the production soundtrack. As the quality of the extra sound effects grew, however, it became clear that cutting in new sound effects would make a much more dramatic and pristine final sound mix than most of the production recorded sounds. A new labor force emerged, editors dedicated only to cutting sound.

The only footsteps heard in these first sound pictures were the actual footsteps recorded on the set. By the mid-1930s, editors were cutting in footstep sound effects (also known as "footfalls") from the growing new sound libraries to various sequences on an as-needed basis. The technique of cutting in new sound effects grew to the point that most sound editors commonly cut footsteps to all characters throughout the entire picture, all pulled from the studio's sound library. It became more and more difficult to find just the right kinds of sounds in the sound library to meet the growing demand to cover subtle movements and props.

Foley spent most of his time walking the actor's performances over again, using the direct-to-picture technique. By now, Foley and his crew had slowly transformed a small sound stage into a full-time direct-to-picture facility (dedicated to sound effects only), with music being recorded on its own dedicated scoring stage. The film projector was synchronized to an optical film recorder (a specially built 35-mm camera adapted for photographing sound via light impulses) in the machine room as Foley stood in the middle of the sound stage floor, watching the projection screen and performing the selected actor in whatever footsteps and/or movements were made.

The recording mixer was seated behind what was referred to as a control desk (known today as a mixing console), where he or she carefully raised or lowered the volume level, sending the signal back into the machine room to the optical film recorder, watched by the recordist, who carefully monitored the sound quality that came to it.

Of course it was not possible to roll back the recording and listen to the performance for approval. Remember, these still were the days of optical sound. The sound image that had just been recorded went to the film laboratory and was developed before it could be heard. Even if it could be listened to, it could not be backed up and played. Rock-and-roll transport technology was still years in the future.

Sound craftspeople at Universal simply referred to the direct-to-sound stage as Foley's room, but it was when Desilu Studios built its own direct-to-sound stage facility that they officially honored Jack Foley by naming their stage the *Foley stage*. The term stuck and today it is used all over the world.

In those early years many sound editors performed their own custom effects needs, but, as films became able to have customized footsteps from beginning to end, a special performer was needed to walk the entire picture, thereby guaranteeing continuity to footstep characterization and style. A few sound editors spent more time walking Foley cues for other editors, slowly evolving into full-time Foley artists.

During Jack Foley's 40-year career at Universal, he became the footstep performer of choice for movie stars on a regular basis, each of which had individual characteristics. Foley referred to Rock Hudson's footsteps as "deliberate," James Cagney's were "clipped," Audie Murphy's were "springy," Marlon Brando's were "soft," and John Saxon's were "nervous."

Sometimes the amount of sound work to perform would be so heavy that Jack would get his prop man involved, pressing him into walking with him or performing a piece of movement while he concentrated on the primary sound. When Walter Brennan was not busy working on his own picture as an actor, he often spent time walking cues with Foley over at Universal. It was Foley who suggested Brennan put a rock in his shoe, thereby giving Brennan his famous limp.

"You can't just walk the footsteps," recalls Joe Sikorski, a veteran sound editor of nearly 400 pictures and colleague of Jack Foley during the 1950s. "When Jack performed a scene he got into the actor's head, becoming the character. You have to act the part, getting into the spirit of the story. It makes a big difference."

For the epic battle sequence in *Spartacus*, Foley was faced with the unique and exciting challenge in the scene where 10,000 battle-hardened Roman troops pressed forward in a deliberate rhythm as they approached the ridge where Kirk Douglas and the slave army stood. After consultation with director Stanley Kubrick, and knowing

Figure 17.1 Jack Foley had a love and passion for life, which was exactly the way he approached his work. A robust man with an extremely talented mind, Foley always strove to support the storytelling of the film through his "sync-to-picture" customized approach, which the world now refers to as "Foley." (Photo courtesy of the Foley Estate.)

that trumpet brass and heavy drums would be used in the music score, Foley hit upon the idea of putting together hundreds of metal curtain rings and keys strung out on looped cords. He and his assistants stood together on the Foley stage and rhythmically shook the rings in sync to the soldier's feet, creating the extremely effective and frightening effect, uniquely underlining the military might of Rome.

MODERN FOLEY

Alas, the last of the old studio Foley stages has been torn down and rebuilt to service the demands of modern film. Today's Foley stages have evolved into efficient and precisely engineered environments, capable of recording either in analog or digital to a myriad of formats, but most of them lack that really lived-in world that made great audio character.

A talented workforce of specialists known as "Foley artists" (a.k.a. "Foley walkers" or "steppers," now considered demeaning terms by many Foley practitioners) spend a huge portion of their lives living in these acoustical cave-like stages amid an apparent eclectic junkyard.

Figure 17.2 Director Robert Wise made a clean-room bio-suit and stainless steel security pylon available for Joe Sikorski to perform the custom sound effect "Foley cues" for the 1970 techno-thriller *The Andromeda Strain.* (Photo courtesy of the Joe Sikorski.)

These remarkable sound effects warriors immerse themselves in an amazing type of consciousness, consumed by attentive study of how people walk and move and realistic recreation of sounds that replicate a real-life auditory experience for the audience. Foley artists must create sounds with various available props on hand that are made to sound like other props that are not on hand or don't exist to create a sound never before heard.

The most dramatic bodyfall impacts are also created on the Foley stage. Very few recordings in the field can equal the replication of a Foley artist. Years ago, David Carman, a humor illustrator, and his wife visited our sound facility in North Hollywood. I gave them an audio demonstration, playing the various sound effects that make the dramatic magic used to acoustically sell the action. One such effect was cue 1030-02, "Groundfalls" (sound cue #39 of the provided audio CD). As I played the series of vicious bodyfalls, David asked how we could make such wicked-sounding impacts.

Teasing, I replied deadpan, "My Foley artist, Johnny Post, lines up all the assistants in a row, and for each take he picks them up one by one and slams them to the concrete. Kind of tough on the body, that's why we go through so many." A couple of months later I received the following illustration that is Figure 16.3. Copies hang in many Foley stage recording booths in Los Angeles.

Figure 17.3 Bodyfall.

John Post is considered a grand old gentleman of the Foley art form. I have lost count of how many aspiring young Foley apprentices John has taken under his wing and trained. What he can do with a bowl of vegetables is truly disgusting, not to mention what he can do with an old broken camera, a leaf rake, or an old rotary phone mechanism—all to create some new high-tech prop gadget on screen.

Post is one of the most creative and resourceful sound men I have ever had the pleasure to work with. He could pick up an ordinary object sitting in the corner of the room and perform sounds that you would never imagine could be made with them. I once watched him perform a couple romping on a brass bed (I leave that to your imagination) and all he used was his foot flexing a metal leaf rake on a trash can lid. He inspired us all how to creatively think, to achieve the sounds we needed with everyday things that lay around us.

Many Foley artists are former dancers, giving them the added advantage of having a natural or trained discipline for rhythm and tempo. Some Foley artists, especially in the early days, came from the ranks of sound editors, already possessing an inbred understanding of what action on the screen is needed to be covered. This background is especially valuable for those hired to walk lower-budget films, where full coverage is not possible. Both the supervising sound editor and the Foley artist must understand and agree on what action to cover, and what action to sacrifice when there just isn't sufficient time to physically perform everything.

It is not enough to know that Foley artists perform their craft in specially engineered recording studios outfitted with pits and surfaces. Whether one is a supervising sound editor, Foley supervisor, or a freelance Foley artist, traveling to the various Foley stage facilities and researching them carefully is a valuable experience. I have taken many walk-through tours with facility executives anxious to expose their studio services to potential clients. Most of these tours were extremely shallow, because most of those who tour a Foley stage really do not understand the true art form in the first place. They usually consisted of walking into a studio with the executive giving a cursory gesture while naming the latest technological buzzwords and always reciting the productions that just used their stages. When I got back to my shop, I always felt like I had heard a great deal of publicity, but really came away with little more substance than before I arrived.

Taking a tour is an extremely important beginning, especially for understanding the capabilities of the sound facility and for building a political and/or business relationship with executive management. Ask for a facility credit list, handy during meetings with your client (producer). Discuss the pictures or projects each stage has done. Find out what Foley artists have used the facility recently. Talk to these artists about their experience on the stage in which you are interested, and, if possible, hear a playback of their work. This gives a good idea of the kinds of results you can expect.

Look the credit list over thoroughly. Serious facilities are very careful to split out credits into the various services they offer, taking great care not to take undue credit for certain services on pictures that are not theirs. For instance, I noticed that one facility credit listed a picture in such a way as to give the impression that they had handled the Foley, ADR, and the re-recording mixing. I knew for a fact that another studio had actually performed the final re-recording mixing, and so I inquired about that accreditation. The facility executive was caught off-guard, quickly explaining that they had only contracted the Foley stage work. I nodded with understanding as I commented that he might redo the credit list and split the work out accordingly in the future. It may seem superficial and unimportant while reading this, but a precise and verifiable credit list is an important first impression for those deciding which sound facility to contract. If one item on the credit list of your career resumé can be called into correction when a potential client checks you out, it can cast doubt over your entire resumé.

Once you have had the facility tour and collected all the available printed information from the facility (including their latest rate card), politely ask if it would be all right to visit the stage on your own, both when a Foley session in progress and when the stage is dark (meaning, not working). This way, at your own leisure, you can walk around the Foley pits, study the acoustics, and visit the prop room.

IT'S REALLY THE PITS

You always can tell if a Foley stage was designed by an architect or by a Foley artist. Most architects do not have adequate experience or understanding in what Foley artists want or need, and, more often than not, they only research the cursory needs of the recording engineers and acoustical engineering. Granted, these are vital needs. Not addressing them properly is facility suicide, but many Foley artists are distressed that so few facilities have consulted them prior to construction, since the stage is their workplace.

Most of the Foley stages I have worked with over the years had to undergo one or more retro-fittings after discovering their original design did not accommodate the Foley artists' natural work flow or was not isolated enough from noise for modern

Figure 17.4 The "pits" of a typical small Foley stage. The Foley artist stands in these variously surfaced pits, performing footsteps in sync with the actors while they watch them on screen. Most Foley stages are equipped with both film and video projection. (Photo by David Yewdall.)

sensitive digital technologies. They rebuilt the pits, changed the order of surface assignments, and grounded the concrete to solid earth. This last issue is of extreme importance, as it dictates whether your concrete surface actually sounds like solid concrete. Oddly enough, most Foley stages suffer from a hollow-sounding concrete surface because they are not solidly connected to the ground.

When I contract for a new job, I run the picture with the producer, director, and picture editor with at least a cursory overview. I have learned consciously to notice how much concrete surface work I must deal with in Foley. If the picture is a western, it doesn't matter. If the picture is a science-fiction space opera, it doesn't matter. However, if the picture is a police drama or gangster film, concrete surfaces abound. Mentally I strike from consideration the Foley stages that I know have hollow-sounding concrete surfaces, because it will never sound right when we mix the final soundtrack.

Back in the mid-1980s I did a Christmas movie-of-the-week for a major studio. Part of the agreement was to use the studio's sound facilities. Since it was my first sound job using its stages, the sound director decided to visit me on the Foley stage to see how things were going. He asked me how I liked it. I told him, not very much. He recoiled in shock and asked why. I pointed out through the recording booth windows that the concrete sounded hollow. He charged through the soundproof access door and walked out onto the concrete surface, pacing back and forth. What was the matter with it? It sounded fine to him. I told the sound director that it did not do any good to try to assess the quality of the concrete surface out there; he had to stand back with us in the recording booth and listen through the monitor speakers as the Foley artist performed the footsteps. The sound director stood out on the floor defiantly and asked what good that would do. I explained it made all the difference in the world—*what you hear with your ears is not necessarily what the microphone hears.*

The sound director came back to the recording booth, and I asked my Foley artist, Joan Rowe, to walk around on the concrete surface. The sound director stood there in shock as he heard how hollow and unnatural it sounded. He turned to his mixer and demanded why he had not been told about this problem before. The mixer replied that they had complained on numerous occasions, but that perhaps it took an off-the-lot client to get the front office to pay attention and do something about it. A couple of months later I was told that a construction team was over at the studio, jackhammering the floor out and extending the foundation deep into the earth itself. When you return to revisit the Foley stage facility you are considering, walk around on it by yourself, and take the time to write detailed notes. Draw a layout map of the pits. It is crucial to know which pits are adjacent to each other, as it makes a difference in how you program your show for Foley cues. If you are doing a western and the hollow wood boardwalk pit is not next to the dirt pit, there will be no continuous cue for the character as he steps out of the saloon doors, crosses to the edge of the boardwalk, and steps off into the street to mount his horse. To cue such action in one fluid move, the Foley artist must be able to step directly from the hollow wood surface pit into the dirt pit. Now you begin to see the need for a well-thought-through Foley pit layout.

Note the surface of each pit. Sketch the hard surface floors that surround the pits and make a note of each one's type. You should have bare concrete (connected to solid earth), a hardwood floor, linoleum and/or tile, hard carpet, and marble at the very least. The better Foley stages have more variations, including flagstone patio surface, brick, variations of carpet, marble, hardwood, and others.

One of the first surfaces I always look for is a strip of asphalt—real asphalt! A well-thought-out Foley stage floor has a long strip, at least 10' to 12' long by approximately 2' wide, of solidly embedded concrete, with a same-size strip of asphalt alongside it. It is annoying when concrete is made to sound like asphalt because no asphalt strip is available for on-stage use. These kinds of subtle substitutes really make a Foley track jump off the screen and say, "Hey, this does not connect!"

If viewers are distracted enough to realize that certain sounds are obviously Foley, then the Foley crew has failed. Foley, like any other sound process in the final re-recording mix, should be a seamless art form.

The other important built-in is the water pit. No two stages have the same facilities when it comes to water. Before the advent of decent water pits, water almost always was cut in hard effects from the studio's sound effects library. On shows that needed more customized detailing, Foley artists brought in various tubs and children's blow-up vinyl pools. The problem with these techniques, of course, is that the Foley artist and recording mixer constantly must listen for vinyl rubs or unnatural water slaps that do not match the picture. Not only does this dramatically slow down the work, but not enough sensation of depth and mass of water can be obtained to simulate anything more than splashing or shallows.

Only big pictures with substantial sound budgets could afford to pay for a major 4'-deep portable pool to be set up on the Foley stage, as was done on Goldwyn's Foley stage for the film *Golden Seal*. Naturally, a major commitment was made to the Foley budget while the stage was tied up with this pool in place (at least a 15'-diameter commitment to floor space was necessary for weeks). A professional construction team set it up with extra attention to heavy-duty bracing to avoid a catastrophic accident should the pool break and flood the sound facility floors.

Today, almost all major Foley stages have variations of a water pit. Water pits should be built flush to the floor and extend down into the earth three and a half feet. The audio engineer told me that the concrete foundation went several feet deeper, ensuring a solid grounding with the earth for all the pits and floor surfaces.

Invariably, almost all Foley stages with permanently built water pits suffer from the same problem: precise attention was not paid to the slope and surface of the edges of the water pit. Although these pits are deep and can hold enough water to adequately duplicate mass and heft of water for almost any Foley cue, they still suffer the slap effect at the top edges. I have yet to see a water pit with a sloped textured edge.

If your project has hollow wood floor needs, check the hollow wood floor boardwalk pit. I do not know why, but several Foley stages use 2' × 4' wood planks. This size is far too thick to get a desired hollow resonance. Make sure that the boardwalk pit uses 1' × 4' non-hardwood planks, such as common pinewood. Walk on it slowly, listen to each plank, and test each edge. Foley artists often get a hammer and adjust these planks so that one or more of them has loose nails, allowing the artist to deliberately work loose-nail creaks into the performance if appropriate. This technique works well when a character is poking around an old abandoned house or going up rickety stairs.

Figure 17.5 The water pit on the Foley stage at 20th Century Fox. Notice how the Foley artists use various fabric wrapped over the flat tile surfaces to defeat the unwanted "slappy" effects that bare tile would yield. (Photo by John LeBlanc.)

It is vital to be able to control just how much nail creak you work into the track; a little goes a long way.

Many stages have at least one metal deck, and, by laying other materials on top of it or placing the microphone lower to the floor or underneath it, you add a wide variety of textures. Roger Corman's *Battle Beyond the Stars* was an action-adventure space opera with various spaceships and futuristic sets. The entire picture had been filmed in Venice, California, in his renowned lumberyard facility, and the spaceship interiors were crossbreeds of plywood, cardboard, styrofoam, and milk crates—none of which sounded like metal at all. We knew we would walk the Foley at Ryder Sound's Stage 4, which had a smooth metal deck set flush to the concrete floor as well as a very nice roll-around metal ladder.

I knew, however, we would need much more than that. Contacting Bob Kizer, the picture editor (the same R.J. "Bob" Kizer we spoke about in the last chapter; he was a picture editor before he evolved into a world-class ADR supervisor), I apprised him of the problem. "Could you ask Roger to cough up an additional fifty dollars so I could have something made to order?"

The next day, cash in hand, I dropped by the nearest welding shop and sketched out a 3′ × 2′ metal diamond deck contraption with angle iron underneath to support human weight. The deck was to sit on four 6″ high steel tube legs and solidly welded in place so the microphone could be positioned under the diamond deck for an entirely different kind of metal sound as desired. Listen to cue #43 on the audio CD provided with this book to listen to two examples of metal sounds.

Figure 17.6 For *Battle Beyond the Stars*, I had a steel diamond deck prepared with 6″ steel pipe legs. Recording microphones could be used under as well as above the deck for an entirely different sound. For this cue, a chain-link fence gate was laid atop the diamond deck to make the "mushy" metal surfaces to Camen's ship. (Photo by David Yewdall.)

By positioning this deck platform onto the concrete floor or onto the existing smooth metal deck of the stage, we could achieve numerous characterizations to the metal footsteps. We pulled a 3′ section of chain-link fence out of the prop room and laid it over the diamond deck for an even stranger type of spaceship deck quality. For years that metal diamond deck has been floating around town from one Foley stage to another. Every time I needed it, an "all points bulletin" had to be sent out, as I never had any idea who had it at any given time.

Listen to the sound cue on the DVD provided with this book of VARIOUS FOLEY FOOTSTEP CUES performed on various types of described surfaces.

Prop Room

Another important place to search when checking out a Foley stage is to poke around the prop room. You can always tell the amount of professionalism and forethought given the building of a Foley stage by whether a real prop room was designed into the facility. If a stage has a prop room that is just a closet down the hall, work progress slows down, costing hundreds of dollars in additional hours taken by the Foley artist repeatedly leaving the stage to access the prop room and storage areas.

The prop room should be directly accessible to the stage itself, and large enough to amass a full and continuous collection of props (basically useless junk that makes neat sounds). This junk needs to be organized and departmentalized to accommodate easy acquisition. Everyone greatly underestimates an adequately sized room. Only a Foley artist can properly advise an architect how to design a proper prop room, complete with appropriate shelving, small prop drawers, and bins for storage. Smart sound facilities will have a convenient and adequate size prop room and will actively collect

Figure 17.7 The prop resources at the Foley stage at 20th Century Fox are immense—they *have* to be. (Photo by John LeBlanc.)

various props for it (a never-ending task). Every project will have its own requirements and challenges.

One major studio had employed a sound man by the name of Jimmy MacDonald. Over the course of 35 years MacDonald had custom-made several thousand devices and props for the studio's Foley stage. He was literally the backbone for the studio's reputation for unique sounds as custom performed for their famous cartoons and animated features. Over the decades Jimmy's masterful craftspersonship continued to make these ingenious and valuable tools of the sound creation trade. Studio carpenters built a wall with hundreds of various sized drawers with identification tags so efficient and detailed that each prop or group of similar devices could be carefully stored and protected for years of service, allowing quick access by a Foley artist without spending valuable time hunting through the entire prop department looking for what is needed.

In the mid-1980s, when the studio was wavering about whether or not to shut down their aging sound facility or spend millions to redevelop it, they brought in a young man to head the sound department and infuse new blood and new thinking. With hardly any practical experience in the disciplines and art form of sound, the new department head walked through the studio's aging Foley stage to recommend changes. All he saw was a huge room filled with junk. He ordered the place cleaned up, which meant throwing out nearly a thousand of Jimmy MacDonald's valuable sound props. Some were salvaged by quick-thinking Foley artists and mixers who knew their value, some were sent to Florida for an exhibit, but so many were lost due to ignorance. The great sadness is that, with that unfortunate action, a large part of a man's life and contribution to the motion picture industry was swept away. It is difficult to say for how many more decades Jimmy's devices would have still been creating magic. If the young department head only had called a meeting of respected professional Foley artists and recording mixers for advice on assessment, reconstruction, and policy, the entire industry would still have the entire collection of Jimmy's sound effect devices.

Numerous excellent props have been painstakingly collected over the years from old radio studios by several Foley facilities specially built for making custom sound effects in the days of live broadcasts. One of my favorite sounds that is very hard to record in the atmospheric bedlam of the real world is the classic rusty spring of a screen door. Austin Beck, owner of Audio Effects and veteran of the days of live radio, acquired numerous props from an NBC radio studio, including half-scale doors, sliding wood windows, and thick metal hatches mounted on roll-around platforms. The metal spring in the screen door had been allowed to properly rust and age for years and was used to customize the most unbelievable sounds.

In the final shoot-out scene in Carol Franklin's film, *One False Move*, Michael Beach (Pluto) is mortally wounded by Bill Paxton in an exchange of gunfire, staggers out the back screen door and collapses to the ground in a slow, dramatic death scene. All the country insects and birds had quieted, reacting to the sudden outburst of gunfire. Music did not intrude; no one spoke; the moment was still, electrified with the energy and shock of the moment. The screen door slowly swung back and gently bumped closed. No one would ever suspect that it was anything but production track, but it was not. It was Austin Beck's NBC half-pint screen-door prop.

Foley artists appreciate a well-equipped prop room; although they are known to cart around boxes and suitcases of their own shoes and favorite props, they always

Figure 17.8 Bottles, dishes, utensils, pots, pans—all variations of historic periods and types. (Photo by John LeBlanc.)

Figure 17.9 Various locks and dead bolts mounted on a practical door give the right resonance and make it quick and easy for a Foley artist to perform such sounds. (Photo by John LeBlanc.)

Figure 17.10 You are going to need a lot of shoes—all types of soles, all types of characters. (Photo by John LeBlanc.)

want to know that they are working in a facility able to supplement their own props with a collection of prop odds and ends on stage. A Foley artist's boxes of props are the arsenal of tools that achieve countless sound effects. With so many modern films using pistols and automatic firearms, a Foley artist needs a variety of empty shell casings at the ready. Some artists keep a container filled with a dozen or so .45 or 9 mm brass shell casings, a dozen or so magnum .44 shell casings, and a dozen or so 30-06 or .308 shell casings. With these basic variants, a Foley artist can handle shell-casing drops as well as single shots or automatic ejection clatters for any type of gunfight thrown their way.

Every Foley artist looks like a shoe salesman from skid row. The shoes in their boxes do not look nice and new. Most look as if the Foley artist had plucked them off street urchins themselves. These shoes are usually taped over to lessen squeaky soles; they have been squashed and folded over, and any semblance of polish has been gone for years. If Foley artists do not have at least 10 pairs of shoes in their bags of goodies, they are not serious enough about their work. They should be able to take one look at a character and, regardless of the shoes worn, reach into their boxes to pluck out just the right pair for the job.

We attached sponges to the bottom of John Post's shoes so he would sound like squishy-footed mutants in *Deathsport*. The steel plates wrapped with medical tape on the bottoms of the motorcycle boots worn by Joan Rowe added a certain lethality to Dolph Lundgren in *The Punisher*.

Lead Foley artist Dan O'Connell understands the world of audio illusion. From conceptual detailing for feature projects such as *Mouse Hunt*, *Total Recall*, *Star Trek II, III,* and *IV*, and *Dune*, to heavy-duty action pictures such as *The Rock*, *Cliffhanger*, *Con-Air*, and *Armageddon*, to historical pieces such as *Glory*, *Last of the Mohicans*, and *Dances with Wolves*, Dan O'Connell has developed a powerful and respected resumé for handling comedy, to fantasy, to heavy drama. In his studio in North Hollywood (One Step Up, Inc.), Dan and his associates revel in developing that sound that directors and

Figure 17.11 Lead Foley artist Dan O'Connell works with his favorite bolt-action prop rifle, specially loosened and taped up to maximize the desired weapon movement jiggles. Dan also carries a belt of empty 50 caliber brass shell casings and nylon straps to recreate gear movement. (Photo by David Yewdall.)

producers always ask for—something that the viewing audience has never heard before.

> You have to have a passion about your work. Without passion you are just making so much noise to fill the soundtrack, instead of developing the story point with just the right nuance. We assist the director in telling his story in ways that he and the actors cannot. Try distilling the in-the-pit-of-your-stomach terror of an unseen spirit that is flexing the bedroom door of your bedroom through a spoken narrative. What's the actor going to do, sit up in bed and say "Gee, I'm terrified?" He or she is so scared they can't talk—are you kidding? We make the audience experience the terror along with the frightened actor through created sound inventions—that's what we do.

Supervising Foley Editor

If the project is big enough and a supervising sound editor has the budget, a supervising Foley editor may be hired to oversee all Foley requirements.

The Foley supervisor sits down and runs the picture with the supervising sound editor, spotting and discussing specific cues that must be addressed. Then the Foley supervisor programs the entire show for both footsteps and props. When I am contracting a show to supervise, I will personally go to the stage to work with the Foley artists and mixer to establish the surfaces and props for that particular movie, but I do not sit around and watch every single cue being done.

If I cannot afford a dedicated Foley supervisor, I would rather let the professional lead Foley artist work as a team with his or her second Foley artist and Foley mixer to expedite the work and not slow down the process with excessive presence.

If the movie has special sound effect challenges that require a cue-by-cue decision and finesse, of course, I will stay and work with them to help develop and perform the right sounds. I do go to the Foley stage when they call and tell me that they are ready to play the reel for me. I'll review the work in a playback with them and point out the changes that I want.

I am very particular about surface texture. If I don't like how the character of the surface is playing, I'll have them redo it. Most of the time, I have already had a thorough briefing with the Foley mixer and Foley artists, so we have already gone over those kinds of issues. My lead Foley artist will demonstrate his or her intent for the various characters and surface textures that I have listed in the cue sheets, so before I return to the cutting room we all know exactly what is going to work and what doesn't. If I need to sit on the stage and oversee my Foley artists perform each and every cue then we hired the wrong crew.

I had this backfire on me once, however. I was completing the final re-recording mix of *Dreamscape* over at another studio and I had to start my Foley artist crew on night sessions on John Carpenter's car thriller, *Christine*. It was a very busy season that year, and the Foley stage at Goldwyn Studios was booked up. The only way we could squeeze in Foley sessions was to schedule them at night. I asked my lead Foley artist, John Post, if night sessions would be acceptable; he said yes.

The evening of the first session, I was still tied up with other matters back at the cutting room and could not shake free. John had helmed most of my important projects before, so I felt very comfortable with him starting on his own, even though he had never screened any of the film prior to the Foley session. Why should I worry? After all, I had Charlene Richards, one of the best Foley mixers in the business, handling the console. Several hours later, I called to see how things were going. Charlene informed me everything was fine, aside from the fact that the cue sheets did not match anything, but not to worry, as they were rewriting them as they went. I was not immediately suspicious with that disclaimer, but asked if I could speak to John Post. Charlene patched me straight onto the stage to speak to John, who welcomed a break to catch his breath.

John told me not to worry, everything was going fine, but, wow, there certainly was a lot of action in this movie. John asked if I had all those fancy helicopters in my sound library. My thought process skipped a groove. Helicopters? I asked him what he saw on the screen. John said he had never seen helicopters fly between and around buildings like that. I did not waste a moment. "Put me through to the projectionist."

When the projectionist answered the phone, I told him to look at the film rack and tell me what he saw. A loud unpleasant exclamation burst forth. The daytime Foley sessions had been working on *Blue Thunder*. The projectionist had picked up and mounted reel 1 of the wrong film, and John Post had been busy creating worthless Foley cues for 3 hours!

Back then we did not have any head or tail titles for a film until well into the final re-recording phase of the mix. The only way to tell one show from another was by paying strict attention to the handwritten labels on the ends of the film leaders themselves, which obviously that projectionist had failed to do.

Emphasis on Foley Creation

Charles L. "Chuck" Campbell received his first theatrical screen credit on a 1971 motion picture docu-feature entitled *The Hellstrom Chronicles.*

> It was an amazing project to work on. Much of the picture was shot with macro-lenses, so we, the audience, are watching the insect vs. mankind sequences on their level. We had to come up with all sorts of sounds that did not exist or would be virtually impossible to record, like insect leg movements, time-lapse photography of plants growing, opening in daylight, closing at night. I spent hours on the Foley stage to oversee and help make the kinds of sounds that we knew we would need.

Campbell supervised the sound editing on two of Robert Zemeckis's early films, *I Wanna Hold Your Hand* and *Used Cars*, which attracted the attention of Steven Spielberg. Spielberg was impressed with the detailing that Chuck brought to those films and in turn, asked him to supervise the sound editorial chores on *E.T. the Extra-Terrestrial*. "Needless to say, it was a huge break for me. As is my style, I put major emphasis on creating much of the sound effect design on the Foley stage. I personally oversee it so that I can have immediate input and help the Foley artists focus on achieving the necessary sound cues."

Campbell's attention to detail and almost fanatical use of the Foley stage and its artists helped redefine for many of his peers the importance of Foley. Many re-recording mixers were using Foley as simply a filler (many still consider it such); if the production track or the cut hard effects were not making the action work, only then would they reach for the Foley pots.

Rather than using Foley as a last resort, Campbell shoved his Foley work into a dominant position.

> I approach the creation of each sound effect from a storyteller's point of view. What is the meaning, the important piece of action that is going on? The sound must support the action, or it is inappropriate. That is one of the big reasons that I create the sound cues that I want in Foley. If I have them in Foley, why would I waste time and valuable editorial resources recutting them from a sound effect library? I just customized them exactly as I want them for that piece of action for that film.

This philosophy and technique served him and his partner, Lou Edemann, well. Campbell won the Academy Award for Best Sound Effects Editing three times (*E.T. the Extra-Terrestrial*, *Back to the Future*, and *Who Framed Roger Rabbit?*) as well as the British Academy Award for Best Sound Editing for *Empire of the Sun*. In recent years, Charles has served as supervising sound editor on *Catch Me If You Can* and *The Terminal*.

Selection of Lead Foley Artist

It usually falls to the supervising sound editor to hire Foley artists. If the supervising sound editor has a dedicated Foley supervisor on board, then it would be wise to

Figure 17.12 The lead Foley artist studies a sequence just prior to performing the cue on the Foley stage at 20th Century Fox.

include the supervising Foley editor in the decision-making process of hiring the lead Foley artist.

If you are responsible for selecting the lead Foley artist, two issues will guide you into the proper selection. The first one is simple: first know your scheduled Foley dates (actual days booked at a particular facility for recording the Foley performances to picture). This narrows the selection of Foley artists at your disposal because many of them already may have booked Foley commitments. The second issue is the strengths and weaknesses of the various Foley artists available for your sessions. Some Foley artists are extremely good with footsteps. They may have a real talent for characterization and texture, having less difficulty with nonrhythmic syncopated footsteps such as steeplechase sequences, jumping, dodging, or stutter-steps. If you are forced to do a walk-and-hang (often referred sarcastically as "hang-and-pray") Foley job, hire a Foley artist with a strong reputation for being able to walk footsteps in precise sync. (I discuss the pros and cons of the walk-and-hang technique later.)

Some Foley artists are known for their creative abilities with props, especially in making surrogate sounds for objects too big and awkward to get into a Foley stage or not at the immediate disposal of the Foley artist. Rarely do you find a Foley artist skilled at both props and footsteps, and those who are are seldom available because of such high demand.

TELEVISION BREAKS THE SOUND BARRIER

Until a few years ago, television sound was not taken very seriously. Most re-recording stages that mixed television series or movies-of-the-week kept a stereo pair of small speakers on the overbridge of the mixing console so they could do a simulated TV playback of the soundtrack. This way, they would be confident that the audio material would play through the little tin speakers of the home set.

Sound editors and Foley artists were looked upon in a feature versus television caste system, and often were deemed incapable of handling feature standard work if they worked on too much TV. I was one of those employers who glanced over resumés and made snap judgments based on seeing too much episodic television. Shame on me, and shame on those who still practice this artistic bigotry.

Since the early 1980s, home televisions have evolved into home entertainment centers as consumers became very discerning and more audio aware. Major home theatre-style set-ups, once erected only by the audio/visual enthusiasts with expert knowledge of how to build their own home systems, are now within instant reach of anyone with enough cash for a ready-made system. Major electronics stores have hit-teams that sell you the kitchen-sink system, and another team moves it to your residence and sets it up. Consumer awareness and desire to have such prowess in the home are added to the fact that we are now able to produce soundtracks with as great, and in some cases greater, dynamics and vitality than those produced for your local cinema.

Donald Flick, the sound editor who cut the launch sequence of *Apollo 13*, believed that the film sounded bigger and better in my home, played from a DVD through my customized system, than he remembered it sounding in the theatre. What does this mean to today's television producers or directors? The television show or direct-to-video movie has just grown a pair of lungs and insists that you think theatrical in audio standards. Never again should the flippant excuse be used, "It's good enough for television."

Along with this new attitude has cropped up an entirely new cadre of television sound artisans, not only regarding program content, but also challenging and continually excelling in its medium's format. One such Foley artist who has done sensationally well in television is Casey Crabtree. Casey has specialized in creating Foley for television, both episodic such as *ER, Smallville, Brimstone,* and *Third Rock From the Sun,* as well as movies-of-the-week and miniseries such as *Amelia Earhart, Peter the Great, It, Ellis Island, Keys to Tulsa;* and to name a few feature films, *Police Academy, Bad Lieutenant, Coronado, Thank Heaven, Dancing at the Blue Iguana.*

"With today's compressed schedules, editors rely on Foley more and more. I create absolutely anything. I have created car crashes, sword fights, lumbering tanks crushing through the battlefield—I even created an entire ten-story building collapsing—on the Foley stage," recalls Casey. "I am particularly proud of my horses. I create horse hooves and movements that are so real the editors want me to do all of it on the Foley stage because it sounds better than any effects that they could cut by hand."

I must admit I took the "horse" statement as being a little too self-assured, since I have been cutting horse hooves longer than I would like to recount. Casey grinned as she detected my skepticism. She proudly had her crew pull a Foley session reel from an episode of Bruce Campbell's *The Adventures of Brisco County Jr.* I was impressed. Her horses sounded so natural and real—hooves, texture of the ground, saddle movement, bridle jingles—as good as anything I would want for a feature film, and this was episodic television.

"For ER I did absolutely everything. I have my own prop 'Crash Cart' with all the devices and good sounding junk that I used to recreate virtually everything from

Figure 17.13 Casey Crabtree performs an "ambu" bag as an on-screen medical technician struggles to maintain life support of a patient for the hit television series *ER*.

squirting blood vessels to syringes to re-breathers to blood pressure wraps. I even did the pocket pager beeps."

   Although Casey performs her craft on any Foley stage the producer requests, she is quick to point out that every stage has its own voice:

> You can do the same kind of action on four different Foley stages, and you will get four different audio characterizations and colorations. Of course, I have my favorite Foley stages as well as my favorite Foley mixers, and I will discuss the options with the client accordingly. Ultimately, it is their decision where their facility deal is going to be, and I will abide by that.
>
> I had done several episodes of one particular television show over at Film Leaders, and then the producer switched to another Foley stage for one reason or another. They got the material to the stage and did not like how it sounded—not my performance, but the characterization and color of how my performance was reproduced through the microphones of the Foley stage. There is an acoustical imprint or influence that a stage itself has. You have to factor that knowledge into the equation as well.

OBSERVING THE FOLEY STAGE IN ACTION

Visit the Foley stage when it is working. Unless the stage is closed because of a film's sensitivity, most Foley stages do not mind visitation from qualified professionals (or serious students of sound) for observation purposes. You learn virtually everything you want to know about the stage by quietly watching the recording mixer and artists at work. Watch how they pay attention to the recording levels and the critical placement of the microphones. Although today's Foley artists adjust the microphone positioning themselves (except on special occasions), the recording mixer should be very attentive to how each cue sounds. If the mixer is not willing to jump up and run in to readjust the microphone stand, then that should be a red flag to his or her commitment to quality.

Observe how mixer and Foley artist work together. Are they working as a team or as separate individuals just making their way through the session? The respect and professional dedication a mixer has for the Foley artist are of paramount importance. The Foley artist could be working as hard as possible, trying to add all kinds of character to the cue, but if the mixer is not applying at least an equal dedication to what the Foley artist is doing, the cue will sound bland and flat.

Watch the mixer carefully and observe the routine. Is the mixer taking notes on the Foley cue sheet supplied by the Foley supervising editor? Is the mixer exercising common sense and flexibility as changes arise or if the Foley artist requests them?

Do not be afraid to ask the mixer questions about particular preferences. Most mixers have different priorities regarding your cue sheets and notes that make their jobs more efficient. Listen to what the mixer says; if you do decide to use this particular Foley stage, and if this mixer will be on your show, take his or her advice and factor it into your preparation.

The worst thing you can do is not work with and collaborate with a mixer. If a mixer feels that he or she is being forced to effect a particular style or procedure without good reason, the Foley stage experience can be very painful. To get the collaboration of the mixer, explain the shortcomings and budgetary realities and constraints you are facing, and you will get a sympathetic ear. Encourage the mixer and lead Foley artist to suggest where you might cut corners. They are sources of good advice and pointers on joining forces to accomplish your job within constraints.

Pay attention to the quality of the sound recording. Does it sound harsh and edgy, or full and lush? Ask for explanations if you are unsure. Embrace the professionals you have hired and pull from their mental knowledge to enhance each cue and each track to augment the audio that you want. It will help you better understand what you need to ask to get you what you want.

A big problem that the smaller Foley stages may have is inadequate acoustical engineering. Many times a recording mixer needs to go to the thermostat and turn off the air conditioner because the microphones are picking up too much low-end rumble. This is a sure sign of poorly designed bass trapping (special acoustical engineering to isolate and vastly diminish the low-end rumble) in the air ducts that feed the stage itself. Other low-end problems arise from insufficient isolation from nearby street traffic or overhead aircraft. The Foley crew and I have had to wait on many occasions for a passing jet or a heavy tractor-trailer because the stage walls or ground foundation were not properly isolated during construction.

A few years ago, this was not such a problem. The standard microphone was a directional Sennheisser, and the recording levels were meant to be recorded as close to final intended level requirements as possible. In 1980, +6 dB recording was adopted for the Foley sessions on *The Thing*. By recording the Foley at a higher level (+6 dB) and then lowering it later in the final mix, the combined bias hiss of all the Foley channels being played back together was remarkably reduced, making for a much cleaner sounding final re-recording mix. With the success of this elevated recording technique on *The Thing*, it instantly became an industry standard.

Digital technologies have accelerated the performance demands of today's Foley stages. Many stages abandoned the traditional Sennheisers for more sensitive and fuller-sounding microphones, such as Neumann, AKG, and Schoepps. These sensitive and ultra-clean microphones uncover hosts of flaws in acoustical engineering and construction shortcomings no matter whether or not the stages were built for the express use of Foley/ADR recording. If not positioned correctly, they literally pick up the heartbeat of a Foley artist. While doing the sound for *Once upon a Forest*, an animal handler brought in several birds of prey so we could record wild tracks of wing flaps and bird vocals. The handler held the feet of a turkey buzzard and lifted the bird gently upward, fooling it into thinking it needed to fly. The giant 6' wingspan spread and gave wonderful single flaps. After doing this routine several times, both bird and handler were tired and paused a moment to rest. The microphone picked up fast heartbeats from the throat of the bird itself!

Make sure you step back into the machine room and take careful note of the various types of recording and signal processing equipment. Most Foley stages can record to various mediums, but the recording platform of choice is Pro Tools. We use QuickTime video picture, as it is much easier to scrub the image back and forth over the cue to determine exact sync. A great benefit of nonlinear digital editing is that now all Foley tracks can be heard playing against one another at the same time during playback of cut sequences than in the days when we could only record to a 4-track 35-mm fullcoat.

Figure 17.14 Supervising Foley editor/Foley artist Vanessa Ament discusses the strategies of what they need to create with her Foley mixer, Karin Roulo (on the left) who is handling the recording session on action-thriller *Chain Reaction*. Sandy Garcia is the Foley recordist (in back on the right). (Photo by David Yewdall.)

The Foley Stage Recordist

Most Foley stages have a recordist working with the recording mixer. The recordist works all day with high-quality headsets over both ears. While loading the recording machine, he or she makes labels, keeps notes, and alerts the recording mixer if any dropouts, static, or distortion are heard from the playback head. In addition, the recordist also handles machine malfunctions, fields incoming phone calls, and alerts the mixer if the session is in jeopardy of running into meal penalties or overtime. The recordist's responsibility also includes proper set-up and monitoring of the signal-processing equipment, such as Dolby SR noise reduction cards when and if they are needed.

The recordist also ensures that precise lineup tones (at least 30 seconds) are laid down at the head of each roll of stock. When a roll is completed, the recordist makes sure that it either goes to the transfer department with clear and precise notes on making the transfers, whether to another audio medium or burning the session folder and audio files onto a CD-R or DVD-R for the Foley editors to take back to editorial and make precise sync adjustments later.

Some Foley stages have the recordist regenerating new cue sheets to reflect what is actually being recorded and onto which channel. This practice is based on sloppy Foley cueing done by inexperienced editors who do not understand Foley protocol and procedure. Unfortunately, this extra work diverts the energies and attentions of the recordist away from the primary job of monitoring quality control as outlined above.

CUEING THE FOLEY

The best way to cue Foley is to pull out the trusty 8-channel cue sheets and write it up by hand. Print neatly! Remember, too, your recording mixer must be able to read this cue sheet in dim light, so do not use pencil.

Foley Cue Sheet Log

The cue sheet is not meant to go to the dubbing stage later; it is simply a road map of intent and layout by which the recording mixer navigates. As the recording mixer executes each cue and the Foley artist is satisfied with the performance, the mixer makes a checkmark by the cue, thereby confirming that the cue was actually done.

As the Foley artist and recording mixer work their way through the reel, they may wish to make changes in your layout, usually to accommodate an item the Foley artist wishes to add; perhaps they feel the need to separate cues you had assumed would be done simultaneously. For instance, you may have made notes in a prop channel, such as Foley-7, that you need Jesse James to draw his pistol, snap open the cylinder, and reload six fresh cartridges. Because of intricate maneuvers with entirely different props to simulate the weapon, your Foley artist might tell the mixer that the holster draw and bullet inserts will be done in channel 7 (Foley tracks are referred to as channels), but that he or she wants to redo the gun movement (the subtle metallic

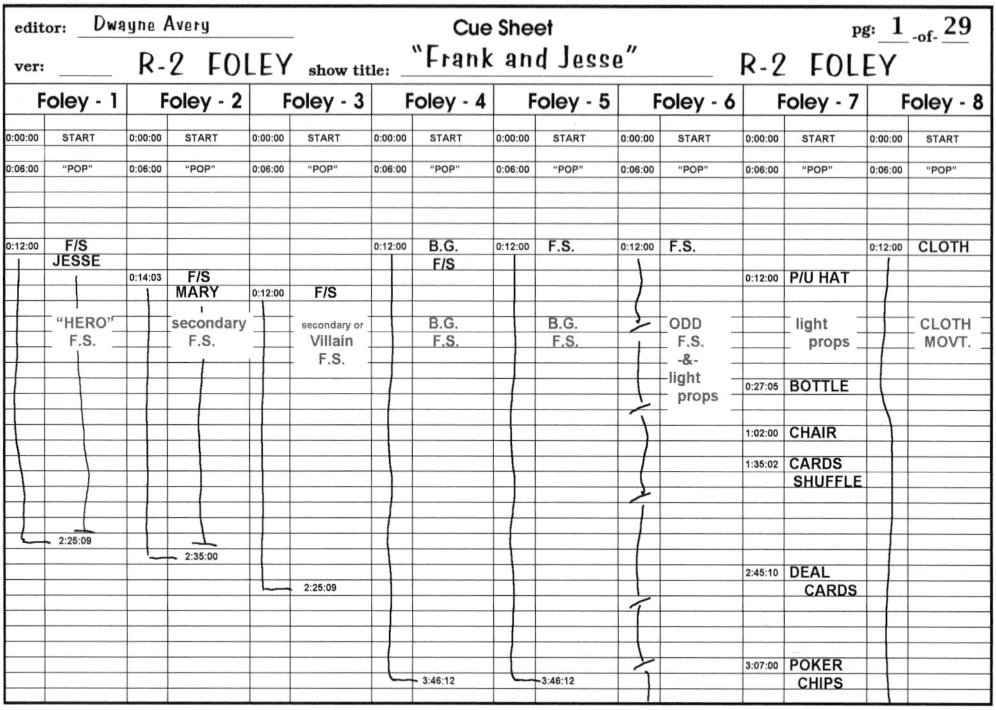

editor: Dwayne Avery		Cue Sheet				pg: 1 -of- 29	
ver: ___ R-2 FOLEY		show title: "Frank and Jesse"				R-2 FOLEY	
Foley - 1	**Foley - 2**	**Foley - 3**	**Foley - 4**	**Foley - 5**	**Foley - 6**	**Foley - 7**	**Foley - 8**
0:00:00 START	0:00:00 START	0:00:00 START	0:00:00 START	0:00:00 START	0:00:00 START	0:00:00 START	0:00:00 START
0:06:00 "POP"	0:06:00 "POP"	0:06:00 "POP"	0:06:00 "POP"	0:06:00 "POP"	0:06:00 "POP"	0:06:00 "POP"	0:06:00 "POP"
0:12:00 F/S JESSE			0:12:00 B.G. F/S	0:12:00 F.S.	0:12:00 F.S.		0:12:00 CLOTH
	0:14:03 F/S MARY					0:12:00 P/U HAT	
		0:12:00 F/S					
"HERO" F.S.	secondary F.S.	secondary or Villain F.S.	B.G. F.S.	B.G. F.S.	ODD F.S. -&- light props	light props	CLOTH MOVT.
						0:27:05 BOTTLE	
						1:02:00 CHAIR	
						1:35:02 CARDS SHUFFLE	
2:25:09	2:35:00	2:25:09				2:45:10 DEAL CARDS	
			3:46:12	3:46:12		3:07:00 POKER CHIPS	

Figure 17.15 Typical Foley cue sheet; we start with 8-channel sheets.

rattle) and the cylinder snap open movement in channel 8 to separate the two bits of action.

Plotting out Foley is extremely important. Cues of different character cannot be jumbled one after another without realistic separation. Be very predictable and consistent, think ahead to the eventual predubbing process on the re-recording stage, and put yourself in the chair of the sound effects mixer. The standard rule is as follows: hero footsteps in the first channel; second hero (or first villain, depending) in the second channel; secondary individual performances in the next channels; then background extras using one or more channels; next, several channels of props—and remember to keep each performance isolated for the sound effects mixer.

Most of your work, unless the budgets are large enough and the Foley schedule long enough, fits most effectively in the 8-channel format. This format fit all analog and most digital tape formats perfectly—8 channels fit into two rolls of 4-channel 35-mm fullcoats perfectly—or one 8-channel DA-88. Thinking in groups of 4 and 8 channels was the most logical.

Today, it does not really matter. Recording in Pro Tools we record in selected Record channel, then drag the renamed cue down into an appropriate channel for playback and get it out of the way. Later, when the Foley editor cuts it up and splits it off for perspective, no matter how many channels you end up with in the session is going to expand de facto because of perspective split editing later. You just want to use the Foley cue sheet as a road map, a blueprint of what you need the Foley crew to perform and supply to sound editorial.

The Practice Foley Boot Camp

The Foley exercise cues on the interactive DVD included with this book will empower you with a real-life experience of what it's like to be on a professional Foley stage. This is an opportunity to become familiar with exactly what would be expected from you on the Foley stage including cue sheet layout strategies and individual video cues, complete with Colin-Broad streamers. You will not hear three beeps prior to the first frame of the cue, as you do with ADR—but the streaming system is incredibly helpful to assist the Foley artist for precise in-and-out points. Go to button #8 on the main menu—the Art of Foley. The third button on the submenu will take you into a Foley boot camp exercise series of cues.

Aspiring Foley artists who wish to train and prepare themselves for the technique and expectations of their efforts on a professional Foley stage will probably want to acquire a dedicated Foley boot camp DVD, which is available separately from this book. It has dozens of Foley cues—two feature films, various footstep challenges, cloth movement, and various props cues to problem solve. All of the cues have Colin-Broad streamers as well as cue sheets to review so you can compare what you see to the layout strategies. This DVD is not just for the Foley artist; it would be a very valuable experience for the aspiring director and producer, so that those who have the budget and schedule decisions can better understand what is possible and what they should plan for—months, perhaps even a year, before the film ever reaches the supervising sound editor and Foley crew.

Techniques to Consider

Most Foley expertise you acquire is simply a matter of hands-on experience, getting in and doing it, trying different things, listening to how they sound in playback.

Self-Awareness Tips

You must learn from the start, when around these highly sensitive microphones, to breathe very lightly—not an easy task if you have just completed a rather strenuous cue. I often hold my breath or take very shallow breaths, holding my mouth open so as not to cause any wheezing sounds, for fear the microphone will pick it up.

After a recording mixer reports that a cue was ruined by some extraneous noise (which you probably caused) and it must be done over, you learn to cross the room noiselessly, pretending to be a feather, or you breathe with such a shallow intake as to redefine stealth.

I spent most of the time with my pants off while I was on the Foley stage. (Remember Foley is performed on a dark stage.) I wore black close-fitting cotton bikini shorts or a competition swimsuit. The reason was really quite simple—I could not risk unwanted cloth movement. As your ears become more discerning, you discover how intrusive various cloth materials are. If you wish to perform various props and/or non-cloth movement cues as cleanly as possible, you will do anything to achieve the desired level of sonic isolation necessary. Many female Foley artists wear leotards, aerobic exercise garments with little if any excess.

Grassy Surrogate

One of the best ways to simulate grass is to unwind 100 feet or so of old ¼″ recording tape. Place the small pile in the dirt pit. When bunched together or pulled apart for thinner textures, walking through grass, or leaf movement on bushes, is simulated amazingly well.

Snow

Probably the substance that most closely matches the sound of snow is cornstarch. Lay an old bedsheet down over the dirt pit or on a section of the concrete floor, then pour several boxes of cornstarch into the center of the sheet, making a bed approximately 1″ thick. With the microphone stand positioned close in and the microphone itself lowered fairly near to the floor, the result is an amazing snow compaction crunch. Most Foley stages are equipped with two stands with identical microphones. As you experiment with placement and balance, you will find that having the second microphone placed back and a little higher affords the recording mixer an excellent opportunity to audition and choose the better sounding angle or to mix the two microphone sources together for a unique blend.

The only drawback to tromping footsteps through the cornstarch, as you will experience when you spend a good part of the day performing in the dirt pit, is that you kick up a lot of dust and powder particles. It is unavoidable. Hopefully, the Foley stage is equipped with powerful exhaust fans that can be turned on during breaks to filter the air or keep surgical filter masks available. Check the sensitivity of the smoke sensors on the stage, as they often get clogged and silently alert the local fire department to come unnecessarily.

Safety with Glass

You may need to wear a surgical mask if the film you are walking has a great deal of either snow or dirt effects to perform. A smart Foley artist keeps a pair of safety goggles in the box, especially for performing potentially hazardous cues such as broken glass or fire. For *The Philadelphia Experiment*, we purchased 100 6′-long, 25-watt light bulbs and mounted them in 100 closely drilled holes on a 2′ × 12′ board. When we performed the sequence in the picture where the actor smashes vacuum-tube arrays with a fire axe, we had our biggest and strongest assistant kneel down to support the board in a vertical position. He wore heavy leather construction gloves and safety goggles. For added protection, we draped a section of carpet over him to shield him from the shower of glass shards. I also wore safety goggles, but I wore black dress gloves so as not to make undo noise.

Because we could not accurately estimate the dynamic strength of the recording, we brought in a back-up ¼″ Nagra recorder. This gave us not only a direct recording to 35-mm stripe, but a protection ¼″ recorder in the machine room recording at a tape speed of 7.5 ips and a second ¼″ recorder on the stage itself recording at 15 ips. The ¼″ Nagra recording at 15 ips captured the most desirable effect as I swung a steel bar down through the 100 light bulbs, resulting in an incredible explosion of delicate glass and vacuum ruptures. I have been ribbed for years by Foley artists who claim that, every so often, they still find shards of those light bulbs.

Fire

Fire is another tricky and potentially dangerous medium to work with on a Foley stage. While performing some of his own Foley cues for *Raiders of the Lost Ark*, Richard Anderson used a can of Benzine to record the little fire raceways in the Nepal barroom sequence when Harrison Ford (Indiana Jones) is confronted by Ronald Lacey and his henchmen. After a few moments, the fire suddenly got out of control, and, as Richard quietly tried to suppress it, the flame nonetheless spread out quickly, engulfing his shoe as it raced up his leg.

In typical Richard Anderson fashion, he did not utter one word or exclamation, but pointed for his partner to grab the fire extinguisher. It had been moved before lunch, however, and was no longer in its place. Steve Flick dashed through the sound-proof door to find one as Richard breathlessly jumped around trying to put out the growing threat. He saw the 3′-deep water pit and jumped in—only it was not full of water, and in a seemingly magical single motion jumped instantly out again. He grabbed the drapes under the ledge of the screen and used them to smother the flames just as Steve Flick appeared through the doorway with another fire extinguisher at the ready.

Figure 17.16 At the North Carolina School of the Arts–School of Filmmaking, David Yewdall teaches one of the most aggressive hands-on Foley classes at any film school. Here he is teaching open flame Foley and the correct safety techniques vital to avoid accidents and disasters. (Photo by Lisa Audrey Yewdall.)

Because of the increased hazard and potential injuries posed by performing various types of fire on a Foley stage, most sound facilities either discourage or forbid anything more than matches and a lighter. The days of burning flares and destroying blood bags with fire on stage (as I did for John Carpenter's *The Thing*) are rare and few between. This is why I teach careful and exceptional planning with the sound facility and with the studio fire department in attendance. The supervising sound editor should plan for these sound cues to be performed and recorded in any venue other than the Foley stage, whenever possible. Naturally, the sync-to-picture advantage of being able to perform cues such as the actor carrying and waving a torch around is vital to do in the controlled environment of a Foley stage. Even with the studio fire department supervising during custom recording of a blowtorch in *Jingle All the Way*, the glowing metal of a 55-gallon drum reached a certain dangerous hue, and the fire captain stepped in to say enough.

The Most Terrifying Sound Effects in the World Come from Your Refrigerator!

When it comes to slimy entrails and unspeakable dripping remnants, few have done it longer or better than John Post. Considered the inspirational sponsor and teacher of virtually half the Foley artist cadre of Hollywood, as stated earlier, John has trained more than his share of aspiring sound effects creators. As of the writing of this book, John is in his fifth decade of working the pits and creating the audio illusions that make his work legendary.

I always liked working with John. He brought a whole different performance to even the simple act of walking. Many Foley artists made footfalls on the right surface and in sync with the action on-screen, but Johnny took the creation to a whole new level. It was not just a footfall on the correct surface—the footstep had character, texture, and often gave an entire spin on the story. I remember being on the re-recording stage when the director stood up and paused the mixing process. He asked the mixers to back up and replay the footsteps of the actress crossing a room. After we played the cue again, the director turned to us with an amazed expression. He was fascinated about how John Post had completely changed the performance of the scene. Before John performed the footsteps, the actress simply crossed the room. During the Foley session, however, John built in a hesitation by the actress on the off-screen angle, then continued her footsteps with a light delicacy that bespoke insecurity. This not only completely changed the on-screen perception of the actress's thoughts and feelings, but also greatly improved the tension of the moment. John's very act of craftspersonship separates the mechanical process from art. He always approaches his Foley responsibilities as part of the storytelling process. Many agree that John Post knew how to walk women's footsteps better than women. Listen to the sound cue of *Autopsy* with the picture of John Post on the DVD included with this book under the menu button FOLEY MISC. It is John Post performing the original autopsy sound effect cue for *The Thing*. This recording has been used in perhaps a hundred or more motion pictures and/or television shows since.

As a general rule, I do not reveal how an artist makes magic. Since this book is about sharing and inspiration, however, I will divulge to you how John Post made this famous sound. John set up a large heavy bowl on the Foley stage. He then broke half

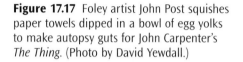
Figure 17.17 Foley artist John Post squishes paper towels dipped in a bowl of egg yolks to make autopsy guts for John Carpenter's *The Thing*. (Photo by David Yewdall.)

a dozen eggs and mixed them thoroughly, just as if he was preparing a scrambled-egg breakfast. After the Foley mixer received a volume level test and readjusted the microphone positioning, John dipped several sheets of paper towels into the eggs until they were completely saturated. He then lifted the paper towels out of the brew and voice slated what he was doing. John proceeded to play with the paper towels, squeezing them, pulling them through his tightened fingers, manipulating the egg to replicate that to which our ears and imagination responded. If you wish to hear this fun and disgusting creation, you can find it on the DVD provided with this book under the Foley demo button on the main menu. Listen to the actual recording cue, with John Post slating the variations of his creation.

Hush Up!

You learn very early as you work on a Foley stage or out in the field, recording sound effects, to keep your mouth shut—even when the unexpected happens. If that crystal bowl slips out of your hands and smashes to the floor, you want a clean and pristine recording of a crystal-bowl smash, untouched by a vocal outburst of surprise or anger. After all, it may end up in the library as one of the proudest accidental sound effects. Every sound editor has a private collection of special sounds attributable to this useful advice.

Zip Drips

Another classic sound is the zip-drip effect. This tasty little sweetener effect often is performed to add spice, such as the sizzling power line that extended over the downtown square in *Back to the Future* after Christopher Lloyd (Dr. Emmett Brown) made the fateful connection allowing lightning to energize the car that sent Michael J. Fox forward into the future. The Foley artist, John Roesch, burned a piece of plastic wrap from a clothing bag, causing the melted globule to fall past the microphone, making a zip-drip flight.

The same technique was used when I supervised *The Thing* four years earlier, only I burned the plastic fin of a throwing dart. As I studied the frame-by-frame action of Kurt Russell lighting a flare before descending into the ice cavern of the camp, I saw a small spark fly off the striker. I wanted to sweeten this little anomaly with something tasty, as there was a moment before the three men turned to go below. We recorded several zip drips for this, but as I played them against the action, I noticed that, because of the Doppler effect caused by the globule approaching and passing the microphone so quickly, it made the zip by sound ascending, instead of descending as you might expect. (If you listen closely to the above-mentioned sequence in *Back to the Future*, you will notice that the globules falling from the power line sound ascending, instead of descending.) Wanting the spark from the flare to have a descending feel, I simply took the recording of the zip drip and made a new transfer, playing the original recording backward. It may seem like a small, insignificant bother, but this kind of attention to detail adds to a more pleasing overall performance, regardless of whether the audience is aware of the detail.

For years we have been brainwashed about how dumb the population out there is. What a bunch of hooey! The audience is NOT dumb. They are very intelligent and sophisticated, and they notice absolutely everything.

EDITING FOLEY

In the days of magnetic film, we had transportation runners wheeling hand dollies into the editorial rooms stacked high with hundreds of thousand-foot rolls of 35-mm stripe weighing hundreds of pounds. Each roll represented a single Foley channel of a single reel of a movie. These were called "string-offs" because they were transferred one channel at a time to one roll of film at a time. We threaded up each roll on the Moviola and interlocked the start mark with the Academy start frame of the Foley string-off.

For hours we rolled back and forth, checking and correcting sync, cutting out frames to condense, adding frames of blank film to expand. Our Rivas splicers clacked and whacked every few seconds with another cut decision. It was not unusual to use up an entire roll of splicing tape on one channel roll of Foley. Back then, one roll of 35-mm white perforated splicing tape cost over $15. Each foot of 35-mm magnetic stripe film cost 2.5¢ (from the manufacturer) and as much as 7¢ a foot for the labor to transfer it. That means that every foot of stripe was costing approximately a dime. If we held the show to 8 Foley tracks per reel, we burned off at least 80,000 feet of Foley stripe transfer. Some sound facilities were using an average of 22 to 44 channels of Foley for action features.

The Foley cutter is just as much an artist as the person performing Foley on stage. An interesting axiom is that precisely cut Foley sometimes does not play as well as creatively cut Foley. While cutting Foley on *Predator 2*, during the sequence where Glover and Paxton chase the alien up to the rooftop, I cut each and every step in precise sync. The men burst out of the room, into the hallway, slamming up against the wall, turning and running down the hall, turning and vaulting up steel stairs, steeplechase-style running and maneuvering. I cut it all in exact sync, using three rolls of splicing tape per Foley roll. Then I played it at real time. It felt funny. I knew it was cut in exact sync, but exact sync wasn't evoking the passion and rhythm of the sequence.

I pulled it apart and spent another day just cutting movements and turns to accent the sweep and moment of the action. I discovered that, by changing the footsteps that had been performed, by moving the order around so that a more forceful footfall was replaced by a lighter one, and the heavier one placed in a more strategic spot to emphasize a particular change of body direction, the performance took on a whole different spin. Suddenly, power and energy backed up the visuals on the screen.

One of the harder techniques to master is cutting footsteps in precise sync when you cannot see the feet. Most beginners think this is easy stuff. After all, you cannot see the feet, so just let the footsteps roll. It doesn't play quite right, however. To cut footsteps when all you see are talking heads and torsos, watch the shoulders of the actors. Flip frame slowly. Each frame of walking has a natural blur to it, except when the foot has just impacted the ground. That one frame has a perfect focus. To that frame you sync the footstep sound. If the footsteps still feel odd, try changing feet. Sometimes sliding down the left foot impact sound and syncing it to the right footstep makes all the difference.

Some editors like to cut sync on footsteps one frame prior to focus frame (visual impact). Because light travels faster than sound, some think it gives a better appearance of sync when playing at normal speed as heard in the theatre.

Before I start cutting, I magnify the waveforms of the tracks so high that they become blocks of color. This way, I can see all of the most sensitive and subtle recordings without having to take the time to play it all. I will highlight and cut out all of the strips of silence in between the individual cues, then highlight and rename the regions. This way I can highlight and cut all the strips of silence between individual cues, then highlight and rename the regions.

For many Foley artists who develop the rich footstep movement and prop creations prevalent in today's entertainment, the term "Foley" itself is no longer enough. Years ago, the process helped fill in the subtle, but important, footsteps and movement the production track lacked. Today, the Foley artist creates sounds that Foley walkers never dreamed about 15 or 20 years ago. On *Extreme Measures*, Foley artists created the entire subway train, complete with the feel of massive tonnage, steel wheels shrieking on rails, cavernous echo—all of it! This is no longer Foley. This is custom sound effects creation at its most liberated.

Pro Tools—One Artist's Recording Technique

Recording straight to hard disk using Pro Tools is the industry standard, especially as the D to A converters have improved with the HD interfaces. The technique is easy, and with a little practice you will quickly develop your own preference for naming Foley cues and how to manage your track assignments.

Refer to Chapter 18 regarding setting up a new Pro Tools session. Once you have created your session, draw down from File in the menu bar and select New Track.... I usually start by creating 18 tracks. The first track I rename Guide, which is where I

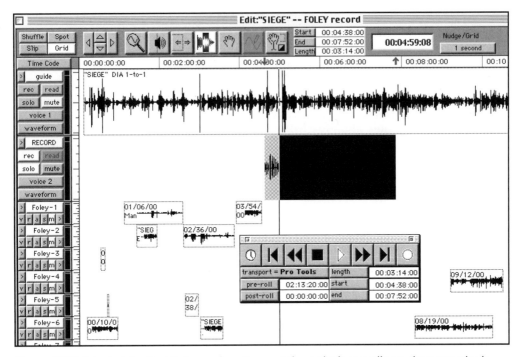

Figure 17.18 A typical Pro Tool Foley session. Here, a Foley artist is recording a character who is walking up a spiral staircase.

import the editor's cut work track, or 1-to-1. It is a good idea to have the editor's work track at the ready in case the Foley artist would like to listen to it, to get a sense of what he or she might need to do, such as evaluate a surface. I usually leave this track in the Mute mode unless the Foley artist wants to review it.

Rename the second audio channel Record. This is where you will record all of the incoming Foley performances. Think of this as a scratchpad, a place to record, dump it out if you do not like it, or keep it and rename it before you pull the cue down into the Foley channel where it will reside for subsequent editing and final predubbing.

Rename the rest of the audio channels Foley-1, Foley-2, Foley-3, and so forth. This gives you 16 Foley tracks. Remember what we talked about—thinking in groups of 4 and 8? Unless you are getting into complex action, 16 channels of Foley should be plenty. If it turns out you need more, no big deal, you can add more as you need them. I always do.

Open the Show Mix Window under Display in the menu bar. Make sure that your Input channel assignment for the Record channel is the same channel as the line input feed that carries the signal that the stage microphone(s) are plugged into.

Make sure you engage the rec button on the Record channel. This is an arming safety. As we talked about in Chapter 15, you will not record anything if this button is not on.

Personally, I record in Grid mode. Note the highlighted rectangular box in the upper left-hand corner of the session window with the word "Grid." This means that I will record either exact second to exact second, or I can record exact frame to exact frame. I like to record in Grid mode with the Nudge/Grid reference (shown on the upper right-hand corner of the session window) in the 1 Second option. This makes it extremely easy to accurately move cues up or down from one audio channel to another channel without loosing sync, once I have recorded the cue into the session.

Now select Show Transport Window under Display in the menu bar. The Transport Window will appear. This is your tape recorder complete with all the controls to interlock, record, play, stop, etc.

Using the Line tool, highlight from just in front of the spot you wish the Foley artist's performance to be recorded to a couple of seconds past the Out cue advertised on the Foley cue sheet. Pro Tools will automatically kick into Record mode when the time code hits this highlighted area and will kick out when it reaches the end.

You do not *have* to highlight the cue area. If you would rather, you can simply place the record head line at the spot you wish to record, and later stop recording by hitting the Stop button on the Transport Window when you wish to stop.

Either way, you need to rewind the videotape approximately 10 seconds prior to the start point you wish to record. This pre-roll is not only to allow the session to interlock with the time code but it allows your Foley artist to get focused on the action that he or she is about to perform, especially when it comes to rhythmic footsteps.

Once you have run the sequence for the Foley artist and he or she is ready to perform, take the cursor and press the button on the far right-hand side of the Transport Window. This is the Record Arming switch. Once you have armed the Transport Window you are ready to roll. Make sure that you are interlocked with the time code signal by pressing Apple/keystroke "J." The little window at the bottom left-hand corner of your session window will show Waiting for Sync. The little clock window on the far left-hand side of the Transport Window will glow blue.

Roll the videotape. The time code will be seen by the Pro Tools session and will interlock. The record/playback head (line) will start scrolling toward the top of your highlighted cue. When it hits the cue area the session will jump into Record mode.

Once you have finished the cue, the recording will either stop on its own (if you use the highlighted method) or you will hit the Stop button.

Tap twice on the audio cue that you have just recorded. It will probably say "Record-01." Now enter what you want the cue to be called. I use a technique of entering a reference number in case I have to rebuild sync positions. If you will note, the cue started at the 38th second of the 4th minute. So, I enter 04/38/00 prior to a short-action name. Should something happen to my original session, I can easily make a new session and throw the cues very quickly into performed sync locations by using the minute/second/frame designations. Pro Tools protocol will not allow you to use a colon in the name, as you would write out a time code number, so I use a slash instead.

Once I have named my cue I will use the Hand tool and grab the cue and drag it down into the Foley channel that I intend for it to reside. On to the next cue.

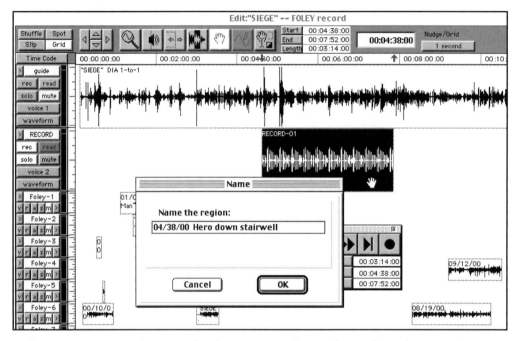

Figure 17.19 Once you have completed a cue, tap on the waveform twice and rename the cue.

Importing Foley Stems into Pro Tools for Track Stripping

If you are stuck using a Foley stage that still uses DA-88 tapes for recording Foley, or you may have a stage that is still using recording analog 2" 2-track with Dolby SR noise reduction, then you may want to follow the following technique.

Whatever the reason, you may receive material that will need to be imported into a Foley session as stems. The stem technique is extremely wasteful when it comes to disk space. It chews it up at 5 megabytes per minute, per channel. Which means that if you have a 24-channel Foley session of an A-B reel of film, you are looking at 2 to 2.5 gigabytes of memory *per reel*. Most of the timelines a of the stems are empty blank space, with a few cues of Foley every so often. If you are blessed with unlimited memory resources, you do not have a problem, but many craftspeople do not have unlimited memory allocations. Even more important is the archival space that may be necessary to waste afterwards.

When I receive Foley sessions as stems, the first thing I do is import them into a Foley session. If you are transferring from a source medium, slave the session to the time code of the source medium (DA-88 or 24-track, etc.). The Foley stems will lay into your Foley session in sync. Once you have finished, go to the head and look at the first 6-second position in the time code. There should be a pop there. If there is no pop, then you have no exact frame reference to start with. Your better Foley stages will always put a reference pop in their sessions.

To better look for any subtle recordings, increase the waveform signature by tapping on the up arrow (the four-arrow array in the upper left-hand corner

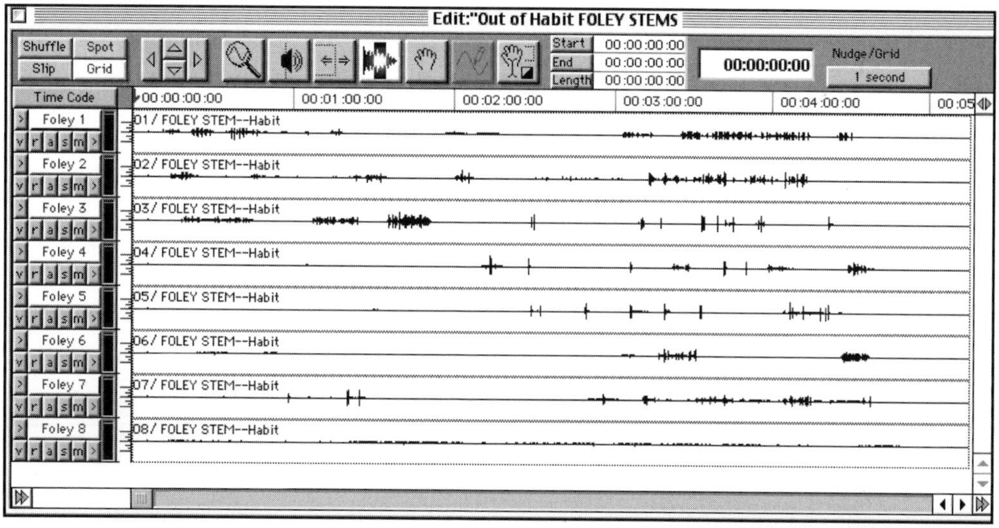

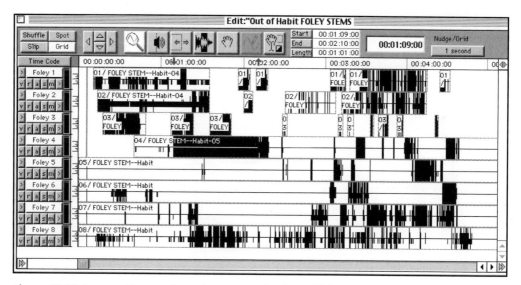

Figure 17.20 Foley stems are imported into a Foley session, ready to work with.

Figure 17.21 Increase the waveform signature to clearly see if there are any subtle Foley cues lurking about.

of your session window, next to the magnifying glass). Tap on this several times until the track becomes thick black. Any subtle recordings will appear clearly now, and it makes it very easy for you to determine what wasted areas you wish to eliminate.

Software writers at Digidesign will scoff and ask me why I do not use their Strip Silence option under Edit in the menu bar. Well, I have used it, and even changing the

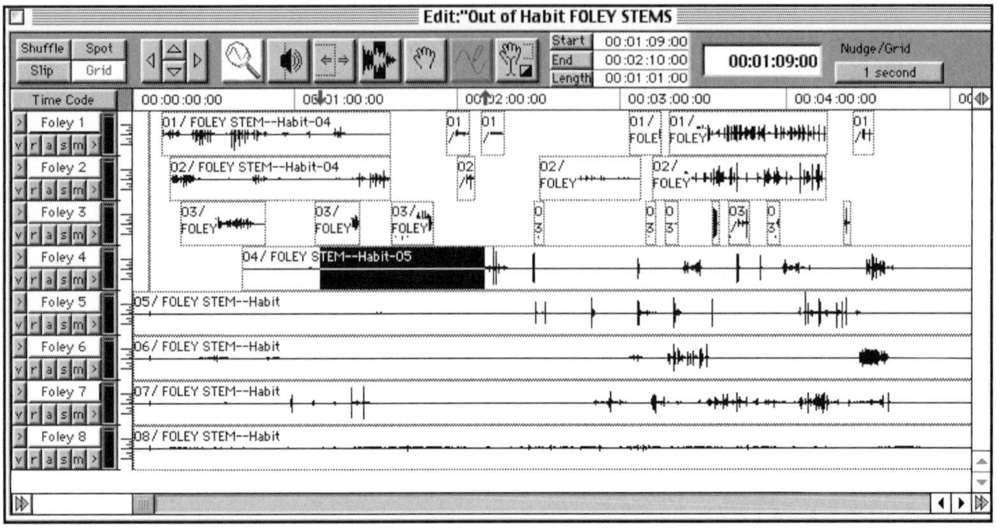

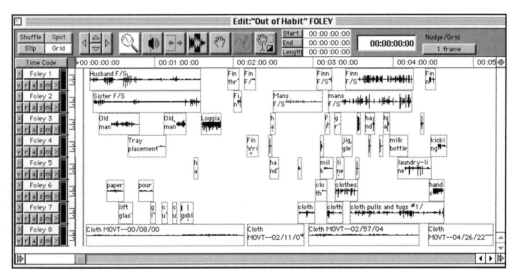

Figure 17.22 Highlighting empty track areas in GRID mode with a 1-second Nudge/Grid setting, erase the wasted silent sections.

Figure 17.23 Refer to the Foley cue sheets for reference, then tap on each cue and rename the region.

presets to open the pre- and post-roll sensitivities, I have still experienced clipped overtones and giblet cut-up cues that are really inappropriate. I find it safer just to take a few moments and do the job manually. Like all good art form, good craftspersonship is done by human tactile interaction. And, like all programmed parameters, computers only do things literally. They do not judge or evaluate and then make their own educated or creative decisions.

Now I will quickly go through and decide which areas of silence I wish to eliminate. It is important to work in Grid mode with a 1 Second Nudge/Grid option for fast re-syncing. Highlight the areas of silence you want to do away with and delete.

Once you have done that, tap twice on each cue and rename it. Once you have renamed the cues, highlight all the audio cues in the session. Then go up to the bar above the region list with the Audio designation and open that menu. Come down to Export Selected as Files and a menu will come up asking you what audio format you want, what sample rate, etc. You need to choose a target folder to put these new audio cues. Once you have set the parameters of the export, initiate the transfer.

The session will output each cut region as a new audio file, named with the new name that you gave the cut region in the session. Once the process is complete (and it does not take very long, especially when using a Mac G4) go back up to the Audio bar and import these new files. They will line up as bold black titles against the non-bold cut region names. The bold black titled audio cues are your new files. Now is when the Grid mode of 1 second really pays off. You can quickly grab and pull in and snap to sync each bold titled audio file against its cut region counterpart very quickly.

Once you have done this, you can save and close your session. Open up your session folder where the original Foley stems reside and drag them into your computer's Trash barrel and flush them away. Take a moment to be sure that all you are throwing away are the original stems and not your newly created audio files. You will probably discover that you have reduced your drive space consumption for the Foley session by at least 60 percent, often times as high as 80 percent. This makes it far more efficient to work with, both for you as well as shipping data and archival.

IT WILL ALL COME TOGETHER

If you have not worked on the creation of audio art, undoubtedly it is difficult to understand its techniques and philosophical issues, but, as you learn the process by which the soundtrack evolves, you eventually will come to understand. Some of it will make sense to you as you read about it here. Other parts will evolve into a sharp focus of understanding as you practice one or more aspects of sound creation. Then at the strangest moments, when you least expect it, often quite humorous to those around you, you will swear you had an epiphany induced by extraterrestrial intervention. It was that way for me, like a bolt of lightning: suddenly two points of technicality collided to bring forth conceptual understanding, and then my mind became a sponge, soaking it up.

Remember this—the best Foley, just like great dialog editing, is a transparent art form. If the audience is aware of what we do, we have pulled its attention out of the film reality we are creating, and therefore we have failed. So go forth and make Jack Foley proud of you!

Chapter 18
Nonlinear
The Digital Workstation

I slip into my ergonomic workstation seat with self-adjusting hydro lifts to support my back and correct my posture. I flip on the system. My liquid helium hard drive cylinders glow to life. My system is not considered to be bulked up with memory, but I do like to have 30.5 terabytes of instant access, especially on the larger feature films. At times I can remember when we still struggled with 24-byte 96-kHz sampling rate sound files. Drive management was so much more difficult then—only a couple of terabyte drives at our disposal. That was when data was stuck on rigid surfaces that spun at high rates of speed. Now with liquid helium, fragmentation doesn't exist anymore because nothing moves, in the old sense of the word, and thus the concept of a computer crash has ceased to exist.

I slip on the infrared wristband and boot up the newly installed Pro Tools 14.2 software. The blue laser of my optical computer drive flashes to life and stabilizes.

The Neurosine plug-in is becoming easier to work with. Its creative freedom has taught me to just lean back, relax my head into the neck pad of my ergo lounger, and simply think through the process. I do not have to manipulate a track ball or use a freehand pencil pad to articulate my DSP wishes, as we had to do a few years back. Just a short time ago, I used to have to watch each process unfold on my plasma monitor screen, but I have learned to trust my hearing more than my vision, so I simply close my eyes to begin my day's work.

The wristband interfaces with my nervous system straight into the audio software linkages, and the computer instantly extrapolates what I think. It took awhile for the computer and me to bond—I even chose the Hal alert kit that Apple had included in this custom package—so now I really feel like I belong to the world of a space odyssey—at least the one that I get work in now. The personal filter files disregard the vast amount of brain noise, allowing only the focused solution-seeking elements of neuro-transmission. In short, I am a creative person with a busy brain stem who also tends to be a little scatterbrained, but the Neurosine plug-in has really helped me focus when I need to.

I call up an old recording Dr. Regusters of the Jet Propulsion Laboratory had made in the Congo many years ago. I go to work on separating the loud and hashy presence of the atmospheric insects from the distant cry of a Mokele-mbembe, a fascinating sauropod recording from deep in the Congo jungle.

Within an instant, the holographic dynamic pattern hovers over the center of my workstation as well as in the center of my mind's eye. I study it carefully. Sound technology has changed so much with the advent of select timbre analysis. The traditional two-dimensional thinking had gone as far as it could. Now we realize that the three-dimensional study and manipulation of sound have changed everything.

I see the insect noise in my head and wish an overview of the exact components. Suddenly, color values are applied to all points in the timbre analysis, rendering what looks like a magnificent galaxy filled with trillions of multicolored stars. My brain rotates the overview so I can study the interwoven blends of colors. Like peeling an onion, my thought pattern separates and assigns to the digital clipboard each color value that does not fit the desired outcome. Bit by bit the insect hash layers diminish.

I invert the audio envelope, like turning a positive into a negative, much like how the old re-recording sound mixers used a universal dip filter to isolate and then revert to ferret out the precise scope of an offending noise.

The insect hash is totally gone; now all I hear is the gentle sway of tall dried grass, the lap of the lakeshore water, and every so often the mournful cry of the Mokele. My mind sweeps in closer on the image of its timbre. Now it is easy to isolate it from the grass and water lap. I do not want to lose the other sounds completely, so I mentally ask the computer to Save As and file it away under Africa, Grass, Regusters, and Water.

There, rotating in all its glory, is the undulating timbre wave of one of the most magnificent and lonely cries that natural history has probably ever heard. My wish to do so prompts the enrichment plug-in to fill in the missing gaps the algorithm note was lacking. "Yes, please save." I mentally thought. The revised audio file disappears into the vast molecular storage structure of cold liquid helium.

I feel a hand on my shoulder. I open my eyes to see my good friend and dialog editor, Dwayne Avery. Oh, I must have been napping. I rub my eyes and wonder what happened to my wristband. I see that I was sitting in my stiff so-called lumbar-support chair. I swear, whoever does invent the ergonomic editing chair will make a fortune— and where did my Pro Tools 14.2 go? Oh yes, we are still some years away from that but these very technologies are in development right now. Some of it is a lot closer than you may think.

PRACTICAL PHILOSOPHY

Each chapter of this book could easily be expanded into a complete book of its own; therefore the focus is toward the practical art form and technique to empower you, whether you are the writer, director, producer, or picture editor beginning to venture into the hands-on applications of working with sound, or you're simply fascinated by the audio arts.

With that in mind, I turn the focus toward a basic overview of the nonlinear digital audio workstation and a few software programs that will launch you in the right direction.

At first glance, the tidal wave of hardware and software can be daunting and intimidating, even to the experienced craftsperson. With very few exceptions, those individuals who truly understand digital applications and can work software proficiently do not necessarily make artistically talented sound artists. Those who are great sound editors or create audio works of art often struggle just to move around in the vastly complex world of computer technologies. It is a very odd phenomenon, but one I have seen time and time again—it goes back to the issue of left-brain/right-brain function.

I have had film school students who had taken a course in Pro Tools and had been taught all kinds of tricks and shortcuts, but not the basic sound-editing disciplines and techniques. Yes, I use some simple keystroke shortcuts with digital software, but readily acknowledge that I shun the super-shortcut tricks. Those who have the most trouble with edit sessions and especially with exactitudes to synchronization can trace the roots of their nemesis directly back to the use of super-shortcuts. These techniques only work in ideal situations, where each preceding step is followed exactly and everyone does his or her job correctly. As has been demonstrated repeatedly, just the opposite prevails. The very art of editing is to problem solve in addition to asserting one's own creative voice. How can one possibly hope to use super-shortcuts in a flawless manner amid the production and postproduction tempest?

NONLINEAR EDITING PLATFORMS

With few cosmetic differences, most nonlinear sound editing platforms work pretty much the same way. Many have their own proprietary something or others and a few excel in exceptional signal processing prowess over their competitors. But when it comes right down to it, if you understand the basic techniques of how to set up sessions, what drives sync for these sessions, and how to route a signal path and the basic principles of audio signal processing, then you can move back and forth through the various manufacturers fairly easily.

Think of the nonlinear audio workstation as a digital Moviola, a digital synchronizer, a digital Rivas splicer, and all the other audio tools used by sound craftspeople through the decades since Alexander Graham Bell invented the telephone. For the sake of streamlining this chapter as we discuss the nonlinear world of sound editing, and because Pro Tools is the dominant nonlinear audio workstation platform in the motion picture business, we will discuss the nonlinear issues through the procedures and protocols of Pro Tools.

This book does not try to instruct in the full use of this software program; that would be a big fat volume of its own and not what the mission of this book is about. This chapter is a basic get-started primer to get you on track and heading in the right direction. By the time you finish digesting this chapter you should be ready to tackle the owner's manual and/or the Digidesign Pro Tools PDF versions on line. Check them out; they are a great source of information and detailed explanation of your nonlinear system, and after reading this chapter, it will actually start to make sense.

Remember that virtually all audio software and hardware have been designed and text manuals written for music users. The vast majority of the consumer market for these products is not the sound editing market, but music composers, music editors, and music developers and the thousands of hope-to-be music composers. Hence, the user manuals talk in music terms.

A reason that user's manuals are seemingly impossible to read and understand is that they are written with the supposition that you are a computer-techie who already knows how to use computers or basic software. Most problems I hear include "I can't get it open!" or "How do you get the software to see a file?" or "How do I get from here to there?" and the proverbial, "Someone has deleted my session!" Therefore, I include basic highlights that should problem solve many of the get-started questions.

This book is not going to deal with the volatile and ever-changing keeping-up-with-the-digital-Joneses syndrome. As for this chapter, before you jump in the deep end, you first have to learn how to swim. Once again, let me remind you that a computer is only as smart as you tell it. When you call it stupid, you are really calling yourself stupid. You were the one who did not set the disk allocation logically. You were the one that did not set the session set-up window correctly, and who was it that forgot to target where to put the Save As option and now you can't find it? . . . I think you get the idea.

Nonlinear Audio Signal Path

As touched on briefly in Chapter 11, you must create a clean signal path from your audio file source, through your sound interface (whatever system you decide to use that requires a hardware interface; some do not), through the computer, back through the interface, out through your workstation mixer, out to your speaker amplifiers (if you are not using self-powered speakers), and ultimately to the monitor speakers.

You must have a clean input path where you can digitize (record) monaural, stereophonic, quadraphonic, or as many tracks as you have interface inputs to accommodate—bringing an analog world into the digital realm as an audio file format that your workstation recognizes and uses. You also must have the ability to transfer material digitally (known as D-to-D) from DAT cassettes, such as a DAT recorder, using AES/EBU ins and outs or a coaxial digital processing cable or digital optical cable. Many beginners do not understand that they must use a high-quality digital coaxial cable for D-to-D work, often mistakenly using common RCA connectors.

When it comes to your signal path, whether it is a digital or an analog signal—spending a few extra dollars to have the best quality connectors and speaker cable for your gear can only make the signal path cleaner and easier to listen to and allow you to relax and be assured that you are not adding noise and audio gunk to your recordings or downloads.

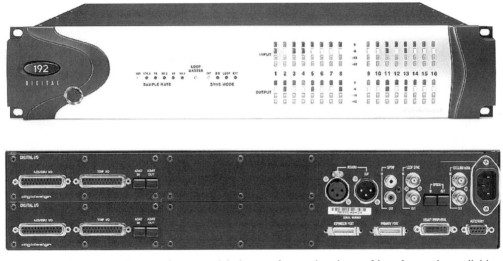

Figure 18.1 The Digidesign Interface 192 Digital. One of several variants of interface units available for postproduction sound work.

The Interface I/O

The 192 I/O, the flagship of the Pro Tools HD interface family, is the best-sounding audio interface ever offered from Digidesign. In addition to support for up to 16 channels of analog and digital input and output, the 192 I/O features a wide range of analog and digital I/O options to choose from, including 8 channels of high-definition, pristine-quality analog I/O, 8 channels of AES/EBU, 8 channels of TDIF, 16 channels of ADAT, and 2 additional channels of AES/EBU or S/PDIF digital I/O. The Pro Tools HD Interface handles 8 discrete channels of either analog or digital audio signal.

In designing the Pro Tools HD environment, Digidesign offers a work environment that not only supports today's common standards of 48 kHz and 44.1 kHz, but the emerging use of 96 kHz, all the way up to a stunning 192 kHz. In addition, Pro Tools HD 192 I/O also supports 176.4-kHz and 88.2-kHz sample rates.

You already know that with 24-bit resolution, and now with the higher sampling rates, you will be able to capture every nuance of sound with the utmost clarity and precision.

192 Expansion Cards

Along with its outstanding sonic specs, 192 I/O includes an additional I/O option bay, allowing you to add more inputs or outputs, and making it one of the most unique and flexible audio interfaces on the market. To expand the analog I/O capacity of 192 I/O, you can add either a 192 AD card, providing 8 more channels of high-definition analog input, or the 192 DA card, which gives you 8 additional channels of analog output. 192 I/O can also be outfitted with the 192 digital card, which adds 8 channels of AES/EBU, TDIF, and ADAT I/O connections.

Speakers

Choose your speakers carefully. This is where so many sound designers and sound editors make a common mistake. You can beef up your workstation suite with powerful subwoofers and all kinds of tricked-out gear. When you play your sessions, you are rocking and rolling, literally sending earthquake-like shudders through the studio's framework. You finish cutting your helicopter chase sequence, absolutely convinced that you aced a sequence that will garnish an Academy Award nomination. Then you get to the re-recording stage and experience total shock when it does not play back anything like you remember cutting it.

The reason is simple. You colorized your workstation environment to have acoustical fun, not to develop and cut serious sound for film and video applications. You must think transparent. I say this to designer and editing colleagues alike. You want a workstation environment that reproduces your work as identically as possible to how it will sound when you get it to the re-recording stage. Keep all your ultra-subwoofer toys at home for personal use and fun, not at work when you are developing serious product. On the other hand, you do not want a speaker system lacking the rich low ends your material must have.

SETTING UP AN ORGANIZED DESKTOP

I can always tell how organized a sound editor is by looking at how he or she sets up the desktop of the computer. The ones with troubles tend to have a cluttered desktop. Poor desktop layout slows down your work and frustrates you. I keep my desktop divided into two basic parts. The hard-drive icons always boot up on the right side of the screen; therefore I leave that side strictly for hard drives and nothing else.

I make a folder that I leave on the left side of the desktop and name it "Sessions." Each evening, before shutting down for the day, I copy the sessions on which I have worked into this folder, giving each session a current date or code designation. The first time your external hard drive crashes with irreparable damage or melts down, you adopt this technique instantly. I make a couple of other work-in-progress-type folders, which hold word-processing documents regarding work, sound design layout charts, spotting notes, EDL lists, and so forth. I keep all other folders in the lower center of my screen. The desktop is organized, easy to read.

Keep an organized desktop and drive management routine, and you will lose very little work and endure a lot less anguish.

DRIVE MANAGEMENT

The oft-repeated adage "garbage in, garbage out" also applies to the building and maintaining of your internal and external hard drives.

One of my hard drives on *Starship Troopers* was named 149 A. No matter what project, I always placed my Pro Tools edit sessions on the first drive of my SCSI chain. I placed some sound files on this drive, but basically kept the bulk of the sound library files on the following drives. I made individual folders that designated the reel of the

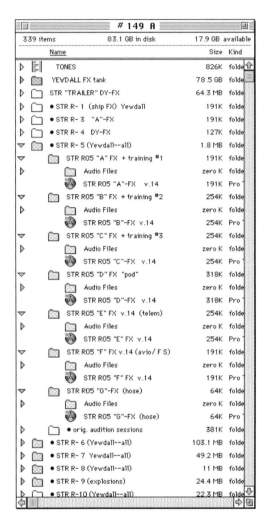

Figure 18.2 Drive 149 A. Fast and efficient work starts with good disk management. Neat, efficient layout makes it easy to find things and helps to defeat drive conflicts and corruption.

project, using an abbreviation of the project, followed by the reel number. In the example displayed in the 149 A chart in Figure 18.2, I have opened the folder for reel 5 of *Starship Troopers*. In naming the file, I held down the Option key and pressed the 8 key to make a bullet prior to the name. Using bullets ensures that bullet folders group together when read under the View menu designation of By Name. This gives the folder the name of STR R05 (Yewdall—all).

149 A Hard Drive

Because we had quite a team of sound editors on *Starship Troopers*, with many specialty assignments, I needed to make it clear that the materials in this folder were my sessions and not those of Warren Hamilton, Jr., Charles Maynes, or Greg Hedgepath.

One of the most important things you must consider when organizing work and designating files is working on the heart-attack principle. Here you are, working on a motion picture with a production budget in excess of $150 million. After a grueling day's work, you have a heart attack, a stroke, an auto accident, and you are in the hospital in a coma or otherwise incapacitated. As cold and unfeeling as it may sound, someone must be able to boot up your computer with as little trouble as possible and carry on with your work with little lost time. Developing good disk management technique and discipline goes a long way toward helping others, should the need arise.

Inside the STR R05 (Yewdall—all) file is where I keep all my Pro Tools sessions involved with reel 5. *Starship Troopers* was such a gargantuan project that I needed a dedicated external hard drive just to keep the fade files from bloating up my session drive. This is not the case for most projects, as you keep your fade file folders in the Pro Tools session folder.

The second folder from the top is named YEWDALL FX tank. This is the first of several folders, as well as external hard drives, where I kept sound effect audio files.

Tones Folder

Inside the tones folder are the basic audio files ensuring consistently clean head and tail pops, correct line-up tone, ADR blips, and a slug of blank (an audio file with no sound that sound editors often use for making notes to themselves or other editors on the Pro Tools session). This note will show up on the computer-generated cue sheet and is perfect for making editor's notes to the re-recording mixer.

Carefully measure the pop audio file. As discussed earlier, many editors do not think that a video (30 fps) session shows frames shorter than film sessions (24 fps). Before you commence using someone else's tones folder and are not intimately familiar with the material, take the time to drag the pop audio file into your session, set the feet.frame designation under the Display menu, and actually check the precise length of the pop.

You should also drag the 1 kHz at –18 line-up tone out on the session, then digitally output the signal to your DAT recorder. It is important that you output the signal digitally, to ensure that you can calibrate properly. You will not be able to assure yourself of signal path impedance if you output the signal in analog.

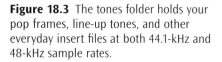

Figure 18.3 The tones folder holds your pop frames, line-up tones, and other everyday insert files at both 44.1-kHz and 48-kHz sample rates.

If the line-up tone audio file is advertised at –18, then it should read exactly –18 on the digital meter of your DAT recorder. If it does not, you should find out why. As discussed in Chapter 6, –18 dB is not necessarily an industry standard, but whatever the house standard, the line-up tone audio files in the tones folder should reflect that.

Notice that there are two sets of pops as well as two sets of 1-kHz tone; each has been made in both 48-kHz and 44.1-kHz sampling rates so that you can work in either sample format. We place a 1-kHz tone in every channel of your session, usually placed at the end of the session several seconds after the tail pop. Many of us use the technique of staggering these tones 2 seconds apart, so that the machine-room engineer can scan the meter and watch each channel pop up to –18 on the peak meter and confirm that the signal path is playing at the correct level.

We also have a track of ADR blips. I make my ADR blips by taking 1 frame of 1-kHz tone and then I make an *extremely* short fade-in and fade-out on the tone, thus taking the digital harshness off the blip. I then import the softened blip into a Pro Tools session where I set the counter to feet and frames (and not time code). I place three rhythmic blips in a row, exactly 1 foot (24 frames) apart. I then highlight from the leading edge of the first blip through the three blips and to the leading edge of 4 feet. This will yield three rhythmic blips with 23 frames of silence before the end of that audio file. I then bounce to disk (see Bounce to Disk later in this chapter) to make a new file (i.e., ADR blips).

Building Your Audio File Drives

To make your audio files efficient and easy to access, you must plan to make them so. Some editors simply make a file folder they call "Load," which is supposed to hold all the audio files needed for the particular reel on which they are working. This method works fine if you are working on only one reel and if you have a precise cut list to work from with no deviations.

If you are working on more than one reel, if you have been given creative license, if you think creatively rather than methodically, you will desire the alphabetical file system. I set my drives up in such a manner that the main library resides in an alphabetical format.

Sound Library Drive

The most important way to facilitate smooth, efficient performance of your hard drives is to practice good drive management techniques. For those confused by conflicting advice regarding the use of an optimization program, nonlinear picture editing platforms such as Final Cut Pro or the Avid work more efficiently if the files are fragmented, thus the contradictory advice from those who might tell you not to defragment your audio workstation hard drives. The contrary is true when it comes to Pro Tools and how it functions. I defragment my hard drives at least every other week, and, when I am working on extremely complex sound effects pictures, I let my Norton Utilities speed disk function defragment my hard drives every few days.

Sometimes, defragmenting hard drives with Norton Utilities has led to damage or data loss in the audio file directories. A good maintenance software very useful in

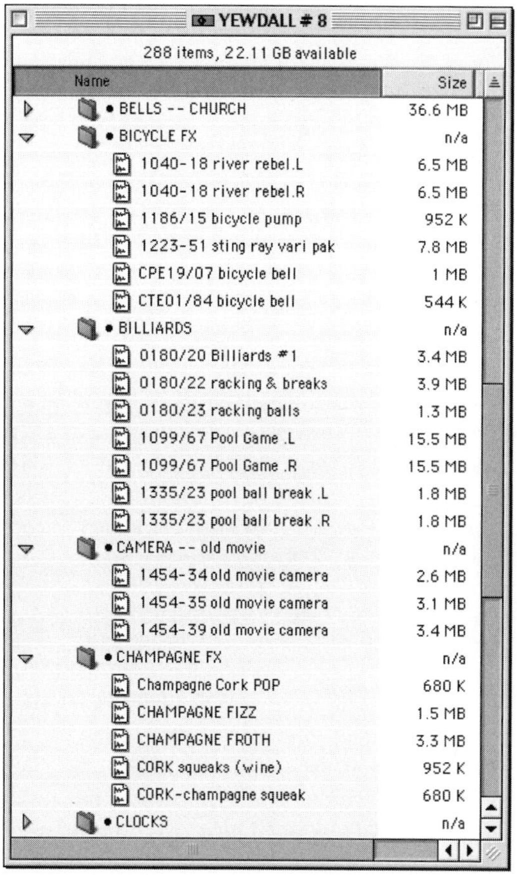

Figure 18.4 A typical sound effect access drive. This is the alphabetical file system. Personally, I use a bullet and a space prior to the file name. This guarantees that all of these file folders will line up to the bottom of the list.

protecting audio file directories is DiskWarrior. Run this application before you defragment your drives, and you will notice dramatically less file corruption.

For a step-by-step narration of the Pro Tools get-started presentation outlined above, you can interact with the DVD provided with this book—choose button number nine on the main menu, STUDIO FACILITIES -&- SYSTEMS. The second button on the submenu will take you through the presentation.

This chapter is meant only as an introduction. One could easily fill an entire book trying to properly discuss and review the use and techniques of Pro Tools and Nuendo software. There is a lot more information on the Interactive DVD that is included with this book. Go to button number nine—NONLINEAR EDITING & MIXING on the main menu. For a more extensive version of this chapter, see the book's website at *http://textbooks.elsevier.com/companions/9780240808659*.

The first button on the submenu will take you to another submenu regarding EUPHONIX -&- NEUNDO USER PROFILES. You can view four really informative user profile videos. Button two will take you through a narrated step-by-step tour of Nuendo software and a few of the plug-ins Nuendo offers. Button three will take you through a narrated step-by-step tour of Pro Tools 7.2 as well as an overview of many of the plug-ins available. Button four will take you on a short but fascinating narrated overview of the Pro Tools Icon system.

Nuendo 3—Media Production System

After you read this section on Nuendo, you really need to review the four video demos on the interactive DVD that accompanies this book with user profiles of three master craftspeople in Hollywood and London who are using Nuendo software in conjunction with the Euphonix Mixing console.

Nuendo 3 is one of the most flexible and technologically advanced postproduction, recording, and surround systems available on the market today. Extraordinary sound quality and a host of unrivalled features, paired with a totally open architecture engineered to accommodate the audio industry's prevailing software and hardware standards, make Nuendo the system of choice for discerning professional users. Its system performance is readily scaled using any standard computer components. This gives you the computing power you need to rise to the challenge of handling complex projects entailing hundreds of tracks, innumerable effects and even the most intricate mixer configurations, all at a remarkably affordable price.

- Recording, editing, and mixing with up to 192-kHz/24-bit processing power (pristine 32-bit floating-point internal resolution)
- Intuitive handling and extensive customization options to accelerate workflow
- Projects port readily to and from all standard audio and video cutting systems
- Powerful multichannel capability throughout the signal path
- Awesome-sounding 32-bit audio engine optimized for multiprocessor operation
- Up to 192 physical inputs/outputs alongside freely selectable audio hardware
- Smooth, seamless integration into LAN and WAN environments
- Cross-platform product (Mac OS X/Windows XP)

Like many DAW systems, Nuendo has two main windows, an Edit window and a Mix window. Figure 18.5 is an example of an Edit window. On the top left is a blue hardware control button which allows for multiple sessions being open at the same time; the session that has this button highlighted actually is controlling the hardware, but all open sessions have full editing capability and cut and paste functionality among each other, a great tool for reconfirming a picture.

Below this button is an inspector panel that gives an overview of all the details that belong to the current highlighted track.

To the right of the inspector panel are the track names and track headers, which show and control automation states, locking and unlocking, solo control, mute control, all the sublevels of automation, and level indication. The view above is a collapse view only showing the minimal amount of detail.

The Transport window shows you your basic tape-machine-style transport buttons as well as jog and shuttle controls, in and out markers, pre-/post-roll amounts, sync status, memory location points, and computer performance.

As this program is a host-based system, the power of the host computer is of great significance.

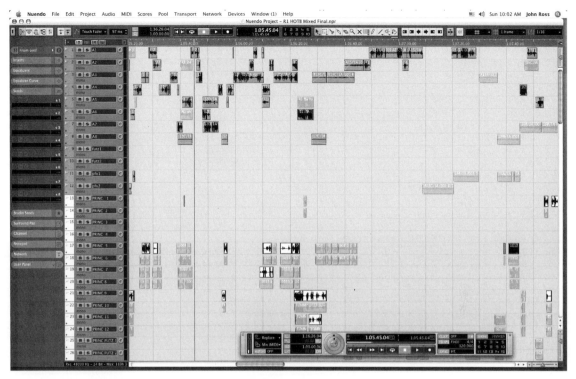

Figure 18.5 Sound library drive.

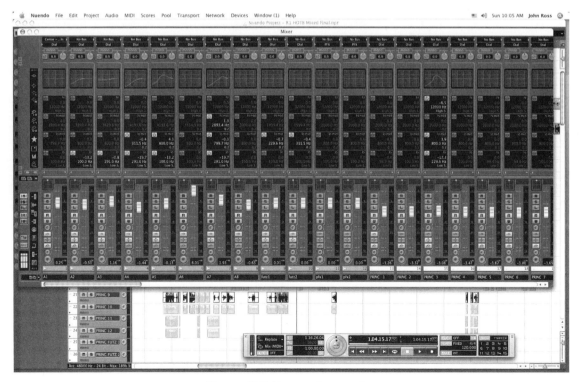

Figure 18.6 New session warning.

Figure 18.7 New session menu.

Figure 18.8 New tracks.

One can control the amount of DSP type functionality by using better and faster computing power, which is moving like a runaway train today.

With a dual-core AMD system, today track counts well over 200 with a plentiful amount of plug in are not uncommon on a single system.

Below is the Mixer window. This window can be viewed in many different ways; here are a few of many examples.

The Mixer from the top down first shows your input source, the amount and configuration of which are set up in the VST connections page, or I/O page as some systems call it. Below that are the output assign and the trim and phase knob, consistent with what you would find on any high-quality mixing console.

The section below this can display EQs (in a few view types), plug-in insert points 1–8, aux sends 1–8, or elaborate metering and panning. Below this panel is the fader panel that has metering, panning, automation states, record arming, input monitoring, plug-in, and EQ bypass switches mute and solo. There are many sublevels and far more detail in these windows than what I am currently describing, but for a basic overview these are the main points.

Figure 18.9 shows the VST connections or I/O page that allows you to create and map inputs and outputs to the hardware you have in your system, as well as create

Bus Name	Speakers	Audio Device	Device Port
▼ ◁ Mon	5.1	Not Connected	
—○ Left		(ASIO HDSP MADI/AES–32)	Pending
—○ Right		(ASIO HDSP MADI/AES–32)	Pending
—○ Center		(ASIO HDSP MADI/AES–32)	Pending
—○ LFE		(ASIO HDSP MADI/AES–32)	Pending
—○ Left Surround		(ASIO HDSP MADI/AES–32)	Pending
—○ Right Surround		(ASIO HDSP MADI/AES–32)	Pending
▼ Dial	5.1	Not Connected	
—○ Left		(ASIO HDSP MADI/AES–32)	Pending
—○ Right		(ASIO HDSP MADI/AES–32)	Pending
—○ Center		(ASIO HDSP MADI/AES–32)	Pending
—○ LFE		(ASIO HDSP MADI/AES–32)	Pending
—○ Left Surround		(ASIO HDSP MADI/AES–32)	Pending
—○ Right Surround		(ASIO HDSP MADI/AES–32)	Pending
▼ Grp	5.1	Not Connected	
—○ Left		(ASIO HDSP MADI/AES–32)	Pending
—○ Right		(ASIO HDSP MADI/AES–32)	Pending
—○ Center		(ASIO HDSP MADI/AES–32)	Pending
—○ LFE		(ASIO HDSP MADI/AES–32)	Pending
—○ Left Surround		(ASIO HDSP MADI/AES–32)	Pending
—○ Right Surround		(ASIO HDSP MADI/AES–32)	Pending
▼ MX	5.1	Not Connected	
—○ Left		(ASIO HDSP MADI/AES–32)	Pending
—○ Right		(ASIO HDSP MADI/AES–32)	Pending
—○ Center		(ASIO HDSP MADI/AES–32)	Pending
—○ LFE		(ASIO HDSP MADI/AES–32)	Pending
—○ Left Surround		(ASIO HDSP MADI/AES–32)	Pending
—○ Right Surround		(ASIO HDSP MADI/AES–32)	Pending
▼ TC	Mono	Not Connected	
—○ Mono		(ASIO HDSP MADI/AES–32)	Pending
▼ PFX	LRC	MOTU 828mk2	
—○ Left			Main OUT L MOTU 828
—○ Right			Main OUT R MOTU 828
—○ Center			Line 3 OUT MOTU 828

Figure 18.9 New track creating.

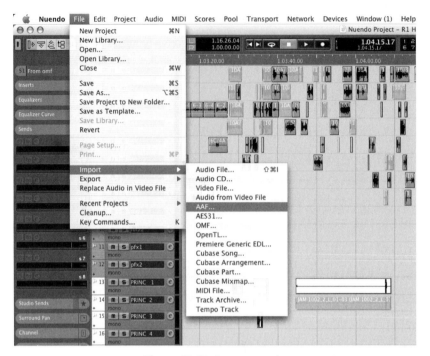

Figure 18.10 Rename track.

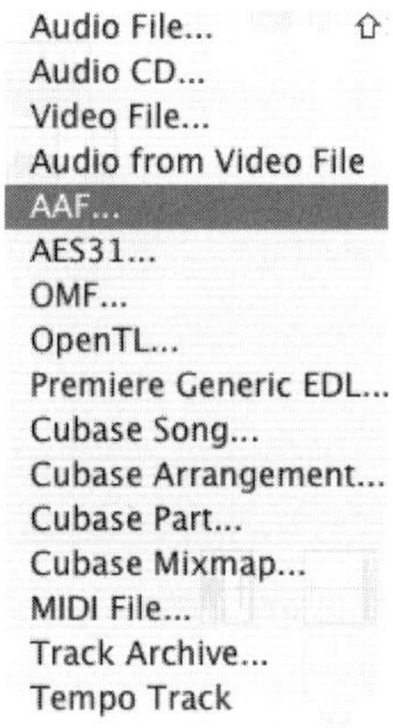

Figure 18.11 Track header.

bussing for FX, groupers, and I/O for external processing boxes. The amount of physical I/O or inputs and outputs is determined by the choice of hardware. It can be as small as the 2-channel system on a laptop or as elaborate as a multi-card Madi system with 192 inputs and outputs.

Here are the Import Selection options (Figures 18.10 and 18.11). This system can import and export AAF and OMF for working with other editing systems and picture editing workstations as well as AES31 and a host of options, including HD picture when paired with a Decklink card for picture I/O.

Media	Used	Status	Info				Type	Date		Origin Time	Image	Path
▼ 🗁 Audio		Record										
008 10A_2_4.bwf	5	▦	48.000 kHz	24 bits	Mono	1.50 m	Broadcast Wave File	2006-07-24	06:52:52	0.00.00.00		[HOME OF THE BRAVE] /Volumes/WORKGROUP:424SERVER/Mix I
A1_02	1		48.000 kHz	24 bits	Mono	2.467 s	Broadcast Wave File	2006-08-01	13:22:07	1.18.41.06		[HOME OF THE BRAVE] /Volumes/WORKGROUP:424SERVER/Mix I
REEL 1 LOCK v1L			48.000 kHz	24 bits	Mono	17:33 m	Wave File	8/9/06	7:14 PM	0.00.00.00		[HOME OF THE BRAVE] /Volumes/WORKGROUP:424SERVER/Mix I
HOTB R1 LOCK V2_L			48.000 kHz	24 bits	Mono	17:33 m	Wave File	8/9/06	7:14 PM	0.00.00.00		[HOME OF THE BRAVE] /Volumes/WORKGROUP:424SERVER/Mix I
work 1_01	1		48.000 kHz	24 bits	Mono	8.144 s	Broadcast Wave File	2006-07-21	17:52:22	1.07.55.12		[HOME OF THE BRAVE] /Volumes/WORKGROUP:424SERVER/Mix I
Will 1092_01.R	1		48.000 kHz	24 bits	Mono	3.434 s	Broadcast Wave File	2006-07-14	16:17:12	1.14.58.16		[HOME OF THE BRAVE] /Volumes/WORKGROUP:424SERVER/Mix I
Will 1092_01.L	1		48.000 kHz	24 bits	Mono	3.434 s	Broadcast Wave File	2006-07-14	16:17:12	1.14.58.16		[HOME OF THE BRAVE] /Volumes/WORKGROUP:424SERVER/Mix I
Will 1091_02.R	1		48.000 kHz	24 bits	Mono	4.243 s	Broadcast Wave File	2006-07-14	16:16:21	1.14.56.03		[HOME OF THE BRAVE] /Volumes/WORKGROUP:424SERVER/Mix I
Will 1091_02.L	1		48.000 kHz	24 bits	Mono	4.243 s	Broadcast Wave File	2006-07-14	16:16:21	1.14.56.03		[HOME OF THE BRAVE] /Volumes/WORKGROUP:424SERVER/Mix I
Will 1091_01.R	1		48.000 kHz	24 bits	Mono	5.507 s	Broadcast Wave File	2006-07-14	16:15:29	1.14.56.03		[HOME OF THE BRAVE] /Volumes/WORKGROUP:424SERVER/Mix I
Will 1091_01.L	1		48.000 kHz	24 bits	Mono	5.507 s	Broadcast Wave File	2006-07-14	16:15:29	1.14.56.03		[HOME OF THE BRAVE] /Volumes/WORKGROUP:424SERVER/Mix I
Vanessa 1194_01.R	3		48.000 kHz	24 bits	Mono	17.721 s	Broadcast Wave File	2006-07-14	15:04:26	1.14.21.19		[HOME OF THE BRAVE] /Volumes/WORKGROUP:424SERVER/Mix I
Vanessa 1077_02.R	9		48.000 kHz	24 bits	Mono	14.928 s	Broadcast Wave File	2006-07-14	15:02:45	1.12.45.01		[HOME OF THE BRAVE] /Volumes/WORKGROUP:424SERVER/Mix I
Vanessa 1077_02.L	10		48.000 kHz	24 bits	Mono	14.928 s	Broadcast Wave File	2006-07-14	15:02:45	1.12.45.01		[HOME OF THE BRAVE] /Volumes/WORKGROUP:424SERVER/Mix I
Vanessa 1077_01.R	2		48.000 kHz	24 bits	Mono	17.146 s	Broadcast Wave File	2006-07-14	15:01:10	1.12.45.01		[HOME OF THE BRAVE] /Volumes/WORKGROUP:424SERVER/Mix I
Vanessa 1077_01.L	2		48.000 kHz	24 bits	Mono	17.146 s	Broadcast Wave File	2006-07-14	15:01:10	1.12.45.01		[HOME OF THE BRAVE] /Volumes/WORKGROUP:424SERVER/Mix I
Vanessa 1063_01.R	1		48.000 kHz	24 bits	Mono	4.928 s	Broadcast Wave File	2006-07-14	14:59:36	1.11.01.15		[HOME OF THE BRAVE] /Volumes/WORKGROUP:424SERVER/Mix I
Vanessa 1063_01.L	1		48.000 kHz	24 bits	Mono	4.928 s	Broadcast Wave File	2006-07-14	14:59:36	1.11.01.15		[HOME OF THE BRAVE] /Volumes/WORKGROUP:424SERVER/Mix I
Vanessa 1060_01.R	13		48.000 kHz	24 bits	Mono	29.166 s	Broadcast Wave File	2006-07-14	14:57:07	1.10.55.11		[HOME OF THE BRAVE] /Volumes/WORKGROUP:424SERVER/Mix I
Vanessa 1060_01.L	13		48.000 kHz	24 bits	Mono	29.166 s	Broadcast Wave File	2006-07-14	14:57:07	1.10.55.11		[HOME OF THE BRAVE] /Volumes/WORKGROUP:424SERVER/Mix I
Vanessa 1057_02.R	1		48.000 kHz	24 bits	Mono	4.133 s	Broadcast Wave File	2006-07-14	14:53:55	1.10.40.15		[HOME OF THE BRAVE] /Volumes/WORKGROUP:424SERVER/Mix I
Vanessa 1057_02.L	1	▦	48.000 kHz	24 bits	Mono	4.083 s	Broadcast Wave File	2006-07-14	14:53:55	1.10.40.15		[HOME OF THE BRAVE] /Volumes/WORKGROUP:424SERVER/Mix I
Vanessa 1057_01.R	1		48.000 kHz	24 bits	Mono	3.272 s	Broadcast Wave File	2006-07-14	14:53:35	1.10.40.15		[HOME OF THE BRAVE] /Volumes/WORKGROUP:424SERVER/Mix I
Vanessa 1057_01.L	1		48.000 kHz	24 bits	Mono	3.272 s	Broadcast Wave File	2006-07-14	14:53:35	1.10.40.15		[HOME OF THE BRAVE] /Volumes/WORKGROUP:424SERVER/Mix I
Vanessa 1037_02.R	2		48.000 kHz	24 bits	Mono	4.159 s	Broadcast Wave File	2006-07-14	14:51:56	1.07.25.23		[HOME OF THE BRAVE] /Volumes/WORKGROUP:424SERVER/Mix I
Vanessa 1037_02.L	2		48.000 kHz	24 bits	Mono	4.159 s	Broadcast Wave File	2006-07-14	14:51:56	1.07.25.23		[HOME OF THE BRAVE] /Volumes/WORKGROUP:424SERVER/Mix I
Vanessa 1014_03.R	3		48.000 kHz	24 bits	Mono	11.357 s	Broadcast Wave File	2006-07-14	14:50:02	1.05.05.12		[HOME OF THE BRAVE] /Volumes/WORKGROUP:424SERVER/Mix I
Vanessa 1014_03.L	3		48.000 kHz	24 bits	Mono	11.357 s	Broadcast Wave File	2006-07-14	14:50:02	1.05.05.12		[HOME OF THE BRAVE] /Volumes/WORKGROUP:424SERVER/Mix I

Figure 18.12 Import session 15414.

R1 HOTB Mixed Final.npr	Shared		Bay 2
A1	–		Bay 2
A2	–		Bay 2
A3	–		Bay 2
A4	–		Bay 2
A5	–		Bay 2
A6	–		Bay 2
A7	–		Bay 2
A8	–		Bay 2
futz1	–		Bay 2
futz2	–		Bay 2
pfx1	–		Bay 2
pfx2	–		Bay 2
PRINC 1	–		Bay 2
PRINC 2	–		Bay 2
PRINC 3	–		Bay 2
PRINC 4	–		Bay 2
PRINC 5	–		Bay 2
PRINC 6	–		Bay 2
PRINC 7	–		Bay 2
PRINC 8	–		Bay 2
PRINC 9	–		Bay 2
PRINC 10	–		Bay 2
PRINC 11	–		Bay 2
PRINC 12	–		Bay 2
PRINC FUTZ 1	–		Bay 2
PRINC FUTZ 2	–		Bay 2
GR 1	–		Bay 2
GR 2	–		Bay 2
GR 3	–		Bay 2
GR 4	–		Bay 2

Figure 18.13 Import audio window.

Above is a view of the Pool window (Figures 18.12 and 18.13). This is where all the media for a project is housed and managed; you can insert media from here as well as format convert and search and audition. This system will search as well as play media across a network allowing for extensive sharing capability across networks and facilities.

A view of the specific project-sharing window is shown in Figure 18.14. This allows you to publish a project on a network and for other people who are allowed by the owner of that project to access and work on that project in real time.

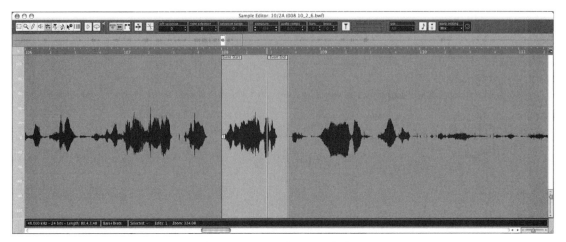

Figure 18.14 Workspace window.

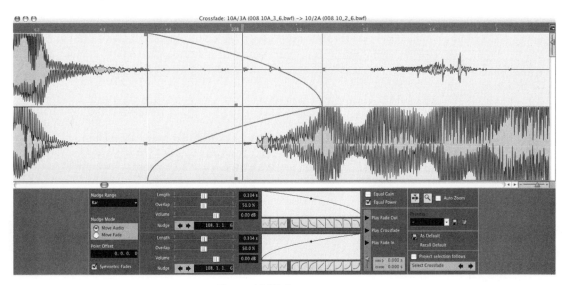

Figure 18.15 Set-up menu.

Above are shots of both the extensive waveform editor and the cross-fade editor (Figure 18.15). Nuendo 3 marks another milestone advance in the evolution of Steinberg's celebrated Media Production System. It offers a multitude of new features, including AAF support, optimized media management, Pull Up/Down, and Warp to Picture, as well as numerous new recording and surround production functions. And with the release of version 3.2, Nuendo even boasts a full-fledged control room section unlike anything found on any other software mixer.

Figure 18.16 Hardware set-up.

Control Room and Headphone Bus
Nuendo 3.2 sports dedicated output busses for control room and headphone monitoring. Control room settings do not influence the main mix output.

Four Separate Monitor Set-ups
Four freely configurable monitor set-ups let you quickly toggle among different auditioning systems. Options include fold-back as well as useful solo functions such as Solo to Center and Back to Front for surround environments.

Inputs for External Sources
You can quickly select up to six playback inputs for external signal sources such as DAT, CD, and tape decks, and route them to any desired studio, headphones, or control room bus.

Four Studio Busses
You are free to create individual submixes for up to four separate studios. Every audio, group, or effect channel in the Nuendo mixer offers new studio sends with dedicated volume and panorama controls as well as a Pre-Fader/Post-Fader switch.

Talkback Function
The talkback circuit lets you communicate directly with speakers or artists in each of the connected studios. Automatic dimming prevents feedback. You also have a switch available for manual dimming. Simply press it to instantly reduce the control room level.

Separate Click Bus

A dedicated click bus lets you patch the metronome signal to any studio, headphone, or control room bus, whereby volume and panorama may be adjusted individually.

Key Command for Main Mix to Studio Bus

A simple key command is all it takes to route the main mix to each studio. Once this is accomplished, you will find it easy to accommodate the speaker/artist's wishes and adjust the mix accordingly.

In the interactive DVD provided in this book, choose button #9 on the main menu, NONLINEAR SYSTEMS. The first button on the submenu, EUPHONIX & NUENDO USER PROFILES, will take you to another submenu. You have five choices:

- 15-minute video user profile of John Ross
- 20-minute video user profile of Richard Meredith
- 13-minute video user profile of Steve Tushar
- 8-minute video user profile of Fernand Box
- Step-by-step narrated panel presentation of the material presented in the text

Chapter 19
The Music Composer
Audio Collaboration or Mud and Destruction

"Music is nothing more than organized sound effects, and sound
effects are nothing more than disorganized music."

– David Lewis Yewdall, M.P.S.E., lecturing at the
Sibelius Academy, Helsinki, Finland

I remember, growing up, going to the local cinema to see the week's double feature. I
sat transfixed, totally in awe of the epic spectacle of Charlton Heston dividing the Red
Sea, painting the Sistine Chapel, driving the Moors out of Spain, protecting the foggy
Norman bogs from raiders of the North lands, or defending the walls of Peking from
the Boxer Rebellion. The musical scores raised me to a new level of inspiration and
majesty. Who are these musical dreamers that reach into my very soul and manipulate
my emotions?

Names like Erich Wolfgang Korngold (*The Sea Hawk, Of Human Bondage, The
Adventures of Robin Hood, Deception, Captain Blood*); Miklós Rózsa (*El Cid, Ben-Hur,
Ivanhoe, Men of the Fighting Lady, The Asphalt Jungle*); Dimitri Tiomkin (*Duel in the Sun,
55 Days in Peking, Giant, Big Country, The Guns of Navarone, Dial "M" for Murder*); Jerry
Goldsmith (*Lilies of the Field, The Sand Pebbles, Planet of the Apes, Patton, Chinatown*); Elmer
Bernstein (*To Kill a Mockingbird, The Hallelujah Trail, Hawaii, The Magnificent Seven, The
Great Escape*); Alfred Newman (*The Robe, How the West Was Won, Airport, Demetrius and
the Gladiators*); Maurice Jarre (*Lawrence of Arabia, Doctor Zhivago, The Train, Grand Prix*)
all thrilled me, lifted up and inspired me, made me want to come back and see it all
over again and be bathed in the lush glory of it all.

There was Bernard Herrmann, a category unto himself. No one else had a style
like him. Who would soon forget the haunting scores to pictures like *Citizen Kane, Jane
Eyre, The Naked and the Dead,* and *The Day the Earth Stood Still*? Sometimes I wonder

how successful Alfred Hitchcock films would have been without Herrmann handling the musical scores for *North by Northwest, Vertigo, The Man Who Knew Too Much,* and *Psycho,* and he got to show off his flair for instrumental humor in *The Trouble With Harry.*

Other contemporaries wrote their own great works: Ennio Morricone, Brian May, Bill Conti, Lalo Schifrin, and Henry Mancini are just a few of the great music composers who added musical magic to dozens of major and well-loved motion pictures.

The filmography of music composers is truly a bookshelf unto itself. Music is the most powerful and manipulative art form. It does not require translation for foreign sales; it does not require subtitles to explain itself or establishing shots to orient the listener. With a single note, music can reach into the heart and soul of the audience to set the mood, telegraph danger, or evoke romantic passions. Music whips up our emotions; reveals the guilty; sweeps us into the complex whirlpools of love, pain, anger, fear, patriotism, and joy, often at the same time.

If music is so powerful and omnipotent in films, why do we need dialog and sound effects? Many composers have asked that very question. Some would be perfectly content to return to the days of flickering images on the wall with insert cards for bits of dialog and story exposition while the only audio track would be their music.

CHALLENGES OF WRITING FOR THE SCREEN

An important lesson a music composer learns is that writing music for the screen is very different from writing music that is a total performance unto itself. When writing for the screen, the composer must understand that he or she is sharing the audio track with two other major concerns—spoken dialog and sound effects. These factors are now working together as part of a collaborative trio, rather than each singing its own aria.

When I was preparing a film for the Sundance Film Festival, the director was scrambling to complete his project with the few dollars left. He could not afford an established music composer, but found a promising new music group who wanted to break into writing for the movies. The musicians delivered their music cues in 2-channel stereo on DAT. They were so interested in the opportunity that they personally brought the tape to me.

I loaded the cues into the Pro Tools session and laced them up into sync, according to the director's notes. It was immediately evident that the music cues were unacceptable. From a technical point of view, the recordings had been overloaded—a common mistake of rock groups who think that volume is achieved by crashing the upper limits of the digital peak meter. At the very least, the cues needed to be transferred from the master and lowered to −6 dB.

The lead guitarist informed me they had no master; they performed straight to a DAT tape. I explained the virtues of recording to a multichannel master first, where one can record each element of the music group onto its own stereo pair of channels and then control the mix-down later. They were faced with having to re-perform the cues over again. It was just as well, as I showed them where the levels had flattened out in what I call the "aircraft carrier effect," where they had run out of digital zeros and ones. Surely they did not want their music to suffer dynamic flatness and distortion.

That was only a technical problem, however. A deeper, more important issue was at hand. They had written the music as if they were performing a solo act at a rock concert, full out, with no regard for anything else happening on the screen. What did they expect would happen to their music when dialog was spoken? What did they expect would happen to their music when the comic and raucous car sound effects were played? They had not considered that.

I took a piece of paper and drew a giant circle. I told them to think of this as the total amount of audio energy that can play on the screen at any given moment. It was like that peak meter where their music clashed. There just wasn't any more level to be had; the digital ones and zeros were all used up. That is the same principle by which we mix a motion picture—whether in analog or digital, it does not matter.

I drew pie slices out of the circle. In one pie slice, I wrote "Music," in another I wrote "Sound Effects," in the third I wrote "Dialog." Remember, the dialog track will always and must always play. On rare occasions, the filmmaker may decide to stylize particular moments of the film, in which case the dialog track shuts down, and either a combination of conceptual sound effects and music or simply music alone plays out. Such scenes can be extremely effective, but an entire motion picture cannot be made this way. Such moments are the exceptions, not the rule. For the majority of a film's soundtrack, the dialog track is dominant; therefore, any music score that steps on a dialog line or makes it unintelligible is likely to be dropped or lowered so much that the composer will surely rewrite it rather than have it sound so squashed.

The smart composer knows this and carefully writes the music so it can expand, stretch, or envelop when not in competition with dialog cues; the composer also pulls back and writes music that compliments or enhances the dialog in a collaborative fashion.

The same is true when it comes to sound effects, only with a different and competitive edge. Unlike the dialog track, which always plays, the sound effects track is not constantly heard. For decades, sound effects editors and music composers have been clashing and competing for dominance. Those on both sides have healthy creative egos and know their contribution is vital to a film's successful soundtrack. Some individual artists, however, such as the rock group mentioned above who had never written for the screen, are beset by ignorance. Almost all these difficulties can be eliminated by a collaborative effort between music and sound editorial far in advance of the re-recording stage. As discussed later, this process seems obvious, but is very seldom practiced, for a number of reasons.

One of the most common errors music composers make is that they often "sting" sound effect moments, probably the greatest contributor to sound effects and music colliding in competition on the dubbing stage. Stinging sound effect cues is what is done for silent movies, where no other soundtrack element exists other than music. In the silent days, some of the major movie theatres had custom Wurlitzer organs with the capacity to generate a whole array of sound effects in addition to music. The organ could produce gunshots, booms, pealing bells, and even horse hooves for the inevitable chase.

Another sting effect conflict occurs when explosions are planned in a sequence. Often, the temptation for the music composer is to sting the explosions. This obviously leads to a clash between sound effects and music as they simultaneously attempt to share the same slice of that energy pie. Either music or sound effects, or both, suffer. The smart music composer recognizes that sound effects must work in sync with the event on the screen. On the other hand, music does not need to be frame accurate. Knowing this, the composer may write a stinger that hits just prior to, or just after, leaving a "hole," where the sound effect can properly live and play fully. This technique enhances not only the effect, but the musical emotion of the moment. The intelligent composer also chooses the instruments according to what kind of timbre and frequency textures the sound effects possess. It makes no sense to compose a musical passage using bass violas with low-end dominance to play against the thunderous cascade of a volcanic eruption where rock and lava are flowing. Sound effects must work with low-end and mid-range as a foundation. Wise instrument choices are those that get up out of the competitive regions—instruments that "cut" through the wall of sound effects surely produced by sound editorial, instruments that allow the music to survive and live alongside its sound effect track comrades.

Study the work of John Williams. He can write big lush scores that still compete with big sound effects. This is accomplished because of his intelligent selection of when to push big and when to retract selective pieces and his experienced picks of which instruments fulfill the musical moment and best survive the re-recording mix without needing pull back and emasculation.

Some modern composers use their own brand of sound effects, working them into the very musical score itself. Nagging incidents do occur when a music composer actually scores the picture in a deliberate attempt to torpedo the sound effects track, sometimes out of ego, other times out of ignorance or fear of collaboration. Some of these basic competitions are never overcome entirely. Nonetheless, we must continue to focus on what is good for the film, what serves the need of the film's soundtrack at each moment in time.

SET THE MUSIC COMPOSER EARLY

The smart producer sets a music composer far in advance of the actual work. This accomplishes two things. First, it assures the producer of the desired composer, rather than using one hired at the last minute because the initial choice was booked up and unavailable. Second, the producer can use what I call the "Debra Hill logic." In the early 1980s, I was contracted to supervise the sound for *The Dead Zone* directed by David Cronenberg and produced by Debra Hill. I had supervised the sound on several other projects Debra produced and she knew how I worked. I received a call from her, to fly me to Toronto and look at the director's cut of the picture. At the time, I thought it was a waste of money. The film would be coming down to my shop in just over a month anyway, so why spend the dollars?

Debra matter of factly replied that creativity does not happen instantly, that it takes time to ferment and percolate. Since she had a fixed and finite budget, she could put my subconscious to work, problem solving and creating at no cost until the film was turned over to me several weeks later. I never forgot that, or how true it is. By the time *The Dead Zone* was turned over, I was ready to hit the Moviola designing.

Setting the music composer as far in advance as possible and submitting work-in-progress videotapes allow the composer the same advantages to write a far more creative score than having to deliver the score overnight. A person asked to create instantaneously does not have time to develop new ideas; he or she simply falls back on the experiences of what was done before and creates variations to make it work. Hence, sometimes you hear a score written by a particular music composer with strains and elements that sound much like something written by the same person for a previous picture or sounding incomplete because the full time was not able to be allotted to the details of instrument usage.

Listen to several of James Horner's scores. Though I enjoy the style of his music, you will quickly see how he recycles his own material. I often hear strains and/or passages of *Star Trek II: The Wrath of Khan* in many other scores he has since written. Listen to the opening music to *Millennium Man* and then play the opening score to *A Beautiful Mind*. It is the same music, simply re-massaged. There are so many others who are guilty of it as well; it's just that these examples are so obvious.

BASIC MECHANICS

During the picture-editing process, temp music is pulled from audio CDs or other tape sources to be cut in along the cut picture, to relate a scene's intent or a mood by music. If a music composer is already set for a film, he or she is included in the preliminary process, discussing styles and possible temp pieces. During this time, the composer already draws certain concepts and ideas to ultimately yield an interesting and successful musical score.

Most composers have a music editor with whom they are accustomed to working, and, in turn, the music editor is set for a film project as soon as the music composer is committed. The music editor handles and takes care of the management of the score, freeing the composer to focus on the singular and crucial task of creating the music itself.

One famous composer cannot even read music. He also is incapable of personally setting his themes to paper. As creative and wonderfully rich as his scores are, he either whistles or hums his creation to the orchestrater, who, in turn, sets it to paper. This is not to imply that his work is not good nor that he is incompetent. On the contrary, his work is delightful and always in demand. It is just an additional hurdle he must overcome, along with the usual daily requirements that haunt all composers.

When the picture is locked and ready for turnover, the music composer and music editor have one or more music spotting sessions. The picture editor, director, and producer sit with the composer and music editor and run the film, discussing the kind of music required, the intent of the score, and its desired effect on the audience. Most music editors use a stopwatch to time the start and end points, taking careful notes for the composer to review later. Other music editors take advantage of the computer that drives the Final Cut Pro or Avid, having the counter set to zero at the beginning of each cue point. Instead of feet and frames, the calibration is set for minutes and seconds. At the end of the session, the music editor has compiled the list of music cues and their running times. This immediately assists the composer in scheduling musicians and a scoring stage.

Sometimes the music composer is involved in writing special cues for "source music" (music that comes from practical props in the film, such as radio, jukebox, TV, or Muzak in an elevator or waiting room). Such music often is licensed, broken down into a few parts based on how many seconds the piece is played in the film. Obviously, the cost of licensed music differs wildly, depending on the fame and importance of the piece or artist. We often heard the song "Bad to the Bone" used as temp music in a film, but rarely do we see it licensed for the actual soundtrack.

On major pictures, a composer may be contracted to produce a score electronically first (known as "synth" scores) so that studio executives can get a feel for the music and screen it with test audiences. With motion picture budgets soaring high for the mega-blockbusters, and with the knowledge that a music score can make or break a picture, it does not seem unreasonable to have an electronic version produced first, as long as it is paid for in the budget. With digital emulators and synthesizers today, music scores sound extremely "real," and although they do not have the timbre and depth of a full orchestra, they bring the intent of the composer's design into a crisp focus. Once the studio approves and signs off on the "synth" score, arrangements are made for a scoring stage and musicians for a series of scoring sessions, where the music is rehearsed and recorded for final mastering.

Although music cues have nicknames or pet designations, for organizational reasons music cues are generally referred to by reel and position. Therefore the fourth music cue in reel 5 will be listed as 5-M-4.

BASIL POLEDOURIS

Basil Poledouris first trained to be a concert pianist, then studied opera because of its theatrical drama. He eventually discovered this thing called "film," which had all the theatricality of opera—the staging, the drama, and close-ups! "It really excited me," remarks Basil. "Two of the most formative influences on the way I write music were Miklós Rózsa and Alfred Newman. I like the spectacle of it, the largeness—the scope. The sound of an acoustical orchestra, it is very thrilling!"

Somehow it was more dramatic, more immediate. "All I've ever wanted to do is write film scores, and to this day that's all I have done. Oh, I've taken a couple of excursions outside of film, like the opening ceremonies for the Olympics, which is more like a ballet. It was really a dance with ancient Greek athletes sort of portraying it. The other outing was the *Conan: Sword and Sorcerer Show* that was at Universal Studios for years."

As only fitting, Basil had written the score for both *Conan the Barbarian* in 1980 and *Conan the Destroyer* in 1983. Some composers write a film score for the album and not for the movie; Basil considers his work of writing music for film an end unto itself:

> There's no guarantee that you'll get an album out of the movie. You have to write for the film, otherwise you are not doing justice to the picture. The key to composing good music

Figure 19.1 Music composer Basil Poledouris in his studio in Venice, California, transposes his new theme concept via emulators and synthesizers into his Pro Tools HD workstation for audition purposes. (Photo by David Yewdall.)

for the screen is to focus on the dramatic reinterpretation of the film itself. When I work on a picture, I try to interpret the story musically. There, by definition, I have to follow what is there, up on the screen. You can't tell a different story. Oh, you can tell it from a slightly different point of view, and that's often what I will end up doing, especially if the director has that intention, but you are still telling the same story.

Basil's personal style has served him well, having written scores for *The Hunt for Red October, Free Willy, Les Misérables, Under Siege 2, Robocop, Wind, Big Wednesday, Quigley Down Under, Breakdown, Red Dawn, Starship Troopers, Cecil B. Demented, For the Love of the Game,* and *Bunyan and Babe* to name just a few. Each one dictated a different style, demanding a fresh approach and precise awareness of the subject on screen.

There is a very fine line between being aware of your work, without being self-conscious. We all walk that thin line, when we're in it. You don't want to be too aware of what you are doing, because then it becomes too intellectualized. You can overthink the process to the point that it becomes truly manipulative, because then you're thinking about how it's going to affect the audience—as opposed to how it affects you, as an artist, and then you are just retelling that affect.

Collaboration between the music composer and the sound effects team truly improves the final effort. Of all the films to which we give the lip service—"Oh, yeah, we're gonna work closely with the sound effect editors," *Wind* is the only picture that we really did. It takes two things to truly bring a music and effects collaborative effort together.

First, it takes the willingness of both the music composer and the sound effects editing team to want to do this. To set up the communication lines, asking what the other side is doing in a particular sequence or even to ask if it might be possible to get a DAT layback of some of the key sounds that the sound effects editors are using so that a composer can listen to the frequencies and harmonics. It makes a tremendous difference in how I might handle a particular music cue, as well as what instruments I choose to use.

Second, it takes time to collaborate. It was always difficult to encourage real collaboration when we worked back on film, let alone today with nonlinear technology and highly compressed postproduction schedules. The lightning speed delivery expectations have completely spun out of control.

It is not unusual for the producer to call me up before breakfast, telling me they have a problem. Another cue, either rewritten or new, is necessary and, by the way, they need it on the stage to mix into the film just after lunch. How can one possibly hope to exercise collaboration with sound effects like that? You can't. What has to happen is the producer and director have to continually be brought into equation. They have to be made cognizant that they are the key to really encouraging and making intercollaboration work. If they understood how much positive impact it has on their soundtrack, and therefore on their film, then more producers and directors would be making the collaboration concept a much higher priority.

After being contracted to score a new film, the music composer first must determine what it is about, not just as a filmmatic story, but as it translates to the needs of the music composition.

Sometimes it is very obvious. When I write a score, I usually try to make a metaphor out of the movie. That is where I really start my work. Then I will sit and think it through, saying, "What if it were this, instead of that? What if it were about something completely different? What if it were me in that situation? How would I feel or respond?" It's just a way to trigger, emotionally in me, something in my own experience that I relate to, such as bugs, from *Starship Troopers*. Bugs, in and of themselves, do not scare me, so I have to sit and transpose. What really terrifies me is something like the Orwellian rats in *1984*. Whatever it is, I find something within me from a personal experience.

The very next step I will do is to sit at the piano and just free-associate, to think about a character, an event, or a philosophical concept in the film, and I then just start improvising. I don't even want to be held up by writing it down on paper or recording my improvisational sessions. Then there comes a time when I will know it is time to set it down, whether on tape or just start writing. It may come to me at two or three in the morning, and when it comes I have to get up and start working. Sometimes I will have fuller orchestration ideas, and I will fill it out earlier on with synthesizers.

The key is to capture the mood, the color of the sequence, for which you write. Basil continues:

Many times I find that I am actually scoring the director, when I am writing the music. I have worked for the same director on more than one film, and I find that their personal themes and styles remain consistent. The material that they are attracted to is something that lives within them. I know what Paul Verhoeven's mind is like, I know his approach and take on how a particular scene will be, for the most part. That's not to say that sometimes he throws up some startling aspects, but Paul will usually go for the throat. You never need to be embarrassed about going over the top with Verhoeven. Rarely has he ever said that something is too much.

Randal Kleiser (*Blue Lagoon*), on the other hand, wants a sort of Gestalt between the audience and the film. Things are left—open. Not neutral, exactly. Just not so reinforced, musically, that the audience can only perceive it as one thing or the other.

John Milius is another director who is very clear. He wants the music to speak very directly, mostly melodic. John is a romantic at heart. Bille August is another romantic director; it's just that he achieves his romanticism by keeping a restraint on it, a restraint that creates this kind of tension. On the other hand, Milius does not hold back, he just goes for it.

John McTiernan is more interested in tension, on keeping the camera moving constantly, never letting the audience rest. On *The Hunt for Red October*, it was more than just developing a tension. John wanted the music to represent a culture. The whole Russian state was sort of poured into the building of the submarine *Red October*, which was the ultimate machine that had been produced at that time.

During the filming of *The Hunt for Red October*, the Soviet Union collapsed, which could not help but cause a change in inflection, a spin different from if that country had held her hard-line existence when the film was released to theatres. Basil remembers the effect these historical developments had on his music for the film:

> The Soviet Union's collapse did have an influence, how could it not have? I think it caused the producers to turn the film more into a mystery, rather than a straight ahead defection. The book was very clear about the captain's actions in turning the submarine over to the Americans, and that, of course, is still there. But as the Soviet Union collapsed so suddenly, the producers wanted to slant it as more of a sympathetic mystery. The film had already been shot. We were deep in postproduction when the Soviet Union ceased to exist politically. It was not a matter of re-shooting anything, but through the editing and how the music would be scored, we could give the story a different slant, a different reality.
>
> Early on, we thought that the music would be more confrontational—there were the Russians, and there were the Americans. If I were to use role models of style, there would be Prokofiev and Aaron Copeland. Early on, Copelandesque parts went by the board, as it was really Ramius's story, and the action music was sort of rhythmic with a Russian choir. From the beginning, McTiernan had Russian choir elements in mind. He built it into his temp music tracks. Since the beginning of the film is rather lengthy, from the time that *Red October* leaves port, to the time we go to Washington and set up Jack Ryan and the metal fatigue issues, McTiernan did not want the audience to forget that there is a Russian submarine out there.

Basil asked McTiernan about *Red October*'s Russian translation, which proved to have a tremendous influence on how Basil wrote the theme. The very lilt of the pronunciation of the words in Russian gave Basil the famous emphasis that underlined the theme. Basil explains:

> Latin does the same thing to me. We used a lot of Latin in *Conan the Barbarian*, which greatly influenced how I wrote it. The stress and the syllables. It scans differently than English, and it gives songs a melodic feel that says French, Italian, or Russian. It cannot help but influence how I write.
>
> For acoustic instruments, nothing sounds better than recording analog at 15 ips with Dolby SR. The richness of basses, cellos, the horns—there is a lushness that comes from saturation of the tape.

On November 8, 2006, the entertainment industry lost a great and inspiring talent when Basil Poledouris passed away from cancer. He will live on through his exceptional achievements, which include *Robocop, Conan the Barbarian, The Hunt for Red Octoer*, and *Starship Troopers*.

PHILOSOPHY OF FILM SCORING

Mel Lewis graduated from the North Carolina School of the Arts in 2001, but has, as of mid-summer of 2006 already scored 22 feature film scores, all in distribution! Now working in Los Angeles, Mel has shown his incredible ability to not only be prolific,

Figure 19.2 Mel Lewis, one of the more prolific composers, works a lot of sound effect elements and primal sounds into his work.

but the ability to tune in to the vision of the director with a clarity of interpretation. Mel admits:

> It allows me to hit the pavement running. Instead of wasting time with a preconception before the director has a chance to share how *he* hears the film, I let my inner voice imprint my interpretation of what the director imparts to me—and then I get my mind around the sound experience as a whole—not just music as one of the elements.
>
> A soundtrack is often referred to as the commercial recording of music of a movie. However, the primary and often ignored definition of soundtrack is the complete audio components—dialogue, sound effects, and music. These elements I propose to be viewed as Plato's three sources of human behavior—knowledge, instinct, and emotion. Knowledge as dialog gives the apprehender information to reason in the head. Sound effects as instinct is the impulse or appetite found in the gut. Music as emotion instills the spirit found in the heart.
>
> Music's primary function is therefore emotional, not thoughtful or instinctual. In other words, music communicates through melody, harmony, and rhythm to suggest a feeling. So often I hear amateur composers scoring the other elements (FX and dialogue) of the soundtrack or literally reinforcing the visual picture. Music should not tell you what is happening or what title a person has but what they are feeling or what we should be feeling about the person. This emotion approach can be either subjective or objective.
>
> A subjective example is in *Silence of the Lambs* where Hannibal Lector is in a cell listening to Bach's *Goldberg Variations* reflecting his sophisticated yet serene state. As he proceeds to murder a guard the Bach music continues, representing the subjective aspect of Hannibal's emotional state despite the demonic act. Remember it? Of course not. The producers had it removed for fear of the act being literally interpreted as elaborate and beautiful as Bach's music. The solution was to put in "horror" music to objectify the act as evil rather than risk the misinterpretation of the music's intention. The producers don't want us to become Hannibal Lector, but for us to realize he is bad.

A Personal View of Film Scoring

A perspective from Mel Lewis, composer:

Hollywood film music began with Western classical music traditions. Due to the exciting innovations in mass media, I find film music taking on an evolution incorporating electronic sounds and capabilities as well as addressing non-Western cultural music. The electronic palette, African rhythms, and world instruments are a few of the new sources for my inspiration.

The advent of electronics in music has brought as many opportunities as well as disastrous misuses. "Drum machine have no soul" is one of my favorite quotes in regard to electronics as having no emotion. This opinion presupposes using programmed and dull repetitive "presets" rather than utilizing the novel sound and parameters in a musical context. Computers as drum machines are not an end in themselves but a means or more specifically a tool for composition. Preconceived perceptions of instrumental sounds can now be manipulated to yield novel colors from traditional sounds. A few examples include reversing the sound wave of a violin, affecting the sound by the addition of delay or sampling one specific element of the sound which creates a new sounding instrument once divorced from its previously conceived context.

Although there is a lot of trial and error in making electronics work successfully to create an emotion, the end result is a more singular refined piece.

African rhythms, more than bringing a new feel to film music, gives a new approach to music conception. The Western music that we are used to follows a linear progression much like a book. When you write there are words (notes) arranged into coherent sentences (melodies with harmonic structure) which are then divided into paragraphs (themes). Contrary to this logical or intellectual progression emphasizing melody and harmony, African music take a more circular or instinctual approach rooted in rhythm. Percussion instruments with different timbre perform specific rhythmic patterns or motives that interact to form a detailed fabric. Because the motives remain constant, these rhythmic building blocks are no longer linear or directional as melodies and harmony in Western music but can be viewed instead as past and present material that coexists in an environment that is circular.

With this approach to writing, focus is placed on the interaction of ideas rather than a directional anticipation of what is to come. We experience or feel the music that changes due to the ebb and flow of the patterns rather than think about what is coming next. Changes in volume as well as removal or addition of instruments highlight particular motives and give the fabric a variety. What is so fascinating to me is the simplicity of this construction but yet how complex and rhythmically advanced the music can become due to the interaction of patterns.

It is as if I was told to remove the intellectual process of writing and instead feel the tendencies in the patterns and what aspects highlight emotional shifts. Maybe African music is a signal to get back to emotional basics.

World instruments also give a more singular emotional response for the listener. What has continued to surprise me is the emotional weight that an instrument sound choice can have before even using melody, harmony, or rhythm. It is as if the sound wave itself presents a character. The sounds of western music have evolved into a universally accepted orchestra. World instruments are unique from this universal orchestra in that they present nationalistic sounds particular to a culture. Where the orchestral instruments are perfect in their note performance, the world instruments offer unique nuances, giving character that can be interpreted as more real. For example, the Japanese *shakuhachi* is performed and looks similar to a flute but has a vast array of performance techniques that vary the attack or sustain as well as the color of the sound.

Exposure to these as instruments as well as the African music techniques have given me the task I believe to capture this whole stylistic kaleidoscope and reflect the new collective reality of the world.

THE MUSIC EDITOR

After cutting music for the past 36 years, Ken Hall knows a thing or two about film music, whether for the big screen or for television. Ken's original training was responsible for the foundation of his professionalism. Ken explains:

> I was extremely lucky to break into music by learning my craft with the legendary music director, Lionel Newman. It was the greatest training ground in all of music editorial. You learned how to do bar breakdowns, how to do tie-ins and tie-outs. You learned cuing the Newman system. This kind of training was just unheard of in those days. You were taught how to subdivide bars. A guy could be in 7/8 or 5/8 flip-flop patterns. For instance, if you are in a 7/8 bar, there are seven eighth-notes, but the composer may have written it in a quarter and a quarter and three-eighths—"daa, daa, da-da-da." Or he might have written it "da-da-da, daa, daa"—three eights and two quarters, and so forth. You had to prepare the groundwork for the composer before we got to the scoring stage. That was the job of a music editor, and this kind of training was invaluable to anyone who expected to excel in this field.

Ken cut television music until theatrical composers became aware of his personal style and abilities. Shortly thereafter, Ken broke into working on theatrical films. Just prior to leaving 20th Century Fox, he handled the music cutting chores on the *Swiss Family Robinson* television series, as well as cutting theatrical work, such as *Silver Streak* with Henry Mancini, and bringing Dino De Laurentiis's remake of *King Kong* into the studio with composer John Barry. Over the years, Ken has worked with top film music composers, such as Lalo Schifrin, Jerry Goldsmith, John Williams, Bill Conti, and Henry Mancini—all names at that time that led Ken to believe he could break out on his own, offering his own independent music editorial service. It was a big gamble, but he knew he had to try. He sold his house to finance his independent music editorial service. The business succeeded, and he developed a reputation for excellence and dependable service.

Years later, Kenny met with Jerry Goldsmith about handling the music editing for *Poltergeist*. Near the end of the picture, John Williams called Kenny Hall, informing him that Spielberg had another picture: *E.T. the Extra-Terrestrial*. Ken continues:

> Steven Spielberg is probably one of the most articulate directors that I have ever worked with. He knows exactly what he wants, and, more importantly, he knows exactly how to communicate with his craftspeople the way he wants to achieve it. Those two pictures changed my career forever.

As for Jerry Goldsmith, a composer with whom Ken Hall has worked for more than 70 pictures, his output had anything but slowed down up until the time of his passing in 2004, with over 250 film scores to his resumé, including *The Omen* (which earned Jerry an Academy Award), *Alien, Outland, First Blood, Explorers, Twilight Zone: The Movie, The Ghost and the Darkness, L.A. Confidential, Air Force One,* and *Mulan*. Goldsmith is fearless when it comes to working with unusual instruments, even going so far as to use bits of props in conjunction with traditional instruments, as well as fixing bits of wood and plastic chips to the strings of a piano to give an eerie and unusual sound.

Ken Hall knows that thorough note taking is vital to successful, efficient development of a musical score:

> After the spotting session, Jerry and I will talk briefly about the movie and a few preliminary ideas. I will write up formal notes based on the notes that I took during the spotting session. I will list the start and stop times of each cue throughout the picture, making any sub notes that the director has talked about—his intentions and personal thoughts. Jerry gives me a lot of latitude, allowing me to speak out during the spotting sessions. I try to give a tiny synopsis of the action of each scene alongside the notes for each particular music cue. Then I time the picture, using the cue system. We use video now, it's faster than film, but I time the cues to a hundredth of a second. I list the cues in footage, not in time code.
>
> So many composers will get in and just start writing music. Jerry doesn't do that. He doesn't start writing cues until he is satisfied with the material. Jerry has banks of keyboards in his studio in Beverly Hills; he can create an entire orchestra. He'll have the director come over and run various cues. They always love it. Many times I'll get lucky and be invited over to experience the first musical themes or sometimes I'll just hear cues over the phone.

Preparations are crucial. The hourly cost of a scoring stage adds up; the cost of the musicians per session multiplies. Ken goes on:

> Jerry cannot be distracted by those kinds of things. I not only attend the recording sessions on the scoring stage, but I am present at the mix-down sessions later. Jerry might want to add something through the Auricle, so I'm still hooked up with the mixing board. Then we mix-down to whatever format the producer requires from our 48 channels of digital.
>
> We usually mix-down to 5 channels—1, 2, 3 across the front and split surround. The re-recording mixer will often add a boom channel during the final mixing process. Jerry rarely shows up for the final re-recording process. It's my job to supervise the music mixing process during the final mix.

During the final mix of *Twilight Zone: The Motion Picture*, Ken and I had a heated discussion; although I can't remember exactly which particular segment of film was in dispute, it certainly related to the theoretical dominance of music over sound effects, or of sound effects over music. Kenny Hall turned and snapped at all of us, "Well, when the audience leaves the theatre, they certainly aren't whistling the sound effects, now are they?"

That statement upset me for years, yet the more I wrestle with it, the more I have come to side with Kenny. That's not to say that music and sound effects should not work harder to collaborate instead of creating mud and destruction. The re-recording stage becomes a highly charged emotional battlefield. All parties present have spent weeks, some months, and a few even years, working on a project that is now focused on this final creative process, and motivations and protective instincts are in play.

THE DELICATE GAME OF INSIGHT

Often, the composer finds that he or she must be especially insightful when scoring a picture. Sometimes the director tells the composer exactly what to do, and then, when the composer actually does the work as instructed, it gets rejected and thrown out. This sounds like an oxymoron, but many who have worked as supervising sound editors have seen this strange phenomenon. The composer and supervising sound editor must develop a sixth sense when working with a director, understanding that the director often gets scored, not the film. Sometimes you must listen to the director's requests, agree completely with no hesitation or doubt, and then write (or design) what you know they really need, not what they articulated.

For some reason, regardless of whether directors and producers know it, an unconscious atmosphere of "misspeak" develops. Many of us talk about it, but no one fully understands why it happens. When you realize it is present, trust your inner instincts and tastes, all the while with the complete outward appearance of following the director's or producer's request to the letter.

I have been on projects where the director made a very big deal about a particular item. He harped on it all through the spotting sessions, all through the weeks of cutting. We got to the dubbing stage, and suddenly he said, "Why'd you do that?"

"Because you asked for it," I insisted.

"That's not what I meant!" he defiantly exclaimed.

What do you do? In the case of one film I was working on, the producer fired the picture editor, and the director "retired" from the project. The producer hired a "film doctor" editor to complete the picture successfully. Usually, this does not happen. Usually, you are the one left holding the bag, working late into the night, back-peddling to make the changes.

SIMILAR ISSUES AFFECTING THE CREATIVE EFFORT

One problem plaguing the postproduction industry is the false notion that a shortened and accelerated schedule saves money. So many times we are presented with a post-production schedule and budget that looks good on paper (i.e., it appeals to business affairs at the studio or to the independent film company), but in application it falls apart. This truncated philosophy mostly stems from ignorance of how the process really works, not from the *perception* of how it works.

I became involved with several completion bond companies. My sound editorial firm had contracted to handle the post-sound services for film projects that were already over budget, with complete decision making and financial dealings taken over by the completion bond company. More than once, a bond executive took me aside after a roundtable discussion with the producer(s) and director, to ask what I really thought. Could I live up to a chiseled-in-stone contract now controlled by the completion bond company? Not one extra penny would be spent for creative achievement, although they expected that with the price tag they would authorize. I found it very interesting that, before bonding a picture, many completion bond executives flipped to the postproduction part of a film budget to see how realistic the producer had been about allocated monies. If completion bond companies know what is realistic, though, why do we still have so many pictures run way over budget?

Resource assets of both sound editorial time and budget monies are diffused by the production of the plethora of temp material. Motion pictures have grown so expensive to make, the financial gamble so intense, that studios and executives want to take every possible step to ensure they make films with an eye focused on the audience, doing everything they can to broaden box office appeal.

This double-edged sword often spells doom for the outcome of the final soundtrack. Without anyone noticing, monies are drained by the development of temp music and sound effects for the temp dubs needed for test screenings, especially screenings for studio executives and distributors. Emphasis has shifted from making temp dubs in order to test the picture for an objective audience to selling the director's work to the studio to secure the next project. Many of us worked on pictures that exhausted their assets even before the real turnover for final preparation occurred.

Basil knows the scenario all too well.

> Aside from the syndrome of this false sense of savings from compressed schedules, one of the biggest problems that we often face is a director who cannot make up his or her mind, and the process just goes on and on and on, and there is a release date fast approaching. I think that digital technology has made a false promise that it will be quicker as well as cheaper. I have it here in my own studio. My place is loaded with digital equipment. It changes every two or three months. There is the latest this and the newest that, but when it comes down to it, the most important piece of equipment in my studio is me. Without a musical idea, the million dollars' worth of stuff in here to produce music is not worth a penny.

INDEX-LINKING FOREIGN SALES

With today's motion pictures costing nearly nine times the average budget of films made when I started in the industry, the studios understandably are concerned about making a profit. An important and proven way for them to hedge their bets is to develop ancillary sales through music. Music publication rights, sales of music scores on audiotape or CD, and licensing fees make a major contribution toward recouping a picture's budget.

No studio executive openly admits it. Many are not even aware of it. However, with the foreign box-office share rising from 40 percent 20 years ago, to well past 60 percent by the mid-1990s, a quiet understanding has arisen that the value of the licensing fee of a motion picture in foreign markets is directly index-linked to how much music is in the movie.

George Lucas made it fashionable to fit as many licensed songs into a film soundtrack as possible with his 1973 hit, *American Graffiti*. Others did the same with their coming-of-age films such as Rob Reiner's *Stand by Me* or other popular trash-the-dormitory films. It seems a movie cannot be made unless it has at least a dozen songs, either custom-written for the film (which the studio hopes become hit singles in their own right) or oldies-but-goodies licensed to spruce up and flavor it.

Music composers are pressured to write increasingly more music for a picture than traditional artistic requirements anticipated. I know composers who felt that a music cue was not only unnecessary in a particular sequence, but actually inappropriate. The executive's insistence nonetheless overruled, and the composer was compelled to write the music cue(s) anyway.

In one case a few years ago, I supervised the sound on a film that had 105 minutes of music in it—the film only ran 95 minutes! The producer and I had worked together on several previous pictures, so when I asked him why so much music, he was surprisingly open and candid with me. He admitted that in serving the index-linked issue for foreign territory sales, he feared the picture was too weak to make its money back on a domestic release alone.

Regardless of the reasons why so much music is in motion pictures today, whether the driving force is creative or purely related to dollars and cents, music is without question the greatest audio force that issues from the silver screen. It necessarily tells a story as much as breathing sustains life. Embrace it with a passion, as the art form itself can create great passions.

Chapter 20
The Re-recording Stage
Predubbing and the Final Mix

> "Rolling the first rehearsal on a dubbing stage is weeks of blood,
> sweat, and tears followed by seconds of sheer terror!"
>
> – *David Lewis Yewdall*, M.P.S.E., *commenting on Roger
> Corman's 3-day mixing schedules*

By the time Arnold Schwarzenegger had completed principal photography on *Predator*, he was well on his way to becoming a big-screen veteran of numerous action-adventure and fantasy motion pictures, most of which bristled with special effects and robust soundtracks (*Conan the Barbarian, Commando, Red Sonja,* and *The Running Man*). Inevitably, though, when he screened the finished pictures, they sounded nothing like he remembered during principal photography. Arnold soon realized that something very powerful and magical happened to a picture between the time shooting wrapped and the time of the cast-and-crew screening, and he was determined to figure out what that was—this thing called postproduction.

Arnold followed *Predator* through the postproduction process filled with cutting-edge CGI (computer-generated image) special effects as well as a high-energy soundtrack of music and dynamic sound effects. He thought that if he understood the magical contributions of postproduction, he could select those future entertainment projects with the most potential. He would become empowered.

Indeed, several months later Arnold found himself on the Zanuck Stage at 20th Century Fox with the re-recording mixers as they painstakingly worked through the umpteenth predub of sound effects for the destruction of a rebel camp. The tail pop "bleeped," and the mixer leaned over and pressed the talk-back button to speak to the recordist in the machine room. He told him to take this predub down and to put up a fresh roll for the next dedicated sound effect pass. Knowing it would take the crew several minutes, the mixer pushed his chair back from the giant dubbing console and glanced at Schwarzenegger, who was taking in the entire mixing process. "Well, Arnold, whad'ya think of postproduction now?"

Arnold considered the question, and then, in his Bavarian accent, replied, "Well, I'll tell you. I spent weeks in the jungle, hot and dirty and being eaten alive by insects—and now, here we are, for weeks going back and forth and back and forth on the console—I think I liked the jungle better."

RE-RECORDING

Re-recording is the process in which separate elements of various audio cues are mixed together in a combined format, and set down for preservation in a form either by mechanical or electronic means for reproduction. In other words, re-recording, otherwise referred to as "mixing" or "dubbing," is where you bring carefully prepared tracks from sound editorial and music and weave them together into a lush, seamless soundtrack.

With a little variation, the basic layout of mixing stages is the same. The stage cavity, or the physical internal size of the stage itself, however, varies dramatically in height, width, and length, determining the spatial volume. Sound facilities that cater to theatrical release product generally have larger stages, duplicating the average size of the movie theatres where the film likely will be shown. Sound facilities that derive their business from television format product have smaller dubbing stages, as there is no need to duplicate the theatrical environment when mixing for home television presentation, whether for network, cable broadcast, or direct-to-video product. In all cases, though, these rooms have been carefully acoustically engineered to deliver a true reproduction of the soundtrack without adding room colorization that does not exist in the actual track.

The mixing console (or the board) is situated approximately two-thirds the distance from the screen to the back wall of the dub stage. The size and prowess of the mixing console also reflect the kind of dub stage, theatrical or television. A theatrical stage has a powerful analog or digital console able to service 100 to 300 audio inputs at once. The console shown in Figure 20.1 is a Neve Logic 2 console. This particular console has 144 inputs with 68 outs. The board is not as long as traditional consoles, which can stretch between 30 to 40 feet. Digital consoles do not need to be as long because they go down as well as side by side. Each fader module controls more than one audio input in a layered assignment configuration, allowing mixing consoles to be much bigger in their input capacity without being as wide as a football field. This input expansion is not reserved only for digital consoles.

I can tell how mindful a sound facility is to the needs of the supervising sound editor and the music editor by whether it has included supervisor desks on either end of the console. As a supervising sound editor, I want to be seated right next to the effects mixer, who is usually working on the right third of the console, so that I can talk to the head mixer and effect mixer in a quiet and unobtrusive manner. In this position, I also am able to maintain a constant eye on the proceedings and to make editorial update needs or channel assignment notations in my own paperwork without being disruptive. Supervising sound editor Greg Hedgepath has his sound effects session called up on one of the two Pro Tools stations on stage. This places him in an ideal position to communicate with the mixers as they mix the material, as well as to

Figure 20.1 Re-recording mixer John S. Boyd, twice nominated for an Academy Award for Best Sound for *Empire of the Sun* and *Who Framed Roger Rabbit?*, works on a Neve Logic 2 console. (Photo by David Yewdall.)

Figure 20.2 Head mixer André Perreault (*center*) helms the mixing chores of *The Wood* with his sound effect mixer; Stan Kastner working the material on his left. Supervising sound editor, Greg Hedgepath (*foreground*) checks over the channel assignments. (Photo by David Yewdall.)

make any fixes or additions right on the spot. It also saves the effort of taking down a reel and sending it back to editorial for a quick fix that can be made in moments.

The same is true for the music editor. He or she wants to sit next to the music mixer, who is usually situated on the left third of the console. From this position, the editor not only can communicate with the mixer quietly, but also can listen to the audio reproduction from the speakers in the same basic position as the music mixer. Just behind the console is the credenza, a bank of rack-mounted gear and patch bays easily utilized by the mixers by just turning about in their chairs. When I walk onto an unfamiliar stage, I first glance at the console to see the platform used by the sound house,

Figure 20.3 The credenza holds outboard signal processing gear and signal path patch bays just behind the mixing console in reach of the re-recording mixers.

but I next study the credenza very closely. Here, one can see what kind of extra bells-and-whistles gear the mixer has at command without resorting to equipment rentals from an outside supplier, which obviously affects the hourly stage rental rate. Looking over the patch bay in the credenza, an experienced eye gets an immediate feel for the layout and prowess of the machine room as well as for the contemporary facets of the stage engineering.

THE CREDENZA

Fancy face plates and sexy color schemes do not impress me. Many modern equipment manufacturers go to a great deal of trouble to give their equipment sex appeal through clever design or flashy image. The experienced craftsperson knows better, recognizing established names and precise tools that are the mainstays of the outboard gear arsenal that produces the firepower for the mixer.

The mixing console is either hard-wired to a patch bay in the stage credenza or hard-wired to a patch bay up in the machine room. Either way, the patch bay is critical to giving full flexibility to the mixer or recordist when patching the signal path of any kind of playback equipment (film, tape, or digital hard drive) to the mixing console. The mixer can then assign sends and returns to and from other gear, whether internal or outboard, to enhance, harmonize, add echo, vocord, compress, dip filter, and many other functions not inherent in the fader slide assemblies of the console.

Once the signal path has passed through the fader assembly, the mixer assigns the signal to follow a specific bus back to the machine room, where the mixed signal is then recorded to a specific channel of film, tape, or a direct-to-disk digital drive.

It Can Seem Overwhelming

The first time you approach a mixing console can be very intimidating, especially if it is a feature film mixing stage, where you have a console with three mixers operating it.

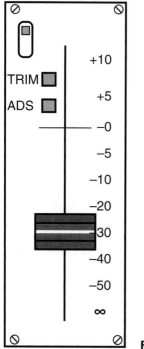

Figure 20.4 Fader pot.

Take a moment and look at it carefully. It is all about signal path, groupings, and routing. You see a desk with dozens of automated faders and a sea of tall slender knobs for equalization. First of all, you can reduce the complexity down tremendously when you realize that the console is composed of dozens of fader/EQ components that are all the same. If you analyze and understand channel 1, then you understand the majority of the rest of the board.

These fader/EQ components are long computer board-style assemblies that fasten into place by a couple of set screws and can be removed and replaced in a few short minutes. The two basic components of the fader/EQ assembly are the fader (volume control) and the parametric equalizer.

The fader is a sliding volume control that moves forward (away from the re-recording mixer) to increase volume or back (toward the re-recording mixer) to reduce volume. Almost all fader controls today are automated, that is, they can be engaged to remember the re-recording mixer's moves and will play back those moves exactly the same unless the move program data is updated by use of the mixing console's software.

You will note that the fader moves forward, or up, hence the cliché that you hear on the re-recording stage all the time, "Up is louder."

In front of (or above) the fader is the equalization array. This is usually a classic GML parametric configuration such as shown in Figure 20.5. Some low-end parametric assemblies only offer three bands of influence. The one shown is a four band, and others may have as many as five or six. Each area (the low frequency, low-mid range, high-mid range, and high end) has its own volume attenuation as well as a frequency

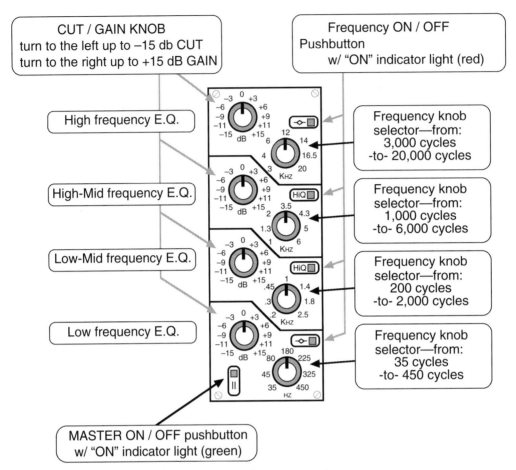

CUT / GAIN KNOB
turn to the left up to −15 db CUT
turn to the right up to +15 dB GAIN

Frequency ON / OFF
Pushbutton
w/ "ON" indicator light (red)

High frequency E.Q.

Frequency knob
selector—from:
3,000 cycles
-to- 20,000 cycles

High-Mid frequency E.Q.

Frequency knob
selector—from:
1,000 cycles
-to- 6,000 cycles

Low-Mid frequency E.Q.

Frequency knob
selector—from:
200 cycles
-to- 2,000 cycles

Low frequency E.Q.

Frequency knob
selector—from:
35 cycles
-to- 450 cycles

MASTER ON / OFF pushbutton
w/ "ON" indicator light (green)

Figure 20.5 Parametric equalizer.

selector, showing the apex of influence. The next thing to understand is that a three position console, supporting the music mixer (usually on the left side), the head mixer (usually in the center), and the effect mixer (usually on the right side) is really three consoles that for the majority of the time work as three separate consoles that happen to be connected together as one.

Each mixer is paying attention to his or her own assignments (dialog, music, and effects) and the designated audio signals are passing their own sections of the console onto either their own dedicated recorder or onto to their own dedicated channel assignments of a multi-track machine or nonlinear workstation. They just happen to be interlocked together and playing through the same speakers, which gives the illusion that it is all one soundtrack, at least for the present.

After the supervising sound editor, editor, director, producer(s), executive producers, studio executives, and distribution executives have signed off on the final mix—only then will the Dolby, SDDS, and DTS techs be brought in to oversee the two-track print master and the various digital format masters. Only then will the soundtracks

Figure 20.6 The mixing team on the John Ford Re-recording Stage at 20th Century Fox. Head mixer Paul Massey oversees the progress as David Giammarco, the sound effects mixer, works in the foreground on material that supervising sound editor Hamilton Sterling has brought to mix on *For Your Consideration* directed by Christopher Guest. (Photo by John LeBlanc.)

(dialog, music, and effects) truly reside together as a single theatrical soundtrack. But that will only come after weeks of blood, sweat, and tears and other unmentionable events have taken place.

THE MIXERS

Head Mixer

With few exceptions, the head mixer is also the dialog mixer, usually running the stage from the center seat. This gives the head mixer ideal physical positioning in the dubbing stage cavity to listen to and evaluate the mix. Almost always, the head mixer is involved with each step of the predubbing process. Only with the mega-soundtracks now being predubbed on two or more stages simultaneously is the head mixer not a part of each predubbing pass before the entire reel is mounted for a rehearsal for final mix.

During the final mix, the head mixer intercedes and instructs the music mixer and sound effects mixer to raise, lower, or tweak certain cues. Mixing teams often stay together for years because they reach a level of unspoken communication as they come to know each member's tastes and work habits. The head mixer has the last word in the balance and dynamic strategies of the final mix.

Effects Mixer

Most sound effects mixers work from the right chair. During the predubbing process, they often work with the head mixer as a team. During the dialog predub, the effects mixer may help the dialog mixer with extra peripheral tracks if the cut dialog track preparation is unusually wide. By doing this, the dialog mixer can concentrate on the primary on-screen spoken words. On lower-budget projects, where stage time utilization is at a premium, the effects mixer may run backgrounds or even Foley as the dialog mixer predubs the dialog tracks. In this way, the dialog mixer knows how far to push the equalization or to change the level to clean the production tracks. He or she knows what to count on from backgrounds or Foley to bridge an awkward moment and make the audio action seamless.

When the dialog predubs are completed, the head mixer then assists the effects mixer in sound effects predubbing. At this point, the effects mixer runs the stage, as the sound effects predubs are his or her responsibility. The dialog (head) mixer helps the effects mixer in any way to make the most expeditious use of stage time, as only so much time is budgeted and the clock is ticking.

Music Mixer

The music mixer rarely comes onto the stage during the predubbing process. The music mixer may be involved in music mix-downs, where an analog 2" 24-track or a digital multichannel session master may need to be re-recorded down to mix down cues for the music editor to cut into sync to picture. He or she may be asked to mix the music down to 6- or 8-channel Pro Tools sessions. There are still some music mixers that do not like mixing straight to a nonlinear platform, insisting instead on mixing down to a 6-channel 35-mm fullcoat or 6 or 8 channels of a 2" 24-track tape, and then having the transfer department handle the transfer chores to a nonlinear audio format.

Times Have Changed

In the old days, the head mixer was God. Directors did not oversee the mixing process as they do today; the head of the sound department for the studio did that. The director would turn over the director's cut of the picture and move on to another project. He or she would see the finished film and mixed soundtrack several months later.

Head mixers dictated what kind of material went into a soundtrack and what would be left out. Often, the supervising sound editor was an editorial extension of the will of the head mixer. When a head mixer did not like the material, it would be bounced off the stage, and the director would tell the sound editors to cut something different; sometimes the director would dictate the desired sound effects series. This is unheard of today. Not only do directors follow the process through to the end, often inclusive of the print master, but they have a great deal of say in the vision and texture of the soundtrack.

Supervising sound editors are no longer just an extension of the head mixer, but come onto the stage with a precise design and vision they already have been developing; from the Foley artist and sound designer on up through their sound editorial staff, they have taken a far more commanding role in the creative process.

Many film projects are brought to a particular stage and mixing team by the supervising sound editor, thereby making the mixing crew beholden to his or her design and concept wishes. This is a bad thing; although, in many instances, a greater degree of collaborative effort does occur between sound editorial and re-recording mixers with an already established relationship. Many signal-processing tasks once strictly the domain of mixers are now being handled by sound designers and even sound editors, who are given free rein to use their digital processing plug-ins.

Whole concepts now come to the stage virtually predubbed in effect groupings. Whip pans on lasers and ricos are just not cost-effective to pan-pot on the re-recording stage by the sound effects mixer, and in some cases so many sound effects must move so fast that a mixer just cannot pan-pot them properly in real time. These kinds of whip pans are built in by the sound editor at the workstation level. (The lasers from *Starship Troopers* discussed in Chapter 13 is a case in point.)

As discussed in prior chapters, supervising sound editors and their sound designers handle more and more signal processing, including equalization and filtering. Just a few years ago, these acts would have been grounds for union fines and grievances; now they take place every day in every sound facility. Some sound editorial services are even doing their own predubbing, bringing whole sections of predubbed material rather than hundreds of tracks of raw sound. Some of this is due to financial and schedule considerations, some due to sound design conceptuality.

A Vital Collaboration

And then, every once in a blue moon, you just find yourself working with a mixer who talks a good game, but when the chips are down he just "once-easy-overs" your stuff and basically mushes out any design hopes that you have built into your material, or he or she just does not have the passion to go the extra distance to really make it sing.

While supervising the sound editorial and mixing of *Near Dark*, Katherine Bigelow's first feature film as director, we were predubbing the dialog, which needed a lot of extra massaging with equalization and signal processing gear. It takes a little work to make a silk purse out of a sow's ear of mediocre location mish-mash. Katherine was a superb quick study, anxious to learn anything and everything she could to empower herself to be a better director.

I was becoming increasingly annoyed at the lack of assistance that the lead mixer was giving to help her out, both for the dialog track of her present film and to her personally for her future pictures.

I went out into the lobby and grabbed the phone and called my shop. I told my first assistant to build a bogus set of sound units, complete with intercut mag stripe (with no sound at all) and a full cue sheet advertising dozens of seemingly important cues.

The predub pass showed up at the stage by mid-afternoon, and with the usual set-up time the machine-room crew mounted the units within 20 minutes. The head mixer got a full green-light status, so he rolled picture. The first cue passed through with no audio being heard.

Standard procedure was to back up and try it again, checking your console to make sure that nothing was muted, turned off, and mis routed. The cue went through again, and of course, with no audible result. The mixer turned to his credenza to make sure that the patch cords were firmly in place and in the right order. All of this takes time, precious time; the clock on a dubbing stage is always ticking and every tick costs money.

The mixer rolled the projector again and the cue went by again, and again (of course) there was no audio. The mixer glanced at me. I shrugged innocently. He pressed the talk-back button to speak to his machine room, "Is effects 4 in mag?"

The recordist had to get up out of his booth and walk around into the machine room to physically find "effects 4" and see if the mag track was on over the playback head. Now, just by looking at the mag track itself, the recordist assumes that there is sound on it. Wouldn't you? Then he walked all the way back into his booth to answer back, "Yes, it's in mag."

The mixer rolled the cue again, with the same silent results. He hit the talk-back button, "Bloop the track."

The recordist had to walk around into the machine room, grab the "tone loop" off the hook, find "effects 4," work the tone loop mag in between the mag track and the head, and pull it up and down to cause the tone to rub against the mag track. Loud "vrip-vrip-vrip" of tone modulation blasted out the speaker. That meant the patch cords were good, the routing was good, nothing was muted, and we were getting signal. The mixer shot a suspicious glance over at me. I shrugged. Standard procedure when you did not get a proper playback of a cue was to make a note and bring it back as a sweetener later, so I turned and scribbled a seemingly legitimate note to bring "effects 4" as a sweetener later.

The mixer pushed on to the next cue. The next cue did not play. Again, the mixer stopped to check the signal path for "effects 5" as he had before. Again, he ran the cue and again it played nothing. He shot me another suspicious scowl. I just gazed at him with an innocent expression. Again he had to have his recordist walk back and "bloop" the track, and again the "vrip-vrip-vrip" tone pounded the room. I shrugged and turned to write another bogus notation for a sweetener. The mixer rolled to the next cue, and again it passed over the heads without any audio response. By now the mixer had had enough. He yanked back all of his faders with a smack and whirled around to me, "Okay, Yewdall—WHAT?!"

I quietly put my pencil down and folded my hands while Katherine watched. My eyes met the mixer's rage and I quietly, but firmly, replied, "Let's understand one another. This is a collaborative effort. I am only as good as how you make my material sound and you are only as good as the material I bring you. God blessed you with the arms of an orangutan and I would think that you could at least reach up to your parametrics and help the director achieve her vision."

The mixer leaped up and stomped off the stage to the head of the sound department, with the expectation that I would get chewed out and hopefully removed from the project. Instead I was called into the head of the sound department's office to watch the mixer get chewed out and be reminded of how the winds of postproduction power had shifted.

The mixer and I walked back to the stage together to forge a working agreement about how we could both survive together and deliver the best soundtrack possible to a new rising director.

PREDUBS: TACTICAL FLOW

Predubbing is the art of keeping options open. You want to distill the hundreds of your prepared sound elements down into more polished (not final polish) groupings. By doing this, you can put up all your basic elements, such as dialog, ADR, Group Walla,

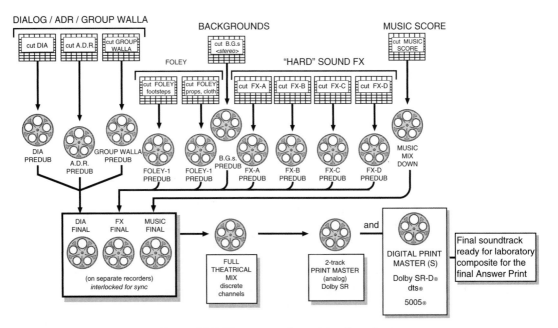

Figure 20.7 The re-recording mixing flow chart.

Foley, backgrounds, sound effects, and music, so that you can rehearse and "final" the reel as one complete soundtrack.

Re-Recording Mixing Flowchart

As shown in Figure 20.7, predubbing is broken into logical groupings. Because dialog is the most important component of a film soundtrack and must sound as smooth and seamless as possible, predub it first, especially if you have a limited amount of time in the schedule for predubbing. Ideally, we always would have enough time to predub all our cut material fully and properly. Not only is this not the case, it is the exception.

Since I could write an entire book on mixing encompassing budgeting, scheduling, and techniques, here I simply discuss one fairly common formula. Four-week dubbing schedules are normal for medium-budget feature films in Hollywood. Naturally, tactics differ, depending on whether you use the single mixer approach or the mixer team approach. This example is of a mixer team approach, using a two-mixer formula. Provided that sound editorial was not put into an insane schedule crunch and that the normal mixing protocol can be implemented, I generally find the following to be a safe, tried-and-proven battle plan.

Four-Week Mixing Schedule

- Dialog predubbing: 5 days (dialog with BGs); 4 days (if dialog only)
- Background (BG) predubbing: 2 days
- Foley predubbing: 2 days
- Sound effects predubbing: 3 days

- Final mix: 7 days
- Playback and fixes: 1 day
- Print master: 1 day
- Foreign M&E (music and effects): 1 day

Please note that this schedule does not allow for a digital sound mix and mastering process. This gets you through predubbing, final mix, continuity playback along with a conservative amount of fixes (if you have a greater list, add additional days to your mixing schedule), print master, and foreign M&E for the analog version.

This is a guide used over and over in generalities. The what-ifs factor a hundred variants, and no two motion pictures are ever the same. You will have a mixer who prefers to predub dialog along with the Foley, rather than a mixer who wants backgrounds. Then you will have the purist mixer who wants it to be predubbed without anything camouflaging the material. (I endorse the purist philosophy, by the way.)

A client discusses the mixing schedule for his or her project with me. Naturally, this conversation is held months after the film has been scheduled and budgeted, so it is not a discussion about how to schedule the mixing process. Rather, it becomes a retrofit of "This is all that we have budgeted for—how do you think we should utilize it?"

With this is mind, I always counsel that more possible predubbing makes the final mixing process go much smoother and more quickly. You can adopt one of two tactics in deciding how to balance the number of days to predub, as opposed to how many days to final. First, you can take a 15-day mixing schedule and set aside 5 days for predubbing (at a lower per-hour rate) and have 10 days to final (at a higher per-hour rate). The producer and director like the idea of having a full day per reel to final; that is how the big shows are done, so they want the same. This means much less material is predubbed, and that, during the final mix, you stop more often to reset equalization or fix transitions between sound cues because not enough time was devoted to predub the material properly. With the stage cost at full rate, tensions on the stage quickly develop.

The second, more logical approach is to give a larger portion of the 15 days to predubbing. I have often suggested that 9 days be devoted to predubbing, meaning you must final two reels a day. This is often done, as the smart client knows, and if the material was more thoroughly predubbed, the final mixing goes much smoother and more quickly. As discussed in Chapter 4, the success or failure of a soundtrack is in your hands long before postproduction sound craftspeople ever get a chance to touch it.

That does not mean that good soundtracks are not achieved in shorter schedules or for fewer budget dollars. *One False Move* is a perfect example of this. This picture had only 9 days to mix, inclusive of predubbing. *One False Move* looks like a much more expensive movie than its budget would suggest. Jeffrey Perkins at International Recording was set as the head re-recording mixer. He had won the Academy Award for Best Sound on *Dances with Wolves*, and both Carl Franklin (director) and Jesse Beaton (producer) of *One False Move* considered it a fabulous opportunity to have Jeffrey handle the mixing chores. The dubbing schedule happened to fall in the slow period during the Cannes Film Festival, which gave the added value of a lower hourly stage rate.

Even so, the schedule was only 9 days, all inclusive. Jeffrey and I had not worked together before, and such a short schedule concerned him. I offered to go over to International to talk with him about dubbing tactics. I grabbed the cue sheet envelope for reel 7 on my way out the door, as I thought he would learn more about what to expect in sound editing preparation by seeing the cue sheets laid out.

I spread the cue sheets to reel 7 across his dubbing console, starting with dialog and ADR, then Foley, backgrounds, and finally sound effects. Jeffrey began to relax, seeing how I had not spread the sound assembly too wide, should we have to forego some predubbing needs, hang the cut material, and final the reel from raw cut sound units.

The first thing we both agreed to was persuading the client to take 1 day from final mixing and use it for predubbing. We knew it would make for an easier and faster final mix. Jeffrey prioritized what he would predub, first, second, third. When we ran out of time and had to commence finals, at least the priority chores would be completed.

As it turned out, we did not need to compromise anything on the re-recording mix of *One False Move*. Although the mixing schedule was extremely tight, the client listened to our advice and counseling and, for the most part, took it. All the cut material ended up being predubbed. Nothing was left to hang raw. We set a methodical schedule for finals, and, with very little exception, lived up to it. We predubbed, executed the final mix as well as shot the 2-track print master, and made the M&E in 9 days.

THE NEW CENTURIONS OF THE CONSOLE

Today's technologies dictate the evolution of how we may do things—new tools, new protocols, new delivery requirements—but not the change of an art form. If you learn your art form you will always be the artist—understanding how to create an audio event that moves an audience in a desired emotional way. All of us are and will always be learning new tools, many of which we have discussed in the previous chapters of this book. But the disciplines—how and why we work with the audio medium the way we do to create our art form—do not change.

The reality is that the majority of sound re-recording is not executed in the traditional theatrical rooms, but in smaller venues. Most of these rooms have been sleekly designed to offer a lot of bang-for-the-buck, keeping the overhead nut as low as possible without sacrificing or compromising the audio art form that the mixer(s) continually strive to achieve.

One such new talent is Zach Seivers, a very bright and talented mixer. Zach explains:

> Being able to adapt and evolve is probably the most important trait a person entering the industry can have. Producers have to answer to the bottom line. Ultimately, at the end of the day, the job has to be done professionally, efficiently, and under budget.
>
> The tools and techniques one adopts can put that person years ahead of the competition. With just a little bit of ingenuity and willingness to step outside the standards and conventions everyone else is following, it's possible to discover a whole new and better way

Figure 20.8 Zach Seivers, re-recording a feature film in his 5.1 room at Herzog-Cowen in North Hollywood. (Photo by John LeBlanc.)

of doing things. Just think, what would have happened if 10 years ago Pro Tools wasn't adopted to edit, design, and eventually mix sound for films? We most definitely wouldn't have the kinds of soundtracks we do today!

Creating a soundtrack on a low budget is much more challenging than when you have money to throw at the problem, as we discussed in Chapter 14. The partner to the editorial team who has to figure out how to bring the material to the mixing console in such a way that it can be mixed within the budget and time restraints is, of course, the re-recording mixer. Without question, the collaboration and interdependency with each other, the sound editor and the re-recording mixer, is magnified when there is no latitude to waste money.

Most of these new mixing venues are strictly run by a single mixer, mainly for budgetary reasons. That said, there is something to be said for the single-mixer style of re-recording a track. The mixer knows every detail, every option in the dialog production material as he or she balances backgrounds, Foley, and sound effects against the music score because he or she has predubbed the dialog track and knows what is and is not there for use.

It is a natural evolution that sound designer/editors are mixing more and more of their own material. Many do their own predubbing, taking their material to a re-recording stage only for the final mixing process.

More and more are becoming editor/mixers, not just because technology has offered a more fluid and seamless transition from the spotting notes to the final mix stems, but the obvious continuity of creative vision, where a supervising sound editor may end up mixing his or her own show. There is a lot to be said for this, but it cannot be realistically accomplished on the superfast postproduction schedules that studios often crush the sound crews to achieve. During most of the re-recording process of *Dante's Peak* there were four separate re-recording stages working on various predubbing and finaling processes simultaneously.

Figure 20.9 Close view of the automated console, with the Pro Tools session on the monitor to the re-recording mixer's left. (Photo by John LeBlanc.)

WHO REALLY RUNS THE MIX?

It never fails to amaze me who really has the last word on a dubbing stage. On the miniseries *Amerika*, Jim Troutman had to work on both Stages 2 and 3 of Ryder Sound simultaneously. His re-recording mixers down on Stage 3 were predubbing, while another team of mixers made the final mix upstairs on Stage 2. Ray and Joe had just completed predubbing the action sequences on a particular reel and were about to play it back to check, when a tall gentleman in a business suit entered, patted Jim Troutman on the shoulder, and sat in a nearby make-up chair. The two mixers glanced at the executive-looking man with slight concern, then commenced the playback.

When lights came up at the end of the reel, Jim asked the businessman what he thought. He shrugged and was a little timid to give his opinion. With a little encouragement, he spoke his mind, "I thought the guns were a little low and mushy during the shoot-out."

Immediately, the mixers spun the reel down to the scene, took the safeties off the predub with the gun effects, and started remixing the weapon fire. That finished, they asked what else bothered him. Cue by cue, they coaxed his ideas and concerns, immediately running down to each item and making appropriate fixes. After speaking his mind, he stood up and smiled, patted Jim on the shoulder again with appreciation for letting him sit in, then left.

Once the door closed, the mixers turned to Jim, "Who was that?!"

Jim smiled. "Who, John? Oh, he's my accountant." The two mixers sat frozen in disbelief, then started laughing in relief.

Not all control stories end with relief and humor. I supervised a science-fiction fantasy that was filled with politics and egocentric behavior. Reel 5 was a major special-effects-filled action reel. Everyone had arrived promptly to start rehearsals at 9:00 a.m., as it promised to be a long day. To stay on schedule, we would need to final reel 5 and get at least halfway through reel 6.

Everyone had arrived, everyone, that is, except for the producer. The mixing team had gotten right in and commenced rehearsing the reel. At the end of the first rehearsal pass, the head mixer glanced about, looking for the producer. He still had not arrived. The reel was spun back to heads and they commenced another rehearsal pass. By 11:00 a.m. the crew had completed four rehearsal passes of the reel, and still the producer was not there. The head mixer looked to me, "We're starting to get stale. Let's make this reel. He'll be walkin' through the door any minute." I agreed. The mixer pressed the talk-back button and informed his recordist to put the three Magna-Tech film recorders on the line and to remove the record safeties. We rolled. Foot by foot, the mixers ground through the reel. The last shot flickered off the screen, and 3 feet later the tail pop beeped.

Suddenly, the stage door burst open as the producer entered, "Hey, guys, what are we doing?"

"We've just finaled reel 5 and are about to do a playback," the head mixer replied matter-of-factly.

The producer's demeanor dropped like a dark shroud. "Really? Well, let's hear this playback."

You could just feel it coming. The machine room equipment wound down and stopped as the Academy leader passed by and reel 5 rolled. Almost every 10 feet the producer had a grumbling comment to make. At first the head mixer was jotting down notes, but after the first 200 feet he set his pencil down.

As the reel finished, the lights came up. The producer engaged in a nonstop dissertation about how the mixing crew had completely missed the whole meaning and artistic depth of the reel. I studied the head mixer as he listened to the producer talk. Finally, the head mixer had had enough. He turned and hit the talk-back button, telling the recordist to rerack at Picture Start and prepare to refinal the reel—they would be starting over.

Satisfied that he was proving his command and control, the producer rose and headed out the side door to get a cup of coffee and a donut. I watched the head mixer as he quietly leaned over to the console mike. He pressed the talk-back button and whispered, "Take these three rolls down and put them aside. Put up three fresh rolls for the new take." He noticed me eavesdropping and winked.

We worked hard on the new final of reel 5, slugging it out for the next two and a half days. We had given up any hope of keeping to the original dubbing schedule, as the issue of politics and egocentric behavior had gone way over the top. I knew the stage alone was costing $700 per hour. Over the course of the extra two and a half days, the overage bill for the stage would easily run close to $16,000.

Finally, the last scene flickered away, and the tail pop beeped. The producer rose from his make-up chair and strode toward the side door to get a fresh cup of coffee. "Awright guys, let's do a playback of that!"

I watched the head mixer as he leaned close to the console mike and alerted the recordist, "Take these three rolls off and put the other three rolls from the other day back up. Thank you." He calmly turned to meet my gaze with a grin.

The producer returned, and the lights lowered. For 10 minutes, reel 5 blazed across the screen, playing the original mix done 3 days before. The producer slapped the armrest of his chair, "Now that is how I wanted this reel to sound!"

PROPER ETIQUETTE AND PROTOCOL

Protocol is the code of correct conduct and etiquette observed by all who enter and spend any amount of time, either as visitor or client-user, on a re-recording stage. It is vitally important that you pay strict attention to the protocol and etiquette understood in the professional veteran's world. Just because you may be the director or producer does not mean you are suddenly an expert in how to mix sound. Clients often are on the stage during predubbing processes when they really should not be there. They speak up and make predubbing level decisions without a true understanding of what goes into making the material and particularly what it takes to predub the material properly to achieve the designed effect.

One particular director who makes huge budget pictures thinks he truly understands how good sound is made. I had spent weeks designing and cutting intricate interwoven sound effect cues, which, once mixed together, would create the audio event making the sequence work. The sound effects mixer has never heard these sounds before, and I spread several layers of cue sheets across his console. One vehicle alone required 48 soundtracks to work together simultaneously. The mixer muted all but the first stereo pair, so that he could get a feel for the material. Instantly, the director jumped up, "That's not big enough; it needs more depth, more meat to it."

Knowing his reputation during the predubbing process from other sound editors, I turned to him, "This sequence is a symphony of sound. Our effect mixer has simply introduced himself to the first viola. Why don't you wait until he has tuned the entire orchestra before you start criticizing?" Booking the dubbing stage does not necessarily give the client keys to the kingdom. On countless occasions, the producer books a sound facility and proceeds to push the dubbing crew to the brink of mutiny. The adage that money talks is not an excuse to use to disregard protocol and etiquette.

I was dubbing a temp mix for a test audience screening on a Wesley Snipes picture. It wasn't that the director and his committee of producers had nitpicked and noodled the temp mix to death. It wasn't that the schedule was grueling and demanding. All postproduction professionals understand compressed schedules and high expectation demands. It was the attitude of the three producers, the inflection and tone of their comments, that ate away at the head mixer.

During a reel change break, I overheard the head mixer talking to the facility director in the hall. Once the temp mix was finished, the mixer would have nothing to do with any further temp dub or the final mix for this picture, regardless of its high profile. The facility director was not about to force his Academy Award–winning mixer to do something that he did not want to do, so he informed the client that the stage had just been block-booked by another studio, forcing the client to look elsewhere for sound facility services.

Usually, the etiquette problem is much simpler than that. It boils down to who should speak up on a re-recording stage and who should remain quiet and watch politely, taking anything that must be said out to the hallway for private interaction with the director or producer.

Teaching proper protocol and etiquette is extremely difficult because the handling of dubbing chores has changed so much that entire groups of young sound editors and sound designers are denied the re-recording stage experience. A few years ago, before the advent of nonlinear sound editing, access to the re-recording stage was far more open, an arena in which to learn. You prepared your material, brought it to the stage, and watched the mixer run it through the console and work with it. You watched the mixer's style and technique. You learned why you should prepare material a certain way, what made it easier or harder for the mixer, and what caused a breakdown in the collaborative process.

I always had the sound editor, who personally cut the material, come to the stage to sit with the mixers and me. After all, this was the person who knew the material best. We also would call back to the shop late in the afternoon for the entire crew to sit in on the playback of each reel on stage. The sound crew felt a part of the process, a process that today inhibits such togetherness. Somehow we must find a way to get editorial talent back on the dubbing stage. Somehow we must make the re-recording experience more available to up-and-coming audio craftspeople, who must learn and understand the intricacies of the mixing process.

PRINT MASTERING

Upon completion of the final mix are three 35-mm rolls of fullcoat per reel, or there are discrete digital stems to a master hard drive in the machine room. The three basic elements of the mix—dialog, music, and sound effects—are on their own separate rolls. When you lace these three rolls together in sync and set the line-up tones so the outputs are level matched, the combined playback of these three rolls produces a single continual soundtrack. If not mixing to 35-mm film fullcoat, MMR-8s, or Pro Tools HD, you can mix to a hard drive inside the mixing console system, if the console is so equipped. Regardless of the medium, the re-recording mixers still want dialog, music, and effects in their own controlled channels.

Once the final mix is complete, the head mixer sets up the room for a playback of the entire picture. Many times, as you mix a film reel by reel, you feel you have a handle on the continuity flow and pace; however, only by having a continuity playback running of the entire film with the final mix will you truly know what you have. Much can be learned during a continuity playback, and you will often make notes to change certain cues or passages for various reasons.

Several days prior to completing the final mix, the producer arranges with Dolby or for a tech engineer to be on hand with the matrixing box and supervise the print mastering of the final mix. Although many theatres can play digital stereo soundtracks, such as Dolby SR-D, SDDS, or DTS, always have the analog stereo mix on the print.

Do not attempt to have discrete optical tracks for the component channels; Dolby and Ultra Stereo offer a matrix process that encodes, combining the left, center, right, and split surround channels of the final mix into 2 channels. When the film is projected in the theatre, this matrixed 2-channel soundtrack is fed into a Dolby decoder box prior to the speaker amplification, where the 2 matrixed channels are decoded back out into the proper left, center, right, and surround channels. On many occasions a theatre that offers a digital sound presentation has a technical malfunction with the digital equipment for some reason. Sensors in the projection equipment detect the malfunction and automatically switch over to the analog 2-track matrixed track.

The tech engineer sets up the matrix encoding equipment and sits with the head mixer, paying strict attention to peak levels on extremely loud passages. The analog soundtrack is an optical track and has a peak level that must be carefully adjusted, what used to be called "making optical."

There may be moments in the print-mastering process where the tech engineer will ask the mixer to back up and lower a particular cue or passage because it passed the maximum and clashed.

For some, the print-mastering phase is the last authorship of the soundtrack. Many a smart music composer who has not been on stage for the final mix always shows up for the print master; he or she knows that changes and level balances are still possible, and many films end up with a different balanced soundtrack than the final mix. Hence, the supervising sound editor never leaves the print-mastering process as just a transfer job left to others.

Pull-Ups

An overlooked finalizing task that must be done before the soundtrack can be shipped to the laboratory is having the pull-ups added. A pull-up, technically, is the first 26 frames of sound of the reel that has been attached to the end of a previous reel. This makes smoother changes in theatrical projection when one projector is finished and must change over to the next projector.

Because of electronic editing, precise pull-ups have become a fairly sloppy procedure. I see more and more mixers electronically shooting the pull-ups. This indicates laziness on the part of the supervising sound editor, rather than being the fault of the re-recording mixer.

You do not need to put pull-ups on every reel, unless the show was mixed prebuilt in an A-B configuration. If the print master is in A-B, then, of course, every reel needs to have a pull-up.

The mixer has the print master of the following reel mounted. The line-up tones are critical, and great pains are taken to ensure that the "X-Copy" transfer of the print master is an exact duplicate. The mixer includes the head pop and several feet of the opening shot. The recordist makes sure that each pull-up is carefully tagged to show from which reel it came. The supervising sound editor and assistant usually cut the pull-ups in the change room of the sound facility, as the print master should not be moved off-site for contract and insurance reasons. If the show was not mixed in A-B configuration, then the supervisor and assistant should do so now.

Electronic editing unfortunately made many editing services extremely sloppy in the head-and-tail-pop disciplines. I have seen pops slurred in replication over several frames. The worst I have seen was a head pop that slurred 8 frames. Now where in the world do you get a precise position for sync?

If you pay close, disciplined attention to the head and tail pops, you will have an easy time finding the precise perforations between which to cut. You can take satisfaction and ease in being 1/96th-of-a-second accurate, rather than trying to decide which frame pop to believe.

First, I take the roll of pull-ups the mixer transferred for me. I place it in a synchronizer and roll down until I pass a reel designation label; shortly thereafter are tones and then the head pop. I stop and carefully rock the film back and forth under the sound head, being absolutely assured of the leading edge of the pop. With a black Sharpie I mark the leading edge, then count 4 perforations and mark the back edge. I rock the film back and forth gently to see if the back edge is truly 4 perforations long. I open the synchronizer gang and pick the film out, then roll the synchronizer so the 0 frame is at the top. I zero the counter and then roll down to 9 feet. I place the marked pop over the 0 frame, then roll down to 12+00.

This is the exact leading edge of the soundtrack for this reel—this is where I mark the frame line. Just in front of the frame line, I write from which reel this piece of sound comes. I then cut off 3 or 4 feet of the incoming sound and hang it in the trim bin until I need it. After I prepare all my pull-up sections, I commence building the A-B rolls.

I always roll the picture in the first gang alongside the print master. This way, I physically can see and verify the relationship of picture to soundtrack. I always locate the head pop first. I seat it exactly on the 0 of the synchronizer, with the footage counter at 9 feet. I then roll backward toward the start mark. Head start marks are often one or two perforations out of sync. This is not connected to how the recordist is doing his or her job. It is related to the way the film machines settle in when put on the line. That is why the 9-foot head pop is critical because its position is the only true sync start mark. From it, you can back up and correct the position of the start mark label.

Once this is done, I roll down through the reel to the last frame of picture. Be sure you are using a 2,000-foot split reel or 2,000-foot projection reel on which to wind the reels. I mark the frame line and mark past it with a wavy line to denote waste. I then take the next reel and seat the head pop at 9+00. I roll down to 12+00 and mark the top of the frame. Using a straight-edged (not an angle!) Rivas butt splicer, I cut the 2 frame lines, then splice the backside of the fullcoat with white 35-mm perforated splicing tape. Never use a splicer that punches its own holes in splicing tape during this procedure—never, never!

I then continue to roll down through the second reel, now attached to the first, until I reach the last frame of picture. I mark the bottom of the frame line of the last frame. I then pull the pull-up of the next reel and cut the frame line I had marked on it. I carefully make sure that the cuts are clean and without any burrs or lifts. I flip the film over and splice the back with white 35-mm splicing tape. It is only necessary to cut 26 frames of pull-up, but I have cut 2 feet, 8 frames for over 20 years. I then cut in an 8-frame piece of blank fullcoat, which I took off the end of the roll, where it is truly blank and has not been touched by a recording head. The 2.5 feet of pull-up and 8 frames of blank equal 3 feet. The tail pop comes next. Now that the A-B configurations as well as the pull-ups have been built, you are ready to ship the print master to the optical house to shoot the optical master for the laboratory.

Various Formats: A Who's Who

In theatrical presentation, in addition to the 2-track analog matrixed-encoded optical track, there are three basic digital formats that dominate the American theatre. Dolby SR-D, SDDS, and DTS cover the majority of presentation formats. With the advent of

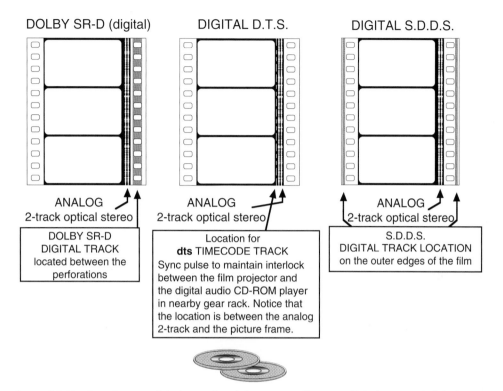

Figure 20.10 Three 35-mm digital soundtrack formats: Dolby SR-D, digital DTS, and digital SDDS.

digital stereo, the need to blow up 35-mm prints to 70 mm just to make bigger 6-track stereo presentations became unnecessary.

DTS is now offering an opportunity to present a multichannel stereo soundtrack to 16-mm film. The proprietary DTS time-code-style sync signal is placed on the 16-mm print, which in turns drives the outboard CD-style playback unit, much the same as their theatrical 35-mm cousin. Figure 20.10 shows where the various audio formats reside on a 35-mm print. DTS does not have its digital track on the film; rather, it has a control track that sits just inside the optical 2-track analog track and the picture mask. This control track maintains sync between the film and a CD that plays separately in a separate piece of gear nearby. The CD has the actual audio soundtrack of the movie.

Note that the SDDS digital tracks are on either side of the 35-mm print, outside the perforations. The DTS time code control track lies snugly between the optical analog track in the traditional mask and picture, with the Dolby SR-D digital track between the perforations.

By combining all the audio formats on the same release print, it does not matter which audio playback system a theatre is using; one of the formats of sound will suit the presentation capabilities of that exhibitor.

Figure 20.11 Actual image of various 35-mm digital sound formats on one print.

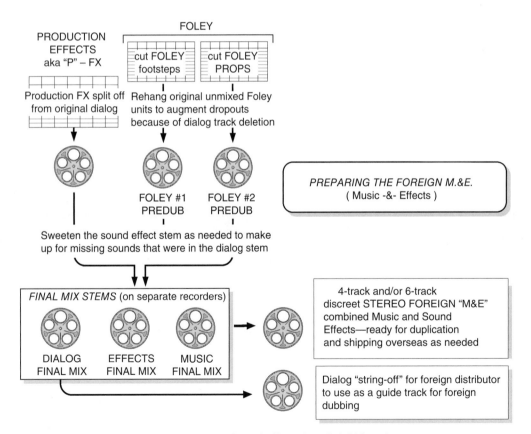

Figure 20.12 The music and effects (M&E) dubbing chart.

Foreign M&E

Once the print master is complete, the next step is to satisfy the foreign market. You must produce a full and complete soundtrack without any holes or sound events missing, yet also without any track of English dialog. This mainly is why each component of dialog, music, and sound effects has been carefully kept on its own roll or separate channel. However, just keeping the components separated is not enough. This is where the cautious preparation of the dialog editor (discussed in Chapter 14) pays off. If he or she has done the work properly, the mixer need only mute the dialog track and make sure that the P-FX track, which the dialog editor so carefully prepared, is open and running so those production effects may be included in the foreign M&E.

Preparing Foreign M&E

The mixer laces the Foley back up, as he or she may need to use more, especially footsteps and cloth movement, than was used in the final domestic mix. When the English dialog is muted, more than just flapping lips go with it. Cloth rustle, footsteps, ambience—an entire texture goes with it. The only thing remaining from the dialog track is the P-FX that was carefully protected for the foreign M&E.

We have a saying in postproduction sound. If you can get it by Munich, then your M&E track is A-Okay. The German film market is the toughest on quality control approval of M&E tracks. One of the harshest lessons a producer ever has in the education of his or her soundtrack preparation is when he or she does not care about guaranteeing a quality M&E. When an M&E track is bounced, with fault found in the craftspersonship, the foreign distributors must have it fixed by their own sound services, and the bill is paid by you, not them. It either comes out as a direct billing or is deducted from licensing fees.

The mixer combines the music and sound effects onto one mixed roll of film. The mixer makes a transfer of the dialog channel (called the dialog stem) as a separate roll of film so that foreign territories can produce their own dialog channel to replace the English words, if desired.

Chapter 21
Emerging Technologies
Sound Restoration
and Colorization

5.1 TO 6.1 AND HIGHER

What Is 5.1?

Back in mid-1990s, a young sound department trainee burst into my room. He was all excited as he announced that the decision had been made to mix the soundtrack we were working on in "five-point-one"! Wasn't that great?! I smiled at the news. He spun on his heels and disappeared down the hall to tell the rest of his friends.

My smile vanished as I sat there, stumped at the announcement. What the devil was "five-point-one"? This was the new breakthrough sound technology that everybody was talking about around town. Gee, I was going to have to learn a whole new way of doing things. I decided that I did not want to disclose my ignorance too blatantly, so I slipped down the hall and knocked on the door of our resident engineer.

"I hate to admit this, but I don't know what five-point-one is. Could you explain it to me?"

His eyebrows shot up. "Oh, you're going to love it! The sound comes out of the left speaker, the center speaker, the right speaker, as well as split surrounds, and we have a subwoofer."

I waited for the shoe to drop. "Yeah—what else?"

He shrugged. "Isn't that great?"

I studied his face suspiciously. "That's five-point-one?"

"Yeah."

I turned and paced back to my room. We've been doing that for the last 30 years! It's called *theatrical format*! What is so new about this?! Of course what was so important about it was that it was an encode that would allow the home consumer to have true dedicated audio signals assigned to the proper speakers in their home entertainment system to replicate the theatrical presentation with a compression that would allow

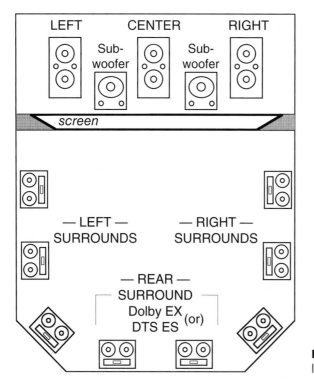

Figure 21.1 The theatrical speaker layout.

this enormous amount of audio information to take up less space on a DVD. It would mirror what we have been doing for cinema for the last three decades. Okay, that's a good thing. So let's just remove the idea that it is a *new sound system*—it is not. It is a new sound *delivery format*, a better way to bring the big theatrical sound to the consumer.

So, first we should review is the speaker layout for theatrical presentation.

Center speaker is where all dialog (except for more recent mixing philosophy) emanates.

Subwoofers (also known as "baby booms") are low-frequency speakers that sit in between the left-and-center and center-and-right speakers. These speakers reproduce very low-frequency audio signals; some of them are subharmonic and are meant to be felt and not just heard.

Left speaker and right speaker is where the stereophonic presentation of sound effects and music live (with occasional hard-left or hard-right placement of dialog).

Left surround speaker and right surround speaker is where a growing taste in aggressive 360-degree sound experience is rapidly evolving. Both music and sound effects come from the surround speakers. Since the movie *Explorers* (1984), the surround speakers have been dedicated left and dedicated right, allowing wonderful abilities to truly surround the audience and develop an ambience envelope that the audience sits within to enjoy the full soundtrack experience.

The **dedicated speaker** is placed at the rear of the theatre, thanks to the introduction of Dolby EX. It is meant for the hard assignment of sound effects that will perform behind the audience—for further envelopment—as well as pop-scare effects and dramatic swoop from rear to front aspect audio events.

Everyone knows that the home theatre has literally skyrocketed both in technology as well as the ability, in many cases, to present the theatrical experience more vibrantly (in the audio sense) than the hometown cinema. This literal tidal wave of home entertainment theatre development has demanded an audio encoding system that could properly place the prescribed audio channels to the correct speakers and do it with as little fuss or muss (as well as technical understanding) on the part of the consumer as possible.

Many home systems use a separate speaker on either side of their big screen television screens instead of the built-in speakers. The dialog is phantomed from the left and right speakers, creating an illusion of a center channel. More and more consumers are now buying a special center channel speaker and placing it either on top or just below the television screen, thus having a dedicated dialog signal assignment. This makes for a much fuller and more natural front dialog track experience than the phantom technique.

For many years home systems have had a surround system, where both the left and right rear speakers were fed by the same surround speaker signal, just as theatrical presentation was prior to the movie *Explorers*. But more and more consumers are taking advantage of the split-surround option and incorporating that into their home system as well.

A favorite of many consumers, especially those who love to irritate their neighbors, is the subwoofer speaker additive. They come in all prices and sizes, up to a 3,000-watt subwoofer that can just about move walls. This full-speaker system, for consumer venues, is what the 1 in 5.1 is all about.

Now, with Dolby EX and DTS-ES, the 5.1 rises one more notch, allowing consumers to place a dedicated rear surround channel just like they experience in the theatre. Technically, this raises the encode designation to 6.1, rather than 5.1, though this term has not officially taken hold as of the writing of this book. The truth of the matter is, variations have provided us with 7.1, and only technical variations will dictate how far this will evolve. Several years ago Tom Hollman (THX) told me that he was working on 10.1. Ten years from now I can just see two consumers standing around the off-the-shelf purchase shelf at their nearest dealer, arguing whether the 20.1 or 22.1 version is more satisfying for total immersion entertainment!

Channel Assignments
Channel 1: Center speaker (front)
Channel 2: Left speaker (front)
Channel 3: Right speaker (front)
Channel 4: Left-surround speaker(s) (rear left)

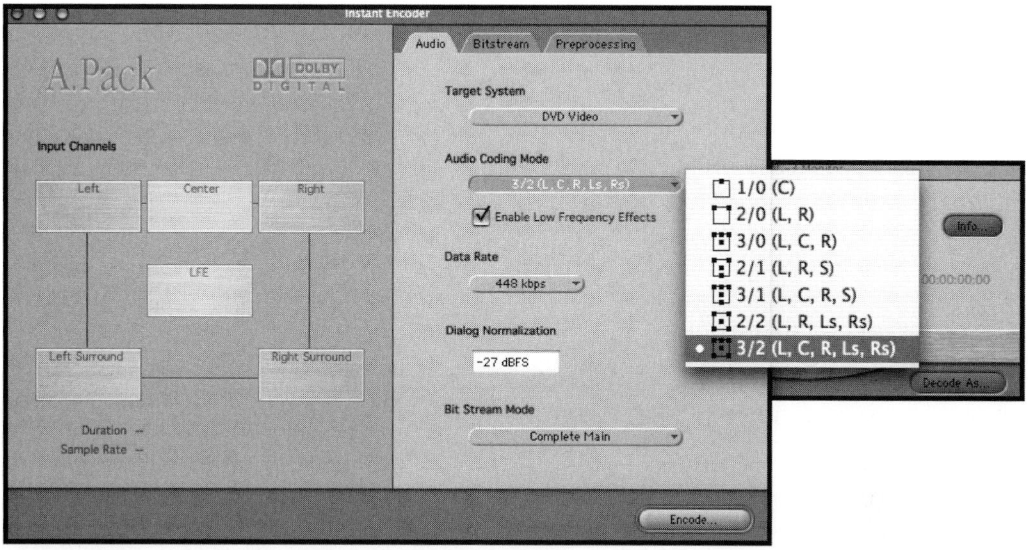

Figure 21.2 Dolby encode software that the user can matrix-encode his or her audio channels into any playback configuration listed in the submenu. The user simply presses the speaker button icon on the left and assigns the proper audio file to it.

Channel 5: Right-surround speaker(s) (rear right)
Channel 6: Rear (Dolby EX) speaker (rear center)
Channel .1: Subwoofer (low-frequency effect)

THE QC GAME

One would not know it by looking at the sleek disk products coming out onto the market, but there are huge issues when it comes to quality control.

All DVD authoring facilities have a QC department, of course, but only a small percentage of DVD authoring is done with proper 5.1 playback room environments. Some DVD authoring companies simply have their QC techs (usually underpaid get-start trainees) handle the QC evaluation by listening to the soundtrack through headsets. As incredibly stupid as this sounds, it is no joke. You are going to have someone listen to and properly evaluate a 5.1 soundtrack (review Figure 20.2) through a left-right set of headsets?! I know, I know, the market advertises headsets claiming to play proper spatial 5.1 environment, but they simply do not.

You have just spent umpteen million dollars producing this motion picture; you have hired the best sound team you could to record the production sound, the best team you could to handle the post-edit challenges and sound design, and the best re-recording sound team you could to mix it. They worked thousands of hours to produce the best sound experience that they could, and now—now, you are going to entrust a quality evaluation to an underpaid get start trainee using HEADSETS! After all that, you really need to have someone listen to and evaluate a 5.1 soundtrack (review Figure

20.2) with proper equipment. Go ahead—play Russian roulette if you want to—but NOT ME!

To add insult to injury, there is a general plus or minus 4-frame sync acceptability. A top Hollywood film laboratory vice president actually admitted this to me, quote: "Plus or minus 4 frames is acceptable to us." Ever wonder why those lips seem a little "rubbery" to you? Now you know. And I am not just talking about low-budget product. One major studio subcontracted their DVD authoring for a huge-budget picture to an independent firm and discovered that the DVD had been mastered with the audio channel assignments directed to the wrong speakers. This was a huge budget picture, by the way. The studio had to buy back all the DVDs and remaster, which cost them an extra several million dollars.

Here is a bit of warning for those who thought it was perfectly safe to watch DVDs on your computer. Much to the chagrin of a major (and I mean major) studio executive who watched a test DVD of his $100+ million epic motion picture on his personal computer, he found out that the DVD authoring service had contracted a virus in their system which was transplanted onto the DVD and as he watched the movie the virus transplanted itself into his own computer hard drive, eating away and destroying his computer files.

Unfortunately the world of DVD authoring is so misunderstood, like so many technical disciplines that are misunderstood, that there are few in the business who really know their own business. The before-mentioned studio put its foot down about the independent contractor that misassigned the audio channels of its major motion picture. The studio execs decided to build their own in-house state-of-the-art operation. Good idea, except for one problem: they did not hire the right person to head it up.

Over time the work literally was outsourced to independent contractors again because of mismanagement and technical ineptitude from the inside. A doctor may be a doctor by virtue of the initials M.D., but you do not hire a podiatrist when you need a brain surgeon. Consequently the studio found itself back where it started. Once again, quality and craftspersonship are being destroyed by throat-cutting and low-ball bidding, by studio decision makers who think they know what is going on and how it should be done (and seldom do) making decisions based on who-knows-who relationships and low-bid greed, rather than keeping the eye on the art form.

TOTAL IMMERSION OPPORTUNITIES

In addition to the obvious soundtrack mastering of linear entertainment product, such as authoring DVD media of motion pictures, rock videos, and the like, the need for sound event designers and audio authoring is rapidly expanding.

One of the most exciting emerging technologies for the future generation of entertainment venues is the total immersion experience. This is the next quantum step, with photo-realistic visuals fed to you via wraparound goggles, spherical-audio that is event linked to visual action and touch/temperature sensations phantomed throughout your nervous system—driven by complex algorithmic interdependent software that obey the laws of physics.

Interactive programs have evolved from crude digital color-block figures to mirroring reality. The technologies that need to drive the serious replication of such high-level audio-visual experiences require faster computers and mammoth amounts of high-speed access compressed visual and audio files. With every passing week the computers get faster, and the drive storage media get bigger, faster, and less expensive.

Several serious developers, thanks to Department of Defense dollars, are emerging with almost unbelievable audio-visual "scapes" that defy the boundaries of tomorrow's entertainment possibilities. The promises of 1980's *Brainstorm* and Isaac Asimov's remote viewing from *I Robot* as well as countless science-fiction prognosticators of the past 100 years are finally coming to fruition.

Software programs have pushed the boundaries of realism, such as the seascape software that can replicate ocean waves as real as nature makes them. The operator simply fills in parameter requirements, such as water temperature, wind direction and speed, longitude and latitude, and the sea will act and react exactly as the laws of physics dictate. Another software program can replicate any kind of ship. The operator enters parameters such as historic era, wood, metal, displacement, size, cargo weight, design, etc. The ship will replicate out and ride the ocean wave program, obeying the laws of physics as its size and displacement require.

New body-scanning platforms can scan the human body down to a hair follicle and enter the images into the computer for action manipulation in real time, bringing forth a whole new reality of opportunities. You can now create whole epic scenes, limited only by the power of your imagination and your understanding of how to enter parameters into the multitude of programs that will work in concert to create the future vision that you have in mind. Today's war cry is: "If you can think it, you can make it!"

There will be an exploding market for the new "total immersion" sound designer who will be hired, along with his or her team of sound creators—what we may have once called the sound editor. These craftspeople, who will specialize on their own assignment audio events, which once created and factored into the entire audio construct of the project, will work in concert with each other—all obeying the laws of physics along with the virtual real visual replications to create the brave new worlds. After we come home from a long day at the office, we will want to unwind and relax by "jumping" into various "total immersion" entertainment scenarios.

Various new sensor interactive technologies are currently being developed that will allow you to "feel" the visual realities. You are already able to turn your head and change the aspect of your view, turning to see a big oak tree with its leaves rustling in the warm afternoon breeze. Now with 360-degree spherical-binaural audio, you will be interlinked to visual events that will play for you the realistic sound of deciduous leaves fluttering in the breeze; and through a device such as a wristband, embedded signals in the program will phantom the sensation of a warm gust of wind across your body. You will feel pressure as well as temperature in addition to seeing photo-realistic visuals and spherical sound.

Practical Application for Training Purposes

The armed forces believed that they could possibly save as many as 50 percent of their wounded if they could just train their combat personnel not to fear the act of being shot or seriously injured in action. They had a scenario developed for total immersion interactive, whereby their soldiers train in ambush scenarios with enemy forces. Realistic spherical-audio sells the distant weapon fire and the incoming flight of deadly bullet rounds. The phantom bullets strike the body, the first in the upper shoulder, the second in the left thigh. The sharp zip of other bullets flies past the trainee, striking and ricocheting off various surfaces (exactly linked and replicating the trainee's surroundings) around the soldier.

Now the wounded trainee has experienced as realistically as possible (short of really being shot) what it is like to be hit by incoming fire. Instead of reacting with the emotional side of our psyche, "Oh my God, I'm shot—therefore I am going to die," the trainee is now trained to think, "Damn it! I've been hit! Now I have to problem solve how to survive!"

Mental attitude makes all the difference in the world. Our self-disciplined intellectual position will hold back the emotional side and discard the primal fears and spur the will to live.

Entertainment in Total Immersion

In the world of entertainment, one can just imagine the limitless applications to nervous system stimulation as triggered by nervous system events embedded in the total immersion program. New audio technologies are now being perfected that will change everything. What if I could give you a microphone and tell you that you do not have to try and mimic or sound like Clark Gable or Cary Grant, all you have to do is perform the dialog line with that certain lilt and timing of pace and performance. Your spoken words would then be brought into a special audio software and processed through the "Clark Gable" or "Cary Grant" plug-ins and out will come, voice printable, Clark Gable or Cary Grant.

Science fiction? Not at all. In fact, as of the writing of this book, a number of first step tests have already been accomplished. By the time this book is ready for its third edition I am sure that I will be updating this segment of the chapter to outline the specifics of the various software applications and how to use them.

This, of course, will change everything. Up to now, the visual cut-paste technique of integrating deceased celebrities into commercials and motion pictures (e.g., *Forrest Gump*, beer commercials with John Wayne, and Fred Astaire dancing with a vacuum cleaner) has been dependent on original footage. Yes, we have been able to morph the actor's face to be absolutely accurate for some time; that is no trick at all. It is the human voice that has eluded us, and the use of voice mimics to impersonate the deceased actor has always been just detectable enough to make it useless for serious celebrity replication. With the advent of this new audio technology, however, the shutters will be thrown back on all of the projects that have wanted to bring an actor back to life to perform in a project and give a performance that he or she had never given before. We are literally on the eve of a new evolution of entertainment opportunities utilizing these new technological breakthroughs.

These new opportunities (as well as the responsibilities) are staggering. By combining the technologies, one could create a total immersion entertainment venue whereby you could come home from a stressful day and decide that you want to put your total immersion gear on and activate, say, a Renaissance Faire program that would take you into an evening-long, totally realistic experience of being at a fifteenth-century festival on a nice spring afternoon with, of course, a spherical audio experience.

It only stands to reason that the more aggressive opportunists will develop programs where you could come home and put your total immersion gear on and make passionate love to Marilyn Monroe or Tom Cruise (depending on your sex and/or preference) or whoever else is literally on the menu.

Needless to say, there will be obvious exploitation used with this new technology as well as amazing mind-blowing opportunities to do things we could not otherwise do, such as a total immersion space walk or participate alongside Mel Gibson in the Battle of Sterling or scuba dive amid the coral reefs. Can you imagine what it would be like to turn an otherwise boring afternoon (say that you are snowed in at home or maybe you are just grounded by your parents) into an interactive educational scenario, such as sit around in a toga in the Roman Senate or participate in the lively debates in the House of Lords during Cromwell's time? Or be aboard the frigate *USS Bonhomme Richard* under the command of John Paul Jones in the fierce night engagement with the Serapis off the Yorkshire coast at Flamborough Head? You are a member of the crew helping to man the cannons and fight hand-to-hand combat in the grappling embrace of the two ships. Entertaining and extremely educational at the same time—what a concept!

All of this is going to need a new generation of sound craftspeople, developing and pushing the boundaries of how to design, develop, and bring to the consumer the most amazing audio event experiences you can possibly imagine.

AUDIO RESTORATION

To the inexperienced, "audio restoration" probably sounds like some salvation service, with medieval monks hunkered around their individual workstations working on would-be lost sound files. I doubt that they are monks, but this wonderful and amazing aspect of our industry is woefully misunderstood by far too many who may very well find that they desperately need this kind of work. Though there are a number of off-the-shelf programs with no-noise, broadband, declick, or other algorithmic spectrographic resynthesizer applications, only experienced and well-trained veterans can properly empower the use of such software. There is nothing worse than a bull swinging a sledgehammer in a china closet rather than a Dutch master painter using a sable brush!

There are few very fine audio restoration services. To salvage nearly 85 percent of the production track of *Frank & Jesse*, and clean out dominant fluorescent ballast hums from over 50 percent of *Doctor Jekyll and Ms Hyde*, as well as on several other occasions, I have personally used John Polito of Audio Mechanics (Burbank, California), one of the world's leaders among a multitude of audio restoration services.

Figure 21.3 Audio Mechanics' 5.1 mastering studio.

Audio Mechanics features two mastering rooms designed for 5.1 from the ground up: a live room and vocal booth for recording and ADR, and a stereo mastering control room. Their rooms are a well-thought-out design with complete audio/video/data integration among all rooms and facility-wide Equi-Tech balanced power to eliminate grounding problems. The centralized equipment room allows rooms to share resources efficiently and quickly recover from equipment failures.

This state-of-the-art 5.1 mastering room features instant room tuning presets to adapt to the project: a "flat" setting for music mastering; a Dolby-certified film setting for print mastering; a screen-compensation EQ setting for the center channel when the Stuart screen is lowered for picture projection; and a delay compensation for the digital video projector.

Up to 50 different room tunings can be stored to simulate various listening environments. The speaker system features an ITU placement of five matched dual-15″ Pelonis Series mains, based on a Tannoy 15″ dual concentric phase linear driver integrated with a super-fast low-frequency driver and a super tweeter that extends the frequency response up to 80 kHz. JBL dual-18″ sub-woofer delivers a thundering "point-one punch." The room is not only gorgeous, but the sound is amazing, and the imaging is perfect. Like all great craftspersonship, it is all about the *details*.

Figure 21.4 shows a view of the rear wall of the room featuring a rear-center channel soffit and Pelonis Edge technology bass trapping with a first-ever acoustic RPG Peg-Board, utilizing a mathematically randomized hole pattern to permit near perfect bass absorption along with an evenly distributed diffusion above 500 Hz.

The tools required for sound restoration and noise removal are extremely sophisticated and infinitely complex. Without the proper experience and talent, results can vary from mediocre to just plain awful. Audio Mechanics has more combined experience and talent with these tools than anyone in the world, and their track record proves

Figure 21.4 Reverse view of Audio Mechanics' 5.1 mastering studio.

Figure 21.5 Audio mechanic logo.

it. Producers, directors, mixing engineers, and dialog editors come to Audio Mechanics because they know they will get the best results attainable.

Sound Preservation and Restoration

Research evaluation is the most important step in preservation. The three Rs of restoration—research, research, research! Any information you can gather about the original sound production, the genealogy, quality, and condition of existing elements, will enable you to pick the best possible elements for the restoration. The goal is to find the best sounding, most original element. Oftentimes the best element will be one that is not readily available. The engineer should evaluate the elements' physical condition and audio quality, and document the findings. Select the best element or elements for transfer.

Transfer (the second most important step in preservation). Always use the best playback electronics and digital converters available. Prepare the element by carefully inspecting and, if necessary, cleaning and repairing. Mechanical modification of playback equipment can be used to accommodate shrinkage, warping, vinegar syndrome, reduced sprockets, roller heads, etc.

Listening environment (always important). The quality of listening environment is as important as the talent of the engineer. Care must be taken to make the listening environment appropriate for the type of work being performed. Use high-quality speakers and amplifiers appropriate for the type of sound work being performed. Make sure that the acoustics of the room are optimized. Just as important as the room itself, the engineer must know how the room translates to the environment the sound will be heard in.

Remastering (clean up, conform to picture, remix). Ninety-nine percent of remastering is now performed with digital tools. The current standard for digital audio restoration is 48 kHz/24-bit, but the industry is moving towards 96 kHz/24-bit. Digital tools are available to reduce hum, buzz, frame noise, perforation noise, crackle, pops, bad edits, dropouts, hiss, camera noise, some types of distortion, and various types of broadband noise including hiss, traffic noise, ambient room noise, motor noise. High-quality digital filters and equalizers can help balance the overall sonic spectrum. Digital audio tools are only as good as the engineer who is using them.

The experience and aesthetics of the engineer directly relate to the quality of the end result. Knowledge of the history of the original elements guides the engineer's decision process. For example, the restoration process would be quite different for a mono soundtrack with Academy pre-emphasis than it would be with a stereo LCRS format. Knowing whether a mono show was originally a variable-density track versus a variable-area track will also affect key decisions early on in the process. For picture-related projects, ensure that the restored audio runs in sync with picture. It may seem obvious, but make sure you are using a frame-accurate picture reference when checking sync. Oftentimes there are different versions of the picture available. The intended listening environment will determine the final audio levels.

Theatrical environments have a worldwide listening standard of 0 VU = 85 dB. This means that the sound level of a film should sound about the same in any movie theater. The music industry has not adopted a listening standard, so the level depends on the genre and delivery media. Until recently, digital audio final masters were delivered on digital audiotape. DAT, DA-88, DA-98HR (24-bit), and DigiBeta were used for film; while 1630, DAT, and Exabyte were used for the music industry. The problem with these formats is that they had to be transferred in real time and the shelf life of the tapes was anywhere from 1 to 10 years. High error rates were sometimes experienced within a single year. The industry has been moving toward optical disk and file transfer over the Internet for final digital delivery, with a preference for audio data files that can be copied and verified faster than real time.

The music industry uses Red Book audio CD-R with an optional PMCD format (Pre-Master CD), and recently DDP files (Disk Description Protocol) that can be transferred and verified over the Internet or via data CD-ROM or DVD-ROM. The film and video industries have been converging on Broadcast Wave Files audio files (BWF) on DVD-R, removable SCSI drives, FireWire drives, or transferred directly over the Internet via FTP. Higher capacity optical disk storage has recently become available with HD-DVD and Blu-ray (a.k.a. ProData for data storage).

Archiving (re-mastered and original elements). *Save your original elements!* Technology is continually evolving. Elements that seem hopelessly lost today may be able to be resuscitated 5 or 10 years from now. Save both the original elements and the raw digital transfer of the elements. The film industry routinely transfers the final restored audio to several formats. Analog archival formats include 35-mm variable area optical soundtracks and 35-mm Dolby SR magnetic tracks on polyester stock. Digital formats include BWF files on archival grade DVD-R, and digital Linear Tape-Open (LTO).

DVD-ROM is a good choice because a high-quality archive-grade DVD-R has a long expected shelf life of 50+ years. They are, however, very sensitive to mishandling and scratch easily, which can cause a loss of data. LTO tape is popular because it is an open standard with backwards compatibility written into its specifications. It is widely supported and not owned by any single manufacturer, so it is less likely to become obsolete quickly in the ever-changing digital frontier.

Even though LTO is digital tape with a fairly poor shelf life, solutions exist to allow easy migration to newer and higher capacity tapes. Software verifies the data during migration. The music industry vaults their masters in whatever format is delivered. Because the manufactured optical disks are digital clones of the original master, they can rely on a built-in automatic redundant worldwide archive. Live data storage servers are another option for digital archiving masters. RAID storage (Redundant Array of Independent Disks) is perhaps the most proactive way to digitally archive audio. RAID is a self-healing format. Because RAID disks are always online, a computer can continually verify the data. If a drive in the array fails, a new unformatted drive can be put in its place and the RAID will automatically fill the drive with the data required to make the data redundantly complete. RAID storage is much more expensive than DVD-R and LTO.

A wise digital archivist would adopt two or more digital archiving formats, and create multiple copies of each using media from multiple manufacturers. Geographically separating multiple copies should also be adopted as a precaution in the unlikely event of a disaster.

John Polito has been at the forefront of digital sound restoration since its inception. After graduating in 1987 from Stanford University with honors in music and digital signal processing, Polito joined Sonic Solutions and helped define the field of digital sound restoration by assisting in the development of the first digital audio workstation for sound restoration. In 1991 he started Audio Mechanics, considered to be a world's leading sound restoration facility, with a reputation for maintaining the highest quality standards the field has to offer. For further information on Audio Mechanics as well as how to contact John Polito personally, please visit www.audiomechanics.com.

For a further demonstration of the audio work that John Polito has shared with us in this chapter, go to the interactive DVD provided with this book. Choose button #10 RESTORATION & COLORIZATION and a submenu will appear. Choose the AUDIO MECHANICS demo button and you can hear comparisons and examples for yourself.

Restoration and Colorization

Colorization in a book on sound? Yes, it might seem odd at first, but this entire chapter is about the ever-evolving world of emerging technologies and the future that we, craftspeople as well as producers and product users, are swiftly hurtling toward like a mammoth black hole in the galaxy of the entertainment arts.

Inexorabilis—the disciplines and artistic concepts come colliding together like two separate galaxies that criss-cross each other's determined path. Though you have read my touting that sound is more important than the visual image in a motion picture, I

Figure 21.6 Legend logo.

am the first to speak an opinion with regard to the colorization of film. A staunch resistor was I—until in late 1989 I saw one film, one film only that changed my thinking. John Wayne's *The Sands of Iwo Jima* was amazingly better than any of the childish smudge coloring that I had seen up until that time.

Then, out of the blue, I happened to have a fateful conversation with an old colleague whom I had worked with a number of years ago at another cutting-edge firm (no longer in existence). I asked Susan Olney where she was working. She told me she was vice president of operations at an amazing, cutting-edge technology company based in San Diego, California.

In a few short conversations I found myself talking to Barry Sandrew, president and COO of Legend Films. Our conversation was almost like two lost brothers finding each other after years of separation. I told him that the only colorization effort I ever saw that gave me cause to pause was *Sands of Iwo Jima*. He chuckled as he responded, "That was my work."

Well, of course it was. It had to be. As the conversation continued it became extremely obvious to me that the evolution of our art forms are, in fact, inexorably drawing all of us into a singularity of purpose and dedication—art form and the highest standards of craftspersonship to create artificial reality.

Barry sent me several DVD demos, parts of which I am pleased to share with you, as they are on the interactive DVD that comes with this book. Under button #10, RESTORATION & COLORIZATION, choose the LEGEND FILMS DEMO and I am sure that like myself, you will be amazed by what you will see. The interview of Ray Harryhausen is especially compelling in dispelling the standard artistic argument that we always hear *against* colorization, and he should know—he was there, he worked with these directors and artists. I cannot think of a professional and respected voice who can give a reason to rethink and appreciate this amazing process.

COLORIZATION: A BIASED PERSPECTIVE FROM THE INSIDE*

The technology of colorization has changed considerably since it first arrived on the scene in August 1985 when Markle and Hunt at Colorization Inc. released the 1937 production of *Topper*, the first colorized feature film. They used a system in which analog chroma signals were digitally drawn over and mixed with analog black-and-white video images. To put it more simply, colors were superimposed on an existing monochrome standard video resolution image much like placing various colored filters over the image.

Today, Legend Films, a leader in all-digital colorization, is working with black-and-white and color feature film at the highest film resolutions and applying long-form

*The text for this entire section was provided by Barry B. Sandrew, PhD, Legend Films, Inc.

and short-form nondegrading restoration and a spectrum of color special effects with a brilliance and quality never before attainable. These technological advances are largely the result of my work in digital imaging and specifically digital colorization over the past 20 years.

However, the overall workflow and processing protocol for restoration and colorization evolved over several years beginning in 2001 by a very talented team of colleagues at Legend Films who built a machine that colorizes feature films, commercials, music videos, and new feature film special effects in the most efficient and cost-effective manner in the industry. Historical accounts of colorization from its genesis in the late 1980s and early 1990s is replete with a handful of highly vocal, high-profile Hollywood celebrities who adopted a vehemently anti-colorization stance. Some became so obsessed with the cause that it appeared their life's mission to rid the world of this new technology that was to them so evil and so vile that its riddance would somehow deliver them salvation in the afterlife.

Others much less vocal understood that the purpose of U.S. copyright law was to eventually make vintage films freely available to the general public after the copyright holder held the title as a protected monopoly for a fixed period of time. These laws are the same as patent laws, which eventually make inventions, drugs, and other innovations free to the public for competitive exploitation and derivation. There was a significant majority who saw colorization as a legitimate and creative derivative work and who recognized that colorization was actually bringing new life to many vintage black-and-white classics that were until then collecting dust on studio shelves or viewable on television only in the early morning hours. I believe the most balanced and accurate account of the technological evolution of colorization as well as the political and economic perspectives underlying the colorization controversy can be found in a critical essay by Gary R. Edgerton, "The Germans Wore Gray, You Wore Blue," in *IEEE Spectrum* (Winter 2000). (Gary R. Edgerton is a professor and chair of the Communication and Theatre Arts Department at Old Dominion University.)

For me, one of many significant revelations in the *IEEE Spectrum* article is that the colorization controversy might have been largely avoided had Colorization Inc. continued the joint venture relationship they had already developed with Frank Capra to colorize three of his classics, including *It's a Wonderful Life*. When Markle discovered *It's a Wonderful Life* was in the public domain he dismissed Capra's involvement in the colorization of the Christmas classic and took on the project himself, seriously alienating Capra.

Edgerton, wrote the following, which is an extract from an R. Lindsey, May 19, 1985, *New York Times* article (pp. C1, C23)—"Frank Capra's Films Lead Fresh Lives."

Capra did indeed sign a contract with Colorization, Inc. in 1984, which became public knowledge only after he began waging his highly visible campaign against the colorizing of *It's a Wonderful Life* in May 1985, when he felt obliged to maintain that the pact was "invalid because it was not countersigned by his son, Frank Capra, Jr., president of the family's film production company." Capra went to the press in the first place because Markle and Holmes discovered that the 1946 copyright to the film had lapsed into the public domain in 1974, and they responded by returning Capra's initial investment, eliminating his financial participation, and refusing outright to allow the director to exercise artistic control over the color conversion of his films.

As a consequence, Colorization, Inc. alienated a well-known and respected Hollywood insider whose public relations value to the company far outstripped any short-term financial gain with *It's a Wonderful Life*, especially in light of the subsequent controversy and Frank Capra's prominent role in getting it all started. Capra, for his part, followed a strategy of criticizing color conversion mostly on aesthetic grounds, while also stating that he "wanted to avoid litigation . . . at [his] age" and "instead [would] mobiliz[e] Hollywood['s] labor unions to oppose" colorized movies' without performers and technicians being paid for them again.

Edgerton succinctly sums up the controversy: "All told, the bottom-line motivation behind the colorization controversy was chiefly a struggle for profits by virtually all parties involved, although the issue of 'creative rights' was certainly a major concern for a few select DGA spokespersons such as Jimmy Stewart, John Huston, and Woody Allen, among others."

The rest of Edgerton's article is historically spot-on accurate. However, in his conclusion Edgerton writes:

> In retrospect, the controversy peaked with the colorization of *Casablanca* and then gradually faded away. Ted Turner recognized as early as 1989 that "the colorization of movies . . . [was] pretty much a dead issue" (G., Dawson "Ted Turner: Let Others Tinker with the Message, He Transforms the Medium Itself," *American Film*, Jan/Feb 1989:36–39, 52). Television audiences quickly lost interest in colorized product as the novelty wore off completely by the early 1990s.

While certainly a reasonable conclusion for Edgerton to make in 2000 when he wrote the *IEEE Spectrum* article, I'm confident it will be judged premature given significant changes in the attitude of the entertainment industry, the emerging spectrum of digital-distribution channels available for entertainment of all types, and the advent of Legend Film's technological advances in both restoration and colorization.

From Brains to Hollywood

I first learned that people were creating colorized versions of black-and-white classic feature films in 1986 when I was a neuroscientist at Massachusetts General Hospital engaged in basic brain research and medical imaging. My interest in colorization at the time was purely academic in nature. Indeed, a process that could create colorized black-and-white feature films where color never existed intrigued me. From the lay literature I understood the early colorization effort was accomplished using an analog video process. Consequently I did not delve much further into the early process because at the time I was not experienced in analog video but firmly entrenched in high-resolution digital imaging. When I saw the results of the analog process I was less than impressed with the quality but certainly impressed with the technological and innovative effort.

Digging further into the business rationale for colorization it was clear why the technology had become attractive even if the aesthetic value of the process was questionable. While the black-and-white version of a vintage film remains in public domain, the colorized version becomes a creative derivative work that (back in 1986) was eligible for a new 75-year copyright.

Coincidently, in the summer of 1986 George Jensen, an entrepreneur from Pennsylvania with the entertainment company American Film Technologies, approached me to develop an all-digital process for colorizing vintage black-and-white films which he hoped would become a major improvement over the current analog process. American Film Technologies had financed several failed development trials in an effort to create a digital colorization process that might capture the market. When approached by George to provide an alternative solution I suggested a novel direction to the problem that was significantly different from any of the failed attempts.

Given my background in digital imaging and my credibility credentials in academia, American Film Technologies decided to offer me a chance to develop their system. I considered the opportunity sufficiently low risk to leave academia for a period of time and take on an R&D project with company stock, a considerably higher salary than one can expect at a teaching hospital, and all the potential rewards of a successful entertainment startup company.

Part of my decision was based on the fact that George Jensen had assembled an impressive group of Hollywood talent, such as Emmy-nominated Peter Engle (executive producer, *Saved by the Bell*) and two-time Oscar winner Al Kasha (Best Song, honoring "The Morning After" from *The Poseidon Adventure* and "We May Never Love Like This Again" from *The Towering Inferno*), as well as Bernie Weitzman, former vice president/business manager for Desilu Studios and vice president of operations for Universal Studios. This brought me additional confidence that the company was heading toward the mainstream entertainment industry. I saw George Jensen as a visionary in that he realized one could colorize a huge library of proven classic black-and-white films in the public domain and in the process become a Hollywood mogul based solely on technology.

The problem that stood in his way was the development of advanced digital-imaging technology and the acquisition of original 35-mm film elements that would be acceptable in overall image quality to capture digitally for colorization and VHS release. His search for a superior, all-digital process ended soon after we met. My lack of experience in analog video was a huge advantage because I believe I would have been biased toward developing a more advanced analog solution and ultimately the system would have been less successful. Instead, I started from scratch and created a digital colorization process that was technologically much different from existing systems but markedly superior in final product.

I believe my strength was coming at the problem from a totally different and perhaps naïve perspective. I was not a video engineer and had very little knowledge of the field. Consequently, there were some in the entertainment industry that told me my concept wouldn't work and advised me to go back to studying brains.

The Early Digital Process

Colorization was a designer-created color transform function or look-up table that was applied to underlying luminance or gray scale values of user-defined masks. Each mask identified objects and regions within each frame. In other words, instead of simply superimposing color over the black-and-white image like the old analog processes, the color was actually embedded in the image, replacing the various levels of black and white with color. This permitted a great deal of control over color within each frame and automated the change of color from one frame to the next based on changes in luminance. Once a designer created a reference frame for a cut it was the colorist's job to make certain the masks were adjusted accurately from frame to frame. The colorists had no color decisions to make because the designer-created look-up tables intimately linked the color to the underlying gray scale. All that the colorist was required to do was manually modify the masks to fit the underlying gray scale as it changed due to movement every 24th of a second from frame to frame. However, because each mask in each frame had to be viewed by the colorist and possibly manually modified, the number of masks allowable within each frame had to be limited.

Of course from a production-cost standpoint the more masks in a frame the more the colorists had to address and the longer each frame took to be manually modified the greater the cost to colorize. Consequently, using this method, the number of mask regions per frame in the American Film Technologies system was ultimately limited to 16. Because the process was highly labor intensive the user interface was designed to be very simple and very fast so that process could be outsourced to a cheaper labor market.

Within 5 months I had a working prototype and a demo sufficient to premier at a Hollywood press conference. The late Sid Luft, Judy Garland's ex-husband and manager, became a great personal friend and major supporter of colorization. He provided American Film Technologies with some of our early black-and-white material from Judy Garland concerts and television shows which we incorporated into a demo. Most of the material originated on relatively poor-quality 2" videotape but the digital color was such an advancement over the analog process that it appeared stunning to us. Apparently it also appeared stunning to the press at a conference held across the street from Universal Studios in April 1987. When Frank Sinatra appeared with baby blue eyes you could hear the amazed reaction of those assembled.

The majority of articles that resulted from that press conference were favorable and indicated that colorization had finally come of age. In reality we had a long way to go. The real proof of concept didn't happen until November 1987 when we successfully produced the first all-digital colorized film, *Bells of St. Mary's,* for Republic Pictures. Much of the technology was refined and developed during that period of production and during the production of several feature films thereafter.

American Film Technologies took over the colorization industry within one year following the release of *Bells of St. Mary's* though Jensen's vision of creating a library of colorized films never really materialized. We learned that the best 35-mm prints at the time were held by the studios or by a very close-knit subculture of film collectors, so we became largely dependent on the major studios as work-for-hire clients. Those clients included Republic Pictures, Gaumont, Universal, Disney, Warner Bros., CBS, ABC, MGM, Turner Broadcasting, and many others.

In the early 1990s American Film Technologies and its competitors eventually faded away because each company overbuilt for what was essentially a limited market. Once Turner completed colorizing his "A" and "B" movie hit list, colorization essentially dried up. I believe that both the technology and the industry premiered and peaked 20 years too early. Today there is affordable computer horsepower to automate much of the process at the highest resolutions and in high-definition as well as film

Figure 21.7 Barry B. Sandrew, Ph.D., president and COO of Legend Films.

color space. In addition, using reliable outsourcing resources, particularly in India, virtual private networks can make it seem as though a colorization studio in Patna, India is next door to our design studio in San Diego. The affordability and, most important, quality of colorization product has advanced to a technological plateau.

The Rationale for Colorization Today

The early days of colorization were a wakeup call to studio asset management directors and archivists, many of whom saw their studio libraries neglected for over half a century. However, the very early studio asset managers and archivists (if they existed) were not at fault. Indeed it was a matter of budget, studio culture, and lack of foresight. As a result over half of the films that were ever produced in the United States are gone today. Not because they have deteriorated over time, though this was also a contributing factor, but because the studios threw many of their film negatives *in the trash*!

There were actually rational excuses for this mass destruction of our film heritage. No one in the 1920s through the late 1940s saw the enormous impact of television on our lives and culture. Certainly, the idea of tape recorders in every home and later DVD players and soon high-def DVD players was as distant as a man landing on the moon . . . probably more so because digital video entertainment in the home could hardly be envisioned. No one anticipated Blockbuster, Hollywood Video, or Netflix, where films of every genre and era can be rented. There was no sign that the cable industry and the telcos would be laying the groundwork for downloading high-definition films to home digital disk recorders and viewable on the average consumer's 50-inch high-definition monitor with 5.1 surround sound, as they are today.

In the early years, studio feature films had a theatrical run and those films that had a significant return on the studio investment were likely saved. Those that did not were eventually thrown out to make shelf space for newer films. The idea of films having an after-life was foreign to only the most Nostradamus-like among studio executives. It's ironic that it took colorization, with all its controversy, to focus mass attention on the need to restore and preserve our film heritage. With so many diverse digital distribution outlets for entertainment product today and a renewed desire for proven vintage entertainment, the studios now have a great incentive to restore their classic black-and-white film libraries. Several have called on Legend Films to colorize selected classic black-and-white titles in an effort to make them more attractive to new generations of audiences.

Indeed, by now much of the furor over colorization has subsided and special effects specialists, archivists, creative producers, and iconic Hollywood talent are embracing the process. Digital distribution outlets cry for content that is economical yet proven profitable. What better time for colorization to reemerge, and now in high definition. The studios realize that new film production is typically high cost, high risk, and low margin. Colorization of proven evergreen (having timeless value) classic feature films is low cost, low risk, and high margin over time.

Legend Films, Inc.: Building a System for the 21st Century

In 2000 I met Jeff Yapp, former president of International Home Video at 20th Century Fox Home Entertainment and later president of Hollywood Entertainment (Hollywood Video stores). He was a major proponent of colorization for at least a decade before I met him and he always pointed to the old but valuable 20th Century Fox Home Entertainment collection of colorized Shirley Temple films that were re-released in the late 1990s as fully remastered for broadcast and VHS sales. Those colorized classics turned into one of 20th Century Fox Home Entertainment's most successful home video campaigns. Jeff understood the added value of colorization if it could be done correctly, at high-definition, and with a color vibrancy and quality never before seen. He asked whether I could create a more automated method of colorization that would be "light years ahead of the look of the old colorization processes." Fully equipped with the latest and most economical computer horsepower, major advances in software development, and broadband connectivity, I was 100 percent certain it could be done.

Restoration of the black-and-white digitized film is the first step in the colorization process. In order to create the best-looking colorized product, it is essential to start with the best black-and-white elements with the best dynamic range. We search for the best quality 35-mm elements and then digitally capture every frame in high-definition or various film formats. While the colorization is ongoing we put each frame through the Legend Films' proprietary restoration process. The software is semi-automated, using sophisticated pattern recognition algorithms, and the user interface is designed to be easily adaptable to unskilled outsourcing labor markets.

The colorization system had to be sophisticated enough to do the heavy lifting of correct mask placement from frame to frame with little decision making or direction

Figure 21.8 Barry Sandrew going over Q&A colorization points to David G. Martin, CEO and Sean Compton, QA Manager on 20th Century Fox Home Entertainment's *Heidi.*

by the actual colorist. Speed, efficiency, and, most of all, quality were the essential ingredients. With the cost of high-powered technology at an all-time low, and with reliable PC networking I went to work. The result was a semi-automated colorization system, in which there were no color restrictions, and the number of masks per frame could be essentially unlimited. Legend Films currently has 10 international patents that are either published or pending along with a full-time R&D team that is constantly evolving the system to meet and overcome new production challenges.

One objective was to create an intuitive user interface that would make much of the sophisticated technology underlying the color design, colorization, and restoration software transparent to the user and consequently built for unfettered creative design as well as speed and efficiency.

In the case of a feature film, the entire movie is captured digitally in high-definition or film resolution. The resulting digital frames are then dissected into cuts, scenes, characters, locations, etc. Once the entire film is broken down into its smallest components, a series of design frames is selected to serve as a color storyboard for the film. The design process involves applying many different colors for various levels of shadows, mid-tones, and highlights. With 16 bits of black and white or 64,000 levels of gray scale available for each frame, the amount of color detail that can be applied is enormous. At American Film Technologies only 256 gray scale values were available for each frame. In the case of color film, Legend Films can apply color effects at a resolution of 48 bits of color or 16-log bits per red, green, and blue channel. Pure hues are not common in nature, but in earlier digital colorization processes, single hue values were the only way to apply color to various luminance levels.

In the Legend Films process, color is dithered in a manner that mixes hues and saturations semi-randomly in a manner that makes them appear natural, particularly for flesh color and different lighting situations. While this sounds complicated, the design process is actually unencumbered by the underlying technology, allowing the designer to focus on the creative aspects of the colorization process rather than keeping track of masks or how the computer interprets the data. Once the designer has established the color design, it becomes locked into a cut and scene so that no additional color decisions need to be made during the actual colorization process. The color automatically adjusts according to luminance levels.

A second key ingredient of the Legend Films' color effects process is a method of applying color effects from frame to frame in a manner that requires little skill other than an eye for detail. Once the color design is established for the entire film, at least one frame per cut in the film is masked using the lookup tables appropriate for that cut. This key frame is used as a reference to move the color masks appropriately from one frame to the next. This process of moving masks from one subsequent frame to the next has been largely automated in the Legend system using many sophisticated pattern recognition algorithms that are activated with the press of a space bar. Making the process even easier, only the foreground objects (i.e., objects that move independently of the background) are addressed at this stage. The backgrounds are colorized and applied automatically in a separate step. The only labor-intensive aspect of this process is the high level of quality assurance we demand for each frame. This requires that a colorist monitor the computer automation and make slight adjustments when necessary. Any adjustments that the colorist makes updates the computer to recognize those errors in future frames so in effect it learns from prior mistakes. As a consequence of this proprietary computer intelligence and automation, the colorization software is readily adaptable to any economical labor market regardless of skill level. In fact, a person can be trained to become a colorist in little more than a day, although it takes a few weeks to become proficient.

The third key ingredient of the Legend colorization process is the automated nature of background color effects. Each cut in the film is processed using Legend's proprietary utility software to remove the foreground objects. The background frames for the entire cut are then reduced to a single visual database that includes all information pertaining to the background, including offsets, movement, and parallax distortion. The designer uses this visual database to design and subsequently apply highly detailed background color automatically to each frame of the cut where the foreground objects have already been colorized. This sophisticated utility enhancement dramatically cuts down the time required for colorizing, essentially removing the task of colorizing the background from frame to frame. Since backgrounds are handled in design, the colorist need only focus on foreground objects and the designer can place as much detail as he or she wishes within the background element. Complex pans and dollies are handled in the same manner.

Once the color of the foreground and background elements are combined, the entire movie is rendered into 48-bit color images and reconstructed using SMPTE time code for eventual layoff to high-definition or 35-mm film.

Colorization—A Legitimate Art Form

In 2006, colorization matured into a legitimate art form. It provides a new way of looking at vintage films and is a powerful tool in the hands of talented color designers

Frame from *Reefer Madness*

Captured image from acquired 35-mm print

After digital restoration

The underlying technology retains film grain and avoids artifacts without filtering.

To see the colorization step, you need to review the interactive DVD (button 10) RESTORATION -&-COLORIZATION—to fully enjoy and appreciate the *colorization* step after the B-&-W restoration.

Figure 21.9 *Reefer* restored two-panel black and white only presentation.

for realizing what many creative contributors to our film heritage intended in their work.

A color designer typically looks at an entire film and creates a color storyboard that influences the way the film will ultimately look like in color. Our designers are experienced in many aspects of production including color theory, set design, matte design, costumes, and cinematographic direction. Their study and background research of each film is exhaustive prior to the beginning of the design process. Once into the film, the designer uses visual cues in an attempt to interpret what the original director had intended in each shot.

If the shot focuses on a particular individual, object, or region the focal length of that shot within the context of the dialog and storyline will often provide the reason it was framed in a particular way. Using color the designer can push back all or parts of the background or bring forward all or parts of the object, person, or region of interest that is necessary to achieve the desired effect.

The designer can also enhance the mood by the use of warm colors and/or cold colors as well as enhance the intended character of particular actors with flesh tones and highlights. Lighting can be used in a spectrum of ways to increase tension or create a more passive or romantic mood in a shot. Certainly the possibilities for influencing the audience's reaction, mood, and perception of scenes are enormous when using color appropriately.

India Is the Future

To paraphrase Legend Films' Thomas L. Friedman (*The World Is Flat: A Brief History of the Twenty-first Century*, 2006), the world of entertainment production is getting flatter by the day. Outsourcing to Canada was yesterday; today it's China and India. I've become particularly enamored with India because we've maintained a highly efficient and professional production facility there for the past three years. I never would have considered maintaining a satellite production studio halfway around the world in Patna, India, and $12\frac{1}{2}$ hours ahead of us; but with broadband connectivity and a virtual private network, Legend Films is functioning 24 hours a day. We receive color data from India every morning that is applied to our high-definition frames in San Diego. We review that work during the day and send QC notes for fixes, which follow the next day. The work ethic and work quality of this largely English-speaking part of the world has been a major asset to Legend Films.

Our primary studio in India is partitioned into 16 smaller studios with 10 to 15 colorist workstations in each. High-quality infrared cameras are mounted in each studio so that we can see the work being done and communicate with the colorists over any production issues. The result is that Uno/Legend Studio in Patna and Legend Films in San Diego are one virtual studio that works in sync around the clock, around the world. We are now adding an additional studio in India at Suresh Productions in Hyderabad to increase our overall output and offer a more complete service package globally to filmmakers. The new facility acts as a third element of the Legend virtual studio working in tandem with our Patna studio. It concentrates on film restoration but also has digital intermediates and color-grading capabilities as well as the most advanced high-definition telecine, editing, and laser film scanning equipment. The

Figure 21.10 Special FX wizard, Ray Harryhausen, directs the color design for Marian Cooper's *She* with Creative Director, Rosemary Honath.

facility also includes a complete soundstage resource as well as audio suites for voice looping and sound effect sweetening.

Hyderabad is one of the major centers of the film industry in India and as such has a large middle-class and rather affluent and highly educated population. The world is changing and professionals in all aspects of the entertainment industry, particularly in production, must be aware of this change. Don't be in denial.

The Second Coming of Colorization

In the past three years we have restored and colorized more than 50 films in high-definition or film resolution and we currently have another 50 in the pipeline. 20th Century Fox Home Entertainment has elected to use the Legend Films' process to revitalize the entire Shirley Temple catalog of films that were originally colorized in the 1980s—and early 1990s. We've also colorized *The Mark of Zorro* and *Miracle on 34th Street* for 2005 and 2006 releases, respectively, for 20th Century Fox Home Entertainment.

Many in the creative community of vintage Hollywood are looking to correct the gaps in available technology when their films were first produced. Other contemporary producers, directors, and special effects supervisors are using colorization to bring cost savings to what are already skyrocketing production costs.

Ray Harryhausen

Even when color film was first available the cost often outweighed the value since, unlike today, the theatergoing audience back then was quite accustomed to black-and-white films. A case in point is Marian C. Cooper's sci-fi classic, *She*. Cooper intended that the film was to be originally shot in color, and both the sets and costumes were obviously designed for color film. However, RKO cut Cooper's budget just before production and he had to settle for black and white.

It wasn't until 2006 that Ray Harryhausen chose Legend Films' advanced colorization technology to re-release *She* in the form that Cooper envisioned it—in vibrant color! Ray spent days in our design studio working with our creative director to select appropriate colors for the background mattes so that they retained or in most cases enhanced the realism of a shot. He knew exactly what Cooper would have been looking for had he been sitting in the designer's chair. The result is outstanding and, because of Ray's involvement and creative input, the film is one of the most important colorization projects ever produced.

Ray Harryhausen has become a staunch proponent of Legend Films' colorization process and has asked both Warner Bros. and Sony Home Entertainment to allow him to work with Legend to colorize his black-and-white classics, including *Mighty Joe Young*, *Beast from 20,000 Fathoms*, *20 Million Miles to Earth*, *It Came from Beneath the Sea*, and *Earth vs the Flying Saucers*. When he originally produced these films, he envisioned them in color but was constrained by studio budgets and the status of film technology at the time. He told me that it was difficult to do realistic composites with the existing color film stock. Today, using Legend Films technology he can design his iconic fantasy monster films into the color versions he originally intended.

The Aviator

Martin Scorsese used Legend Films to produce the *Hell's Angels* opening scene in *The Aviator*. He also used Legend's technology to colorize portions of *The Outlaw* with Jane Russell and many of the dogfight scenes in *Hell's Angels*. While many of the dogfight scenes were done using models, other scenes were simply colorized footage of the *Hell's Angels* feature film. Obviously those scenes would have been very difficult to reproduce as new footage. For a tiny fraction of the cost to recreate the models and live-action footage of key scenes, he received from Legend Films all the colorized footage he needed which Rob Legato, FX supervisor, blended seamlessly into *The Aviator*.

Jane Russell

I remember showing Jane Russell the seductive scene in *The Outlaw* that made her a star and was used in Scorsese's *The Aviator*. Of course it was the first time she had seen it in color. Although the scene was only about 8 to 10 seconds long and she was viewing it on my 15″ laptop, she loved the way her red lips looked, the natural flesh color of her face, and the accuracy of her hair color and its highlights. She later did a running commentary of *The Outlaw* for the Legend Films colorized DVD library in which she was very frank, with typically Jane Russell sass, reminiscing about her experiences with Howard Hughes. That Legend Films' title is scheduled for an April 2007 release date.

Whenever I speak to Jane she expressed a very strong desire to colorize *The Pink Fuzzy Nightgown* (1957) owned by MGM. That was the last starring film role for the Hollywood icon, which she co-produced with her former husband, Bob Waterfield. Jane considered that film her favorite starring role next to *Gentlemen Prefer Blondes*. The film was originally intended to be a film noir, which Jane wanted directed and shot in black and white. She was fortunate to have that option. However, it evolved into a comedy and looking back, she has always regretted her decision to shoot it in black and white, and today is lobbying the studio to allow her to design the film in color using the Legend Films' process. Colorization and her personal involvement in reviving the title will add considerable asset value to a film that is certainly not a revenue-producer at the moment. To have Jane Russell color design and provide commentary on one of her favorite films was fulfillment of a longheld wish by a beloved and significant Hollywood icon.

Terry Moore

Terry Moore is an actress who was married to Howard Hughes and starred in films such as *Mighty Joe Young, Shack Out on 101, Why Must I Die, Man on a Tightrope*. She was nominated for a best supporting actress Academy Award for her role in *Come Back, Little Sheba*. Terry is a dynamo who, at 76, is probably more active today than ever in her career. She became a "believer" in colorization and a very dear friend of mine when Legend Films colorized *A Christmas Wish* in which she co-starred with Jimmy Durante.

During that process she provided running commentary on the colorized version for our DVD release in 2004. She was so engaged with the process that she commented that Howard Hughes would have loved the Legend Films' technology and would have wanted to redo his black-and-white classics. Terry and Jane are happy that we were able to accommodate Hughes with our colorized version of *The Outlaw*. The two Hollywood stars collaborated on the video commentary for the Legend Films DVD of *The Outlaw* in which Moore interviews Russell and the two compare notes on Howard Hughes. They are certain he would have colorized that film if he was alive today.

Shirley Temple Black

What can you say about Shirley Temple Black? I had the awesome privilege of visiting her at her home in the San Francisco Bay area 3 years ago. I wanted her to compare how the 1990s colorization of *Heidi* looked (that had been sold for the past 10 years on VHS) and how it looked in the 2003 colorization by Legend Films in high definition. We set up a high-def workstation in her house and set it up in her living room. I'll never forget Shirley's reaction when she saw the switch from black-and-white to color. She initially said, "That looks really good in black-and-white," but when the color popped in she said, "Wow, that looks great!" I believe she understood at that moment that colorization using advanced technology brings new life to great classics.

Shirley and Legend soon entered into a partnership to restore and colorize original Shirley Temple films and TV programs that she always showed to her kids during birthday parties but which were stored in her basement after they were grown. Shirley had dupe negatives of her *Baby Burlesk* shorts, the very first films in which she appeared when she was 3 and 4 years old. She also had 11 hours of *The Shirley Temple Storybook*, which were produced when she was a young woman. She acted with Jonathan Winters, Imogene Coco, and many other famous comedians and actors of the day in the most popular children's stories.

Those 11 hours were the last starring and producing project in which she was involved. The classic TV programs are rich in color and held up well as quad tapes. We restored each 1-hour show and released both the *Baby Burlesk* and *Shirley Temple Storybook* as a set that is currently being sold as *The Shirley Temple Storybook Collection*.

Conclusion

While there will always be detractors, the fact that we fully restore and improve the original high-resolution, black-and-white digitized film elements in the process of colorization should satisfy most purists. Furthermore, we always provide the restored black-and-white version along with the colorized version on each Legend Films DVD.

In a very real sense, colorization and the increased revenue it generates subsidize the restoration of the original black-and-white feature film.

> The bottom line: Colorization applied to public domain vintage films is a derivative work that deserves attention, as a valid interpretation of earlier studios' work-for-hire. In that regard it is separate and distinct from the original work and should be allowed to stand on its own. In 2006, colorization has matured to a level where it is a legitimate art form. It is a new way of looking at vintage films and a powerful tool in the hands of a knowledgeable color designer for commercials, music videos, and contemporary feature film special effects.
>
> *– Barry B. Sandrew,* PhD, *president, and COO of Legend Films*

You can review the video demo which includes Ray Harryhausen sharing his views and commitment to colorization as well as the numerous comparisons that have been discussed by Barry Sandrew on the interactive DVD included with this book. Choose button #10, RESTORATION and COLORIZATION; choose LEGEND FILMS VIDEO DEMO, and I am sure that you will also enjoy the LEGEND FILMS GALLERY of comparison stills.

IT IS ALL UP TO YOU

Your creativity and your dedication to your art form are limited only by your imagination and your personal commitment to quality in whatever craft you choose.

Thank you for your patience and open mindedness in reading this chapter as well as the entire book.

Now go forth and be creative.

Chapter 22
The Venerable Nagra
IV-S (Analog)

I have been pleasantly surprised at the number of e-mails that I have gotten over the last few years, even up to a few days ago, before I updated this chapter from sound craftspeople as well as several directors and producers who have thanked me for including a comprehensive chapter on the Nagra IV-S. Therefore, I have decided not to delete it from this edition. (For information about the digital direct-to-disk Nagra V, see this book's Website at *textbooks.elsevier.com/9780240808659.*)

THE PRACTICAL NAGRA

The title of this book is the *Practical Art of Motion Picture Sound*. Practical is a code by which the Nagra operates, as it still remains the highest bang-for-the-buck quality audio recorder available for production sound recording. Trust me when I tell you this, but in the heat of combat, when the production dollars are flowing like a sieve, when the proprietary DAT battery packs have taken a nose dive, when the extremes of high or low temperatures are turning your digital gear into inoperable lock-up, when the moisture of predawn dew or the blistering winds of Death Valley are turning all of your perfect preproduction plans of genius into just the mere desire to survive the day of shooting with any kind of track at all—that is when you stride back to your vehicle and pull out the Nagra. To hell with the producer's or director's craving for techno-fads or the perception of cutting-edge digital promises. You know what the Nagra will deliver under arduous conditions.

Nagras are tough, durable, and extremely forgiving. These remarkable recorders were invented by the Polish audio designer, Stephan Kudelski, and have been manufactured at the Kudelski/Nagra factory in Cheseaux, Switzerland, since the early 1960s. The Nagra audio recorder has attained legendary status, its very name being synonymous with field audio recording for sync sound. Though DAT recorders have come into extremely wide use in the film industry, most of your professional sound mixers keep the Nagra close at hand. Your really good sound mixers use the analog Nagra in concert with digital recording equipment, thereby creating a greater collaborative alliance between the two technologies.

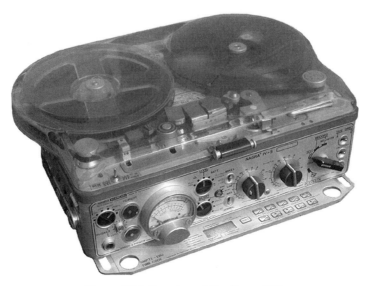

Figure 22.1 Overview of the Nagra IV-S.

Figure 22.1 shows the Nagra IV-S with the 7"-reel expansion and the oversize lid conversion. This allows the use of standard ¼" stock on 7" reels with the lid closed. Note that the width of the 7" reels is wider than the basic Nagra body. Originally the Nagra was designed to use the 5" reels. Nagra even went on to design an adaptation kit that attaches to the unit with pulley belts so that the sound mixer could use 10" reels if desired (though this adaptation is seldom used). This particular model also has a slim pull-out time code panel that tucks neatly under the unit between the leg stumps.

There is an interesting rising interest in recording in analog on the Nagra again— no doubt due to comparison test recordings (such as the comparison recording included on the DVD of this book) along with the recording mixer's evaluation of the quality of sound vs. dollars spent. I hear reports of many Nagras being bought on eBay, and even though this is a great way to buy and sell goods directly from others, one should be aware of one very important fact. Nagras were built in two standards, CCIR and NAB.

We all know NAB is the Western standard for calibrations. CCIR is the Eastern European equivalent, and those who do not remember to check whether the Nagra under consideration is NAB or CCIR may discover that they have a beautifully conditioned Nagra that is CCIR instead of NAB.

CCIR models can be converted to NAB by sending it to a qualified tech maintenance service company and authorizing them to make the conversion. The cost of a conversion seems to be hovering around $1,000 (as of this writing) which is not a bad price if you consider the overall value received, as one considers the sale price of a used Nagra IV-S and the workhorse value it will deliver.

Figure 22.2 D-cell batteries are used in the Nagra IV-S.

You can use a CCIR Nagra perfectly fine *if* you transfer back from the same machine to whatever source, film mag, or nonlinear digitization or whatever. But you cannot record with a CCIR model and ship the tape to any postproduction facility without conversion to NAB. The truth is, many of the reports are that most of these CCIR units have been maintained in fabulous shape, so, if you find a particularly great bargain on a CCIR unit, you may want to go ahead and acquire it and spend the extra thousand dollars to convert it. That, of course, is a decision you will have to make.

THE BATTERY SUPPLY

One of the best engineering designs of the Nagra is the practicality of power. It does not run on a proprietary battery design, like so many systems today. It runs on the classic D-cell battery, a standard power unit found everywhere. Unlike many new technology devices that work only an hour or two on their special-made batteries, the Nagra can work like a race horse for days on one set of 12 D-cell batteries (Figure 22.2).

When you have checked the strength of your battery supply (as explained later) and have decided to put in a fresh set of D-cells, you need to flip the Power Source selector switch (item 1 in Figure 22.3) to EXT (external). Make sure that the Main function selector bar (item 4 in Figure 22.3) is turned to the OFF position, horizontal, or 9 o'clock position. This will ensure that no power is flowing through the unit. Never, ever change out batteries when the Main Function selector bar is turned up to Test!

Make sure the lid of the unit is secured and carefully turn it over. I like to use a hand towel as a protective surface, no matter where I am recording. On the underside you will see a rectangular stainless steel cover held in place on the back edge by two small stainless steel clips and locked down in front by two quarter-turn screws. Notice that the edge of the screws has a flattened side to them. It is a good idea to carry a coin, as the two lock-down screws of the battery well cover are designed perfectly for a nickel (though any coin will do). Place the coin in the screws and turn until the flattened edge of each screw is aligned with the edge of the battery well housing. Lift the lid up and out and place it to one side.

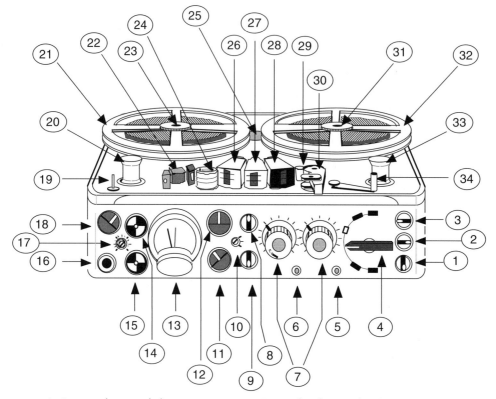

1. Power selector switch
2. Line & phones switch-to meter
3. Tape/direct switch to headsets
4. Main function selector
5. Meter light button
6. Reference oscillator button
7. Potentiometer (volume) channel control
8. Microphone/line input selector switch
9. NRS (noise reduction)/normal switch
10. Mono/stereo Input selector
11. Filter selector
12. Meter level selector
13. Modulometer
14. Pilot "flag" indicator
15. Speed/power "flag" indicator
16. Headset ¼" connector (stereo)
17. Headset volume control
18. Headset input selector
19. Rewind/fast forward switch
20. Tension roller for the supply reel
21. Supply reel (fresh ¼" stock)
22. Erase head
23. Lock-down "keeper" (supply reel side)
24. Stabilizer roller (with a 50 or 60 Hz stroboscope)
25. Tape speed selector
26. Record head (two channels)
27. Pilot head
28. Playback head (two channels)
29. Capstan
30. Pinch roller arm
31. Lock-down "keeper" (take-up reel side)
32. Take-up reel
33. Tension roller for the take-up reel
34. Clutch control lever

Figure 22.3 Nagra IV-S designation chart.

Always use Duracell batteries. No, I do not own any stock in the company. I give you this advice from years of experience. They are recommended for good reason—they endure. With good operational procedure protocol your fresh change of batteries can last for days, even weeks if you use good power management. I had one set actually last 6 months, but that is extremely rare.

Take a moment to check that the six spring-action contact terminals on the sides of the battery well are clean and free of any battery corrosion or fouling dirt or debris. On earlier Nagra models, the three positive side contact terminals are spring-action fuses. You should take a moment to remove each one and closely inspect it. If they need to be changed out, you need to use 2.5 A 5 × 20 mm replacements. Be careful to insert them correctly or they could burn out. Of course, you will know very quickly that your fuse was replaced improperly when you turn the Nagra over and try to power it up again and nothing happens. Be sure you place the batteries into the trough guides facing the correct direction. If you do not place them all in facing the correct direction the power flow will be wrong.

Once you have properly placed the new batteries in, replace the stainless steel cover and using your coin again, twist the lock screws 90 degrees to secure it in place. Turn the unit over and flip the Power Source selector switch back to BATT (internal batteries). Turn the Main Function selector bar up to Test, thereby powering up the Nagra electronics. Just off center of the Front Control Panel is the Level selector; rotate the selector to BATT. The modulometer needle should flip all the way over to the right side of the meter. If it does not, you need to go back and check your batteries and/or fuses to understand why.

If you use an older Nagra that has a Volt/Cell option on the Level selector you can get an exact measurement of the battery power by turning the Level selector to this option. The modulometer needle should drop back to about midpoint on the meter. A fresh battery should read 1.5 volts or better. As the batteries diminish in strength you will notice that the voltage strength will drop bit by bit. It is unwise to use the batteries if their voltage strength has dropped under 1.2. Time to change them out with a fresh set.

On the Nagra IV-S you do not have a Volt/Cell selection. That function is incorporated in the BATT position and shows up on the modulometer in the short third-level set of numbers to the right side. The same indication of voltage strength applies.

Remember that all batteries, no matter what make or model, are going to suffer in cold conditions, so it is a good idea to keep your batteries in a warm and temperature-protected spot. I always keep a packing blanket as part of my kit to wrap the Nagra, leaving a flap over it for easy access. When I can, I also use two pairs of battery-powered electrical socks (to place under the Nagra) to ensure stable battery power. Go to your favorite sporting goods store and shop as if you were going duck hunting and need to keep warm; you will think of and find a multitude of helpful devices and aids.

THE PARTS

The designation chart (by number) shown in Figure 22.3 will help you through the rest of this chapter because it identifies which part, switch, or selector procedure is being described.

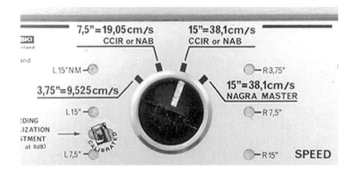

Figure 22.4 The tape speed selector is nestled underneath and between the take-up reels.

Figure 22.5 The tape path: clean and simple.

Speed and Equalization Selector

It is a good idea to decide what tape speed you want to record at before you thread up a fresh roll of stock. It is a pain to get to this selector once you have threaded your tape stock, as you can see in Figure 22.5.

This decision goes back to everything we have discussed throughout this book, so I am not going to belabor that point.

The Nagra records at the following tape speeds:

$3^3/_4$ ips = 9.525 centimeters per second
$7^1/_2$ ips = 19.05 centimeters per second
15 ips = 38.1 centimeters per second

The Nagra IV-S also has a setting for 15 ips Nagra Master. This setting allows the equalization curve as if you were recording at $7\frac{1}{2}$ ips, giving all the benefits of compensating for a high-frequency loss.

Note the "calibrated" sticker over the bias equalization adjustment, just to the lower left of the Speed selector. Unless you wish to become responsible to be your own audio tech engineer and recalibrate your equipment, you would be wise not to tinker with or try to recalibrate your machine yourself. That kind of work should be handled by a professional audio engineer who does maintenance work on Nagras for a living. Your job is to go out and capture the audio recordings—practice your art form. The audio engineer's job is to maintain your equipment when needed and keep you recording true and clear.

Once you have decided on the tape speed you wish to run at, leave it. It is a really bad idea to change tape speeds during the recording process of a job.

Tape Thread Path

The Nagra has to be the easiest tape path for loading. Open up the head/transport mechanism by grasping the Clutch control lever (item 34 in Figure 22.3) and pulling it outward, toward you. This is a three-position lever. With the Clutch lever pulled all the way out, the head/transport mechanism will open up, allowing a clear path for the $\frac{1}{4}$" tape stock to run from the far-left tension roller across to the far-right tension roller without obstruction.

Place your fresh roll of $\frac{1}{4}$" tape stock on the left transport spindle (item 21 in Figure 22.3) with the fresh roll of tape unwinding counterclockwise. You will see that there are three small stainless steel pins that the $\frac{1}{4}$" hub must seat precisely onto for proper stability. Once the reel is seated correctly, screw down the Lock-Down keeper (item 23 in Figure 22.3). Mind that you do not misplace these little elusive jewels, as they are not cheap to replace. A clever trick many mixers use is to slide the two keepers over the upright handle of the Clutch control lever, acting as a hook to keep them from being misplaced until they need to screw them back on to hold the $\frac{1}{4}$" reels in place. Now pull the $\frac{1}{4}$" tape toward you, pull it around the supply reel Tension roller (item 20 in Figure 22.3), then straight across past the head stack and around the take-up reel Tension roller (item 33 in Figure 22.3). Note that as you pull the tape up and into the take-up reel, you will see a slot to insert the headend of the tape. Be careful not to inadvertently flip the tape stock over as it will cause the tape to wind onto the take-up reel with a half twist. This can be easily loaded incorrectly, so you should try it a few times to get the hang of it.

I personally pull the end of the stock into the slot and then spin the take-up reel three or four turns to hold it in place. I keep either a razor blade or a small pair of scissors in my recording kit, which I use to trim the head end excess flush to the take-up reel hub. The reason you want to do this is when you close the lid of the Nagra and begin recording, you will have no excess $\frac{1}{4}$" stock sticking up and scraping the underside of the lid, which can cause unwanted noise. Once you are satisfied with the tape being securely loaded and the excess stock trimmed away, grasp the Clutch control lever (item 33 in Figure 22.3) and push it in toward the Tension roller. The head/transport mechanism will rotate into place, properly pinching the $\frac{1}{4}$" tape against the Capstan (item 29 in Figure 22.3) and Pinch roller lever (item 30 in Figure 22.3).

If your Nagra is equipped with a playback shield (which may cover the pilot and playback heads or just the playback head), be sure that it was flipped open when you loaded the tape. Believe it or not, I have seen several rolls of transfers where the mixer was listening directly from microphone and had no idea that he had loaded the tape *over* the playback shield, therefore causing a misalignment over the record head with poor results.

Once you are satisfied that the tape is loaded correctly, flip your playback shield up into position (if your Nagra is equipped with one). Note the tension rollers when you roll tape (for Record or Playback). They will undulate, wobble back and forth for a brief moment as they bring the feed and take-up transportation of the $\frac{1}{4}$" stock past the head stack array and Capstan/Pinch roller. They should settle down quickly. Sometimes they continue to vacillate. Turn your hands over and use your thumb nails to gently drag on the top of them, which should encourage them to stop undulating. Most of the time this will occur during the first rolling of the morning (temperature acclimation stiffness or such; who knows?). You must settle the Tension rollers down or you will suffer major wow-and-flutter as they yank and slack out on the $\frac{1}{4}$" tape that is being pulled across the Capstan.

If the Tension rollers continue to be a problem more than once or twice where they tend to undulate even after you attempt to settle them, it means your Nagra probably needs an adjustment by your audio tech contractor. Just to make sure it is not something on the deck that is inhibiting smooth operation, you should keep a can of compressed air in your kit. Using the nozzle extension, place it under the bottom edge of the rollers and give each Tension roller a blast, just to be assured that no foreign matter is causing the excessive undulations that can easily be blown away.

Rewind Switch

Rewinding
This is a good time to comment about the rewind and fast forward capabilities of the Nagra (Figure 22.6). If you need to rewind your tape to listen to a previous take you accomplish this maneuver by grasping the Clutch control lever (item 34 in Figure 22.3) and opening up the head/transport mechanism. Turn (item 4 in Figure 22.3) the Main

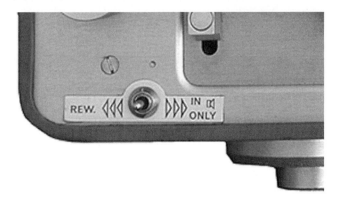

Figure 22.6 The Rewind/Fast Forward switch, located on the upper left-hand edge of the deck.

function selector up one click to Test. Turning the Main function selector up to Test powers up the unit, allowing the motors to work in rewind mode if necessary.

It is a good technique not to rewind with the Playback shield in an upright position. Flip the shield back so the $1/4$" tape will not rewind against the heads, effectively sandpapering the tape emulsion unnecessarily.

Keep your right index finger in place just to the side of the take-up reel (but not actually touching it) to guard against runaway tape when you stop rewinding. Now click the Rewind/Fast forward switch (item 19 in Figure 22.3) to the left. The Nagra will instantly start rewinding.

Personally, I use my left thumb to guide the rewinding tape in close, but not actually touching the playback head. In this manner I can hear important audio points of reference as the tape rewinds and makes it very easy to rewind virtually exactly where you want to be for playback. When you wish to stop, simply click the Rewind/ Fast Forward switch straight up and the left motor will stop. This is where your right index finger comes in handy as a gentle brake. If you do not encourage the take-up reel (gently) to stop, it will unwind a bunch of recorded tape off the right side of the machine.

Close the Clutch control lever, closing the head/transport mechanism. Flip the Playback shield back up into position. Turn the Main function selector back down to the horizontal position. You can now play back the tape by turning the Main function selector down to either of the two Playback positions.

Fast Forwarding

The Nagra does not fast forward at the speed it can rewind. The idea of fast forward is simply running twice as fast as normal speed. When you have the Nagra in playback mode, you can click the Rewind/Fast Forward switch to the right and the Nagra will accelerate the playback speed. It helps a little bit. You have to understand that the Nagra is not designed for high-speed wind and rewind, but to record at a very high resolution and ship the reels "tails out" to the lab. It is just as simple and as practical as that.

Head Stack and Transport

The head stack is beautifully designed with very easy access to clean the heads. I always take a moment to inspect and clean the head stack before I load another roll of $1/4$" tape. Do not use consumer cotton-tipped ear swabs, as they fleece and leave stringy cotton remnants on the heads. (Remember, it takes only the slightest speck of foreign matter to ruin your recording). Try to use a foamed-tip video cleaning swab if you can, but I also find the use of a cotton-tipped cleaning stick, such as the Realistic brand at Radio Shack, to work very well. This cotton tip does not unravel and leave remnants. Use denatured alcohol. If you have to use isopropyl you must wait a few moments for the heads to fully dry out before loading up a fresh roll of stock. Make sure that you clean everything along the tape path. Look for grit and excess magnetic emulsion, an extremely fine dark shedding of the stock from the physical rubbing across the heads.

The degauss Erase head (item 22 in Figure 22.3) is on the far left in Figure 22.7. Do not depend on this head as a bulk degausser; it is meant to erase field-strength. If

Figure 22.7 Transport assembly in open position.

you are using recycled $\frac{1}{4}$" stock (which you should never use for important production dialog), you need to have them bulk degaussed through a heavy-duty magnetic unit prior to going out to record.

The Stabilizer Roller

The Stabilizer roller (item 24 in Figure 22.3) sits right next to the Record head and serves two important functions. First, it guides the $\frac{1}{4}$" tape around at the proper angle to seat against the Record head for proper recording, and second, it has an interesting gear-like adornment on top with either a "50" or a "60" (European 50 cycle or American 60 cycle). As the machine is running up to speed you can lean over and look down at this spinning top, and under AC light (burning at either 50 cycle or 60 cycle), squint slightly, and if the machine is running at proper speed, the "gear" will appear to be holding still. If the machine is running fast or slow, the "gear" will appear to drift around. This is an indication that you should have your machine checked.

The Record Head

The Record head (item 26 in Figure 22.3) records 2 channels of analog audio.

The Pilot Head

The Pilot head (item 27 in Figure 22.3) records the sync signal down the center (in between left and right audio channel).

The Playback Head

The Playback head (item 28 in Figure 22.3) plays back the 2 channels of analog audio that is recorded by the Record head. As stated before, most of the more recent machines are equipped with a hinged Playback shield. Note that the photo above (Figure 22.7) has the shield covering both the Pilot and Playback heads. Some machines have Play-

Figure 22.8 Transport assembly in "closed" position.

back shields that only cover the Playback head. These shields help guard against RF radio signal interference.

The Capstan and Pinch Roller

The Capstan (item 29 in Figure 22.3) is extremely important. This little spinning metal post is the precise speed mechanism that literally drags your ¼" tape across the heads at precisely the right speed. It is dependent on the Pinch roller; when the Clutch control lever is pushed forward into position (as it is in Figure 22.8), the Pinch roller arm is rotated into position, with the Roller (made out of a hard rubber-like synthetic material) perfectly pressing a smooth and even surface firmly against the Capstan. If you do not take great care in the delicate cleaning of this roller, making sure that there is no build-up of oxide, grit, or other foreign matter, the Pinch roller will not properly track the ¼" tape and it will result in improper tape speed and can cause the tape to "walk" up the Capstan, causing the tape stock to ride out of alignment with the Record, Pilot, and Playback heads. Be extremely careful not to cause any kind of dimple, nick, or scratch on the Pinch roller. It is exactly these kinds of wounds that will lead to catastrophic performance as just described.

On the far right of Figure 22.8, you can see the Clutch control lever (item 34 in Figure 22.3) in the open position. Note the position of the Stabilizer roller (item 24 in Figure 22.3). When the Clutch control lever is pushed in, the Stabilizer roller moves forward, pressing in against the ¼" tape to make it track in across the Record head at just the right angle. Note the 90-degree rotation of the Pinch roller arm up against the Capstan. When the Nagra is not in motion, the Pinch roller rests slightly relaxed off the tape. It pinches in on the tape stock when in the Record or Playback mode.

Front Control Panel

Figure 22.9 shows the full-frontal view of the front control panel. As you come across other Nagra models, you will notice that certain controls and indicators are located differently. Unlike the other versions, the IV-S has its Pilot and Speed/Power flag indi-

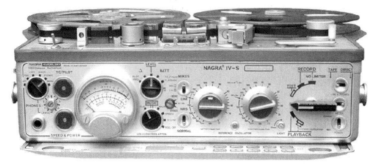

Figure 22.9 Front control panel, full view.

cators located to the left side of the modulometer, rather than on the far right, just to the side of the Main function selector bar. Some versions have their Tape/Direct, Line & phones and power switch array to the left of the Main function selector bar, whereas the IV-S has those switches to the right of the Main function selector bar. These differences are strictly cosmetic and have evolved over years of refining the sound mixer's eye-hand coordination efficiency with the machine.

Right Side of Front Control Panel

Power Selector Switch
The Power selector switch is shown as item 1. Since the Nagra can work on an external power converter power pack from an AC outlet, you need to tell the machine whether it is using the AC power pack or internal battery power. Up is AC power pack; down is internal batteries.

Tape/Direct Switch
Put your headsets on and flip the Tape/Direct switch (item 3 in Figure 22.3) to the right (Direct) and you will be listening directly from the microphones. You will need to do this when the $\frac{1}{4}$" tape is not in motion in either the Record or Playback mode. When you are monitoring for levels in standby (Test) mode you will only be able to hear in the Direct position.

Once you have engaged the machine to record you will want to flip the Tape/Direct switch to the left (Tape), so you can hear what you are actually recording. Believe me, there are times, due to oxide build-up, incorrect threading of the machine, or some other problem, you will hear your incoming signal just fine when in Direct mode, but you are not actually recording properly. You will not know this unless you are monitoring in playback mode, with the Tape/Direct switch flipped to Tape position.

Most mixers will flip the switch back and forth during the recording to A-B the signal, in other words, to see if they are getting a true or transparent replication from the microphones onto the tape oxide.

Line & Phones Switch
The Line & Phones switch (item 2 in Figure 22.3) will allow you to A-B compare by use of the meter (item 13 in Figure 22.3, the modulometer). This switch is a momentary

Figure 22.10 Front control panel, right side.

contact switch, so when you let go of it, it will automatically return to the Direct position. I personally do not use this option very much, as my ears will tell me so much more about the clarity and coloration of the A-B comparison using the Tape/Direct option instead; but I could see its use if you are doing Line Input line-up tones and want to see how accurately your tape oxide is mirroring the incoming signal.

Main Function Selector Bar

When the Main function selector bar (item 4 in Figure 22.3) is in the horizontal position, as shown in the full view of the Nagra panel (Figure 22.10), all electrical power to the Nagra is turned off. There is no power running through any electronic components and the batteries are not being drained.

Because it takes a few moments for the electronics to warm up to optimum capacity, you never want to just flip the selector bar straight up into a Record mode from the off position. The first few seconds of the recording will sound dreadful—sounding like a breaking-up distorted awakening. This is why recording mixers will anticipate the assistant director's call to make the shot. Most good mixers are already rolling when the AD calls out, "Roll sound"—usually because the mixer is also responsible for sounding the warning bell and turning on the red light. Once the AD calls for "Light and bell," the mixer usually flips the warning on and rolls the recorder. To anticipate this, the recording mixer gets into a rhythm which starts with knowing when to warm up his Nagra by flipping the Main Function selector bar up to the Test position. In a matter of 4 to 6 seconds, you will hear the signal from your microphones well up and the signal becomes clear. From this moment on you are free and ready to roll sound and record confidently.

Roll to Record

There are two Record positions. The first position records with a limiter. This limiter compresses the volume signal when it peaks too high, thereby guarding against distortion and spiked explosive moments that oversaturate the stock. That is all well and good for documentary and other monitoring missions where you cannot ask for a second take because you peaked out. However, recording with a limiter also means you are going to have an audio track that may (and probably will) have periodic compressed areas that are not at all desirable in a theatrical film. That is why you have the second recording position, the 12 o'clock, straight up position. You will now be recording in the no limiter position, thereby turning off the compressing limiter option. Now you are on your own, but of course that is why you are the recording mixer.

Roll for Playback

To listen to recorded material in a Playback mode is accomplished simply enough by clicking the Main function selector bar downward to either the first or second Playback position. The difference between these two options is that the first position will give you playback signal through the headsets only. It is important to note that the internal resolver (to maintain sync speed) function is turned off during playback in this position.

To play back the audio signal with the internal resolver in an active mode, you need to turn the Main function selector bar down to the second playback position (marked with a double-cone icon). This second position will send the signal to the headsets and also to the built-in speaker that is mounted on the right flank of the unit. This speaker should not be expected to yield full fidelity as you will hear through full-spectrum monitor speakers later, but they are meant to give you a guidance in that what you have done is clear and acceptable sound; or, if you *do* have distortion issues, to address what you are doing wrong and correct it.

Light Button

Pressing this small button (item 5 in Figure 22.3) will turn on the light in the modu-lometer so you can read it under poorly lit conditions. This is a momentary button, so when you take your finger off of it the light will shut off. If, on the other hand, you wish to have the light remain on, push and pivot the button to the right. The meter light will remain on until you pivot the button back to the left. Try not to leave the light on too long as it does accelerate the wear and tear on the batteries.

Reference Oscillator Button

Press this momentary contact button (item 6 in Figure 22.3) and the built-in Reference Tone Oscillator will activate. You will want to press and hold this button down for 10 to 20 seconds to lay down the −8 dB reference line-up tone at the head of each roll of tape.

When the mixer ends each recorded take, he or she will press this button twice to leave two short beeps to mark the end of each take. Later in sound transfer, the transfer engineer can spin the tape at high speed, holding his or her thumb against the tape, nudging it partially in toward the playback head (without touching it) and this reference tone signal is strong enough to be heard as fleeting blips going by. The transfer engineer can count those blips flying by as he or she looks at the sound report and counts down (or up, depending on winding direction) to quickly locate the precise take required.

Volume Control "Potentiometers"

These two knobs (item 7 in Figure 22.3) are the volume control pots, or what Nagra likes to call the potentiometers. Channel 1 (left) has a small crescent latch built into it. If you move the latch down you will unlock the two knobs so they can work independently. If you move the latch up, you will lock the two knobs together. In this manner, if you move one, the other will move in precise linked calibration. This is very useful if you wish to have channel 2 (right) record the same incoming signal as channel 1 (known as 2-track mono), but at a lower level (e.g., –10 dB). Unlock the two knobs. Turn them both completely to the left until they are at Off. Now move the crescent lock upward to link the two knobs together.

If you feed an incoming line-up tone into the Nagra from your outboard mixer or from a portable reference generator, you can quickly calibrate an exact –dB setting. Turn channel 1 up until the two needles on the meter (modulometer) reads 0. Obviously channel 2 has come up to the exact same position because the two pots are locked together. Now move the crescent lock-down to unlock the two channels. Move the channel 2 (right) knob to the left until the red needle (channel 2) backs down to the – 10 dB position on the meter. Now move the crescent lock up to lock the two volume pots back together again.

Now you have channel 1 and channel 2 locked together in precise relationship with each other, only –10 dB apart. This works wonders when you have sudden volume bursts, such as gunshots, screams, door slams, or other sudden concussionary sounds that will blow out and distort channel 1. Later in the postproduction phase, the dialog editor will take the channel 2 transfer of the blown-out channel 1 performance and integrate it into the dialog (or P-FX track) to utilize the nondistorted version.

Linking the two channels is also mandatory in true stereophonic recordings, where the two channels have to be in precise left-right balance to effectively create the envelope of the audio field presence.

Personally I like to simplify the signal path in recording. I feel that the more you run the audio signal through things, the more you are going to add noise and/or hiss. Be careful not to send a weak or artificially lowered signal into your Nagra if you are using an outboard mixer. Beginners often make the mistake of having too low a level feed into the mixer (using the line input mode) which compels them to turn the poten-

Figure 22.11 Front control panel, center.

tiometer volume pots up too high in order to boost the signal. By doing this you will dramatically increase hiss and excessive ground noise rumble. That is why you want reference tones and known levels that can be read on meters and matched accordingly. If you are having to turn your volume controls over past the 2 o'clock position you are risking unwanted hiss and noise—so beware.

Center Controls of Front Control Panel

The Meter Selector

The Meter selector (item 12 in Figure 22.3) tells the meter (modulometer) (item 13 in Figure 22.3) what it is you wish to view. This selector is your gateway to check the performance of the machine and/or incoming or outgoing signals as read on the meter. Different models of Nagras have different variations on possibilities to meter. Some Nagras have options to measure Compression, Volt/Cell, and Bias, for instance. The Nagra IV-S shown here has been greatly simplified, excluding the need for some settings found on older models.

Pilot Frequency

This setting is used in conjunction with the built-in QFMS frequency meter, between the pilot signal—recorded or played back on the pilot track and a 50 or 60 Hz internal reference. The red needle may deviate as much as plus or minus 4 percent as it compares the pilot signal versus a 60 Hz crystal. The green needle will show on the dB scale the signal from the channel with the greatest amplitude.

This setting measures on a 0 to 100 percent scale; groove depth of a record made from recorded signals in accordance with NAB weighting; 100 percent corresponding to a 50 μm vertical deviation of the cutting stylus. The green needle, as with the Pilot Frequency setting, will show on the dB scale the signal from the channel with the greatest amplitude.

Level

This straight up position will allow you to monitor the two audio input levels of channels 1 (left) and 2 (right). Note the top dB scale on the modulometer (see Figure 22.12 in the next section). The modulometer is a peak meter. Unlike its cousin the VU meter, which shows an averaging of the signal, a peak meter shows the exact peaks of the loudest amplitude of the signal. It is important to know that 8 dB on the Nagra's modulometer equals 0 level on a VU meter. The 0 level shown on the modulometer is, therefore, 8 dB hotter than on other tape recorders using the standard VU meter system.

With this in mind, your normal dialog recording should be bouncing around –5 to –10 dB (or around the straight-up area on the meter). This gives you a nice amount of head room for loud sudden sounds, such as screams, door slams, crashes, and impacts, etc. If your dialog is recording as high as 0 dB on the modulometer, it will be far too hot when you transfer to the audio signal to another medium, for that would be equivalent to a +8 to +10 dB peak which is *really* hot!

You should reserve the need to record above 0 dB for exceptional situations, such as momentary sounds (e.g., gunshots or door slam-type sounds), and *only* momentary.

Battery

Flip the selector to the BATT position and you will be able to see how your batteries are doing. This is your Battery reserve level and is read on the bottom scale, the short one on the right side of the modulometer window. Remember, as discussed earlier under The Battery Supply, a fresh battery array will read 1.5 volts or better. As the power drops down close to 1.2 volts it is time to change out to a fresh set.

TC/Pilot Playback

This selection will measure the sync signal on the tape. The strength will be read on the center scale (with Pilot above it) of the modulometer window. The red needle will read −4 to +4 percent on the scale, the frequency shift between the pilot signal recorded or played back on the pilot track and a 50 or 60 Hz internal reference. The green needle will read on the 0 to 100 percent scale, the level of the signals recorded or played back on the pilot track; 100 percent corresponds to a frequency deviation of ±40 percent. This setting is used more often by your tech maintenance person when your Nagra goes into the shop for its checkup.

M Setting

This setting will read the current through the motor. The red needle will read on the 0 to 100 percent scale; 100 percent corresponding to 250 mA.

Filter Selector

The Filter selector (item 11 in Figure 22.3) is where you choose what kind of frequency attenuation you wish to record. On the Nagra IV-S most mixers will record at either flat (which is most of the time), or for exterior work they find a need to flip the Filter selector down to S + LFA2 (Speech plus Low Frequency Attenuation 2). This will help with some wind noise and low-end rumble issues. With today's microphone wind abatement technologies, there is little need to have to resort to the second setting unless you hear a great deal of low-end rumble. When in doubt, record flat. Postproduction may very well want the low-end frequencies that you rolled out of a recording. They can always remove it later; they cannot reinstate it naturally if you canceled it out of the equation.

> **Flat:** Linear response curve.
>
> **Music:** High-pass filter, −3 dB at 40 Hz.
>
> **M + LFA:** Music and low frequency attenuation, −7 dB at 40 Hz and −3 dB at 400 Hz.
>
> **Speech:** High-pass speech filter, −3 dB at 80 Hz.
>
> **S + LFA2:** Speech filter and low-frequency attenuation, −7.5 dB at 80 Hz and −3 dB at 400 Hz.
>
> **Roll off:** Strong low-frequency attenuation, −10 dB at 100 Hz and −3 dB at 400 Hz.

Note: Most older Nagras may show these filter settings as LFA1, LFA2, FLAT, HP1, HP1 + LFA1, and HP2 (High Pass). Those Nagras that have LFA1 and LFA2 offer two roll-off variations. You need to listen through your headphones to the subtle differences and decide what feels best for your needs. Most mixers use two basic settings—flat for interior work and HP1 + LFA1 (denoted with a box around it) for exterior work. These two settings will usually achieve a consistent response for your production track throughout the shoot.

Mikes/Line Selector Switch

The Mikes/Line selector switch is shown as item 8 in Figure 22.3. If you are recording with microphones, you will obviously switch it up to Mikes. If you are recording with an outboard mixer or making a machine-to-machine transfer, you will need to flip this switch down to the Line position. Remember that you do not plug line inputs into the XLR inputs on the left flank side of the Nagra. To do so will cause you to double-phantom your microphones, as your outboard mixing panel is sending a phantom power signal and by going through the microphone XLR inputs of the Nagra defaults through the phantom power supply, causing a distorted signal. This will be covered later when we talk about the Tuchel In & Out connectors and XLR Microphone Inputs.

Noise Reduction Switch

If you intend to utilize the internal noise reduction system (item 9) or if you intend to utilize an outboard noise reduction system (by coming into the left flank Tuchel connector marked EXT.NRS) you need to flip the switch up to NRS. If you do not want to use NRS simply flip the switch down to the Normal position.

Mono-Stereo Selector

Set the Mono-Stereo selector (item 10 in Figure 22.3) in the configuration that you wish to import your signal. In the Mono mode the 2 coupled inputs are connected to the 2 channels. In the Stereo mode each input is connected to the corresponding channel for dedicated control. In the ST.HS (Stereo High Sensitivity) mode each input is connected to the corresponding channel as in the Stereo mode, but the sensitivity of the input signal is +6 dB higher. This gives you a little extra firepower if you need it without cranking the Volume Control Potentiometers up too high and building up unwanted bias floor hiss. Of course it will add a little more extra bias hiss. More volume cannot help but do that, but it is better than just cranking up the volume controls to maximum. This is especially useful for subtle stereophonic backgrounds and nonclose proximity audio events.

Left Side of Front Control Panel

Headphone Jack and Headphone Controls

The lower left corner of the Nagra has a $\frac{1}{4}$″ stereo jack for your headsets. Just above it and to the right is the volume control setting. You simply turn the flat-edged screw using the 0 to 7 level calibration. Older Nagra models have the volume control located just below and to the right of the plug input, right next to the modulometer. Other Nagra models use the upper left-hand corner selector switch as a volume control selector with a 0 to 5 level setting.

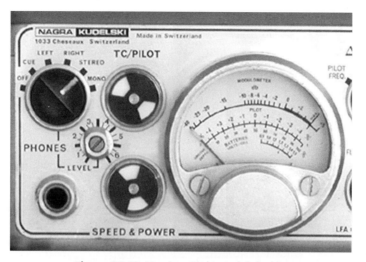

Figure 22.12 Front control panel, left side.

In the model shown in Figure 22.12, the upper-left selector is the Headset input selector. You can turn your headsets off by clicking the selector all the way to the left. Click it to the right one stop for the Cue option. Click it one more stop to the right to hear the left channel only. Click it one more stop to the right to listen to right channel only. Click it one more stop to the right to listen to full Stereo. If you wish to listen in flat monaural through both ears, click the selector to the far right to Mono.

If you are recording Stereo or two separate microphones as monaural feeds and are concerned about phasing issues, you can click the selector to the right to the Mono position and the two channels will be folded down together. If you have phasing issues you will immediately experience a fully swimming quality to the signal and you will immediately know that you need to make an adjustment. Some Nagra models have been outfitted with a very convenient momentary contact switch. You merely press it and both channels automatically fold down so that you can easily A-B compare between discrete 2 channel and folded mono. Both procedures accomplish the same result ultimately.

Pilot Flag Indicator

The Pilot flag (item 14 in Figure 22.3) shows completely black when the unit is at rest. When you roll in the Record mode, two little white flags will flip open and hold steady when it reads the incoming sync signal. As you record these two flags hold perfectly still until you shut down. If they flicker, it means you are getting a bad sync signal and you will probably not be able to warrant good lip sync. If you are using an external sync source, check the jumper cable for it might be loose or the contact is not clean.

Speed and Power Indicator

The speed and power indicator (item 15 in Figure 22.3) works just like the Pilot indicator. When you roll, this flag indicator will flip on and hold steady. It tells you that your speed is constant and that your power is good. If the flag flickers or goes out, you know

Figure 22.13 Left flank Input panel.

that you are not going to have proper lip sync. Naughty, naughty—you have not kept good account of your battery power and they have dipped below the safe level that we have talked about in this chapter. Check your batteries by flipping the Meter selector to BATT and, if your batteries are croaking, of course, replace them. But, if your batteries are fine and the flags continue to flicker, cease using the machine. Get your backup unit out and immediately send your Nagra to your maintenance tech to be checked out.

The Modulometer
See the preceding paragraphs for discussion on this function.

The Tuchel In and Out Connectors

Line Inputs (Tuchel 7-Pin Connector)
Figure 22.13 shows the left flank side of the Nagra, or the Input side. Notice that the outboard Line inputs and outputs use Tuchel (pronounced too-shell) connectors and are located on the left side of the panel (Figure 22.14). The Microphone inputs, using XLR female input connectors along with their counterpart phantom power settings, are on the right side of the panel.

If you are transferring from another machine or using an outboard mixer to control your microphones and slating chores, you will patch into the Nagra using a Tuchel 7-pin connector. If you need to make or have a Tuchel connector cable made, a schematic of the pin assignment configuration is shown in Figure 22.15.

Remember, when you use the Tuchel connection for an outboard mixer or input from another machine you must go to the front panel of the Nagra and flip the Mike/ Line switch (item 8 in Figure 22.3) down to Line.

EXT.NRS (Tuchel 7-Pin Connector)
If you are utilizing an outboard noise reduction system, you will connect the system via the Tuchel 7-pin connector into this screw socket. You must then go to the front panel of the Nagra and flip the switch (item 9 in Figure 22.3) up to NRS. This will send the signal out to the outboard noise reduction gear and return it back into the Nagra after the noise reduction encode is effected.

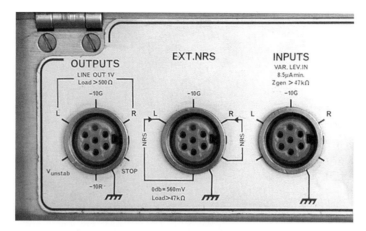

Figure 22.14 Closer view of the Tuchel inputs.

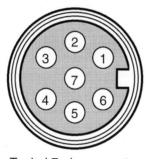

Tuchel 7-pin connector   **Figure 22.15** Tuchel schematic.

Line Outputs (Tuchel 7-Pin Connector)

If you are using the Nagra as a transfer machine you may output the signal either through the Tuchel 7-pin connector on the far left of the left-side panel or from the banana plug options (see the following list) on the right-side panel.

Should you need to custom fabricate your own connector cables, Nagra wiring assignment specifications are listed next. The illustration of the Tuchel connector in Figure 22.15 shows the external view of chassis connector or plug from the soldering side.

Outputs

1. Channel 2 (right) output: output voltage is 1 V at 0 dB, minimum impedance load 500 Ω (Ohms).
2. −10 G: −10 V stabilized voltage output, maximum current 100 mA for all −10 V terminals.
3. Channel 1 output (left) identical to channel 2.
4. Vunstab: unstabilized power supply voltage.

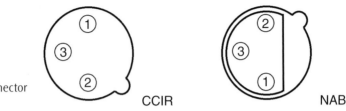

Figure 22.16 XLR connector schematic.

5. −10 R: −10 V stabilized voltage output available on record only, maximum current 100 mA for all −10 V terminals.
6. Stop: input for the motor stop control (connect to −10 V to stop).
7. Ground.

EXT.NRS (Noise Reduction System)

1. External noise reduction system output channel 2 (right).
2. −10 G: −10 V stabilized voltage output, maximum current 100 mA for all −10 V terminals.
3. External system output, channel 1 (left).
4. External system input, channel 1 (left) minimum input impedance 47 Ω.
5. External system input, channel 2 (right) minimum input impedance 47 Ω.
6. Ground (common).

Inputs

1. Channel 2 (right) input, impedance variable from 0 to 5 kΩ when switch 11 is on ST. HS, current drive with minimum source impedance 47 kΩ; current to obtain 0 dB at maximum sensitivity 7.8 μA.
2. −10 G: −10 V stabilized voltage output, maximum current 100 mA for all −10 V terminals.
3. Channel 1 (left) input, identical to channel 2.
4. Ground for input signals.

The Microphone XLR Connector

The first thing you will want to take note of is the difference between the NAB wiring scheme and the CCIR scheme (Figure 22.16). Again, Nagra wiring assignment specifications are listed should you need to custom fabricate your own connector cables. The illustration of the XLR connectors shows the two standard wiring schemes as external views of the chassis connector or plug from the soldering side.

The Microphone XLR Inputs

The two microphone XLR inputs, unlike previous monaural models, record on two dedicated channels. I know that seems very obvious, but you have to remember that the previous Nagras were, in fact, monaural machines; even though they had two microphone inputs, they combined both signals into a single channel. Per industry standard configuration: Left is channel 1 and right is channel 2.

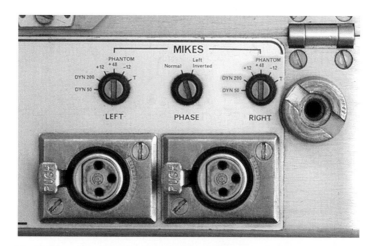

Figure 22.17 Close-up view of microphone XLR inputs and Phantom power selectors.

The Phantom Power Selectors

Nagra includes a six-option Phantom power supply for each input.

DYN 50: If you are using a dynamic microphone with an impedance of 50 Ω, 0.1 mV/μbar sensitivity.

DYN 200: If you are using a dynamic microphone with an impedance of 200 Ω, 0.2 mV/μbar sensitivity.

+12: If you are using a condenser microphone with a 0.1 mV/μbar sensitivity and require +12 V phantom powering.

+48: If you are using a condenser microphone with a 0.1 mV/μbar sensitivity and require +48 V phantom powering.

–12: If you are using a condenser microphone with a 0.1 mV/μbar sensitivity and require –12 V phantom powering.

T: If you are using a condenser microphone with a 3 mV/μbar sensitivity and require +12 V T-powering (Tonaderspeisung).

The Phase Selector

Occasionally you may have microphones that do not have matching wiring schematics and you may need to invert the phase of one mike to properly record against another one. If you flip the screw slot switch (located between the two Phantom power selectors) to the right you will invert the phase of channel 1 (left).

The Output Side

Figure 22.18 shows the right flank side of the Nagra, or the Output side. Notice that the grill on the left part is where the built-in loudspeaker is. This speaker only works when the Main Function selector bar is turned all the way down to the second Playback position with the double-cone icon. On the Nagra IV-S the speaker volume is controlled by the Volume Potentiometers. On older Nagra models, there is a volume control screw,

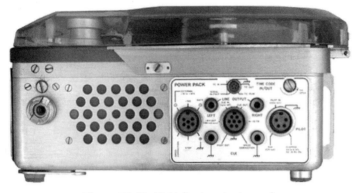

Figure 22.18 Right flank output panel.

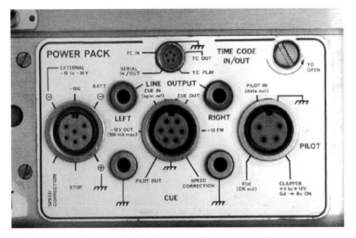

Figure 22.19 Close-up of output panel.

sometimes located on the left flank side of the Nagra just below the Phantom power selector; other models have it just to the left of the loudspeaker up near the shoulder strap bolt.

External Power Pack—6-Pin Tuchel

The Nagra can work off of a 50 or 60 Hz AC power adapter that comes with the Nagra package. The power pack uses a 6-pin Tuchel connector to attach rigidly into the screw socket to feed the machine (Figure 22.19). You must go to the front panel of the Nagra and flip the Power switch (item 1 in Figure 22.3) up to External.

You will find that most mixers are very reluctant to try to use the power pack out in the field, feeding from an unknown and/or suspicious power source. It works fine for interior and stage work where known power feeds are dependable.

Line Outputs (via Banana Jacks)

Output transfers can be efficiently made using banana jacks, feeding from the left and right banana ports just below and to either side of the 5-pin Lemo Time Code

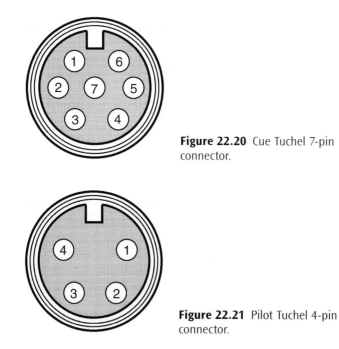

Figure 22.20 Cue Tuchel 7-pin connector.

Figure 22.21 Pilot Tuchel 4-pin connector.

connector. The ground banana jack ports are on either side of the Cue 7-pin Tuchel connector.

Cue Tuchel 7-pin connector: This connector is for recording and playback on the pilot track. The illustration of the Tuchel connector in Figure 22.20 shows the external view of the chassis connector, or plug, from the soldering side.

1. Modulation signal input.
2. −10 V stabilized voltage output, maximum current 100 mA for all −10 V terminals.
3. Pilot signal input.
4. −10 V stabilized voltage available on Record only, maximum current 100 mA for all −10 V terminals.
5. Voltage terminal to activate the FM modulator.
6. Signal output (direct or recorded).
7. Ground.

Pilot Tuchel 4-pin connector: This connector receives signal input for the pilot track. The illustration of the Tuchel connector in Figure 22.21 shows the external view of the chassis connector or plug from the soldering side.

1. Ground.
2. Clapper: reference oscillator or crystal pilot generator control input.
3. Xtal: 50 or 60 Hz internal crystal pilot generator Output.
4. Pilot In: pilot signal Input.

Figure 22.22 Time Code panel.

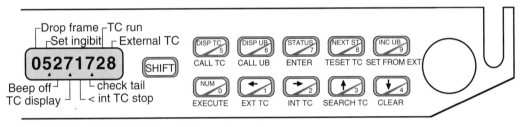

Figure 22.23 Pull-out Time Code panel.

Time Code In/Out
This 5-pin Lemo connector can either import an external Time Code signal or output the Time Code signal generated from the internal generator.

The Time Code Option

Some Nagra models, including the one featured in this chapter, are equipped with a pancake thin Time Code panel, which slides forward from the underside (Figure 22.23), tucked neatly between the two front stumpy feet on a scissor fold-out mechanism.

The Nagra can accept an external time code signal (via the Time Code connector on the right flank panel) or it will default to using its own generated time code signal. When using a Smart Slate, plug the Time Code wireless transmitter into the Time Code In/Out connector on the right-side output panel. The Smart Slate will display whatever time code the Nagra is generating for visual reference by the camera when the clapper assistant holds out the slate to snap sync. The illuminated red numbers make it easy for the assistant picture editor to sync the dailies later in picture editorial.

If you want to check the time code status, press the Status/7 button. Unless you want to record in a Drop frame mode, there should not be the little marker under where "Drop frame" is shown on the far left-hand side of the display. If there is a marker, it indicates that you are recording "Drop Frame Time Code," which is not what you want if you are recording for film projects. Press Next Status/8 button to check the frame rate. It should read "30 Fr." Thirty frames per second NDF (nondrop frame) is the industry standard for film cameras running 24 or 30 fps.

To clear the Time Code panel of previous programming, press the following buttons in this order: Shift, Status/7, Num/0, ≥/2, Num/0, Num/0, Shift, Num/0 (or, if you wish to read the words under the buttons: Shift, Enter, Execute, INT TC, Execute, Execute, Shift, Execute).

To program the user bits for use in the date format, press: Num/0, ≤/1, Num/0, DISP UB/6, Shift, Execute.

To enter the time of day, press the buttons: DISP TC/5, NUM/0, then the Hour, Hour, Minute, Minute, then Num/0, Num/0, Num/0, Num/0, Shift, Enter.

To enter the date, press the buttons: DISP UB/6, Num/0—then the Day, Day, Month, Month, Year, Year—then Num/0, Num/0, Shift, Enter.

To display this new Time Code, press the button: DISP TC/5.

To program the Nagra for Record Run time code (or code that advances only while the machine is in Record mode), press: Shift, Enter, Num/0, ≤/1, Num/0, Num/0, Shift, Execute.

Note that the last feature is only on machines with software version 1.95 or above. To check what software version is on your Nagra, press the button Status/7, and then repeat pressing the button Next Status/8. To return the machine to a regular time code mode, follow the instructions for clearing the time code panel and setting the time of day again.

AUDIO TECH MAINTENANCE

The following is a list of authorized Nagra IV-S sound service centers that render outstanding services in the United States.

Nagra USA, Inc.
Nancy Belt, General Manager, 357 Riverside Drive, Suite 230C, Nashville, TN, (615) 726-5191

California
Alternative Audio Services, 5750 Camelia Avenue, North Hollywood, CA 91601, (818) 764-5164
Dan Dugan Sound Design, 290 Napoleon Street, San Francisco, CA 94124, (415) 821-9776
Location Sound Services, 10639 Riverside Drive, North Hollywood, CA 91602, (818) 980-9891
The Sound Check, 5435 Cahuenga Boulevard, North Hollywood, CA 91601, (818) 766-2920

Maryland
Vark Audio, 8101 MacArthur Boulevard, Cabin John, MD 20818, (301) 229-0288

New York
Audio Services, 353 West 48th Street, New York, NY 10036, (212) 977-5151
Professional Sound Services, 311 West 43rd Street, New York, NY 10036, (212) 586-1033

Tennessee
Trew Audio, 240 Great Circle Road, Nashville, TN 37228, (615) 256-3542

Glossary

AB stereo—Also known as time-delay stereo, time-difference stereo. Two-channel stereo recording technique which benefits mainly from the differences in time delay between the microphones (channels). Omnidirectional microphones are used in most cases.

acetate base—The transparent cellulose acetate plastic film which forms the foundation, the base, or backing for the magnetic medium that is placed on the tape or film by the manufacturer.

acoustics—A science dealing with the production, effects, and transmission of sound waves; the transmission of sound waves through various mediums, including reflection, refraction, diffraction, absorption, and interference.
   The characteristics of auditoriums, theatres, studio stages as well as their design.

ADC (analog-to-digital converter)—An electronic device used at the input of digital audio equipment to convert analog electronic signals to digital values whose numbers represent the level and frequency information contained in the original analog signal.

ADR—Automated Dialog Replacement.

AES—Audio Engineering Society (a professional organization).

alignment—For film and tape recorders, referring to the correct adjustment of the record and playback head position with respect to the exact attitude of the film or tape path, and also adjusts the electronics for the ideal frequency response.

ambience—The distinctive acoustics of a given location being recorded; the environmental sounds that create a mood and a sense of place. The resulting audio sources (e.g., fluorescent ballast hums, distant traffic, air conditioning ducts, etc.) create relatively constant characteristics that reverberate off the walls, ceiling, pavement, and so on.

amplification—Increase in signal level, amplitude, or magnitude.

analog—Electrical signal that continuously varies in strength. Not digital. Magnetic and optical sound recording and playback systems are analog.

anechoic chamber—A testing room free from echo. Usually used to test microphones and other audio equipment that must be free from reverberation. Special acoustical surface and angular walls are vital to deaden the environment of the testing chamber.

articulation—A quantitative measurement of the intelligibility of human speech, where 100 percent is completely understandable. For the typical sound reinforcement or communications system no more than a 15 percent articulation loss is acceptable.

asperity noise—Otherwise called hiss; caused by minute imperfections in the surface of the recording tape. The cheaper the tape, the higher the degree of imperfections in the surface, thus the higher the danger of tape hiss.

attenuate—To reduce a signal's strength. Attenuator: A device that reduces or weakens the amplitude of a signal. Used on volume control, also called a fader.

audio analyzer—A test instrument used by motion picture theatre sound engineers. The device contains terminations of various values capable of carrying up to 150 watts of audio power. Included is an AC voltmeter for measuring the frequency response of amplifiers, equalizers, filters, and the overall frequency response of the sound system.

audio fatigue—A hearing weariness brought on by a constant sustaining soundtrack that does not let up in intensity, both in volume as well as complex detailed make-up, which oversaturates the ears as well as the viewer's brain to assimilate such long durations. First signs are tingling and fuzzy sensation in the ears, followed by a shutting down of brain attention, thereby protecting itself from constant bombardment.

audio frequency—Any frequency within the range of normal audio sounds, whose sound waves undulate roughly 20 to 20,000 Hz (Hz = cycles per second).

back-up—This term is most commonly used to describe having a protection redundancy recorder to guard against accidental erasure or loss of material, as in a DAT back-up recorder to the primary nonlinear Pro Tools recording session or 24-track or DA-88 recorder. Such protection can also be made after a recording or edit session, as in making a back-up of the hard drive at the end of the day, or making a DVD-RAM back-up from the Deva's internal hard drive to ship to editorial.

balanced—See *cable, balanced*.

balanced connectors—Microphone cable connections in which both conductors are electronically symmetrical with the case and cable shield (ground).

balance stripe—Also known as guide stripe or balance track. A narrow stripe of magnetic material identical to the primary magnetic stripe that the audio signal will be recorded on and reproduced from. This balance stripe is not used for sound recording, but is used to maintain a level contact with the sound head.

bandwidth—Refers to the space in the frequency response of a device through which audio signals can pass (between lower and upper frequency limits, those points where the signal level has rolled off 3 dB).

bias—A direct current (DC) or high-frequency alternating current (AC) signal fed to a magnetic recording head with the audio signal in order to minimize distortion. (AC bias ordinarily provides higher fidelity.)

bit rate—The amount of the binary information code included in the audio file; the number of bits assigned to each sample (not the sampling rate) limits the dynamic range. If you are working in a 16-bit system, you have 65,636 possible volume levels to work with in each sample of the recording. If you try to drive the signal to 65,637, you will experience clipping and distortion because no more 1s and 0s are left to use. The volume-level saturation geometrically increases as you work at a higher bit rate. If you were working in a 20-bit system, you would have 1,048,576 choices, and working in 24-bit would give you 16,777,216 for each sample.

blooping ink—An opaque paint-like ink that an editor can apply over splices to protect the join in the optical track from making popping or snapping sounds when it runs over the optical reader head of the projector.

BNC connector—Coaxial connector for RF connections.

boom—(microphone boom) A telescopic arm to which a microphone (and hanger) are attached. The boom is held up over the head of the actors by the boom operator to place the microphone in an ideal out-of-camera position to record the action in the scene.

boom operator—Person who operates an overhead microphone unit, such as a microphone boom, to place the microphone in the most desirable position to capture the best quality recording.

bounce-to-disk—A process by which an editor can choose which channels of an edit session he or she wishes to combine in a mix-down, creating either a new monaural or stereo audio file. This process is done inside the computer using the editorial software and does not involve outputting any audio signal out of the computer to achieve a new mixed combine.

boundary microphone—Also known as pressure zone microphone (PZM). In a boundary microphone, the capsule is fitted flush in a surface which is large and flat compared to the wavelength. This produces the ideal semi-omnidirectional pick-up pattern.

cable, balanced—An audio cable with three wires; two wires carry the signal, high (+) and low (−), and the third is a shield which is connected to the chassis or system ground. The signal leads are both of equal potential difference from the ground; hence are balanced with respect to the ground, which is sometimes referred to as "floating."

cable, unbalanced—An audio cable with two wires. There is no third shield and is not connected to the chassis or system ground. Therefore, the signal leads are unbalanced.

cable attenuation—Also known as cable loss. Attenuation which a signal experiences when it is transmitted via a cable. It is dependent above all on the length of the cable and the frequency of the transmitted signal. Given in dB/m.

cable length—The cable length is usually measured between the anti-kink sleeves of the cable (cable length without connectors).

capacity—Short for ampere-hour capacity; that is, the charge that can be delivered by a rechargeable battery. This value can be used to calculate the operating time of a unit which is powered by the rechargeable battery.

capstan—Rotating shaft used with a pinch roller which pulls magnetic tape stock through a tape deck mechanism at an exact rate of speed. This is necessary because, unlike film, there are no perforations to engage with sprockets.

cardioid response—A heart-shaped microphone pick-up, directional in various degrees of configuration; sound waves coming to the microphone's rear and sides are rejected and those directly in front of it are received giving it its directional qualities.

CCIR (Comité Consultatif Internationale Pour la Radio)—The French term basically means International Radio Consultative Committee, and the organization influences Central and Eastern Europe. These standards affect equalization standard settings on equipment and will not play back correctly on NAB (Western hemisphere) equipment.

click track—In motion picture or television sound recordings, an electronic metronome is applied to the audio recording so that musicians can synchronize the musical tempo with the visual action or frame rate. The channel carrying the metronome signal is known as the click track.

clipping—Occurs when the capabilities of an amplifier are exceeded. The result is very audible distortion, also visible on an oscilloscope.

colorization—Distortion of frequency response by resonances at particular frequencies.

compander—The combination of a compressor and an expander used together to achieve noise reduction and/or increase the dynamic range capabilities of recorders or audio systems.

compressor—(compression) A process whereby the dynamic range of the audio signal is reduced. This is accomplished by making louder parts of the signal quieter and/or quieter parts louder, as desired.

condenser mike—A microphone in which sound strikes an electronically charged diaphragm, which acts like a variable capacitor as it moves near a fixed plate of opposite polarity. Ultra-low moving mass ensures extended frequency response. Condenser mikes require phantom power to operate.

connector—Type of pin device at the end of a cable to either send (male) or receive (female) audio signals, power, sync pulse, and so on (e.g., XLR, Tuchel, phono jack, Lemo, etc.).

cross-talk—Audible signal that spills over from one line to an adjacent line.

cue control—A device on the recording machine for finding a desired cue or audio even selection while winding (or rewinding) at high speed.

DAT (digital audio tape)—Specifically, 4-mm high-density magnetic tape loaded in a small cassette unit. Maximum length of DAT tapes is 120 minutes (at 48 kHz sampling rate).

dB (decibel)—A measurement of relative intensity of power or voltage based on an algorithmic scale.

decoder—A device that reads the encoded signal or pulse and turns it into some form of control or usable information signal (e.g., 2-track printmaster decoded in the theatre into its six component signal streams).

degaussed—A device with a powerful electric coil magnet that can be turned on and off for bulk degaussing purposes. The film or tape roll must be moved in a rotating motion as it is moved into and out of the magnetic influence, thereby degaussing the magnetic stock properly and not causing spikes or uneven erased areas.

digital—A system whereby a continuously variable analog signal is sampled at regular intervals (usually 44,100 to 48,000 times a second). Each sample is assigned a numerical value, encoded into discrete binary bits (1s and 0s to represent quantities) that establish a mathematical model of the original sound. Advanced method of recording which involves a sequence of pulses or on/off signals rather than a continuous variable or analog signal.

directivity index—Index for the dependency of the pick-up pattern on the frequency. The lower this is, the better the quality of the microphone.

discrete—A single audio channel carrying a signal with no attachment or dependency on any other channel—not a matrixed multichannel signal.

distortion—Undesired qualities in the sound signal, usually introduced by electrically generated devices or changes in the relative levels of the different frequencies involved; overloading the saturation maximums allowable for clear audio recording.

distortion during playback—A modification of the original audio signal appearing in the output of audio equipment that had not been present in the input during the recording process. The most common way of expressing distortion is in percentage of original signal as total harmonic distortion (THD).

distortion while recording—An audio signal from the microphone to the recorded medium (analog or DAT) is distorting due to either overloading the record level beyond the capacity of the tape to accept the signal, or by using underqualified pre-amplification power or overamplification (i.e., double-phantom powering a microphone).

diversity reception—Reception technique to reduce signal cancellation caused by reflection. The signal is received several times and the best signal is chosen for amplification.

drop frame—(1) Hole in the reception caused by the cancellation of the high frequency at the antenna. The receiver hisses and speech reception is disturbed. (2) Drop-frame time code is so named because the counting sequence skips, or drops 2 frames, every minute except at the 10 s of minutes. (See Chapter 6.)

dropout—Loss of a portion of the signal caused by lack of oxide on the portion of the tape, or by dirt or grease covering the portion of the tape, or by an interruption of the signal from the microphone to the record head. It is a term also used when a nonlinear session is locked to time code and is either recording or in playback mode and the time code reader (e.g., slave driver) loses the steady flow of time code data and suddenly stops because there is no time code stream to lock onto and follow.

DSP (digital signal processing) functions—Refers to special algorithmic software plug-ins for audio signal processing equipment and digital audio workstations for altering audio signals in a myriad of ways.

dual diaphragm—Special capsule design in condenser microphones. This allows the pick-up pattern to be adjusted from omnidirectional through cardioid to figure-of-eight by means of the diaphragm bias.

dummy head stereo—Head-based, 2-channel recording technique using a (plastic) separator body in the shape of a head between the two microphones.

dynamics—Term used to describe the intentional design of an audio event (or mix) to build in strategic quiet passages to help the perception of louder passages being bigger than they otherwise may appear. To strategically design in high and low points into a soundtrack so that the audience will not suffer from audio fatigue, greatly increasing the listening value, making an audio roller coaster ride.

dynamics range—The way in which sound volume varies; the difference (in decibels) between the loudest and quietest portions of the audio signal, or between the maximum signal level of the audio performance and the noise floor of the electronic equipment.

EDL (edit decision list)—A list of decisions which describe a series of edits. The EDL contains an ordered list of reel and timecode data representing where each video clip can be obtained in order to conform the final cut.

emulsion—Magnetic batch mixture coating that is adhered to the base stock of film or tape for eventual audio recording and playback purposes.

encode (encoder, encoded)—Device which brings in electronic signals and alters the character or superimposes other information onto it (e.g., multichannel matrix encoding or noise-reduction encoding, etc.).

ENG—Electronic news gathering.

exciter lamp—A lamp housing in the optical head of a projector or Moviola whose light passes through the optical soundtrack image of the film and impinges on a photoelectric cell, causing current fluctuations that accurately reproduce the analog audio signal for playback.

feedback—In a PA system consisting of a microphone, amplifier, and loudspeaker, feedback is the ringing or howling caused by amplified sound from the loudspeaker being picked up by the microphone and being recycled through the system and re-amplified, played through the speaker and being picked up by the microphone again, etc.

flutter—Rapid change in frequency of an audio or video signal due to variations in tape or disk speed. Wow is usually considered a lower frequency speed variation. See *wow*.

Foley—A process whereby a Foley artist can perform custom sync-to-picture audio events by watching the projected image of action and simultaneously performing the desired sound event in sync. Originally developed by Jack Foley at Universal Studios, and eventually named in his honor at Desilu Studios. Foley sound is usually associated with footsteps, prop movement unique to the film, and cloth movement.

frequency—Number of times a signal vibrates each second, expressed as cycles per second (cps) or hertz (Hz).

frequency response—(audio and video systems) The frequency range over which signals are reproduced within a specified amplitude range. Generally expressed in dB versus Hz; example: 100 to 5,000 Hz ± 5 dB.

fullcoat—Audio film stock where the magnetic emulsion covers the entire surface of the film, from edge-to-edge over the perforations.

gain—Amount of signal amplification.

gain brain—A signal processing device that can be adjusted to be less or more sensitive to the dynamics of an incoming audio signal, and then lift and compress the volume of that signal according to the operator's need both in preset decibel expansion as well as duration of sensitivity.

generation loss—Every time an audio or video signal is copied, whether it is transferred from one medium to another or 1-to-1 duplicate copies are made, there is always a generation loss. Generation loss is more pronounced in analog form than in digital form. There is a myth that digital does not suffer from generation loss. This is simply not true. Every time you make a copy of a signal, there will be some degradation.

graphic equalizer—A multi-band fixed area of frequency influences that can be boosted or attenuated as needed. Thirty-band graphic equalizers are the most popular for post-production work, with ±6 dB shifts with 6 dB boosters to make them 12 dB shifts per channel.

Group Walla—A sound effect for the murmur of a crowd in the background. The word walla comes from early radio broadcasts when background dialogue was created by recording a group of people repeating "walla walla walla."

harmonic distortion—Unwanted signal components within a spectrum as multiples of the fundamental frequency. If this frequency is 1 kHz, the distortion produces signal components at, for example, 2 or 3 or 4 kHz (these components are given in percentage of the useful signal).

head room—The amount of safe recording range above the established 0 VU (and whatever designation as equivalent on the digital peak meter—e.g., –18 to –22 dB) reserved for more robust audio event moments where additional momentary increased volume is desired, but before you hit distortion or maximum.

head stack—A rigidly fixed array of erase, record, and playback heads (or record, pilot sync, and playback heads) that are aligned precisely together to appropriately write or read audio information. Head stacks are often modular and can be removed and changed out with other variations, such as the Magna-Tech multichannel combinations or the Stellavox interchangeable head-stack arrays.

high pass filter—A high pass filter is a filter that allows only those frequencies above a so-called limit frequency (called the crossover point or cutoff) to pass. In electroacoustics, high pass filters are often called low cut filters, bass filters, bass cut filters, bass roll-off filters, or rumble filters. High pass filters on microphones are usually used to reduce the effects of handling noise, pops, rumble (e.g., stage rumble), and low-frequency vibrations, or to reduce the proximity effect in close mike situations.

hirose connector—Also known as HRS connector. Commonly used plug connector between a pocket transmitter and a clip-on microphone. Unfortunately without a fixed standard.

Hz (hertz)—The unit of measurement for frequency; 1 Hz is equal to one cycle per second.

image frequency—Undesired carrier frequency, produced by the conversion of the receiving frequency into the intermediate frequency. The result is a second reception frequency as a mirror image around the intermediate frequency.

image rejection—The ratio of actual receiving frequency to image frequency. Given in dB.

impedance—Resistance to the flow of an electrical current, expressed as high or low impedance. Hi-Z or low-Z, measured in ohms (Ω). A lower value means you can run longer lengths of cable without loss of signal integrity.

Impedance expresses the AC resistance of a microphone or a set of headphones. It is dependent on frequency and is given at 1 kHz as the so-called nominal impedance. In recent years, an industrial standard has developed, setting the impedance of headphones at 50 or 600 Ω. With microphones, the input impedance of the following microphone amplifier should have at least three times the value of the nominal impedance, in order to prevent it from unnecessarily attenuating the microphone signal.

inputs—The program that enters a unit or system; a connector or receptacle into which a signal is fed.

interlock—To sync up two or more recorders or playback machines, either by mechanical or electronic means so that they will run in exact sync with each other.

jack plug or **socket**—A common audio connector in the consumer electronics and music industries. Available in various diameters; in the hi-fi segment, $\frac{1}{8}''$ and $\frac{1}{4}''$ are widely used. Poles range from 1 to 4 (examples: headphone jack or jack of an electric guitar).

jam sync—A process of synchronizing a time code generator with time code being played on a tape, and then reentering that time code onto the tape. Done to extend code or to replace bad code dropouts without disturbing the continuous count of time code.

KEM—Flatbed picture editing machine. The film (both picture and sound) are mounted on cores and placed flat on aluminum plates that are synchronized together using sprocketed rollers that can interlock to run in sync or disengage to run each roll of film independently for ease of editing.

kHz (kilohertz)—One thousand times 1 Hz (hertz).

layback—To transfer from one medium to another medium, usually in multichannel form, usually involving time code lock-up to maintain synchronization. This term is usually used when describing transferring a nonlinear edit session from the computer software from which the picture and/or sound edit session was created to another medium for presentation purposes (e.g., 24-track analog tape, multichannel perforated 35-mm film, 2-, 8-, 16-, 24-, 32-, or 48-channel digital tape, or to any kind of video medium). See *output*.

LED (light emitting diodes)—semiconductor diodes that typically emit a single waveength of light when charged with electricity. LEDs require relatively little power to operate and last for decades.

limiter—An automatic control to reduce volume when the audio signal rises above a level that would introduce significant distortion.

lobar (pick-up pattern)—A microphone with a lobar polar pattern has the highest possible directivity. A lobar pick-up pattern is achieved with a shotgun microphone.

M&E—Music and effects.

M-S stereo—In the M-S stereo technique, one microphone with any pick-up pattern picks up the sound from the front (middle) while another microphone with a figure-of-eight pick-up pattern is positioned at right angles to it (side). The M-S stereo technique produces an optimum mono signal, and can be used to infinitely change the included angle.

Magna-Tech—A rugged rack-mounted film recording and playback machine. Extremely accurate and practical. One to 6 channels capable, using mag stripe (for mono) and full-coat for multichannel. Uses 60 cycle stepping motors for sync accuracy; pushbutton choice of American 24 fps or European 25 fps standards.

MIDI (musical instrument digital interface)—A communication system between musical synthesizers.

monaural (monophonic)—A single audio channel, not stereophonic.

monitor—To watch, to listen; to oversee and be vigilant about quality control of something, as in "she monitored the digitization process."

monitors—(1) One or more television monitors to view visual images. A specialized highly calibrated television monitor for professional use to judge color values and quality control. (2) A pair (or set, as in 5.1 audio imaging field) of audio speakers of high quality standard to accurately reproduce an audio signal for professional use.

moving-coil (dynamic) microphone—The moving-coil microphone is the most frequently used dynamic microphone. It makes use of magnetic induction to represent sound: a coil connected to the diaphragm moves in a magnetic field and induces a voltage that corresponds to the curve of the sound. The microphone never needs external operating voltage.

Moviola—An upright picture-and-sound editing machine used between the 1920s and the mid-1990s. Ultimately replaced by nonlinear digital workstations, except in rare cases.

NAB—National Association of Broadcasters.

noise cancellation—A microphone designed to cancel ambient noise so that it will not be recorded. The housing of the microphone allows noise to reach both sides of the diaphragm simultaneously, thereby canceling each other out.

noise gate—A signal processing device that can be adjusted to various calibrated sensitivities to compress or cut out noise peaks that are stronger than some specific desired maximums of the desired signal, thus limiting unwanted audio anomalies from the audio track.

nondrop—Unlike drop frame time code that skips, or drops, 2 frames every minute, nondrop time code does not drop or skip anything.

ohm (Ω)—The unit of measure of electrical resistance or impedance.

OMF—Open Media Framework is a file format technology designed to allow media-handling applications to communicate in a platform-independent manner, to speak a common language. The goal of OMF is to allow any OMF-compatible application that handles audio, video, picture, or other media to communicate with any other OMF-compatible application. It is most often used to take a Final Cut Pro or Avid picture-edited session and to convert that session into a Pro Tools session. OMF translates simple single, continuous time code. OMF translates any number of audio tracks. It translates clip names (region names) and can translate it sample accurate (precision sync).

omnidirectional—Picking up signal equally from all directions.

optical head—See *exciter lamp.*

output—Signal delivered from any audio or video device; also a jack, connector, or circuit which feeds the signal to another device such as a speaker or headset.

overtones—Individual component frequencies in a sound which when added to the fundamental signal, helps to define its spatial quality (e.g., cathedral expanse).

pad—Attenuator, usually with an attenuation of 10 to 20 dB. Used in both audio and RF technology.

pan pot—A multichannel volume controller. In this case the pan pot does not control how loud the signal will be, as it usually rides in line with the volume fader control, but controls the spatial placement of the sound, whether it will favor to left or to right speaker; or if hooked up to the surround speakers, the pan pot can literally fly sounds around the room by the placement of the joystick during the performance of the audio cue. See *phantom imaging.*

parametric equalizer—Unlike the graphic equalizer whose bands are precisely fixed to control exact sectors, a mixing console parametric equalizer has three or more (usually four to five) ranges of influence. Low frequency—lower mid-range—upper mid-range—high end. Each influence can be adjusted in attenuation or amplification by dB steps or by fractions of dB. Each influence can also be adjusted on how broad a frequency range in that influence the user may want to affect. The user may want it to be quite broad or the user may want to narrow the swath for fine surgical work. The usual attenuation/amplification can be as much as ±24 dB.

peak meter—Unlike the VU meter which shows an average of the modulation volume, a peak meter shows the maximum amplitude hits, moment to moment. Some meters will hold that level for a fraction of a second for easier reading, unless superseded by a louder level.

phantom imaging—Sound that is reproduced through two or more speakers that, through the use of multiple speakers and deriving audio material from these speakers in a varying percentage balance, is imaged in a part of the listening envelope where there is no speaker (i.e., right and left channels phantom a center channel by giving certain parts of the signal program identical elements that will cause perceived central derivation).

phantom power—A method of remotely powering the preamplifier or impedance converter which is built into many condenser microphones by sending voltage along the audio cable. Phantom power is usually from 6 to 48 volts DC and is run along the same conductors that carry the audio signal. The electrical power is separated from the audio by using capacitors and special transformers.

phase—Timing relationship between two signals.

phase matching—In playback, a swimming sensation when two identical audio signals are lined up *almost* identically. This swimming sensation tells the dialog editor that his replacement reprint of production audio is perfectly in sync with the work track.

phasing—In recording, two identical audio signals (from two separate microphone input sources) that cancel each other out. This is most often noticed in two microphones that are not placed in an X-Y pattern. The two microphone diaphragm capsules are separated too much, and as a moving sound source, such as a car passing by changes from the source striking diaphragm 1 first a millisecond before striking diaphragm 2 to favoring diaphragm 2 first before striking diaphragm 1; the signal is in a moment of transition and winks out.

pick-up pattern—Also known as polar pattern, directivity. Directions from which a microphone is sensitive to sound waves. Pick-up patterns vary with each mike element and mike design. The two most common patterns are omnidirectional and unidirectional. According to their acoustic design, microphones differ in their sensitivity towards sound from different directions. Pressure microphones have a sensitivity that is largely independent of direction (omnidirectional pick-up pattern). Pressure gradient microphones have the pick-up patterns wide cardioid, cardioid, super-cardioid, or figure-of-eight. Interference microphones can be used to achieve a further concentration of the pick-up pattern (lobar pick-up pattern). As a special case, dummy head microphones achieve the pick-up pattern of the human ear/head (dummy head stereo).

pink noise—Pink noise is an electronic signal that has equal energy levels at all frequencies across the range from 20 Hz to 20 kHz.

PNO (program number)—An abbreviated term used on DAT recording machines that can lay down a tape location reference, using 1 to 99 for the number of countable cues.

polarization voltage—Also known as bias. A condenser microphone needs a polarizing voltage in order to generate the signal voltage which follows the audio signal.

polar pattern—A graph of a transducer's directional characteristics measured in a 360-degree pattern, and usually at several different frequencies. Speaker polar patterns indicate relative output level, whereas microphone polar patterns indicate relative sensitivity.

pop—(1) One frame of 1 kHz tone placed at the 2 frame of an Academy leader at the top of the reel (6 seconds from the Picture Start frame). This 1/24th of a second pop or beep is used as head line-up for sync relative to a unit of sound or a mixed predub or final mixed track. One frame of pop is also placed 2 seconds (or 3 feet in 35-mm terms) from the last frame of picture (also known as LFOP). (2) A thump or explosive breathy impact produced when a puff of air from the actor strikes the microphone diaphragm. This most often occurs with the P, T, and B consonants of speech.

pop filter—(1) A foam or cloth shield placed over a microphone to avoid popping consonant sounds from suddenly impacting the microphone diaphragm. Stretched nylon hose over a metal ring (such as a bent wire clothes hanger can make a very effective pop filter in a pinch). (2) An electronic filter than can attenuate low frequencies where the popping sound exists (a high pass filter with its cutoff at approximately 70 to 100 Hz).

postconform—To postconform means that you are going use the EDL (edit decision list) generated by the nonlinear editing software (picture editing) to use with transfer equipment that will automatically ask for certain production audio tapes (whether analog or digital), then have the time code driven audio deck automatically spin down to and transfer only the sections of the tape required (along with prescribed pre- and postroll handles). These transfers would be transferred into perfect sync into a nonlinear sound editing software session. This procedure is used if (1) the picture editor's audio material is not trustworthy to warrant using the OMF method, and/or (2) if the original production audio tapes used time code as a sync reference, thereby having the time code signal on the tapes to follow. Often this procedure is used with video transfer tapes that are made at the laboratory during the original telecine process—but what good is it to postconform from a medium that is already in question, as it is not the original material and is already de facto suffering from generation loss?

preamp (preamplifier)—An amplifier that strengthens weak signals such as those from a microphone, magnetic playback head, photo cell, or a phonograph pick-up to a level sufficient to drive a power amplifier.

presence peak—An increase in microphone output in the presence frequency range of 2 to 10 kHz. A presence peak increases clarity, articulation, or apparent closeness.

pressure gradient microphone—Also known as pressure gradient receiver, directional microphone. In the pressure gradient microphone, both faces of the diaphragm are exposed to the sound field. In an ideal pressure gradient microphone, the voltage given off by the microphone depends only on the difference in pressure between front and back. This results in a figure-of-eight pick-up pattern. By adding time-delay elements, one-sided pick-up patterns can be achieved; for example, wide cardioid, cardioid, and super-cardioid.

pressure microphone—Also known as pressure receiver, omnidirectional microphone. In a pressure microphone, only the front of the diaphragm is exposed to the sound field. The voltage given off by the microphone depends only on the sound pressure at the front and is therefore essentially nondirectional (see *omnidirectional*). Depending on the diameter of its diaphragm, the pressure microphone becomes, to a certain degree, unidirectional with increasing frequency.

print thru—Print thru is an analog issue. As the analog tape passes over the head stack, the recorded audio signal is laid on. The tape continues around the tension roller and winds onto the take-up reel. If the recorded audio was very loud the highly saturated recorded molecules on the tape, due to the very loud signals that registered in the upper maximums of the head room on the peak meter, are vibrating much stronger than quieter passages. As the take-up reel revolves and winds yet other layers of tape over these highly agitated passages, the excited magnetic molecules will affect the layers on either side of the tape, both prior to and following, causing influences of phantom audio imaging, known as print thru. This gives you a faint reproduction of that sound approximately 1 second between each phantom prior to and following the actual recording.

proximity effect—Every directional microphone (pressure gradient microphone) has the property of providing a pronounced boost in low-frequency output when placed close to the sound source (less than 20 cm). This has physical reasons and is partly decisive for the sound of a vocal microphone.

quadraphonic—Four cardioid microphone capsules aligned at precise 90-degree angles to each other so that when reproduced in a listening environment with four audio speakers in proper spatial positioning, the signal will produce a realistic 360-degree envelope that will replicate the original environmental reality.

response—The sensitivity, frequency, and polar characteristics of a microphone.

reverberation—The sum of many reflections of a sound in a recording environment that is enclosed.

Rivas tape splicer—A precision film tape splicer (16-mm or 35-mm) that uses pre-perforated splicing tape for exact alignment. Clear tape is used for picture and white base perforated tape is used for the sound. Rivas is the name of a particular manufacturer.

sample rate—The number of measured moments in a second that digital data numbers represent the level and frequency information that models the audio signal. The two basic industry standards for sample rates are 44.1 kHz (44,100) and 48 kHz (48,000) times per second. Played in real time, these moments render a recreation of the sound. Look for the sample rate standards to rise to 96 kHz and possibly as high as 192 kHz within a decade.

session—(1) A contiguous length of time that a group assembles together to perform and/ or record, or for a picture or sound editor and the director (and any other participants) to work in a scheduled length of time. (2) In nonlinear terms a software icon that contains all of the edit decision data that the picture or sound editor has worked with to create either a picture or sound reel of action. This icon session knows, through the editor's input, where in the computer hard drives all of the digitized media material resides.

shotgun mike—Slang term for a highly directional tube-like cardioid microphone. This interference microphone uses a lobar pick-up pattern. Especially useful for reducing ambient noise in ENG applications.

sibilance—In speech, the overemphasis of "s" and "ch" sounds in speech which causes undesirable sharp and shrilly spikes.

signal-to-noise ratio (SNR)—The ratio of audio information of a signal that has unwanted hiss, rumble, hum, and other background noises in balance to the desired signal. Measured in dB. The ratio of the largest possible output voltage to the smallest possible output voltage of an electroacoustic transmission device. The signal-to-noise ratio is the difference between the reference sound level of 94 dB (equivalent to 1 Pa) and the equivalent noise level. Studio condenser microphones generally have a signal-to-noise ratio of 74 to 64 dB (CCIR) or 84 to 74 dB (A).

signal cancellation—One audio signal is combined with another audio signal that has varying degree of identical information in it (being recorded at the exact same time) will cancel out its counterpart in the first signal (like taking an image of something as a positive image and aligning it with its identical image in negative form, the two cancel each other out and become nothing). The audio signal material from the first source that does not have a counterpart in the second signal will be all that remains.

sine wave (sinusoidal)—A signal wave signature that has a magnitude that varies as the sine of an independent variable. (See Chapter 6, Figure 6.9.)

slate—Slang term, "sticks." Rectangular surface (black or white background) on which the slate assistant can write, for the camera to see just prior to snapping sync. Information such as production title, company, date, camera roll, sound roll, director's name, cameraman's name, as well as the scene number, angle designation, and take number can clearly be seen. At the top of the slate is a hinged bar (usually painted with alternating black and white angled stripes for ease in designating the exact frame of sync) and when the slate assistant is told to "Mark it," claps the hinged bar down onto the slate, causing an audible snap for the microphone to hear.

smart slate—The smart slate works identically as the conventional slate, in that information is handwritten onto the white slate surface. The difference being that the smart slate has a wireless receiver that reads the running time code transmitted from the audio recorder and displays it in large red LED numbers. These numbers run until the slate assistant claps the hinged bar down onto the slate, causing the two electrical contacts on the inside surfaces to touch and freeze the time code so the picture assistant can sync dailies back at picture editorial.

SMPTE—Society of Motion Picture and Television Engineers.

square wave—A signal wave signature that is periodic and equal to one constant on one half of the period and a different constant (which may be zero) on the other half. (See Chapter 6, Figure 6.9.)

SRT—Standard reference tape.

stereo—The audio signal is recorded using two discrete channels in parallel that when played back will yield a spatial presence with a balance left and right signal. Movement of audio generating sources within the program will appear to move from left to right or right to left as the two microphones were set up to record them. See also *quadraphonic*.

supervising sound editor—The individual who is responsible for and heads the postproduction sound editorial team and various audio facility services to bring together a polished production dialog track, sound design, custom performed and edited Foley, and stereo backgrounds. He or she also oversees the mixing of the final re-recording process with the cut music sessions. The supervising sound editor is solely responsible to the director and producer and often is the contractor of the post-sound edit process.

sync (synch)—The exact alignment of the audio event to the corresponding frame of visual action.

sync block—See *synchronizer*.

sync generator—A pulse generator producing the sync signals necessary to integrate the functioning of various pieces of sound, camera, or video equipment in relationship to each other.

synchronizer—Also known as a sync block. When working with picture and sound 16-mm and 35-mm film, the most accurate synchronization device is the synchronizer, which comprises up to six side-by-side sprocketed wheels (known as gangs) that are coupled to each other with a solid metal rod. When one wheel turns, the others turn exactly the same because they are physically coupled together. Each full rotation equals 1 foot of film. These wheels have sprocket teeth on the perimeter edge, precisely engaging into the perforation holes of the film stock, forcing the film to remain in rigid synchronization due to locking arms that are lowered and clicked into place. Each locking arm has two rollers with grooved glides that allow the sprocket wheel teeth to pass through; yet the roller holds the film place against the wheel, so the film does not slip and slide out of sync with the picture or other mag stripe strand of film.

Magnetic heads can be lowered down onto the magnetic film strands so that the sound can be heard. The heads feed the signal into a table-top amplifier. The synchronizer does two things: First, it keeps the picture and parallel tracks of sound in sync to one another. Second, the synchronizer keeps track of the position of the film by the use of a precision foot-and-frame counter. This counter can be zeroed-out by the editor when he or she has locked the strands of film into the synchronizer in the desired line-up positions (usually using a start mark or frame designation marking).

Even in today's nonlinear digital domain editing environment, going back to film, whether by negative cutting or use in the post-sound mixing process, the film synchronizer is the ultimate and most accurate way to guarantee sync in the film industry. (See Chapter 13, Figure 13.9.)

THD (total harmonic distortion)—Total harmonic distortion is a measure of nonlinear harmonic distortion and is given in percentage. Nonlinear harmonic distortions are signals which were not present in the original before the signal was converted by the headphones. These unwanted signals are caused by the diaphragm, whose movements do not precisely move in time with the electric signals that cause it to move. Unfortunately, this is a feature of all electroacoustic transducers. Although it cannot be completely eliminated, suitable steps can be taken to minimize it. However, the user is not interested in why this distortion takes place but in how great the level of distortion must be for it to become perceptible. According to the findings of several research projects, a total harmonic distortion of 1 percent in the frequency range of 100 to 2,000 Hz is imperceptible. Below 100 Hz, the perceptibility threshold lies at 10 percent.

time code—"Electronic perforations." A numbering system developed by SMPTE that assigns a number to each frame—the frame address denoted by hours, minutes, seconds, and frames. There is a visual time code for visual reference as well as an audio time code which matches its visual reference.

transducer—A device that converts one form of energy to another form. A microphone transducer converts acoustical sound energy into electrical signal energy.

transfer bay—An array of equipment (usually in a dedicated room) that can transfer audio or video medium from one source to another source. Such transfer bays have calibration tools and meters so that accurate and precise 1-to-1s can be made to the closest tolerances.

VITC (pronounced vit-see; vertical interval time code)—This time code reference is recorded in the video frame line vertical interval. Computers can read this time code very accurately.

VU meter (volume unit meter)—Used in most American equipment for measuring audio signal levels. It averages the sound, showing a percentage modulation and is not linear in dB, unlike the peak meter.

watt—A unit of measure for electrical or acoustical power.

wavelength—Provided that the wave is perfectly regular (e.g., a sine wave), this is the distance between successive peaks.

wow—A cyclic fluctuation in pitch due to mechanical malfunction (usually tension rollers) or in constant speed of the transport capstan, as in wow-and-flutter.

XLR—Professional connector (having three or more conductor pins) with an outer shell which shields the connection and makes a solid male/female lock. Most commonly used for balanced audio signals for microphone and line feeds. The XLR-type connector is sometimes called a "cannon" connector, so named for the original manufacturer.

X-Y pattern—A pair of cardioid microphones or mike elements aimed at crossed directions, with the two microphone diaphragms as close together as possible, putting the two signals in phase.

About the Interactive DVD

This book includes an interactive DVD that I hope you will find both informative and a whole lot of fun. The DVD is loaded with audio material that you will want to take time to listen to, appreciate, and study. We recommend that you use a DVD player on your home or school entertainment system with a speaker array that will replicate the soundtracks appropriately. Even though you can use the DVD drive on your personal computer, you will not receive the fullness of the sound because conventional system monitor speakers cannot reproduce it.

When the DVD is started, the main menu will come up on your screen. There are ten primary button choices:

1. Sound: An Overview
2. Equipment Review
3. Production Recording
4. Dialog Editing
5. Custom Recording FX
6. Backgrounds and FX
7. ADR and Looping
8. The Art of Foley
9. Nonlinear Editing and Mixing Systems
10. Sound Restoration and Colorization Technologies

Each one of the primary buttons leads you to a submenu that will help you navigate to the material you wish to review:

1. Sound: An Overview
   A. Our Beginnings—and Bruce Campbell
   B. The Disciplines of Film
   C. Picture Editorial Protocols
   D. Re-recording Flow Charts: Strategy
   E. The Sound Format Protocols
   F. The Editor's Photo Gallery
   G. Terms and Definitions
2. Equipment Review
   A. Microphones—Cable and Wireless, Smart Slate, and Wind Control Accessories
   B. Field Production Sound Mixers
   C. Field Production Sound Recorders

3. Production Recording
   A. The Sound Report
   B. *Bad* and *Proper* Information Header
   C. The Mixer's Information Header
   D. Simple 2-track Protocol
   E. Sound Mixers in Action Photo Gallery
   F. How We Shoot a Musical—*Playback*!

4. Dialog Editing
   A. The Code Book—EDL and OMF
   B. Dialog Session Layout
   C. Dialog Equalization Comparisons
   D. Demo Sequence—Original Editor's Cut
   E. Demo Sequence—Re-Cut Dialog
   F. Demo Sequence—Backgrounds
   G. Demo Sequence—Hard FX
   H. Demo Sequence—Final Mix

5. Custom Recording FX
   A. Custom FX Reformists
   B. Comparison Recording Test
   C. Recording a Vehicle Series
   D. Recording an Aircraft Series
   E. Recording Guns
   F. Recording Animals
   G. Mastering FX and the Library

6. Backgrounds and FX
   A. Evolution of Sound FX and the Importance of Knowing Your History
   B. Backgrounds Tell a Story
   C. *Prisoner of War* directed by Scott Byrns: FX, Backgrounds, Foley Stems, and Final Mix
   D. Layering the Big Sound
   E. *Starship Troopers* R-7: Yewdall's invasion of Klendatho

7. ADR and Looping
   A. ADR—Cue Sheets (2 types) Recording and Audio File Protocol
   B. ADR Practice Boot Camp
      • Feature film scene sequence in its entirety
      • ADR sheets
      • 18 individual ADR cues (each ADR video clip is looped four times for convenient individual practice with industry standard 3-beep and Colin-Broad streamer cues exactly as it would work with "loop record" option)

8. The Art of Foley
   A. Foley Artists in Action
   B. Foley Cue Sheets and Recording
   C. Foley Boot Camp Practice Cues
      • Foley cue sheets
      • Foley exercise cues with Colin-Broad streamers (separate cues for footsteps, props, and cloth)

9. Nonlinear Editing and Mixing Systems
   A. Euphonix and Nuendo User Profiles
   B. Nuendo 3.2 Charts and Plug-In Charts
   C. Pro Tools version 7.2 Charts and Plug-In Charts
   D. Pro Tools Icon System Overview

10. Sound Restoration and Colorization Technologies
    A. Audio Mechanics—Studio Photos
    B. Audio Mechanics—Audio Demos
    C. Legend Films—Restoration and Colorization Sample Photos
    D. Legend Films
       • Video presentation of the process featuring an interview with Ray Harryhausen and his new venture and collaboration in helping the directors of classic films finally fulfill their visions.

Some of the submenus have submenus of their own to help you further navigate and choose what you want to view and/or work with. In addition to video clips and sequences, there are numerous slide show presentations, many that have audio files attached.

The slide show presentations are easy to use. After navigating through the main menu and submenu items, simply press the activate button and the slide show will begin. Most of the photographs and charts have been authored to pause indefinitely, until you use the chapter skip button, which will advance the slide show to the next image. A few sequences, particularly those that have audio files attached, will automatically advance from one photo or chart to the next until that particular narration or sample sound cue is complete.

Many of the photographs and charts presented in the book are also on the DVD in their original color versions. Additionally, there are literally hundreds of photographs and charts on the DVD that are not in the book.

To truly take advantage of the DVD's cavernous collection of information, leave no stone unturned. For instance, by navigating to a submenu under "The Disciplines of Film," you would find How to Bias Mag Stock. This is a very easy step-by-step narrated slide show that carefully walks you through the often misunderstood but crucial technique of setting the bias strength correctly for each and every roll of magnetic stock. This very detailed and illustrated color instruction is not even discussed in the book, but is provided to you in a very easy-to-understand presentation.

ADR-Looping Boot Camp Exercise Cues
Here are the exact dialog cues that you can practice under ADR practice Boot Camp.

431 Maria "Hey."
432 Louie "Oww!"
433 Maria "Oh! . . . oh!—oh, are you alright?" (*nervous chuckles—breath*)
434 Louie "You sure you don't want to talk about this?
435 Maria (*exhale*) "Louie, I don't see any reason for us to keep fooling ourselves."
436 Louie (*catch breath*) "I think you are fooling yourself."
437 Maria "Please don't make this any harder than it is."

438	Maria	(*exhale*) "So—what is it?"
439	Louie	"It's your, uh—your . . ." (*breath*)
440	Louie	"Uh—crank—alternating . . ."
441	Louie	". . . shaft-a-nator . . . thingy."
442	Louie	(*embarrassed chuckling*)
443	Maria	"You have no idea, do you?" (*chuckles—vocal tickle*)
444	Louie	"Uh, not a clue." (*chuckles*)
445	Louie	"Uh—you want a ride?"
446	Maria	"Yeah, right." (*add breaths*)

If you find these ADR-looping exercise cues extremely helpful and wish to try other variations, you can acquire a dedicated interactive DVD—ADR-Looping Boot Camp (full version) that has nearly a hundred cues from five different scenes from two different feature films. The DVD is also available through Elsevier/Focal Press.

Foley Boot Camp Exercise Cues

There are eight individual video streams. Each stream contains several Foley cues. These cues are complete with Colin-Broad streamers that correspond to the Foley cue sheets you can view on the DVD. You will have three dedicated video cues devoted to *footstep* cues and four dedicated video cues devoted to individual *prop* movement creations.

If you find these Foley exercise cues helpful and wish to try other variations, you can acquire a dedicated interactive DVD—Foley Boot Camp (full version) that has nearly a hundred cues from two different feature films. The DVD is also available through Elsevier/Focal Press.

Enjoy—and be audio empowered!

Index

Limited Warranty and Disclaimer of Liability